REAL WORLD
ADOBE® PHOTOSHOP® CS4
FOR PHOTOGRAPHERS
INDUSTRIAL-STRENGTH IMAGING TECHNIQUES

CONRAD CHAVEZ
DAVID BLATNER

PEACHPIT PRESS
BERKELEY, CALIFORNIA

Real World Adobe Photoshop CS4 for Photographers

Conrad Chavez and David Blatner

Peachpit Press
1249 Eighth Street
Berkeley, CA 94710
510/524-2178
510/524-2221 (fax)

Peachpit Press is a division of Pearson Education.
Real World Adobe Photoshop CS4 for Photographers is published in association with Adobe Press.

For the latest on Adobe Press books, go to www.adobepress.com
To report errors, please send a note to errata@peachpit.com

Project Editor: Susan Rimerman
Production Editor: Lisa Brazieal
Copy Editor: Rebecca Pepper
Composition: Conrad Chavez, Danielle Foster
Indexer: Rebecca Plunkett
Cover Illustration: John Weber

ISBN-13: 978-0-321-60451-4
ISBN-10:   0-321-60451-2
9 8 7 6 5 4 3 2 1
Printed and bound in the United States of America

For Bruce

1954–2006

Longtime coauthor, friend, expert, mentor, demystifier
www.brucefraserlegacy.com

&

For Fay, Harry, Ann, Abe, Katie, and Rita,
who laid the foundation in my family. *—David*

For my mother, Aida, who makes it all possible. *—Conrad*

CONTENTS

Chapter 4: Color Settings 49

Chapter 5: Building a Digital Workflow 101

INTRODUCTION
Photoshop in the Real World

If you're checking out this book because you want to produce embossed type, fractalized tree branches, or 3D logos in Adobe Photoshop, you're in the wrong place. There are at least a dozen good books on those subjects. But if you're looking to move photographic images through Photoshop—importing digital captures or scans, bending them to your will, and creating world-class results—this is the book for you. Its *raison d'être* is to answer the questions that people in production environments ask every single day.

- How can I quickly and efficiently process the 500 images coming from my digital camera?

- How should I set up my computer for Photoshop?

- What settings should I use in the Color Settings dialog?

- How do I bring out shadow details in my images without blowing away the highlights?

- What methods are available to neutralize color casts?

- How do I calibrate my monitor? (And should I?)

Our Goals for This Book

This book isn't just about Photoshop. It's also about photography and about images. We believe that photographers understand tone and color as well as any other skilled group of professionals, and one of our aims has been to help photographers translate their own understanding of images into the digital world of Photoshop.

Digital imaging has undoubtedly changed the practice of photography, but images still come from an intentional act on the part of the image maker, and that isn't going to change, whether the photons are captured by goo smeared on celluloid or by photoelectric sensors. What has changed is how a photographer gets from camera to the final print (if it's even a print)—once chemical, now digital. And Photoshop is at the center of this workflow.

When you're in a crunch, you've got to have an intuitive, almost instinctive feel for what's going on in Photoshop so you can finesse it to your needs. Canned techniques just don't cut it. For that reason, you'll find a fair amount of conceptual discussion here, describing how Photoshop thinks about images and suggesting how you might think about them as well.

Our goal is not to detract from the way you've been doing things. It's to show you how those approaches can be incorporated with new tools and pushed to the limit.

This Edition

Photoshop CS4 has not only added even more features but exists in a more specialized version: Photoshop CS4 Extended. If we were to cover every feature of Photoshop CS4 and Photoshop CS4 Extended in detail, you'd have to back a semi-trailer up to the store to take this book home.

Our solution is to focus the book more tightly on high-quality photographic editing and output for print and online use, hence the new name: *Real World Adobe Photoshop for Photographers*. The flip side of this change is that this book does not go into detail about topics that stray too far from photography. If you need information about the Photoshop Extended features that enhance medical or engineering workflows, or you want to know about designing Web pages in Photoshop, you'll want to reach for a more specialized book on the subject. (We do cover a few Photoshop Extended features that help photographers, such as using image stacks for noise reduction.)

Photoshop has changed over the years, and so have we. Many techniques we once thought brilliant have been superseded by the new features in each Photoshop upgrade. This is a good thing—you'll find that some techniques that required arcane, clever combinations of obscure Photoshop features are now condensed into convenient one-step tools that work just as well. We've tried to tell you whenever that's happened.

UPGRADING TO A NEW VERSION

Like death and taxes, upgrading your software is both inevitable and not fun, until you actually start enjoying the new features. Sooner or later you'll be faced with new challenges, unfamiliar options, and a new bottle of aspirin. Fortunately, we have some tips that can help ease the transition.

Migrating Your Existing Settings to CS4

The joy of discovering new features in an upgraded application is often tempered by the frustration of realizing that none of your meticulously crafted personal customizations are in your freshly installed virgin upgrade. Do you really have to go in and reconfigure every last preference and preset in Photoshop? The answer is, probably not. You can get your workflow back a lot faster if you proceed with a little patience and preparation, instead of upgrading and instantly throwing out the old version.

Preferences. There's no way to directly transfer your current preferences to the new version. Instead of writing down all of your settings, take a screen shot of each pane of the Photoshop Preferences dialog and refer to them as you set up the new version of Photoshop. You can use Adobe Bridge CS4 to browse your screen shots so that you can easily cycle through them as you adjust each preference in the new version of Photoshop.

TIP: Don't delete your old copy of Photoshop until you've copied your existing settings and moved all of your favorite plug-ins to the new Photoshop folder.

Presets and Other Customizations. Your actions, keyboard shortcuts, and other user presets are stored in specific locations in your user account on your computer; you can copy the CS3 versions of those files to the locations where Photoshop CS4 will find them. To find these locations, consult the Adobe document *Functions, Names, and Locations of Preference Files in*

Photoshop. As we write this, the Photoshop CS4 version of that document is at www.adobe.com/go/kb405012 and the Photoshop CS3 version is at www.adobe.com/go/kb401600.

Some presets may not work correctly if the features they're based on were changed in Photoshop CS4, so pay careful attention to how everything works as you begin using your migrated presets in your daily work. If you notice any serious problems with a particular preset, it's best to delete its preset file from the Adobe Photoshop CS4 Settings folder and re-create the preset in Photoshop CS4.

Plug-Ins. Photoshop plug-ins are installed into the Plug-ins folder inside the application folder for each version of Photoshop. This means that plug-ins don't automatically appear in a newer version of Photoshop—you have to move them manually. Before you delete your old Photoshop folder, find each non-Adobe plug-in and drag it to the corresponding folder in the Photoshop CS4 Plug-ins folder. If you move a plug-in to a newer version of Photoshop and it isn't compatible, Photoshop displays an alert telling you that the plug-in wasn't loaded. At that point, you need to get a newer version of that plug-in.

If you upgrade to Photoshop CS4 on an Intel-based Mac and your old plug-ins don't run, you'll likely need to upgrade to Intel-compatible versions of the plug-ins. If you're desperate to run those plug-ins now, try running Photoshop CS4 in the Rosetta compatibility environment: Select the Photoshop application icon in the Finder, choose File > Get Info, and turn on the Run in Rosetta check box. Unfortunately, Photoshop CS4 runs much slower in Rosetta.

What's New in Adobe Photoshop CS4

Here are some of the most important changes in Photoshop CS4. We're not listing every new feature, just the ones you should know about before jumping into the rest of the book.

Performance. Photoshop CS4 takes advantage of OpenGL and graphics card processors, which gives you faster and smoother visual feedback. Photoshop is now fully compatible with 64-bit Windows Vista.

Updated User Interface. Again?!? There are those who complain that the Photoshop user interface is rearranged with every upgrade, but this version's update isn't just for show. To us, a big benefit of the change is to accommodate tabbed documents and n-up views (such as viewing four documents as four panes in a single window). We cheer these changes because they greatly simplify managing multiple windows.

Adobe Bridge CS4. The file browser and organizer for Photoshop (and the rest of the Adobe Creative Suite), Bridge CS4 is faster than Bridge CS3 and better organized. Bridge CS4 also makes it easier to create output that involves many images, such as generating contact sheets and web galleries.

Adobe Camera Raw 5. The most amazing new feature in Camera Raw 5 is the support for local corrections. For example, you can lighten just a small area of an image.

Modeless Color Corrections. You no longer have to lock yourself away in dialog boxes when color correcting, because the options are now presented in the modeless Adjustments panel. If you've mastered the special keyboard tricks for dialog boxes such as Curves, we caution you that many of them have had to change as a result of moving these functions into panels.

Masks Panel. You can manage masks more easily with the new Masks panel. For example, instead of running a filter to feather a mask edge, just drag the new Feather slider. And instead of using Levels to lower the density of a mask, just drag the Density slider. Unlike the old techniques, these new features are nondestructive, so you can easily dial them back at any time.

Other New Hotness. Photoshop CS4 offers many other small changes, such as better Dodge and Burn tools, a Vibrance adjustment layer (safer than Saturation), and improved layer blending, including the ability to extend depth of field using multiple images. There's also content-aware scaling, which can resize images and reposition important content without distorting it.

You'll find the performance changes outlined in Chapter 1, the Bridge and Camera Raw changes in Chapter 5, the user-interface changes in Chapter 6, the color workflow changes in Chapter 7, and the masking changes in Chapter 8. Extended depth of field and content-aware scaling are covered in Chapter 11.

THANK YOU!

We'd like to give special thanks to a few of the many people who helped make what you hold in your hands: Susan Rimerman, our editor of this ninth edition, who was forever helpful and patient; production heroine extraordinaire Lisa Brazieal, Rebecca Pepper, Danielle Foster, Pamela Pfiffner, and our other friends at Peachpit who took our work and made it fly.

A huge thank you must go to Thomas and John Knoll. There would be no Photoshop without them. We'd also like to thank John Nack, Bryan O'Neill Hughes, and the Photoshop team, who have been generous with their time and knowledge for so many years. We would also like to extend our appreciation to Scott Byer, Marc Pawliger, Chris Cox, Eric Chan, Jeff Tranberry, and others for their remarkable openness and generosity. They have shared their inside knowledge not only with us, but with the world through their blogs and in the Adobe user forums.

If we see further than others, it's because we stand on the shoulders of Photoshop giants, including Ben Willmore, Julianne Kost, Katrin Eismann, Jeff Schewe, Martin Evening, Andrew Rodney, Stephen Johnson, Michael Ninness, Greg Gorman, Russell Brown, Scott Kelby, and Deke McClelland, pixel-meisters all.

And most of all, we owe a monumental debt of thanks to Bruce Fraser, who co-wrote the first seven editions of this book with David. He provided irreplaceable guidance and clarity to the entire digital imaging community.

CONRAD. I sincerely thank my family and friends for their support and patience during the long and demanding process of updating this book. In addition, I thank the Photoshop development team and the exceedingly creative user community for continually expanding the boundaries of what Photoshop can do, and in turn expanding the possibilities of photography.

DAVID. My deepest appreciation to Debbie Carlson, my friend and partner, and to Conrad Chavez, who stepped into a difficult task with courage and pulled off a great update. My sincere appreciation to my two sons, Gabriel and Daniel, who constantly remind me that life is more than pixels and vectors.

CHAPTER ONE

Building a Photoshop System

Adobe Photoshop is about as rich a program as you'll ever encounter, and much of this book focuses on ways to help you be more efficient in your use of it. But no quantity of tips, tricks, and work-arounds can compensate for hardware that's inadequate for the task or a poorly configured system. So in this chapter, we look at building an environment in which Photoshop—and you—can excel.

When buying a computer, consumers tend to fixate on raw processor speed. However, Photoshop also makes heavy demands on random access memory (RAM) and hard drives. Whatever system you choose, it will be most productive with Photoshop when the capabilities of the processor, RAM, and disks are balanced so that none of the three is an unnecessary bottleneck for the other parts.

CHOOSING A PLATFORM

Discussions of Macs versus PCs usually tend to degenerate into "my dad can beat up your dad"—spats that produce a lot of heat but little light. Most of the hardware and software you'll need is platform-independent, and we're firmly convinced that when you look at the big picture, price and performance are about the same on the two platforms. The Mac tends to be simpler to operate and easier to maintain. The PC has a greater range of hardware options and general business software.

The bottom line: If you're happy with your current hardware platform, there's probably no reason to switch. You may, however, want to think about upgrading if your machine is more than three or four years old. Photoshop CS4 and the latest operating systems make heavy demands on hardware.

If you're planning to upgrade to Windows Vista or Mac OS X 10.5, do yourself a favor—get a machine that was designed with the new operating system in mind. You'll save yourself a ton of time and frustration by doing so. It's possible to run Photoshop CS4 on fairly old machines—the minimum Mac OS requirement is Mac OS X 10.4.11, and the minimum Windows requirement is Windows XP with Service Pack 3—but we can tell you from bitter experience that it can be an uphill struggle. If your time is worth anything to you, trying to run an application like Photoshop CS4 on an outdated machine is a false economy.

Mac. Many Photoshop operations involve major number crunching, so the speed of your Mac's processor makes a big difference. Photoshop CS4 unequivocally demands at least a G5—it won't run at all on anything less. Although the G5 towers were powerhouses in their day, the multiple-core, Intel-based Macs now outpace them.

Windows. Photoshop CS4 requires a Pentium 4-class machine, but it's distinctly happier on an Intel Core 2 Duo or Intel Xeon. If you have a 64-bit machine and want to take advantage of more than 2 GB of RAM, Windows Vista 64 is highly recommended.

If you decide to switch from one platform to the other, you probably won't have to buy Photoshop all over again. Contact Adobe customer service—they should be able to transfer your Photoshop license to the other platform for a minimal fee.

PROCESSORS AND CORES

Photoshop loves a speedy central processing unit (CPU), particularly as you pile on the megapixels, layers, and Smart Objects. CPU makers used to boost performance by increasing the CPU speed in gigahertz (GHz), but started hitting a wall in terms of heat and power consumption. In recent years, CPU design has shifted from speeding up one processor core to including multiple processor cores in a single CPU. Now it's easier to find a computer with two 2 GHz cores than with one 4 GHz core.

Photoshop has recognized multiple processors for several versions now. However, it's important to understand that two 2 GHz cores are not exactly as fast as one 4 GHz core. Overhead is involved in splitting the workload across the cores, and it takes time to move data between the cores. Some operations aren't even practical to split across cores. Today's four-core and eight-core computers can in some cases process data faster than the memory bus can deliver more pixels to be processed, resulting in cores that wait for things to do. Multiple cores are beneficial when you have multiple applications that each require high CPU usage, or multiple processes that don't depend on each other, such as rendering video frames.

Multiple cores are most effective when doing a lot of processing on a relatively small data set. However, editing a Photoshop document usually involves moving high volumes of image data between the CPU, RAM, and disks, so the transfer speed between those components is a common bottleneck. To make the most of a multiple-core computer with Photoshop, you need enough RAM to minimize disk access. When disk access is inevitably required, you want disks that are fast enough to minimize delays in getting data to the RAM and CPU. If you're talking only about Photoshop, the speed gain of an eight-core computer versus a four-core computer is not necessarily proportional to the price difference between them. This could quickly change as motherboard designs and operating systems are updated. If you're trying to make a purchase decision, be suspicious of specs that quote CPU speed improvements alone without accounting for the other components. We advise you to research Photoshop-specific performance benchmarks for any computer you're thinking about buying.

64-BIT PROCESSING

Many people anticipate huge performance gains from the newer CPUs that can process 64 bits of data at a time, compared to the 32-bit CPUs that have been in use for years. Sounds twice as fast, right? Well, not automatically. To get the most out of a 64-bit CPU, you also need to have the following:

A 64-bit Operating System. For example, it isn't enough to have Windows Vista; you need the 64-bit version of Windows Vista. (Photoshop CS4 doesn't officially support 64-bit Windows XP.) On the Mac, it's a little more complicated. Mac OS X 10.5 is the first Mac operating system to have 64-bit support throughout the system, and Adobe had originally planned to make the Mac version of Photoshop CS4 support 64-bit operation. However, because Apple unexpectedly removed their 64-bit support for legacy (Carbon) applications, Adobe won't be able to provide a 64-bit Mac version of Photoshop until after CS4.

Well Over 4 GB of RAM. One of the biggest benefits of 64-bit computing is that Photoshop can directly use more than the roughly 3 GB of RAM that it can use under 32-bit computing. If this appeals to you, don't upgrade to just 4 GB or you won't see much difference. Aim for 8 GB to start, and go higher if your files are big enough to need it.

In 64-bit Windows Vista, the edition you use determines the maximum amount of RAM the system recognizes, ranging from the 8 GB supported by the Home Basic edition to the 128 GB limit of the Ultimate edition.

Really Big Files. The ability of a 64-bit processor to directly address much more RAM speeds up the processing of very large files. If you work with Photoshop files that are over 1 GB in size, you should see major performance gains from 64-bit Photoshop. But if you mainly make simple edits to 5-megapixel JPEG camera files without using many layers, masks, or Smart Objects, 64-bit Photoshop probably won't feel much faster.

Choosing 64-bit over 32-bit computing is like driving a 64-passenger bus instead of a 32-passenger bus. The 64-passenger bus can *potentially* move twice as many people in a single trip. But if you rarely carry that many people, the 64-passenger bus is no faster than the 32-passenger bus, and because it's bigger, it may actually cost you a bit more in overhead when it isn't being used to capacity. A 64-bit system can actually be slower than 32-bit when editing small files or when not much RAM is installed.

RAM

The old adage that you can never be too thin, too rich, or have too much RAM holds true for Photoshop CS4, just as it did for previous versions. Just how much RAM you need depends on your typical file sizes and work habits. We don't recommend even *trying* to run Photoshop on a system with less than 1 GB of RAM, and more, *much* more, is better. The absolute minimum amount of RAM for Photoshop CS4, according to Adobe, is 512 MB. That may be doable . . . but it'll feel like mopping a floor with a toothbrush. For editing digital camera photos, think of 2 GB of installed RAM as a baseline,

TIP: If you have a Mac with a 64-bit processor and have a legitimate need to run 64-bit Photoshop CS4 now, you could try running the Windows version of Photoshop CS4 in 64-bit Windows Vista under Boot Camp. Yes, we realize this isn't an ideal 64-bit solution for Mac users (like us).

TIP: If you have more than 1 GB of RAM installed, you may be able to enhance performance by installing the Bigger Tiles plug-in, which processes image data in larger chunks. The plug-in is inside the Optional Plug-Ins package on the Photoshop install disk. To install, remove the tilde (~) character from the file name and restart Photoshop.

4 GB as a workable amount, and much more than 4 GB if you want to edit very large files or take advantage of 64-bit Photoshop.

We used to have various rules about how much RAM is enough, but as Photoshop has added more features that use scratch-disk space, the old rules have largely gone out the window. The key idea is that Photoshop uses RAM as a cache for its scratch disk: If what it needs at any given moment is in its RAM cache, it can fetch it quicker. But unless you work only on small, flat files, at some point Photoshop will call on its scratch disk. Generally, the more megapixels, layers, Smart Objects, and Smart Filters you use, the more RAM you'll need.

32-Bit Hardware. Photoshop can use as much as 2 GB of RAM when running on a 32-bit system. However, if you have 2 GB of RAM installed, you won't want Photoshop to use all of it. Otherwise there won't be any RAM left for the system, causing it to use the virtual memory on disk, which is much slower. For this reason, you can use the Performance pane in the Preferences dialog to set an upper limit on how much RAM Photoshop is allowed to use (see "RAM Allocation" later in this chapter).

64-Bit Hardware. When running on 64-bit hardware with a 32-bit operating system, Photoshop CS4 can, in theory, directly use up to 3.5 GB of RAM (in practice it uses 3072 MB directly). If you're working on huge images, you may see benefits from even more RAM. When more than 4 GB of RAM is installed, Photoshop lets the operating system buffer scratch data into RAM instead of writing it directly to disk. We talk about 64-bit operating systems in "64-Bit Processing," earlier in this chapter.

Photoshop doesn't normally use those buffers because doing so can be slower than using a scratch file on disk; the way operating systems use virtual memory is not optimal for the way Photoshop needs to use virtual memory. But if you have enough RAM to hold most or all of your scratch data, it becomes faster to let Windows or Mac OS X use extra RAM above 4 GB as a cache for scratch data. As you add RAM to your computer, you should see corresponding improvements in performance up to about 8 GB, the point of diminishing returns. You have to be working with files large enough to make good use of all that RAM—if you're editing 300-by-200-pixel Web images with no layers, adding another 4 GB of RAM won't make Photoshop run any faster.

TIP: Some have asked if setting up a RAM disk as a scratch disk will make Photoshop run faster. There's no reason to do that, because as we explain on this page, Photoshop can work with your operating system to use the available RAM above 4 GB as if it was a RAM disk for scratch data.

NOTE: 64-bit Windows Vista won't see more than 4 GB of RAM unless your PC motherboard's chipset supports the x64 instruction set and at least 8 GB of RAM, and your BIOS must also support a feature called Memory Remapping.

A reliable way to figure whether you'll benefit from more RAM is to keep an eye on the Efficiency indicator while you work. To turn on the Efficiency indicator, click the third option from the left in the Status bar at the bottom of a document window and choose Efficiency from the Show submenu (see **Figure 1-1**). If the Efficiency reading drops below 100 percent, more RAM would help. (If you've already maxed out your machine with as much RAM as Photoshop can address, and your efficiency is still below 100 percent, see "Scratch Disk Space," later in this chapter.) If the Efficiency display always says 100 percent, you won't get any benefit from adding more RAM, but if you want to allocate 100 percent of the available RAM to Photoshop, it's best to install more than 5 GB of RAM.

Figure 1-1 To help monitor RAM usage, click the black triangle in the Status bar and choose Efficiency.

TIP: In Mac OS X 10.5, caching should work properly without having to use the VMBuffering plug-ins.

Virtual Memory Buffering Plug-Ins in Mac OS X. While Mac OS X lets Photoshop use your extra RAM as a fast cache if you have more than 4 GB of RAM installed, there is a catch. In Mac OS X 10.3 or 10.4, the caching behavior may cause Photoshop to pause for a few seconds, which can mess you up if you're painting, for example. For this reason, Adobe provides two plug-ins, ForceVMBuffering.plugin and DisableVMBuffering.plugin, that let you control whether OS X uses high RAM for direct caching. How do you decide which one to use? It comes down to whether you're more interested in responsive painting or quickly handling very large files. Use the following guidelines:

- If you have more than 4 GB of RAM and you use the ForceVMBuffering plug-in, Photoshop will be as fast as it can be with very large files, but you may experience pauses when painting.

- If you have more than 4 GB of RAM and you use the DisableVMBuffering plug-in, you shouldn't experience pauses when painting, but you won't see optimal Photoshop performance with very large files.

- If you have 4 GB of RAM or less installed, don't bother installing either plug-in, because you won't have the amount of RAM that brings the extra Mac OS X caching into play.

If you need these plug-ins, download them from the Adobe Web site. Go to www.adobe.com/support/downloads, click Photoshop-Macintosh, and look for Adobe Photoshop CS3 VM Buffering Optional Extensions. Installation instructions are in the ReadMe document.

RAM Allocation. Both Mac OS X and Windows XP automatically adjust the amount of RAM each application gets. Photoshop takes a certain amount of RAM when you start it, and if it needs more, the system hands it over. However, you *don't* want Photoshop to use all the RAM on your system—that starves the OS of the RAM it needs to run the machine, causing everything to slow down. The system will start using virtual memory on disk out of desperation.

In Mac OS X, use the Performance pane in the Preferences dialog to set an upper limit on how much RAM Photoshop uses (see **Figure 1-2**). The Performance pane suggests an ideal range of RAM for you to let Photoshop use. It also defaults to an amount of RAM that's a good starting point for most users under most conditions. If you have a large amount of RAM—3 GB or more—you can try increasing that percentage, but if you go too far, you'll hear the hard disk start to thrash whenever the operating system or another application needs to grab some RAM.

Mac OS X actually gives you an extra clue: When an application is waiting for the computer, you see the all-too-familiar spinning wristwatch cursor, but when the operating system is the one causing the delay, you see a spinning multicolored wheel, sometimes called the "Spinning Beach Ball." If you see the wheel in Mac OS X, or you hear the hard disk thrashing on either platform when you're working on an image that should fit into RAM, you may need to lower the memory allocation a little.

You can fine-tune your settings based upon your own system, the amount of installed RAM, and the way you use Photoshop. Depending upon the number of system processes and applications you typically run, you can try increasing the RAM allocation incrementally while checking the available unused RAM with a system utility. On the Mac, you can use Activity Monitor (built into OS X) to watch RAM usage. On Windows you can watch Performance Monitor, which is also built in. Because a 32-bit system

TIP: There is a common misconception that the presence of the Memory Usage preference means that Photoshop makes you allocate RAM manually. This is untrue. Photoshop automatically uses any RAM the system lets it have. The only function of the Memory Usage preference is to *limit* the maximum amount of RAM Photoshop uses, in case you need to leave more RAM free for the system and other applications you need to run at the same time.

TIP: If you get an "out of memory" alert, try choosing a command from the Edit > Purge submenu: Clipboard, Histories, Pattern, Undo, or All. If a Purge command is dimmed, it means that particular buffer is already empty, so there's nothing there to purge.

is limited to 2 GB of RAM, you must never allocate 100 percent of RAM to Photoshop on a 32-bit system—always leave a few hundred megabytes free to avoid starving the system. Even on a 64-bit system with well over 4 GB of RAM, Adobe recommends that you allocate just short of 100 percent (remember, on 64-bit hardware Photoshop can still use RAM above 4 GB as a fast cache).

Figure 1-2 Allocating RAM to Photoshop using the Memory Usage preference

On a computer with 2 GB of RAM, Photoshop sees all available RAM. Because the operating system needs part of that 2 GB to run, allocate 70 percent or less of available RAM.

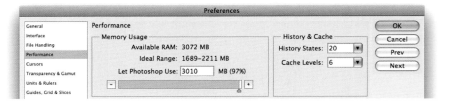

On a computer with 7 GB of RAM, 32-bit Photoshop sees 3 GB. Because 4 GB of additional RAM is available to the operating system, it's OK to set Photoshop to use almost 100 percent of 3 GB.

Note that a few Photoshop filters (Lens Flare, for instance) require that you have enough physical RAM to load the entire image into memory. Even though Photoshop has a virtual-memory scheme, if you don't have enough actual RAM to process the whole image, these effects just won't work.

Image Cache. The Cache Levels setting in the Memory and Image Cache panel of the Preferences dialog (see **Figure 1-3**) also has an impact on RAM usage. Increasing the Image Cache value speeds screen redrawing when you're working with larger files that contain a lot of layers. However, the Image Cache doesn't do much for small files. The default setting is 6 levels. If you routinely work with larger, multilayered files, try increasing the cache level to 8. If you work with smaller files, try reducing it.

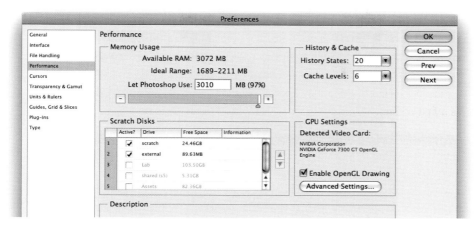

Figure 1-3 Preferences you can use to optimize performance for your computer

VIRTUAL MEMORY

Virtual memory is a programming trick that fools the computer into thinking it has more RAM than it really does. It works by reserving a specially marked amount of space on your hard drive that gets treated as RAM. The real, physical RAM is then used as a cache for the virtual memory stored on the disk. If the data that the computer is looking for is cached in RAM, your computer won't slow down, but if the computer has to go searching on the hard disk instead, things can slow down a lot.

Operating systems create one or more virtual memory *swap files* on your hard disk that serve as virtual memory to let multiple applications grab RAM as needed. On top of this, Photoshop has its own virtual memory scheme that it uses to let you do things that wouldn't fit in physical RAM, such as storing 1000 history states for a 300 MB image (which we don't actually recommend doing). To get optimum performance, you need to configure both the operating system's virtual memory scheme and the Photoshop scratch disk space so they play nicely together.

The Photoshop Scratch File and the Operating System Swap File. Both Windows and Mac OS X use the startup disk for the swap file unless you specified otherwise. On Windows XP, you can change the swap file setting by bringing up Properties for My Computer, selecting the Performance tab, clicking the Virtual Memory button, and selecting the Change option. This lets you specify maximum and minimum swap-file sizes and which drive gets used. On Windows Vista, it's under the Advanced tab.

TIP: We often slip into talking about virtual memory as if it always happens on the hard drive, but if you have more than 4 GB of RAM installed, remember that Photoshop may be using your unused RAM as a fast virtual memory buffer.

In Mac OS X, the procedure for pointing the swap file at a drive other than the startup disk is way more complex, so much so that it's crazy to try to move it when it's so much easier to move the Photoshop scratch disk setting instead (see "Scratch Disk Space" later in this chapter).

Photoshop performs much better if you assign the Photoshop scratch disk to a different physical mechanism than the operating system swap file, so a second hard drive is always desirable. This way, the same set of read-write heads doesn't scurry around like gerbils on espresso while trying to serve the dual demands of the operating system swap file and the Photoshop scratch space. If all you have is one single hard disk, you'll have to let Photoshop and the operating system fight it out. You can minimize conflicts by being careful with your Memory Usage preference setting.

TIP: Although the Photoshop scratch file preference is called Scratch Disk, you can assign the scratch file to any volume. A volume can be an entire disk, one partition of a disk, or a number of disks seen as one RAID. For performance reasons, don't set the Scratch Disk preference to a slow disk, removable media, or a volume on the network.

Setting Up Photoshop Scratch Disks. To tell Photoshop where to store its scratch data, open the Preferences dialog and in the Scratch Disks options, check the Active? check box for any volumes that you want to use for that purpose (see Figure 1-3). Photoshop starts with the volume at the top of the list. If the scratch data uses up the first scratch disk, Photoshop extends it into the checked scratch disks from top to bottom. To move a disk up or down in the list, click a disk to highlight it, and then click the arrows to the right of the list's scroll bar.

If you store the Photoshop scratch file on a disk where you want to store other files, it's best for the Photoshop scratch file to be in its own partition that contains no other files and does not contain the operating system swap file. If the Photoshop scratch file is mixed with other files, that volume may become fragmented and slow down Photoshop. A dedicated partition is much easier to maintain. If you need to defragment it, you can do so very easily simply by reinitializing the partition (erasing everything inside the partition)—you don't need to run a fancy disk optimizer.

Scratch Disk Space. The space you set aside for a scratch disk should at least equal the amount of RAM you've allocated to Photoshop, as it uses RAM as a cache for the scratch disk space. That means if you've given Photoshop 120 MB of RAM, you must also have 120 MB of free disk space. If you have less, Photoshop will use only an amount of RAM equivalent to the free space on the scratch disk. In practice, you'll likely need more and, if you work with layered, high-bit files or many history states, much more. A good scratch disk is large (many gigabytes) and fast.

Photoshop constantly optimizes the scratch space. If you consider constant disk access (often called *disk thrashing*) to be a warning that things are about to get very slow, you should learn to accept it as normal Photoshop behavior. People are often especially concerned when they see disk access immediately after opening a file. This, too, is normal: Photoshop is simply setting itself up to be more efficient down the line. Photoshop has a couple of ways to tell you how much of the scratch disk is involved.

In the lower left corner of the document window, there's a pop-up menu that shows, among other things, document size, scratch size, and efficiency (see **Figure 1-4**). If you set this to Scratch Sizes, the first number shows the amount of RAM being used by all open documents, and the second number shows the amount of RAM currently allocated to Photoshop. If the first number is bigger than the second, Photoshop is using virtual memory. When the indicator is set to Efficiency, a reading of less than 100 percent indicates that virtual memory is coming into play.

TIP: Any Status bar readout can also be displayed in the Info panel by changing the Info panel options. This is useful if the Status bar is hidden because you're in Full Screen mode.

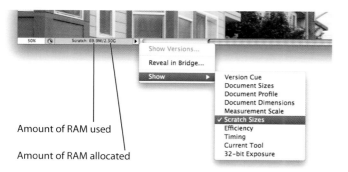

Amount of RAM used

Amount of RAM allocated

Figure 1-4 The Scratch Sizes indicator

RAID. Using a striped Redundant Array of Independent Disks (RAID) can be a very worthwhile way to set up a scratch disk, particularly if you often edit images that are too large for your available RAM. Photoshop can write to a RAID much faster than to a single disk, so your performance will improve. Opening and saving large files is also faster with a RAID. But if you have a choice between buying RAM and buying a fast hard drive, get more RAM first, unless opening and saving large files already constitutes a significant bottleneck in your workflow.

MONITORS AND VIDEO CARDS

TIP: There is a myth that if two different monitor brands have the same LCD panel in them, they'll perform identically. In reality, a panel's color performance can be significantly altered by how each company chooses to tune the backlight brightness range and the electronics driving the panel.

Liquid crystal display (LCD) monitors have essentially replaced bulky cathode ray tube (CRT) monitors in most studios. When you shop for a monitor for Photoshop use, the primary criterion is whether the monitor accurately reproduces a wide range of color after calibration. Unfortunately, you can't find that out by reading technical specifications such as contrast ratio and maximum brightness. Contrast ratios are not standardized among manufacturers and often don't take calibration into account. Maximum brightness is meaningless for photo editing, because what you are really interested in is whether the monitor can give you a good black level so that you can judge shadow detail. To do this, a monitor must reach the optimal brightness range for calibration, typically between 100 and 120 candelas per square meter (cd/m^2). But because monitor companies like to brag about brightness, some inexpensive LCD monitors can't be turned down that far!

TIP The new OpenGL support in Photoshop CS4 does *not* accelerate image processing or speed up image display. It makes image display smoother, and through the new display features, more interactive and convenient. The good news? If you don't have an OpenGL video card, you aren't missing out in terms of performance.

Because much of the information available about monitors is unreliable or irrelevant to Photoshop work (mostly written from the point of view of office work or gaming), the best way to shop for a Photoshop monitor is to get recommendations from photographers, prepress professionals, and online professional photography forums you trust.

Video Card. For pure two-dimensional (2D) image editing, you probably won't benefit from spending more money on the kind of high-end three-dimensional (3D) video card that makes gamers happy. The bottleneck in redrawing Photoshop images is almost never the video system—it's getting the image data out of RAM (or even worse, from disk) to the video system.

That said, Photoshop CS4 is the first version of Photoshop that can take advantage of a video card's graphics processing unit (GPU) for some display (not image-processing) operations. If you have the right video card, you'll see new, smoother panning and zooming options in Photoshop CS4, such as free rotation of the canvas. We cover these features in Chapter 6, "Essential Photoshop Tips and Tricks." To be able to use these new GPU-assisted features, aim for a video card that's compatible with OpenGL 2.0 and Shader Model 3.0 and has at least 128 MB of video RAM. The video cards in many recent computers easily surpass these specs, though some low-end models do not. It's a good idea to have at least 512 MB of video RAM if you'll be using large or multiple monitors, editing multiple large documents, or working in 3D.

Monitor Calibration and Profiling. If you want to be reasonably confident in what you see on screen (and we certainly are), good monitor calibration and profiling is essential. The free, eyeball-based, software-only monitor calibrators, such as the Apple Display Calibrator Assistant, are better than nothing, but unless you work in a cave, you'll find it's extremely difficult to get consistent results, because your eyes—and hence your "monitor calibration"—adapt to changing lighting conditions.

We believe that every serious Photoshop user would be better served by using a hardware color-calibration puck to measure the behavior of the monitor, along with its accompanying software, which will set the monitor to a known condition and write a monitor profile. There are several good, relatively inexpensive hardware-based monitor calibration packages available. We like the Eye-One Display from GretagMacbeth, BasICColor Display, or the DataColor Spyder. All of these can calibrate both CRT and LCD monitors, and any of them will do a better job of keeping your displays accurately profiled than any of the eyeball-based tools. We talk more about calibration and profiling in Chapter 4, "Color Settings."

While manufacture of high-end CRTs has essentially ceased, they still have their die-hard fans. If you're still trying to eke out another year of use from your beloved CRT, keep an eye on its brightness level when you recalibrate it. When a CRT's brightness level drops below 95 cd/m^2 after you set the black level, it's about time to start budgeting for a new LCD monitor.

Multiple-Monitor Support. Any Mac that supports multiple monitors can properly apply the specific color profile for each display, and therefore you should generate a separate profile for each display that you want to use for critical color evaluation. However, some Windows video cards that support multiple monitors report themselves to the operating system as a single device with which only one display profile can be associated. Before buying a video card to use with Photoshop in Windows, it's best to assume nothing and do plenty of research.

We don't have much experience with multiple-monitor Windows setups, but we do know that, aside from the profiling issue, they are nearly as easy to set up in Windows as they are on the Mac. If your Windows video card doesn't support separate profiles for each monitor connected to it, you can at least display the Photoshop document window on your best, profiled monitor and arrange your Photoshop panels on another monitor.

TIP: Looking for Adobe Gamma calibration software? Starting with Photoshop CS3, Adobe Gamma is no longer included (or recommended). If you still have an old copy of Adobe Gamma, avoid using it, especially on an LCD monitor. Get a hardware calibrator instead.

Notebook Displays. Displays on notebook computers lag behind desktop monitors in quality, because notebook displays need to be thin, light, and low-power. If your only Photoshop computer is a notebook, consider connecting a good external monitor when you're at your desk. An external monitor port is built into many notebooks, and you'll love the extra work area. If you must use the notebook's built-in display to evaluate color—for example, on a photo shoot in the field—it's especially critical that you create a monitor profile for it using a hardware calibrator. That still won't make a notebook display as good as a desktop monitor, but at least it will be as accurate as it's ever going to be.

Some newer LED-backlit LCD notebook monitors, such as the display on the Apple MacBook Pro, are capable of a wider color gamut than the older, more common LCD notebook monitors that use fluorescent backlights. However, as we write this, even a calibrated LED-backlit notebook monitor can't match the performance of a calibrated high-quality desktop monitor.

CHAPTER TWO

Image Essentials

Computers know nothing about images, or tone, color, truth, beauty, or art. They're just very complicated adding machines that crunch numbers. Every piece of data we store on a computer consists of numbers. All the commands we send to the computer are translated into numbers. Even this text we wrote is made up of numbers.

Fortunately, you don't have to learn hexadecimal or binary math to use Photoshop—we authors are living, math-challenged proof of that. But if you want to put Photoshop under your control, rather than flailing around and occasionally getting good results by happy accident, you do need to understand the basic concepts that Adobe Photoshop and other image editors use to represent photographs using numbers.

We'll try to keep it simple. If you want to avoid heavily pixelated output and wildly unpredictable color shifts, you will want to understand the essential lessons in this chapter.

Pixels and Paths

When you get down to the nitty-gritty, there are essentially two ways to make computers display pictures. In Photoshop terminology, the distinction is between pixels and paths. Other terms you may hear are *raster* (rasters are rows or lines, not reggae artists) and *vector* (see **Figure 2-1**). We call the stuff made up of pixels *images* and the stuff made of vectors *artwork*.

Pixel-Based Images. Digital images are simply collections of pixels laid out in a big grid. No matter what the picture is—whether it's a modernist painting of a giraffe or a photograph of your mother—it's always described using rows of pixels. This is the only way to represent the fine natural details and subtle gradations of photorealistic images. If a graphic came from a capture device (such as a digital still or video camera, or a scanner), or a painting or image-editing program (such as Photoshop), chances are it's an image made up of pixels.

Vector Artwork. Vector artwork, also known as *object-oriented graphics*, describes graphics using instructions instead of rows of dots. Vector graphics just say, "Draw a rectangle this big and put it here." This is a more efficient and space-saving method for describing certain simple types of graphics, such as lines, hard-edged curves, and text. Vector graphics can have a variety of attributes—line weight, type formatting, fill color, graduated fills, and so on—but subtle details can be difficult to render.

Vector graphics primarily come from drawing programs such as Adobe Illustrator and computer-aided design (CAD) programs. You might also get vector artwork from other programs, such as a program that makes graphs.

Figure 2-1 The individual pixels of an image become increasingly visible as you enlarge the graphic. Vector-based artwork maintains smooth lines at any size.

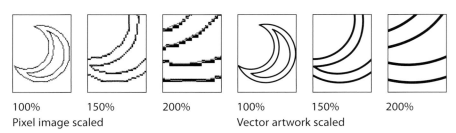

100%   150%   200%   100%   150%   200%
Pixel image scaled   Vector artwork scaled

Crossing the Line. Neither pixel images nor vector graphics are best for everything, so many applications are centered around editing one type of graphic while letting you include the other. For example, Photoshop is all about editing pixels but includes a pen tool, shape layers, and type layers that let you draw vector graphics and editable text and store them as part of a Photoshop document. Similarly, although the tools in Illustrator, Adobe Flash, and the Adobe InDesign page layout program are all vector-based, all let you include images in documents, such as photographs from Photoshop.

Once you've experienced the creative convenience of combining pixel-based images and vector-based artwork and text, you need a universal format that can store both types. Although anything you can create in Photoshop can be stored in the Photoshop file format (PSD), not all programs can read Photoshop files. With the Adobe Portable Document Format (PDF), you can store both images and artwork in one file that can be exchanged easily among programs and platforms. Photoshop can save a Photoshop PDF file, which can store all the features of a Photoshop image while also preserving vector artwork and text and is readable by many other programs.

Words, Words, Words

While terminology might not keep you up at night, we in the writin' business have to worry about things as simple as the meaning of the term *bitmap*.

Photoshop uses the term *bitmap* to refer to images containing only black and white (no grays, no colors). But in general use around the industry, bitmap often means any image that's made up of pixels. In this book, we've settled on calling documents that comprise pixels *images*, and calling documents that comprise vectors *artwork*.

Pixels and Images

To use Photoshop effectively, you need to understand the basic attributes of pixel-based images: dimension, bit depth, and color model (which Photoshop refers to as *image mode*).

Dimension

Pixel-based images are rectangular grids made up of little squares, like floor tiles; those little squares are individual pixels (see **Figure 2-2**). The dimensions of the pixel grid (*pixel dimensions*) refer to the number of pixels along its width and height. The grid of pixels that makes up your computer screen might be 1680 by 1050 pixels, while an image reduced for display on a Web page may be 600 by 400 pixels.

Figure 2-2 The grid of squares that makes up an image. The nonprinting pixel grid lines are visible in Photoshop CS4 when you zoom in over 500 percent.

TIP: A Photoshop document has a maximum size of 300,000 by 300,000 pixels. You may not be able to buy a camera that makes an image that large. It's more likely that you'd hit that limit by using the Auto-Align feature to stitch very large images out of many small ones.

The original pixel dimensions of an image are determined by the capabilities of the sensor in the digital camera or scanner that you use to create the image. For example, a 10-megapixel digital camera may produce an image that's 3888 by 2592 pixels. The more pixels there are in an image, the more disk space it uses, and the more processing time it needs.

Pixel dimensions aren't the same as resolution. You can't actually know the resolution (pixels per inch) of your 3888-by-2592-pixel image until you declare how large you're printing it. We'll talk about this more in "Resolution," later in this chapter.

Bit Depth

Bit depth tells Photoshop how many shades or colors the image can contain. For example, in a 1-bit image (one in which each pixel is represented by 1 bit of information—either a 1 or a 0) each pixel is either on or off, which usually means it's black or white. (Of course, if you printed with red ink on blue paper, the pixels would be either red or blue.)

With 2 bits per pixel, there are four possible combinations (00, 01, 10, and 11), hence four possible values and four possible colors or gray levels (see **Figure 2-3**). Eight bits of information give you 256 possible values; in 8-bit/channel RGB images, each pixel actually has three 8-bit values—one each for red, green, and blue—for a total of 24 bits per pixel. (In 8-bit/channel CMYK [cyan, magenta, yellow, and black] there are four channels rather than three, so a CMYK pixel takes 32 bits to describe.)

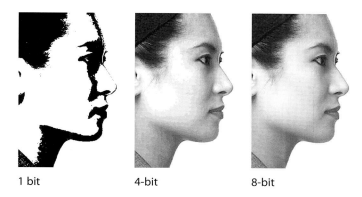

1 bit   4-bit   8-bit

Figure 2-3 Bit depth

In Photoshop, you can work with bit depths up to 32 floating-point bits per channel in HDR (High Dynamic Range) mode. Most image editing is done at 8 bits per channel (24-bit RGB and 32-bit CMYK), while some high-end photographers have 16 bit/channel (48-bit RGB) workflows.

How many bits are enough? A bit depth of 8 bits per channel provides 16.7 million possible RGB color definitions, which is much more than the number of unique colors the human eye can distinguish, and certainly much more than the number of unique colors we can print.

Why capture many more colors than we can print, or even see? The simple answer is that the larger number of bits gives us more editing flexibility. As you'll see in Chapter 7, "Image Adjustment Fundamentals," every edit opens up gaps between some adjacent pixel values and smooshes others together, reducing the total number of shades.

Image Mode

Pixel dimensions and bit depth each tell part of the story, but the third essential attribute of images, the *image mode*, is the one that dictates whether all those numbers represent either shades of gray or colors, and how many.

In general, the numbers that describe pixels relate to tonal values, with lower numbers representing darker tones and higher ones representing brighter tones. In an 8 bit/channel grayscale image (256 levels per channel), 0 represents solid black, 255 represents pure white, and the intermediate numbers represent intermediate shades of gray.

In the color image modes, the numbers represent shades of a primary color rather than shades of gray. So an RGB image is actually made up of three grayscale channels: one representing red values, one representing green values, and one representing blue values (see **Figure 2-4**). A CMYK image has four grayscale channels: one each for cyan, magenta, yellow, and black.

Figure 2-4 Color images (like the one in the top-left corner) can be described with RGB data (top) or CMYK data (bottom). Note that for press reproduction, the red, green, and blue channels in this figure had to be simulated using cyan, magenta, and yellow press inks.

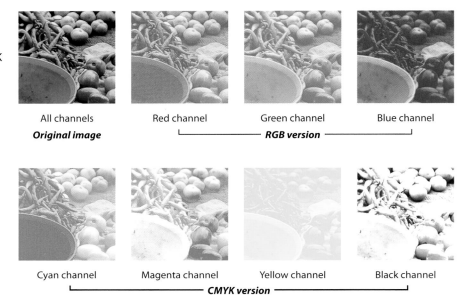

All channels
Original image

Red channel   Green channel   Blue channel
└──────────────── ***RGB version*** ────────────────┘

Cyan channel   Magenta channel   Yellow channel   Black channel
└──────────────── ***CMYK version*** ────────────────┘

Indexed Color mode is an exception—its colors are not built using channels. In Indexed Color mode, each value represents a color from a *lookup table*, a list of up to 256 colors actually used in the image. Many Photoshop features don't work in Indexed Color mode because of the arbitrary nature and limited number of colors available in the lookup table. For example, you can't easily make a color area more blue, because the blue shades you want may not exist in the lookup table. Indexed color images have become much less common because indexed-color GIF files are increasingly being replaced by 24-bit JPEG and PNG images.

RESOLUTION

Resolution is one of the most widely used and yet least understood words in desktop publishing. People use it when they talk about scanners and printers, images and monitors, and halftones. Then they wonder why they're confused. Fortunately, it isn't that hard to sort out all of the different meanings of resolution.

An image in its pure digital state has no physical size—it's just a bunch of pixels without any real-world measurement attached to them. Resolution answers the question "How small are the tiny squares that make up this picture?" Once you bring an image into the physical world, the number of pixels across the width and height take up a specific amount of physical space in print or on screen, and that determines the resolution.

The resolution of an image is the number of pixels per unit of measurement—usually the number of pixels per inch (ppi) or pixels per centimeter (ppcm). If your image is 72 pixels wide and you tell it to be 72 pixels per inch, then it's an inch wide. If you print it at half the size, you'll still have the same number of pixels, but they'll be crammed into half the space, so each inch will contain 144 pixels, or 144 ppi (see **Figure 2-5**). Print it at 300 percent of the original size, and the resolution goes down to 24 ppi.

TIP: This scaling example assumes that the image is not resampled—that the number of pixels remains the same. We talk about the effect of resampling later in this chapter.

Figure 2-5 Scaling and resolution

50 percent
(144 ppi)

Original (72 ppi)

300 percent (24 ppi)

You can look at resolution in another way: If you know an image's size and resolution, you can figure out its dimensions. When you scan a picture that is 3 inches on each side at 100 pixels per inch, you know that the image has 300 pixels on each side (100 per inch). If you then scan it at 300 pixels per inch, the dimensions shoot up to 900 pixels on each side.

How Resolution Changes During Production

One source of confusion is that people often lock onto a single resolution value, like "300 dpi," and assume that something's wrong if they don't see that value from start to finish, but that's not how it is. It's useful to think of resolution at various stages of production: sampling resolution, document resolution, effective resolution, and device resolution (see **Figure 2-6**).

Sampling Resolution. If you're using a scanner, sampling resolution describes how precisely an image was scanned, in samples per inch (spi). You set the sampling resolution in your scanning software. For digital still and video cameras, "samples per inch" is meaningless—if your camera takes images that are 4256 pixels wide by 2832 pixels tall (12 megapixels), a landscape photo 3 miles wide will produce the same 4256-by-2832-pixel frame as a close-up of a 3-inch-wide flower.

Document Resolution. When you save an image from software such as Photoshop, the resolution value saved into the file is its *document resolution*. Changing this value doesn't change the image quality unless the image is resampled at the same time (see "Resampling" later in this chapter). When you don't resample, a 4256 by 2832 pixel image still has 4256 by 2832 pixels, whether you set it to 72 ppi or 300 ppi, because the total number of pixels in the image doesn't change. Does this mean that file resolution isn't important? Not until you start thinking about final output, and at that point it does matter.

Effective Resolution. When you place one document inside another and resize the first document, its pixels may be stretched or compressed. This is its *effective resolution*—the resolution of the image after it's been scaled to its final print size. The document resolution inside the file still exists, but the new size changes the density of the pixels.

Device Resolution. Device resolution is the resolution of the final output device. For example, a monitor might have a device resolution of 100 ppi, and a platemaker might be 2400 dpi. This kind of resolution is not stored in the file; in fact, it hardly has anything to do with the file at all.

In printing, the effective resolution of an image typically doesn't need to be as high as the device resolution. For example, while an inkjet printer might print at 5760 dpi, the optimum image resolution for printing photographic images might be 360 ppi, because printers mix very tiny dots to build larger

TIP: When you open a digital camera file in Photoshop, it may report a specific resolution, such as 72 ppi, but bear in mind that this may be an arbitrary value that the camera wrote into the image's resolution field just to have a number in there.

TIP: In Photoshop, effective resolution comes into play when you resize a Smart Object. In Adobe InDesign, resizing a placed image changes its effective resolution, and you can view this in the InDesign Info panel.

groupings that form tones and colors. Inkjet printers mix device-resolution ink dots to build areas of color. Printing presses use device-resolution ink dots to build halftone cells; the 2400 dpi dots on such a device may be grouped into halftone cells at 150 lines per inch (lpi), for example.

When you create images for the Web, you don't know the final device resolution. Someone might view your Web page on a 20-inch desktop monitor at 1680 by 1050 pixels, while another might have a 15-inch desktop monitor at 1024 by 768. There's only one measurement you can rely on: the image dimensions in pixels, such as 600 by 400 pixels.

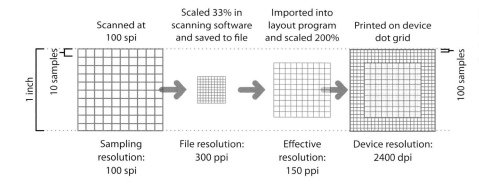

Scanned at 100 spi

Scaled 33% in scanning software and saved to file

Imported into layout program and scaled 200%

Printed on device dot grid

1 inch

10 samples

100 samples

Sampling resolution: 100 spi

File resolution: 300 ppi

Effective resolution: 150 ppi

Device resolution: 2400 dpi

Figure 2-6. How the meaning of resolution changes as you move an image from capture to output

Dot's Not Quite What I Meant

When we talk about the bits of an image, we call them *pixels*, *samples*, or *dots*, and we feel that all three terms are necessary for clarity.

The term *samples* comes from what a scanner or digital camera does: It samples an image—checking what color it finds—at each photo receptor on the sensor. The term *pixel* is a contraction that specifies the most basic *picture element* in an image. Most of the time, we'll talk about images in *pixels per inch* (ppi), which is also how Photoshop labels resolution readouts in its documents.

We reserve the term *dots per inch* for use when speaking of printed output, because pixels per inch do not necessarily equal dots per inch (see Figure 2-6). For example, it is very common to print an 8-by-10-inch image with a document resolution of 300 ppi to a platemaker operating at 2400 dpi. When you print that 8-by-10-inch image, 300 ppi is the document resolution, and at the exact same moment, 2400 dpi is its output resolution.

How Much Resolution Is Enough?

When it comes to image resolution, bigger isn't necessarily better. The higher the resolution of an image, the longer it takes to open, edit, save, or print. If your output requires only 300 dpi images but you use 1200 dpi photographs in a document just because you can, chances are you're going to wait longer at every step of your workflow and your hard disks will fill up much faster.

But smaller isn't necessarily better. If your image resolution is too low, your image will look pixelated (see Figure 2-5): You'll start seeing the pixels themselves, or adverse effects from excessively large pixels. Loss of detail and mottling are the two worst offenders in this category.

Maybe you thought you could save time by reducing your images to 150 ppi. But if the client rejects the job because the image is too pixelated, any savings are more than wiped out. So if bigger isn't better, and too small is even worse, how much is enough? How much image data do you need? The first consideration is image mode: The requirements are very different for line art than for grayscale and color.

Press Halftones

TIP: If a lot of this halftone talk is going over your head, we recommend a book that David and Conrad coauthored with Steve Roth and Glenn Fleishman called *Real World Scanning and Halftones,* 3rd Edition.

In general, when printing grayscale and color images to halftoning devices such as platesetters, image resolution should be no more than twice the screen frequency of the halftones. For instance, if you're printing a halftone image at 133 lpi, the image resolution doesn't need to be higher than 266 ppi (see **Figures 2-7** and **2-8**). Under some well-controlled printing conditions and high-quality substrates, it may be possible to see the difference between 2 and 2.5 times the screen frequency, but it will be difficult. When you output an image resolution that's more than 2.5 times the screen frequency to a PostScript-language output device, you're basically wasting data: Due to the unnecessary resolution, your images will take more disk space to store and back up, more time to process during editing and production, and more time to transmit across the network or to your printer. Because of this, Photoshop warns you when you try to output an image that's unusually large.

2:1 sampling ratio, 266 ppi

1.5:1 sampling ratio, 200 ppi

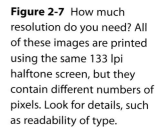

Figure 2-7 How much resolution do you need? All of these images are printed using the same 133 lpi halftone screen, but they contain different numbers of pixels. Look for details, such as readability of type.

1.2:1 sampling ratio, 160 ppi

1:1 sampling ratio, 133 ppi

Desktop Printers

Many inkjet and laser printers don't use halftone dots. Instead, they lay down dots using a technique called error diffusion. (See Chapter 12, "Image Storage and Output," for more on the differences between halftone and diffusion dithers.) These printers use device-resolution dots to build larger areas of color. Many inkjet printers today exceed resolutions of 4000 or 5000 dots per inch, and there is no reason to send those printers an image at half or ever a quarter of that resolution, with the possible exception of line art.

Most of the time we print at between 240 and 360 ppi, depending on the print size and the degree of detail in the image. We've gotten good results in the range between 180 ppi for very large prints and 480 ppi for small prints.

Line Art

For bilevel (black-and-white, 1-bit, bitmap-mode) images, the resolution never needs to be higher than that of the printer you're using. This is one situation where image pixels per inch equate to printer dots per inch. If you're printing to a 600 dpi desktop laser printer, there's no reason to have more than 600 pixels per inch in your image (the printer can output only

TIP: For more about the resolution and appearance of line-art images, see Chapter 11, "Essential Image Techniques."

600 dots per inch, so any extras just get thrown away). However, when you print to a 2400 dpi platesetter, that 600 ppi image will appear jagged.

If you're printing line art on press, plan on using an image resolution of *at least* 800 ppi—preferably 1000 ppi or more. Lower resolutions often show jaggies and broken lines. On newsprint or very porous paper, you may get away with a lower resolution, such as 400 or 600 ppi, because the jaggies will disappear with the spreading ink. But unless you have considerable experience with the print process at hand, you can't tell until the job has run, so err on the side of caution.

Figure 2-8 Resolution of line art

144 ppi   300 ppi   800 ppi   1200 ppi

Tuning Resolution for Printing Conditions

Whether you're printing on a press or a desktop printer, guidelines for proper resolution often assume high-quality printing conditions. When you're working out the correct resolution for a print job, take into account your printing process and paper stock. For example, when we say that for a press, you should aim for an effective resolution of around 2 to 2.5 times the halftone screen frequency, you may be able to use a lower multiplier if you're printing on a paper stock with high dot gain (where the ink spreads out), such as newsprint. Similarly, while 360 ppi might be appropriate for exhibition-quality glossy inkjet prints, you can try 240 ppi or less if you're printing on inexpensive matte paper. It all comes down to how well the medium can reproduce details.

Content also comes into play. Most pictures of people look fine at resolutions below the guideline, but if an image has fine details, such as tree branches or fine diagonal or curved lines, it might do best at or above the guideline.

Ultimately, there is no absolute index for quality; the final judge of quality is the client. For critical prepress jobs, plan to prepare Kodak Approval or other high-quality, dot-based proofs of different images using a range of resolutions to test where the quality trade-off works for the client.

Web and Video

It's generally misleading to think in terms of resolution when you prepare images for use on screen. All that really matters are the pixel dimensions, such as setting an image to 600 by 400 pixels. The dots-per-inch value varies depending on each individual monitor, so you can't rely on dpi when sizing for the screen. For example, you can find a 1280-by-900 pixel display on both 13-inch and 15-inch notebook computers, so the dpi value will be different on each display because the same number of pixels covers a different area. In addition, resolution can also change if you change the display settings of a monitor. For these reasons, the old advice that Mac monitors are 72 dpi and Windows monitors are 96 dpi became an obsolete myth a long time ago. Because digital cameras and scanners can produce far more pixels than you need on screen, you typically need to downsample an image before using it on a Web page or other video-based output. (We discuss this in more detail in the next section.)

USING THE IMAGE SIZE DIALOG

The Image Size dialog is always a big source of confusion, because the results you get depend not only on which buttons you click and which fields you type numbers into, but also on the order in which you do so. The Image Size dialog is split into the two sets of numbers that determine an image's resolution: its pixel dimensions, and its size if it's printed.

Pixel Dimensions. The best way to specify an image's size is by its pixel dimensions—these tell you exactly how much data you have to work with. The Pixel Dimensions section shows you both the dimensions and the file's size, in megabytes (or kilobytes, if it's under 1 MB).

Document Size. A bitmapped image has no inherent size; it's just pixels on a grid. The Document Size section lets you state a size and resolution, so that when you import the file into some other program, it knows what the image's size will be when it's printed.

The Resample Image check box affects resizing in a fundamental way. When you turn this option on, Photoshop lets you change the image's pixel dimensions; when it's off, the pixel dimensions are locked. Leave Resample Image off if you don't want to increase (upsample) or decrease (downsample) the number of pixels that make up the image. The Resample Image pop-up menu at the bottom of the dialog becomes available when Resample Image is checked. For more information about how these options affect an image, see "Resampling," later in this chapter.

Setting Size Options in the Right Sequence

One point of potential confusion is that whenever you make a change to one field in the Image Size dialog, some fields change and others don't. Sometimes editing a value wipes out another value you entered earlier! Without an understanding of how the Image Size options interact, you can sometimes feel like a frustrated safecracker. There actually is logic behind it; here's our quick cheat sheet to getting what you want (see **Figure 2-9**):

- To lock down the current file size and the current number of pixels in the image, turn off Resample Image. Now edit the Document Size as needed. When Resample Image is off, changing either Resolution or Width and Height always changes the other option so that the file size and total number of pixels remain constant.

- To "up-res" (upsample) for large-format prints, turn on Resample Image and choose Bicubic Smoother from the Resample Image pop-up menu. Then enter the Document Size and Resolution appropriate for the print size and printer you're using. Don't touch Pixel Dimensions.

- To resize an image for print while locking down the current resolution, turn on Resample Image and pick an appropriate option from the Resample Image pop-up menu. Then change the Document Size Height and Width as needed. Don't change anything else.

- To resample an image for the Web or video, turn on Resample Image and pick an appropriate option from the Resample Image pop-up menu. Now enter the Pixel Dimensions required by your project, but don't touch anything else. We mean it—editing anything in the Document Size section will screw up the Pixel Dimensions values.

TIP: When using the Image Size dialog for straight photographic editing, you'll almost always want the Constrain Proportions option to be on. Scale Styles comes into play only if you've applied something from the Style panel; otherwise Scale Styles has no effect.

With Resample Image turned off, the image's Resolution and Document Size (physical dimensions) are interdependent, while the pixel dimensions, file size, and details in the image don't change.

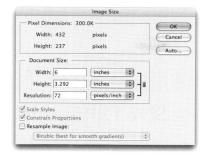

Figure 2-9 How the Image Size dialog works

With the units pop-up menu set to "percent," the Width and Height represent the scaling (200 percent) relative to the original (100 percent) physical dimensions. The resolution drops because the Resample Image check box is off, so the same number of pixels will cover more ground, causing each pixel to become larger.

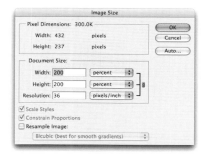

Turning on Resample Image lets you change the number of pixels in the image, so the Pixel Dimensions become editable. In addition, this allows Resolution to be adjusted independently from Width and Height in the Document Size section. This also guarantees that the file size will change, so watch the file size display at the top of the dialog.

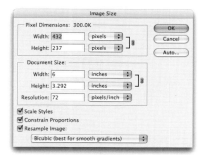

With Resample Image on, changing any attribute alters the pixel dimensions and the file size. The more you increase (or decrease) the pixel dimensions, the more pixels are made up (or discarded), altering the details in the image.

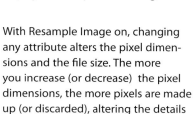
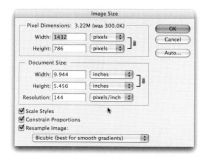

Scaling by Percentage

The word *percent* appears in both the Pixel Dimensions and the Document Size pop-up menus. Percent isn't an absolute size; it's based on the current size of the image you're working on. For example, if you have a 2-by-2-inch image and you type in "200 percent" for Document Size Width and Height, the result will be a 4-by-4-inch image. The resulting number of pixels in the image depends on whether Resample Image is on or off.

We find this especially helpful when we have to re-create an image that was scaled "for position only" in a layout program. First we write down the scaling values on a piece of paper, and then we open the image in Photoshop and type the percentages into the Image Size dialog.

The best way to learn how the Image Size dialog works, though, is to open an image, note the starting values, and play around with it. So get going!

RESAMPLING

One of the most important issues in working with images—and, unfortunately, one which few people seem to understand—is how the resolution can change relative to (or independently of) the physical size of your image.

TIP: If you're trying to use the Image Size dialog to both scale by percentage and resample to a different resolution, you may find it easier to do these two steps separately: First apply the percentage scaling, click OK, then open Image Size again and resample.

There are two ways you can change resolution: scaling and resampling. Figure 2-5 is an example of simple scaling—it doesn't change the pixel dimensions, just the resolution. On the other hand, resampling changes the pixel dimensions, as shown in **Figure 2-10**.

Photoshop gives you both options. If you scale an image down without changing the resolution, Photoshop has to throw away a bunch of pixels; that's called *downsampling*. If you double the size to 4 by 4 inches by *upsampling*, the program has to add more pixels by *interpolating* between the other pixels in the image.

Upsampling vs. Downsampling

We used to avoid upsampling when our images mostly came from scanned film, but in the digital age there is no longer a hard-and-fast rule. Digital captures have no film grain, and excellent noise-reduction software is available, which makes digital camera images more amenable to upsampling

Communicating Image Size

There are different ways of talking about the same essential concept: *how much information* the file contains. Here's a quick rundown of your options.

Pixel Dimensions. As we've mentioned, pixel dimensions are the width and height of an image in pixels. It's the standard measurement for Web and video. It's also a useful indicator of what physical sizes are possible. For example, an image from a 6-megapixel camera may be 2048 by 3076 pixels. What does that tell you? With experience, you'd know that the file size, at 8 bits per channel, is 18 MB, and that at 225 ppi you could print a full-bleed letter-size page. Later in this chapter, we discuss ways you can figure all this out for yourself.

Physical Dimensions and Resolution. A wordier but less ambiguous way to discuss resolution is to cite physical dimensions and resolution. For example, you might say a file is 4 by 5 inches at 225 ppi. This makes the most sense to someone doing page layout, because he or she will typically be concerned with the amount of detail that will end up on the printed page.

File Size. A third way to discuss resolution is by the file's size on disk. You can quickly get a sense of the content difference between two files when we tell you that the first is 900 KB and the second is 12 MB. While many digital veterans think only in terms of file size, there is some ambiguity in this measurement. How many pixels are in an 18 MB file? It depends . . . on whether the file is RGB or CMYK, 8 or 16 bits per channel, flattened or layered, TIFF or JPEG, compressed or not. Changing any of these variables could radically change the file size. When someone specifies a file size, such as 18 MB, be sure to ask for the rest of the specs: Do they want an 18 MB *flattened 8-bit RGB TIFF* file?

Megapixels. Digital cameras (or more precisely, their sensors) are rated in megapixels, which is the total number of pixels you get by multiplying the number of pixels on each side of the image. For example, if a camera produces files that are 4256 by 2832 pixels, multiplying 4256 by 2832 equals 12,052,992 pixels. That works out to 12 megapixels, because "mega" means *million* here.

Single-Side Dimension. People who work with continuous-tone film recorders, such as those used to transfer digitally edited footage back to movie film, talk about resolution in terms of the dimension of one side—typically the width—of the image. For instance, they might ask for "a 4 K file," or exactly 4096 pixels across, since in this case K means 1024 pixels. The other dimension is typically determined by the aspect ratio of the film.

Res. More commonly used in Europe when discussing capture resolution on drum scanners, *res* is the number of pixels per millimeter. For example, a file scanned at res 12 is scanned at 12 sample points (pixels) per millimeter, or 120 sample points per centimeter. That's about 304.8 sample points per inch.

than film scans ever were. We often upsample digital camera captures by 200 percent, and sometimes more. Upsampling never adds details that weren't there in the capture, so when possible it's still better to have enough pixels for the job in the first place.

Figure 2-10 Upsampling creates more resolution but can't create more detail or sharpness. Resampling from the high-quality original image always works best.

| 72-by-72 pixel Web site image printed at 1 by 1 inch (72 ppi) | Web image scaled up 300 percent, resampling off (24 ppi) | Web image scaled up 300 percent, resampling on (266 ppi) | Upsampled from original 8-megapixel camera file (266 ppi) |

Downsampling is simpler, because it just throws away data in a more or less intelligent manner. In fact, it's a common and necessary practice: Today's digital cameras can record more pixels than you'd need for an image that's less than a full page in size, or for a Web page. We downsample to the optimal resolution before printing to save processing time and storage space.

Resampling methods. Photoshop offers five resampling methods. You choose one in the General pane of the Preferences dialog or in the Image Size dialog (see **Figure 2-11**). The resampling method you choose in the Preferences dialog affects when you resample outside the Image Size dialog, such as when you use the Free Transform tool. Each method has its strengths and weaknesses, and we use each of them in different situations.

- Nearest Neighbor is the most basic, and it's very fast: To create a new pixel, Photoshop simply looks at the pixel next to it and copies its value. Unfortunately, the results are usually lousy for photographic content. Nearest Neighbor works best when the image has hard, straight edges and when you only want to make the existing pixels look bigger.

- Bilinear is more complex and produces better quality: The program sets the color or gray value of each pixel according to the pixels surrounding it. Some pictures can be upsampled pretty well with bilinear interpolation, but one of the bicubic options usually looks better.

- Bicubic creates better effects than Nearest Neighbor or Bilinear. Like Bilinear, it looks at surrounding pixels, but its equation is much more complex and calculation-intensive, producing smoother gradations.

Bitmaps and File Size

Big files take a long time to open, edit, print, or save. Many people who complain about how slow editing is in Photoshop are simply working with files much bigger than they need. Save yourself the complaining and minimize your file size when you can. Here's a quick rundown of how each attribute of a pixel-based image affects file size.

Dimensions and Resolution. When you increase the number of pixels, you increase the file's size by the square of the value. So if you double the resolution, you quadruple the file size (double the height multiplied by double the width). There can easily be a multimegabyte difference between a 300 ppi image and a 225 ppi image. (And remember that a 225 ppi image is almost always plenty of resolution for a 150 lpi halftone screen.)

Bit Depth. Increasing bit depth increases file size by a simple multiplier. Therefore, a 24-bit image is three times as large as an 8-bit image, and 24 times as large as a 1-bit image.

Image Mode. Changing the image mode can increase file size when the new image mode uses more bits, more channels, or both. For example, going from RGB to CMYK mode adds a fourth 8-bit channel.

Now that you know the main factors that affect the size of images, you can calculate file size using the following formula:

File size in kilobytes = $Resolution^2 \times Width \times Height \times Bits\ per\ sample \div 8192$

For example, if you have a 4-by-5-inch, 1-bit image at 300 ppi, you know that the file size is 220 KB ($300^2 \times 4 \times 5 \times 1 \div 8192$). A 24-bit image of the same size would be 5273 KB (just about 5 MB). This formula works because 8192 is the number of bits in a kilobyte.

Other Features. Of course, that formula applies only to flattened files. When you start adding layers, layer masks, and alpha channels, it becomes quite difficult to figure file size. Each channel or mask adds another 8 or 16 bits to the bit depth (depending on whether the document was in 8-bit/channel or 16-bit/channel mode). Layers are much harder to figure because Photoshop divides each layer into tiles. Empty tiles take up almost no space, but if a tile contains just one pixel, it takes up the same amount of space as a tile that's full of pixels.

Compression. If the file is saved in a compressed format, its file size will be smaller than indicated by the formula above. It's important to bear in mind that the file size that Photoshop reports in the Info panel or status bar is always the amount of RAM that the uncompressed, flattened image will occupy. We'll discuss compression options and file formats in much greater detail in Chapter 12, "Image Storage and Output."

TIP: You don't have to figure out file size by solving a formula. Instead, let the computer do it for you. The New Document and Image Size dialogs are very handy calculators for figuring dimensions, resolution, and file size. Simply type in the values you want, and the top of the Image Size dialog shows you how big the file will be (see Figure 2-9).

- Bicubic Smoother is specifically designed for upsampling. As its name suggests, it gives a smoother result that handles subsequent sharpening better than the Bicubic sampling method does.

- Bicubic Sharper is designed for downsampling. It does a better job of preserving detail than the Bicubic method does.

The differences between these resampling methods are often subtle. As a starting point, use Bicubic Smoother for upsampling (but don't expect miracles) and Bicubic Sharper for downsampling, but always test different resampling options when working with critical images.

Figure 2-11 Where to find resampling (interpolation) methods in Photoshop

In the General pane of the Preferences dialog

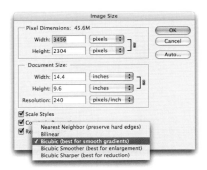

In the Resample Image pop-up at the bottom of the Image Size dialog

IMAGE MODE

As we said earlier, a pixel can have a value of 165, but that doesn't mean anything until you know the image's mode. That 165 could represent a level of gray or a particular color, or it might be only one member of a set of three or four other 8-bit values. Fortunately, Photoshop makes it easy to see the image mode of a file, and you can convert it to a different mode if you want.

Ultimately, an image mode is simply a method of organizing the bits to describe a color. In a perfect world, you could say to a printer, "I'd like this box to be navy blue," and they'd know exactly what you were talking about. However, even we can't agree on what navy blue looks like, much less you and your printer. So color scientists created a whole mess of ways for us to describe colors—to each other and to a computer—with some precision.

Photoshop reads and writes only a handful of the many different color modes these scientists came up with. Fortunately, these modes are the most important of the bunch, at least for those in the world of graphic arts. Each of the following image modes appears on the Mode menu in Photoshop.

Bitmap

As far as Photoshop is concerned, Bitmap means one thing: an image that contains only black or white (no shades of gray)—technically, a 1-bit image. Compared to other image modes, the kinds of image editing you can do are severely limited in Bitmap mode. For instance, you can't use any filters, and you can't use tools such as the Smudge tool, the Blur tool, or the Dodge/ Burn tool. Those features are designed to finesse shades of gray and color, which simply don't exist in Bitmap mode.

Grayscale

Grayscale files in Photoshop can use 8, 16, or 32 bits to represent gray shades. If a file uses a different number of bits, it's rounded up. For example, if you open a 10-bit grayscale file in Photoshop, it's opened and saved as a 16-bit file.

In an 8-bit grayscale image, each pixel has a value from 0 (black) to 255 (white), so there are a maximum of 256 levels of gray possible. In a 16-bit grayscale image, each pixel has a value from 0 (black) to 32,768 (white), for a theoretical maximum of 32,769 possible gray shades.

Few capture devices can actually deliver all those gray shades, so 16-bit files usually have a lot of redundancy. But that redundancy translates into editing headroom, so if your camera or scanner can capture 12 or more bits per pixel, it's often worthwhile to bring the high-bit data into Photoshop.

Duotone

When you print a grayscale image on a printing press, those 256 levels of gray often get reduced to 100 or so because of the limitations of the press. People get around this by printing the image with more than one color of

TIP: If you're going to work with layers, it's best to do so after you've completed all image mode conversions, because some image mode changes flatten layered images. If flattening isn't required, a mode change may still change the appearance of the image due to the different nature of channels in the new image mode.

ink, increasing the tonal range of the printed image. This is called printing a *duotone* (for two inks), a *tritone* (for three inks), or a *quadtone* (for four inks).

The extra colors aren't typically used to simulate colors in the image; rather, they're used to extend the dynamic range of the underlying grayscale image. Those expensive Ansel Adams books on your coffee table were very likely printed using three or four (or even five or six) *different* black and gray inks.

TIP: As we mentioned in the preface, you can download the free online chapter from www.peachpit.com/realworldphotoshop_cs4.

Photoshop has a special image mode for duotones, tritones, and quadtones, and even though the file may appear to be in color, each pixel is still saved using only 8 bits of information. The trick is that Photoshop saves a set of contrast curves for each ink along with the 8-bit grayscale image. Creating a good duotone is as much art as science. For more information, see our online chapter, "Spot Colors and Duotones."

Indexed Color

Indexed Color mode is like a paint-by-numbers approach. It uses 8 bits to store a table of 256 colors, and a pixel in the image can use any of the 256 colors in the table. For example, instead of defining a pixel's color as Red 32, Green 140, Blue 96, as it might be in RGB mode, in Indexed Color mode a pixel simply says "I'm using the 35th color in the table." Photoshop then finds out which color is 35th and uses it for that pixel. You can completely change the look of the image by loading a different table.

While indexed color can save disk space (it requires only 8 bits per sample point), it gives your image only 256 different colors. That's not a lot when you compare it to the millions of colors you can get in RGB. But back when video cards and network speeds were very limited, the small size of indexed-color images outweighed the lack of subtle color variations, so indexed color was popular as part of the GIF standard for Web graphics.

Most Photoshop editing tools don't work in Indexed Color mode because it can't store enough colors to create gradual variations in color and tone. Do your major image edits in RGB mode first.

RGB

Every color computer monitor and television in the world displays color using the RGB image mode, in which every color is produced with varying amounts of red, green, and blue light. (These colors are called *additive prima-*

ries because the more red, green, or blue light you add, the closer to white you get.) In Photoshop, files saved in RGB mode typically use a set of three 8-bit grayscale files, so we say that RGB files are *24-bit* files. Digital cameras and scanners capture images in RGB format, and we prefer to work in RGB mode when editing color images.

CMYK

Traditional full-color printing presses reproduce colors using just four inks: cyan, magenta, yellow, and black, simulating all other colors using various combinations of those inks. When you see the image on your RGB monitor, Photoshop converts the CMYK values to RGB values on the fly for display.

If you reuse images from old press runs, they may be CMYK files, because drum scanning to a CMYK file used to be the most common way to obtain a color image for use in prepress. These days, you're more likely to start out with an RGB file from a digital camera or desktop scanner, so for many pre-press jobs you'll have to convert those RGB images to CMYK. We discuss Photoshop's tools for doing so in Chapter 4, "Color Settings."

TIP: A great philosophical debate rages on the issue of whether it's better to work in RGB or in CMYK for prepress work. Here's our advice: If someone gives you a CMYK image, edit that image in CMYK. In all other cases, we recommend staying in RGB for as long as possible.

Lab

The problem with RGB and CMYK modes is that a given RGB or CMYK specification doesn't really describe a *color*. Rather, it's a set of instructions that a specific output device uses to produce a color. The problem is that different devices produce different colors from the same RGB or CMYK specifications. If you've ever seen a wall full of television screens at a department store, you've seen what we're talking about: The same image—with the same RGB values—looks different on each screen. Similarly, if you've ever sat through a printing-press run, you know that the 50th impression probably isn't exactly the same color as the 5000th or the 50,000th. So while a pixel in a scanned image may have a particular RGB or CMYK value, you can't tell what that color really looks like. RGB and CMYK are both *device-specific* color modes.

However, a class of *device-independent* or *perceptually based* modes has been developed over the years. All of them are based, more or less, on a color space defined by the Commission Internationale de l'Éclairage (CIE) in 1931. The Lab mode in Photoshop is one such derivative.

A file saved in Lab mode describes what a color looks like under rigidly specified conditions; it's up to you (or Photoshop, or your color management software) to decide what RGB or CMYK values are needed to create that color on your chosen output device.

Lab doesn't describe a color by the components that make it up (RGB or CMYK, for instance). Instead, it describes *what a color looks like.* Device-independent color spaces are at the heart of the various color management systems now available that improve color correspondence between your screen, color printouts, and final printed output. Photoshop uses Lab mode as a reference when switching between CMYK and RGB modes, taking the values in your RGB Setup and CMYK Setup dialogs into account (see Chapter 4, "Color Settings," for more information on this conversion).

Lab is considerably less intuitive than the other color modes. The Lightness channel is relatively easy to understand, but the a★ and b★ channels (pronounced "A-star" and "B-star") are less so. The a★ channel represents how red or green a color is—negative values represent greens, positive ones represent magentas—and the b★ channel represents how blue or yellow the color is—negative values represent blue, positive ones represent yellow. Neutrals and near-neutrals always have values close to zero in both channels. Most hard-core Photoshop geeks have a few tricks that rely on Lab mode, but many of them can be accomplished more easily by using blending modes instead. Luminosity blending, for example, produces results that are extremely similar to those obtained when working in the Lightness channel in Lab mode.

Multichannel

The last image mode that Photoshop offers is Multichannel mode. This is a generic mode: Like RGB or CMYK, Multichannel mode has more than one 8-bit channel; however, you can set the color and name of each channel to anything you like.

Today, many scientific and astronomical images are made in "false color"—the channels may be a combination of radar, infrared, and ultraviolet, in addition to various colors of visible light. Some adventurous digital photographers use Multichannel mode to combine infrared and visible-spectrum photographs into composite images of surreal beauty.

CHAPTER THREE

Color Essentials

People have many different ways of thinking about, talking about, and working with color, but there's a notion that comes up again and again—that we can create any color by combining three primary colors. Art directors may feel comfortable specifying color changes with the terms *hue*, *lightness*, and *saturation*. Those who came to color through the computer may be more at home with levels of RGB. Scientists think about color in all sorts of strange ways, including CIE Lab, HSB (hue, saturation, and brightness), and LCH (lightness, chroma, and hue). And dyed-in-the-wool prepress folks think in CMYK dot percentages.

Although Adobe Photoshop tries to accommodate all these ways of thinking about color, many Photoshop users find themselves locked into seeing color in only one way, such as RGB. This is natural and understandable; we all have one way of thinking about color that matches the kind of work we do or how we learned. If you learn about other three-component ways to see color, you can unlock much more of the power of Photoshop.

"Wait a minute," you say. "CMYK has four constituents, not three!" Well, for now just trust us and set this issue aside. We promise to deal with it later.

In this chapter, we take a hard look at some fundamental color relationships and how Photoshop presents them. This stuff might seem a little theoretical at times, but we urge you to slog through it; it's essential for our later discussions about tonal and color correction.

Primary Colors

You might have learned the concept of *primary* colors in grade school, and conveniently, that concept is still helpful now. When we work with primary colors, we're talking about three colors that we can combine to make all the other colors. Ignoring for the moment which specific colors constitute the primaries, there are two fundamental principles of primary colors.

- They are the irreducible components of color.

- The primary colors, combined in varying proportions, can produce an entire spectrum of color.

The *secondary* colors, by the way, are made by combining two primary colors and excluding the third. What makes the primary colors special—indeed, what makes them primary colors—is human physiology rather than any special property inherent in those wavelengths of light.

Additive and Subtractive Color

Before becoming preoccupied with the behavior of spherical objects like apples and planets, Sir Isaac Newton performed some experiments with light and prisms. Like others, he found that he could break white light down into red, green, and blue components. His breakthrough was the discovery that he could *reconstitute* white light by recombining those red, green, and blue components. Red, green, and blue—the primary colors of light—are known as the *additive primary* colors because as you add color, the result becomes more white (the absence of colored light is black; see **Figure 3-1**). This is how computer monitors and televisions produce color.

But color on the printed page works differently. Unlike a television, the page doesn't emit light; it just reflects whatever light hits it. To print colors, you don't work with the light directly. Instead, you use pigments (like ink, dye, toner, or wax) that *absorb* some colors of light and reflect others.

The primary colors of pigments are cyan, yellow, and magenta. We call these the *subtractive primary* colors because as you add pigments to a white page, they subtract (absorb) more light, and the reflected color becomes darker. (We sometimes find it easier to remember: You *add* additive colors to get white, and you *subtract* subtractive colors to get white.) Cyan absorbs all the red light, magenta absorbs all the green light, and yellow absorbs all the blue light. If you add the maximum intensities of cyan, magenta, and yellow, you get black—in theory (see Figure 3-1). In practice, it produces a muddy brown mess. There are a couple of reasons for this.

Imperfect Pigments. If we had perfect CMY pigments, we wouldn't have to add black (K) as a fourth color. But in reality, cyan pigments always contain a little red, our magentas always contain a little green, and our yellows always contain a trace of blue. Moreover, there's a limit to how much ink we can apply to the paper without dissolving it. So when we print in color, we add black to help reproduce dark colors and to achieve acceptable density on press. See Chapter 4, "Color Settings," for more on this.

Imperfect Conversions. If we had to deal only with CMY, life would be a lot simpler. However, a large part of the problem of reproducing color images in print is that digital cameras and scanners deal with light, so they see color in RGB, and we have to translate those values into CMYK to print them. Unfortunately, this conversion is a thorny one, as we discuss in the next chapter.

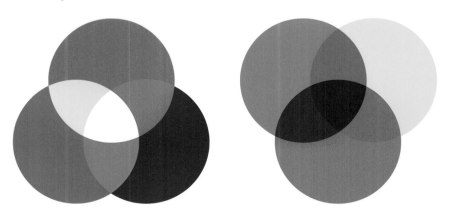

Figure 3-1 Additive and subtractive primaries

THE COLOR WHEEL

Before moving on to weightier matters such as gravity, calculus, and his impending thirtieth birthday, Sir Isaac Newton provided the world of color with one more key concept: If you take the colors of the spectrum and arrange them around the circumference of a wheel, the relationships among primaries become much clearer (see **Figure 3-2**).

Figure 3-2 The color wheel

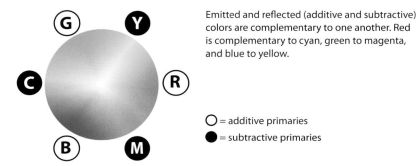

Emitted and reflected (additive and subtractive) colors are complementary to one another. Red is complementary to cyan, green to magenta, and blue to yellow.

○ = additive primaries
● = subtractive primaries

What's important to notice about this color wheel is that the additive and subtractive primary colors are opposite each other, equidistant around the wheel. These relationships are key to understanding how color works. For instance, cyan sits opposite red on the color wheel because it is, in fact, the opposite of red: Cyan pigments appear cyan because they absorb red light and reflect blue and green. Cyan is the absence of red. Colors that lie directly opposite each other on the wheel are known as *complementary* colors.

Saturation and Brightness

So far, we've talked about color in terms of three primary colors. But there are other ways of specifying color in terms of three ingredients. The most familiar one uses the terms *hue* (the property we refer to when we talk about "red" or "orange"), *saturation* (the "purity" of the color), and *brightness*.

Newton's basic two-dimensional color wheel lets us see the relationships between different hues, but to describe colors more fully, we need a more complex, three-dimensional model. We can find one of these in the HSB color cylinder (see **Figure 3-3**).

In the HSB cylinder, you can see that the hues are arranged around the edge of the wheel, and that colors become progressively weaker as we move into the center—the farther in you go, the less saturated or pure the color is.

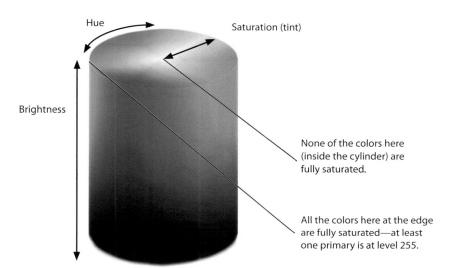

Hue

Saturation (tint)

Brightness

None of the colors here (inside the cylinder) are fully saturated.

All the colors here at the edge are fully saturated—at least one primary is at level 255.

Figure 3-3 The HSB color cylinder

Tristimulus Models and Color Spaces

Ignoring the inconvenience of CMYK, all the ways we've discussed of specifying and thinking about color involve three primary ingredients. Color scientists call these *tristimulus models*. (A *color model* is simply a way of thinking about color and representing it numerically. A tristimulus model represents colors by using three numbers.) If you go deep into the physiology of color, you'll find that our perceptual systems are actually wired in terms of three different responses to light that combine to produce the sensation of color. So the tristimulus approach isn't merely a mathematical convenience—it's inherent in how we see.

Tristimulus models have another useful property. Because they specify everything in terms of three ingredients, you can easily view them as three-dimensional objects with *x*, *y*, and *z* axes. Each color has a location in this three-dimensional object, specified by the three values. These three-dimensional models are called *color spaces*. The cylinder in Figure 3-3 is an example of a color space expressed as a 3D model. However, the simple HSB model can't really describe how you see colors. For instance, you know that cyan appears much lighter than blue, but in the HSB cylinder, they both have the same brightness and saturation values. Therefore, while some 3D representations are helpful, we have to go further to understand how to work with color.

How Colors Affect Each Other

There are a lot of times in Photoshop when we find ourselves working with one color space but thinking about the changes in terms of another color space. As you'll see in Chapter 7, "Image Adjustment Fundamentals," we often recommend that you use curves to adjust RGB values, but that you base your changes on the resulting CMYK percentages as displayed in the Info panel. You'll work faster if you understand how editing colors in one color space affects the way they appear in another color space. Here are some ways to think about RGB, CMY, and HSB colors and how they relate to each other.

Tone. One of the least understood—yet most important—effects of adding colors together is that adding or removing primaries affects not only hue and saturation but also tone. When you increase any RGB component to change the hue—adding light—the color gets lighter. The reverse is true with CMY because you're adding ink, making the color darker.

Hue. Every color, except the primaries, contains opposing primary colors. In RGB mode, red is "pure," but orange contains red alongside a good dose of green (and possibly some blue, too). In CMYK, magenta is pure, and red is not—it contains some amount of yellow in addition to magenta. So to change a color's hue, you add or subtract primary colors. In the process, you will probably affect the color's tone—adding or removing light (or ink) so the color gets lighter or darker.

Saturation. A saturated RGB color is made up of only one or two primaries; the third primary is always zero. When you add a trace of the third color—to change the hue, for instance—you desaturate the color. Because desaturation introduces another primary, the original color becomes less pure.

Likewise, if you increase the saturation of a color using the Hue/Saturation dialog (or any other), you're removing one of the other primaries, increasing color purity. If you get out to the edge, where one of the primaries is maxed out and the other two are still changing, you'll change the hue and the tone.

TIP: To see which primaries carry detail in an image, view each image channel in the Channels panel (Window > Channels).

There's another important consideration pertaining to saturated colors. When you saturate a color in an RGB image, detail exists in only one of the three channels. One of the others is always solid white, and the third is always solid black. All the detail is being carried by one channel, which is why saturated colors in images are hard to handle.

Color Relationships at a Glance

It's worth spending some time to understand the color relationships we're discussing in this chapter. We all have a favorite color space, but if you can learn to view color in more than one way—understanding how to achieve the same results by manipulating CMY, RGB, and HSB—you'll find the world of color correction much less alien, and you'll be much more able to select the right tool for the job.

We suggest memorizing these fundamentals (see **Figure 3-4**):

- 100 percent cyan = 0 red
- 100 percent magenta = 0 green
- 100 percent yellow = 0 blue
- Increasing RGB values reduces corresponding CMY values, and vice versa.
- Reducing saturation (making a color more gray) means introducing the complementary color. For example, to desaturate red you add cyan.
- The complement of a primary color is produced by combining equal amounts of the other two primary colors.
- Lightening or darkening a saturated color desaturates that color.
- Changing the hue of a color often changes lightness as well.
- Saturation changes can cause hue changes.

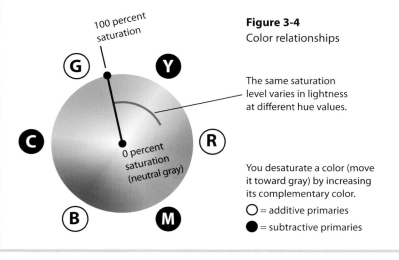

Figure 3-4
Color relationships

The same saturation level varies in lightness at different hue values.

You desaturate a color (move it toward gray) by increasing its complementary color.

○ = additive primaries
● = subtractive primaries

Neutrals. A color made up of equal values of red, green, and blue is always a neutral gray (though you may have to do quite a bit of work to make it come out that way onscreen or—once you've converted it to CMYK—on press). The "darkness" of the gray depends on how much red, green, and blue there is; more light makes for a lighter gray. This is useful in a number of situations, including making monitor adjustments and correcting color casts. For a quick summary of relationships among the color spaces, see the sidebar "Color Relationships at a Glance."

DEVICE-INDEPENDENT LAB COLOR

Basically, the problem with HSB, RGB, and CMY (and even CMYK) is that they don't describe how a color looks; they describe only the color's ingredients. You've probably walked into a television store and seen about a hundred televisions on the wall, each of them receiving the same color information. But none of them displays the colors in the same way.

In fact, if you send the same RGB values to ten different monitors, or the same CMYK values to ten different presses, you'll probably end up with ten different colors (see **Figure 3-5**). We call RGB and CMYK *device dependent*, because the color you end up with varies from device to device.

Figure 3-5 Device-dependent color and color gamuts

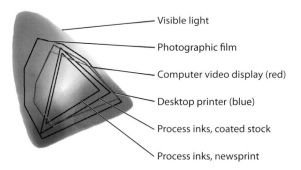

As you can see, Photoshop has a problem in trying to display colors properly on your monitor: It doesn't know what the colors should *look like* to you. It doesn't know what those RGB or CMYK values really mean.

Plus, the program has to take all the little quirks of human vision into account. For instance, our eyes are more sensitive to some colors and brightness levels than to others, and we're more sensitive to small changes in bright colors than we are to small changes in dark ones (if you've had trouble teasing all the subtle shadow details out of your images, this can be one reason for that). RGB and CMYK values alone don't give Photoshop enough information for it to know what color is actually being described.

Fortunately, there's CIE Lab, which appears on the Mode menu simply as Lab. Lab is designed to describe what colors look like regardless of the device they're displayed on, so we call Lab *device independent.*

Whereas in HSB the hues are represented as being placed around a wheel, Lab color uses a more accurate but significantly less intuitive arrangement. In Lab, the third axis (which lies perpendicular to the page and is roughly equivalent to brightness in HSB) is the luminance axis—it represents how bright the color appears to the human eye. But unlike brightness in HSB, it takes into account the fact that we see green as brighter than blue.

Lab color can be an intimidating subject, but for the purposes of color correction, there are really only three things you need to know.

- HSB, HSL (hue, saturation, and lightness), and LCH are based on the way we think about color, and RGB and CMYK are based on the ways devices such as monitors and printers produce color, but Lab is based on the way humans actually see color. A Lab specification describes the color that most people will see when they look at an object under specified lighting conditions.

- Photoshop uses Lab as a reference when it does mode changes. For instance, when you switch from RGB mode to CMYK mode, Photoshop uses Lab to decide what *color* is being specified by each device-dependent RGB value, and then it comes up with the right device-dependent CMYK equivalent. This idea is critical to the concept of color management.

- Finally, don't feel dumb if you find it hard to understand Lab color. It *is* difficult to visualize, because it's an abstract mathematical construct. It uses differing amounts of three primaries to specify colors, but those primaries don't really correspond to anything we can actually experience, as we can with RGB or HSB.

Colors in the Real World

Some color-correction tasks aren't straightforward. For example, it's difficult to adjust saturation in an image by manipulating RGB or CMYK values directly. But because you have Photoshop, you can use Photoshop tools that let you apply changes using hue, saturation, and brightness, and Photoshop will do the math to alter the underlying RGB or CMYK data.

Even with the help of Photoshop, you face two fairly large problems. First, when you convert an image between color modes, you lose some image information; if your images start with 256 shades of each color, some get lost due to rounding errors during the conversion.

The second problem is that the color spaces in which most of your images are stored, RGB and CMYK, are device dependent: The color you'll get varies depending on the device you send it to. Worse, some devices have a much wider range of colors that they can reproduce—called the color gamut (see Figure 3-5 earlier in this chapter). For example, a digital camera sensor can record a wider range of colors than a color monitor can display, and the monitor displays a wider range of colors than you can reproduce with ink on paper, so no matter what you do, some of the colors captured by the camera simply can't be reproduced in print.

Fortunately, Photoshop lets you specify the gamut of your monitor and your CMYK output devices; we'll show you how to set that up in the next chapter, "Color Settings." In Chapter 7, "Image Adjustment Fundamentals," we'll show you how to use Photoshop to predict the color values and appearance of a color in those other gamuts.

CHAPTER FOUR
Color Settings

We consider every topic in this book to be important, but color management is one of those subjects that can quickly make anyone feel stupid. If you're under the delusion that you can use Adobe Photoshop *without* using color management, this chapter is a must-read. Without understanding how Photoshop handles color behind the scenes, there's no way to get great color (or black-and-white) images out of this program.

Although the color management system in Photoshop uses mathematics that approach rocket science, using the tools that control the system is fairly simple. You just need to understand a few key concepts, learn where the buttons are, and use common sense in deciding when to push them.

In the last chapter, we broke the sad news that RGB and CMYK are very ambiguous ways of specifying color, since the actual color you get will vary from device to device. In this chapter, we'll look at the features Photoshop offers to make what you see on the screen at least resemble, if not actually match, what you get in your printed output.

Writing just a chapter about color management doesn't do justice to the subject. If you read this chapter and find that you need more detailed information, pick up the book *Real World Color Management* (Peachpit Press) by color management guru Bruce Fraser, along with Chris Murphy and Fred Bunting.

What Is Color Management Anyway?

Color management can be an intimidating subject for photographers. With such a dry name, color management is often perceived as a technical chore to be avoided whenever possible. But hardware and software vendors have devoted a great deal of time and resources to working color management into every nook and cranny of digital photography, so it must be important, right? Right: Color management exists because it solves a problem. But what problem does it solve?

You may already know that colors don't look the same from camera to display to printer for all kinds of reasons, from simple production variations to the fact that some devices (like displays) use additive color and others (like printers) use subtractive color, a fundamentally incompatible conflict. This is the problem color management tries to solve, and it does so by creating a common foundation that color hardware and software can use to make color more consistent.

Ultimately, color management is about reconciling color differences. You could try doing this manually by fiddling with your monitor and printer controls, but it would mean that your files would display and print properly only with the specific hardware and software you currently have in front of you. If you upgrade any of your equipment or send the file to someone else, the file won't look the same because it won't have been tweaked for the new equipment.

A color management system is a much better solution because it uses standardized *profiles* that describe how your hardware and software reproduce color. When you want to display or print image colors properly on a system with different hardware or software, as long as you have profiles that describe the hardware and software being used, the color management system can make the adjustments necessary to reproduce the image colors consistently. If you think of a display and a printer as using different color "languages," you can think of a color management system as a sort of translation layer between your image and the system it's on, and profiles as language phrase books used to translate colors from one device to another.

Yes, color management can be a challenge to understand, but the effort is well worth it. Even understanding just the basic ideas of color management can give you skills that save you time and frustration when trying to get colors to reproduce consistently in many environments.

Color Management Is About Answering Simple Questions

To simplify the way you think of color management, it helps to remember that ultimately, what you're trying to do is answer a few questions about the image in front of you:

- How is this image supposed to look?

- Where did this image come from? (Under what viewing conditions was this image edited?)

- Where is this image going? (What are the editing or output conditions where the image is going next? How should the colors be preserved under those conditions?)

These questions may seem random now, but you'll soon see that if you keep these questions in mind when you're trying to decide which button to push in a cryptic color management dialog, you'll find it much easier to think through your answer. We will come back to them.

Color Management Is About Relationships

Those new to color management sometimes become fixated on the individual pieces of the system, such as a monitor or a printer. But focusing on an individual piece misses the point. Because the goal is to keep colors consistent among different parts of a workflow, what you really want to pay attention to are the *relationships* between those parts. The questions we just posed help you find out about relationships within a workflow.

Profiles are a way of recording and communicating those relationships. For example, when you calibrate a monitor to specific viewing conditions, such as a color temperature of 6500 Kelvins, or K, at gamma 2.2, a monitor typically can't achieve that standard exactly. The monitor profile fills the gap, telling the system how much to alter the display signal so that the image on the monitor does meet the standard. This means that the profile has recorded the relationship (the difference) between the monitor's performance and the desired standard and has communicated it to the system. The system can then make up (compensate for) the difference. As a result, you see a consistent representation of the colors in the image.

COLOR MANAGEMENT SYSTEMS EXPLAINED

A color management system (CMS) is software that does its best to maintain the appearance of colors when reproduced on different devices. We stress the word *appearance* because it's simply impossible to reproduce many of the colors found in the world in print, or even on a color monitor.

Color management often gets dressed up in much fancier clothing, but it really does only two things:

- It lets you assign a specific color appearance to RGB or CMYK numbers that would otherwise be ambiguous.

- It maintains that color appearance as consistently as possible as you send images to different displays and output devices.

No matter how complicated color management options might appear, when you examine them more closely, they always serve those two purposes.

Parts of a Color Management System

All color management systems employ three basic components:

- The *color-matching engine* (sometimes known as the *color-matching method*, or CMM) is the software that converts color meanings between different device-specific color spaces, like a universal translator between your color devices. You can choose a different CMM than the very good Adobe Color Engine (ACE), but you probably won't ever need to. The only reason we can see for using a different engine is if you absolutely must obtain exactly the same conversions from non-Adobe products.

- The *reference color space* (also known as the *profile connection space*, or PCS) is a device-independent, perceptually based color space. Most current CMSs use a CIE-defined color space, such as CIE Lab or CIE XYZ. You never have to work directly with the reference color space; it's the theory behind how the software works. Think of it as the common ground for all color devices—a space that can represent any color.

- A *profile* describes the behavior of a device like a scanner, monitor, or printer. For instance, a profile can tell the CMS, "This is the reddest red that this device can output." A profile can also define a *virtual color space* that's unrelated to any particular device (the Adobe RGB space is an example of this; we'll see how it's useful later on). Profiles are the key to color management. Without a profile, 100 percent red has no specific meaning; with a profile, the color management system can say, "Oh, this color is supposed to be red in the specific way that red appears on that printer." Profiles conform to the standard ICC (International Color Consortium) specification that lets them work with all CMSs on all platforms. ColorSync profiles on the Mac and .icm or .icc profiles in Windows both follow the ICC spec and work on both platforms.

Fortunately, you have to work only with the last of the three components: profiles. You'll run into profiles if your images come from many sources or go to many different types of output media, while the CMM and reference color space may never need to be changed and are usually invisible to you.

Conveying Color Meaning with Profiles

The key concept in using a CMS is conveying color meaning—making those ambiguous RGB and CMYK values unambiguous. If a CMS knows what RGB values a scanner produces when it scans specific colors, and it knows what colors a display produces when we send it specific RGB numbers, it can calculate the new RGB numbers it needs to send to the display to make it reproduce the colors represented by the scanner's RGB numbers.

Profile Embedding. When you embed a profile in an image, you aren't changing the image itself, and you're not changing the color values. All you're doing is including extra information that tells color management–savvy applications how to reproduce the colors you saw using the color values in the file. This is possible because a profile designates a specific color appearance for the RGB or CMYK numbers. With a profile, color values are no longer ambiguous—they gain a context to refer to.

TIP: *Embedded* and *tagged* mean the same thing: A color profile is included inside the file. When Photoshop reports that an image is *untagged*, it means no profile is embedded.

Source and Destination Profiles. When you ask the color management system to make a conversion—to change the numbers in the file—the CMS needs to know where the RGB or CMYK color values came from and where you want to send them. You can give the CMS this information by specifying a source profile and a destination profile.

For example, imagine that a color management system works with words rather than colors. The purpose of the CMS would be to translate words from one language to another. If you just feed it a bunch of words, it can't do anything. But if you give it the words and tell it that they were written by a French person (the source), it can suddenly understand what the words are saying. If you then tell it that you speak German (the destination), it can translate the meaning faithfully for you.

The Process. When you scan artwork, you get RGB data. For Photoshop to know what specific colors those RGB values should represent, Photoshop needs to read the profile that describes how the scanner (the source) saw the colors. If the scanning software embeds a profile describing its colors, all you have to do is open the image; Photoshop will just read the profile that's already in the image. You can then start editing the file, or you can first convert it from the scanner's color space to a more standard color space like sRGB or Adobe RGB, which you would set as the destination color space.

When you print the image, the CMS converts the image's colors into a form the printer driver can accept. This color conversion happens whether or not you're aware of it. If you don't take control of the color conversion, the standard color handoff from Photoshop to the printer driver software may result in mediocre printed colors. If you do take control over the conversion, the Print dialog in Photoshop lets you choose a printer (destination) profile that describes exactly what colors are possible using that specific printer, paper, and ink. Photoshop performs that color conversion on the way to the printer without permanently altering the image file, which remains in its current color space. This more manual approach to printing gives you printed colors that are as consistent as possible with what you saw onscreen. For more information, see "Converting Colors When You Print" later in this chapter

This is really the only thing CMSs do. They convert color data from one color space (one "language") to another, using profiles to preserve the intended appearance of the colors throughout the workflow. Pretty much everything you do with a CMS involves asking it to make the colors in a source as consistent as possible with those in the destination, and this two-step is integral to the way Photoshop handles color.

There's one more wrinkle, in that the source and destination typically aren't very similar in size or in shape. In addition, when you print, it's just about guaranteed that the destination will not be able to reproduce as many colors as the source. (A printer using CMYK inks simply can't reproduce anywhere near the number of colors that a computer monitor can reproduce.) When this is true, a lot of colors will have nowhere to go—they can't be

TIP: When a profile is embedded in an image and you start to convert the image colors to a different profile, Photoshop automatically recognizes the embedded profile as the default source profile. You have to specify only the destination profile, which would typically represent your final output.

reproduced by the destination device. To deal with these mismatches, CMSs provide for rendering intents, which we'll cover later in this chapter.

Identifying a Document's Color Profile

Photoshop makes it easy to tell which profile an image uses. The tools that do this aren't visible by default, but before you read any more of this book, you might want to turn on some of these readouts (see **Figure 4-1**):

Status bar. To display the document profile in the Status bar, click the black triangle next to the Status bar at the bottom of a document window. If you have multiple floating document windows, each window's Status bar will show the profile for the document, which is especially useful if you've opened copies of the same document that have different document profiles.

Info Panel. Click the options menu icon in the top left corner of the Info panel, choose Panel Options, turn on Document Profile, and click OK. Now the document profile will appear in the Info panel. The Info panel shows the profile only for the frontmost window.

TIP: If you see a number sign (#) at the end of a window's title bar, that indicates an untagged document. An asterisk (*) at the end of the title bar indicates a document that's tagged with a profile different from the current working space. If neither character appears, the document is tagged with the working space profile.

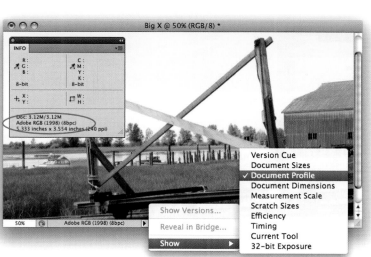

Figure 4-1 You can display a document's profile in the Info panel, as well as in the Status bar at the bottom of a document window.

Comparing Color Spaces

There are a couple of ways to observe the kinds of discrepancies a color management system must deal with to maintain consistent color. You can look at 3D plots that tell you how big each color space is, and you can preview how an image will look in another color space.

TIP: To overlay a second profile's gamut plot over an existing one, in the Apple ColorSync Utility, right-click or Control-click the first profile's plot, choose Hold for Comparison, and then select the second profile.

You might have come across two-dimensional plots of color gamuts (see **Figure 4-2**). But 2D plots can be misleading. A color space is actually three-dimensional, because it isn't just about the range of colors. It's also about the range of tones from light to dark, as in the HSB color cylinder you saw back in Figure 3-3. In other words, brightness is the third dimension. For this reason, 3D plots are much more informative (see Figure 4-2). For example, you'll find that while RGB devices can generally reproduce more colors than CMYK devices, especially at brighter luminance levels, CMYK devices can often reproduce more dark colors than RGB devices can. If you bear in mind that you increase RGB saturation by adding light and you increase print saturation by adding ink, this makes perfect sense.

Figure 4-2 2D gamut plots can be misleading; to get the complete picture, rotate the plots in 3D.

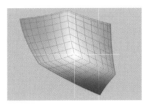 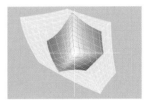 

This 2D plot is the color gamut of the Adobe RGB profile, as displayed in Apple ColorSync Utility.

In the 2D plot, Adobe RGB appears to fully contain the CMYK gamut of the U. S. Sheetfed Coated v2 profile.

But rotating the comparison in 3D reveals that this CMYK profile's gamut exceeds that of Adobe RGB in the shadows.

Another way to compare color spaces is to preview how an image looks in the destination color space. This is called *soft-proofing*. For example, you can open an image embedded with an sRGB document profile and preview how it will look in a specific CMYK press profile, without actually altering the image. You can also soft-proof how that image would look in any other color space for which you have a profile, such as a different printer or display standard. For example, you can view a Mac image under default Windows display conditions. For information about setting up and using soft-proofing, see "Soft-Proofing Other Color Spaces" later in this chapter.

Document, Device, and Working Spaces

The idea of a color space is easy to understand, since it's essentially the range of colors you get. What's more challenging is the idea of multiple color spaces, particularly within a single color mode. Let's look at some of the questions behind the various color spaces.

What's the Difference Between Document, Device, and Working Spaces? These are all color spaces that are simply used in different ways. One way to think about this is that they go from general to specific:

- The *working space* that you set in the Edit > Color Settings dialog is the default color space you set in Photoshop. If you start a new document or open a document that doesn't have a profile, the working space is the profile that will be associated with the image. It also means that if you're always opening images that already contain the right profile, the working space never comes into play. You'll notice that there are four working spaces in the Color Settings dialog—that's because each color mode gets its own default. RGB has its own working space, CMYK has its own, and so on. When picking an RGB working space, it's usually best to choose one that's built into Photoshop; for more information see "About the Built-In RGB Working Spaces" later in this chapter.

- The *document color space* is just another way of saying "the profile that's embedded inside an image." If there is no profile embedded in an image, you can either let your Photoshop default working space take over, manually assign a profile to it, or tell Photoshop to leave it untagged (that is, don't color-manage the document). Photoshop handles document profiles very intelligently: If you have five documents open and each has its own correct but very different profile, there won't be any need to apply the working space to any of them, and in addition, Photoshop will maintain each document's profile separately. Photoshop won't let one document's profile affect another document.

- A *device color space* represents the range of color produced by a device you use to create or output images. On the creation side, it could be a digital camera or scanner. On the output side, it could be a printer. As we've discussed, device color spaces are valuable for precisely describing the colors of the device that an image came from or is going to, but they are not good for editing, so you'll typically run into device color spaces (device profiles) when you first create or finally output an image.

In a typical image-processing workflow among color spaces, an image begins its life containing a device-specific source profile and gets converted to a standard, perceptually uniform workspace (such as Adobe RGB or

TIP: The working space is most important when you open untagged images, because the working space is essentially a default color space for documents that aren't already tagged with a profile. If you usually work with tagged images, the working space may not come into play often.

TIP: The one device profile Photoshop uses all the time is the display profile describing your monitor. That's why it's so important to calibrate your monitor and generate a profile for it.

sRGB) for editing and archival storage. Media-specific copies of the image are then converted to the color spaces for the media where they'll be used (the Web, print, video, and so on).

Why Do We Need More Than One Kind of RGB or CMYK? Different devices reproduce different ranges of color, so if you used an RGB space that was relatively small, like sRGB, it wouldn't be big enough to preserve the colors from a higher-quality source, such as a professional camera. In that case you might consider using a larger color space to archive the original.

So Why Not Just Use One Color Space Big Enough to Contain All of the Others? The only problem with using very large color spaces, such as ProPhoto RGB, is that most people still edit 8 bit/channel images. Eight bits isn't quite enough to stretch across the wide-gamut color spaces, so when you edit an 8 bit/channel image in ProPhoto RGB, instead of smooth color transitions you might see banding or steps. Editing in very large color spaces is more practical if you edit images that have 16 or more bits per channel. That's kind of an advanced technique, though, because you have to be comfortable with how to convert both to 8 bits per channel and to the color spaces that your final images need.

Choosing Your Working Spaces

You set up your working spaces in the Color Settings dialog (Edit > Color Settings; see **Figure 4-3**). The simplest way to use Color Settings is to choose a preset from the Settings pop-up menu. Because the choices in that pop-up menu are presets, when you choose one it changes many options in the dialog. If one works for you as it is, just choose it and you're done. Or you can choose a preset as a good starting point, and then fine-tune it.

For RGB, remember that working spaces are just defaults, affecting only images that aren't tagged. If most of the images you open already have correct profiles embedded in them, you won't have to obsess over getting the working spaces exactly right. That said, it's best to pick one for each color mode that matches your primary workflow, such as prepress or Web design. For CMYK, there are still workflows that don't require profiles to be embedded in images, and in those workflows it's important that the CMYK working space be set to the profile for your press conditions.

About the Built-In RGB Working Spaces

The RGB working spaces built into Photoshop are designed to provide a good environment for editing images. As such, they have two important properties that aren't shared by the vast majority of device spaces.

- Gray balance. The built-in working spaces are *gray-balanced*, meaning simply that equal amounts of R, G, and B always produce a neutral gray. This is hardly ever the case with device (scanner, camera, display, printer) spaces. Since one of the easiest ways to bring color into line is to find something that should be neutral and make it so, gray balance is an extremely useful property.

- Perceptual uniformity. The built-in working spaces are approximately *perceptually uniform*, meaning that changing each channel's numeric values in the image by the same increment results in about the same degree of visual change, no matter whether it's in the highlights, the midtones, the shadows, the pastels, or the saturated colors. Again, device spaces generally don't work that way.

All color-space conversions entail some data loss, but the conversion from capture (camera or scanner) to working space is, in our experience, invariably worthwhile, and when it's done in 16-bit/channel mode, the loss is so trivial it's just about undetectable. Even in 8-bit/channel mode, you're likely to produce much better results editing in a working space rather than a device space. The idealized properties of the built-in RGB working spaces also makes them useful for creating and archiving master images, from which you can make copies that you convert for specific types of output.

Why Not Just Use Lab? After all, Lab is, by design, a device-independent, perceptually uniform color space. But Lab has at least two properties that make it less than ideal as a standard editing space.

First, Lab is pretty nonintuitive when it comes to making color corrections—small adjustments to a* and b* values often produce large changes in unexpected directions. A bigger problem, however, is that Lab, by definition, contains all the colors you can see, and as a corollary, it also contains many "colors" you can't see.

When we use 8 bits per channel to represent this whole range of color, the distance from one value to the next becomes uncomfortably large. And since any real image from a scanner or digital camera contains a much smaller range of color than Lab represents, you waste bits on colors you can't capture, display, print, or even see. If you work with 16 bit/channel images, the gamut problem is much less of an issue, but editing in Lab is still not particularly friendly, and conversions from capture space to Lab generally involve more data loss due to quantization error than the conversion to RGB working spaces.

Figure 4-3 The Color
Settings dialog

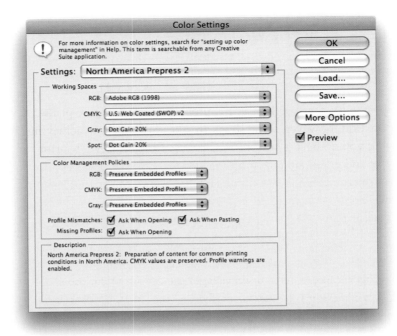

Choosing an RGB Working Space

If you're doing prepress or other high-quality printing, Adobe RGB is the one working space that's big enough not to clip U.S. Sheetfed Coated v2 (a typical CMYK color space) very much, and yet it is also constrained enough to work well as an editing space for 8 bit/channel images. If your work is aimed primarily at the Web or video, sRGB is the natural choice. If you print to printers with larger gamuts than a CMYK press has, and you're comfortable with 16 bit/channel editing and handling color space conversions, ProPhoto RGB is a definite option for you.

David likes to keep things simple and uses Adobe RGB virtually all of the time. Conrad uses different working spaces depending on the project. It isn't absolutely necessary to load these as working spaces in Color Settings—you can always use the Assign Profile command (see "Assign Profile" later in this chapter) to assign a profile other than the working space to an image—but if you're going to be working with a bunch of images in the same space, it makes life slightly easier to load that space as the working space.

Choosing a CMYK Working Space

Unlike RGB working spaces, which may be entirely abstract and not based on any real device, CMYK working spaces always reflect some real combination of ink (or toner, or dye) and paper. The ideal situation is to have a custom ICC profile for the specific CMYK process to which you're printing. In the real world, however, some shops are ahead of others in achieving this workflow. If you do have a custom ICC profile for your CMYK print process or for an industry-standard proofing system such as Kodak Approval or Creo Spectrum, click the More Options button and load that profile into the CMYK pop-up menu in the Color Settings dialog.

By default, your choices of CMYK working space are limited to the press profiles that are installed by Photoshop, plus Custom CMYK, which users of older versions of Photoshop may recognize as the old "Built-in" panel of Photoshop 5's CMYK Setup. Mac users also get the option to choose ColorSync CMYK, which, with the advent of Tiger (Mac OS X 10.4), is hardwired to Generic CMYK, a profile that represents no printing condition known to humankind and so is best ignored.

If you're using an accurate CMYK profile, either as a working space or as a profile in tagged CMYK images, you shouldn't have to worry about dot gain, gray component replacement (GCR), and so on. Because a properly created profile represents the output conditions, all output characteristics should already be accounted for by the profile. Choose Load Custom CMYK from the CMYK working space pop-up menu to select your CMYK profile.

If you're still working with a printer who is more comfortable with the old-style Photoshop CMYK setups, they're still available. Choosing Custom CMYK from the CMYK pop-up menu opens the Custom CMYK dialog; the settings for that dialog should be supplied by your printer. Today's profiling technologies are far superior to the old manual methods, so use a CMYK profile when available.

Choosing a Gray Working Space

Grayscale profiles are independent of RGB or CMYK. However, note that grayscale profiles contain only tone reproduction information; they have no information about the color of the black ink or of the paper.

TIP: Some Mac users naturally gravitate to using Apple RGB as a working space because it has the word *Apple* in it. This is wrong. Apple RGB is based on the early 13-inch Apple RGB High-Resolution monitor (640 by 480 pixels), which hasn't been produced in more than 15 years. Any of the default RGB working spaces is better. ColorMatch RGB also represents a long-dead brand of CRT monitor.

TIP: When you build your own CMYK profiles for a press or proofer, it's always a good idea to build a family of profiles with different black generations. Some profiling tools will even let you take an existing profile and regenerate it with new black generation settings.

When Color Settings is displayed with Fewer Options, you can choose among grayscale dot gains of 10, 15, 20, 25, or 30 percent, depending on your printing conditions. You can also choose either gamma 1.8 or 2.2, which are good choices for grayscale images destined for the screen or for unknown printing conditions. Of course, there's nothing to prevent you from using these gamma values for print images, or the dot-gain curves for onscreen use, but generally speaking, gammas are designed for onscreen use and dot-gain curves are designed for print.

When to Reveal the Hidden Options

Photoshop presents a short list of options in the Color Settings dialog by default, to keep from overwhelming you with choices. If you click More Options, you'll not only see the dialog expand with additional features, but you'll find more profiles listed in the Working Space pop-up menus. Some of them are holdovers from previous versions of Photoshop, included only to support old images you might open. The rest are all the profiles you've installed on your computer, such as profiles for your desktop printer.

For RGB, most people are best served by using one of the working spaces on the "short list" in the shorter Color Settings dialog. The need to use or define a custom RGB working space should be rare.

As we've discussed, for CMYK, you do want to have a custom CMYK profile for your printing conditions. You don't need to click More Options to see your custom CMYK profile, since you can select the profile straight from your disk by choosing Load CMYK.

Custom Gray and Spot Color Spaces

As with Custom CMYK, you can choose Custom Dot Gain (see **Figure 4-4**) from the Gray pop-up menu in the Working Spaces section of the Color Settings dialog. This is necessary only if you're doing grayscale work and don't already have a grayscale profile to load. Two reasons to edit a custom gray working space are to enter custom dot-gain values or to load the black channel from your CMYK profile so that you can use it for grayscale images. (There's also a Custom Gamma option, but it's rarely needed.) To save your gray settings as a grayscale profile, choose Save Gray from the Gray working spaces pop-up menu.

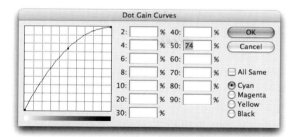

Figure 4-4 To build a custom dot-gain curve, enter the measured dot area for a swatch. You can enter a single value for the 50 percent dot or take more measurements to increase accuracy.

The Custom Dot Gain command in the Spot working spaces pop-up menu is essentially the same as the grayscale option of the same name, and you can use it if you want a dot-gain curve other than the many already available in that pop-up menu. As with grayscale settings, spot color settings know nothing about the actual color of the ink and paper, and they contain no information about the way the spot ink interacts with other inks.

HANDLING COLOR-SPACE CONVERSIONS

Now that you've been introduced to the parts that make up a color management system, you're ready to think through what happens as you move documents through your workflow. If you intend to use Photoshop to its fullest potential, you'll be doing color-space conversions at some point. The three main tools you'll use are the Color Settings dialog for your defaults, the profile alerts when opening a document, the Convert to Profile and Assign Profile commands for converting colors at any time, and the Print dialog when you're sending output directly to a printer.

Setting Up Conversion Defaults (Policies)

You can set color-conversion defaults for each color mode and control how the documents you open relate to your working spaces. Adobe has given these the bureaucratic-sounding name *color management policies*. Don't let the name intimidate you; to set them up, just answer these questions:

- What do you want Photoshop to do when you open or import an image that's missing a profile?

- What do you want Photoshop to do when you open an image that has a different profile than the working space you chose?

• Do you want Photoshop to let you know when a profile is missing or doesn't match your working space?

Now let's see how the pop-up menus and check boxes in the Color Management Policies section (see **Figure 4-5**) answer those questions.

Handling Existing Profiles. The three pop-up menus all do the same thing: They tell Photoshop what to do if the incoming image already has an embedded profile. When you have no doubt that incoming images are embedded with the correct profiles, Preserve Embedded Profiles is the safest choice, especially in a color-managed workflow. Consider choosing Convert to Working RGB/CMYK/Gray when you expect to receive many images with different profiles and you'd like to standardize them to your working space by converting their colors as you open them. In today's color-managed workflows, you typically do not want to choose Off unless you have a very good reason for deleting the profiles of all incoming images. When this option is set to Off, Photoshop also does not embed profiles by default when you choose the New (document) or Save As commands.

TIP: If you're working with images from many different sources, it's a good idea to turn on the profile displays in the Status bar and Info panel. Then keep an eye out for documents that open up in unexpected color spaces. This is especially useful if you've turned off the mismatch warnings.

Figure 4-5 Color Management Policies let you tell Photoshop how documents you open should relate to your working space.

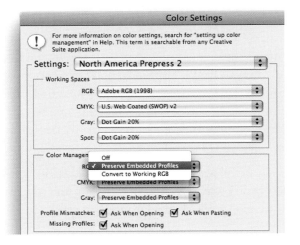

Getting Notified. The check boxes in the Color Management Policies section are concerned with one thing: Do you want Photoshop to ask you what to do when an incoming image doesn't match your color settings? If the answer is yes, check the boxes, and you'll get to approve every potential conversion. Although this lets you maintain control, if you work with many images the alert may appear with annoying frequency. If the answer is no, leave the boxes unchecked, and when there's a mismatch or missing profile

Photoshop will simply execute the default handling you set up with the pop-up menus above the check boxes. Unchecking the boxes works best if you trust that incoming images should always do what the pop-up menus say in the event of a mismatch, because Photoshop is going to do that every time, without asking you.

Let's walk through an example. Suppose you turn off the check boxes, your RGB working space is Adobe RGB, and you set the RGB policy to Convert to Working RGB. Now let's say you open an sRGB image. The profile mismatch with your RGB working space causes Photoshop to implement your policy. Because you told Photoshop to convert images with mismatched profiles to your RGB working space, and you turned off the check boxes, Photoshop will go ahead and convert the sRGB image colors to Adobe RGB without telling you. If you had turned on the check boxes, Photoshop would have asked you before performing the conversion.

Handling Color When Opening an Image

The color management policies we just discussed control how color conversions occur as you open an image. If you checked the Ask When Opening check boxes in the Color Settings dialog, you'll have the opportunity to confirm the color management policy you set for the image's working space; if you didn't check the boxes, Photoshop will silently execute the policy (for example, converting the image colors into your working space). If you turned on Ask When Pasting, you'll also have an opportunity to control the conversion of images you paste or drag into an open Photoshop document.

Responding to Warning Dialogs. If you turned on the Missing Profiles or Profile Mismatch check boxes in Color Management Policies, you'll see an alert dialog whenever you open or import a document that has no profile or a different profile than your working space.

- Embedded Profile Mismatch means the incoming image has a different profile than your working space (see **Figure 4-6**). That doesn't necessarily mean anything's wrong. A profile is already embedded in the image, so the only question is whether you have a reason to change it. If you don't have a good reason to change it, select "Use the embedded profile" and move on. If your project requires that all images be saved in a specific color space, such as sRGB for digital video or a specific CMYK press profile, and you've already set your working space to that

TIP: Clicking the More Options button reveals additional controls; see "The Obscure Color Settings Options" later in this chapter.

TIP: If you're working with a consistent set of images and yet you always run into the same mismatch or missing profile alerts, and you always answer them the same way, that's a clue that you might want to edit your color management policies to handle those profiles automatically and turn off the warnings.

profile, select "Convert document colors to the working space." The last option, "Discard the embedded profile," may be used in prepress workflows where profiles aren't used. Otherwise, avoid that option in color-managed workflows, except when you're opening a printer profiling target. If you're not sure, click "Use the embedded profile," click OK to go ahead and open it, and then see "When You Have No Idea What to Do" later in this chapter to work out how to handle the image.

Figure 4-6 The Embedded Profile Mismatch warning offers three choices for handling images for which the embedded profile differs from the working space.

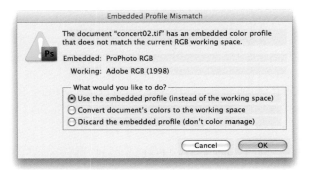

• Missing Profile means what it says: The incoming file doesn't have an embedded profile (see **Figure 4-7**). If you are using a traditional non-color-managed CMYK workflow where profiles are not used, you'll probably choose "Leave as is." If you want to start color-managing the file, you get to assign a profile—either the current working space, or any profile on your computer—by choosing one from the "Assign profile" pop-up menu. If you need more help figuring out the right answer to a missing profile warning, click "Leave as is," click OK, and then see "When You Have No Idea What to Do" later in this chapter.

"And then convert document to working space" is a check box in the Missing Profile dialog. It's useful when an image was previously edited in a color space that didn't match your working space. It lets you first assign the previous color space of the image so that the colors look normal. Then, by checking the box, you can convert the image into your working space. If you know that the image with the missing profile was previously edited in your working space, you don't need this check box, because you can simply select "Assign working space."

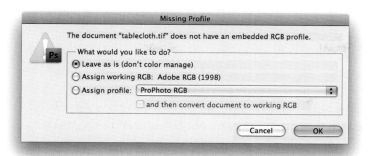

Figure 4-7 The Missing Profile warning offers three choices for handling images that don't contain an embedded profile.

Be aware that if you choose "Discard the embedded profile" or "Leave as is," not only will the document be opened without a profile, but Photoshop will not embed a profile into the document when you save it. If you want a profile to be embedded without converting the colors, choose "Use the embedded profile" or an "Assign profile" option, depending on the alert.

- Paste Profile Mismatch may appear if you paste from a document that uses a different color space than the one you're pasting into (see **Figure 4-8**). Because it's coming from the Clipboard and not from a saved file, assigning isn't possible; the only option is whether or not to convert. In a color-managed workflow, you typically want to click Convert so that the appearance of the pasted data doesn't change.

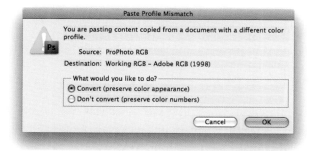

Figure 4-8 The Paste Profile Mismatch warning lets you choose whether to paste the numeric values or the perceived colors that those values represent.

Converting Colors for Output

When you print, the Print dialog uses the document space as the starting point and gives you the opportunity to convert to a print profile or any other profile. We cover this more specifically in "Converting Colors When You Print," later in this chapter.

TIP: Colors in images you edit in Photoshop may look different in applications that don't support color management. For those applications, you may need to use the Convert to Profile command to convert images to a more common color space. For example, all images published on Web pages should be converted to sRGB.

There may be times when you need to convert colors for a Photoshop document for someone else to print. Since you're not going through the Print dialog yourself, you'd use the Convert to Profile command instead (see "Convert to Profile" later in this chapter). For example, you might be sending an image to a publication that requires that images be converted to their CMYK printer profile, while the document space of your images is Adobe RGB. To take care of this, you'd duplicate the original document and convert the copy's colors to the printer's CMYK profile.

When you use the Save for Web and Devices command, a Convert to sRGB check box in that dialog lets you convert colors to sRGB, so that you don't have to remember to use Convert to Profile in advance.

Storing and Finding Color Profiles in Mac OS X

Mac OS X offers a bewildering variety of places to store profiles. You'll find them in the System\Library\ColorSync\Profiles folder, in the Library\ColorSync\Profiles folder, in the Library\ColorSync\Profiles\Displays folder, in the Library\Application Support\Adobe\Color\Profiles folder, in the Library\Application Support\Adobe\Color\Profiles\Recommended folder, in the Users\(username)\Library\ColorSync\Profiles folder, and in some cases, buried several levels deep in subfolders in the Library\Printers folder.

Here's the deal: There are really only three places where you probably want to store profiles. If you want to make a profile available to all user accounts on a Mac, save it in the Library\ColorSync\Profiles folder. Don't try to put it in the System\Library\ColorSync\Profiles folder, because you're not supposed to manually edit the OS X System folder—that's why the other Profiles folders exist.

If you want to make a profile available only to your user account, save it in the Users\(username)\Library\ColorSync\Profiles folder. (If you're the only user, you may as well save all your profiles there.)

If you want to make a profile available from the Color Settings dialog in Photoshop when the Advanced check box is unchecked, save it in the Library\Application Support\Adobe\Color\Profiles folder.

Rendering Intents

Each device has a fixed range of color that it can reproduce, dictated by the laws of physics. Your monitor can't reproduce a more saturated red than the red produced by the color filter or phosphor that a monitor uses to produce red. Your printer can't reproduce a cyan more saturated than the printer's cyan ink, or a white brighter than the white of the paper. The range of color a device can reproduce is called the *color gamut*. Colors present in the source space that aren't reproducible in the destination space are called *out-of-gamut* colors. Since you can't reproduce those colors in the destination space, you have to replace them with some other colors.

The ICC profile specification includes four different methods of handling out-of-gamut colors, called *rendering intents*. (You might see them referred to in Photoshop as simply "intents.") The four rendering intents act as follows:

- Perceptual. The Perceptual intent fits the gamut of the source space into the gamut of the destination space so that the overall color relationships, and hence the overall image appearance, are preserved, even though all the colors in the image may change somewhat in lightness and saturation. It's a good choice for images that contain significant out-of-gamut colors.

- Saturation. The Saturation intent maps fully saturated colors in the source to fully saturated colors in the destination without concerning itself with hue or lightness. It's mostly good for pie charts and such, where you just want vivid colors. However, you can also try it as an alternative method of perceptual rendering. It may be worth previewing a conversion using Saturation rendering to see if it does something useful. For more information on doing that, see "Soft-Proofing Other Color Spaces," later in this chapter.

- Relative Colorimetric. The Relative Colorimetric intent maps white in the source to white in the destination, so that white on your output is the white of the paper rather than the white of the source space, which may be different. It then reproduces all the in-gamut colors exactly, clipping out-of-gamut colors to the closest reproducible hue. For images that don't contain significant out-of-gamut colors, it's often a better choice than Perceptual because it preserves more of the original colors. But if an image has many out-of-gamut colors, they're simply clipped, so Perceptual might be a better choice for those types of images.

- Absolute Colorimetric. The Absolute Colorimetric intent is the same as Relative Colorimetric, except that it doesn't scale source white to destination white. If your source space has a bluish white and your output is

TIP: For photographic images, the two most commonly used intents are Relative Colorimetric and Perceptual. On a critical image, it's best to see how it looks both ways to find out which intent works better for that image.

on a yellowish-white paper, Absolute Colorimetric rendering makes the printer lay down some cyan ink in the white areas to simulate the white of the original. It's generally used only for proofing (see "Soft-Proofing Other Color Spaces" later in this chapter).

Embedding Profiles

Embedding a profile simply means you're including it in a document when you save it. In the Save As dialog (see **Figure 4-9**), the Embed Color Profile check box embeds the profile. When you create a Web image, the File > Save for Web & Devices dialog contains an Embed Color Profile check box. If you save or export a file and the profile option is unavailable, it means you've selected a format (such as GIF or BMP) that can't embed a profile.

Figure 4-9 To include a profile as you save a document, turn on the Embed Color Profile check box near the bottom of the Save As dialog. Photoshop always tells you which profile will be embedded.

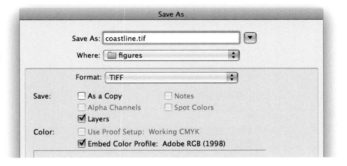

When Not to Embed Profiles

We've been pushing embedded profiles so hard that you might think we always do it. Well, mostly, but there are a few cases where we don't.

For example, we didn't embed profiles in any of the CMYK images we used in this book, because they were all going to the same printing condition, and we set InDesign's CMYK working space to the profile that describes that printing condition. Our CMYK profile is about 2.8 MB, so by not embedding it in every image, we saved a huge amount of disk space and FTP transmission time. The CMYK numbers are unambiguous, because they're governed by the working space profile for the InDesign document.

For Web images, we usually don't embed profiles. Instead, we convert the images to sRGB and leave it at that. Most of the few Web browsers that use ICC profiles have that feature turned off by default, and when fast page loading is a priority, including profiles works against that goal by increasing the file size of images. We're keeping an eye on this, though; as typical Internet speeds increase and browsers mature, it may become more practical to include profiles in Web images. For now, we include profiles only if we know that the primary audience of the Web page uses a browser that's color-managed by default (such as Safari), or if the image is so large that including a profile would be a relatively small part of its file size.

When we work with profiling targets, the whole point of the exercise is to find out what colors the device in question produces when we feed it the numbers in the target, so there's no point in making any assumptions about the appearance represented by the numbers. Therefore, no profile.

Last but not least, if you're working in a closed-loop CMYK workflow, where you just don't want the CMYK numbers to change when sent to your printing process, there's no point in embedding a profile.

In all other situations, we strongly recommend embedding profiles in your images. This conveys your color intentions clearly to all the devices and all the people in your workflow. If you don't, the people downstream have to guess your intentions, causing extra work and frustration for all concerned.

Using Color Settings Presets

In the Settings pop-up menu at the top of the Color Settings dialog, you can choose a single preset that sets working spaces, policies, and warnings for you all at once (see **Figure 4-10**). The real power of the Settings pop-up menu isn't in the settings Photoshop provides, which is why we haven't really brought them up until now. Instead, it's in the ability it gives you to save your own settings to disk and then recall them quickly later. Even better, although you can always load a Color Settings preset from anywhere on your hard drive (using the Load button), if you save your settings in the right place, they become available from the Settings pop-up menu. (In Mac OS X, the "right place" is inside the Library\Application Support\Adobe\Color\Settings folder; in Windows, it's inside Program Files\Common Files\Adobe\Color\Settings.)

Figure 4-10 In the Color Settings dialog, clicking the More Options button extends the dialog and the choices in the pop-up menus.

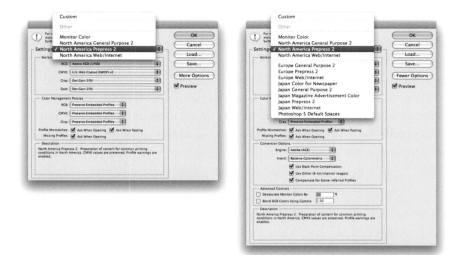

Saving presets that appear in the Settings menu offers an easy way to configure Photoshop for an entire workgroup. And if you own the entire Creative Suite, you can even synchronize the color settings to the same preset across all the Creative Suite applications: In Bridge, choose Edit > Creative Suite Color Settings, and click Synchronize Color Settings.

The presets that Adobe offers fall into two broad categories: those that ignore color management and those that use it. As you can probably guess, we fall squarely into the "use it" camp.

General Purpose 2. The three General Purpose 2 presets (North America, Europe, and Japan) set the RGB working space to sRGB; they set the CMYK working space to U.S. Web Coated (SWOP) v.2 (North America), Euroscale Coated v2 (Europe), or Japan Color 2001 Coated (Japan); they set the Gray working space to Dot Gain 20%; and they set all the policies to Preserve Embedded Profiles while disabling the profile warnings.

What's the "2" all about? These presets are an improvement over the General Purpose Default settings that first appeared in Photoshop CS. The version 2 settings preserve embedded profiles for all color modes (which means the image is displayed in the same way it was when it was last saved), and they no longer use a different default rendering intent than all the other presets. The default rendering intent for all Photoshop CS4 presets is Relative Colorimetric with black-point compensation.

Prepress 2. The three prepress settings—Europe, Japan, and North America Prepress 2—tell Photoshop to use color management wherever possible and to turn on all the alerts for missing and mismatched profiles. They differ only in their choice of CMYK profiles and the dot gain for grayscale and spot colors (20 percent in the United States and 15 percent in Europe and Japan). If your work is destined for a printing press and you don't have a custom profile for your printing or proofing conditions, one of these choices may be a good starting point.

The North America and Japan Prepress 2 presets are identical to the prepress defaults that shipped with Photoshop CS. The Europe Prepress 2 preset uses the Europe ISO Coated FOGRA27 CMYK profile as the CMYK working space instead of the older Euroscale Coated v2, which, unlike the new profile, wasn't readily traceable to any standardized printing condition, so we have to consider it an improvement.

Monitor Color. As its name suggests, Monitor Color loads your monitor profile as the RGB working space and tells Photoshop not to use color management, setting all policies to Off. It treats all your documents as though they are in the working space for that color mode, ignoring any embedded profiles. For some inexplicable reason, though, it turns on the Profile Mismatches: Ask When Opening warning, which makes no sense, since the profile will be ignored anyway.

Web/Internet. If you prepare images *exclusively* for the World Wide Web, the new Web/Internet presets (one each for North America, Europe, and Japan) may be quite useful. The Web is, of course, the same in Japan as it is in North America or Europe: The only difference between the three presets is the CMYK working space, which is U.S. Web Coated (SWOP) v2 for North America, Japan Color 2001 Coated for Japan, and Europe ISO Coated FOGRA27 for Europe.

The dangerous aspect of the Web/Internet presets is that they set the policy for RGB to Convert to Working RGB. That's probably OK if all your work is destined for the Web, but since it automatically converts every RGB file to sRGB, you'll be unhappy when larger-gamut RGB images destined for print get squashed into sRGB! At least the profile mismatch warnings are turned on for this preset; pay attention when they appear.

TIP: If you are working with a printer who provides a Color Settings preset optimized for their prepress workflow, install their preset and choose it in the Color Settings dialog.

TIP: If you want a Color Settings preset to appear in the short version of the Settings pop-up menu, move it into the Recommended folder inside the Settings folder (at the location described on the right). If there are presets you don't want to see, remove them from the Settings folder or the Recommended folder.

The Obscure Color Settings Options

When you click the More Options button in the Color Settings dialog, you gain access to the Conversion Options and Advanced Controls, as well as to a wider range of profiles (we've discussed these earlier in this chapter). The Conversion Options can be useful in typical workflows, but the Advanced Controls are a grab bag of options that may be useful to a very small number of serious players and are dangerous for almost everyone else.

Conversion Options and Advanced Controls

TIP: The terms *color management module* (CMM) and *color management engine* (CME) mean the same thing.

The Conversion Options section of the dialog lets you control useful things like the default rendering intent in Photoshop and the color management module (CMM)—things you may never need to change (see **Figure 4-11**).

Engine. The Engine pop-up menu lets you select the CMM that Photoshop uses for all its color-space calculations. The options that appear on the menu depend on which CMMs are installed on your system. Unless you have really pressing reasons to use a different CMM, we recommend sticking with the Adobe (ACE) engine. When the engines work correctly, there is only a tiny change in pixel values among the different engines; except for the bugs, we've never noticed a visual difference. Mac users will notice separate entries for the Apple CMM and Apple ColorSync; Apple CMM means that the Apple CMM will always be used.

Intent. The Intent pop-up menu lets you choose the default rendering intent that Photoshop uses when you convert colors as you open a document or change the color mode on the Image > Mode submenu (such as when you convert from RGB to CMYK). It also affects Photoshop's calculation of color value readouts for color modes other than the document's, such as in the Info panel and the Color Picker.

While it's nice to be able to set the default rendering intent, intent is best treated as an image-specific and conversion-specific decision. In many places in Photoshop you can preview and change the rendering intent to suit the needs of the image at hand.

Use Black Point Compensation. The Use Black Point Compensation option, when selected, maps the black of the source profile to the black of the destination profile, ensuring that the entire dynamic range of the output device is used. In many cases you'll find no difference whether it's turned on or off, because it depends on the contents of the particular profiles involved. We recommend that you leave Use Black Point Compensation turned on at all times.

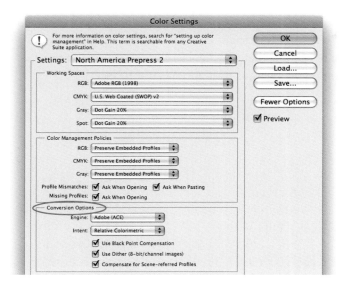

Figure 4-11 The Conversion Options let you fine-tune how Photoshop performs color conversions.

Use Dither (8-Bit/Channel Images). All color-space conversions in Photoshop are performed in a high-bit space. When Use Dither is turned on, Photoshop adds a small amount of noise when the 8-bit channels are converted into the high-bit space, making banding or posterization much less likely to occur (that's a good thing). But if your final output will be JPEG, this tiny dithering may cause a larger file size (because it adds discrete colors into the image), and if you're using Photoshop for scientific work, where you need to perform quantitative analysis on colors, you should turn this off, as it will introduce noise in your data. Otherwise, leave it on.

Compensate for Scene-Referred Profiles. If you use Photoshop to create documents for the Adobe After Effects motion-graphics application and After Effects is set to its default color management settings, you'll want to turn this option on. For everyone else, it doesn't matter how you set it.

The Advanced options are named Advanced for a reason; most users should not need to touch them.

Desaturate Monitor Colors By. Unless you're working with a very large space, like ProPhoto RGB, avoid touching this option. Monitor display is

TIP: If you use Desaturate Monitor Colors By, always remember to turn it back off before you return to normal work; otherwise you'll find yourself producing unexpectedly colorful imagery!

always Relative Colorimetric, so any working space colors that are outside the monitor's gamut must be clipped to the nearest equivalent the monitor can display. This option scales down the saturation of display colors to try to get around the problem. Even then, we don't use it—we find that the problem is much less severe than theory would lead one to expect. If you do want to try it, a setting in the 12 to 15 percent range seems somewhat useful for Kodak ProPhoto RGB.

Blend RGB Colors Using Gamma. To see the effect of this option, paint a bright green stroke on a red background with the check box turned off, and then again with the check box turned on and the value set to a gamma of 1.0. With the check box turned off, the edges of the stroke have a brownish hue, as they would if you were painting with paint. With it turned on, the edges are yellowish, as they would be if you were painting with light. You can think of the behavior with the check box off as artistically correct, and with it turned on as colorimetrically correct.

Photoshop and Your Monitor

Photoshop displays *everything* through your monitor profile. If your monitor profile doesn't accurately describe the actual behavior of your monitor, your judgments about your images won't be accurate, which means your corrections will also be inaccurate. We're guessing that's not what you want.

Photoshop uses the monitor's profile to transform color data on the fly as it gets sent to the video card so that the monitor displays the color correctly. The great benefit of this approach is that it makes it possible for people using very different monitors on different platforms to view the same image as consistently as possible. This makes monitor calibration a mission-critical necessity! (The only time this behavior doesn't happen is if you set the working space to Monitor RGB, which we don't recommend.)

To make this magic happen for you, you need an accurate profile for each monitor. To display color accurately, Photoshop needs to know how your monitor behaves—what color white it produces, what sort of tonal response it has, and what actual colors it produces when it's fed pure R, G, or B. Photoshop gets this information from the display profile. Although a default display profile is assigned to your monitor by your operating system, you'll get the best results from a profile customized for your specific monitor.

Color Settings and the Color Picker

Why are we talking about the Color Picker in this chapter? Simply put, a great many people overlook the fact that the Color Picker is subject to the choices you make in Color Settings, because the numbers that appear in the Color Picker for all the color modes other than the current document's mode are the product of color-space conversions made using the default profiles, engine, and rendering intent.

We've lost count of the number of e-mails we've received from confused users who tried to specify black as 0C 0M 0Y 100K in an RGB document and then got bent out of shape because:

- The resulting color was dark gray.
- It picked up a bunch of C, M, and Y on conversion to CMYK.

Well, 100K isn't black, because black ink isn't perfectly black or perfectly opaque—if it were, we'd never need to lay down more than 100 percent total ink. If you specify 0C 0M 0Y 100K in the Color Picker and then look at the RGB values, or at the Lightness value in Lab, you'll find that they aren't zero. And unless your CMYK working space uses maximum GCR, 0C 0M 0Y 100K isn't a "legal" value for a converted RGB 000 black—you'll almost always want to add some amount of CMY to increase the density.

The Color Picker is governed by two simple rules:

- The "real" color being specified is represented by the numbers relevant to the color mode of the current document, which may not be the numbers you're entering. If you enter CMYK numbers while working on an RGB document, the color you're actually specifying will be represented by the numbers that appear in the RGB fields, and vice versa.
- When you specify color in a mode other than the document's, the actual color is calculated by taking the color values you entered and converting them to the document's mode using the working space profile for the mode you specified as the source profile, the document's profile as the destination profile, and the rendering intent specified in Color Settings.

When you think about it, it's hard to imagine how this could work any other way, but how may of us think that way in the Color Picker?

TIP: To see which monitor profile Photoshop is using, choose Edit > Color Settings, click the RGB pop-up menu, and look at the Monitor RGB command. Photoshop always uses the monitor profile used by the operating system. In Mac OS X, this is in the Displays preference; in Windows it's in the Display Properties control panel.

You also have to maintain your monitor profile. Monitors drift over time, and though LCDs tend to drift much more slowly than CRTs, a profile that was accurate when it was created may not be accurate a week or a month later. Professionals whose jobs depend on accurate color may decide to update their monitor profile every week or two; some people go for a month or more before updating the profile.

There are two distinct ways to compensate for monitor drift.

- You can adjust the monitor hardware itself to bring its behavior into agreement with a specific standard, a process called *calibration*.

- You can create a profile that describes the behavior of the monitor, a process technically known as *profiling* or *characterization*. A profile basically describes the difference between the standard and what the hardware can actually achieve, so that the color management system can make up the difference when sending the image to the video card.

In practice, most monitor profiling tools do both, and they make no clear distinction between the two. (This is why many people refer to the entire process as "calibrating your monitor," even though that's really only the first part of the process.) The practical distinction boils down to the aim points you choose, and how much of each you end up doing depends on the adjustments offered by the monitor.

Calibration Parameters

Monitor profiling packages typically ask for the following parameters:

- White luminance: The brightness of pure white on the monitor, specified in candelas per square meter (cd/m^2), or foot-lamberts.

- White point: The color of the monitor's white, specified either in Kelvins or as a daylight temperature such as D50 or D65 (see the sidebar "How White Are Your Whites?" later in this chapter). For practical monitor calibration purposes, you can treat 5000 K and D50, or 6500 K and D65, as interchangeable.

- The tone response curve, usually specified as a gamma value.

Some packages also let you set a separate black luminance value, but only for CRT displays. LCD displays have a fixed contrast ratio, so the black luminance depends entirely on the white luminance.

Creating a Consistent Viewing Environment

Three factors combine to produce the sensation we describe as color: the object, the light source that illuminates that object, and the observer. You are the observer, and your color vision is subject to subtle changes brought on by everything from your diet to your level of sleep. The other factors that affect your color vision are, fortunately, easier to control:

Lighting. Consistent lighting is vital if you want to create a calibrated system. In the United States, color transparencies and print proofs are almost always evaluated using light with a controlled color temperature of 5000 K. In Europe and Asia, 6500 K is the standard—it's a little more blue.

You need a consistent lighting environment for viewing your prints; otherwise the light falling on the print you're evaluating will constantly change. You can brick up all the windows in the room and install D50 lighting everywhere, but for most of us that's impractical. An easier way is to orient your monitor away from direct window light, turn off the standard room lights for color-critical evaluations, and instead use a relatively inexpensive 4700 K Solux desk lamp for evaluating photographs and prints.

Theoretically, the ideal working environment is one that has low ambient light (almost dark). This maximizes the apparent dynamic range of the monitor and ensures that no stray light is distorting your color perception. However, some shops have noted a significant drop in productivity when they force their employees to work in dark, windowless rooms.

Consistency is more important than the absolute color temperature of the light source. If you work in a studio with a skylight and floor-to-ceiling windows, the color of the light will change over the course of the day, and your perception of color will change along with it. In a situation like that, you really need to create an area where you can view prints and transparencies under a light source that's shielded from the ambient light. A hood to shield the monitor from stray reflections is also very worthwhile—a cardboard box spray-painted matte black may not be elegant, but it's every bit as effective as more expensive solutions, and it doesn't distort the color the way most antiglare shields do.

Context. Your color perception is dramatically affected by surrounding colors. Again, you can go to extremes and paint all your walls neutral gray. It's easier and more important, however, to make your desktop pattern a neutral 50 percent gray. Pink-marble, green-plaid, or family-snapshot desktop patterns may seem fun and harmless, but they'll seriously interfere with your color judgment. We also recommend not wearing Hawaiian shirts when you're making critical color judgments. Designer black, you'll be happy to know, is just great.

Display Adjustments

The ability to calibrate a display depends on the controls that can affect its behavior. You can calibrate any display by changing the lookup tables in the video card that drives it, but the glaring weakness in this approach is that most video card lookup tables (LUTs) use 8 bits per channel. Just as with image editing, making adjustments always results in fewer levels than when you started, so when you only have 8 bits per channel, you need to preserve levels by putting the 8 bits per channel through as few adjustments as possible.

General LCD Monitors. Most professional LCD monitors have no physical adjustments other than the brightness of the backlight. With this type of display, it makes the most sense to profile its native, unadjusted behavior and let the color management system—which typically uses 20 bits per channel instead of the video card LUT's 8 bits—do the work of correcting the displayed colors. We provide some guidance on setting the backlight level in "Setting Aim Points," later in this chapter.

Some LCD monitors have additional color controls like those found on CRTs, which let you adjust options such as white point, contrast, and individual RGB levels. Don't use them! They're only there to pad out the feature list and provide the same convenience as CRT monitors, but in a color-critical workflow they'll probably degrade image quality, not enhance it. This is because those controls typically add an 8-bit adjustment step to your calibration and profiling routine, and as we've said, you don't want to add more conversions. Even if you did, you wouldn't want them happening at only 8 bits per channel. Just leave such a monitor at its native settings, adjust only the backlight, and let your calibration and profiling package do the rest.

High-End LCD Monitors. Some high-end LCD monitors—notably the EIZO FlexScan and ColorEdge series—contain their own lookup tables, independent of the video card, with 10, 12, or even 14 bits of precision. The extra bits don't let the monitor display more colors—the operating system pipeline through which applications communicate with the display is only 8 bits per channel wide—but they do let you calibrate the display to a specific white point and gamma without incurring the losses inherent in doing so in the 8-bit video card LUT. For these displays, we recommend a white point of D65, native gamma if it's an option, and gamma 2.2 if it isn't.

LED-Backlit Monitors. These monitors use arrays of LEDs for the backlight instead of a fluorescent tube. Some LED backlights use white LEDs, but better models use separate arrays of red, green, and blue LEDs, which are capable of much larger gamuts than fluorescent-backlit displays. If your LCD has a white-LED backlight, expect to calibrate it like a fluorescent-backlit LCD—you'll probably be able to calibrate only the display brightness, leaving everything else up to the profiling step. With the superior RGB-array LED backlights, you should be able to adjust the white point by varying the strength of the red, green, and blue LEDs. RGB-array LEDs are found in desktop monitors, while notebooks and other compact displays use white LEDs because they are smaller and lighter, though less adjustable.

CRT Monitors. High-end CRT displays are essentially no longer made, but there are still CRTs in good working order out in the field. For CRT displays which allow separate control over the RGB guns, we recommend adjusting the three RGB gains to achieve the desired white point and destination luminance. The gamma value, however, can be achieved only by adjusting the video card LUT during the profiling stage. If the profiling package offers native gamma as an option, use it. Otherwise we recommend choosing gamma 2.2 because it's closer to the native gamma of CRT displays than any of the other likely choices and hence involves smaller tweaks to the video card LUT than other gamma settings do.

Profiling Tools

If you're serious about working visually with Photoshop (rather than just going by the numbers), you'll get the best results if you use a profiling package that includes a hardware measurement device. Various eyeball-based profiling utilities (such as Apple Display Calibrator software) are available, but they have two major drawbacks:

- Most are designed for CRT displays and don't do a good job of estimating the tonal response of LCDs.

- They use your eyeballs as the measurement device. Our eyes are highly adaptable, which is great for a mammal living on planet Earth but distinctly suboptimal when the goal is to set the monitor to a known state. Human eyes involuntarily and uncontrollably adapt as ambient lighting conditions change, so they aren't accurate enough for consistent color.

Colorimeters and spectrophotometers have none of the eye's wonderful adaptability, so they always produce the same answer when fed the same

TIP: Adobe Gamma was an eyeball-based calibrator included with earlier versions of Photoshop. If you still have it, don't use it on LCDs. Adobe Gamma was designed for CRT monitors, and the mechanism it uses for estimating gamma doesn't work well on LCD monitors.

stimulus. For monitor calibration and profiling, that's a big advantage! If you must use eyeball-based tools, these guidelines may help improve the results:

- Minimize your eyes' adaptability by profiling under the same lighting conditions each time you make a profile. Ideally, the monitor should be the brightest thing in your field of view. (This is always true, but it's particularly critical during profiling—see the sidebar "Creating a Consistent Viewing Environment.")

- Warm up the display for at least a half an hour before profiling.

- Many eyeball-based profiling tools take an existing profile as their starting point. Often, if you take an existing display profile built with the eyeball-based tool as your starting point, the end result is very bad indeed. Start with a known good profile.

Many people are reluctant to spend money on display profiling hardware and software. Unless you've trained yourself to color-correct by reading the Info panel, trying to save money by doing calibration and profiling by eye is a classic example of being penny wise and pound foolish. As with most things, when it comes to monitor-profiling tools you tend to get what you pay for, but even the least expensive instrumented package will return more accurate and more consistent results than any of the visual tools.

Setting Aim Points

TIP: How do you know when your monitor is worn out? One measure is when it no longer reaches the target white luminance value of your profiling package. If you aren't using a hardware calibrator, another less precise way to tell is if the monitor doesn't seem bright enough when you turn up the contrast all the way.

Use the capabilities of your monitor as a guide in setting aim points for calibration and profiling. The goal is to change the video card LUT as little as possible so that you get the full 256 shades per channel that the operating system allows you to send to the monitor.

Aim Points and the Working Space. Some beginners think they need to calibrate and profile their monitor to the same specs as their working space. That's a mistake; the white point and gamma of your display are entirely independent of the white point and gamma of your working space. The color management system translates working space white point and gamma seamlessly to those of your display. The goal in setting white point and gamma for the display is simply to make the display behave as well as it can.

Monitor Brightness (White Luminance). How bright should your monitor be? Here are some factors that will help you set the appropriate level:

- The monitor should be bright enough to provide comfortable viewing. Reasonable starting points are around 80 to 95 cd/m^2 for CRT and around 120 cd/m^2 for LCDs.

- For an LCD monitor, you probably won't be turning the monitor brightness up all the way. For one thing, changing the brightness level typically changes the black level as well. Today's LCD monitors are capable of such high brightness that some less expensive monitors can't be made dark enough for a good black level. And anyway, full brightness wears out the backlight more quickly.

- Don't aim for a brightness lower than 75 cd/m^2 or you'll affect the accurate reproduction of highlights. If a monitor can't achieve at least 75 cd/m^2 after profiling, it's a candidate for replacement.

White Point. On the few high-end displays with genuinely adjustable white points, we recommend adjusting the display to a D65/6500 K white point. For more information, see the sidebar "How White Are Your Whites?" If the white point isn't adjustable in the display itself, as is the case with most LCDs, we recommend profiling with the native white point—it's usually very close to D65 anyway.

Gamma. We prefer to use native gamma as the aim point. If native gamma isn't an option, we use gamma 2.2, which is close to the native response of most monitors. (Actually, the tonal response curve of an LCD monitor doesn't really match a gamma curve, but if gamma is the only option, gamma 2.2 is still the best alternative.)

Perhaps in recognition of the fact that LCDs don't really follow a gamma curve, some profiling packages now offer more exotic tone-response curves. With "standard" LCDs that don't have their own internal LUTs, we still prefer using native gamma if possible. But if that isn't an option, or if you're using a display with internal LUTs that the profiling software can address, we encourage you to investigate these options. We've obtained good results using the L* curve in Integrated Color Corporation ColorEyes, and with the DICOM curve in NEC's SpectraView II.

If You Just Want to Go by the Numbers. It's possible to do good work with Photoshop using an uncalibrated, unprofiled monitor. But to do this, you can't trust monitor colors at all. Instead go by the numbers, reading RGB levels and the CMYK dot percentages in the Info panel. Even with a calibrated monitor, it's a good idea to keep an eye on those numbers.

TIP: if your prints are always dark compared to your monitor, your monitor brightness may be set too high relative to the real-world brightness of the paper you're using. Try regenerating the monitor profile at a lower monitor brightness level.

To set your monitor up for this old workflow, open the Color Settings dialog, select the RGB pop-up menu in the Working Spaces section, and choose Monitor RGB. We don't advocate this—we prefer the benefits of visual feedback—but it is possible, particularly if you're working in a closed-loop environment where you always go to the same output conditions. Of course, if you do this, you may as well ignore the rest of this chapter.

ASSIGN PROFILE AND CONVERT TO PROFILE

Earlier we talked about how the settings in the Color Settings dialog control color conversion as you open or import a document. In a document that's already open, you apply profiles and color conversions using the Assign Profile and Convert to Profile commands on the Edit menu.

If you aren't sure when you should assign and when you should convert, you're not alone. What it comes down to is this:

*   Do you need to tag the image with a specific profile without altering the color values at all? If so, you want to use the Assign Profile command.

*   Do you need to change the image's color values into another color space (such as converting RGB to CMYK, or Adobe RGB to sRGB) while keeping the image appearance as consistent as possible with the way it currently looks? If so, you want to use the Convert to Profile command.

Assigning profiles is like attaching labels, while converting is a fundamental change. If you're still having trouble with the concept, here's an analogy. Wearing a police uniform is like *assigning* a profile: It doesn't turn a person into a police officer, but it does make it possible for others to recognize him or her as a police officer. A police officer is a police officer even when not wearing a uniform, but without the uniform (when the profile is missing), nobody can see that the person is a police officer. When someone walks into a police academy and trains to become a police officer, that's *conversion*—the person started as a civilian and is now a police officer. If the officer always wears a uniform in public, that's like *embedding* a profile; it's with the officer wherever he or she goes, enabling instant identification and avoiding ambiguity.

How White Are Your Whites?

One of the aim points for monitor calibration and profiling is the white point. The basic advice is to choose a white point that's consistent with your proofing conditions. In the past, that meant the prepress proofing standard you are using, but Web designers and video editors may want to be consistent with sRGB instead. Unfortunately, setting the white point is not as straightforward as entering the numbers.

For example, you may be advised to calibrate to a white point of D50 and a gamma of 1.8 to match the proofing illuminant and dot gain of the commercial printing industry. But when you attempt to compare an image on the monitor side by side with a print in a D50 light box, highlights on the monitor may appear redder than those on the hard copy, even when both monitor and light box are calibrated to D50 and balanced to the same level of illumination.

We're not exactly sure what causes this widely reported phenomenon, but part of the explanation may be that, although a theoretically ideal D50 illuminant produces a continuous spectrum, the light sources in both the lamps in light boxes and the phosphors or color filters in monitors produce spiky, discontinuous output that's concentrated in fairly narrow bands. This would affect the many different combinations of wavelengths that produce the tristimulus values that add up to a D50 white point.

There may also be a perceptual effect in play. One of the well-known tricks our eyes play on us is called "discounting the illuminant." If we look at a red apple under red light, we still see it as red rather than white, because we know it's red and we discount the red light. But when we look at a monitor, we can't discount the illuminant because the image *is* the illuminant!

One solution that some find to be effective is to separate the monitor and the light box—for example, you can work with the monitor in front of you and the light box behind you, switching from one to the other. Many find that calibrating the monitor to D65 rather than D50 creates a much better match with a D50 light box, and this may be the simplest solution. Another factor that nudges us toward D65 and away from D50 is that whenever we measure the color temperature of daylight within a thousand meters of sea level, we invariably find that it's much closer to D65 than to D50. Our eyes seem to adapt easily to a D65 monitor white.

While this subject needs more research, we've come to the conclusion that it makes more sense to calibrate the monitor to D65 than to D50. Most LCDs have a native white point of D65 anyway, so for LCDs, just use this native white point. If you're happy with a D50 monitor white, don't fix what isn't broken, but if you're running into any of the aforementioned issues, we strongly recommend that you try D65 instead.

Assign Profile

Assign Profile lets you tag an image with a specified profile or untag an image by removing its profile. It doesn't do any conversions; it simply attaches a description (an interpretation, as it were) to the numbers in the image, or removes one (see **Figure 4-12**).

Figure 4-12 The Assign Profile dialog

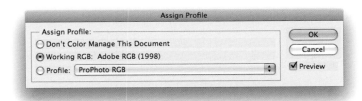

We mainly find Assign Profile useful when we're trying to decide what profile should be attached to an untagged document. Unlike the profile assignment in the Missing Profile dialog, Assign Profile lets you preview the results of applying various profiles. This gives you the opportunity to make an educated guess rather than a blind one.

The Assign Profile dialog offers three options, which are identical to the first three options in the Missing Profile warning (see "Color Management Policies," earlier in this chapter).

- Don't Color Manage This Document. This option tells Photoshop to treat it as an untagged document. The numbers in the file are preserved and are interpreted according to the current working space, and the embedded profile is stripped out. If you're delivering final CMYK to shops that are scared or confused by color management, or if you've inadvertently embedded a profile in a calibration target, you can use this option to strip out the profile.

- Working RGB or Working CMYK. This option tags the document with the profile of the current working space. As with the previous option, the numbers in the file are preserved but reinterpreted according to the current working space. The difference is that the document is treated as tagged, so it keeps that profile if you later change the working space. If you've opened an untagged document and decided that it really does belong in the working space, use this option to make sure that it stays in the working space.

- Profile. Profile lets you tag the document with a profile other than the default working space profile. Again, the numbers in the image are preserved, but in this case they're interpreted according to the profile you assigned. For example, if you scan an image using software that doesn't embed a profile, but you have a profile for your scanner, you can use this option to assign color meaning to the image you've just scanned. You'll then probably want to use Convert to Profile (coming up next) to move the image into a more reasonable editing space, like AdobeRGB.

TIP: We always use the time-saving Preview check box in the Assign Profile and Convert to Profile dialogs, since the whole point is to make sure the image looks right after we're done.

Convert to Profile

Convert to Profile, as its name suggests, lets you convert a document from its profile space (or, in the case of an untagged document, the current working space) to any other profiled space, with full control over how the conversion is done (see **Figure 4-13**).

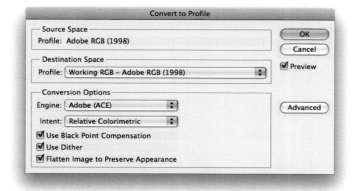

Figure 4-13 The Convert to Profile dialog gives you full control over color conversions. You can choose the destination space, engine, and rendering intent.

The Convert to Profile dialog displays the source profile and lets you specify a destination profile and other options. It includes the Preview check box so that you can see the effects of the conversion before you actually do it.

The engine, rendering intent, black-point compensation, and dithering options all work identically to those in the Color Settings dialog (see "Conversion Options and Advanced Controls," earlier in this chapter).

The Flatten Image to Preserve Appearance option is there as a convenience, for when you want to produce a final flat file for output. When we use Convert to Profile, we usually make a duplicate of the layered file first (choose

Image > Duplicate) and then run Convert to Profile on the duplicate, with Flatten Image turned on—that way we keep our layered master files intact.

Photoshop CS4 adds an Advanced button to the Convert to Profile dialog box. Clicking it reveals additional options for the Destination Space. Instead of seeing all your profiles in one list that can become rather long, available profiles are divided into categories. Also, you can now convert to Multi-channel, Device Link, and other profile categories that don't correspond to standard RGB or CMYK channels. Device Link profiles let you convert directly from one device profile to another, such as between two press profiles; this can preserve image quality because it bypasses the intermediate conversion to Lab color that usually happens when Photoshop converts between color modes. In Mac OS X, Abstract profiles are about special effects, not image quality; these options are provided by Apple ColorSync, and chances are, you'd rather create these effects in Photoshop itself.

We use Convert to Profile instead of choosing an Image > Mode command for most conversions (whether converting RGB to CMYK, cross-rendering CMYK to CMYK, or whatever), because it offers more control, and especially because we can preview different rendering intents. Rendering intents know only about the color gamut of the source color space—they don't know anything about how much of that gamut is actually used by the source image—so applying perceptual rendering to an image that contains no significant out-of-gamut colors compresses the gamut unnecessarily. With Convert to Profile, you can see how the different rendering intents will affect a particular image and choose accordingly.

Soft-Proofing Other Color Spaces

If you're sane, you probably want to get some sense of what your images are going to look like before you commit to a $50,000 print run. There are three ways to proof your pictures: traditional (print film negatives and create a laminated proof such as a Matchprint), on a color printer (such as one of the new breed of inkjet printers), or onscreen. Proofing images onscreen is called *soft-proofing*, and Photoshop offers soft-proofing capabilities limited only by the accuracy of the profiles involved.

One of the hardest and most important tasks in Photoshop is proofing your final output on your screen or on a color printer. Photoshop gives you very fine control over both. We discuss this in more detail in "Optimizing an Image for Print" in Chapter 8, "The Digital Darkroom," but here's the quick version:

- The Proof Setup command (View > Proof Setup) gives you full control over onscreen proofing simulations. You can simultaneously view the same file with different simulations in different windows.

- You can view how different rendering intents will convert an image to a destination space before actually making the conversion.

- You can see how an image prepared for one output process will behave when sent to another output process without adjustment: This is particularly useful when you're faced with the prospect of repurposing CMYK files made for one printing condition to work with another.

- You can work inside an accurate output simulation to optimize your image for a particular output process.

For this to work, you *must* calibrate and profile your monitor, and we highly recommend that you also take steps to control your viewing environment (see the sidebar "Creating a Consistent Viewing Environment," later in this chapter).

In Photoshop, soft-proofing has its own set of controls separate from the Color Settings dialog. These allow you to preview your output accurately, whether it's RGB or CMYK. This is a huge advantage for those who print to RGB devices such as film recorders or to photorealistic inkjet printers that pretend to be RGB devices. Soft-proofing is also a big improvement for those who print CMYK. We can soft-proof different conversions to CMYK while we're still working in RGB and have them accurately depicted onscreen. For example, you can quickly see how the same image would look on newsprint and in your glossy brochure.

The View > Proof Colors command lets you turn soft-proofing on and off. Soft-proofing changes only the onscreen display for the current document window, without altering other windows or saved image data. By default, Proof Colors works as follows:

- It first simulates the conversion from the document's space to working CMYK, using the rendering intent and black-point compensation settings specified in Color Settings.

TIP: You can open several windows for the same image (by choosing Window > Arrange > New Window) and apply different soft-proofing settings to each window. This lets you see how the image will appear under different output scenarios. You can use this feature to adjust the unproofed image while watching the effect on multiple soft-proofed views of the same image.

- It renders that simulation to the monitor, using relative colorimetric rendering. If Use Black Point Compensation is turned on in Color Settings, it's also applied to the rendering from the proof space to the monitor.

The default Proof Setup settings probably don't represent the output you're trying to preview, so to really benefit from soft-proofing, you need to be more specific. Your first stop is the Proof Setup submenu (see **Figure 4-14**), which governs exactly what Proof Colors shows you. If your actual output conditions are represented by one of the menu items, choose it so that Proof Setup will use those conditions when it shows you the soft-proof.

Figure 4-14 The Proof Setup submenu lets you choose a wide variety of soft-proofing options, including your own custom settings.

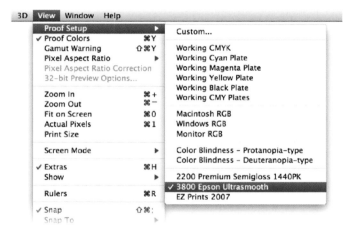

However, chances are that the output conditions listed by default on the Proof Setup submenu aren't specific enough to represent your output conditions. To unleash the power of soft-proofing, you need to use the Customize Proof Condition dialog, which gives you the tools you need to nail your soft-proofs precisely and list them on the Proof Setup submenu.

Customize Proof Condition Dialog

The Customize Proof Condition dialog lets you independently control the rendering from the document's space to the proof space, and from the proof space to the screen. It allows you to preview accurately just about any conceivable kind of output for which you have a profile. You can open the Customize Proof Condition dialog (see **Figure 4-15**) by choosing View > Proof Setup > Custom.

When You Have No Idea What to Do

Assign Profile and Convert to Profile can be intimidating to new (and even not so new) Photoshop users. If you're staring at the dialog but the answer isn't obvious, how do you figure out what it is? It all goes back to the three questions we posed early on (see "Color Management Is About Answering Simple Questions," earlier in this chapter).

- **How is this image supposed to look?** When a profile is missing and a known good image looks way off, you can often fix it instantly by assigning the correct profile to it. If you open an untagged image and you immediately see that it looks wrong, the next question to ask is *how* it looks wrong. For example, if an image appears unusually desaturated and weak, that's often a clue that it was edited in a larger color space than the one you're using to view it. Assigning a larger color space, such as Adobe RGB or ProPhoto RGB, may snap the image back to life.

- **Where did this image come from?** Because a profile represents the color space where an image was last edited, if you know what that environment was, assigning that profile will most likely display the image colors properly. For example, if you receive an untagged image from an old CMYK print job, assigning the profile for that job should display the image as it originally appeared. (In this specific example, though, if the prepress workflow is designed for untagged CMYK files, it may be better to click Don't Color Manage or Leave As Is and instead change your CMYK working space to that job's CMYK profile. This way, you can view the images as intended and without attaching profiles to them.)

- **Where is this image going?** For Convert to Profile, the right answer comes from knowing the destination of the image. And it might not be about the final destination. If you're about to edit an image you intend to use as a full-resolution RGB master, you'll probably want to convert it to a great editing space, like Adobe RGB or ProPhoto RGB. If you're already working with a master image and are now getting a duplicate ready for final output, you'll convert it to the appropriate color space, such as CMYK for prepress or sRGB for the Web or video.

Custom Proof Condition. The Custom Proof Condition pop-up menu lets you recall setups that you've saved in the special Proofing folder. (On Mac OS X, this folder is in harddrive\Library\Application Support\Adobe\Color\Proofing. In Windows, it's in the Program Files\Common Files\Adobe\Color\Proofing folder.) You can save proof setups anywhere on your hard disk by clicking Save, and load them by clicking the Load button, but the setups you save in the Proofing folder appear on the list automatically. (Even better, they also appear at the bottom of the Proof Setup submenu, where you can choose them directly.)

Device to Simulate. The Device to Simulate pop-up menu lets you specify the proofing space you want to simulate. You can choose any profile, but if you choose an input profile (for a scanner or digital camera), the Preserve Numbers check box becomes checked and dimmed, and all the other controls become unavailable. Generally, you'll want to choose an RGB, CMYK, or grayscale output profile.

Preserve RGB/CMYK/Gray Numbers. The Preserve Numbers check box tells Photoshop to show you what your file would look like if you sent it to the output device without performing a color-space conversion. It's available only when the image is in the same color mode as the selected profile (such as when both are in RGB); when you turn it on, the Rendering Intent pop-up menu becomes unavailable, since no conversion is requested.

Figure 4-15 You can control color conversions from the document space to the proofing space and from the proofing space to the monitor.

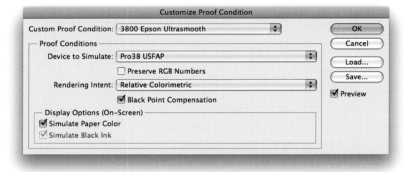

This feature is particularly useful when you have a CMYK file that was prepared for some other printing process. It shows you how the CMYK data will work on your output, which can help you decide whether you need to edit the image, convert it to a different CMYK space, or just send it as is. It's also useful for seeing just how crummy your image will look if you send it to your desktop inkjet printer without converting it to the proper profile (see "Converting Colors When You Print," later in this chapter).

Rendering Intent. The Rendering Intent pop-up menu lets you specify the rendering intent you want to use in the conversion from the document's space to the proof space. Since the correct intent depends on individual images, it's good to be able to test it. It defaults to the rendering intent specified in the Color Settings dialog. If you change it, it remembers your change. Saving a new proof condition also saves your selected rendering intent, so if you're continually being tripped up by the wrong intent, you can just save a proof setup with your preferred rendering intent and make sure to use it.

Black Point Compensation. When turned on, this option applies black-point compensation when converting from the document's space to the proof space. Keep this option turned on; the only exceptions are some obscure printing workflows that will tell you when it should be turned off.

Display Options (On Screen). The check boxes in the Display Options section—Simulate Paper Color and Simulate Black Ink—control the rendering of the image from the proofing space to the monitor. When both Simulate Paper Color and Simulate Black Ink are turned off, Photoshop does a relative colorimetric rendering (with black-point compensation if that option is turned on in Color Settings). This rendering maps paper white to monitor white and ink black to monitor black using the entire dynamic range of the monitor. If you're using a generic monitor profile, this is probably as good as you'll get (of course, with a canned monitor profile, you can't trust anything you see onscreen anyway). With a good monitor profile, though, you should check out the alternatives.

- When you turn on Simulate Black Ink, Photoshop turns off black-point compensation when rendering from the proofing space to the monitor, so the black you see on the monitor is the actual black you'll get on output (within limits). If you're printing to a low-dynamic-range process, such as newsprint or inkjet on uncoated paper, Simulate Black Ink will give you a much better idea of the actual blacks you'll get in print.

- Turning on the Simulate Paper Color check box makes Photoshop do an absolute colorimetric rendering from the proof space to the display. (Simulate Black Ink becomes checked and dimmed, since black-point compensation is always disabled in absolute colorimetric conversions.) In theory at least, turning on Simulate Paper Color should give you the most accurate soft proof possible.

  In practice, the most obvious effect of selecting Simulate Paper Color isn't that it simulates the color of the paper, but rather that you see the compressed dynamic range of print. If you look at the image while

TIP: Most monitor profiles have a "black hole" black point. The black ink simulation will be off by the amount that real monitor black differs from the monitor profile's black point. On a well-calibrated monitor, the inaccuracy is very slight.

turning on Simulate Paper Color, the effect is dramatic—so much so that we look away from the monitor when we turn it on, then wait a few seconds before looking at the image to allow our eyes to adapt to the new white point. More importantly, we also make sure that we hide all white user interface elements, so that our eyes *can* adapt.

Obviously, the quality of the soft-proofing simulation depends on the accuracy of your monitor calibration and on the quality of your profiles. But we believe that the relationship between the image on the screen and the final printed output is, like all proofing relationships, one that you must learn. We've never seen a proofing system, short of an actual press proof, that really matches the final printed piece—laminated film proofs, for example, often show greater contrast than the press sheet, and may have a slight color cast too, but most people in the print industry have learned to discount the slight differences between proof and finished piece.

It's also worth bearing in mind the limitations of the color science on which the whole ICC color management effort is based. We still have a great deal to learn about color perception, and while the science we have works surprisingly well in many situations, it's only a model. The bottom line is that each of the different soft-proofing renderings to the monitor can tell you something about your printed images. We recommend that you experiment with the settings and learn what works for you and what doesn't.

Proof Setup Submenu

The Proof Setup submenu (under the View menu) contains several other useful commands. For instance, when you're viewing an RGB or grayscale image, you can view the individual CMYK plates (or the CMY progressive) you'd get if you converted to CMYK via the Image > Mode command. You can also use these commands to view the individual plates in CMYK files, but it's much faster and easier to either use the keyboard shortcuts to display individual channels or click on the eyeball icon in the Channels panel.

The next set of commands—Macintosh RGB, Windows RGB, and Monitor RGB—is available only for RGB, grayscale, and indexed color images, not for CMYK or Lab. They show you how your image would appear on a "typical" Mac monitor (as defined by the Apple RGB profile), on a "typical" Windows monitor (as defined by the sRGB profile), and on your personal monitor (as defined by your monitor profile) if you displayed it on these monitors with no color management. These commands might be useful when producing Web graphics, for instance. The rest of the menu lists custom proof setups saved in the Proofing folder.

The soft-proofing features let you see how your image will actually appear in the output, so you can optimize the image for the best possible rendition in the selected output space. They also help you see if the same master file can produce acceptable results in all the output conditions to which you plan on sending it, relying on color management to handle the various conversions. So whether you're a driven artist seeking perfection or a lowly production grunt doing the impossible on a daily basis, the soft-proofing tools in Photoshop will become an invaluable addition to your toolbox.

Converting Colors When You Print

In the Print dialog, Photoshop can convert colors as it sends an image to a printer. We prefer this to letting the printer driver do the conversion. It's convenient because you don't have to convert a duplicate document first. You can either convert from the document space to a selected printer profile using a selected rendering intent or from the document space to a selected Proof Setup space using the rendering intent specified in Proof Setup, and then to the printer profile. The second method lets you print an RGB file to a composite printer and make the printer simulate the CMYK output you've been soft-proofing—that is, it gives you a hard copy of your soft-proofed image without your having to first convert the image to final output CMYK.

The Print Dialog in Photoshop

We cover most of the Print dialog in Chapter 12, "Image Storage and Output"; however, we'll cover the color management aspects of the dialog here.

To use the color management features in the Print dialog (File > Print), choose Color Management from the unnamed pop-up menu that appears at the top of the options group on the right (see **Figure 4-16**). The Color Management options let you control the data that's sent to the printer and choose whether to let Photoshop do the conversion to the printer space.

Color-Space Buttons. The first two buttons let you choose the Document space (to reproduce the image as well as your printer can) or the Proof space (to produce a hard copy of your soft-proof simulation). If the image window from which you're printing has a custom proof setup, it will appear as the Proof option; otherwise the choice reads Profile N/A. This is slightly misleading, because if you click the Proof radio button, it actually enables the Proof Setup Preset menu in Options, described later in this section.

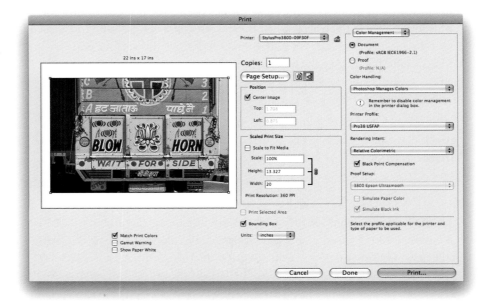

Figure 4-16 The Print dialog supports print preview and soft-proofing.

Color Handling. The Color Handling pop-up menu (see **Figure 4-17**) determines what options are available in the rest of the Options section.

- Printer Manages Colors sends unconverted source data, letting the printer driver convert colors to the printer space. Color-managing CMYK images on PostScript printers requires PostScript 3—on a PostScript Level 2 printer, choose Lab Color instead. PostScript color management varies enormously. We don't recommend this method, because Photoshop converts colors better than most printer drivers.

- Photoshop Manages Colors enables the Printer Profile menu. Photoshop converts the data sent to the printer to the profile space described by the profile chosen from the Printer Profile menu, using the rendering intent specified in the Rendering Intent pop-up menu.

- Separations is available only for CMYK documents. It sends the individual plates to the printer, unmodified, as four separate pages. If you choose Separations, you may want to choose Output from the pop-up menu at the top right of the Print dialog, so you can specify options such as crop and registration marks.

- No Color Management is almost the same as Printer Manages Colors—it sends the numbers in the document to the printer, but it doesn't include the profile that describes them. We use this option for printing profiling targets.

Figure 4-17 The Color Handling pop-up menu

Printer Profile. The Printer Profile menu is enabled only when you choose Photoshop Manages Colors from the Color Handling pop-up menu. Choose the profile that describes the printer to which you're printing and the paper and ink the printer is using.

Rendering Intent. The Rendering Intent menu is enabled when you choose either Printer Manages Colors or Photoshop Manages Colors from the Color Handling menu, but in our experience, it behaves reliably only in the former case. Choose the rendering intent that works best for the image by previewing the print using Proof Setup. (The Black Point Compensation check box is enabled only when Photoshop Manages Colors is selected in the Color Handling menu. As previously noted, we leave it turned on.)

Proof Setup. The Proof Setup menu is available with all Color Handling pop-up menu choices except Separations and is enabled when you click the Proof radio button. Photoshop executes the conversion specified in the selected Proof Setup preset before sending the data to the printer using the options controlled by the Color Handling menu.

It also disables the Rendering Intent menu. The rendering of the simulated proof space to the printer space is controlled instead by the Simulate Paper Color and Simulate Black Ink check boxes. When both are unselected, Photoshop converts the simulated proof data to the printer space using relative colorimetric rendering with black-point compensation. Checking Simulate Black Ink turns off the black-point compensation, while checking Simulate Paper Color makes Photoshop use absolute colorimetric rendering instead, forcing the printer to reproduce the actual "paper white" and actual "ink black" of the simulated proof.

TIP: The Match Print Colors and Show Paper White check boxes in the Print dialog don't affect the color conversion to the printer. All they do is apply the Printer Profile you selected in the Print dialog to the proxy image, so that the Print dialog can display a more accurate preview of the colors that will print. Match Print Colors and Gamut Warning are based on that selected profile.

In our experience, this feature works well when Photoshop Manages Colors is selected in the Color Handling menu, but it can produce random results when any of the other alternatives are selected. By all means, experiment, but don't say we didn't warn you!

The Printer Driver's Print Dialog

Photoshop applies all of the Print dialog Color Management options to the data it sends to the printer driver. You won't see any trace of the Photoshop options in the printer driver's Print dialog, which appears after you click the Print button in the Photoshop Print dialog. If you use the Photoshop Print dialog to convert image colors, make sure you don't have another conversion specified in the printer driver's Print dialog, or you'll get a double correction and a nasty print. In the printer driver, look for a color management option such as Off, None, or No Color Adjustment, and choose it to make sure that the driver doesn't sabotage you with an unwanted extra conversion.

PRINTING TO DESKTOP PRINTERS

TIP: On professional desktop printers such as the Epson Stylus Pro line, we recommend using Photoshop-managed color output, described in "Converting Colors When You Print" earlier in this chapter: In the Print dialog in Photoshop, choose Photoshop Manages Colors; choose the right printer profile, and turn off color management in the printer driver's Print dialog.

The way Photoshop prints to a desktop printer depends on the color mode in which it expects to receive data. Photographic printers are true RGB devices—they expose photosensitive paper using red, green, and blue lasers or LEDs—so the CMYK color mode simply doesn't apply. Inkjet printers use cyan, magenta, yellow, and black inks (plus additional inks to extend gamut and detail), which in theory at least makes them CMYK devices. But in practice, unless you're printing through a PostScript raster image processor (RIP), desktop inkjet printer drivers are built to receive only RGB data. This is because traditionally, operating system-level graphics languages have not been able to send CMYK to printers. Photoshop itself can send CMYK to these printers, but the printer driver will immediately convert it to RGB before doing anything else with it.

A PostScript RIP may seem to allow more control over the printing process by letting you control the individual inks, but that usually isn't the case. PostScript RIPs that use the printer's native screening algorithms usually send RGB to that part of the print process; those that truly provide ink-level control use their own screening, which may not look better than the printer's native screening. A PostScript RIP makes sense from a workflow standpoint if you're using a desktop printer as a proofer for prepress, but if your desktop print is your final output, use your printer's own RGB driver or a specialized RIP designed for photo output, such as Colorbyte's ImagePrint.

RGB Output. If you're printing RGB, you can skip the entire CMYK section in this chapter. You should, however, read the sections "Choosing an RGB Working Space," "Soft-Proofing Other Color Spaces," and "Converting Colors When You Print" carefully. We recommend using ICC profiles for your printer. If you print using the printer vendor's inks and papers, the canned profiles that come with the printer may work well. If you're using third-party inks and papers, though, a custom profile will improve your output immensely. Inexpensive scanner-based profiling packages such as the PANTONE huey can work well with inkjet printers and can pay for themselves in savings on ink and paper. Don't use your RGB printer profile as an RGB working space, because RGB printer spaces aren't gray-balanced or perceptually uniform, making editing difficult. Instead, use a working space such as ProPhoto RGB, and fine-tune your image for output using Proof Setup to create a simulation of the printed output.

CMYK Output. If you're printing CMYK through a PostScript RIP, almost everything we say in this chapter about press CMYK applies equally to desktop printers.

Isolating Variables

All color management operations depend on a minimum of two profiles. Simply viewing a document requires a profile that describes the document and one that describes the current display. Other operations involve three or even more profiles. If you run into issues that don't appear to be a result of operator error, it's likely that one or more of the profiles involved is a weak link. Use a process of elimination to troubleshoot problems. Test each profile in isolation and change one thing at a time. You're likely to find the culprit much quicker than you would by flailing around and changing multiple parameters willy-nilly.

Color management isn't a panacea, and it doesn't remove the need for intelligent human color correction. It's just a useful tool that provides a solid floor for you to stand on when you make your (hopefully intelligent, certainly human) corrections.

Canned vs. Custom Profiles

Canned profiles—profiles supplied by a third party that are based on something other than measurements of your specific device—have earned a bad reputation, often deservedly so. But under the right circumstances, generic ICC profiles can be very useful. It's true that each combination of printing press, ink, and paper is unique. However, virtually all press operators pride themselves on their ability to match a contract proof such as an Imation Matchprint or Fuji ColorArt. If they couldn't, color printing would be almost impossible.

Proofer Profiles. Proofing systems are generally very consistent from shop to shop. This makes them good candidates for canned profiles—stable, repeatable, consistent output processes like contract proofers simply don't need custom profiles. You need to make sure that the profile you choose has the correct ink limits, black generation, and substrate for your job, but as long as you pay attention to these variables, you can produce excellent results using generic proofer profiles.

Sheetfed Press. Although sheetfed presses vary a little more than do proofing systems, we've seen excellent results from generic sheetfed press profiles too, providing the paper stock isn't too weird. Bear in mind that the press operator has a great deal of control over the final result—a profile has to be only a reasonable match to the press.

Desktop Printers. Whether you use a desktop color printer for proofing or for exhibition-quality prints, having custom-built profiles for your ink and paper combinations helps ensure that your printer is reproducing color to the best of its ability.

CHAPTER FIVE

Building a Digital Workflow

In a previous edition of this book, we said it was only a matter of when, not if, digital would replace film for most applications. Now we look back on that statement and laugh, because in the short time between these editions, the transition from film to digital is essentially complete. In addition, photographers have latched onto the idea of processing files of raw data straight from the camera's sensor because it provides a level of control and potential quality comparable to developing and printing your own film.

That said, anyone who has made the switch from film to digital can tell you that the time savings of digital photography (compared to film) is often offset by new tasks that photographers didn't have to worry about before. Having total control over the processing of every image means a photographer must now set aside the time and acquire the skills to do it right, instead of sending film to the lab to be developed or printed and getting something else done in the meantime. Digital storage is so cheap and capacious that a typical shoot now produces far more frames than it would have using film. But that also means there are many more frames to cull and process afterward, burdening the photographer further.

The good news is that Adobe Photoshop CS4 benefits from what everyone learned during the earlier stages of the transition to serious digital photography. Photoshop CS4, along with the Adobe Bridge and Adobe Camera Raw software included with it, can fulfill the key tasks of a high-volume digital camera workflow from beginning to end—something that wasn't possible in previous versions. Also, Adobe has added so many useful features to Camera Raw 5 that in some cases you may not even need to open the images in Photoshop.

CHOOSING A DIGITAL WORKFLOW

The Photoshop/Bridge/Camera Raw combo handles most digital imaging workflows quite well, whether you're processing raw files from the latest digital SLR camera or scanning your archives of film. To get the most out of all these programs you bought, it helps to think of them as a team. Toward that end, let's meet the players:

- Adobe Bridge CS4. Browses folders and lets you perform all kinds of metadata and file system-related tasks on them, including comparing images, adding keywords, rating, and batch-renaming files. Bridge CS4 integrates the generation of slide shows and Web sites, and the ability to batch output to PDF contact sheets or Web galleries.

- Adobe Camera Raw 5. Converts raw digital camera images to RGB files Photoshop can use. But it's more than just a converter: Because it acts on raw camera data, its adjustments are of a very high quality. In addition, because the adjustments are held in metadata before the conversion, you can make any number of edits to the original without degrading it. Despite its name, Camera Raw can also apply metadata-based edits to JPEG and TIFF files. Camera Raw 5 adds local adjustments, leaving even fewer reasons to go to Photoshop.

- Adobe Photoshop CS4. Photoshop is the ultimate traditional pixel-based image editor, but since you bought this book, you know that. In the past, all image edits happened in Photoshop, but now that the Camera Raw feature set has expanded, you may want to have Photoshop perform only those pixel-level edits that Camera Raw can't handle.

Camera Raw and Bridge have gotten so capable that we can't describe them in detail in this book and still have room to cover Photoshop, so we've focused only on the features that will make you most productive. For the most thorough and detailed description of Camera Raw, we recommend that you check out the book *Real World Camera Raw with Adobe Photoshop CS4* by Jeff Schewe.

Key Tasks in a Digital Workflow

In today's digital workflow, the images you shoot or scan typically need to be processed through the following tasks:

1. Bring the images into your computer. For raw files from a digital camera, you can use Adobe Photo Downloader, included with Bridge. Part of this step involves letting Bridge cache image thumbnails, previews, and metadata, which also gives you an opportunity to verify that the images were copied successfully.

2. Rate and label your highest-priority images, if you have more images than time. You can do this in Bridge and Camera Raw.

3. Correct the images. If they're raw images, TIFF, or JPEG files, Adobe Camera Raw may be the fastest way to make fundamental corrections to tone and color (see "Fundamental Image Corrections" below). Edits you can't do in Camera Raw can be done in Photoshop after you make the fundamental corrections in Camera Raw.

4. Make your images easy to find. Add keywords and other metadata in Bridge or Photoshop to make it easier for Bridge to locate a specific image. The earlier you do this, the better; some photographers prefer to make this step 2 or 3 unless they are very short on time.

5. Process the images. Use Camera Raw to convert selected originals to the final format, such as TIFF for print or JPEG for the Web. In many cases the next format may not be the final format; for example, you can open a raw file from Camera Raw into Photoshop for further editing and then produce the final image from Photoshop.

Fundamental Image Corrections

To create high-quality, professional images, perform the following basic tone and color corrections as needed:

1. Correct the color balance. This is the first step in removing color casts.

2. Set the endpoints of the tonal range (the white point and black point). This is the first step in achieving good tonal contrast, sometimes called making the image "pop."

3. Set the overall brightness level (the midpoint of the tonal curve).

Digital Raw Workflow Quick Start

Figure 5-1 Start by copying raw images to a new folder. To do this from within Bridge, you can launch Adobe Photo Downloader. Bridge will generate thumbnails and previews and read the metadata from each image. This gives you large previews and verifies that the raw images were copied correctly to the computer. Never open or edit images stored on the camera storage media itself—you risk ruining your only copy.

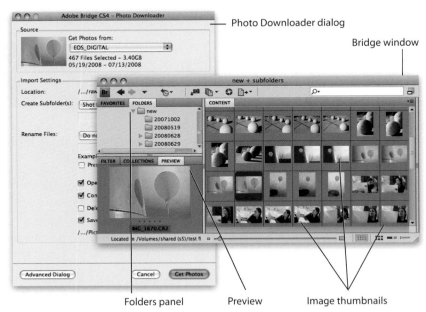

Photo Downloader dialog

Bridge window

Folders panel   Preview   Image thumbnails

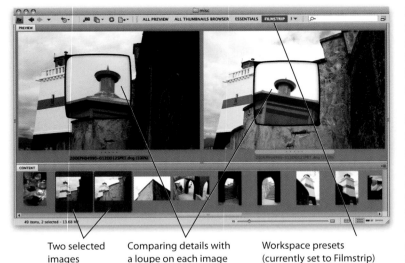

Two selected images

Comparing details with a loupe on each image

Workspace presets (currently set to Filmstrip)

Figure 5-2 Change the view to make images easier to evaluate. Here we clicked Filmstrip at the top of the Bridge window and hid the panes on the left. You can save your own workspaces.

Select multiple images in the Content panel to display multiple previews in the Preview panel. Click a preview to display a movable loupe. Both features make comparing images in detail much simpler. Press + or – to zoom the loupe, or zoom all loupes by also pressing the Command (Mac) or Ctrl (Windows) keys.

Figure 5-3 Double-click an image's thumbnail to launch the Camera Raw plug-in, which allows you to control the conversion of the raw file into any of four RGB working spaces.

The histogram, preview, and RGB readouts all show the results of the conversion from the raw file to the designated RGB working space.

To apply the settings without opening the image, click Done. Click Open to bring the file directly into Photoshop.

Figure 5-4 To apply the last-used settings quickly to other similar images in Bridge, choose Edit > Develop Settings > Previous Conversion.

The settings are recorded in each image's metadata, and are used when you open the images.

You can convert the raw images straight into Photoshop without revisiting the Camera Raw dialog by Shift-double-clicking the selected images.

To process images selected in Bridge using actions you've previously created in Photoshop, choose Tools > Photoshop > Batch.

4. Set the overall contrast level, and then refine image contrast further using a tone curve as needed.

5. As needed, refine local contrast within the image, either overall or in specific areas of the image.

6. Refine the overall image color further by targeting specific color ranges or image areas to correct.

7. Remove defects such as dust, scratches, and chromatic aberrations.

8. Remove image noise, then sharpen the image.

9. Create a copy of the image for final output (such as Web, prepress, stock photos, or video), and archive the original.

Notice that we've listed only the tasks, and not where and how you do them. That's because both Camera Raw and Photoshop provide many of the tools to do these tasks, and you can decide how much of the work you want Camera Raw to perform before handing the files off to Photoshop. We talk about that more specifically in the next section.

The Division of Labor

Camera Raw used to be thought of as a simple plug-in for Photoshop, but as subsequent versions of Camera Raw have allowed more essential corrections to be done to the raw file, more photographers are trying to do as much as they can in Camera Raw before passing the image on to Photoshop. If you need to adjust the white balance on 250 raw camera images, you'll get it done much faster in Camera Raw and Bridge than by wiring up a Photoshop action to batch-process 250 images converted from raw files. This doesn't mean you should always use Camera Raw instead of Photoshop, but it does mean that you should think about how you want to divide the basic correction tasks between them. What follows are some typical workflow alternatives based on a few common scenarios.

Maximum Camera Raw Workflow. In this workflow, you use the Camera Raw feature set as much as you can before passing the images to Photoshop. This workflow has many advantages. You save disk space because corrections are stored as very compact *metadata* (unprocessed instructions) attached to your original image files. This results in smaller files than if you performed the same corrections in a layered Photoshop file. You can potentially save time, because some multistep tasks that require building layers and masks in Photoshop can be performed in Camera Raw just by dragging a slider.

This workflow is best if you have a large number of similar and relatively well-shot images to process very quickly, because applying the same Camera Raw corrections to many files is much faster and easier than taking the same corrections from one layered Photoshop file and applying them to many other files. A disadvantage is that Camera Raw controls, while powerful, aren't pixel-precise, as the controls in Photoshop are. The goal with this workflow is to leave as little work as possible for Photoshop.

Partial Camera Raw Workflow. In this workflow, you use Camera Raw to perform the most basic tone and color corrections on your original files, but you hand the files over to Photoshop for spot removal, noise reduction, and sharpening, even though Camera Raw can perform many of these tasks. Some use this workflow because they're more familiar with Photoshop than with Camera Raw, or because they feel that the corrections they value the most are not yet as precise or controllable in Camera Raw as they are in Photoshop. This workflow can also appeal to those who typically work intensively at the pixel level with just a few images, instead of regularly processing hundreds of images for output.

If you're preparing images for CMYK prepress, another partial Camera Raw workflow is to use Camera Raw to get a raw file into shape (in terms of tone and color) in RGB for an eventual conversion to CMYK in Photoshop, where you plan to do your image fine-tuning in CMYK channels.

Minimal Camera Raw Workflow. In this workflow, you use Camera Raw only to convert a raw image straight to Photoshop without making corrections in Camera Raw. The intention is to do most of the work in Photoshop. Those who use this workflow typically convert their raw file into a 16-bit Photoshop document to preserve quality. A disadvantage of this workflow is that it can create very large files, as most of the corrections happen on heavily layered Photoshop documents. The minimal Camera Raw workflow was probably more common with earlier versions of Camera Raw, but as the capabilities of Camera Raw and the quality of its output have improved, we feel that you can actually preserve more of the original quality of an image by using the maximum Camera Raw workflow—performing as much of the "heavy lifting" as you can in Camera Raw before converting a raw image into a Photoshop or TIFF document.

TIP: If you're processing scanned images, you can still take advantage of Camera Raw workflows, because Camera Raw also processes TIFF and JPEG images. Although the power of Camera Raw with TIFF and JPEG images is limited compared to what it can do with raw files, its batch-processing abilities can save you time.

Copying Files from a Camera

The first thing you've got to do is get your images off the camera and into your computer. There are two parts to this: the hardware you use to connect the computer to the camera, and the software you use to transfer the images from the camera to your computer.

Using Adobe Photo Downloader

Photoshop CS4 comes with the Adobe Photo Downloader utility, which simplifies and automates downloading. Among other things, it can

- Set a folder on your hard disk as a destination for camera images.

- Rename images as you import them, to your specifications.

- Make a backup copy of the images in a different folder or disk.

- Apply a metadata template to all incoming images (we talk about this later, in "Applying Metadata and Keywords"). For example, you can add a copyright notice to every image as it's imported.

Opening Adobe Photo Downloader. You won't find Photo Downloader as a stand-alone application—you launch it from Bridge. To open Photo Downloader, start Bridge and then choose File > Get Photos from Camera.

If an alert appears asking you if you want Photo Downloader to launch whenever you connect a camera or card, you can click No until you make a final decision as to whether you prefer Photo Downloader to other methods. You can always change that setting by opening Bridge preferences, clicking the General tab, and changing the option When a Camera is Connected, Launch Adobe Photo Downloader. Note that other programs or the operating system options may conflict with this option, so even if you've set it, another program might still try to download images.

Dialog Views. You can display the Photo Downloader window as a Standard dialog or as an Advanced dialog (see **Figure 5-5**). The Standard dialog contains most of the features, but we prefer the Advanced dialog because you can do a few more very useful things: see previews of the images you're about to copy, deselect any images you don't want to copy, and apply a metadata template to all incoming images.

Digital Workflow Principles

There are likely as many workflows are there are photographers—maybe more! One of the wonderful things about Bridge, Camera Raw 5, and Photoshop CS4 is the incredible flexibility that they offer in terms of workflow. The price of this flexibility is, of course, complexity. There are multiple ways to accomplish most tasks, and it may not be obvious at first glance which one is optimal in a given situation. Understanding the different ways of accomplishing the basic tasks gives you a tactical approach. But to make a workflow that works, you also need a strategy that tells you how and when to employ those tactics.

Even a single photographer may need more than one workflow. There's the workflow you need when you're on a shoot, the client is looking over your shoulder, and you need to agree on the hero shots before you strike the lighting and move on. There might also be a workflow you'd like to follow when you're reviewing personal work with no deadlines attached. Between these extremes are many points on the continuum.

We can't build your workflow for you, so we'll offer some key principles of workflow efficiency that should always guide you.

- Do things once, early, and efficiently. Make edits as close to the original file as possible. If you exploit the power of Camera Raw to its fullest, many of your images may need little or no postconversion work in Photoshop. When you apply metadata such as copyright information and keywords to your raw file, the metadata is automatically carried through to all the versions that you derive from that raw file, such as TIFF, JPEG, or PSD files.

- Do things automatically. If you notice yourself doing the same task more than a few times, find out if you can automate it using actions (macros) or scripts if you have programming skills. In most cases we convert our raw images using the Batch or Image Processor commands on the Tools > Photoshop submenu in Bridge.

- Be methodical. Start with the general and work toward the specific, solving the biggest problems first. Find and learn best practices so that you can get the major issues out of the way and clean up the details that much sooner. Start with the tasks that can be done to the greatest number of images, then make increasingly more detailed treatments of ever-decreasing numbers of images, reserving the full treatment—careful hand-editing in Camera Raw and Photoshop, applying image-specific keywords, and so on—to those images that truly deserve the attention.

Figure 5-5 The Advanced dialog of the Adobe Photo Downloader. The mouse pointer is about to turn on the check boxes for the two selected images, which are indicated by blue borders.

Setting Photo Downloader Options

TIP: Add your Location folder as a Favorite in Bridge or on your desktop, so that you can always get to it in one click.

Copying images is something you don't want to do more than once, so take a little time to get it right the first time. When you're done setting the following options, click Get Photos to start copying images.

Previews, Source, and Image Selection. In the Advanced dialog of Photo Downloader, check the previews to see if you're downloading what you want. If the previews don't look right, make sure the Source pop-up menu is set correctly, in case there are multiple cameras or cards plugged in to the computer.

If you don't want to download an image, deselect its check box. To change this option for multiple images at once, Command-click (Mac) or Ctrl-click (Windows) the images you want to change (they'll become selected, indicated by blue borders as shown in Figure 5-5), and then change the check box for any selected image. The Check All and UnCheck All buttons at the bottom of the Advanced dialog are shortcuts for changing the check boxes.

Digital Camera Raw Formats

When a camera shoots a raw file, it's so raw that it doesn't even have RGB channels yet. Digital still cameras use color filters over each sensor in an array to split incoming light into its red, green, and blue components, so each sensor captures only one color, depending on which filter covers it. A raw file records the amount of light recorded by each element in the array. When your camera is set to save JPEG files (the default in most digital cameras), the camera's firmware converts the raw image to an RGB JPEG file, using the in-camera settings for white balance, tone, saturation, sharpness, and so on. When you set your camera to save images in its raw format, processing is deferred until you open the image on the computer using a converter like Camera Raw. The only in-camera settings that permanently affect a raw capture are the shutter speed, aperture value, ISO value, and focus. All other settings—white balance, tone curve, color space, contrast, saturation—are written into the capture as *metadata* (unprocessed instructions) alongside the raw information. Camera Raw can use this metadata as guidance in processing the capture into an RGB image, but the settings don't change what's captured. You always have the freedom to reinterpret how the captured photons are converted into an RGB image.

Compared to shooting in JPEG, shooting in raw format offers other key benefits. While a JPEG image records 8 bits per channel, raw data is limited only by the sensor—typically 12 bits or more in today's cameras. And while most cameras let you record color only into the sRGB or Adobe RGB color space when shooting in JPEG, you can convert a raw image directly into any color space your raw converter supports.

Shooting in raw format does have a few disadvantages. Making processing decisions and converting images takes more time. Raw files are also larger than JPEG images, so it may take longer to save them to your camera's storage medium (which will fill faster, too). We're convinced that the flexibility and image quality that's possible with raw files far outweigh the disadvantages. Raw files give you the ability to perform the digital equivalent of developing your own film, so that you have the ultimate control over the look of your images. As Adobe Camera Raw and other raw converters improve, you can potentially extract more quality out of old raw images by editing them in an updated converter.

Camera Raw is listed as one file format choice in the Open dialog in Photoshop, but in reality, each camera produces its own flavor of raw data based on its specific sensor. Camera Raw and its competitors usually need to be updated for the raw formats of new cameras. A list of officially supported cameras appears on Adobe's Web site, at www.adobe.com/products/photoshop/cameraraw. html. Any significant new camera will often be supported in the next release of Camera Raw, which is updated several times a year.

Save Options. The Location is the folder where the images will be copied; click the Choose button to change the folder. If you want Photo Downloader to automatically create subfolders for your shoots, choose a folder-naming option from the Create Subfolder(s) pop-up menu.

To have Photo Downloader automatically rename images as they're copied, choose a renaming option from the Rename Files pop-up menu. In addition to the date-based naming options, the Same As Subfolder option bases the filenames on the name of their subfolder.

The Preserve Current Filename in XMP option applies only if you rename a file. It keeps the original filename in the image's XMP (Extensible Metadata Platform) metadata, and you can view this information in Bridge.

Advanced Options. We recommend checking the Open Adobe Bridge check box, because if it's on, as soon as the images are copied, Adobe Bridge opens to that folder so that you can work with your images right away.

We also like to check the Convert to DNG option, because the DNG (Digital Negative) format packages raw sensor data in one convenient, vendor-independent file, without storing the metadata in separate XMP "sidecar" files that you have to track along with the raw file. For information about the options you find when you click the Settings button, see "The Output Buttons" later in this chapter.

The "Save Copies to" check box creates a second copy of each image in the folder you specify. The best way to use the "Save Copies to" check box is to set the folder to a completely different hard disk. This may seem paranoid, but professional photographers require this level of backup in case something goes horribly wrong, often using a small portable drive as their backup. For example, if a photojournalist copies photos from a card to a laptop, then erases the card so that he or she can take more photos, and then the laptop's hard disk dies (and you *know* that happens), the only existing images of a one-time event may be gone forever.

Apply Metadata. If you've set up metadata templates in advance, you can choose one from the Template to Use pop-up menu. We recommend that you create and apply a template that at least adds your name and copyright information to all images you shoot. For more information about setting these up, see "Using Metadata Templates" later in this chapter.

Camera Transfer Tips

Transferring your images from the camera to the computer is one of the most critical—and often least examined—stages of your workflow. It's critical, however, because at this stage your images exist only on the camera media. Camera media cards aren't dramatically more fragile than other storage media, but at this stage, there's only one copy! Losing previews or Camera Raw settings is irritating, but you can redo the work. If you make mistakes while you copy images to your computer, you can lose images.

The following ground rules have thus far prevented us from losing even a single image.

- Don't use the camera as a card reader. Although you can connect a cable directly to the camera, it's a bad idea for at least three reasons: Cameras are very slow as card readers; when the camera is acting as a card reader, you can't shoot with it; and you're draining the camera's battery.

- Never edit images directly from the camera media. Errors can occur when a computer or other device saves files to a card that a camera expects to be filled only with its own files.

- Don't rely on just one copy of the images. Copy them to two separate drives before you start working. Some photographers copy to two hard drives; others back up a card to one or two optical disks before editing.

- Don't erase your images from the camera media until you've verified the copies. See "Verifying Images," later in this chapter.

- Format media only in the camera in which you're going to use it. Cameras can be very picky about the exact formatting of a card. Formatting a camera card with a computer can confuse a camera and lose images.

Following these rules takes a little additional time up front but much less time than a reshoot would—if reshooting is even a possibility.

After the computer sees the card, you can use any software that transfers the images to your hard disk. The simplest way is to mount the card as a volume on the desktop and drag the images from there to a folder on your hard disk. We recommend using software designed to copy images from a camera, such as the Adobe Photo Downloader, because these utilities provide an opportunity to automate several important tasks as the images are copied.

TIP: Image files on a memory card can be corrupted by something as simple as pulling the card out of the reader without first ejecting it in the software. If you think you've lost images on a card, do not format it! Doing so will permanently delete any recoverable data on the card. Cards from major vendors often include data-recovery software such as PhotoRescue—turn to that software first. If that fails, and the data is truly irreplaceable, several companies offer data recovery from memory cards, usually at a fairly hefty price.

We recommend that you carefully consider your Photo Downloader settings in the context of how you want your overall photo library to be organized. If you work out folder- and file-naming conventions and your standard metadata in advance, your photo library will automatically build itself in an organized fashion. If you just copy images without taking advantage of the automatic organizational options available in today's downloading utilities, you'll have a growing pile of images to rename, annotate, and organize later, and take it from us, that isn't any fun to deal with.

VERIFYING IMAGES

TIP: Professional photographers use the term "selects" (as a noun) to describe the best images from a shoot. If you also use Adobe Lightroom, you'll notice that it calls selects "picks."

Once you've copied the raw files to your hard disk, point Adobe Bridge to the folder containing the raw images. (If you checked the Open Adobe Bridge option in Photo Downloader, this should happen automatically.) If you haven't opened Bridge yet, it's in the Adobe Bridge CS4 folder, inside the Applications folder (Mac) or Program Files folder (Windows).

Bridge is command central for dealing with hundreds of images. You'll use it to make your initial selection; to apply and edit metadata, including Camera Raw settings; and to control the processing of the raw images.

But before you start doing any of these things, give Bridge a few minutes to generate the thumbnails (see **Figure 5-6**) and previews and to read the image metadata. It's a good idea to let it finish building the cache for the folder before starting work.

Figure 5-6 Imported raw files in Adobe Bridge

The reason is simple. While you can identify and open raw images as soon as the thumbnail appears, the thumbnails are generated by the camera, and Bridge simply displays them. To build the high-quality previews, though,

Camera Raw has to actually read the raw data, and that takes time. A good way to inspect the high-quality previews in detail is with the loupe; see "Evaluating and Comparing Images" later in this chapter.

If there's a problem reading the images, it will show up only on the high-quality thumbnail and preview. The initial thumbnails are the camera-generated ones, and they don't indicate that the raw file has been read successfully. The high-quality ones *do* indicate that the raw file has been read successfully, so wait until you see them before you erase the raw image files from the camera media.

If you see a problem at this stage, check the second copy (if you made one) or go back to the camera media if you haven't erased the card already. It's fairly rare for the data to get corrupted in the camera (though it does sometimes happen, particularly in burst-mode shooting), so the first suspect should be the card reader.

REFINING A SHOOT USING BRIDGE

If you already know which shots you want to open in Camera Raw, you can skip this section and go on to the next one. However, there's another option if you usually shoot multiple frames of each subject to ensure that you get the right shot: After you copy images to your hard disk, use Bridge to narrow down your shoot, selecting only the best images to open and edit in Camera Raw and Photoshop. Doing this has several benefits. You can

- Rate images to prioritize them. You can also mark images as rejected so that you can delete them, freeing up disk space.

- Compare multiple images and use a loupe to compare images in detail.

- Stack images to keep related images together.

- Filter your images to display only ones that contain specific metadata, such as a keyword.

If you need to narrow down your shoot before going into Camera Raw, read about the above Bridge features in detail before you start working in Camera Raw. See "Evaluating and Comparing Images" and "Rating and Labeling Images" later in this chapter.

Opening Images into Camera Raw

You can open a supported file with Camera Raw in several ways:

- In Photoshop, choose File > Open, select one or more raw files, and click Open.

- In Bridge, or on your desktop, select at least one raw file and double-click it.

- In Bridge, you can also open a selected, supported file in Camera Raw by pressing Return.

Opening the file from your desktop works as long as Photoshop is the application that is set to open your camera's raw files; if the file icon has an Adobe icon with a "CRW" badge, you should be able to double-click it. A raw file opened in Photoshop automatically opens in Camera Raw.

If you open multiple files in Camera Raw, you'll see the filmstrip, which lets you select which images are affected as you make edits (see "Filmstrip Mode," later in this chapter). You can also use the Synchronize button to spread settings from one image to others inside Camera Raw.

TIP: If you'd rather have Photoshop host Camera Raw by default when you double-click raw files, open the Preferences dialog for Bridge, and in the General pane, turn off the option Double-Click Edits Camera Raw Settings in Bridge.

Photoshop or Bridge? Being able to choose which program hosts Camera Raw has several practical advantages. If Photoshop is busy (such as when it's running a batch process), you can still edit raw files in Camera Raw by opening them from Bridge. Or you might open Camera Raw from Photoshop while Bridge is busy caching a folder full of images. You can even open one Camera Raw instance in Bridge and another in Photoshop simultaneously! Because Bridge needs less RAM than Photoshop, opening Camera Raw from Bridge lets you open more raw images at once than in Photoshop, and keeping Photoshop closed frees up RAM for other memory-intensive programs you may need to run as you edit raw images.

Turning Off Auto Tone Adjustments. If your images in Camera Raw or Bridge appear radically different from how you thought you shot them, Camera Raw may be applying its Auto Tone option by default. Some people love this feature, while others hate it because it tries to "correct" your manual exposure settings such as bracketing. Fortunately, the behavior is easily changed: Open Camera Raw preferences, turn off the check box for Apply Auto Tone Adjustments, and click OK. Then make sure that White Balance is set to As Shot, and choose Save New Camera Raw Defaults from the Camera Raw menu. Note that the defaults are per camera model, so you'll need to do this for each camera model you use. You can still apply autocorrection to an individual image by clicking Auto, or by pressing Command-U in Mac OS X or Ctrl-U in Windows. See "Using Auto Tone Adjustment," later in this chapter, for more details.

It's Not Just for Raw Anymore

Camera Raw 4 and later can open and edit TIFF and JPEG images. This doesn't magically bring the inherent qualities of raw files to TIFF and JPEG files, but it does simplify some tasks. For example, it can sometimes be easier to get rid of a color cast using the White Balance control in Camera Raw rather than playing with the various color-correction features in Photoshop. Another powerful advantage is that you can now use the batch-processing features of Camera Raw and Bridge on TIFF and JPEG files, such as the ability to synchronize nondestructive Camera Raw adjustments instantly across multiple images. This means that photographers who shoot in JPEG can take advantage of the Camera Raw workflow, even if the images themselves are not as flexible as raw files.

By default, TIFF and JPEG images open in Photoshop. To open a TIFF or JPEG image in Camera Raw, Control-click (Mac) or right-click (Windows) an image and choose Open in Camera Raw from the context menu. In Photoshop, you can choose File > Open, select a TIFF or JPEG image, change the Format pop-up menu to Camera Raw, and then click Open, although you can open only one file at a time this way.

Storing Edits as Metadata

Camera Raw stores edits as metadata, either in the image file or in the Camera Raw database. Storing edits as metadata has two advantages: The original image pixels remain untouched, and files are compact. However, until you export an updated version of an edited raw image, you won't see edits made in Camera Raw in other applications unless they can either read and render XMP metadata or (more likely) display the raw file's thumbnail preview.

For TIFF or JPEG files edited in Camera Raw, the situation is a little more complicated. Camera Raw still stores the edits as metadata without changing the pixels, but other applications generally won't be expecting that. For

TIP: All keyboard shortcuts for zooming in Photoshop (seen on the View menu in Photoshop) also work in Camera Raw. For example, press Command-Option-0 (Mac) or Ctrl-Alt-0 (Windows) to display actual pixels. For the Hand tool, hold down the spacebar or press H, and for the Zoom tool press Z. Double-clicking the hand tool fits the entire image into the preview, and double-clicking the Zoom tool zooms to Actual Pixels view.

example, you'll see a TIFF file's Camera Raw edits in Bridge, but in Adobe InDesign you'll see only the original unedited data. To be able to see Camera Raw edits to TIFF and JPEG files in most other applications, use the Save Image button in Camera Raw to render new copies of the files that have the edits "baked in."

CAMERA RAW CONTROLS

The controls along the top and bottom edges of the Camera Raw dialog (see **Figure 5-7**) affect the overall behavior of Camera Raw; the settings in these options don't represent the image you're currently viewing, although they can affect it. The set of tabbed controls along the right side of the dialog does represent the current image; we'll talk about those later in this chapter.

Figure 5-7 The Adobe Camera Raw 5 main controls

Toolbar

Histogram and RGB readout

Camera Raw menu

Zoom controls

Output buttons

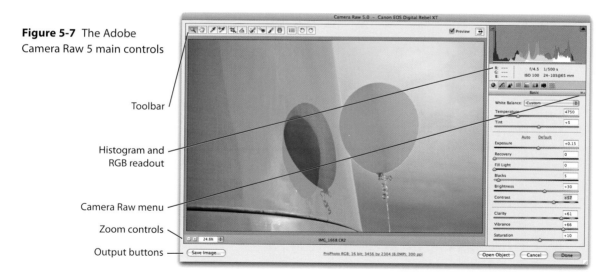

The Toolbar

Many of the tools in the Camera Raw toolbar (see **Figure 5-8**) are also available in Photoshop, but we recommend that you use the Camera Raw version whenever possible because they're nondestructive and apply earlier in the workflow (closer to the source image), which we prefer.

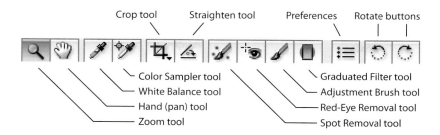

Crop tool   Straighten tool   Preferences   Rotate buttons

Color Sampler tool   Graduated Filter tool
White Balance tool   Adjustment Brush tool
Hand (pan) tool   Red-Eye Removal tool
Zoom tool   Spot Removal tool

Figure 5-8 The Camera Raw toolbar

Zoom and Pan. The Zoom (magnifying glass) and Pan (grabber hand) tools work much like their Photoshop counterparts; see "Navigation Tips" in Chapter 6, "Essential Photoshop Tips and Tricks."

White Balance. The White Balance tool (press I) lets you set the white balance by clicking an area of the image that should be neutral. Unlike the white Eyedropper in Levels or Curves, it doesn't allow you to choose a source color, and it doesn't affect the luminance of the image, only the white balance—the color temperature and tint of the image.

Clicking the White Balance tool provides a very quick way to set color temperature and tint simultaneously, especially if you placed a gray card in the image. You can always fine-tune the results using the individual Temperature and Tint controls in the Basic tab, which we'll cover in due course.

Color Samplers. The Color Sampler tool (press S) lets you place as many as nine individual color samplers, each of which gets its own readout, in the image (see **Figure 5-9**). Combined with the static RGB readout, the Color Sampler tool lets you monitor the values of up to ten different locations in the image, which should be enough for most uses.

TIP: The White Balance tool in Camera Raw works best on a light gray that's close to a diffuse highlight but that still contains detail, rather than on a specular highlight that's pure white. The second-to-lightest gray patch on the 24-patch X-Rite ColorChecker works well, as do bright (but not blown-out) midday clouds.

Color Sampler tool   Color sampler readouts   Mouse pointer's sample

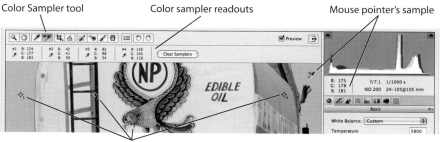

Four color samplers placed on the image

Figure 5-9 The Color Sampler tool

Crop. The Crop tool (press C) lets you drag a cropping rectangle, choose one of several common predefined aspect ratios, or define your own custom aspect ratio from the tool's pull-down menu (see **Figure 5-10**). The same menu allows you to clear the crop. The Camera Raw preview always shows the crop in the context of the whole image, but you'll also see it in filmstrip previews, Bridge previews and thumbnails, and of course in the image itself when you open it in Photoshop.

Figure 5-10 The Crop tool

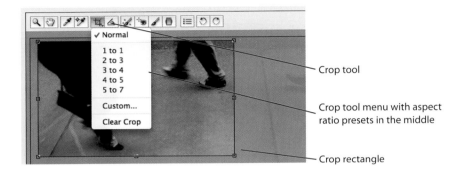

Crop tool

Crop tool menu with aspect ratio presets in the middle

Crop rectangle

Straighten. The Straighten tool (press A) is an huge time-saver for those of us who sometimes fail to keep our horizons horizontal. It should really be called the Straighten and Crop tool because it also automatically applies the crop that maintains the maximum rectangular image when the Crop tool is set to Normal, or a straightened crop of the specified aspect ratio when the Crop tool is set to something else. If there's an existing crop, it's preserved and rotated. Compared to the multistep process required to work out a straighten angle in Photoshop, we much prefer the Straighten tool's one-step simplicity (see **Figure 5-11**).

Figure 5-11 The Straighten tool

Straighten tool

Existing rotated crop rectangle

Dragging the Straighten tool along a line that should be vertical

Rotate Buttons. The Rotate 90 Degrees Left and Right buttons (press L and R, respectively) aren't really tools (see Figure 5-8)—you don't have to do anything inside the image preview. Clicking them or pressing their keyboard shortcuts rotates the image preview. When you click Done in Camera Raw the rotation is applied to the image's thumbnails and previews in Bridge, and is honored whenever you open the raw image in Photoshop.

Spot Removal. The Spot Removal tool (press B) is a spot touch-up tool, similar to the Spot Healing Brush in Photoshop (see "The Healing Brushes and the Patch Tool" in Chapter 11, "Essential Image Techniques"). To retouch a spot, select the Spot Removal tool, position it over the center of the spot you want to remove, and drag until the resulting circle is larger than the spot (see **Figure 5-12**). Press V to toggle the Show Overlay check box to see if the retouch looks good. If it doesn't, drag the green dashed circle to change the retouching source, or drag the red dashed circle to change the retouched spot. You can change the size of the circles by dragging the edge of a circle, or by changing the Radius value in the Spot Removal pane. If you set the Radius when no spots are selected, you'll be setting the default radius. You can tell that a spot is selected when you can see both the source and destination circles. A lone circle is deselected; click inside it to select it.

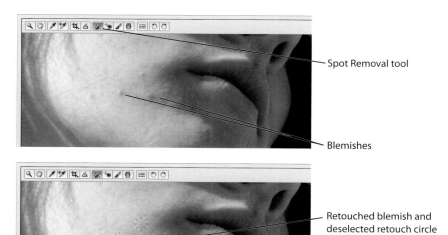

Spot Removal tool

Blemishes

Retouched blemish and deselected retouch circle

Retouched blemish and editing its selected retouch source circle

Figure 5-12 The Spot Removal tool

The Type pop-up menu in the Spot Removal pane determines how the Spot Removal tool works. When set to Heal, the tool tries to smoothly merge the source (the green dashed circle) into the destination (the red dashed circle) by matching texture, lighting, and shading. Heal is the most common choice for this tool, particularly when removing skin blemishes. To exactly copy one spot to another, choose Clone instead.

Though Photoshop has more retouching options, such as the ability to remove long scratches and power lines, there are two good reasons to perform spot retouching in Camera Raw. First, the edits are nondestructive, so you can change them later at any time; in Photoshop, on the other hand, actual pixels are altered in the original image. Second, it follows our recommendation to do any edits you can as early as possible in the digital workflow, so that you have to do them only once.

Red-Eye Removal. The Red-Eye Removal tool (press R) is a quick way to get rid of red-eye from an on-camera flash. Drag a rectangle around an entire eye (it works better if you surround more eye, not less), and Camera Raw detects red-eye and applies the default correction settings (see **Figure 5-13**). As with the Spot Removal tool, you can resize a red-eye rectangle by its edges, reposition it by dragging, add multiple rectangles (most people have more than one eye), and select and deselect rectangles. When a rectangle is selected, you can change the Pupil Size and Darken values in the controls for the tool. Don't make a rectangle much bigger than an eye, or you may have trouble getting the Pupil Size to be small enough.

> **TIP:** With both the Spot Removal and Red-Eye Removal tools, where you click and drag is important. When working with the adjustment shapes each tool leaves behind, click inside a shape to select it, and drag inside a shape to move it. If you drag from the edge of a shape, you change its size.

Figure 5-13 The Red-Eye Removal tool

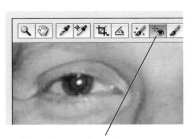
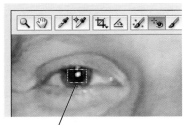

Red-Eye Removal tool

Removed red-eye and selected red-eye removal rectangle

Adjustment Brush. The Adjustment Brush tool (press K) is one of the biggest new features in Camera Raw 5, because you can now apply some types of adjustments to specific areas of an image. It's similar to using a masked adjustment layer in Photoshop (as we discuss in Chapter 8, "The Digital Darkroom"), and in some ways it's both simpler and more powerful: A single Camera Raw adjustment mask can apply multiple adjustment settings at once, such as Exposure, Clarity, and Sharpness. If you need different adjustments in different areas, you can add multiple adjustment masks to a single image in Camera Raw. Instead of managing masks in a Photoshop panel, you manipulate them directly on the image—each mask is marked by a pin (see **Figure 5-14**), like those seen in Google Maps.

Before brushing a new adjustment mask onto an image, make sure the New radio button is selected at the top of the Adjustment Brush controls, and make sure the adjustment sliders are set as desired for this adjustment. It's OK if the sliders aren't perfectly set; you can edit them later.

Below the adjustment sliders are the sliders for the Adjustment Brush tool itself. We recommend setting these more carefully because they set brush-stroke attributes, which can't be edited later except by undoing or erasing. When you hold the Adjustment Brush pointer over the image, the dotted line represents the brush's Size value, and the solid line represents the Feather value. Flow controls the rate of painting, while Density controls the transparency of a brushstroke; lower Flow and Density values let you build effects gradually using repeated brushstrokes. Auto Mask (press M) tries to keep the mask within areas of similar color so that your mask doesn't "color outside the lines." Show Mask (press Y) simply toggles whether the current mask is visible or not. You can also temporarily reveal any mask by holding the pointer over a pin (we're about to talk about those). Clicking the color swatch next to Show Mask lets you edit the display color of the mask.

As soon as you paint a new brushstroke, Camera Raw adds a pin to the image to mark the current mask. A selected pin has a black dot; as long as a pin is selected you're editing that pin's mask (you can edit either the mask brushstrokes or its sliders). The location of the pin marks only your first brushstroke for that mask and doesn't restrict you from adding to the mask anywhere else on the image. It's OK if one mask's brushstrokes overlap another. If you add a brushstroke when no pin is selected, you add a new mask (and pin). For performance and ease of editing, avoid adding too many pins; any regions that need the same adjustment should share the same mask. The Show Pins (press V) check box at the bottom of the Adjustment Brush panel toggles whether pins are visible.

When a pin is selected, dragging the Adjustment Brush sliders affects only that pin's mask. To edit a mask's brushstrokes, click the Add or Erase buttons. Erase remembers its own set of brush slider options; for example, you can set Erase to a different Brush Size than New or Add.

TIP: As in Photoshop, the shortcut for the brush Size slider is pressing the bracket keys, [and] . You can also change the Size by Control-dragging (right-click-dragging in Windows) the Adjustment Brush pointer over the image. Add the Shift key to change the Feather value.

TIP: A negative Clarity value helps soften skin tone for portraits. To approximate the "Soften Skin" feature of the Adjustment Brush in Adobe Lightroom 2, reduce both Clarity and Sharpness.

TIP: To temporarily erase when the Adjustment Brush tool is set to New or Add, hold down Option (Alt in Windows).

Figure 5-14 Adding two Adjustment Brush masks

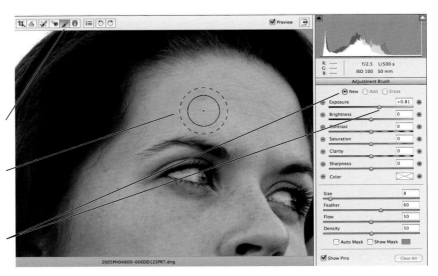

The Adjustment Brush tool is selected.

The outer circle of the Adjustment Brush pointer is the brush Size, and the inner circle is the Feather amount, both set in the lower section of the Adjustment Brush panel.

The New button is selected so that the next brushstroke creates a new mask. This mask is set to increase Exposure.

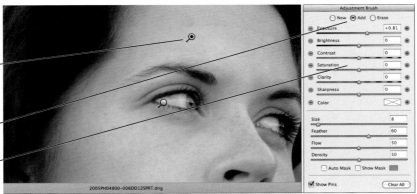

A selected mask appears as a green pin with a dot. The Adjustment Brush settings represent the selected mask. This is the mask that increased Exposure.

The Add button is selected, so the next brushstroke will add to the selected mask.

An unselected mask appears as a gray pin.

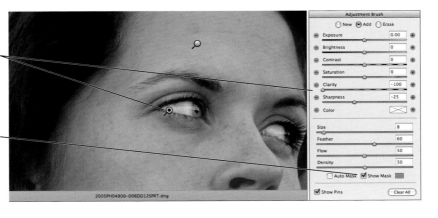

The second pin is selected. Its settings, Clarity -100 and Sharpness -25, are effective for softening the look of skin. The effect of this mask is visible in the middle image above.

The red area indicates this pin's mask, because Show Mask (press Y) is on and the mask color is set to red. The mask shows that the eyes were intentionally excluded from this softening mask.

Graduated Filter. When you make adjustments using the Graduated Filter tool (press G), they're applied through a gradient mask, similar to a graduated filter for a camera lens or a Photoshop adjustment layer with a mask that has a gradient painted in it. The Graduated filter, new in Camera Raw 5, appears as a gradient object that you can resize and rotate (see **Figure 5-15**). Using a Graduated filter is much like using the Adjustment Brush tool, but with a rectangular shape instead of brushstrokes.

Figure 5-15 A Graduated filter

The Graduated Filter tool is selected.

After the overall image is corrected, the sky is too light. We'll create a Graduated filter that reduces the Exposure and slightly boosts the Saturation of the sky.

We drag a Graduated filter overlay down from the top. The adjustment starts at the beginning of the drag (green dot) and fades out at the end of the drag (red dot), primarily affecting the sky, which becomes more dramatic.

You can add multiple Graduated filter overlays to an image. Start a new Graduated filter overlay by making sure New is the selected button at the top of the Graduated Filter panel, and then set the effect of the filter by adjusting the seven sliders. To apply the filter, drag across the image, starting

TIP: In the Adjustment Brush and Graduated Filter tools, circles containing a – (minus sign) and + (plus sign) appear by each slider. Clicking these is a quick way to adjust a slider value by a fairly large increment.

where you want the filter to have maximum effect and ending where you want the filter to fade out completely. You'll find that the starting point of the overlay is green and the endpoint is red.

The selected overlay's controls appear in color; unselected overlay controls are gray. You can edit an existing overlay as long as it is selected and the Edit button is selected at the top of the Graduated Filter panel. As with an adjustment mask, you can edit a selected overlay by changing the sliders in the Graduated Filter panel or by directly manipulating the mask (see **Table 5-1**). Show Overlay (press V) shows or hides the selected overlay.

Table 5-1   Editing a Graduated filter overlay.

To do this to the overlay . . .	. . . do this:
Move entire overlay	Drag the dotted line connecting the endpoints (pointer appears as a four-headed arrow).
Move just one endpoint	Drag an endpoint.
Change the length	Position mouse close to either endpoint so that the pointer turns into a two-headed arrow, then drag.
Rotate	Position mouse along a red or green dotted line so that the pointer turns into a rotate icon, then drag. If you see a two-headed arrow pointer, position mouse farther from the endpoint.

The Preview Controls

Two sets of controls affect the preview image. The Zoom controls determine the viewing size of the preview image, while the Preview check box affects its state.

TIP: If you see a yellow warning triangle in the image area of the Camera Raw dialog, Camera Raw isn't finished processing the image. Don't judge image quality until the yellow warning triangle goes away.

Zoom Level Menu. The Zoom Level menu at the bottom left of the Camera Raw dialog (see Figure 5-7) lets you choose a zoom level for the image preview. We prefer to zoom using the keyboard shortcuts (see the tip earlier in this chapter).

Preview Check Box. The Preview check box (press P) applies only to the current editing tab, toggling between its current settings and those that were in effect when you opened the image. It has no effect on changes you've made in other tabs (see **Figure 5-16**). To see the settings that applied before you opened the image, toggle between Image Settings and Custom Settings on the Settings menu.

Preview check box —— ☑ Preview ⬚ ——Full-Screen Mode button

Figure 5-16
The preview controls

Full-Screen Mode. To make the Camera Raw window fill the entire monitor screen, click the Full-Screen Mode button next to the Preview check box. Camera Raw takes longer to refresh the dialog when it's larger, so if your machine is on the slow side, make the Camera Raw dialog smaller to speed redraw.

The Histogram and RGB Readout

The histogram and RGB readout provide information about the current state of the image (see **Figure 5-17**). It displays the histograms of the red, green, and blue channels that will be created by the current conversion settings, *not* the histogram of the raw image (which would look strange, since digital cameras capture at linear gamma—all the image data would be scrunched over to the left). If you're unfamiliar with histograms, see "Visualizing Tonal Values with the Histogram" in Chapter 7.

Histogram ——————

RGB and EXIF readouts ——

Figure 5-17 The Histogram with RGB and EXIF readouts

RGB Readout. The RGB readout (see Figure 5-17) shows the RGB values for the pixels under the cursor. The values are those that will result from the conversion at the current settings. The RGB readout always reads 5-by-5 *screen* pixels at zoom levels of 100 percent or less, so it may display different values at different zoom levels. When you fit the entire image in the window, you're sampling an average of many pixels. At zoom levels greater than 100 percent, the sample size is always 5-by-5 *image* pixels.

EXIF Readout. To the right of the RGB values is a panel that displays information from the image's EXIF data (see Figure 5-17), if present in the image. If the EXIF readout is blank, the image doesn't contain EXIF data. EXIF data exists in images produced by digital cameras, unless the last person who saved an image chose to strip the EXIF data from the file.

TIP: Want to know how to correct clipped highlights and shadows? See "The Basic Tab," later in this chapter.

Shadow and Highlight Clipping Warnings. The Shadow and Highlight Clipping Warning buttons, at the top left and right corners of the histogram (see **Figure 5-18**), provide a quick way to check for shadow and highlight clipping. The shortcuts are U (for underexposed) and O (for overexposed), respectively. For a more interactive clipping display that's more useful when you're actually making adjustments, hold down the Option key (Mac) or Alt key (Windows) while dragging the Exposure or Blacks slider.

For the histogram and the clipping warnings, the image is measured against the color space selected in the Workflow Options dialog (see "Camera Raw Workflow Options," later in this chapter). For example, colors that don't clip in ProPhoto RGB may clip in sRGB. For meaningful clipping feedback, set Workflow Options to the color space appropriate for your work.

Figure 5-18 Shadow and highlight clipping warnings. Red regions indicate highlight clipping, and blue indicates shadow clipping.

Shadow Clipping Warning button   Highlight Clipping Warning button

The Settings Menu

The Settings pop-up menu lets you change the settings applied to the image (see **Figure 5-19**). The items that always appear are Image Settings, Camera Raw Default, Previous Conversion, and Custom Settings.

Image Settings. If Image Settings is available, you've previously applied edits to the image. If you're working on an image, choosing Image Settings will show you the settings that were in effect before you started editing. If the image is brand new and has never been edited, the Image Settings values equal those of the next item, Camera Raw Defaults.

Camera Raw Defaults. Camera Raw Defaults is what it says—the default settings that apply to all images unless and until you override them. These are also the settings used by Bridge to create high-resolution previews when it sees a folder full of new raw images. If you find that the shipping default settings aren't to your liking, you can create your own Camera Raw Defaults for each supported camera model. If you get yourself in a mess by doing so, you can return Camera Raw to the shipping default settings using the appropriate commands from the Camera Raw menu.

Figure 5-19 The Settings menu is available from the top right corner of the tab group unless a retouch or adjustment tool is displaying options there.

Previous Conversion. Choosing Previous Conversion applies the settings from the last image you opened in Camera Raw to the current image.

Custom Settings. Custom Settings are the current settings you're applying in Camera Raw. As we mentioned previously, you can toggle between Image Settings and Custom Settings to compare your current edits with the ones that were in effect when you opened the image in Camera Raw.

You can also save your own custom settings as presets, which then become available from this menu. It's easy to overlook the mechanism for doing so, though, because it lives on the Camera Raw menu, which—although it's one of the most important of the static controls—is unfortunately an unlabeled button. We'll take a look at this menu in the next section.

Preset Settings. If you last applied Camera Raw settings to the image by choosing a preset, the name of the preset appears here.

Apply Preset Submenu. Presets you've created with Camera Raw appear in this submenu, but it's easier to apply them from the Presets tab.

Clear Imported Settings. Camera Raw and Bridge are no longer the only software that can read and write Camera Raw settings. Adobe Lightroom does it too, since Lightroom and Camera Raw use the same raw-processing engine. However, Lightroom and Camera Raw are not always updated at the

TIP: When the Camera Raw tabs are hidden, bring them back by selecting one of the first six tools on the Camera Raw toolbar.

same time, so occasionally one of them will add controls that aren't available yet in the other. When you open a raw image using software that's missing options that were available in the last application used to edit it, you may find it difficult to control the image because it's influenced by settings you can't change. When that's the case, Clear Imported Settings is a way to set those options to their default values.

Export Settings to XMP. The Export Settings to XMP command offers a way to write a sidecar XMP file when you have the Camera Raw preferences set to save edits in the Camera Raw cache. This offers a way to produce sidecar files when you want to copy the images to removable media for use on another computer while preserving the edits. If the preference is set to use sidecar files, Export Settings will export a sidecar file only if one doesn't already exist. If there's an existing sidecar file, Export Settings does nothing.

Update DNG Previews. When you edit a DNG file, your changes are written to the DNG metadata, but by default, the DNG preview isn't updated. Update DNG Previews rewrites the preview so that you can see the current state of the file in applications that don't render DNG on the fly. If you want DNG previews to update automatically, check the Update JPEG Previews check box in the DNG File Handling section of the Camera Raw Preferences dialog.

Loading and Saving Settings

The Load Settings and Save Settings commands let you load and save settings you make with any of the image-specific controls—the ones located in the tabs below the histogram. When you choose Save Settings, a dialog appears asking you which settings you want to save (see **Figure 5-20**). This means you can save a preset consisting of just a few options. For example, you could create a setting that applies only Color noise reduction.

When you save settings to the default location, they appear on the Settings menu automatically. That location on a Mac is (username)\Library\Application Support\Adobe\Camera Raw\Settings. In Windows, it's Documents and Settings\(username)\Application Data\Adobe\Camera Raw\Settings. These saved settings also appear on the Presets tab and on the Edit > Develop Settings submenu in Bridge. If you save settings anywhere else, you can load them using the Load Settings command in Camera Raw.

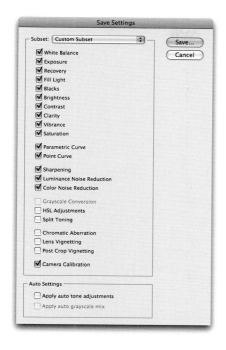

Figure 5-20 The Save
Settings dialog

Camera Raw Preferences

The Camera Raw preferences (see **Figure 5-21**) control many behind-the-scenes behaviors of Camera Raw.

Save Image Settings In. Camera Raw treats raw images as read-only, so your Camera Raw edits for the image get saved either in a sidecar .xmp file—a small file designed to travel with the image—or in the Camera Raw database. Each approach has strengths and weaknesses; choose the one you prefer using the Save Image Settings In option in this dialog.

Saving your edits in the Camera Raw database means that you don't have to keep track of sidecar files or worry about making sure they get renamed along with the image—the Camera Raw database indexes the images by file content rather than name, so if you rename the raw file, the Camera Raw database will still find the correct settings. The major disadvantage is that when you move the images onto a different computer or burn them to a CD or DVD, the edits won't travel with the images.

Figure 5-21 Camera Raw preferences

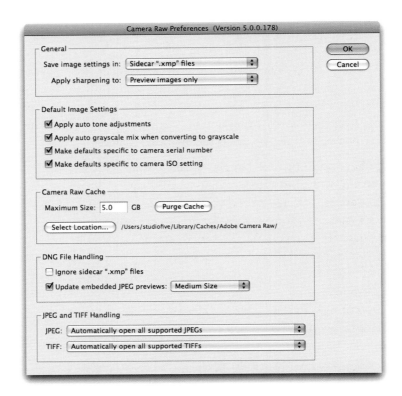

Saving your edits in sidecar files allows the edits to travel with the images. By default, Bridge hides them and automatically keeps them with their respective images when you use Bridge to move or rename them. The only danger is that if you move or rename the images *outside* Bridge, you need to keep track of the sidecars yourself.

A solution to this potentially confusing issue is to convert your raw images to DNG format (see "The Output Buttons," later in this chapter for more on this). Camera Raw treats raw files as read-only because all the vendors' proprietary formats—Canon CRW and CR2, Nikon NEF, Olympus ORF, and so on—are undocumented. Rather than taking the risk of messing up the file by writing metadata such as Camera Raw settings into it, Camera Raw uses sidecar files or its own database. But DNG is a completely documented, open format, so when you use DNG, Camera Raw settings and other metadata get written directly into the DNG file itself.

Apply Sharpening To. Choosing "All images" doesn't mean all images change. It means Camera Raw sharpening values apply to both preview images and to images converted by Camera Raw. If you plan to apply sharpening later in your workflow, such as in Photoshop, it's better to set this to "Preview images only." However, if you're going to export final images from Camera Raw you may want to set this option to "All images"—otherwise no Camera Raw sharpening will be applied to the exported images.

Default Image Settings. Uncheck "Apply auto tone adjustments" if you don't want Camera Raw to automatically adjust each image that you open. "Apply auto grayscale mix when converting to grayscale" is a similar preference for the times when you convert color images to black and white using the Convert to Grayscale check box in the HSL/Grayscale tab (see "The HSL/Grayscale Tab" later in this chapter), but we think you should leave that one on. "Make defaults specific to camera serial number" is useful if you own multiple bodies of the same camera and want different defaults for each camera. Conrad likes to check "Make defaults specific to camera ISO setting," because he has Camera Raw apply higher default noise reduction values to higher ISO settings.

Camera Raw Cache. The Camera Raw cache holds preparsed raw data for the most recently used raw files, which speeds up the following:

• Opening the Camera Raw dialog

• Switching between images in the Camera Raw filmstrip

• Updating the thumbnails in the Camera Raw filmstrip in response to settings changes

• Rebuilding Bridge thumbnails/previews to reflect settings changes

The bigger you make the cache, the more recently viewed images it can display quickly. Nothing is stored exclusively in the Camera Raw cache, so purging it never means you will lose data.

DNG File Handling. The two check boxes under DNG File Handling control the behavior of DNG files only.

• "Ignore sidecar ".xmp" files." This preference addresses a relatively obscure situation that arises only when you have a DNG and a proprietary raw version of the same image in the same folder, and they're identically named except for the extension. If you edit the proprietary

TIP: If you want Camera Raw to use the same JPEG preview size that it applied the last time you chose the Update DNG Previews command, hold Option/Alt while choosing to skip the dialog and apply the last-used preview size.

raw file, Camera Raw also applies the edits to the DNG, to maintain compatibility with older versions of Photoshop CS and Photoshop Elements, which write sidecar files for DNG instead of writing to the DNG file itself. This setting lets you tell Camera Raw to ignore sidecar files and leave the DNG file alone in this situation.

- "Update embedded JPEG previews." This setting controls when the embedded JPEG previews in DNG files get updated. When it's turned on, the embedded preview is updated as soon as you dismiss Camera Raw after editing a DNG file, thereby incurring a speed penalty, since the previews take time to write and save.

You can defer the speed hit by turning this option off. Then, when you want to update the previews, choose Update DNG Previews from the Camera Raw menu, which opens the Update DNG Previews dialog, where you can choose the preview size.

When you choose Full Size, Camera Raw embeds both full-size and medium-size previews. The downside is that full-size previews take longer to build and make a slightly larger file. Bear in mind, though, that you can choose whether Photoshop or Bridge will get tied up generating the previews, so you can continue working in the other application while the one hosting Camera Raw builds the previews.

TIP: The Bridge preference Prefer Camera Raw for JPEG and TIFF Files doesn't affect how those file types open. If the images contain Camera Raw settings, it controls whether Bridge uses Camera Raw settings to render JPEG and TIFF thumbnails.

JPEG and TIFF Handling. These options need a little bit of decoding because the way they work isn't obvious. In Bridge, they control whether Camera Raw or Photoshop opens JPEG and TIFF files when you double-click them or select them and press the Return/Enter key. You get the same three choices for JPEG and TIFF files, so we'll cover them in one list:

- "Disable JPEG/TIFF support." Photoshop will open JPEG/TIFF files.

- "Automatically open JPEGs/TIFFs with settings." If a JPEG/TIFF contains Camera Raw settings (because it was previously edited with Camera Raw), Camera Raw opens it. Otherwise Photoshop opens it. If in Bridge you select a mix of images that have and have not been edited with Camera Raw and open them all simultaneously, Camera Raw will open the ones containing Camera Raw settings and Photoshop will open the rest.

- "Automatically open all supported JPEGs/TIFFs." Camera Raw will open JPEGs/TIFFs whether or not they contain Camera Raw edits.

The Output Buttons

Use the output buttons (see **Figure 5-22**) to tell Camera Raw what to do with your edited file or to close Camera Raw.

Figure 5-22 The output buttons

Save Image. Click Save Image (Command-S in Mac OS X or Ctrl-S in Windows) to export a copy of the raw image as a DNG, TIFF, JPEG, or Photoshop file directly from the Camera Raw dialog without opening the image in Photoshop. Clicking Save Image opens the Save Options dialog, which lets you specify the destination, the file format, any format-specific options such as compression, and the name for the saved file or files. When you click Save in the Save Options dialog, you're returned to Camera Raw, and the file gets saved in the background.

If you don't want the Camera Raw dialog to go away after you're done saving, hold down Option (Mac) or Alt (Windows) to change the Save Image button into the Save button. When you click the Save button, the Save Options dialog doesn't appear; the selected images in Camera Raw are saved using the last settings you used in the Save Options dialog.

Open Image. Click Open Image (Command-O in Mac OS X or Ctrl-O in Windows) to close the Camera Raw dialog and open the image in Photoshop using the settings you applied in Camera Raw. These settings are written to the raw file's metadata, and Bridge's previews and thumbnails are updated to reflect the new settings. When Camera Raw is hosted by Photoshop, Open Image is the default button.

If you want to open selected images in Photoshop, but you don't want the current Camera Raw settings to be saved with the raw files (maybe you're experimenting), press Option (Mac) or Alt (Windows) to change the Open Image button to Open Copies. Finally, if you want to open selected images in Photoshop as Smart Objects (see "Smart Objects" in Chapter 11), press Shift to change the Open Image button to Open Objects.

If this button already says Open Object or Open Objects, the default behavior of the button has been changed. That's set in the Camera Raw Workflow Options dialog, which we will talk about soon.

TIP: The Save button is especially useful when you select multiple images in filmstrip mode, because the conversion of all those images happens in the background. That means you can keep working in Camera Raw while Camera Raw exports image after image.

TIP: You can convert supported formats to DNG by choosing DNG after you click Save Image. This makes Camera Raw a handy DNG converter.

Cancel. Click the Cancel button (press Esc) to ignore any adjustments you've made since opening Camera Raw, close the Camera Raw dialog, and return you to the host application, leaving the raw file settings unchanged. If you have many images open in Camera Raw, all of those images lose all changes you made to them in the current Camera Raw session.

To return all Camera Raw settings to the state they were in when you launched Camera Raw (either Image Settings, if the image had previously had its own Camera Raw settings applied, or Camera Raw Defaults if it hadn't), press Option (Mac) or Alt (Windows) to change the Cancel button to Reset. The Camera Raw dialog stays open after you click Reset.

Done. Click Done (or press Return or Enter) to close the Camera Raw dialog, write the settings you applied in Camera Raw to the raw file's metadata, and return to the host application. Previews and thumbnails in Bridge are updated to reflect the new settings. When Camera Raw is hosted by Bridge, Done is the default button.

CAMERA RAW WORKFLOW OPTIONS

At the bottom of the Camera Raw dialog is blue underlined text that looks like a Web link. You'll notice that the text is a line of image specifications; click the text to open the Workflow Options dialog and change the specs (see **Figure 5-23**). These controls apply to the current image or to all the images being converted in a batch process. The workflow options aren't saved with individual images; the Camera Raw dialog simply continues to use the settings until you change them again.

Figure 5-23 Setting workflow options

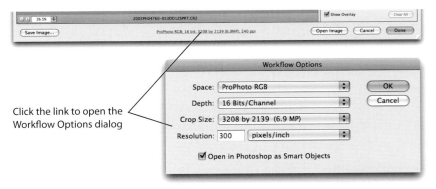

Click the link to open the Workflow Options dialog

Space. Choose a destination RGB color space for the conversion from one of four preset working spaces: Adobe RGB (1998), Colormatch RGB, ProPhoto RGB, or sRGB. Note that the space you choose here determines the boundaries for the clipping warnings in the Camera Raw dialog.

You can't add profiles to the Space menu, but the four RGB choices work well for most jobs. If you're sending images to the Web, sRGB is your choice. For prepress you'll have to convert to CMYK in Photoshop anyway, so choose whichever space your current prepress workflow recommends for editing RGB images before conversion. For fine art or other image master-ing work where you'll do even more fine-tuning in Photoshop before pro-ducing a final file, ProPhoto RGB at 16 Bits/Channel is a good choice.

Depth. We talked about the difference between 8 and 16 bit/channel images in Chapter 2, "Image Essentials." If you feel that an image will need very little further work in Photoshop, you can create smaller files by choosing 8 Bits/Channel . But if you plan to perform further significant adjustments and manipulation in Photoshop, 16 Bits/Channel will provide useful addi-tional headroom so that more of the image's original quality will survive your Photoshop edits.

Crop Size. Choose the pixel dimensions of the converted image. If you see a minus sign (–) after a set of dimensions, choosing those dimensions will downsample the image. Similarly, if you see a plus sign (+) after a set of dimensions, choosing those dimensions will upsample the image. The dimensions in the middle of the list (with no minus or plus sign) represent the number of pixels saved into the image file by the camera.

Resolution. Choose a resolution for the converted image. Changing this value doesn't change the number of pixels in the converted image, only their density. It's like changing the Resolution value in the Image Size command in Photoshop when the Resample Image option is turned off.

If you want to set the image resolution or pixel dimensions with more con-trol than you have in the Workflow Options dialog, leave the settings at their native values, wait until you've opened the image in Photoshop, and then choose the Image > Image Size command in Photoshop.

Open in Photoshop as Smart Objects. This option changes the Open Image button into the Open Object button, so that the selected image in Camera Raw will be passed to Photoshop as a Smart Object (see "Smart Objects" in Chapter 11). This option is off by default, which means the

TIP: To use Camera Raw to resample an image to pixel dimensions that aren't in the Crop Size pop-up menu, use the Crop tool in Camera Raw instead. The Crop tool lets you specify pixel dimensions up to 10,000 by 10,000 pixels, so you can use it to produce a much larger file than the sizes that appear on the Crop Size menu in Camera Raw. The Crop tool method works for downsampling too.

TIP: If you only want to toggle the Open Image/Open Object button temporarily, you don't need to go into the Workflow Options dialog—just hold down the Shift key.

selected image in Camera Raw is converted into a Photoshop document as normal, editable pixels. Conrad leaves this option turned on so that he can change an image's raw conversion settings at any time from inside Photoshop by double-clicking the Smart Object—in other words, a nondestructive raw conversion.

CAMERA RAW IMAGE CONTROL TABS

The image controls—the ones you're likely to change with each image—live in the group of tabs at the right side of the window. The tabs are

TIP: In Mac OS X, Command-Option-8 is the default shortcut for enabling or disabling screen zooming for the visually impaired. If you'd rather use that shortcut for the Presets tab in Camera Raw, open the Keyboard & Mouse system preference, click the Keyboard Shortcuts tab, and change the Turn Zoom On or Off shortcut to a different shortcut (Conrad changed it to Command-Option-9).

- Basic, which deals with color balance, essential tone mapping, and overall image quality

- Tone Curve, where you can fine-tune contrast

- Detail, which provides controls for sharpening and noise reduction

- HSL/Grayscale, where you can adjust specific color ranges or, if you turn on its Convert to Grayscale check box, tonal ranges

- Split Toning, where you can tone highlights and shadows differently to add depth to limited-color images

- Lens Corrections, which can correct chromatic aberration, defringing, and vignetting

- Camera Calibration, which lets you fine-tune the built-in color profiles in Camera Raw to better match the behavior of your camera

- Presets, a list of all of the presets available to Camera Raw

You can switch between tabs by pressing keys 1 through 8 together with the Command and Option keys (Mac) or the Ctrl and Alt keys (Windows). For example, on the Mac press Command-Option-2 for the Tone Curve tab.

These image controls are really the meat and potatoes of Camera Raw, offering very precise control over your raw conversions. The more work you do in Camera Raw, the less work you'll need to do later in Photoshop. If you get your images close to the way you want them in Camera Raw, they'll be able to withstand much more editing in Photoshop—which you may need to do to optimize for a specific output process or to harmonize the appearance of different images you want to combine.

The Basic Tab

The controls in the Basic tab (Command-Option-1 in Mac OS X or Ctrl-Alt-1 in Windows) let you tweak the essential tonal and color qualities of an image, such as white balance and overall contrast (see **Figure 5-24**). Many of the functions here may seem to duplicate similar features in Photoshop, but the more good work you do in Camera Raw, the more time you'll save in Photoshop since Camera Raw is earlier in the image-processing pipeline.

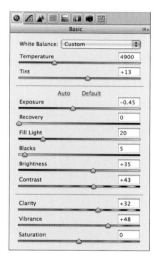

Figure 5-24 The Basic tab

TIP: There are an awful lot of controls in Camera Raw, but unlike Photoshop's controls, Camera Raw's are laid out to make it easy to remember what order to use to preserve the best image quality. You can simply go through the tabs from left to right and, within each tab, adjust the controls from top to bottom.

White Balance. The two controls that set the white balance, Temperature and Tint, are the main tools for adjusting color in the image. Setting the white balance correctly should make the rest of the color more or less fall into place in terms of hue. Note that the "correct white balance" includes (but isn't limited to) "accurate white balance"—you can use white balance as a creative tool, too.

• Temperature. The Temperature control lets you specify the color temperature of the lighting in Kelvins, thereby setting the blue-yellow color balance. Lowering the color temperature makes the image more blue to compensate for the yellower light; raising the color temperature makes the image more yellow to compensate for the bluer light. If this seems counterintuitive—we think of higher color temperatures as bluer and lower ones as yellower—the trick is to remember that the Temperature

TIP: If you can't figure out the white balance for an outdoor shot and the White Balance Eyedropper isn't helping, try choosing Daylight from the White Balance pop-up menu as a starting point. Automatic white balance may not work properly with a scene dominated by a color that isn't neutral, such as a green forest.

TIP: If you did a shoot in lighting conditions that are difficult to white-balance using the sliders, consider using the DNG Profile Editor (covered later in this chapter) to create a custom camera profile for those lighting conditions. Alternatively, you can adjust the sliders in the Camera Calibration tab.

control compensates for the color temperature of the light, so if you tell Camera Raw that the light is bluer, it makes the image yellower.

• Tint. The Tint control lets you fine-tune the color balance along the axis that's perpendicular to the one controlled by the Temperature slider—in practice, it's closer to a green-magenta control than anything else. Negative values add green; positive ones add magenta.

Figure 5-25 shows an image as shot, and with some white-balance adjustments that greatly alter the character of the image. The white-balance controls let you alter the color balance dramatically with virtually no image degradation, which is much harder to achieve once the image is converted to RGB and opened in Photoshop. The freedom with which you can reinterpret the white balance is one of the main advantages of capturing raw rather than JPEG images.

Figure 5-25 White balance

White Balance as shot

White Balance slider dragged left to cool the image

White Balance slider dragged right to warm the image

Tone-Mapping Controls. Learning how the four tone-mapping controls—Exposure, Blacks, Brightness, and Contrast—interact is essential if you want to exercise control over your images' tonal values. It may not be obvious, but the controls work together to produce a five-point curve adjustment.

Exposure and Blacks set the white and black endpoints, respectively. Brightness adjusts the midpoint. Contrast applies an S-curve around the midpoint set by the Brightness, darkening values below the midpoint and brightening those above.

Making Adjustments with Precision and Speed

While it may be obvious that you adjust settings in Camera Raw by dragging the sliders, you can also take advantage of other adjustment tricks. Some give you more precision and others give you more speed.

- You don't have to drag the slider itself. For more precision, position the cursor over the name of an option until the cursor turns into a two-headed arrow, and drag left or right using the entire width of the monitor. This gives you finer control than you get by using the short width of a slider.

- When the cursor is blinking in a field or a value is highlighted, press the up arrow or down arrow keys to adjust the value. The amount of the adjustment varies depending on the option. Add the Shift key to adjust the value by a larger amount.

- Undo works. Even though the Undo command is not available on the Edit menu when Camera Raw is open, you can still undo changes in the Camera Raw image controls by pressing the traditional Undo keyboard shortcut, Command-Z (Mac) or Ctrl-Z (Windows). Press the Undo shortcut again to toggle between the current and previous values. In addition, Camera Raw 4 has multiple undo; just add the Option (Mac) or Alt (Windows) key to the Undo shortcut to move back through Undo steps, or add the Shift key to redo steps you've undone.

TIP: Because half of the linear data in a raw capture describes the brightest f-stop, many digital photographers use the Expose to the Right (ETTR) technique. With ETTR, you set the camera exposure so that as much data as possible is as far to the right of the camera's histogram as possible, but without clipping the highlights. As a result, you'll probably have to lower the brightness of each image in Camera Raw, but it's worth it: ETTR optimizes the signal-to-noise ratio (translation: image noise is less visible).

Let's go into more depth on each of these controls.

- Exposure. The Exposure slider is essentially a white-clipping adjustment, like the white input slider in Curves or Levels in Photoshop. Half of the data in a raw capture is devoted to describing the brightest f-stop, so placing the highlights correctly is your highest priority. First set the Exposure slider, holding down Option (Mac) or Alt (Windows) to see the clipping display, so that clipping happens only on specular highlights. If the overall image becomes too dark, raise Exposure back up and use the Recovery slider to restore highlights (see **Figure 5-26**).

Large increases in exposure value (more than about three-quarters of a stop) can make shadow noise and posterization more visible, because with large positive exposure values you take the relatively few bits devoted to describing the shadows and stretch them further across the tonal scale. If you deliberately underexpose to hold highlight detail, your shadows won't be as clean as they could be. We certainly don't advocate

TIP: Don't forget to use the shadow and highlight clipping warnings (press the U and O keys to toggle them); they help you see whether you need to increase or decrease your Blacks and Exposure values. See "The Histogram and RGB Readout" earlier in this chapter.

overexposure—perfect exposure is always best—but *slight* overexposure is often better than the noise caused by significant underexposure.

- Recovery. The Recovery slider offers the amazing ability to let you recover highlight information from overexposed images. Figure 5-26 shows a fairly typical example of highlight recovery. The actual amount of highlight data you can recover depends on the camera model and on the amount of compromise you're prepared to tolerate in setting the white balance. But it's not at all unusual to recover two-thirds of a stop, and it's often possible to recover more.

Figure 5-26 Exposure and Recovery

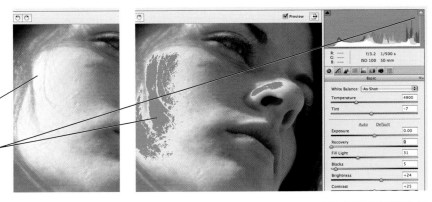

After raising Exposure to lighten the image, important highlights are clipped, or "blown out."

Turning on the Highlight Clipping Warning button in the histogram marks the clipped areas in red.

Increasing Recovery restores the blown highlights.

- Fill Light. The Fill Light slider opens up shadows in a way that isn't easily reproduced by Brightness, Contrast, or the Tone Curves (see **Figure 5-27**). If you try to open up shadows with a curve but find that other key parts of the image lose too much contrast or become too light, Fill Light may do better, since it confines its changes to darker tones, much like the Shadow part of the Shadow/Highlight command in Photoshop.

You may experience a slight delay the first time you drag the Fill Light slider for each image, because it initially generates a mask, which Fill Light uses to restrict the adjustment to the shadows. On a slower machine, drag Fill Light a little, let go, and wait for it to build the mask before tuning your adjustments. You can't see or adjust this invisible mask, but it works well in most cases.

Figure 5-27
Fill Light

Setting Exposure and Brightness for the skin tones makes the stuffed black dog too dark.

Increasing Fill Light opens up shadows with minimal effect on midtones and highlights.

It's normal for noise to exist in the darkest tones of an unprocessed digital image, and Fill Light may reveal that noise if you push it too far. Avoid underexposing images; recording shadows in higher, less noisy tonal levels may give you more leeway when using Fill Light.

- **Blacks.** The Blacks slider is the black-clipping control, like the black input slider in Curves or Levels in Photoshop. The Blacks slider operates on linear-gamma data, however, so small moves make bigger changes than the black input slider in Levels. If you think the default value of 5 is too aggressive, set a lower value and save it as your Camera Raw default.

- **Brightness.** The Brightness slider is like the gray input slider in Levels, redistributing midtone values without moving the black point or white

TIP: Exposure and Blacks are the two most fundamental adjustments because they control the lightest highlight and darkest shadow. If Exposure and Blacks aren't set correctly, you may have trouble getting the other sliders to produce the results you want.

point. Note, however, that when you raise Brightness to values greater than 100, you can drive 8-bit highlight values to 255, which looks a lot like highlight clipping. But if you check the 16-bit values after conversion, you'll probably find that they aren't clipped.

- Contrast. Contrast applies an S-curve to the data, leaving the extreme shadows and highlights alone. Increasing the Contrast value from the default setting of +25 lightens values above the midtones and darkens values below the midtones, while reducing the Contrast value does the reverse. The midpoint around which Contrast adds the S-curve is determined by the Brightness value, so if Contrast isn't doing what you want, make sure Brightness is set correctly.

Intensity Controls. Clarity and Vibrance are versions of Contrast and Saturation that greatly extend your options for correcting images quickly.

TIP: For portraits, you might want to add pop to the image while keeping skin soft. To do this, increase Clarity overall, then use the Adjustment Brush to paint low or negative Clarity values only on skin; we show this technique in Figure 5-14.

- Clarity. The Clarity slider controls local contrast and can help produce that quality some photographers call "pop." Instead of adjusting contrast uniformly, Clarity adjusts contrast among adjacent areas of light and dark within an image (see **Figure 5-28**). Most images benefit from applying a moderate amount of Clarity, but as you increase the value, back off if you start to see unsightly halos around edges. Clarity can noticeably improve images that naturally have low local contrast, such as reflections, foliage, and subjects photographed through haze. Clarity can appear to have a sharpening effect, but it's important to note that it is not a substitute for sharpening. For that, there's the Detail tab.

For portraits, it usually isn't a good idea to increase Clarity, because it tends to accentuate details and texture in an unflattering way for human faces. The good news? In Camera Raw 5 you can set Clarity to a negative value, which has the fortunate side effect of softening skin. To see this effect, try dragging the Clarity slider left instead of right.

Figure 5-28 Increasing Clarity increases local contrast, which can emphasize definition and texture and cut through haze.

You may have used Photoshop to enhance local contrast by setting the Unsharp Mask filter to a high Radius and low Amount value. Clarity is based on the same idea but with some additional intelligence built in.

- Vibrance. The Vibrance slider is intended as a safer version of the Saturation slider. It applies a greater increase in color saturation to colors that are not already saturated (see **Figure 5-29**). For example, if you increase the vibrance of an image that contains both muted and saturated oranges, the muted oranges become more saturated but the bright oranges are prevented from becoming ridiculously saturated. It's a good way to improve color with less of a chance of colors going out of gamut.

  Vibrance has one more key function. The Photoshop team built skin-tone protection into Vibrance, so you can boost image saturation much further before the people in your image acquire radioactive tans.

The colors in the original image are fine, but let's try boosting them.

Figure 5-29 Vibrance and Saturation

Increasing Saturation soon oversaturates the orange shirt, and skin tones are no longer acceptable.

Increasing Vibrance by the same amount still enhances dull colors, but it protects skin tones and colors that are already saturated.

- Saturation. The Saturation slider adjusts color intensity evenly for all colors. While every image-editing program needs a saturation feature, the presence of the more useful Vibrance control means that you may reach for the Saturation slider less often than you used to.

Improving Printed Output. The tonal range and color gamut of print is so much narrower than what your camera and monitor can produce that it isn't unusual to spend a lot of time using layers and masks in Photoshop to shoehorn an image into the gamut of your printed output. You can achieve many of the same goals in Camera Raw by using Recovery, Fill Light, Clarity, and Vibrance. Recovery and Fill Light are quick and reliable ways to move highlight and shadow detail a little closer to the midtones and away from the extreme ends of the tonal scale, which are harder to print. Because compressing detail into the midtones usually means you lose a little contrast, you can then use the intelligent Clarity slider to preserve and enhance contrast in the midtones without pushing those tones back out to the extremes, as the Contrast slider might, and you can use Vibrance similarly for colors.

It may not be possible for you to use Camera Raw to completely prepare an image for printed output—for one thing, you can't load a printer profile and visually check your adjustments against it—but Recovery, Fill Light, Clarity, and Vibrance can reduce the amount of work you have to do with layers and masks in Photoshop to compress an image's tonal and color range.

Using Auto Tone Adjustment

When you click Auto (see **Figure 5-30**) in the Basic tab (it's on by default), Camera Raw works out optimum settings for each image, essentially auto-correcting tone and exposure. Although the word "auto" usually makes us squirm, this feature is more sophisticated than it might seem at first glance.

Figure 5-30 Applying auto tone adjustment

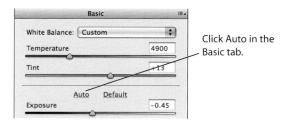

Click Auto in the Basic tab.

TIP: To reset any Camera Raw slider to zero, just double-click the slider.

However, keeping Auto as part of the default setting makes it difficult for you to learn the behavior of a camera, because Camera Raw adjusts each image individually, so you don't get to see a consistent baseline interpretation. Beginners will likely find that Auto provides a quick way to get decent results, but it also makes it much more difficult for them to learn the relationship between shutter speed, aperture setting, and the result. If you don't want Auto to be applied to new images by default, click the Preferences button in the Camera Raw toolbar (Command-K in Mac OS X or Ctrl-K in Windows), and in the Default Image Settings options group, uncheck Apply Auto Tone Adjustments.

Camera Raw + Bridge = Lightroom?

Many Photoshop users ask what value Adobe Photoshop Lightroom adds to a Photoshop workflow that already includes Bridge and Camera Raw, given that Lightroom isn't included with Photoshop and therefore is an extra expense.

Much of the appeal of Lightroom lies in its being an affordable alternative for those who don't need access to the complete Photoshop feature set. The Lightroom user interface puts the image at the center of the screen, surrounded by panels and with few dialogs popping up. Controls are presented as five modules that you can move among freely: Library (like the Content panel in Bridge), Develop (containing Camera Raw controls), Slideshow (a bit better than the Bridge slideshow), Web (where you can export Flash and HTML Web sites to disk or upload them to a server), and Print.

Camera Raw has matured into a powerful image-processing program in its own right. If your images are well lit, focused, and need little retouching, you may be able to produce finished images from Camera Raw without moving them through Photoshop. Because the Develop module in Lightroom includes the Camera Raw engine, it can provide the same level of image processing.

Camera Raw and Bridge are incapable of printing; for those programs, the road to printing still goes through Photoshop. Suddenly you find that you're chaining together three programs to organize, edit, and print your photos. The same goes for building Web galleries. Lightroom accomplishes all of that in one program using its Library, Develop, Web, and Print modules.

Lightroom also removes some of the walls that exist in the Bridge-Camera Raw workflow. Camera Raw exists in a modal dialog, which tends to isolate it from Bridge and Photoshop. In Lightroom, you can switch easily between the Develop module and the Library or any of the other modules.

While Bridge is a type of file browser, Lightroom tracks images in a database called a *catalog*, and you can save multiple catalogs. The database allows Lightroom to do a few things Bridge can't, such as managing images even when their original files are on a volume that isn't currently mounted. Both Bridge and Lightroom let you enter metadata and keywords and then use them to find photos, but because Lightroom uses a database, it's more efficient at searching through images in many different folders on multiple disks.

Despite the similarities between Lightroom and Camera Raw/Bridge, there are quite a few Photoshop users who find Lightroom a valuable addition to their workflow. Some like the smoother integration and the additional power that a database brings to digital asset management. If you're a pro who processes a high volume of images, these Lightroom features may save enough billable hours of labor to pay for the program. If you are a low-volume photographer, Bridge, Camera Raw, and Photoshop may be all you need to get the job done.

Using the Camera Raw Defaults

TIP: The difference between Auto and Default is that Auto tries to calculate settings for each image, while Default applies the same set of values to all images.

Camera Raw contains default settings for images shot by each camera model. They're applied when you view images in Camera Raw or Bridge for the first time (Camera Raw generates the previews for Bridge). You can create your own defaults, and the image metadata will tell Camera Raw which default to use for each camera model. No set of defaults will do equal justice to every image, so the real goal is to find default settings that provide a good starting point for your images. That will still save you time.

If you're editing an image and want to return to the camera defaults, click Default in the Basic tab (see **Figure 5-31**).

Figure 5-31 Applying camera defaults

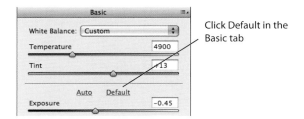

Click Default in the Basic tab

TIP: A common question is how to import images into Camera Raw and Bridge without applying the Auto adjustment. Simply click Default (which neutralizes Auto) and then save new Camera Raw defaults.

If you don't like the Camera Raw defaults, change them. For example, you may find the default Blacks setting of 5 a little too high, or you may notice that you consistently find yourself lowering the Color Noise Reduction slider. So set the controls the way you want them, then choose Save New Camera Raw Defaults from the Camera Raw menu. If you get hopelessly messed up, you can easily set everything back to the shipping defaults and start over by choosing Reset Camera Raw Defaults from the settings menu.

We see a distressingly large number of photographers who convert their raw images at Camera Raw default settings then complain that Camera Raw produces flat, unsaturated results that require a lot of Photoshop work. The defaults in Camera Raw tend to be more conservative than those of proprietary raw converters, which generally aim to match the in-camera JPEG. They often bury shadow detail to hide noise and produce a pleasingly contrasty result. Camera Raw, on the other hand, shows you everything the camera has captured, warts and all, and lets you work with all the bits so that you can create better quality than any automatic converter.

Raw files are always interpreted, as when printing color negative film. There is no definitive way to develop a raw file. The default appearance of images

Workflow Guidelines for Camera Raw Image Controls

There are now so many options in Camera Raw 5 (the Basic tab alone is now loaded with 11, count 'em, 11 sliders) that it can be hard to figure out which slider to move to fix a particular problem. Although it's generally a good idea to move through the sliders from top to bottom, there are some interrelationships to consider among the sliders in the Basic tab and those in other parts of Camera Raw.

- Setting Exposure and Blacks correctly—the clipping points for white and black—defines what's possible with all of the other controls. If you don't get these settings right, your image's total tonal range will be suboptimal, and you'll probably spend extra time wrestling with the other controls to try to compensate for that fundamental problem.

- Similarly, setting White Balance correctly will make it easier to use all of the other color controls in Camera Raw.

- If you find yourself consistently making the exact same color corrections on your processed raws, you may want to visit the Camera Calibration tab to tweak the camera color or use a different camera profile (see "The Camera Calibration Tab," later in this chapter).

- Many people are unclear about the difference between Exposure and Brightness. Exposure affects only the white point, while Brightness only shifts the tonal midpoint up or down. Exposure is more important because it (together with Recovery) determines where highlights get clipped.

- If you set Brightness and Contrast as well as you can in the Basic tab, you may not have to make major moves in the Tone Curve tab.

- Some users ask how they can use the Basic tab in the same way that they use Levels in Photoshop. For the white, black, and gray (middle) slider in Levels, adjust Exposure, Blacks, and Brightness, respectively, in Camera Raw. The controls do not correspond exactly because corrections are applied using Gamma 1.0 in Camera Raw (Photoshop uses the gamma of the working space), but it's as close as you're going to get. Note that in both sets of controls, you can hold down the Option (Mac) or Alt (Windows) key to preview any clipping of highlights or shadows.

in each raw converter reflects the philosophy of the team that created it, and Camera Raw is no exception to that. If you want Camera Raw to render raw files more like the camera manufacturer's raw conversion software or the in-camera JPEG does, Camera Raw 4.5 and later lets you use the new camera profiles by Adobe or even make your own (see "Camera Profiles" and "Using the DNG Profile Editor" later in this chapter). Once you find the look you like, set the Camera Raw defaults (see the discussion in "The Settings Menu" earlier in this chapter) so that your preferred adjustments apply to all the images you download from your camera.

THE TONE CURVE TAB

The Tone Curve tab (Command-Option-2 in Mac OS X or Ctrl-Alt-2 in Windows) offers a luminosity-based curve control that lets you fine-tune the image's tonality (see **Figure 5-32**). If you're used to thinking of the Curves command in Photoshop as the best way to edit images, you may be tempted to skip the slider controls in the Basic tab and use the Tone Curve tab for all your tone-mapping adjustments, but that's not a good idea. To understand *why* it isn't a good idea, you need to know a little about how the Tone Curve tab actually works.

Figure 5-32 The Tone Curve tab, with the Parametric curve shown

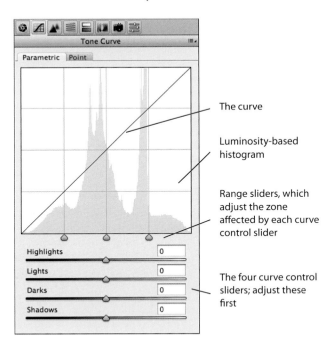

Like the sliders on the Basic tab, the ones on the Tone Curve tab operate on the linear (gamma 1.0) capture—in fact, the slider adjustments and the curve adjustments get concatenated into a single operation during the raw conversion. But the user interface for the Tone Curve tab makes it appear

that the curve is operating on gamma-2.2-encoded data. (If the curve interface corresponded directly to the linear data, the midtone value would be around level 50 and the three-quarter tone would be all the way down at level 10 or so, which would make it pretty hard to edit!)

The key point is that the Tone Curve tab settings are applied in addition to and after the slider adjustments in the Basic tab. Instead of doing all the heavy lifting in the Tone Curve tab, you'll find that it's much easier to use the Basic sliders for rough tonal shaping and the Tone Curve tab for fine-tuning. In other words, instead of trying to do everything in the Tone Curve tab, use it to refine your Basic tab adjustments.

If you've used only Curves in Photoshop or you're upgrading from Camera Raw 3, you'll notice that the default curve-editing tab is Parametric and it doesn't look like the tone curves you're used to. Yes, Parametric is a technical-sounding term, but bear with us—in the end, we think you'll decide that parametric curve editing is actually much easier than the old Point curve interface.

Using Parametric Curves

If you've ever used an audio equalizer (like the one in iTunes, for example), you already have a head start in understanding the Parametric tab. As in an audio equalizer, you get a series of sliders, each corresponding to a tonal range. Just grab the slider representing the range you want to boost or cut, and drag. All right—it isn't quite that simple; for instance, the Camera Raw sliders are horizontal, not vertical like the ones you see in audio equalizers. But the basic idea is the same. We think that the following sequence is the simplest path through the Parametric tab (see **Figure 5-33**). We'll use the example of an image that needs a little more contrast.

1. Drag the Darks and Lights sliders. To increase contrast (which is usually what you'll need to do), drag the Darks slider to the left and drag the Lights slider to the right.

2. If you think that the extreme highlights and shadows still need work, drag the Highlights and Shadows sliders. These sliders affect only the ends of the curves, and not every image needs these adjustments. However, the Highlights and Shadows sliders are a good way to control the tones at the ends of the tonal scale.

TIP: If you've been trained to avoid using the master curve in the Photoshop Curves dialog to edit RGB images, don't worry about that in Camera Raw. In Camera Raw 4.1 (and in Lightroom), the tone curve is engineered to minimize the hue shifts that can occur when you use a single curve to edit RGB images, resulting in a clean tonal edit.

Figure 5-33 Adjusting the
Parametric curve

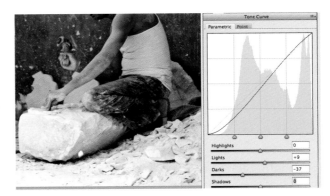

We set the Darks and
Lights sliders first, to
tune the basic S-curve for
midtone contrast.

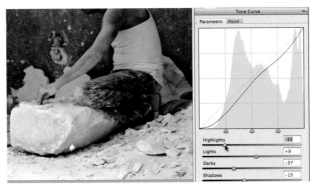

If we need to refine the
extreme ends of the
tonal scale, we drag the
Highlights and Shadows
sliders. Here, we pulled
down the Highlights
slider to see more detail
in the marble.

If the horizontal sliders
aren't affecting the tonal
ranges the way we want,
we adjust the range
sliders under the graph.
We dragged the third
slider to the left to let the
Highlights slider control
a wider range of the lightest tones.

TIP: You can reset any
individual slider by
double-clicking it.

3. With some images, you may find that a slider isn't giving you enough
control in the tonal range you want to adjust. In this case, turn to the
three Range sliders along the bottom of the curve graph. Those three
sliders define the four ranges affected by the four horizontal sliders. For
example, if you wish the Darks slider's effect was a little higher on the
tonal scale, drag the first slider under the graph to the right a little. With

a high-key or low-key image, you may want to shift or expand the tonal range controlled by a particular slider.

To easily remember that sequence, think of it as moving from the inside out: Adjust the inner Darks and Lights sliders first, and then if necessary, adjust the outer Highlights and Shadows sliders. If you've done a good job of setting Exposure, Blacks, Brightness, and Contrast in the Basic tab, you'll probably find that you don't need to move the Parametric sliders very far.

Parametric curves can be easier than point curves because parametric curves work as if the key points are already placed for you, and it's easier to create a curve that avoids posterization. If you need still more control, or you're just too used to placing your own points, you can still use the Point tab.

Using Point Curves

The Point tab is based on the Curves dialog in Photoshop, and they share some features. When you click the Point tab, you'll find that by default, Camera Raw applies a Medium Contrast curve preset (it's selected in the Curve pop-up menu). If you prefer a different default, you can edit the curve points and then save a new Camera Raw default.

To place a new point on the curve, click the curve. A more efficient way to place a point is to position the mouse over a tone in the image you want to adjust and then Command-click (Mac) or Ctrl-click (Windows). This adds a new point on the curve at the tone you clicked. You can preview where on the curve a point will be added if you keep the Command (Mac) or Ctrl (Windows) key pressed as you move the mouse over the image; a small circle appears on the curve, marking the level you're currently mousing over. There are three ways to delete a curve point: Command-click (Mac) or Ctrl-click (Windows) a point, select it, and press the Delete key, or drag it over one of the adjacent curve points.

Control-Tab (on both Mac and Windows) selects the next curve point, and Control-Shift-Tab selects the previous point. To select multiple curve points, Shift-click each one. The up, down, left, and right arrow keys move the selected curve point by one level: add Shift to move in increments of 10 levels. You can also enter numeric values for the selected curve point in the Input and Output entry fields.

To make saved tone curves appear on the Tone Curve menu, save them in (username)\Library\Application Support\Adobe\Camera Raw\Curves (Mac), or Documents and Settings\(username)\Application Data\Adobe\Camera Raw\ Curves (Windows). This is a different folder from the one for all other Camera Raw settings and subsets, but if you save a subset containing only a tone curve, it's saved in this folder automatically. If you save tone curves anywhere else, you can load them using the Load Settings command in Camera Raw (see "Loading and Saving Settings," earlier in this chapter).

Adjustments and Previewing. Here's the most practical way to adjust the curve: Place points by Command-clicking (Mac) or Ctrl-clicking (Windows) the image, and press arrow keys to make adjustments. **Figure 5-34** shows a typical Tone Curve tab adjustment. Adjustments to the Parametric and Tone Curve tabs are cumulative, so if a curve isn't doing what you expect it to, check the other tab to see if there's an existing adjustment there that contradicts what you're trying to do.

Figure 5-34 Adjusting the point curve

We want to bring down the highlights just a bit, so we first Command-click (Mac) or Ctrl-click (Windows) a very light tone to set a point on the curve for that tone.

After dragging down the point we created above, we then add the first two points from the left to improve contrast in the foliage by steepening that part of the curve. The first point is selected (it appears solid), and you can see and edit its Input and Output values below the curve graph. The third and fourth points preserve the contrast in the middle of the curve.

The Detail Tab

The sliders in the Detail tab (Command-Option-3 in Mac OS X or Ctrl-Alt-3 in Windows) let you apply overall sharpening and reduce noise in both the Luminance and Color components of an image (see **Figure 5-35**). To see the effect of the Detail tab, you need to zoom the preview to at least 100 percent. At other magnifications, the actual results of sharpening and noise reduction can't be represented accurately due to image scaling.

Color noise is often more noticeable than luminance noise. If you see color splotches in areas that should be neutral, try turning up Color noise reduction, but not so far that you lose saturation in color details. Luminance noise reduction is more apparent at very high ISO speeds.

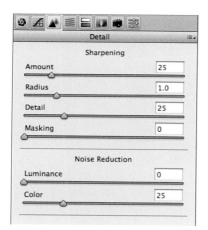

Figure 5-35 The Detail tab

Sharpening

The four Sharpening sliders don't resemble the two prominent sharpening dialogs in Photoshop (Unsharp Mask and Smart Sharpen). The reason for this is that Camera Raw sharpening is based specifically on advanced edge-masking techniques documented by Bruce Fraser and others. Edge masking can restrict sharpening to the edges (where you usually want it) and away from broad areas like skin (where you usually don't want it).

To preview the effect of only the Sharpening slider you're adjusting, set the magnification to 100 percent and then Option-drag (Mac) or Alt-drag (Windows) a Sharpening slider. You'll see a grayscale preview that nicely

TIP: For a deeper explanation of the principles behind edge masking, see "Edge Masking" in Chapter 10. In fact, reading all of Chapter 10 will give you insight into all of the controls in the Detail tab.

isolates the effect for you so you can clearly see what's changing. When previewing the Masking option, your sharpening settings are applied to white areas at full strength, are applied to gray areas at partial strength, and are not applied at all to black areas. You may want to turn off the shadow and highlight clipping warnings so that they don't distract you. In most of our examples, we'll show you the grayscale preview because it makes it easier to see the effects.

Amount. The Amount slider (see **Figure 5-36**) adjusts how much sharpening Camera Raw applies. In most cases, a low to moderate value is appropriate. The Radius, Detail, and Masking sliders use different methods to modify the strength of the Amount value in various parts of the image.

Figure 5-36 Amount set to values of 0 (left) and 85 (right), with all other Sharpening sliders at default values. The rest of the sharpening examples concentrate on the bottom half of this faded mural.

Radius. The Radius slider (see **Figure 5-37**) controls the width of the halo around each detail that's sharpened. If the halos become visible or details start to smear or look like blobs, you've set Radius too high.

Figure 5-37 Radius value shown using the grayscale preview, set to values of 1.0 (default, narrow halos) and 2.5 (wide halos), applied to the bottom half of Figure 5-36

Detail. The Detail slider (see **Figure 5-38**) affects how much the Radius halos are visible on high-frequency details, such as skin pores or other fine textures. A low Detail value filters out Radius halos on those details while letting the Radius value to apply to larger features. To apply Radius to all details without modification, set Detail to its maximum value.

Figure 5-38 Detail value shown using the grayscale preview, set to values of 25 (default, larger details sharpened only) and 90 (most details sharpened)

Masking. The Masking slider (see **Figure 5-39**) affects the degree to which sharpening is restricted to edges only. Edges are considered to be the image areas with highest contrast. At zero, no masking is applied—the current Amount, Radius, and Detail values are applied to the entire image at full strength. As you increase the Masking value, less sharpening is applied to non-edge areas, while edges continue receiving full-strength sharpening. Increasing the Masking value can help you sharpen images that are blurrier than average, because when you increase the Masking value, you can use much higher Amount values without accentuating noise, grain, or other unwanted detail in non-edge areas.

Figure 5-39 Masking shown using the grayscale preview, set to values of 25 (almost no areas masked) and 85 (most areas masked except high-contrast edges)

So how much sharpening is enough? That depends on how you use Camera Raw in your workflow.

- If you use Camera Raw between your camera and Photoshop, you can apply capture sharpening—just enough sharpening to make up for the softness inherent in all image sensors. Then, in Photoshop, apply the appropriate amount of output sharpening to the versions of the image that you prepare for different output media. If you do this, first open the Camera Raw preferences and choose "All images" from the "Apply sharpening to" pop-up menu.

- If you would rather use the Photoshop sharpening controls for all sharpening, open the Camera Raw preferences and choose "Preview images only" from the "Apply sharpening to" pop-up menu. Then don't use the Camera Raw Sharpening controls at all.

- If you intend to use Camera Raw as the final step in your workflow, saving completed images directly from Camera Raw, apply the appropriate amount of sharpening for your final output. If you do this, first open the Camera Raw preferences and choose "All images" from the "Apply sharpening to" pop-up menu.

Reducing Noise

The sensors in today's digital SLR cameras are rather noise-free at low ISO speed settings, but if you shoot at high ISO speed settings or use a digital point-and-shoot camera, noise is likely to be present.

To minimize noise when you shoot digital, never underexpose your images. Noise lives in the shadows, so if you boost shadows in Camera Raw or Photoshop, noise becomes more visible. If you shoot so that an image file is brighter than normal (without clipping highlights), the act of lowering Exposure or Brightness in Camera Raw pushes noise further down into the shadows, hiding it.

TIP: The Color Noise Reduction slider can make a big difference at low values, so you can easily be tempted to turn it up further. Be careful, though—increasing Color noise reduction too far can dull bright colors in important details.

It's difficult to show typical noise scenarios in print because noise that looks objectionable on the displayed RGB file is often invisible by the time the image has been converted to CMYK and printed.

Although the Luminance slider comes first in the Detail tab, we often try the Color Noise Reduction slider first, so that's how we're covering the options here. The Camera Raw defaults agree with us: By default, Luminance is set to 0 and Color is set to 25.

Color Noise Reduction. Color noise appears as random speckles of color rather than gray. In our experience, all cameras need some amount of Color noise reduction (see **Figure 5-40**). While the visibility of color noise varies with ISO speed, the required correction seems to vary less than it does with luminance noise. That means you can generally find a good default value for your camera and then deviate from it only when you see an obvious problem. Now that Camera Raw reads TIFF and JPEG images, it's worth noting that the Color Noise Reduction slider can also work wonders with the visible color grain in scanned color film.

Figure 5-40 Color noise reduction. This is a detail of a digital SLR image shot at ISO 1600. We set the Color slider to 0 and 25 (default).

Luminance Noise Reduction. The Luminance Noise Reduction slider (see **Figure 5-41**) lets you control grayscale noise that makes the image appear grainy—a typical problem when shooting at high ISO speeds. The default setting is zero, which provides no smoothing, but some cameras benefit from a small amount—say 2 to 4—of Luminance noise reduction even at slow speeds, so you may want to experiment to find a good default for your camera. At high ISO speeds—800 and up—you'll typically need to apply luminance smoothing at even higher settings.

At very high settings, the Luminance slider produces images that look like they've been hit with the Median filter, so always check the entire image at 100 percent size or larger before committing to a setting.

Figure 5-41 Luminance noise reduction. With Color set to 25, we set Luminance to 25 and 50. At 50 we're starting to lose image detail, so a value of less than 50 is probably correct.

THE HSL/GRAYSCALE TAB

The controls in the HSL/Grayscale tab (Command-Option-4 in Mac OS X or Ctrl-Alt-4 in Windows) are new in Camera Raw 4. The controls in this tab have two main purposes: to correct specific ranges of color and to convert an image to grayscale while controlling how colors map to gray tones.

Using the HSL Controls

In this tab, HSL stands for hue, saturation, and luminance; see Chapter 3, "Color Essentials," to review those color concepts. When you can't nail the color balance with the Temperature and Tint sliders in Camera Raw, you can turn to these powerful controls. Hue, Saturation, and Luminance each gets a tab of its own, and each of those tabs contains eight sliders (see **Figure 5-42**). That's a lot of sliders, but don't be intimidated, because each tab is simply a variation on the same idea.

Figure 5-42 The HSL/Grayscale tab

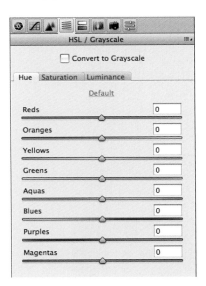

The Hue, Saturation, and Luminance tabs each have sliders for eight color ranges. These ranges were not chosen mathematically but visually—they're colors that typically need correction in photos. To figure out how to use the controls, first identify what's wrong with the color you want to correct in the image in terms of hue, saturation, or luminance (see **Figure 5-43**).

- If a color isn't the right hue, such as grass that's too yellow, go to the Hue tab and then drag that color's slider to shift it to the correct color.

- If a color needs to be less or more vivid, click the Saturation tab and drag that color's slider left to gray down the color, or right to increase saturation. You might use this to make a blue sky more blue.

- If you want a color to be lighter or darker, click the Luminance tab and drag that color's slider left to darken it, or right to lighten it.

If you don't see much of a change, you probably aren't dragging the correct color slider. It's also possible for a slider to change a part of the image you weren't expecting; for example, a black object can change if it has a color cast. To adjust skin tones, try the Oranges and Yellows sliders first.

Figure 5-43 Desaturating one color

This image was white-balanced for the tungsten light bulb in the lamp, which caused the daylight coming in from the window to appear distractingly blue.

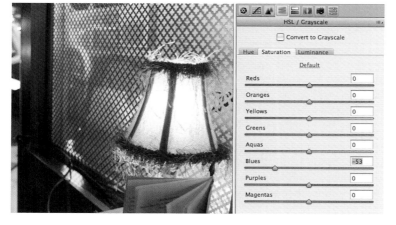

In the HSL/Grayscale tab, we clicked the Saturation tab and lowered the Blues value to make the lighting appear more natural.

Controlling Grayscale Conversions

Although you can convert an image to grayscale by setting Saturation to zero in the Basic tab, the Convert to Grayscale option in the HSL/Grayscale tab is better. It lets you control the lightness of each color when converted to gray.

To convert an image to grayscale, simply turn on the Convert to Grayscale check box at the top of the HSL/Grayscale panel. You'll notice that in addition to the image losing all its color, the Hue, Saturation, and Luminance tabs disappear and are replaced by a single Grayscale Mix tab (see **Figure 5-44**). On top of that, the sliders in the Grayscale Mix tab move around by themselves and take on new values.

What happened? When you turn on the Convert to Grayscale check box, by default Camera Raw calculates how to get the best distribution of tones out of that particular image, and that's why the Grayscale Mix sliders adjust themselves. In many cases, the Auto Grayscale Mix is a great starting point, and you may be satisfied with it. If not, drag the sliders to tweak the results.

Here's how the Grayscale Mix sliders work: When you convert to grayscale, you take away hue and saturation. What's left is the luminance value of each color. However, as you change the saturation of different colors, they occupy different ranges of tones. For instance, at maximum saturation, pure yellow is lighter than any other color. When you convert to grayscale, the resulting distribution of tones can appear unnatural or just weak. The Grayscale Mix sliders let you make specific color ranges lighter or darker in grayscale, so you can get the tone and contrast relationships that bring out the image qualities you want to emphasize. For example, if you drag the Reds slider to the left to darken reds, red lipstick darkens and stands out more effectively. If you've ever placed a color filter in front of a camera lens when shooting black-and-white film, it's the same idea, but with a lot more control.

TIP: If you don't want Camera Raw to calculate grayscale mix values, open Camera Raw preferences and uncheck the "Apply auto grayscale mix when converting to grayscale" check box. If you want to set all of the sliders for the current image to their original values, click Default in the HSL/Grayscale panel.

THE SPLIT TONING TAB

The controls in the Split Toning tab (Command-Option-5 in Mac OS X or Ctrl-Alt-5 in Windows) let you apply different colors to the lighter and darker parts of an image. This is more of a special effect, not an image-correction feature. Here's how to use split toning.

1. Split toning typically starts with a grayscale image (see **Figure 5-45**). If the image in Camera Raw is still in color, you can switch to the HSL/Grayscale tab and turn on the Convert to Grayscale check box, and then return to the Split Toning tab.

2. Drag both Saturation sliders to a value well above zero, or your Hue changes won't be visible. You can leave one of the Saturation sliders at zero if you don't want to apply a color to that tonal range.

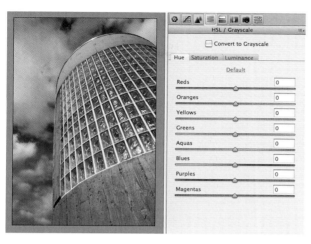

Figure 5-44 Grayscale conversion

This is a color image before being converted to grayscale.

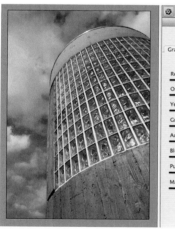

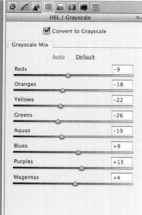

Clicking the Convert to Grayscale check box applies the Auto Grayscale Mix.

We manually customized the grayscale mix by raising the Yellows and lowering the Blues to create more contrast between the building and the sky.

3. Set the Hue sliders to the hues you want for highlights and shadows.

4. Drag the Balance slider to control the point along the whole tonal scale at which the Highlights hue changes over to the Shadows hue.

The one time you may not want to use split toning in Camera Raw is when you want to produce a true multitone image, such as a duotone, tritone, or quadtone. Those are best produced in Photoshop, where you can use the Image > Mode > Duotone command to create and control separate channels for each ink. The results of the Split Toning tab are suitable for reproduction in most other media, such as printing on RGB or CMYK devices and, of course, onscreen media. If you do want to create a multitone image from a raw image, you can use the Convert to Grayscale option and Grayscale Mix in the HSL/Grayscale tab to create a high-quality grayscale, which you can immediately convert to a multitone image in Photoshop.

Figure 5-45 Split toning

Corrected grayscale images are good candidates for split toning.

Adjust the hue and saturation of highlights and shadows. Remember that split toning adjustments take effect only when Saturation is higher than zero.

The Lens Corrections Tab

In the Lens Corrections tab (Command-Option-6 in Mac OS X or Ctrl-Alt-6 in Windows), you can address problems that occasionally show up in digital captures, especially with lower-quality sensors and lenses.

Chromatic Aberration. Chromatic aberration occurs when the lens fails to focus the red, green, and blue wavelengths of the light to exactly the same spot, causing red and cyan color fringes along high-contrast edges. In severe cases, you may also see blue and yellow fringing. It can be found in wide-angle shots and is typically worse at larger apertures (lower f-stop values).

- Fix Red/Cyan Fringe. This slider can reduce or eliminate red/cyan fringes by adjusting the size of the red channel relative to the green channel. Although the red/cyan fringes are usually the most visually obvious, chromatic aberration usually has a blue/yellow component too.

- Fix Blue/Yellow Fringe. This slider can reduce or eliminate blue/yellow fringes by adjusting the size of the blue channel relative to the green channel.

Figure 5-46 shows a chromatic aberration correction.

Figure 5-46 Fixing chromatic aberration

In this corner detail of a digital SLR frame, red and yellow fringes are visible along edges.

Dragging the two Chromatic Aberration sliders minimizes the problem.

TIP: To see color fringes clearly and to judge the optimum settings for the sliders, set the Sharpness slider in the Detail tab to zero. Color fringes are usually most prominent along high-contrast edges, and sharpening makes it harder to see exactly where the color fringes start and end.

TIP: When correcting chromatic aberration, Option/Alt-drag a slider to hide the other channel. This makes it much easier to apply exactly the right amount of correction to both channels. Red/cyan fringing is usually much easier to see than blue/yellow fringing, but chromatic aberration is almost always a combination of both. As with the Detail tab controls, zoom the preview to 100 percent or more when using the Chromatic Aberration sliders.

Defringe. The Defringe option (see **Figure 5-47**) helps minimize color fringing that can occur when sensors are overloaded by light; it typically shows up in high-contrast scenes. You may see it in specular highlights such as chrome or at other times when the raw data is clipped to white, such as sunlight sparkling on the ocean or city lights at night. It's sometimes called *purple fringing*, because that's how it often looks around a highlight.

If you see color fringing, choose Highlight Edges or All Edges from the Defringe pop-up menu, depending on the extent of the color fringing. The color fringe should disappear, and the affected edge should take on the natural color of the objects around it.

Figure 5-47 Defringing

Purple fringing is present in the specular highlights of this metal watchband. You can see that we've already tried a Chromatic Aberration adjustment.

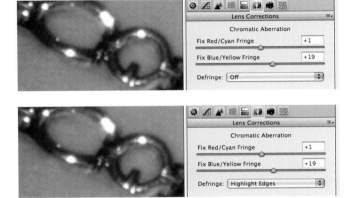

Choosing Highlight Edges from the Defringe pop-up menu reduces the fringing.

Lens Vignetting. Vignetting, where the corners are darker because the lens fails to illuminate the entire sensor area evenly, is a problem you may encounter when shooting wide open.

• Amount. This slider controls the amount of lightening or darkening (negative amounts darken, positive amounts lighten) applied to the corners of the image.

• Midpoint. This slider controls the area to which the Amount adjustment gets applied. Smaller values reduce the area; larger ones increase it.

Post-Crop Vignetting. In earlier versions of Camera Raw, cropping an image also cropped the applied vignette. In Camera Raw 5, you can use the new Post-Crop Vignetting feature to create a vignette that starts from the current crop you've applied to the image. It has the same Amount and Midpoint options as Lens Vignetting, and adds the Roundness and Feather options so that you can control the shape and softness of the vignette edge.

The Camera Calibration Tab

In the Camera Calibration tab (Command-Option-7 in Mac OS X or Ctrl-Alt-7 in Windows) you can fine-tune the default tone and color rendering of raw images (see **Figure 5-48**). If you're wondering why this tab exists in addition to the first three Camera Raw tabs, the reason is that the first three tabs are intended for image-specific corrections. In contrast, the Camera Calibration tab is intended for camera-specific corrections. Not clear yet? Here's an example. If you notice that you always have to add the same amount of red to every image you open from your camera, it might be best to make that correction in the Camera Calibration tab. When the Camera Calibration tab is set up ideally, the default rendering of raw files should require as little adjustment as possible in the first three tabs. The reason the built-in profiles don't always work perfectly is simply because of manufacturing variations in individual cameras. The specific camera Adobe used to make a camera's default profile can't match every sample of that model.

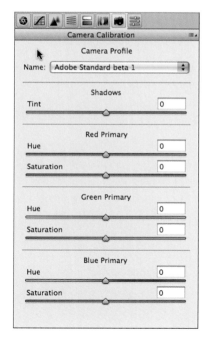

Figure 5-48 The Camera Calibration tab

For Camera Raw 4.4.x or earlier, you adjust the Camera Calibration tab by moving the sliders and then saving the settings as a preset that you can apply to all images from that camera. Color experts such as Bruce Fraser and

Thomas Fors devised ingenious methods and scripts to perform this process precisely, but those methods are no longer necessary: Starting with Camera Raw 4.5, Adobe provides two new and far faster ways to improve the default rendering from your raw files: camera profiles and the DNG Profile Editor.

Because the DNG Profile Editor is such a superior solution, we've decided not to go into detail about using the Camera Calibration sliders. We recommend the following approach to using the Camera Calibration tab:

TIP: Don't look for your camera name in the Camera Profile Name pop-up menu. The profiles in the menu are already camera specific. For example, if you open a Nikon D3 raw file and then a Canon 5D raw file, the Camera Profile Name pop-up menu seems to list identical profiles, such as Adobe Standard, for both cameras. In reality, for each camera Camera Raw uses a different and specifically tuned version of the Adobe Standard profile.

1. In the Camera Profile section, choose the profile that you believe provides the best color.

2. If you feel that the best available profile still isn't right, make sure the sliders are all set to zero and open the DNG Profile Editor.

3. In the DNG Profile Editor, create a camera profile (see "Using the DNG Profile Editor" later in this chapter). You can start from one of the existing profiles and simply tweak the color and tone curve in any way you like, or you can shoot a color checker and let DNG Profile Editor generate a color table for it. Either way, when you're done you can export the profile.

4. After you export the profile to the correct location, return to the Camera Calibration tab in Adobe Camera Raw and choose your new profile.

Camera Profiles

Camera Raw handles color in an ingenious way. For each supported camera, Adobe creates not one but two profiles: one built from a target shot under a D65 (daylight) light source and the other built from the same target shot under an Illuminant A (tungsten) light source. Camera Raw applies the correct profiles for each camera automatically when producing the colorimetric interpretation of the raw image. The White Balance (Color Temperature and Tint) sliders in Camera Raw let you interpolate between, or even extrapolate beyond, the two built-in profiles.

For cameras that write a readable white-balance tag, that white balance is used as the "As Shot" setting for the image; for those that don't, Camera Raw makes highly educated guesses. Either way, you can override the initial settings to produce the white balance you desire.

When you click the Name pop-up menu in the Camera Calibration tab, you see one or more camera profiles. When a camera profile name is ACR followed by a version number, it's an Adobe-generated profile and the version number is the version of Camera Raw where the profile first appeared. Don't be concerned if the profile doesn't match the version of Camera Raw you're currently using, because profiles are not updated unless necessary.

For certain popular cameras, Adobe now provides additional Adobe-created profiles, which you download and install separately. When you install these profiles, they're added to the Camera Profile Name pop-up menu in the Camera Calibration tab. For example, for Canon cameras, the camera profiles are intended to provide a closer match to the look of the JPEG images rendered by the camera, as well as some of the Picture Styles by Canon. You can download these from the Adobe Web site: labs.adobe.com/wiki/index.php/DNG_Profiles.

NOTE: DNG camera profiles are not interchangeable with the ICC profiles used in the rest of a color-managed workflow. For various reasons, the ICC profile specification is not optimal for profiling digital cameras. This also means you can't use the DNG Profile Editor to edit ICC profiles.

Using the DNG Profile Editor

If you don't like how any of the camera profiles render your raw images, you can use the DNG Profile Editor to create your own. If you don't use DNG files, don't worry—you can take camera profiles you create with the DNG Profile Editor and apply them in Camera Raw to the native raw formats of supported cameras. A DNG image is required to generate the profile, but you can easily export one using the Save button in Camera Raw or the free Adobe DNG Converter. You can download the DNG Profile Editor from the same Web link we gave you in "Camera Profiles" above.

NOTE: As we write this, the DNG Profile Editor is in beta, which means it may change after this book goes to press. We recommend that you read the latest instructions available on the Adobe Web site. If the link we provided no longer works, search for the DNG Profile Editor on the Adobe Web site.

There are two ways to make a camera profile. When you think an existing camera profile is pretty close to what you want, use it as a starting point and tweak it. If you're trying to profile color conditions that are not well matched to the default profiles, such as some types of artificial lighting, you can shoot a standard color chart such as the X-Rite ColorChecker (previously known as the GretagMacbeth ColorChecker) and let the DNG Profile Editor generate color tables and export profiles using the chart data.

Starting from an Existing Profile. Start by opening a DNG image in the DNG Profile Editor (see **Figure 5-49**). The image should be a type that you generally wish was rendered differently. In the Color Tables tab, choose the profile you think is the closest to what you want from the Base Profile pop-up menu. If the sample image doesn't look white-balanced, right-click or Control-click (Mac OS X) in a neutral-colored area of the image.

Now identify a color in the image that you'd like to refine, and click it. The color is added to the color list box. When the color is selected, you can use the Hue, Saturation, and Lightness sliders to tune that color just the way you like it. Do this for as many colors as you want.

Figure 5-49 Sampling a color to adjust in the DNG Profile Editor

Click the eyedropper in your DNG sample image to add a control point on the color wheel. Then use the sliders to adjust that color. In this example, skin tones were made less red and more saturated.

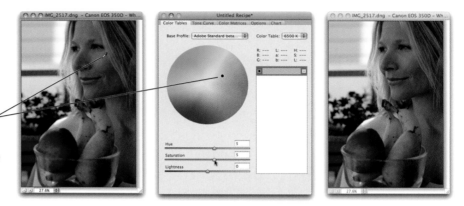

Original image   Color Tables tab   After adjusting the color

You can also adjust the tone curve of a profile by clicking the Tone Curve tab (see **Figure 5-50**) and editing the curve. This works much like the Tone Curve tab in Camera Raw, discussed earlier in this chapter. Modifying the tone curve is appropriate if your exposures for this profile will be consistent, since shot-by-shot tonal adjustments should be done in the Basic tab.

Figure 5-50 Adjusting the Tone Curve tab in the DNG Profile Editor

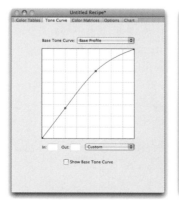

In many cases you won't need to touch the sliders in the Color Matrices tab, which has the same sliders as the Camera Raw Camera Calibration tab. You may want to try them if you're profiling extreme lighting conditions. For example, if you've been shooting in candlelight or with an infrared camera, you might find that the Color Temperature slider in Camera Raw doesn't extend far enough; the Color Matrices sliders may allow you to get there.

The last steps are to save the color recipe and then export a new camera profile from it; see "Saving Recipes and Exporting Profiles" later in this section.

Automatically Generating Color Tables from a Color Chart. Start by shooting a standard 24-patch color chart, such as the X-Rite Color Checker. Shoot it in raw mode (pay attention only to exposure and focus, but not white balance), transfer the file to your computer, and convert the raw file to DNG format. In the DNG Profile Editor, choose File > Open DNG Image and open the chart file. Click the Chart tab (see **Figure 5-51**), make sure the four circles are centered in the four corner boxes of the chart, and click Create Color Table. The DNG Profile Editor switches back to the Color Tables tab, displaying the automatic adjustments that record the difference between the lighting conditions and the true neutral state of the color chart.

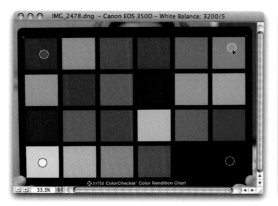

Positioning a circle on a color chart shot under an odd mix of fluorescent light bulbs

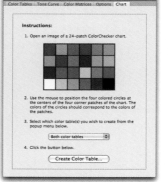

Chart tab in DNG Profile Editor

Figure 5-51 Using a color chart as the basis for a custom camera profile

We haven't mentioned the color tables pop-up menu on the Chart tab, because for basic results you can leave it at "Both color tables." If you want a profile that includes adjustments for color temperatures from tungsten to daylight, as is the case with the profiles Adobe makes, shoot the color chart twice—once at 2850 K (tungsten, specifically Standard Illuminant A) and

TIP: Test your custom camera profile on many images to make sure you aren't making a profile that fixes just one image's specific problems. You can open and view multiple DNG images in the DNG Profile Editor.

TIP: For a consistent lighting situation such as a studio, by making the most of the first three tabs in the DNG Profile Editor you may be able to create a camera profile that requires very little tweaking in Camera Raw, other than white balance.

TIP: When you shoot a color chart, take care to avoid color casts. Watch out for colored reflections from surrounding foliage such as grass and trees, or from surfaces such as backdrops or painted walls. Keep the chart evenly lit. And watch your camera histogram—don't clip the white square!

again at 6500 K (daylight, specifically the D65 standard). In the DNG Profile Editor, open both resulting DNG files and click Create Color Table for each of them. When you generate the final profile (see "Saving Recipes and Exporting Profiles" below), the DNG Profile Editor will take both color tables and interpolate between them for any color temperature in between.

Adobe has done a good enough job with their profiles that you're most likely to use the Chart tab for lighting conditions that aren't very close to the 2850 K or 6500 K sources that Adobe profiles. For example, the Chart tab can be useful for fluorescent and LED lights, since they come in all kinds of temperatures and their output across the color spectrum can be inconsistent and spiky. Before shooting in a room lit by odd bulb types or mixed light sources, you may want to shoot a frame or two of a color checker so that you can later create an editable camera profile of those conditions. We tried this in Figures 5-51 and **5-52**.

Figure 5-52 The color chart's color table, with the results of using the profiles on an image shot in the same position as the color chart under mixed fluorescent lighting

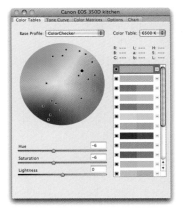  

Color table generated by DNG Profile Editor from the color chart we shot

Adobe Standard profile renders too much green.

The new profile generated from the color chart is more balanced.

Saving Recipes and Exporting Profiles. The DNG Profile Editor can create two kinds of files: recipes (choose File > Save Recipe As) and profiles (choose File > Export Profile). A recipe is a set of color adjustments, including the settings from all of the tabs in the DNG Profile Editor. A profile is a camera profile that works in Camera Raw 4.5 or later, Lightroom 2 or later, or any other raw editor that supports the DNG 1.2 specification. When you export a profile, the DNG Profile Editor combines the currently active recipe with the base profile of the currently active DNG image window. You can use a single recipe to export profiles for different cameras; here's how that works. If you open a recipe in the DNG Profile Editor and then open a DNG image made from a specific Canon camera, you can export a profile based on that combination. If you keep that recipe open and then open a DNG file made from another Canon camera model or a Nikon camera, you can export an additional profile for whichever camera image window is frontmost. All of the profiles should be able to reproduce the results of that recipe, which makes this a great way to make multiple cameras render the same look from the same shoot, such as a wedding.

You can store recipes wherever you like. However, store exported profiles in the following locations, so that Camera Raw can find and load them. If Camera Raw is running, you must restart it to see new or changed profiles.

Mac OS X:
\Library\Application Support\Adobe\CameraRaw\CameraProfiles

Windows 2000 / XP:
C:\Documents and Settings\All Users\Application Support\Adobe\
CameraRaw\CameraProfiles

Windows Vista:
C:\ProgramData\Adobe\CameraRaw\CameraProfiles

Setting a Profile as a Camera Default. The last thing you need to know about camera profiles is how to apply them to all raw images you import. In Camera Raw, verify all of the settings in all Camera Raw tabs to make sure you want them that way for all new raw images you open, then click the Settings menu and choose Save New Camera Raw Defaults. If you work with multiple cameras, you may want to click the Preferences button in Camera Raw (Command-K, or Ctrl-K in Windows) and turn on "Make defaults specific to camera serial number."

> **TIP:** Camera profile editing is not really about achieving accurate color. It's more about getting the colors you *want*—being able to control the interpretation of a raw file and create a certain look that is pleasing to you. It's like choosing color film based on the look you want, but with digital, you get to design your own film!

THE PRESETS TAB

You can store your favorite Camera Raw settings in the Presets tab (Command-Option-8 in Mac OS X if you've disabled the Universal Access shortcut for screen zooming in the System preferences; or Ctrl-Alt-8 in Windows) (see **Figure 5-53**).

Figure 5-53 The Presets tab
and the New Preset dialog

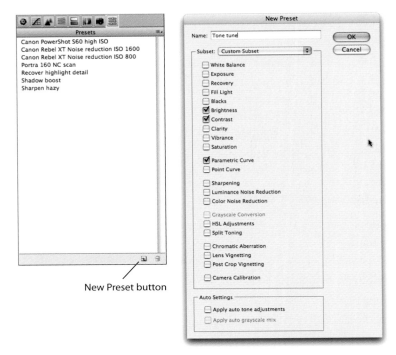

New Preset button

To create a new preset here, first adjust the settings you want to save in any of the other Camera Raw tabs. Then click the New Preset button at the bottom of the Presets tab. In the New Presets dialog, turn on check boxes for the settings you want to save. The Subset pop-up menu can select predefined groups of settings for you; it's also useful when you want to save only a few settings—selecting a subset is faster than manually unchecking a lot of check boxes. Click OK and it's in the list, ready for you to apply to any image.

Although you can also apply a preset by choosing it from the Apply Preset submenu on the Settings menu, it's easier just to click it in the Presets tab. In addition, the Presets tab is easier than a submenu when it comes to trying a few presets, one after the other.

To delete a preset, select it and then click the trash can icon at the bottom of the Presets tab. If you want to rename or manage your presets, they're stored in (username)\Library\Application Support\Adobe\CameraRaw\Settings\ (Mac), and Documents and Settings\(username)\Application Data\ Adobe\CameraRaw\Settings\ (Windows).

FILMSTRIP MODE

If you had to adjust every slider on every image with a lot of images open in Camera Raw, you might conclude that Camera Raw was an instrument of torture rather than a productivity tool. Fortunately, the combination of Camera Raw, Bridge, and Photoshop offers several ways of editing multiple images. One of these is built right into Camera Raw itself: When you select multiple images to open, either in Bridge or in the Open dialog in Photoshop, Camera Raw opens them in filmstrip mode (see **Figure 5-54**). In filmstrip mode, changes you make in the image controls apply to all images selected in the filmstrip.

Filmstrip mode offers a great deal of flexibility. You can select all the open images using the Select All button or by pressing Command-A (Ctrl-A in Windows). You can also select contiguous ranges of images by Shift-clicking, or discontiguous images by Command-clicking (Mac) or Ctrl-clicking (Windows) images. When the focus is on the filmstrip, you can navigate through the images using the up and down arrow keys.

You can click a star rating under each filmstrip, and you can mark images for deletion by pressing the Delete key. Deletion isn't permanent until you exit Camera Raw, although clicking Cancel also cancels the deletion.

TIP: To zoom multiple images at once, select the images in the filmstrip before changing the magnification.

Select All and
Synchronize
buttons   Filmstrip

Selected images
are highlighted

Current image is marked by
a thicker border

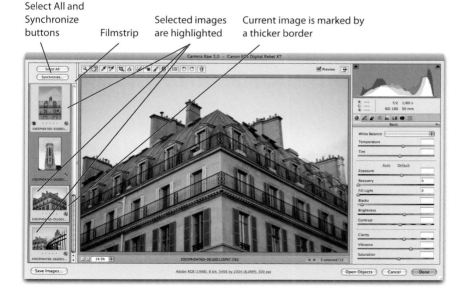

Figure 5-54 Filmstrip mode

Synchronizing Settings in the Filmstrip

When you select more than one image, the Synchronize button becomes available at the top of the filmstrip (see Figure 5-54). This button lets you apply the current image settings to all other selected images. This feature is most useful when you open a set of images that need similar corrections. It's also useful when you've edited one image in Camera Raw and then you realize you want to apply the same edits to other images in the filmstrip.

For example, you can synchronize tonal adjustments, noise reduction, all the settings, or whichever combination of settings is most applicable. A general rule of thumb is to start out by applying the settings that are needed by the largest number of images, then apply the settings needed by the next smallest group, and so on.

To synchronize, select the images that you want to change, and make sure that the currently displayed image contains the settings you want to use as the source for the other images. Click Synchronize, select the options you want to apply to the selected images (see **Figure 5-55**), and click OK.

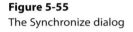
Figure 5-55
The Synchronize dialog

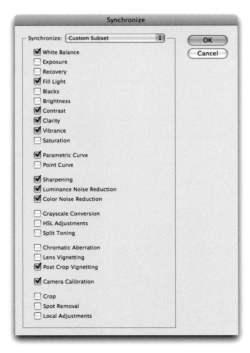

COPYING ADJUSTMENTS TO MORE IMAGES

As an alternative to synchronizing settings among multiple images in the Camera Raw dialog, out in the Content panel in Bridge you can apply Camera Raw settings to any number of other images that need the same edit. You can do this in any of the following ways.

Edit by Example. In the Content panel, select the first of the images that need the same edit and open it in Camera Raw. The choice of host application—Bridge or Photoshop—depends on what else is going on. If Photoshop is busy batch-processing files, host Camera Raw in Bridge. If Bridge is busy building the cache, host Camera Raw in Photoshop. If they're both busy, host Camera Raw in Bridge—Bridge's multithreading lets you work in Camera Raw even while Bridge itself is busy doing other tasks.

Make your edits and then click Done (it's the default option in Camera Raw hosted by Bridge, but not in Camera Raw hosted by Photoshop).

In Bridge, from the Edit > Apply Camera Raw Settings submenu, choose Copy Camera Raw Settings, or press Command-Option-C (Mac) or Ctrl-Alt-C (Windows). Then select all other images that need the same edit and choose Paste Camera Raw Settings or press Command-Option-V (Mac) or Ctrl-Alt-V (Windows). If necessary, select the combination of subsets or settings you want to apply from the Paste Camera Raw Settings dialog first; it's essentially the same as the dialog in Figure 5-55.

TIP: Pasting Camera Raw settings to multiple images is an alternative to working directly in Camera Raw in filmstrip mode.

This approach works well when you need to apply the same settings to a large number of images that are identifiable by relatively small thumbnails, because you can select them quickly. But if you need to edit image by image, the following approaches are better ideas.

Edit by Applying Presets. If you've saved presets for Camera Raw in the Settings folder for Camera Raw (see "Loading and Saving Settings" earlier in this chapter), you can apply them to all the selected images by choosing Edit > Apply Camera Raw Settings, then choosing the settings or settings subsets from the submenu. Saving settings subsets as presets is particularly powerful, because you can simply choose them in succession. Each one affects only the parameters recorded when you saved it, so you can load a preset for White Balance, followed by one for Exposure, Brightness, Contrast, Camera Calibration settings, and so on.

Edit in Camera Raw. The method that offers the most flexibility is to open multiple images in Camera Raw. The number of images you can open in Camera Raw depends on how much RAM is available. As a result, you can open more images in Camera Raw when you host it from Bridge than you can when hosting it from Photoshop, because Bridge doesn't need as much RAM as Photoshop.

That said, it's more practical to work with smaller sets of images. If you open ten or more images, you'll get a dialog asking if you really want to open ten files. We recommend clicking the "Don't show again" check box and cheerfully opening as many images as your machine can reasonably handle without bogging down. Recent machines should be able to open and edit many images without a problem; older machines or ones with inadequate RAM may slow before 100 images are open in Camera Raw.

When you open multiple images, Camera Raw works in filmstrip mode, which contains the Synchronize button so that you can transfer settings from one image to any other images selected in the filmstrip. For details, see "Filmstrip Mode" earlier in this chapter.

Go Back to Square One. When you want to start over, you have three options. Choose Edit > Develop Settings and then choose Camera Raw Defaults, Previous Conversion (the Camera Raw settings last applied to the image), or Clear Settings. The difference between applying the Camera Raw defaults and clearing the Camera Raw settings is rather subtle: When you apply the defaults, Bridge treats the image as having settings applied; when you clear the settings, Bridge treats the image as having no settings applied. The effect on the image is identical in both cases, but when settings are applied, the image's thumbnail displays an icon indicating that (see **Figure 5-56**).

Figure 5-56 The settings icon on a thumbnail

When you choose Camera Raw Defaults or make any other edits to an image, this icon appears. If you don't see this icon, no Camera Raw edits are applied to the image.

Generating Adjusted Images

Because Camera Raw edits are stored only as compact metadata, if you want to be able to use those files in most other programs, you must convert them to a non-raw file format. As with so many other aspects of the digital work-flow that you've seen up to this point, when it comes to this production phase, you've got choices.

- If you need to print an image, or you know that an image needs more work than Camera Raw can handle, you can use Camera Raw to open the image in Photoshop as a new Photoshop document. From there, you can save the image in any file format Photoshop supports.

- If you've completed all of the necessary adjustments and edits in Camera Raw and now all you need is a final file (such as a TIFF or JPEG file), you can save the image directly from Camera Raw and call it done.

- If you need to run Photoshop automation or actions on one or more images, you can use the Tools > Photoshop submenu in Bridge, which includes the powerful Batch command.

We usually convert images edited in Camera Raw in batches using actions rather than simply opening them individually in Photoshop.

Opening in Photoshop with Camera Raw

The most basic way to open a raw image in Photoshop from Bridge is to select the image in Bridge and choose File > Open in Camera Raw or press Command-R (Mac) or Ctrl-R (Windows). In the Camera Raw dialog, verify the blue, underlined workflow options at the bottom of the dialog (if neces-sary, click the underlined text to change them), and when everything's ready, click Open Image (see **Figure 5-57**). For more information about the output options, see "Camera Raw Workflow Options," earlier in this chapter.

Figure 5-57 Camera Raw output buttons

If you want to convert multiple images, select them in Bridge before open-ing Camera Raw. After the Camera Raw dialog opens, be sure to click Select All before clicking Open Images.

If you turned on the Open in Photoshop as Smart Objects check box in the Workflow Options dialog, the Open Image button will say Open Object instead. Whatever the button currently says, you can temporarily switch it to

TIP: We like to open raw images in Photoshop as Smart Objects (clicking the Open Object button in the Camera Raw dialog), because it makes it possible to edit the raw file in that Photoshop document without reimporting it.

the alternate button by holding down the Shift key. For more information about Smart Objects, see "Smart Objects" in Chapter 11.

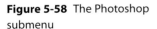 **TIP:** The fastest way to open a selected raw image straight into Camera Raw in Photoshop is to press the Return or Enter key.

When you double-click a raw file in Bridge, Camera Raw opens, hosted by either Bridge or Photoshop. This depends on whether you checked or unchecked the Double-Click Opens Camera Raw Settings in the General pane of the Preferences dialog in Bridge.

You can also drag one or more images from Bridge to the Photoshop icon in the Dock (Mac OS X) or the Taskbar (Windows).

Round-Tripping. If you find yourself working through a list of images between Bridge and Photoshop, here's a way to run the round-trip from the keyboard: In the Content panel in Bridge, press an arrow key to go to the next image, then press Enter or Return to open the image in Photoshop. When you're done with that image in Photoshop, press Command-Option-W (Mac) or Ctrl-Alt-W (Windows) to close the image and return to where you were in Bridge, in one keystroke. That's the Photoshop shortcut for File > Close and Return to Bridge.

Sending Files to Photoshop for Automation

The Tools > Photoshop submenu in Bridge (see **Figure 5-58**) provides access to several useful features that actually hook into commands on the File > Automate and File > Scripts menus in Photoshop. If you have any Photoshop actions that you'd like to run on multiple files selected in Bridge, this is the place to do it. To run any of these automations using images selected in Bridge as the source, you *must* launch them from the Tools menu—if you try to launch them from the File > Automate submenu in Photoshop, you'll find that Bridge is either grayed out or simply unavailable as the source.

Figure 5-58 The Photoshop submenu

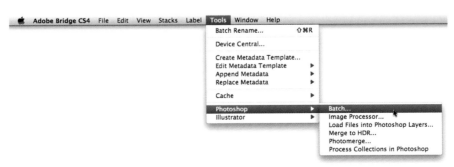

To run a Photoshop Automate or Scripts menu command from Bridge, select images in the Content panel and choose the command from the Tools > Photoshop submenu. Photoshop opens the images using the Camera Raw settings you've applied or the camera-specific default settings (if you haven't applied settings to the image), then processes them using the settings you've specified. You can continue working in Bridge while Photoshop is processing the images. Also, Photoshop CS3 and later queues automations so that you can send a job to Photoshop while the previous job is still running.

We often choose Tools > Photoshop > Batch to run a Photoshop action on files selected in Bridge. For more information on the Batch command, see "Automating Workflows with the Batch Command" later in this chapter.

Saving Files Directly from Camera Raw

Camera Raw has become more powerful than some standalone image editors. It includes local adjustments, spot healing, and cloning, and can apply sharpening using options that exceed some of the options in Photoshop. If you shoot images that are well exposed and focused, some of your images may not even need to continue past Camera Raw to Photoshop. You can simply export those images as final files straight from Camera Raw.

To save files from Camera Raw, select the images you want to save (if you have multiple images open in Camera Raw), and click Save Images (see **Figure 5-59**). Specify settings in the Save Options dialog and click Save. Most of the settings should look familiar: Choose a location for the saved files and customize file naming (see "Renaming Files" later in this chapter). In the Format pop-up menu, choose Digital Negative (DNG), TIFF, JPEG, or Photoshop.

Camera Raw saves files in the background so you can continue to work on other images in the Camera Raw dialog. While Camera Raw is saving in the background, you can close it and do more work in Bridge, or select different images to open Camera Raw again, all without interrupting the background save operation. As Camera Raw saves images in the background, it displays a progress indicator at the bottom of the dialog (see Figure 5-59). Click the underlined status text to open the Camera Raw Save Status dialog. This dialog lists all files remaining to be processed, and you can click Stop to cancel the save.

Figure 5-59 Saving multiple images in the background from Camera Raw

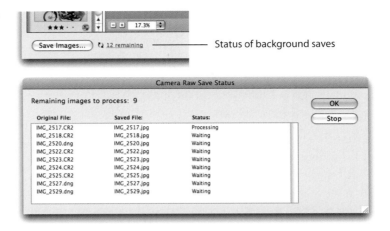

Status of background saves

Using Adobe Bridge

Thus far, we've largely focused on editing individual images in Camera Raw. But if you tried to edit every image individually in Camera Raw, even in filmstrip mode, you probably wouldn't have much time to have a life. Back in the days of film, you didn't scan every image and edit it in Photoshop. Instead, you looked at the film on a light table and picked those images that were worthy of further attention.

That's where Bridge comes in. You can make your initial selects from a shoot by using Bridge as a digital light table. When you want to convert your images, you can host Camera Raw in Bridge and have it convert images in the background. You can also use Bridge to add and edit metadata—one of the first things we do to a new folder of raw images is to add our copyright notices to each image. And although we admit to being less assiduous than we really should be, we also use Bridge to add keywords to images so that we have some hope of finding them again several years hence. See the sidebar "All About Metadata," later in this chapter.

What's New in Bridge CS4

While Bridge CS4 won't fulfill everyone's digital asset management needs, some of the enhancements make it much more effective within a digital image workflow.

It's Faster. There are still people who avoid Bridge due to the performance issues of previous versions. Adobe continues to optimize Bridge, and we think that the benefits of the deep feature set in Bridge outweigh any remaining performance concerns. You'll still wait for it to build the initial cache for image folders, but that's normal for any program that previews images accurately—especially raw images.

It's Easier to Organize and Compare Photos. Several new features make Bridge much more useful when sifting through groups of images. A new Review mode helps you narrow down and compare the best images quickly. Bridge can now automatically stack HDR (high dynamic range) and panoramic images. Bridge workspaces also are much more accessible.

Batch Output Is More Accessible. In previous versions of Bridge and Photoshop, the features that created Web galleries and multiple-page PDF documents were somewhat hidden. Bridge CS4 gives you one-click access to the new Output panel where you can set up and create them quickly.

TIP: On single-monitor systems, we usually keep Bridge hidden or in the background unless we're actually using it. On dual-monitor systems, we'll often keep Bridge open on the second monitor.

Launching Bridge from Photoshop

The simplest way to launch Bridge is the way you launch any other application on your platform of choice. From Photoshop, you have the following additional options:

- Choose File > Browse, or press Command-Option-O (Mac) or Ctrl-Alt-O (Windows).

- Click the Go to Bridge button in the Application bar (see **Figure 5-60**).

- Turn on the Automatically Launch Bridge option in Photoshop General preferences—that way, whenever you launch Photoshop, Bridge automatically launches too.

Figure 5-60 In the Photoshop Application bar, the gray Go to Bridge button is to the right of the Photoshop icon.

Making Key Bridge Workflow Decisions

An efficient workflow requires planning. You can flail around and try everything, but at some point, you have to decide what works and stick with it. The issues in this section are, in our experience, important Bridge workflow aspects to think about in advance.

How Do You Want to Store the Bridge Cache? Certain changes you make to a folder using Bridge, such as sort order and information that can't be stored in XMP files, are stored in the Bridge cache. By default, Bridge stores the cache in one centralized location on your computer, but you can also have Bridge keep folder information in cache files that are stored inside each folder you've managed with Bridge. Each approach has its strengths and weaknesses, but your life will be simpler, and your workflow more robust, if you pick one approach and stick to it. Bridge controls the cache in two places: the Cache pane of the Preferences dialog, and in the Tools > Cache submenu (see "Image Previews and the Cache" later in this chapter).

Where Do You Want to Store Camera Raw Settings for Each Image? Raw files are read-only, but your changes have to be stored somewhere. You can save the Camera Raw settings for each image in the Camera Raw database, in sidecar XMP files, or, in the case of DNG format, in the DNG file.

The Camera Raw database indexes images by their content, not by their filenames, so you can copy, move, or rename them willy-nilly without losing track of your raw settings—but only as long as the images remain on the same computer as the Camera Raw database. Move the raw files to another computer, and their settings will be left behind on the originating computer. If you always remember to use the Export Settings command in Camera Raw to write out a sidecar XMP file for the image, and you always remember to include the sidecar file with the image, there's no problem. But that's a lot of "always remembering."

Bridge does its best to keep track of sidecar XMP files. As long as you copy, move, and rename your raw files only in Bridge, the sidecar files travel with them automatically. But if you copy, move, or rename your raw files *outside* of Bridge, you must keep track of your sidecar files and move them with the images manually. Again, it's not an ideal solution.

A third alternative is to convert raw files to the DNG format. The convenience of having all the metadata, including Camera Raw settings, stored in the file itself outweighs the one-time speed bump entailed in converting the raw files to DNG. But if you want to use your camera vendor's converter, and your camera doesn't write DNG, you should stick with proprietary raw files for your working files, at least for now.

To control how Bridge handles Camera Raw settings, see "Camera Raw Preferences" earlier in this chapter.

How Do You Want to Name Your Files? If you'd like to name your files consistently instead of accepting the rather meaningless default camera filenames, we suggest the following two simple rules:

- Adopt a naming convention that makes sense to you, and stick to it (in other words, be consistent).

- If you want that name to be consistently readable across platforms and operating systems, stick to alphanumeric characters—no spaces (the underscore is a good alternative), and no special characters.

The only place a period should appear is immediately in front of the extension. Some operating systems treat everything following a period as an extension, and promptly hide it, so periods in the middle of filenames can cause those filenames to be truncated. Also, many special characters are reserved for special uses by certain operating systems. Including them in filenames can produce unpredictable results. For example, in Mac OS X, if a filename starts with a period, the system treats it as an invisible file, and it's a good idea to avoid colons or any type of slash character.

It's worth the time to put a lot of thought into your file-naming convention and to test it all the way through your workflow before you use it in production, so that you can watch for potential gotchas. For example, how do you distinguish a raw file from its derivative files, such as a layered Photoshop version for print, a mid-resolution version for HDTV, and a low-resolution sRGB JPEG for the Web? Conrad likes to use a unique date-based base filename for an image (such as 20070418-463) and add a consistent set of characters to tell him which variant it is (such as 20070418-463_PRT.psd and 20070418-463_WEB.jpg).

Another question to consider is how you want the images to sort. Do you want images to list in proper order when you sort by name? Then you'll want to number using leading zeros, and if you use the date in the filename, you'll want to use a year-month-day convention. For example, for June 2, 2007, you'll want to write the date as 2007-06-02, not 6-2-07.

Once you settle on a filename convention, you can craft the Adobe Photo Downloader or Batch Rename dialog to rename incoming files consistently.

What's Your System for Rating and Labeling Images? In Bridge and Camera Raw, the ratings system mimics the old real-world use of a light table by marking the keepers from the first round with a single dot, adding a second dot to the keepers from the second round, and so on. Of course, the primary difference between labels and ratings is that ratings are on a scale while labels aren't. For that reason, we recommend that you reserve ratings for ranking images. It's entirely up to you what the labels mean.

There are different philosophies for rating images. Some photographers always start at one star and use successive passes to narrow down the images by adding additional stars, reserving five stars for only the very best images. Others use three stars as a baseline, with four and five stars marking keepers, and one and two stars marking alternates. Ratings can be read by other software that understands IPTC (International Press Telecommunications Council) metadata, so if you hand off images to someone else down the line, you may want to make sure that you use a ratings system that meshes well with theirs.

Labels are available for purposes that aren't easily taken care of using keywords, ratings, and other metadata, and are often used only temporarily during the editing process. For example, you might use a label to mark just the images you want to upload to an online gallery, or images with unusual lighting conditions that require special attention. For more information, see "Rating and Labeling Images" and "Filtering the Current View" later in this chapter.

Working the Flow. These four issues—Bridge cache, Camera Raw settings, naming conventions, and rating/labeling strategies—are things that can't be changed later without considerable pain. By all means, spend some time trying out the options before setting your strategies in stone, but once you've found the approach that works best for you, don't change it arbitrarily. If you do, you risk losing work, whether it's Camera Raw edits, Bridge thumbnails, or ratings, or simply winding up with a bunch of incomprehensibly named files. Any of these violates the first workflow principle—do things once, early, and efficiently. When you don't, you pay for it with that most precious commodity: your time.

The best way to resolve the four issues is to take a workflow view that's both long and wide. Think of every way that you're likely to use your images at every stage of your workflow, and all of the problems you've encountered in your experience. The more you design workflow standards that take into account your entire workflow and the requirements of yourself and your clients, the more easily you can reduce and avoid unwanted complexity, inconsistency, and unintended consequences.

All About Metadata

Metadata (which literally means "data about data") isn't new. The File Info dialog in Photoshop has allowed you to add metadata such as captions, copyright info, and routing or handling instructions for years. But digital capture brings a much richer set of metadata to the table.

Most current cameras adhere to the EXIF (Exchangeable Image File Format) standard, which supplies with each image a great deal of information on how the camera captured the image, including the camera model, the specific camera body, shutter speed, aperture, focal length, flash setting, and, of course, the date and time. EXIF metadata is generally not editable.

IPTC metadata stores image information that isn't about the camera, such as copyright notices and captions. For more information about IPTC metadata, including specifications and other resource materials, visit www.iptc.org/IPTC4XMP/.

Adjustment metadata, such as Camera Raw settings, tells software how to process and convert images. You can even record every Photoshop operation applied to the image as metadata, using the History Log feature.

Adobe has been assiduous in promoting XMP (eXtensible Metadata Platform), an open, extensible, World Wide Web Consortium (W3C) compliant standard for storing and exchanging metadata. All the Creative Suite applications use XMP, and because XMP is extensible, it's relatively easy to update existing metadata schemes to be XMP-compliant. However, it will probably take some time before all the other applications that use metadata, such as third-party digital raw converters, get updated to handle XMP. But let's be very clear: XMP is not some proprietary Adobe initiative. It's an open, XML-based standard. So if you find that another application is failing to read XMP metadata, contact the publisher and tell them you need them to get with the program!

Right now, metadata is mostly used to help organize and find images, but examples of other innovative uses are starting to appear. For example, Camera Raw can optionally apply different default processing settings depending on the ISO speed setting and even the camera serial number, both found in image metadata. The more information you have about an image, the better your chances of being able to do useful things to it automatically, and the more things you can do automatically, the more time you can spend doing those things that only a human can do, like exercising creative judgment.

Other types of metadata supported by Photoshop and Bridge include GPS information from GPS-enabled cameras and, in Photoshop Extended, DICOM (Digital Imaging and Communications in Medicine) metadata that's extensively used in medical imaging.

USING BRIDGE WINDOWS

In Bridge, you can open as many windows as you like by choosing File > New Window, or pressing Command-N (Mac) or Ctrl-N (Windows). Each window can show the contents of a different folder or volume (subfolders appear as folder icons).

TIP: If you see two numbers separated by a colon in a Bridge window title bar, you're looking at a synchronized window. For example, 2:2 means you're looking at the second of two synchronized windows.

Bridge also offers the synchronized window (see **Figure 5-61**). Choose File > New Window, or press Command-Option-N (Mac) or Ctrl-Alt-N (Windows). The panels of synchronized windows display information about the content of the window that was active when you created the new synchronized window. When two windows are synchronized, selecting different files in one window changes the displayed content in all windows synchronized to the first window. This gives you more flexibility in the content you can display. For example, you can have a synchronized window on a second monitor that contains only the Preview panel, so that you can preview a selected image at a much bigger size than when the Preview panel had to share space with other panels in just one Bridge window.

Figure 5-61 Synchronized windows

An image selected in the Content panel on the left appears in the Preview panel of the separate synchronized window on the right. The synchronized window can be on another monitor.

Window Modes

TIP: You can turn off Compact Window Always on Top from a compact window's menu. But turning this option off can make it easier to lose Compact- and Ultra-Compact-mode windows behind other windows.

A few additional tricks can help you manage your Bridge windows. First, you can, of course, minimize windows to the Dock (Mac) or Taskbar (Windows). Also, you can set windows to either Compact mode or

Ultra-Compact mode. In these modes, Bridge windows by default "float" above Full-mode windows, so they're easily available (see **Figure 5-62**). The compact modes are useful at times when you're in another application and you need Bridge close by, such as when you're laying out a publication in Adobe InDesign and dragging content into it from Bridge.

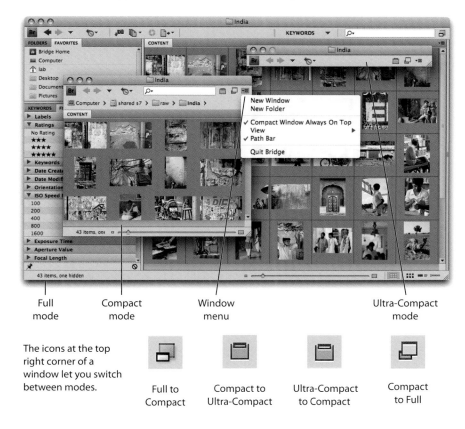

Figure 5-62 Bridge window modes

Full mode   Compact mode   Window menu   Ultra-Compact mode

The icons at the top right corner of a window let you switch between modes.

Full to Compact   Compact to Ultra-Compact   Ultra-Compact to Compact   Compact to Full

You can cycle through all open Full-mode windows by pressing Command-~ (tilde key, Mac) or Alt-Tab (Windows). The shortcut doesn't apply to Compact or Ultra-Compact windows, so it's just as well that they float by default.

You can toggle between Full and Compact modes by pressing Command-Return (Mac) or Ctrl-Enter (Windows). The shortcut toggles between Full and either Compact or Ultra-Compact mode, depending on which of the compact modes you last applied to the window.

TIP: If a Bridge window doesn't respond to a keyboard shortcut, it may not be the foreground window, especially if one of the other windows is in Compact mode. To activate a Full-mode window, select one or more thumbnails in that window (it's not enough to click the window.)

Panels and Workspaces

In Full mode, Bridge windows contains several panels (see **Figure 5-63**) that you can arrange into *workspaces*. Bridge provides several default workspaces that appear across the top of a Full-mode Bridge window—just click one (see **Figure 5-64**). If you make your own workspace (Window > Workspace > New Workspace), it's added to the top of the window.

Figure 5-63 Parts of a Full-mode Bridge window

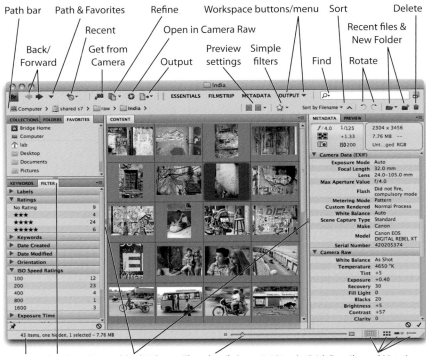

The default workspace is divided into three vertical panes. The Content panel lists the items in the folder or collection you're currently viewing. Other panels provide information about what's selected in the Content panel or let you alter that content. You can arrange panels however you like within the three vertical panes, or drag the dividers to hide any of them.

You can dock panels by dragging their tabs to other panels, resize them by dragging the dividers, and display or hide panels using the View menu commands. You can't drag a panel to another Bridge window, however.

 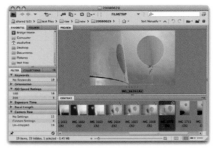

Figure 5-64 Two built-in workspaces: Keywords and Filmstrip

Whenever you create a panel arrangement you like, save it as a workspace. To do this, configure a window the way you want the workspace to appear, then choose Window > Workspace > New Workspace. Specify options (see **Figure 5-65**), and then click Save. If you want the window to always appear in the same place, turn on the Save Window Location as Part of Workspace option (very useful on dual-monitor setups). Bridge adds your saved workspace to the Workspace menu. Your new workspace is added to the workspace buttons at the top of the Bridge window. If you don't see the workspace you want, click the workspace menu (the triangle to the right of the workspace buttons, seen in Figure 5-63), where all workspaces are listed.

TIP: Press the Tab key to hide the side panes so that the center pane fills the window.

Figure 5-65 Saving a workspace

For those of you who have to know where everything gets saved, workspaces are stored in Users\(username)\Library\Application Support\Adobe\Bridge\Workspaces in Mac OS X and in Documents and Settings\(username)\Application Data\Adobe\Bridge\Workspaces in Windows.

Customizing Window Background Colors. You can customize the shade of gray for the overall user interface. Open Bridge preferences, click the General pane, and drag the sliders in the Appearance section (see **Figure 5-66**). The Image Backdrop affects the background color of the Content panel, Preview panel, Review mode, and the Full Screen preview.

Figure 5-66 General
preferences

Bridge Window Tools

Bridge CS4 consolidates the Bridge tools in two narrow strips across the top of the Bridge window, and one strip across the bottom.

TIP: In Windows, you can press Backspace to go up a folder level, just as you can on the Windows desktop. Mac users also need not change: The other Bridge shortcut for going up a level (Command-up arrow) is the same as it is in the Mac OS X Finder.

Navigation Controls and Task-Oriented Buttons. Directly under the menu bar on the right are buttons that are mostly shortcuts to menu commands. Hold your mouse over each button to see its name. These buttons are useful if you're mouse oriented, but we tend to use the keyboard shortcuts for the menu commands they represent. In the middle are the workspaces, which are shortcuts to the workspace names listed on the Window > Workspace submenu. Workspaces you create appear here too.

Path Bar. The first thing in the Path bar (see **Figure 5-67**) is, obviously, the volume path to the currently viewed folder, but the right side of the Path bar contains additional controls for file management. Again, many of these buttons are mouse shortcuts to menu commands.

Figure 5-67 The Path bar

The first square button after the path is notable because it displays the thumbnail preview embedded in a file instead of a preview generated by Bridge. This new option was requested by users to speed the initial display of files—thumbnails display faster when retrieved from the file itself, rather than waiting for Bridge to generate a preview. The downside? You're seeing the camera's interpretation of the raw data, which won't reflect the latest settings applied to the file in Camera Raw. But when you've just downloaded 500 raw images into your computer and need to scroll through them right away to pick an image for a deadline, the important thing is to see what images you have as quickly as you can, not see them perfectly. After you start to color-correct the images, you may want to turn off the embedded thumbnail preview button so you can see up-to-date thumbnails.

If the Path bar displays the international "No" symbol at the end of the path (see Figure 5-67), it means the current view is not of a single folder. For example, View > Show Items from Subfolders may be on, or you might be viewing a collection, which can have files from multiple folders.

Status Bar. The line of text at the bottom left of a Bridge window (see **Figure 5-68**) tells you about the current view, such as how many items are selected. It also tells you that items are hidden; to see the hidden items, choose View > Show Hidden Items. If the Status bar still says there are hidden items, try choosing View > Show Folders or Show Reject Files. Always look in the Status bar if you think a file or folder is missing, because it may be hidden.

TIP: To free up space in the Favorites panel, open the Bridge preferences, click General, and turn off Favorite Items as needed.

Figure 5-68 The Status bar

At the right side of the Status bar are the slider that controls thumbnail size and four shortcut icons for the Grid Lock, As Thumbnails, As Details, and As List commands on the View menu, respectively.

Finding Your Way. While you can use the Folders and Content panels to browse your hard drive or network about as well as you can on the Mac OS X or Windows desktop, Bridge provides many more shortcuts.

The Favorites panel is a place to drag your most frequently opened items (see **Figure 5-69**). We like to store shortcuts to project folders here. Favorites are also listed in the third button from the left at the top of the Bridge window (see Figure 5-63), so if you prefer to reach Favorites there, you can leave the Favorites panel closed.

TIP: When a folder is selected in the Folders panel, you can expand a folder by pressing the right arrow key, or collapse it by pressing the left arrow key.

By the way, you don't have to use the Favorites panel to add a folder or file; you can also right-click or Control-click (Mac) and choose Add to Favorites from the context menu. About the only reason you need to open the Favorites panel is to rearrange the list of favorites.

Figure 5-69 The Favorites panel

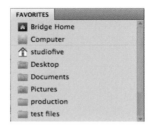

TIP: The Bridge Home icon in the Favorites panel is a great way to find information and tutorials about Photoshop and Creative Suite applications if your computer is connected to the Internet.

The Back and Forward buttons at the top left of the Bridge window work as they do on the desktop or in a Web browser. To the right of that pair of buttons is a button that lists your volumes and Favorites. Next to that is the useful recent files and folders button; recent files are sorted by the applications that can open them. Right below that, the Path bar (see Figure 5-67) shows you the location of the items in the Content panel. At the far right of the Path bar are three buttons; while the two at the end have obvious meaning (create a new folder and delete an item), the third button from the right is another place to select recent files. Using all of these tools should cut down on the time you spend wandering around your disk looking for a file, especially if you add your most frequently used folders to the Favorites.

If you regularly navigate your desktop or Web browser using keyboard shortcuts, you may want to check **Table 5-2** for their Bridge equivalents. Mac OS X and Windows use slightly different shortcuts for desktop navigation, so Bridge tries to forge a middle ground here.

Table 5-2 Keyboard navigation in Bridge. The folder-level shortcuts require that View > Show Folders be turned on.

To do this . . .	. . . press this:
Enter selected folder	Return or Enter
Go up a folder level	Command-up arrow (Mac) or Ctrl-up arrow (Windows)
Go back	Command-left arrow (Mac) or Ctrl-left arrow (Windows)
Go forward	Command-right arrow (Mac) or Ctrl-right arrow (Windows)

TIP: If the Content panel doesn't show a file or folder that you swear should be there, Bridge may not have noticed it yet. Choose View > Refresh, or better yet just press F5.

Escaping the Folder Hierarchy with Collections. There are times when you might want to make a list of files from many different folders. Bridge lets you do this using collections. Choose Window > Collections Panel (see **Figure 5-70**) to manage your collections, where you'll find the usual buttons at the bottom for creating, editing, and deleting the items in the panel. After you create a collection, you can simply go to different folders and drag the files into it. This works best if the Folders, Collections, and Content panels are arranged so you can see all three panels at once.

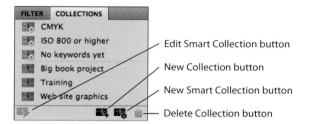

Edit Smart Collection button
New Collection button
New Smart Collection button
Delete Collection button

Figure 5-70 The Collections panel

Bridge also offers Smart Collections, which are listed in the same Collections panel. A Smart Collection is actually a set of search criteria that automatically list any files matching the criteria, and the list updates itself. For example, if you're working on a job destined for prepress and requiring conversion to CMYK, you can make a Smart Collection that looks in a specific folder and keeps a current list of all of the images that are still in RGB mode. Or for a Web site project where images are limited to 600 pixels wide, a Smart Collection could list all of the photos that are over 600 pixels wide. The Edit Smart Collection dialog (see **Figure 5-71**) works much like the Find dialog in Bridge; see "Finding and Filtering Files," later in this chapter.

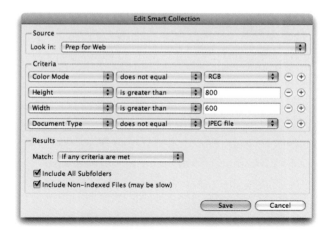

Figure 5-71 The Edit Smart Collections dialog

Seeing Everything in Subfolders. When a folder contains other folders, you might prefer to see everything in the subfolders at once instead of having to go in and out of each folder. In Bridge CS3 there was a button in the Filter panel that would show subfolder contents, but in Bridge CS4 this has changed to the View > Show Items from Subfolders command. This also adds a Parent Folder pane to the Filter panel so that you can easily hide all items except those in the subfolders you selected in the Parent Folder pane.

Finding Out Where It Lives. Sometimes you'll look at a file in a non-folder view (such as a collection or when View > Show Items from Subfolders is on) and wonder where that file is actually stored. Bridge gives you two ways to find out. To display the file in its folder in Bridge, choose File > Reveal in Bridge. If you want to locate its folder on your desktop, choose File > Reveal in Finder (Mac OS X) or File > Reveal in Bridge (Windows).

> **TIP:** We prefer to use the File > Reveal commands by right-clicking or Control-clicking (Mac) the file and choosing the command from the context menu.

MANAGING FILES IN BRIDGE

File management in Bridge isn't that different from file management in your operating system's desktop, but Bridge offers a few additional features—and a few quirks—that you should know about.

Selecting Files

As on your desktop, you can select multiple files or folders contiguously by holding down the Shift key as you click items in the Content panel, or discontiguously using the Command key (Mac OS X) or Ctrl key (Windows).

Manual selection is often the long way to get it done, however. In many cases you can accelerate file selection with help from the other file management tools in Bridge. Here are a few examples.

Select Menu Commands. On the Edit menu, the Select commands offer quick ways to manipulate selections. Select All (Command-A in Mac OS X or Ctrl-A in Windows), Deselect All (just add the Shift key to the Select All shortcut) and Invert Selection (Command-Shift-I in Mac OS X or Ctrl-Shift-A in Windows) do exactly what they say—Invert Selection deselects the files that were selected and selects those that weren't. The two remaining commands, Select Labeled (Command-Option-L in Mac OS X or Ctrl-Shift-L in Windows) and Select Unlabeled (Command-Option-Shift-L in Mac OS X or Ctrl-Alt-Shift-L in Windows) work in conjunction with the Label feature in Bridge, which lets you apply one of five labels, or no label, to images. See "Rating and Labeling Images" later in this chapter.

Sort Menu. If all the files you want to select fall into one of the criteria on the Sort menu on the Path bar, choose that criterion to re-sort the images so they are grouped together for you. For example, if you want to select the most recent files, sort them by Date Modified.

Opening Files from Bridge

In the case of raw images, the subtle difference between the Open command (Command-O in Mac OS X or Ctrl-O in Windows) and the Open in Camera Raw command (Command-R in Mac OS X or Ctrl-R in Windows) is that the former opens the raw image or images in Camera Raw hosted by Photoshop, while the latter opens the raw image or images in Camera Raw hosted by Bridge. There are several easier ways to open images than choosing the menu commands, including context menus and the aforementioned keyboard shortcuts, plus the ones listed in **Table 5-3**.

Table 5-3 Keyboard shortcuts for opening raw images.

To do this . . .	. . . press this:
Open raw images in Camera Raw hosted by Bridge, leaving Photoshop unaffected.	Command-R (Mac OS X) Ctrl-R (Windows)
Open raw images in Camera Raw hosted by Photoshop, bringing Photoshop to the foreground and leaving Bridge visible in the background	Return, Command-down arrow, or Command-O (Mac OS X) Enter, Ctrl-down arrow, or Ctrl-O (Windows)
Open raw images in Camera Raw hosted by Photoshop, bringing Photoshop to the foreground and hiding Bridge	Command-Option-down arrow or Option-Return (Mac OS X) Ctrl-Alt-down arrow or Alt-Enter (Windows)
Open raw images directly into Photoshop, bypassing the Camera Raw dialog, bringing Photoshop to the foreground, and leaving Bridge visible in the background	Command-Shift-down arrow or Shift-Return (Mac OS X) Ctrl-Shift-down arrow or Shift-Enter (Windows)

File Type Associations Preferences. These options let you specify the default application for opening files from Bridge. They apply only to the behavior you get when opening files from Bridge and have no effect on operating system–level behavior (see **Figure 5-72**).

Figure 5-72 The File Type
Associations preferences in
Bridge

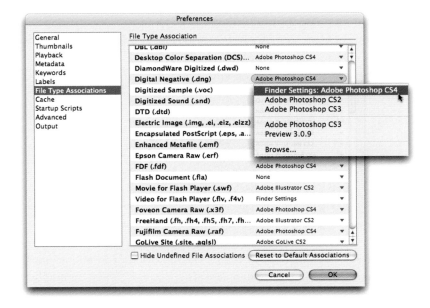

Moving Files

Three submenus on the File menu don't have keyboard shortcuts but are
sometimes useful: Copy To, Move To, and Place. Copy To and Move To are
quick ways to copy or move selected files to folders on your Recent Folders list. Place sends selected files to the target application; the number of
applications you see on the Place menu depends on how many compatible
Creative Suite applications you've installed. If you have only Photoshop,
that's the only application you'll see, and if you have the entire Creative
Suite, you'll see a number of applications on the Place menu. Applications
that don't directly open images, such as InDesign, require that you already
have a document open in the target application before you can place a file
from Bridge. When placing into Photoshop, if you have a document open in
Photoshop, Bridge will place an image into that document, and if there is no
document open, Photoshop simply opens the file.

Sorting Files

By default, Bridge sorts images by filename, so new images appear in the
order in which they were numbered by the camera. However, as we noted

earlier, you can change the sort order by choosing any of the options in the Sort menu on the Path bar (see **Figure 5-73**), or in the View > Sort submenu.

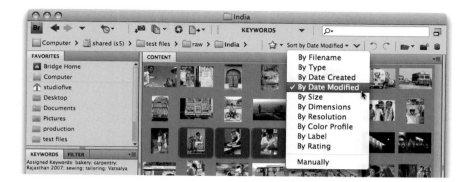

Figure 5-73 Path bar Sort menu

You can also create a custom sort order by dragging the thumbnails around, just as you would chromes on a light table. When you do so, the Manually item on the Sort menu is checked. Your custom sorting order is stored only in the Bridge cache for the folder. If you move or rename the folder, Bridge remembers the sort order. But if you combine images from several folders into a different folder, you have in effect created a new sort order, and it may not be the one you wanted. One way to preserve sort order is to use Batch Rename to rename the images using a numeric sequence (see "Renaming Files," later in this chapter).

Stacking Files

Stacks simplify the Content panel view by grouping similar images (see **Figure 5-74**). For example, if you bracket the exposure of a scene, you can keep all of the bracketed frames in one stack by selecting the images and choosing Stack > Group as Stack or pressing Command-G (Mac) or Ctrl-G (Windows). You can expand or collapse a selected stack by clicking the number in the top left corner of the stack that tells you how many files are in the stack. If you want a particular image to be at the top of a stack, open the stack, select an image, and choose Stack > Promote to Top of Stack.

Bridge CS4 can automatically gather certain types of similar files into stacks if you choose Stacks > Auto-Stack Panorama/HDR. Bridge figures out panoramas by analyzing scene information. It creates HDR stacks by analyzing the scene content and also the EXIF information in images to determine whether you have bracketed using exposure intervals typical of a series shot for later HDR processing.

Figure 5-74 These stacks are handheld panoramas that were automatically stacked by the Auto-Stack Panorama/HDR command.

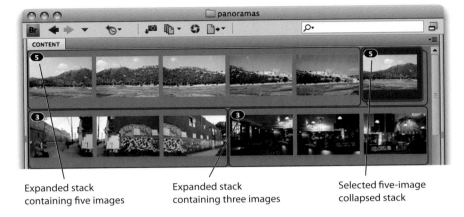

Expanded stack containing five images

Expanded stack containing three images

Selected five-image collapsed stack

Bridge stacks are not to be confused with image stacks in Photoshop CS4 Extended (see "Reducing Noise with Image Stacks" in Chapter 10, "Sharpness, Detail, and Noise Reduction").

Renaming Files

Bridge gives you three ways to rename a selected file:

- Click a filename and wait a second.
- Right-click or Control-click (Mac OS X) a file and choose Rename from the context menu.
- Press F2.

After any of these, type the new name and then press Return or Enter.

Renaming Multiple Selected Files. Use the Batch Rename dialog (press Command-Shift-R in Mac OS X or Ctrl-Shift-R in Windows) to rename selected files and their filename extensions (see **Figure 5-75**). Files are renamed in the order they appear in the Content panel. This means you can change or create a new numbered sequence by manually ordering files in the order you want before you batch-rename them, and then making sure you specified a Sequence Number in the Batch Rename dialog.

The "Preserve current filename in XMP Metadata" option adds a custom metadata tag containing the current filename. If you've already applied

Camera Raw settings before renaming, you can skip this option because the Camera Raw metadata already contains the original filename. But if you're renaming otherwise untouched raw files and you want the original filenames to be retrievable, it's a good idea to turn on this option.

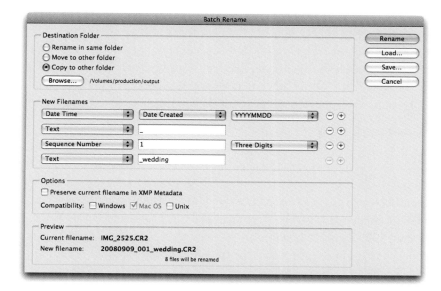

Figure 5-75 The Batch Rename dialog

IMAGE PREVIEWS AND THE CACHE

Image previews are now so commonplace that we don't think about them. Even folders in Mac OS X and Windows can automatically generate thumbnail previews of images. But each preview has to be generated by something. Mac OS X and Windows can display previews because the operating systems have added the ability to read formats such as JPEG natively. Bridge has the same ability for the raw formats it supports.

Generating Image Previews and Thumbnails. Standard image formats such as JPEG already exist as RGB files, so they display quickly and easily. But as we mentioned earlier, raw is not a single format but varies by camera, so a program or operating system that wants to display a new camera's raw format must add support for that specific format. In addition, a raw file hasn't yet been converted to RGB, so it takes longer to display it. To speed up display of raw files and reduce the chance that the file can't be displayed because a program doesn't read the format, a preview image can be associated with a raw file.

An embedded preview image is saved with the file by the camera. This is how you can see the images on the LCD at the back of your camera or in a program such as Adobe Photo Downloader. The preview represents the default rendering of the camera, and depending on how you set your camera, it may not be at full resolution. Unfortunately, as soon as you make any adjustment to a raw file, the built-in preview is immediately out of date. For this reason, raw editors such as Camera Raw can generate an updated preview. Bridge does it by using the Camera Raw engine.

This all seems reasonable: You get a camera-embedded preview right away, and Bridge always retrieves the latest Camera Raw rendering so that thumbnails are kept up to date. Bridge has traditionally made it a priority to keep previews and thumbnails current, starting at import. However, there is a flaw: The time it takes to display a thumbnail, when multiplied by the hundreds of images that can be downloaded from a single shoot, slowed down many photographers, who noticed that other programs could display thumbnails faster. The reason was that the other programs used the camera-generated thumbnails for initial display, so that photographers could immediately start sorting and ranking images.

TIP: Note that the previews are based on the Camera Raw default settings for your camera. If you consistently don't like what you see as Bridge loads your raw images, change the default develop settings for your camera (see "Using the Camera Raw Defaults," earlier in this chapter).

If initial display speed is a concern for you, you can make Bridge CS4 prefer the previews generated by the camera by turning on the first button on the right side of the Path bar (see **Figure 5-76**). It's grouped with another button that provides options for generating updated previews. This gives you the best of both worlds: You can see camera previews for initial speed, then later have Bridge generate up-to-date previews for accuracy. If you aren't in a rush, we recommend using Bridge-generated previews so that you're always looking at the true current state of your images. Speed and quality are also affected by the Do Not Process Files Larger Than value in the Thumbnails pane of the Bridge Preferences dialog; lower the value to increase speed or raise the value to increase quality.

Controlling Preview Sizes. The previews you see in the Preview panel, in Full Screen Preview, or in Slide Show are generated on demand. If you'll soon be doing a lot of work with large preview images or the loupe, you may want Bridge to generate them up front. One way to do this is to click the second icon in the group at the right of the Path bar (see **Figure 5-76**) and choose Generate 100% Previews so that when you view a file, Bridge generates a full-size preview at that time.

Figure 5-76 Preview controls on the Path bar

The Preview Cache. Bridge stores image previews in a cache on your computer and will seem slow when you view images for which a cache hasn't been built yet. As you edit raw files, Bridge updates the previews so that they accurately represent all of the adjustments you've made.

The Bridge cache holds the image thumbnails and previews, custom sort order, and—for file types that can't store metadata either in the file itself or in a sidecar XMP file—label and rating information. For raw files, only the thumbnails, previews, and custom sort order are stored uniquely in the Bridge cache, but since the thumbnails and previews take some time to generate, they're pretty important. You can control how the cache works in the Cache pane of the Preferences dialog.

You can let Bridge keep its cache only in a single, central location, determined by the Location preference (see **Figure 5-77**), or you can have Bridge use decentralized caches, which are stored in each folder you browse with Bridge. The decentralized caches contain only the information about the items in that folder. Turn on the Automatically Export Caches to Folders When Possible check box to enable that option. To manually generate cache files for a folder, open the folder and choose Tools > Cache > Build and Export Cache.

The only advantage offered by using a centralized cache is simplicity—you know where all your cache files are. The significant disadvantages of the centralized cache are

- If you move or rename a folder outside Bridge, the connection to the cache files is lost.

- When you burn a folder full of images to a CD or DVD, you first have to go through the extra step of exporting the cache. If you don't, the recipient of the CD or DVD has to take the time to recache the folder, rebuilding thumbnails and previews, and any custom sort order is lost. By the way, the "When Possible" part of the Automatically Export Caches to Folders When Possible preference refers to the fact that you can't create new cache files on a read-only volume, such as a DVD; cache updates can happen only in the Bridge centralized cache.

Figure 5-77 The Cache preferences in Bridge

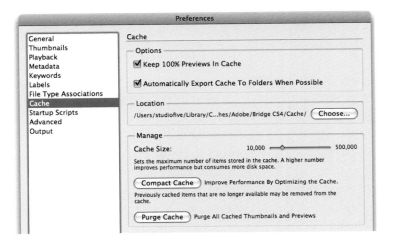

TIP: Using decentralized caches is sometimes referred to as using distributed caches.

TIP: If you change a window view setting (such as View > Show Hidden Files) but the view doesn't change, press F5 (the shortcut for View > Refresh).

Using decentralized caches avoids both problems. The cache files are written directly into the folder to which they pertain and travel with the folder even when it's renamed or moved. But note that if Bridge for some reason can't write a decentralized cache (the volume may be read-only or mounted on a server), it writes to the central cache instead.

The only real downside to using decentralized caches is that every folder that Bridge has opened ends up with two additional files, named .BridgeCache and .BridgeCacheT (the T is for Thumbnails). By default, Bridge hides these files, but you can see them by choosing View > Show Hidden Files. In Windows, it depends on whether you've set your Folder Options to display hidden and system files. If all this file management makes you nervous, by all means use the centralized cache. Otherwise, it's well worth suffering the small inconvenience to obtain the benefits of decentralized caching. (And besides, it's often useful to be able to see the cache files so that you can check that they're present and up to date.)

For Cache Size, we recommend the default size or larger, unless you are running very low on disk space or have a small hard disk, such as in a notebook. The Compact Cache button optimizes the cache, which can be good to do periodically. The Purge Cache button causes Bridge to rebuild thumbnails from scratch, which can help when thumbnails don't seem to reflect the actual contents of files.

Pay Me Now or Pay Me Later. The common thread throughout the thumbnail and preview options is the trade-off between resources and responsiveness. If you go for maximum quality, turning on the options that build a large cache of thumbnails and high-resolution previews in advance, Bridge will go to work building previews as you browse folders and images. Keep in mind, though, that generating high-quality previews and thumbnails essentially generates high-quality JPEG copies of all your images; your CPU will be busy and your preview cache will fill up fast. You can run into performance problems if you are low on disk space or if you have an aging, low-end, or single-core processor that isn't up to the task of generating those previews while you try to do other things. If you don't have fast equipment and lots of disk space, you may have to defer high-quality rendering, keep your cache sizes small, and expect Bridge to hesitate somewhat when you ask for a high-resolution display. It all goes back to what we said in Chapter 1: For Photoshop (and Bridge), it's worth it to have current hardware.

> **TIP:** If you have reason to think that the cache isn't properly displaying the contents of a folder, choose Tools > Cache > Purge Cache for Folder to delete the cache files. You may lose settings that can't be stored in the individual files, such as the folder's sort order.

EVALUATING AND COMPARING IMAGES

Before you can effectively rate and label images in Bridge, you need to be able to evaluate and compare images quickly.

Evaluating Thumbnails. To adjust the thumbnail size, use the zoom slider at the bottom of a Bridge window. In the Content panel you can set Bridge to display more information under each thumbnail. In the Preferences dialog in Bridge, click the Thumbnails panel and turn on up to four additional lines of metadata to display, including keywords and color profiles. If you turn on Show Tooltips, a file properties tool tip pops up as you move the mouse over images (this can be annoying). At any time you can hide all extra information by choosing View > Show Thumbnail Only (Command-Shift-T on the Mac or Ctrl-Shift-T in Windows); this packs more thumbnails into the Content window (see **Figure 5-78**).

> **TIP:** The usual Photoshop zooming shortcuts work on Content panel thumbnails: Command–– (minus sign) to reduce and Command–+ (plus sign) to enlarge in Mac OS X; and in Windows, Ctrl–– (minus sign) to reduce and Ctrl–+ (plus sign) to enlarge.

Figure 5-78 If you don't need to see titles and status icons, choose View > Show Thumbnail Only to display more thumbnails in less space.

Grid Lock (new)

Thumbnails

Details

List (new)

If you use the keyboard or scroll wheel to scroll the Content window and you dislike how thumbnails can be partially hidden at the top or bottom of the Content panel, try Grid Lock (new in Bridge CS4). It ensures that you always see whole thumbnails in the Content panel by automatically scaling thumbnails just enough to make them fit. To use Grid Lock, choose View > Grid Lock or click the Grid Lock button at the bottom of a Bridge window.

TIP: In Full Screen preview, click the image to zoom between 100% and Fit in Window magnifications. Also, the – (minus) and + (plus) keys zoom in and out.

Evaluating a Single Image. To concentrate on one image, select one in the Content panel and press the spacebar (or choose View > Full Screen Preview) to display the image in a full-screen view. From there you can press the left arrow or right arrow to see other files in the same folder. To get out, press Esc or the spacebar.

Comparing Multiple Images. Bridge CS4 expands the ways you can compare images.

TIP: For quick-and-dirty comparisons in the Content window, just increase the size of the thumbnail previews.

• To compare up to nine images at the same time (see **Figure 5-79**), display the Preview panel, make it big, and select more than one image in the Content panel.

Figure 5-79 Four selected image thumbnails in the Content panel on the left, shown larger and side by side in the Preview panel on the right.

- To quickly narrow many images down to a few picks, try Review mode (see **Figure 5-80**), new in Bridge CS4. To enter Review mode press Command-B (Mac OS X) or Ctrl-B (Windows), the shortcut for View > Review Mode. If you select more than four images, they appear as a carousel. There's always one current image (the one where the file-name isn't dimmed), and you cycle through images by pressing the left arrow and right arrow keys or clicking an image. Either way, the goal of Review mode is to drop (deselect) any image you no longer want to consider. To drop the current image, press the down arrow key (if you did this by mistake, press the up arrow key to get it back). When you're down to four images, they appear side by side. Press Esc to get out, and the last images standing remain selected in Bridge for you to label, rate, collect, or keyword.

TIP: You can't zoom images in the Preview panel, but you can click to add a loupe to each image.

Figure 5-80 Full-screen Review mode with loupes

Review mode presents images as a carousel; a loupe checks focus on the eye in the current (frontmost) image

Four images are left in Review mode; two loupes check focus on the eyes in top right and bottom left images

The Loupe. If you're viewing an image in the Preview panel or in Review mode, click to open a loupe (see **Figure 5-80**), which you can drag around an image. Zoom the loupe by pressing the plus (+) or minus (–) key. When you drag the loupe in a way that would push it off the edge of an image, it automatically flips around so that you can still see it. To put the loupe away, click it again—we find that it sometimes takes a couple of tries.

The key (literally) to using multiple loupes is the Command key (Mac) or Ctrl key (Windows). If you have multiple loupes in position in different images and you want to move them all at the same time, Command-drag (Mac) or Ctrl-drag (Windows) any of the loupes. To change the zoom level of all loupes simultaneously, hold down Command (Mac) or Ctrl (Windows) as you press the plus (+) or minus (–) key.

TIP: If you don't want the loupe to come up when you click a preview, open the Preferences dialog for Bridge, and in the General pane, turn off the option Command/Ctrl-Click Opens the Loupe When Previewing or Reviewing.

Rating and Labeling Images

Ratings give you a way to separate keepers from rejects. Labels let you mark images for any reason. Ratings and labels become part of the image's metadata that you can use to search and to filter which images are displayed.

You can get around in the Content panel using the usual keyboard shortcuts—arrow keys and the Home, End, Page Up, and Page Down keys. The fastest way to apply ratings and labels is with the keyboard. Many photographers and photo editors are used to looking at image after image and pressing a key to rate them. All of the ratings and labels shortcuts are listed on the Label menu in Bridge. You can use the same shortcuts in Camera Raw if you've opened multiple images in filmstrip mode. When you see a row of stars under a thumbnail, you can rate by clicking or dragging in the row until you see the number of stars you want.

Bridge and Camera Raw support a special rating called Reject, which came about because many photographers requested a way to mark images that they didn't even want to rate. At first glance it might seem that you could leave the rating blank, but it was not always clear whether no rating meant "have not rated yet" or "do not want." Some photographers used a label to mark rejects, but this also caused problems because labels aren't defined the same way by different users or programs, while ratings are used more consistently. The Reject rating unambiguously solves all of these problems. Reject is also safer than deleting images immediately, in case you change your mind.

Bridge makes it easy to rapidly narrow the field by applying ratings and then using the Filter panel to display files by their rating. You'll usually need multiple passes to complete the process.

Choose a Rating View or Workspace. Bridge CS4 lets you rate images in more views. You can apply ratings in the Content panel, Preview panel, Full Screen preview, Review mode, or Camera Raw. If you want to review images in the Bridge window, you might find that one of the workspaces works best for you; choose one from the top of the Bridge window or create your own. Rating in the Bridge window may be preferable if you'd like to use the Filter panel to show just the images above a certain rating.

Mark the Rejects. Select the first image and decide whether you want to keep using it. If you don't want it, reject it by pressing Option-Delete (Mac) or Alt-Delete (Windows). The word "Reject" will appear in red below the

TIP: To work more efficiently in Camera Raw, apply a label to images you want to process together in Bridge (you can apply a label with a single-key shortcut). Then filter the view to show each labeled group.

TIP: You can rate or label a selected image by pressing a number key alone (without the Command or Ctrl modifier) if you open the Metadata pane of the Preferences dialog and turn on the check box Require the Command/Ctrl key to Apply Labels and Ratings. You might prefer to leave that preference off to avoid applying ratings accidentally through stray keypresses. (You must still press Command/Ctrl to rate images in Camera Raw.)

image (see **Figure 5-81**). Your rejects don't have to be definitive at this point, because they aren't permanently deleted yet. You can add more rejects later or change your mind. Rejects should be images that are just plain unusable—bad compositions, unwanted facial expressions, exposures that can't be saved with any tools, and so on.

Rejects are indicated in red text in the Content panel

Figure 5-81 Marking rejected images

Rate the Rest. In the Filter panel, click to check No Rating (see **Figure 5-81**) and make sure no other rating levels are checked. You are now seeing all of the images that haven't been rated. The great thing about the No Rating filter is that as you rate images they become hidden, so you see only the images that still need to be rated without being distracted by the rest. Of course, if you want to see images that have already been rated, just turn on the Filter panel check boxes for other rating levels.

From here on out, it's pretty easy. Just press the keyboard shortcut for the star rating you want to apply to each image: Press Command (Mac) or Ctrl (Windows) together with a number key from 1 to 5. To remove the rating from selected images, press Command-0 (Mac) or Ctrl-0 (Windows). Those shortcuts apply a specific rating, but if you want to bump an image's current rating up or down, press the Command/Ctrl key along with the comma key (,) to lower the rating by one star, or the period key (.) to raise the rating. It may make more sense to remember those two keys by their Shift meanings, the less-than sign (<) and greater-than sign (>), because that's what they do to the rating. Don't press Shift to apply them, though. To toggle one star on or off, press Command-' (apostrophe) in Mac OS X or Ctrl-' (apostrophe) in Windows. A slower but sometimes convenient alternative is to click and drag in the rating area of the thumbnail—dragging to the right increases the rating, and dragging to the left reduces it.

Don't feel that you have to get all your ratings right the first time. You can always go back and adjust them. Some photographers prefer to rate shots all in one pass. Others use a multiple-pass method, applying one star first, then making another pass to add another star to the standouts, and repeating that until they find their four- or five-star images. It's all up to you.

TIP: The Reject rating is a good safety valve. Instead of trashing unwanted images right away, mark them with the Reject rating. When you're ready to trim down the number of images, set the Filter panel to show only rejects, review them carefully to make sure you aren't going to delete something you want to keep, and then trash them all at once.

TIP: If thumbnails appear without label and rating information under them, check the View menu to make sure that the Show Thumbnail Only command is not checked.

Labels. While the stars are incremental, labels are not—they're simply arbitrary markers. You can apply any of the first four labels by pressing the Command (Mac) or Ctrl (Windows) key together with a number key from 6 to 9 (see **Figure 5-82**). If you don't want to have to press the Command or Ctrl key, open the Preferences dialog in Bridge, click Labels, and turn off Require the Command/Ctrl Key to Apply Labels and Ratings. You can also edit the label text in the Label preferences. Label text is searchable in Bridge.

Figure 5-82 Labeled images in the Content and Filter panels

Labels are less portable than ratings. Your labels will show up as white on any machine that uses a different label definition than yours, which is almost certain to happen if you use something other than the default label definitions (red, yellow, green, blue, and purple) and reasonably likely to happen even if you use the default definitions, since the recipient may not. They can always search for your label text, but it's probably simpler just to use keywords or ratings.

Applying Labels with the Keyboard. Look on the Label menu to see the keyboard shortcuts for each label. Inside Camera Raw, the purple label can be toggled using Command-Shift-0 (Mac) or Ctrl-Shift-0 (Windows).

TIP: To move to another image in the Content view or Camera Raw filmstrip after you rate an image, press an arrow key.

APPLYING METADATA AND KEYWORDS

The key to being efficient with metadata and keywords is the same as it is when applying Camera Raw edits: Select all of the images that need the same treatment, and deal with them all at once. Metadata includes the EXIF data saved into a photo by a camera, IPTC metadata such as captions and keywords, and labels and star ratings. To read more about metadata, see the sidebar "All About Metadata," earlier in this chapter.

Applying Metadata

View and edit metadata in the Metadata panel (see **Figure 5-83**). Bridge and Photoshop give you access to several types of metadata, and not all of them can be edited directly. File Properties describe how the file was saved, so to change them you resave the file from Photoshop. EXIF data records the settings in use when an image was captured, such as shutter speed, so it can't be altered by Bridge or Photoshop after the fact. You can edit other types of metadata, such as IPTC metadata. It's easy to tell which metadata fields you can edit, because they're marked by a pencil icon along the right side.

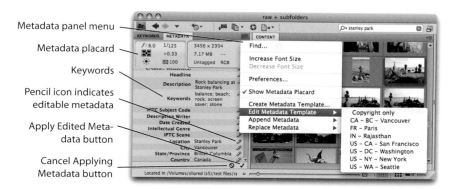

Metadata panel menu
Metadata placard
Keywords
Pencil icon indicates editable metadata
Apply Edited Metadata button
Cancel Applying Metadata button

Figure 5-83 The Metadata panel (top) and Keywords panel (bottom)

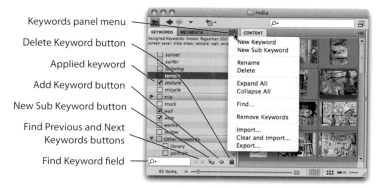

Keywords panel menu
Delete Keyword button
Applied keyword
Add Keyword button
New Sub Keyword button
Find Previous and Next Keywords buttons
Find Keyword field

To enter metadata for one or more images selected in Bridge, click in an editable metadata field, enter the information, and press Tab to advance to the next field. When you're done, click the check mark icon at the lower right of the panel to commit the entries, or press Alt-Return (Mac OS X) or Alt-Enter (Windows). Some metadata fields, such as Description, allow more than one line; in these fields you can enter a line break by pressing Return (Mac) or Enter (Windows); and that's why you can't use those keys to apply changes in multiline fields.

TIP: On Mac desktop keyboards, the main keyboard contains the Return key while the numeric keypad contains the Enter key. On Mac laptop keyboards, press Fn-Return to turn it into an Enter key. Windows keyboards have an Enter key only.

For recurring metadata, such as copyright notices, metadata templates provide a very convenient way to apply them quickly (see "Using Metadata Templates," later in this chapter).

TIP: Trying to figure out where to enter a caption? It usually goes in the Description field.

The Metadata and Keywords Panel Menus. The Metadata and Keywords panel menus (see Figure 5-83) provide commands for managing those panels. They also give you another way to start the Edit > Find command.

Editing the Metadata Panel List. In the Metadata panel menu, the Preferences command takes you directly to the Metadata panel of the Bridge preferences. It's definitely worth taking the few minutes needed to decide which fields you want to display—very few Photoshop users need to see them all! The Show Metadata Placard option displays the section at the top of the Metadata panel that contains EXIF information (and resembles a camera LCD), and the section next to it contains file properties. The Metadata placard duplicates information already shown in the Camera Data EXIF and File Properties sections of the Metadata panel, but if you find the Metadata placard useful as a quick reference, you can leave the option on.

TIP: In the Keywords panel search field, you can type multiple keywords separated by commas. This also works in the Keywords field in the Metadata panel.

One set of metadata you'll notice in the Metadata preferences is the older IIM (Information Interchange Model) set. It's there for compatibility with legacy images but has been superseded by the new IPTC Core schema for XMP metadata. You can read more at www.iptc.org.

Applying Keywords

In the Keywords panel (see **Figure 5-84**), you can apply keywords to selected images by clicking the check boxes for the keywords you want to add. If the keyword isn't in the list, click the New Keyword button to add it. Applying keywords to an image saves them with the IPTC metadata for that image.

Figure 5-84 The results of searching for a keyword. Matches are highlighted; the keyword highlighted in green will be applied if you press Return or Enter.

We prefer to type keywords into the search field at the bottom of the Keywords panel because it has a type-ahead feature: To enter "airliner" in a keyword list that already contains many "air . . . " words, such as "airplane" and "aircraft," you have to type in only "airl" and the Keywords panel will highlight that keyword for you. Now all you have to do is press Return or Enter to apply the selected keyword. You'll find that applying keywords by typing is especially convenient when the keyword list is very long, saving you the time and trouble of scrolling the list. Note that the search field in the Keywords panel searches for keywords in the keyword list, not in images.

If a keyword is highlighted in yellow, it's an alternate match that you must select manually, either by turning on its check box with the mouse or pressing the up arrow and down arrow keys to highlight the keyword in gray and then pressing Return or Enter. If nothing's highlighted, the keyword doesn't exist yet, so simply press Return or Enter to apply the keyword and add it to the list of keywords. You can also move among highlighted alternates by clicking the Find Previous Keyword and Find Next Keyword buttons at the bottom of the Keywords panel, next to the search field.

Keeping Keywords Around. The Keywords panel doesn't permanently list every keyword it comes across; it lists only the keywords used by the files in the current view—you see them in italics. The keywords you see that aren't in italics are *persistent* keywords; they stick around no matter which images you're viewing.

Deleting Keywords from the Keywords Panel and from Images.
Deleting a keyword from the Keywords panel doesn't delete the keyword from any images to which it has been applied; it deletes it only from the panel. As long as a keyword is applied to an image, Bridge keeps that keyword in the list. To remove a keyword from a selected image, you must uncheck it in the Keywords panel. If you want to remove all keywords from an image, select the image and choose Remove Keywords from the Keywords panel menu (see Figure 5-83).

Hierarchical Keywords. Bridge supports hierarchical keywords (see **Figure 5-85**). To create a sub-keyword (child keyword), click the New Sub Keyword button at the bottom of the Keywords panel. A parent keyword appears with a triangle to the left of its name, which you can click to expand and collapse the list of its sub-keywords.

TIP: After you're applied a term in the Keywords panel search field, another way to apply or remove a highlighted keyword is to press the spacebar. Of course, if a cursor is still blinking in the search field, the spacebar types a space.

TIP: You can use the keyboard to turn off a selected keyword's check box in the same way you turn it on: by pressing the Return or Enter key, or the spacebar.

Figure 5-85 Hierarchical keywords

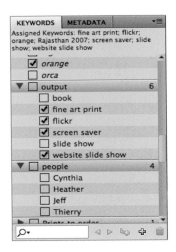

Clicking a parent keyword doesn't apply all of the child keywords, and by default, clicking a sub-keyword doesn't apply the parent keyword. If you want a parent keyword to be applied when you apply one of its child keywords, open Bridge preferences, click the Keywords panel, and turn on the Automatically Apply Parent Keywords option (see **Figure 5-86**). Applying a parent keyword doesn't apply its child keywords by default. To apply both a child keyword and its parent, Shift-click the child keyword's check box.

Figure 5-86 Keywords preferences

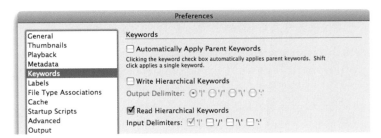

Bridge and Lightroom support hierarchical keywords, but as we write this, not many other programs do. If you send images to colleagues such as stock-photo agencies that might use other software, consult with them before using hierarchical keywords. You may be required to modify how your applications write those keywords into the image metadata. In the Keywords pane of the Bridge Preferences dialog, the options Write Hierarchical Keywords and Read Hierarchical Keywords determine whether keywords written to image metadata are written or read as a hierarchy or as a flat list of keywords. Both options let you customize the character Bridge uses to recognize keyword hierarchies when the character appears between keywords. Setting these options may become easier in the future if hierarchical keywords catch on and standards for handling them emerge.

Using Metadata Templates

Let's face it: Using the Metadata panel is like filling out a form (name, contact info, copyright info, keywords, caption, city, state . . . you get the idea). Forms are no fun. Fortunately, metadata templates go a long way toward making metadata entry much less of a chore.

A metadata template is simply a preset that contains any prefilled metadata you want. We highly recommend that you get to know metadata templates and use them thoughtfully, because they can save you a lot of time. Not only do they save time in a Bridge window, but you can also apply a metadata template as you import images from a camera (see "Copying Files from a Camera" earlier in this chapter) so that the images already have your fundamental metadata before you first view them in Bridge.

Use the Create Metadata Template dialog (see **Figure 5-87**) to make a new metadata template. As with all metadata commands, you can find this command under the Tools menu (choose Tools > Create Metadata Template), or you may find it easier to click the Metadata panel menu and choose the command there (see Figure 5-83). Now you can create your template.

1. To use an existing template as a starting point, choose it from the pop-up menu at the top right corner of the dialog.

2. Enter a Template Name, and fill out any metadata fields that you want to include in the template.

3. Check your spelling. You don't want an error to creep into the hundreds of images that may be edited with a metadata template!

4. Make sure you turn on the check box to the left of any field you want to include in the template. To force a field to be blank, leave it blank and check its check box. Unchecked fields don't affect existing data.

5. Click Save.

TIP: You can temporarily reverse the behavior of the Keywords preference Automatically Apply Parent Keywords by Shift-clicking a sub-keyword's check box. For example, if the preference is on, Shift-clicking a sub-keyword's check box won't apply the parent keyword.

Figure 5-87 The Create
Metadata Template dialog

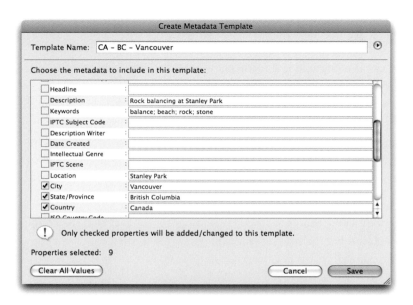

To edit a metadata template, just choose its name from the Edit Metadata
Template submenu (on the same menu as the Create Metadata Template
command).

To apply a metadata template, select the images you want to change. Then
choose the name of the template from the Append Metadata or Replace
Metadata submenu, accessed from the same menu as the Create Metadata
Template command. The difference between Append Metadata and Replace
Metadata requires a little explanation.

Append Metadata. The data in a metadata template field (such as City) is
applied to the image only if the same field in the image is empty. If there's
already data in that field in the image, the template data for that field isn't
applied to the image, which keeps the existing data for that field.

Replace Metadata. The data in a metadata template field always replaces
the data in the same field in an image.

Append Metadata and Replace Metadata change image metadata only for
the fields for which the check box is on. If a field's check box is off in a
metadata template, neither Append nor Replace will change that field.

Looking at Metadata with File Info

The File Info dialog (see **Figure 5-88**) is another way of viewing metadata of files selected in Bridge. It's a relatively inefficient way to apply keywords and other metadata when compared to the Metadata and Keywords panels, but it is still useful for taking image-specific keywords that we don't want to save in a keyword set and adding them to small numbers of images and for examining metadata in something close to raw form. For example, in File Info you can see exactly how the camera encodes things like shutter speed and aperture value by looking in the Advanced pane.

Figure 5-88 The File Info dialog

In Bridge CS4 and Photoshop CS4, you can rearrange the tabs in File Info by dragging them around. Another new CS4 feature is that File Info is now based on Adobe Flash and Adobe Flex technologies, which means that Flash/Flex developers can add their own customized metadata panels for media types that aren't already supported. As a side effect, you can speed up File Info loading by removing some of the modules it uses; in Mac OS X go to Library\Application Support\Adobe\XMP\Custom File Info Panels\2.0\ panels, and in Windows go to C:\Program Files\Common Files\Adobe\ XMP\Custom File Info Panels\2.0\panels.

TIP: To go to the next or previous tab in File Info, press the left arrow or right arrow key. If the tab list is still too wide to see them all, you can resize the window or click the pop-up menu in the top right corner, where all of the tabs are listed, and choose the tab you want to see.

You can choose an existing metadata template from the pop-up menu next to the OK button at the bottom of the File Info dialog. To create a metadata template using the current File Info metadata, choose Export from that pop-up menu; to apply a metadata template, choose Import. In that pop-up menu, Show Templates Folder takes you straight to the Adobe default Metadata Templates folder on your disk.

FINDING AND FILTERING FILES

When you're looking for a file in Bridge, don't think only of the Find command. Bridge provides several approaches to finding files:

- To do a quick search, use the Find field at the top right corner of the Bridge window (new in Bridge CS4). To enter more specific criteria, choose Edit > Find.

- To quickly find files based on criteria in the files' metadata, use the Filter panel. If the criteria you want aren't there, choose Edit > Find.

- To save a search so that you can return to it at any time, create a Smart Collection based on your search criteria.

Indexing. When you first do searches in Bridge, they may take longer than usual as Bridge creates and caches an index of the content within the scope that you specified, such as a folder and its subfolders. The Find dialog lets you skip folders that haven't been indexed, but we usually leave this option off because we can't remember which folders Bridge has indexed, and it won't tell us. The point is, searches should go faster as time goes on. An alternative is to use the Find field

The Find Field

TIP: (Windows only) If you don't see Windows Search options in the Find field, you can download the installer from www.microsoft.com/windows/products/winfamily/desktopsearch/ .

In the Find field at the top right corner of a Bridge window (see **Figure 5-89**), enter a search term, including metadata, and press Return or Enter. The Find field can search using either the index generated by Bridge or the index generated by Spotlight (Mac) or Windows Search (Windows). You make this choice by clicking the magnifying glass icon in the Find field. This not only potentially speeds searches but should make it easier for you to use Bridge to look for any type of file, reducing the need to leave Bridge for your desktop just to use your operating system's search feature.

Figure 5-89 The Find
field and its menu

The Find Command

The Find command lets you perform searches using a wide range of search criteria (see **Figure 5-90**), including a handy selection of metadata fields such as ISO (speed). To use it, choose Edit > Find or press Command-F (Mac OS X) or Ctrl-F (Windows).

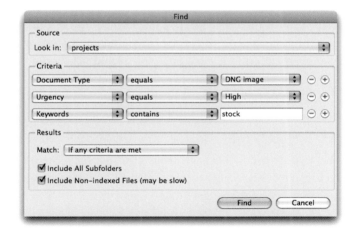

Figure 5-90
The Find dialog

The Find dialog also provides the following important features:

* The Match menu lets you choose whether to find files if any criterion is met (equivalent to an "or" between the criteria) or to find files only if all criteria are met (equivalent to an "and" between the criteria).

- Include All Subfolders does what it says—it extends the search to include any subfolders in the folder specified in the "Look in" menu.

- Include Non-Indexed Files looks at files that have not yet been added to the Bridge cache. Turning this option on may add time to the search, because nonindexed files need to be indexed.

Save as Collection. When you perform a search, you have the option to save the search criteria as a collection. When you click the Save as Collection button, you can save the search results in any folder you want, and optionally add it to your Bridge Favorites.

When you open a collection, the saved search runs and the current results appear. To refine the search, click Search Again; the Find dialog appears so you can edit the criteria.

TIP: To return to the window view before returning search results, choose it from the Recent Folders menu. Or you can choose File > New Window and perform the search in that window.

Smart Collections

We talk about Smart Collections here because a Smart Collection is really a saved search (or like a saved version of the Filter panel). If you've used this type of feature in programs like Apple iTunes, you already know the concept. You don't have to put anything into a Smart Collection, because it fills itself with any item matching the criteria you've specified and automatically removes any item that stops matching the criteria. For example, you could have a Smart Collection that lists only files for which the Copyright Notice metadata is empty, so that you can fill it in; as you fill in those images, they stop appearing in the Smart Collection. You could also keep a Smart Collection of all your five-star images or images rated greater than three stars.

To create a Smart Collection, in the Collections panel click the New Smart Collection button (see **Figure 5-91**), specify options (see "The Find Command," earlier), and click Save. We love Smart Collections.

Figure 5-91
Smart Collections appear in the Collections panel as blue icons with gears

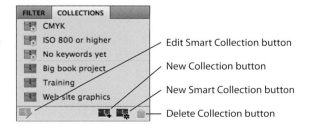

Edit Smart Collection button

New Collection button

New Smart Collection button

Delete Collection button

Exchanging Metadata with Lightroom

Adobe has worked hard to make sure that you can exchange metadata and Camera Raw settings between Bridge CS4 and Adobe Photoshop Lightroom 2. Version numbers are important—as Adobe updates products their feature sets change, and one product may gain features that the other product doesn't know about and can't render or support. Watch your updates and read the ReadMe files to be aware of compatibility changes. As we write this, Camera Raw 5, Bridge CS4, and Lightroom 2 settings are completely compatible.

Even when the versions are compatible and the files are present, you've got two programs writing to the same files, and that can lead to synchronization problems. You sometimes have to be a traffic cop to make sure data goes where it's supposed to. Here are the rules of the road:

Bridge to Lightroom. If you're using DNG files, you're OK because the settings are inside the files that Lightroom will be opening. For other file types, in the General pane of the Camera Raw Preferences dialog, the "Save image settings in" pop-up menu should be set to Sidecar .xmp Files. If it isn't, after you edit images in Camera Raw you must choose Export Settings to XMP from the Camera Raw Settings menu to create the sidecar files. (You don't want to choose Camera Raw Database, because Lightroom doesn't read it.)

If you're in Lightroom and for some reason you don't see changes you made in Bridge, select the out-of-date images in the Library module and choose Metadata > Read Metadata from File.

Lightroom to Bridge. In Lightroom, you may want to choose File > Catalog Settings and turn on Automatically Write Changes into XMP so that you don't have to do it manually. We say you *may* want to choose it, because that option can cause a lot of CPU and disk activity in the background as Lightroom checks and updates every image in your catalog. If that option is off, select the images in the Library module in Lightroom and choose Metadata > Save Metadata to File. That updates the metadata so that Bridge will now see current data.

You might see your Lightroom changes the next time you view that folder in the Content panel in Bridge. If you don't see the changes in Bridge, press F5 (the shortcut for View > Refresh). If that doesn't do it, try purging that folder's cache (choose Tools > Cache > Purge Cache for Folder).

TIP: You can also keep the Lightroom Library view and file metadata up to date using the folder synchronization feature. In the Lightroom Library module, choose Library > Synchronize Folder, make sure Scan for Metadata Updates is checked, and click Synchronize.

Filtering the Current View

The Filter panel (see **Figure 5-92**) lists some of the more useful metadata found in images in the Content panel, such as creation dates, file types, ratings, labels, and keywords so you can quickly show subsets of images. For example, if you want to see only the images in the Content panel that have no keywords, just click to add a check mark to the left of No Keywords in the Filter panel. In the Filter panel menu you can control which categories are visible in the panel.

Figure 5-92 Filter panel

Filter panel menu

Quick Filter menu in Path bar

Results of current filter in Content view

Selected filter criteria

Keep Filter When Browsing button

Cancel Filter button

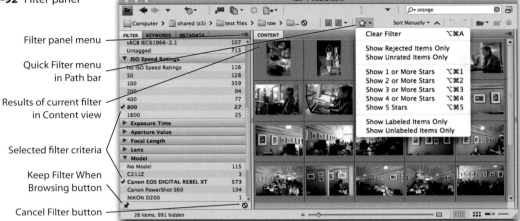

If your filtering needs are simple, try the Filter menu on the Path bar. Click the star button on the Path bar and choose the filter you want from the menu; this modifies the Filter panel settings to match, and the star on the Path bar turns blue. However, it doesn't necessarily work in reverse; if you choose Filter panel settings that don't match up with any of the Filter menu options, the star won't turn blue, even though a filter is active. You can still use the Filter menu on the Path bar to ensure that no filters are active because the first option on that menu is Clear Filter (press Command-Option-A in Mac OS X or press Ctrl-Alt-A in Windows).

PRESENTING YOUR PHOTOS

Whether you're showing images to a client or simply reviewing what you've shot, Bridge provides several ways to make your image library more presentable than it is in the Content and Preview panel. We talked in detail about a few of the following viewing modes in "Evaluating and Comparing Images" earlier in this chapter.

Slideshow. The View > Slideshow command offers an alternative to the Bridge light table metaphor by presenting selected images as a slideshow; you can also enter the slideshow by pressing Command-L (Mac) or Ctrl-L (Windows). While you're in the slideshow, you can rate, rotate, and zoom the image while enjoying the benefits of a large image preview. Press H (with no modifier) to display all the keyboard shortcuts that apply in the slideshow (see **Figure 5-93**).

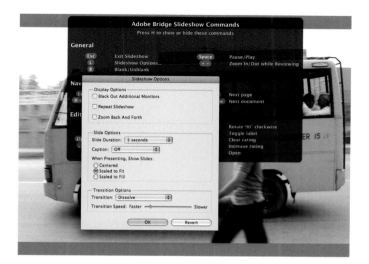

Figure 5-93 A full-screen slideshow with the Slideshow Commands help screen (press H while in the slideshow) and the Slideshow Options dialog (press L in the slideshow)

Choose View > Slideshow Options to adjust how the slideshow displays, such as how the image fits on the screen and whether to display its caption. It's easier to use the Slideshow Options dialog (see Figure 5-93) while the slideshow is running (in the slideshow, press L) because you will see the effects of your changes interactively.

Full Screen Preview. If you want full-screen display but don't need the features of a self-running slideshow (such as transitions), choose View > Full Screen Preview. Full Screen preview can be better if you need to switch frequently between it and the Bridge window, because it opens and closes faster than the Slideshow—just press the spacebar.

Review Mode. To see multiple images in a full-screen display, select them and choose View > Review Mode (see "Evaluating and Comparing Images" earlier in this chapter).

TIP: To zoom in the slideshow, press the – (minus) or + (plus) key. To toggle between the current view and 100 percent (Actual Pixels) magnification, click the image. At magnifications above 100 percent, drag to pan the image.

Preview Panel. If you want to see images larger than you can in the Content panel while being able to continue to work in other panels, you might prefer the Preview panel (see "Evaluating and Comparing Images" earlier in this chapter) instead of a full-screen view. The Preview panel is especially useful when placed in a second synchronized window on another monitor. To do this, choose Window > New Synchronized Window, move the new window to another monitor, and fill it with just the Preview panel. As you select images in the Content panel in the first Bridge window, they'll fill the Preview panel in the second window.

PDF Contact Sheets. In Bridge CS4 and Photoshop CS4 you generate contact sheets from the Output panel in Bridge. To display the Output panel, click Output in the workspace strip at the top of a Bridge window. It's important to note that changes don't appear in real time; you must click Refresh Preview to update the Output Preview panel (or to make the Output Preview panel appear if it isn't already there), and no file is generated until you click Save at the bottom of the Output panel.

Start by clicking PDF and choosing a Template on which to base your design (see **Figure 5-94**), then work your way down the panes in the Output panel. The options are easier to understand if you've created documents using Adobe Acrobat, because most of them map directly to standard PDF options. We go over the options that need the most explanation below.

- Document pane. Choosing a Page Preset sets the Size, Width, Height, and orientation of the page for your contact sheet. Quality controls the compression level of the images you include in the PDF. Setting the Open password will cause a PDF reader to ask for a password when the PDF document is opened, while setting the Permission Password affects whether the PDF reader lets the recipient edit the document.

- Layout. Specify the rows and columns of the contact sheet itself. Rotate for Best Fit means that, for example, if your contact sheet cells are tall but an image is wide, the wide image will be rotated 90 degrees to make the best use of the cell space.

- Overlays. Add filenames and filename extensions to the contact sheet.

- Playback. Control automatic playback in a PDF reader. These options are derived from the playback options you'd find in Acrobat.

TIP: If you preferred the old Contact Sheet, Picture Package, and Web Photo Gallery plug-ins for Photoshop, they are unsupported since their functions were moved to the Output panel. However, they're still available on the Photoshop installer DVD or disk image. Look in the folder /English/ Goodies/Optional plug-ins/ or on the Adobe web site. To install, drag them into the Adobe Photoshop CS4/Plug-Ins folder.

TIP: Any time you want to present a specific subset of images in a slideshow, client presentation, or Web gallery, gather and arrange the images in advance using a collection.

- Watermark. Add a single text watermark at the center of the page. If you want it to cover most of the images, set a big font size.

Figure 5-94 The Output panel for PDF in the right pane, and the Output Preview panel in the middle pane

Web Galleries. In Bridge CS4 and Photoshop CS4, you generate Web galleries from the Output panel in Bridge. Start by clicking Web Gallery and choosing a Template on which to base your design (see **Figure 5-95**). Most of the templates are based on Adobe Flash; if you prefer HTML, choose the HTML Gallery template. Finally, work your way down the panes in the Output panel to set the options below:

- Site Info. Enter the information you'd like to display on the pages of the Web gallery.

- Color Palette. If you want the colors to differ from those in the template, change them here.

- Appearance. Specify the rows and columns of the Web gallery.

- Create Gallery. Set options for the gallery files you save. These options don't affect the visible content of the Web gallery pages in your browser; they set the names of the paths, folders, and files you export.

TIP: Trying to use your mouse's scroll wheel in the Output panel? If it doesn't work, position the mouse over the scroll bar and then try the scroll wheel.

TIP: You can zoom the Output Preview panel. Click to zoom in, and Option-click (Mac OS X) or Alt-click (Windows) to zoom out.

To keep the Web gallery on your machine, click Save to Disk. Click Browse to set the folder location before you click Save.

To send the Web gallery to your Web site using FTP, click Upload and fill out the options. The Gallery Name is actually the name of the folder to be created on the FTP server, so enter a server-friendly name (for example, no spaces or punctuation). In the Folder field, enter the path to the gallery on the server—but be sure to leave out the FTP server domain name and the gallery name, because they have their own fields. Right below the Upload button is a pop-up menu and two buttons; these control FTP presets. To add the current settings to the preset pop-up menu, click the Save Preset Name button. To delete the preset currently selected in the menu, click the trash can button.

Figure 5-95 The Output panel for Web in the right pane, and the Output Preview panel in the middle pane

Save Preset Name button

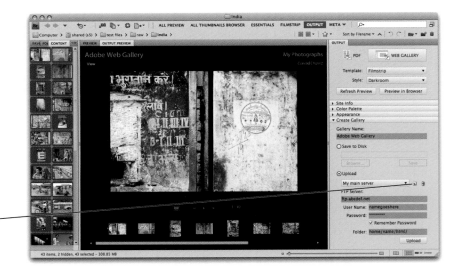

TIP: When you use an automated Web gallery generator, remember to feed it images that are already sharpened and color-corrected for the Web. For example, if you work in Adobe RGB (1998) or ProPhoto RGB, and you forget to convert the images to sRGB color, their colors look flat on the Web.

Output Panel Preferences. If you use the Output panel, you may want to customize its settings. In the Bridge Preferences dialog, click Output and adjust the following options as needed:

- Use Solo Mode for Output Panel Behavior. By default this option is off, which means you can freely open or close any of the panes in the Output panel. If you turn this option on, opening a pane closes the pane that was previously open so that you see only one pane at a time. The advantage of this mode is that the other pane names remain visible more often, so you don't have to scroll as much.

- Convert Multi-Byte Filenames to Full ASCII. If you're uploading the output to a server that doesn't deal well with multibyte filenames (for example, one using accents), this option lets you work with that server.

- Preserve Embedded Color Profile. By default this option is off, which means the Output panel converts all images to sRGB. For most Web galleries and common PDF presentations, this is fine. But if your originals have embedded profiles other than sRGB profiles and you don't want the Output panel to convert them to sRGB, turn this option on.

AUTOMATING WORKFLOWS WITH THE BATCH COMMAND

The Batch command is one of the most powerful features in Photoshop, and a great way to finish off your digital workflow. The Batch command is conceptually very simple. You point it at a batch of images and it runs an action on them, during which it can do one of the following:

- Optionally rename images

- Save new files

- Open images in Photoshop

- Save and close, overwriting the source files

To batch-process files from within Bridge, select the images you want to process and then choose Tools > Photoshop > Batch. To open the Batch dialog from within Photoshop, choose File > Automate > Batch.

The Batch dialog is split into four different sections, each of which controls a different aspect of the batch process's behavior (see **Figure 5-96**).

Play. Choose an action Set, and then choose an Action from that set that will be applied to all the images. We discuss actions and how to create them in more detail later in this chapter, as well as in Chapter 11.

Source. Choose the source of the images on which the batch will be executed, and set some key options we'll explore in a moment. Your choices from this menu are a folder full of images (click the Choose button to choose the specific folder), the currently open files, images imported through the File > Import command in Photoshop, or—when running

TIP: Another shortcut to Output panel is to click the Output button (not the Output workspace button) at the top of a Bridge window; see Figure 5-63.

TIP: We prefer running Batch from Bridge instead of Photoshop because we can take advantage of the metadata filtering, Smart Collections, and search to intelligently and efficiently locate and preview the group of files to send to Photoshop.

Batch from within Bridge—the images that are currently selected in Bridge. For raw images, the source will invariably be a folder or the selected images in Bridge.

Destination. Specify what happens to the processed images. Choose None to leave them open in Photoshop after processing (though keep in mind that leaving many large files open in Photoshop will gobble RAM and slow it down). To save the changed files over the originals and close them, choose Save and Close; Folder lets you designate a folder in which to save the processed images. This section also includes the renaming features offered by the Batch Rename command (see "Renaming Files" earlier in this chapter).

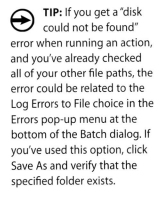

TIP: If you get a "disk could not be found" error when running an action, and you've already checked all of your other file paths, the error could be related to the Log Errors to File choice in the Errors pop-up menu at the bottom of the Batch dialog. If you've used this option, click Save As and verify that the specified folder exists.

When you process raw images, you'll choose None or, much more commonly, Folder. Save and Close can be a "hurt-me" button, because its normal behavior is to overwrite the source image. With raw files, this is usually impossible and always undesirable. Photoshop can't overwrite files in formats it can't write, including most raw image formats, but if you use a camera that records its raw images as TIFFs, there's a real danger of overwriting your raws if you choose Save and Close—so avoid it!

Errors. Choose whether to stop the entire batch when an error is encountered or log the errors to a file. We usually stop on errors when we're debugging an action used in Batch and log them to a file when we're actually running a batch in a production situation. However, when processing raw files, the batch typically either works on all files or fails on all files.

Figure 5-96 The Batch dialog

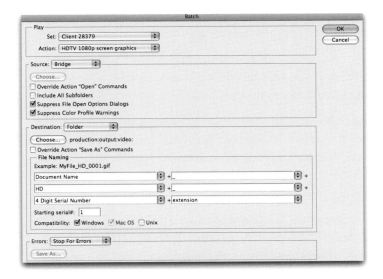

Rules for Batching Files

The difficulties people typically encounter in running the Batch dialog are in the way the selections in the Source and Destination sections interact with the action applied by the batch operation. Here are The Rules (as far as we're concerned, anyway).

Rules for Opening Files. To make sure that the raw files open and are processed the way you want, record an Open step in the action. In the case of raw images, make sure that the Settings menu in Camera Raw is set to Image Settings so that it applies the custom-tailored Camera Raw settings you've made for each image, and make sure that the Camera Raw workflow settings—Space, Bit Depth, Size, and Resolution—are set correctly.

Now comes one of the counterintuitive bits. If you record an Open step in the action, you must turn on the Override Action "Open" Commands option in the Batch dialog. If you don't, the batch will simply keep opening the image you used to record the Open step in the action. Override Action "Open" Commands doesn't override everything in the recorded Open command; it just overrides the specific choice of file to open, while ensuring that the Selected Image and workflow settings get honored.

Some people find this set of behaviors so frustrating and counterintuitive that they latch onto the fact that you can run Batch using an action that doesn't contain an Open step and hence doesn't require messing around with the check box. The problem with doing so is that you lose control over the Camera Raw workflow settings—the batch will just use the last-used settings. So you may expect a folder full of 6144-by-4096-pixel images and get 1536-by-1024-pixel ones instead, or wind up with 8-bit sRGB instead of 16-bit ProPhoto RGB. If you simply follow The Rules, you will have complete control over the workflow settings.

Rules for Saving Files. To make sure that the processed files get saved in the format you want, you need to record a Save step in the action that will be applied in Batch. This Save step dictates the file format (such as TIFF, JPEG, or PSD) and options that go with that format (TIFF compression options, JPEG quality settings, and so on).

Now comes the second counterintuitive bit. You must turn on the option labeled Override Action "Save As" Commands in the Batch dialog, or the files won't get saved where you want them, won't get saved with the names

TIP: If your action keeps naming all of your source files to the same name, re-record the Save As step without touching the filename. If the filename is edited at all when you record a Save As step, Photoshop thinks you want to record that specific filename.

TIP: Always test and debug your actions on expendable copies of images before you run them on the real thing. There's nothing worse than ruining irreplaceable originals with an inadequately tested action. Always set your actions to save processed files to a different folder than the originals. Check the final files, and if something goes horribly wrong you can simply chuck 'em and try again.

you want, or possibly won't even get saved at all! When you turn on this option, the file format and parameters recorded in the action's Save step will be applied when saving the file, but the name and destination will be over-ridden by the options you specify in the Batch dialog.

Rules for Running a Batch Operation. Two other settings commonly trip people up. Unless you turn on the Suppress File Open Options Dialogs check box, the Camera Raw dialog pops up whenever the batch opens a file and waits for you to do something. Turning on this option opens the image directly, bypassing the Camera Raw dialog. The Camera Raw settings for each image are used, but the batch operation isn't interrupted by the dialog.

If the workflow settings recorded in the action result in an image in a color space other than your Photoshop working space, you should also turn on the Suppress Color Profile Warnings check box; otherwise a Profile Mismatch warning may interrupt the batch. You don't want to find that the batch operation you'd set up to generate 2000 Web-ready JPEGs got stalled on the first image with a warning telling you that the file is sRGB when your working space is ProPhoto RGB!

Recording a Batch Action

As a useful example, let's build an action that converts raw files into 16 bit/channel TIFFs with adjustment layers set up for final editing in Photoshop. It's designed for use on "hero" images that merit individual manual edits in Photoshop. It doesn't actually do the editing because that will almost certainly be different for each image in a batch. Instead, it does a lot of the repetitive setup work, so that when you open the image all the necessary adjustment layers are already there, waiting for you to tweak them.

Creating an Action Set. Start by creating a new action set called "Batch Processing" in which to save the actions you'll create in the rest of this section (see **Figure 5-97** and "Actions, Automate, and Scripting," in Chapter 11, "Essential Image Techniques.")

Creating a New Action. Before creating the action, select a raw image in Bridge that has already had custom Camera Raw settings applied. That way, once you've created the action, you can start recording immediately without recording any extraneous steps, such as selecting a file, and you can correctly record the Camera Raw Selected Image setting.

Now click the Create New Action icon in the Actions panel in Photoshop, enter a name (such as "Save for Edit") for the action, and then click Record to close the dialog and start recording the action.

Click the Create New Set button

New set added

Click the Create New Action button

New Action dialog

Action created and ready to record

Figure 5-97 Creating an action set and action

Recording the Open Step. Now that you're recording, switch back to Bridge and open the image in Camera Raw by pressing Command-O (Mac) or Ctrl-O (Windows)—you must open the image in Camera Raw hosted by Photoshop. The Camera Raw dialog will appear (see **Figure 5-98**).

When you use the action in Batch, the Camera Raw dialog won't appear, so it's essential to get the settings right when you record this step. For this example we'll set Camera Raw in the following way:

• From the Space menu, choose ProPhoto RGB, which we prefer for editing images going to high-quality printed (not prepress) output.

• Set the Depth menu to 16 bits per channel for our purposes, though 8 bits per channel would have been fine for a Web graphics action, for instance.

• Set the Size menu to the camera's native resolution (not the sizes with a plus or minus after them).

• Enter 360 pixels per inch in the Resolution field. For this example, our prints are headed for an Epson Stylus Pro 3800 that has an optimal input resolution of 360 ppi; for your own action you'd find out the optimal input resolution of your printer.

TIP: To avoid surprise batch-stopping errors due to causes such as unexpected color modes or bit depths, or being asked to flatten images, consider including some normalizing steps at the beginning of your action. For example, JPEG is only an 8-bit standard with no layer support, so you might start a JPEG conversion action with steps that convert to 8-bit, convert the color profile, and flatten an image before finally saving to JPEG.

Then click OK to open the image. (If the Profile Mismatch warning appears, click OK to dismiss it. This doesn't get recorded in the action, and anyway, you'll suppress the warning when you use the action in Batch.) The image opens, and the Open step appears on the Actions panel.

Figure 5-98 Preparing Camera Raw for a batch process

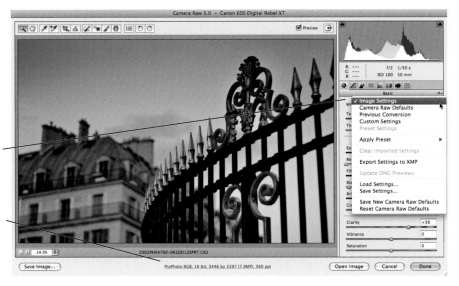

Click the Camera Raw Settings menu and make sure Image Settings is checked.

If the workflow options aren't correct, click the blue link text to change them.

Adding the Edits. This action adds two editing layers to the image before saving and closing: a Curves adjustment layer and a Hue/Saturation adjustment layer. Record them now as follows:

- Add a Levels adjustment layer by choosing Levels from the New Adjustment Layer submenu (under the Layer menu). Just click OK to create a Levels adjustment layer that does not, as yet, apply any adjustments. Remember, you'll make the adjustments on an image-by-image basis in Photoshop; the action just does the grunt work of creating the layers.

- Add two more adjustment layers: a Curves layer, then a Hue/Saturation layer. Click OK when their respective adjustment dialogs appear.

TIP: If a batch action produces one file and keeps saving over it no matter how many images you process, it's probably playing back the filename that was specified when the action was created. Try rerecording the Save As step, making sure not to touch the filename at all.

Recording the Save Step. Choose File > Save As and save it to your test folder for easy disposal after you're finished making and testing the action. Choose TIFF as the format, make sure that the Layers and Embed Color Profile check boxes are turned on (creating untagged ProPhoto RGB files is a very bad idea). Then click Save to advance to the TIFF Options dialog (see Chapter 12, "Image Storage and Output") and make your preferred settings.

The filename and the destination that you enter have no impact on the batch process because you'll use the Batch dialog to specify that. Use an obvious test name such as "test.jpg" and choose a test folder as a destination. Finally, close the image (to record that step in the action as well), and click the Stop button in the Actions panel to stop recording. **Figure 5-99** shows the resulting action in the Actions panel with all the steps expanded.

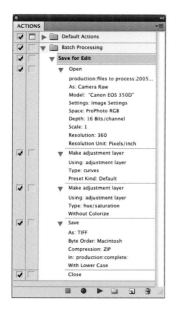

Figure 5-99 The Save for Edit action with its details expanded

When you run this action from the Batch dialog with the necessary overrides applied, filenames and locations will be overridden by the Batch settings. Everything else in the Open and Save steps will be honored.

Stop and Save the Action Set. Finally, click the Stop button in the Actions panel to stop recording. Photoshop doesn't allow you to save individual actions to disk—only action sets. To save an action, select the action set that contains it in the Actions panel and then choose Save Actions from the Actions panel menu (see **Figure 5-100**).

Until you actually use the Save Actions command, actions are recorded only in Preferences in Photoshop, and those are updated only when you choose File > Quit (Mac) or File > Exit (Windows) to close Photoshop normally. If Photoshop is unexpectedly closed for any other reason, such as a crash or power outage, any unsaved actions will be lost. So if your actions are even slightly complex, it's a very good idea to save them before doing anything

TIP: More reasons to save action sets are to back them up, archive versions of them, take them to other machines, send to colleagues, or so that you can transfer them to a reinstalled or upgraded Photoshop.

else. You can save actions anywhere, but if you want them to appear automatically in the Actions panel even if you delete the preferences, save them in the Adobe Photoshop CS4\Presets\Actions folder.

Figure 5-100 Saving an action set

TIP: If your actions call other actions, the other actions must be loaded in the Actions panel in Photoshop, or the calling action will fail when it can't find the action being called. An easy way to handle this is to make sure that any actions on which other actions are dependent are saved in the same set as the actions that depend on them.

When you click a triangle next to an action step to expand it, you can see exactly what's been recorded for each step (see Figure 5-100). When you use this action in Batch with the appropriate overrides selected (see "Rules for Batching Files," earlier in this chapter) the filenames and folder locations you recorded will be overridden by the settings in the Batch dialog, and all the other settings you've recorded here—the Camera Raw workflow settings and the JPEG Save Options—will be honored.

Running Actions on the Batch Dialog

Using the actions we've just shown you in the Batch dialog is really very simple—as long as you remember The Rules! (If you need to take another look, refer back to "Rules for Batching Files," earlier in this chapter.) Play by The Rules, and all will go smoothly. Violate them at your peril.

Other than choosing incorrect settings in the Batch dialog, three common situations can cause a batch operation to fail.

• The destination volume ran out of space for the processed files.

• No source files were selected in Bridge.

- Files with the same names as the ones you're creating already exist in the destination folder.

As we pointed out earlier, the key settings in Batch are the overrides in both the Source and Destination sections of the panel. **Figure 5-101** shows the Batch dialog set up to run the Save for Edit action so that you can avoid the common errors listed above.

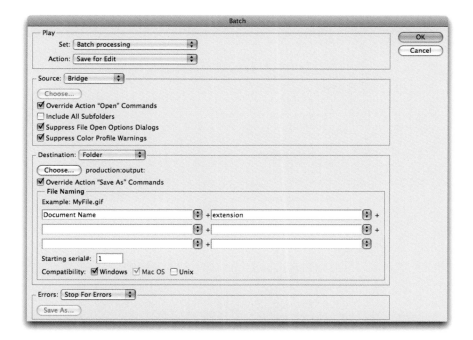

Figure 5-101 The Batch dialog with options specified to run the Save for Edit action

Source Settings. Whenever you run a batch operation using an action that includes an Open step, you must check Override Action "Open" Commands in the Source section. To process raw images, you also need to turn on Suppress File Open Options Dialogs—otherwise the Camera Raw dialog will pop up for every image. And whenever you run an unattended batch operation, it's a good idea to check Suppress Color Profile Warnings so that the batch process doesn't get stuck on a Profile Mismatch warning.

Destination Settings. Whenever you run a batch operation using an action that includes a Save As step, you must turn on Override Action "Save As" Commands in the Destination section; otherwise the files won't get saved.

TIP: In addition to the Batch command (and the Image Processor command we'll discuss soon), any of the commands on the Tools > Photoshop submenu in Bridge can be a useful post-Bridge step in your digital workflow.

THE IMAGE PROCESSOR

You may not have to build a batch action for every mass production task you come across. Some of them can probably be handled by the Image Processor included with Photoshop. You can open it in Bridge by choosing Tools > Photoshop > Image Processor (in Photoshop, choose File > Scripts > Image Processor). The Image Processor dialog (see **Figure 5-102**) presents a simple four-step process for resizing, converting, and saving a set of images in up to three different formats at once. You can also apply an action to every image.

Figure 5-102 The Image Processor dialog

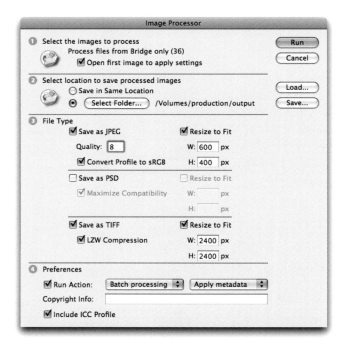

TIP: If you want to run the Image Processor on all of the images in a Bridge window, you don't need to select any. If no images are selected, Image Processor assumes you want to process everything in the Bridge window.

You might be wondering why we dragged you through the Batch dialog when the Image Processor seems to have more image-processing features built right into it. It's the classic trade-off between power and ease of use: Image Processor is an easier way to do certain common tasks, but as you think of more advanced tasks that you could automate you'll find yourself hitting its limitations. For example, the only color conversion you can do is to sRGB, and only for JPEGs. We're big fans of the Image Processor for jobs like a quick batch of JPEGs for a Web site, but a lot of our production tasks can be accomplished only by batch actions.

CHAPTER SIX

Essential Photoshop Tips and Tricks

The biggest speed boost you can give to Adobe Photoshop is to accelerate your own productivity. If you get paid by the hour, rather than by the amount of work accomplished, you may want to skip this chapter. If you want to realize the full potential of Photoshop as a lean, mean, pixel-processing machine, read on! We'll break you of the habit of choosing tools by clicking on their icons, and help you avoid those lengthy mouse voyages up to the menu bar.

Photoshop CS4 brings some of the most sweeping revisions to its user interface thus far, so even Photoshop veterans will want to review this chapter. One of the biggest changes is the ability to take advantage of the graphics processing unit (GPU) in many of today's video cards. GPUs have gotten so powerful that many programs tap into them to take a load off of the central processing unit (CPU), and Photoshop now joins that party. Many of the interactive new navigation tips in this chapter are possible thanks to some help from your video card. (For specifics on which video cards make this possible, see Chapter 1.)

Why would the Photoshop user interface need to be changed? Because the world has changed. Programs now use fewer dialogs and more direct interactivity with objects and views. GPUs make new features possible. The Photoshop team does not change the program for the sake of change; they put in the work only when they sincerely believe that you'll benefit in the long run. We believe that you will.

Window Tips

As applications pile on the panels and options, screen space remains at a premium even as monitor sizes grow. Space is an even bigger challenge if you need to manage multiple windows. Photoshop CS4 makes some radical new changes to window management, most of which we like.

NOTE: In Mac OS X, Photoshop CS4 doesn't include the short-lived Maximize screen mode that debuted in Photoshop CS3. It's been replaced by the application frame.

Use Screen Modes or the Application Frame. Press F to cycle through the available screen modes (see **Figures 6-1 to 6-3**). You can also pick a screen mode from the Screen Mode submenu (under the View menu) or click and hold the Screen Mode icon in the Options bar. Pressing F is so easy that you'll probably go to the View menu only if you're recording an action that plays back a screen mode change.

When users of Photoshop in Windows switch to the Mac, many find it distracting to see the desktop picture and other programs behind their Photoshop windows and panels. To remove this distraction in the Mac version of Photoshop CS4, choose Window > application frame (see **Figure 6-4**). This puts all Photoshop windows and panels inside a sort of master window with a gray background. While it's most common to fill the whole screen with the application frame, in our example we show that the application frame can be made smaller than the screen so that you can have the best of both worlds: a solid gray background for Photoshop while still being able to interact with the desktop for operations such as drag and drop (you can't easily do that with the Full Screen modes).

NOTE: Some Mac users perceive the application frame concept as un-Mac-like, but iPhoto, iDVD, and other Apple programs are presented the same way.

If you're a strict Mac traditionalist, don't worry; the application frame is turned off by default on the Mac. One good reason to use the application frame is to use the n-up view to quickly arrange documents in panes, as we describe later in this section. When the application frame is off, n-up views use regular old floating windows which are harder to keep arranged.

Change the Surrounding Color and Border. All screen modes surround the document with gray except for Full Screen mode, which is black. To change the color, Control-click (Mac) or right-click (Windows) the surrounding area and choose an option from the context menu that appears. You can also change these colors in the Color section of the Interface tab of the Preferences dialog. (You can't change the application frame background color.) Next to the Color section is the Border section, new in Photoshop CS4, where you can specify whether the image edge should be a line or a drop shadow. You can also get rid of the border altogether.

Figure 6-1 Standard screen mode while clicking the Screen Mode button on the Options bar

Figure 6-2 Full Screen with Menu Bar screen mode

Figure 6-3 Full Screen mode; panels are hidden by default but tools are still accessible using shortcuts

Figure 6-4 The application frame almost but not quite maximized, to allow drag and drop with other programs

Multiple Views of the Same Document. Are you often jumping back and forth between two views? For example, between different magnifications, color modes, or preview modes? If so, consider opening a second window by selecting Window > Arrange > New Window and setting it to the alternative view. Whenever you change something in one window, Photoshop updates the other window almost immediately.

Tidy Up Your Windows. The traditional Window > Arrange submenu commands have always been a quick way to cascade or tile multiple document windows. Photoshop CS4 adds a couple of new features here: tabbed windows and n-up windows.

TIP: In Photoshop CS4, you can resize a window, panel, or application frame from any edge—even on the Mac.

⊕ **TIP:** If a document opens zoomed out too far, try closing panels. Photoshop wants to show you the whole document when you first open one, and there's less space to show everything when more panels occupy the workspace.

- Tabbed windows. If you've used tabs in your Web browser, you already know how this works. Instead of having to manage many windows, you collect them into a single window with a tab for each document. To combine windows into tabs, just drag one window's title bar to another window's title bar until you see a thick blue border at the bottom of the destination window, then release the mouse (see **Figure 6-5**). You can pull them apart in the same way. If you have many windows to tab together or many tabs to pull apart, choose Arrange > Consolidate Windows into Tabs or Arrange > Float All in Windows, respectively. You might find it faster to manage these windows through the Arrange Documents button on the Application bar. You can even have tabs within multiple floating windows—handy for multiple monitors.

- N-up windows. *N-up* is a generic way to refer to a view that displays multiple documents side by side, such as 3-up or 8-up views (see **Figure 6-6**). For example, in a 3-up view, three documents appear as three panes in a single window. We find arranging multiple windows to be much easier in Photoshop CS4.

  To use a preset n-up view, select one of the n-up icons from the Arrange Documents icon menu in the application bar. In Mac OS X, if the application frame is off, the documents are arranged as floating windows instead of tabbed panes.

Figure 6-5 Drag one document's title bar to another title bar, and when you see a blue border, release the mouse. The first document becomes a tab in the second document window.

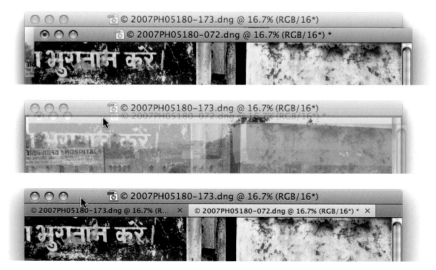

Figure 6-6 The Arrange Documents button in the Application bar lets you create n-up views quickly, such as this 3-up view.

To manually create paned n-up views, drag a document title bar or tab to any edge of any document; when you see a blue border release the mouse. (In Mac OS X, the target document must be in an application frame.)

You can freely combine tabs and an n-up view. In Figure 6-6, a tab for an untitled document shares the left pane with the bicyclist photo. In addition, you can use floating windows along with the application frame.

Flip Through Windows or Tabs. Use your operating system's standard keyboard shortcut to cycle quickly through the open Photoshop windows and tabs—press Command-~ (tilde) in Mac OS X or Ctrl-Tab in Windows. This way you can cycle through every tab in every window without touching the mouse. Add the Shift key to cycle in the opposite order.

From a Document to Its Folder. In Mac OS X, open the folder that contains a saved document by Command-clicking the filename in the document window's title bar and selecting the folder from the pop-up menu that appears. This tells Photoshop to switch to the desktop and open that folder. In Windows, you can reveal a document's file system path by holding the mouse over a document's title bar until a tool tip appears.

TIP: If it takes too long to cycle to a specific document using the keyboard, it may be faster to choose the name of the document from the Window menu.

TIP: If your non-English Mac keyboard has no tilde key, the old Control-Tab shortcut still works in Photoshop CS4.

NOTE: Revealing folder paths works only for saved documents in floating windows, not in tabs.

Navigation Tips

It's funny, but we find that even expert users forget or never learn this basic stuff, so we urge you to read this section even if you think you already know all there is to know about navigating Photoshop. Reviewing this section is mandatory even for Photoshop veterans, thanks to the grab bag of new GPU-assisted navigation goodies brought to us by Photoshop CS4.

Zooming Tips

Images have pixels. Computer monitors have pixels. But how does one type of pixel relate to the other? When one image pixel is displayed on one monitor pixel, you're seeing every detail of the image. In Photoshop, this happens at 100 percent magnification, or the View > Actual Pixels command. This view doesn't necessarily tell you how big the image will appear in print or even on the Web, because different monitors have different resolutions.

At 400 percent, the image is magnified four times, so each image pixel is displayed using 16 monitor pixels (see **Figure 6-7**). At 50 percent, you're seeing only one-quarter of the pixels in the image, because zooming out causes Photoshop to downsample four image pixels to one monitor pixel. At percentages other than 100, then, you're not seeing an accurate view of your image because you aren't seeing the exact number of pixels in the image.

Figure 6-7 How magnification affects the image detail you see

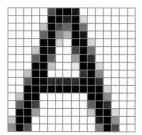 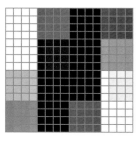 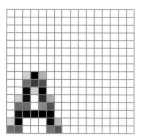

At 100% magnification, (Actual Pixels view) 1 monitor pixel represents 1 image pixel

At 400% magnification, 16 monitor pixels represent 1 image pixel

At 50% magnification, 1 monitor pixel represents 16 image pixels

When you're viewing at an integral multiple of 100 (such as 25, 50, 200, or 400 percent), Photoshop displays image pixels evenly. At 200 percent, four screen pixels (two horizontal, two vertical) equal one image pixel; at 50 percent, four image pixels equal one screen pixel, and so on. However, at magnifications that aren't a factor of two, Photoshop can't cut a screen pixel or an image pixel in half, so instead it fakes the effect using anti-aliasing.

Magnifications other than Actual Pixels (100 percent) can give you a distorted view of resolution-dependent effects such as sharpening. Always return to Actual Pixels magnification to see your image most accurately. You'll be doing this all the time, so learn the shortcuts: Command-Option-0 (zero) (Mac) or Ctrl-Alt-0 (Windows), or double-click the Zoom tool in the Tools panel.

Quick Access to the Zoom Tool. We never select the Zoom tool from the Tool panel because it takes too long. You can temporarily switch to the Zoom tool by holding down Command-spacebar to zoom in or Command-Option-spacebar to zoom out (Mac), or Ctrl-spacebar to zoom in or Ctrl-Alt-spacebar to zoom out (Windows). Each click is the same as choosing Zoom In or Zoom Out from the View menu.

NOTE: Zooming doesn't extend the document under the edges of panels unless you're in one of the Full Screen modes.

Zoom Precisely and Naturally. If you're new to Photoshop, or you're used to older versions, you might have the habit of zooming into an area by clicking over and over again until you hit the right magnification and location. Photoshop gives you not one but two better ways to do this.

Instead of clicking the Zoom tool, drag a rectangle around the area you want to fill; the area you drag magnifies to fill the window. The Zoom tool in Photoshop CS4 also offers *continuous zooming*: Instead of clicking or dragging, hold down the Zoom tool on the area you want to magnify, and Photoshop zooms in smoothly. When you reach the zoom level you want, let go of the mouse button. Continuously zooming out works the same way, but with the addition of the Option key (Mac OS X) or Alt (Windows) key. If you use a Mac laptop with a multitouch trackpad, you can zoom by using the two-finger pinch gesture in Mac OS X.

NOTE: Continuous zooming requires a video card that meets the specifications we described in Chapter 1, "Building a Photoshop System."

Zoom with Keyboard Shortcuts. Zoom in and out by pressing Command-+ (plus sign) or Command-− (minus sign) in Mac OS X, or by pressing Ctrl-+ (plus sign) or Ctrl-− (minus sign) in Windows. By default in Mac OS X, a window resizes when you zoom it; it doesn't resize in Windows by default. If you prefer the opposite behavior, toggle the Zoom Resizes Windows check box in the General Preferences dialog.

Zoom with the Scroll Wheel. If your mouse has a scroll wheel, you can use it to scroll or zoom. To switch between scrolling and zooming, press Option (Mac) or Alt (Windows). To set the default behavior, toggle the Zoom with Scroll Wheel check box in the General Preferences dialog.

TIP: When you zoom in to at least 500% magnification, Photoshop CS4 can display a faint pixel grid to help you tell where pixels start and end, if you have a video card that meets the specifications we described in Chapter 1, "Building a Photoshop System." If you don't like this feature, turn off View > Show > Pixel Grid.

Fit the Image Within the Window. Double-clicking on the Hand tool is the same as clicking Fit Screen in the Options bar when the Zoom tool or Hand tool is selected, or pressing Command-0 (zero) (Mac) or Ctrl-0 (Windows)—it makes the image and the document window as large as possible without going outside the screen's boundaries. The image may not zoom to the full width or height of the monitor if panels are present.

Zoom Numerically. At the bottom left corner of the document window or Navigator panel is the current magnification percentage. This isn't just a display: Double-click to select the whole field, type the zoom percentage you want, then press Return or Enter (see **Figure 6-8**).

Figure 6-8 The zoom field

Type the zoom percentage you want here, then press Return or Enter.

Calibrate the Print Size Command. Generations of Photoshop users have been baffled by the View > Print Size command, because it never seems to match the size of the image when they actually print! In fact, there is a way to make it work. The only way the Print Size command can know the actual print size is to know the resolution of your monitor so that the rulers become accurate. To make Print Size work right, do the following:

1. Open the Displays system preference (Mac) or the Displays control panel (Windows), and note your monitor's current resolution setting (for example, 1280 × 854 pixels).

2. Grab an actual, real-world ruler and measure the width of your monitor image (not the frame in inches). Be careful not to scratch your screen!

3. Divide the horizontal pixel dimension of your monitor by the horizontal real-world dimension of your monitor. For example, my wide-screen LCD monitor is set to 1680 pixels across a physical width of 17 inches, and 1680/17 = 98.8 pixels per inch.

4. Open the Preferences dialog, click Units and Rulers, and enter your pixels per inch value into the Screen Resolution field (see **Figure 6-9**).

Enter the screen resolution of your monitor into this preference in the Units and Rulers pane of the Preferences dialog.

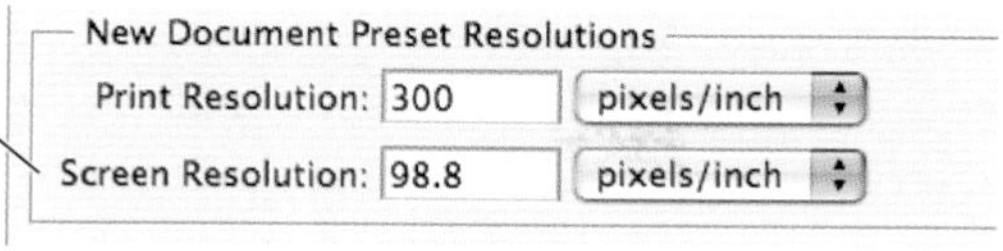

```
┌─ New Document Preset Resolutions ─────────
│   Print Resolution: [300  ]  [pixels/inch ▲▼]
│   Screen Resolution: [98.8 ]  [pixels/inch ▲▼]
```

Figure 6-9 Setting the screen resolution for accurate Print Size

Now when you choose View > Print Size, Photoshop can take into account both your screen resolution and the resolution of the image in the Image > Image Size dialog, and correctly display the printed size of the image. Another wonderful result of all this is that your rulers now match the real world at Print Size magnification. If the rulers don't match exactly, adjust the Screen Resolution field slightly until they do.

Sync Up Your Windows. When you're working in multiple windows, it's often helpful to sync up their views. Several commands on the Window > Arrange submenu automate this process. Match Zoom synchronizes the zoom level, Location synchronizes the positions of images in windows, and the new Rotation command synchronizes the rotated views (more on that soon). The command we find most useful on that submenu is Match All.

TIP: After you match up windows, you can zoom or move them together using the Shift key tip below.

Moving the View

If you're like most Photoshop users, you find yourself moving the image around a lot. There are much better ways than using the window scroll bars, which are so 20th century that we hardly use them anymore.

Faster, More Advanced Window Panning. In addition to the traditional ways to push an image around the screen, Photoshop CS4 adds new GPU-assisted window navigation features such as the following:

- The Hand tool. Hold down the spacebar (to get the Hand tool) and drag. In Full Screen mode, use the Hand tool to slide past the edge of the image into the gray or black area, no matter how far you're zoomed in; going past the edge is something scroll bars can't do. Scrolling past the image edge is useful when you're cropping or retouching close to the edge of an image, and it's a big reason Conrad prefers Full Screen mode over the Standard screen mode.

- Flick panning. Photoshop CS4 features a new panning mode that lets you "toss" an image across the screen. If this sounds strange, it isn't really: If you've thrown the screen around on an iPhone or in Google Earth, you already know this gesture: Drag quickly and release the

TIP: To use the Zoom or Hand tool on every open image window at the same time, hold down the Shift key as you click the Zoom tool or drag the Hand tool. The Options bar includes a Zoom All Windows or Move All Windows check box if you don't want to hold down the Shift key.

mouse button before you stop dragging. The image continues moving across the screen, slowing to a stop. If you prefer the traditional behavior, turn off Enable Flick Panning in the General pane of the Preferences dialog. Flick panning doesn't help much for short moves, but it does save effort in a very large image such as a panorama.

NOTE: Flick panning and bird's-eye view require a video card that meets the specifications we described in Chapter 1, "Building a Photoshop System."

- Bird's-eye view. Hold down the H key and drag; this temporarily zooms out a magnified view and displays a rectangle that represents the part of the image that fits the window at the current magnification. Drag the rectangle to another area of the document and release the mouse to restore the original magnification at the new area (see **Figure 6-10**). If the document is smaller than its window, the same gesture zooms to fill the window. This is much cooler to try than to read about!

Figure 6-10 Bird's-eye view

 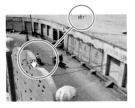 

The original zoomed-in view of the image

Hold down the H key and drag the bird's eye rectangle to a new position on the image.

Release the mouse to snap the view back to the original magnification.

TIP: Rotating the view can be useful when working on a document with upside-down text (as in a card to be folded over) or when you're painting or retouching with a tablet.

- View rotation. Don't confuse view rotation with image rotation. When you rotate the image, it's altered permanently. View rotation changes only the screen display, like magnification. To rotate the view, select the new Rotate View tool (press R) and drag it; you'll see a compass icon in the middle of the window (see **Figure 6-11**) as well as view rotation options in the Options bar. If you use a Mac notebook with a multi-touch trackpad, you can use the Mac OS X two-finger rotation gesture.

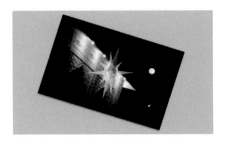

Figure 6-11 View rotation with compass indicator; red points to the original top edge

End Up Down Home. Many people ignore the very helpful Page Up, Page Down, Home, and End keys when working in Photoshop, but we find them invaluable for perusing an image for dust, scratches, or other defects.

When you press Page Up or Page Down, Photoshop scrolls the image by one whole window of pixels up or down. Although there's no Page Left or Page Right button, you can jump one window of pixels to the left or right by pressing Command-Page Up or Command-Page Down in Mac OS X, or Ctrl-Page Up or Ctrl-Page Down in Windows. You can scroll in 10-pixel increments by adding the Shift key to any of these shortcuts.

Also note that pressing the Home button jumps you to the top left corner of the document, and the End button jumps you to the bottom right corner. David often uses this technique when using the Crop tool to quickly adjust the top left and bottom right corners.

TIP: If you're on a laptop, the Page Up, Page Down, Home, and End key functions may be overlaid with the arrow keys. For example, to use Page Up on a Mac , add the Fn key at the bottom left corner of the keyboard, so that you press Fn-up arrow to get Page Up.

Context-Sensitive Menus. When you right-click or Control-click (Mac), Photoshop displays a context-sensitive menu that changes depending on the tool you have selected in the Tool panel. Context menus are so accessible that they're worth trying out with any tool you use (see **Figure 6-12**).

Figure 6-12 The context menu for the Move tool, displaying available layers under the cursor

For brush or retouching tools, the context menu is a quick way to customize the brush. The context menu for the Move tool lets you select a layer; if you have four layers in an image and three of them overlap in one particular area, you can pop up the context menu there to choose which of the three layers you want to select. If the Move tool isn't selected, you can almost always get its context menu by Command-Control-clicking in Mac OS X or Ctrl-right-clicking in Windows.

The context-sensitive menu for the Marquee tool contains a mishmash of features, including Delete Layer, Duplicate Layer, Load Selection, Reselect, Color Range, and Group into New Smart Object (we have no idea why

Adobe picked these and left others out). Many of these features don't have keyboard shortcuts, so the context menu is the fastest way to get to them.

Navigator Panel. If you like to use the Navigator panel (see **Figure 6-13**) to move around in a magnified window, instead try the similar but much more convenient bird's-eye view and continuous zooming features in Photoshop CS4. The only reasons left to prefer the Navigator panel are if your video card won't support the new zoom features, or if you want to have a numeric magnification field to type into when in a Full Screen mode.

Figure 6-13 The Navigator panel

Moving Tips

Before we talk about moving things around, it's useful to understand that in Photoshop, more than one type of move may be available at any one time. For instance, if you've selected an area on a layer, you can move either the selection boundary or the selected content (such as pixels) (see **Figure 6-14**). Your choice will dictate which tool or keyboard shortcut you use.

TIP: With the Move or Path Selection tool, you don't have to worry about positioning the mouse before you drag—just drag anywhere within the document window.

If you simply make a selection and then drag it with one of the selection tools, you move the selection boundary but not the selected layer content. If you want to move the content, use the Move tool (press M). When another tool is selected, you can always get the Move tool temporarily by holding down the Command (Mac) or Ctrl (Windows) key. In Photoshop CS4 you can also use the Move tool temporarily by holding down the V key and then releasing it when you are done. (Note that if you want to move a path or shape, use the Path Selection or Direct Selection tool instead.)

When you move or copy selected pixels with the Move tool, you get a floating selection, which is like a temporary layer that disappears when you deselect. While the selection is still floating, you can use the Edit > Fade command to control how it blends in with the underlying layer.

Original selection | Moving the selection with a selection tool | Moving layer content with the Move tool

Figure 6-14 Moving a selection versus moving layer content

Our selection tips don't apply only to selected pixels. They'll also work on objects like a selected path, a type layer, or the currently selected layer or layer mask in the Layers panel. Most of the tips also work on the selection boundary itself if you choose Edit > Transform Selection first.

Move Precisely. If it's hard to keep your hand steady when working precisely, try using the arrow keys and the Options bar instead of the mouse.

With the Move tool selected, each press of an arrow key moves the layer or selection by 1 pixel. If you add the Shift key, the selection moves 10 pixels. Modifier keys work, too: Hold down the Option key (Mac) or Alt key (Windows) when you first press an arrow key, and the selection is duplicated, floated, and moved 1 pixel (don't keep holding down the Option/Alt key after that unless you want a *lot* of duplicates). Remember that you can always get the Move tool temporarily by adding the Command key (Mac) or Ctrl key (Windows) to any of these shortcuts.

To move an object or layer precisely by entering *x* and *y* coordinates, choose Edit > Free Transform. (If you're moving the selection boundary, choose Select > Transform Selection instead.) Then enter new coordinates in the Options bar.

Move Multiple Layers. To move multiple layers, select more than one layer in the Layers panel and then drag the Move tool. If you haven't selected multiple layers before, it's just like selecting multiple files in a folder on your desktop: Shift-select the first and last layers that you want; or to select a discontiguous range, Command-click (Mac) or Ctrl-click (Windows) each layer you want to add to the selection.

Drag and Drop Selections and Layers. To move selected pixels (or a layer) from one document to another, drag it from one window into the other (if you've got a selection, remember to use the Move tool, or you'll

TIP: If you want to move an entire layer and the layer is already selected in the Layers panel, just drag the Move tool to drag the entire layer right away without any additional selection.

TIP: Is a selection snapping to an edge, and you don't want it to snap? As you drag, press the Control key to temporarily override snap behavior.

just move the selection boundary itself). Again, dragging requires less memory than copying and pasting. If you're trying to copy an entire layer, click its thumbnail in the Layers panel and drag it to the other document's window. Either way, if you want to drop the selection smack in the exact center of the destination document, Shift-drag instead.

Copy Pixels. If you select pixels and choose Edit > Copy, you get only the pixels on the currently active layer(s) (the one(s) selected on the Layers panel). To copy selected pixels across all visible layers, select Copy Merged instead (Command-Shift-C in Mac OS X, Ctrl-Shift-C in Windows).

Some people use this technique to make a merged copy of the entire image (not just a selection). It works, but it's actually more efficient to choose Layer > Duplicate Layers and then choose New from the Destination pop-up menu to merge all layers and send them to a new document in one step. If you're just trying to turn selected pixels into a new layer, press Command-J (Mac OS X) or Ctrl-J (Windows), the shortcut for Layer > New > Layer via Copy—it's more efficient than copying and pasting.

Paste Pixels. In the most common color modes, such as RGB and CMYK, pasting pixels into a document automatically creates a new layer. When a selection is active, you'll also see the Edit > Paste Into command (Command-Shift-V in Mac OS X, or Ctrl-Shift-V in Windows), which adds a new layer with a layer mask based on the selection so that the pixels you're pasting appear only inside the selection. If you add the Shift key to the Paste Into keyboard shortcut, the pixels you're pasting appear only outside the selection, because adding Shift inverts the layer mask that's created.

GUIDES, GRIDS, AND ALIGNMENT TIPS

Moving pixels is all very well and good, but where are you going to move them? If you need to place pixels with precision, you should use the ruler, guides, grids, and alignment features. The ruler is the simplest: You can hide or show it by pressing Command-R (Mac) or Ctrl-R (Windows). Wherever you move your cursor, you can track its position using the tick marks that appear in the rulers (or the coordinates on the Info panel).

Guides. You can add a guide to a page by dragging it out from either the horizontal or vertical ruler (see **Figure 6-15**). Or if you care about specific placement, you can watch the ruler tick marks or the Info panel coordinates,

---

TIP: To drag a layer to another tab, drag from the document window (not the Layers panel) and hold the mouse over the destination tab for a moment until it switches over.

TIP: Making a selection and using the Paste Into command (or the Paste Outside feature that you get by adding the Shift key) lets you create both a layer and a layer mask in one step.

or select View > New Guide so you can type in a numeric position. (If you don't think in inches, you can change the default measurement system; see "Switch Units," later in this chapter.) **Table 6-1** lists a number of grids and guides keystrokes that can help you use these features effortlessly.

Table 6-1 Grids and guides keystrokes.

To do this . . .	. . . press this:
Hide/Show Extras (grids, guides, etc.)	Command-H (Mac) Ctrl-H (Windows)
Hide/Show Guides	Command-' (apostrophe) (Mac) Ctrl-' (Windows)
Hide/Show Grid	Command-Option-' (Mac) Ctrl-Alt-' (Windows)
Snap to Guides	Command-; (semicolon) (Mac) Ctrl-; (Windows)
Lock/Unlock Guides	Command-Option-; (Mac) Ctrl-Alt-; (Windows)

Snap Guides to Ruler Marks. We almost always hold down the Shift key when dragging a guide out from a ruler; that way, the guide automatically snaps to the ruler tick marks. If you find that your guides are slightly sticky as you drag them out without the Shift key held down, check to see what layer you're on. When Snap to Guides is turned on, objects snap to the guides *and* guides snap to the edges and centers of objects on layers.

Switch Guide Direction. Dragged out a horizontal guide when you meant to get a vertical one? No problem: Just Option-click (Mac) or Alt-click (Windows) the guide to switch its orientation (or hold down the Option/Alt key while dragging the guide out of the ruler).

TIP: If you can't move a guide, see if the View > Lock Guides command is on. If it's on, turn it off.

Mirror Guides. If you rotate your image by 90 degrees, or flip it horizontally or vertically, your guides will rotate or flip with it. If you don't want this to happen, choose View > Lock Guides, or press Command-Option-; (Mac) or Command-Alt-; (Windows).

Guides Outside the Image. Just because your pixels stop at the edge of the image doesn't mean your guides have to. You can place guides out on the area surrounding the image and they'll still work. This is just the ticket if you've got a photo that you need to place so that it bleeds off the edge of your image by 0.25 inch.

Change Guides and Grid Specs. Guides are, by default, cyan. Grid lines are, by default, set 1 inch apart. If you don't like these settings, change them in the Guides, Grid & Slices pane of the Preferences dialog, or just double-click any guide with the Move tool.

Smart Guides. If you're working on a highly structured design, you may not need to pull out ruler guides for everything, because Photoshop can sense layer edges and show you when layers are aligned. Choose View > Show > Smart Guides so that when you drag one layer near another, temporary guides appear when any outer edges of the two layers reach the same x or y coordinate (see Figure 6-15), and the selection snaps to the guides.

Figure 6-15 Ruler guides and Smart Guides

Image is already aligned with the vertical ruler guide.

When dragging the type, Smart Guides appear when the type is aligned with the image.

Align and Distribute. Photoshop has alignment and distribution features as powerful as those found in page-layout programs. Alignment lines up layers, and distribution spaces layers evenly between the two outermost selected layers. Here's how you can do all that:

1. Select two or more layers in the Layers panel (see **Figure 6-16**).

TIP: Sometimes it's faster to use Smart Guides than to set up and use the alignment features.

2. To align or distribute specific layers, make sure no pixels are selected by choosing Select > Deselect or pressing its shortcut, Command-D (Mac) or Ctrl-D (Windows).

   To align or distribute layers within a specific area, use the Rectangular Marquee tool to drag a selection boundary. To align or distribute to the canvas size, make sure the Background layer is one of the selected layers, or choose Edit > Select All. When a selection exists, the Layer > Align command changes to Align Layers to Selection.

3. Press V to activate the Move tool, and then click on one of the Align buttons in the Options bar.

Options bar

Figure 6-16 Aligning layers using the Options bar with the Move tool selected

Layers selected in
the Layers panel

Before aligning
and distributing

Tops distributed and
Select All applied

After aligning cen-
ters horizontally

Align or Distribute to a Specific Object. Normally, when you align along the left edges, Photoshop moves all the layers except for the one that has the leftmost data (or the rightmost data when aligning right, and so on). You can force Photoshop to lock one layer and move the others by *linking* the layers: Select the layers, click the Link icon at the bottom of the Layers panel, then click on the layer you want to remain in place. Now when you choose from the Align or Distribute submenu, all the layers move except for the currently selected layer.

When distributing layers vertically, Photoshop distributes layers between the highest and lowest selected layers; when distributing horizontally it distributes between the leftmost and rightmost layers. All the layers in between are moved. For example, if you choose Vertical Centers from the Distribute Linked submenu, Photoshop moves the layers so that there is an equal amount of space from the vertical center point of one layer to that of the next.

TIP: When the Options bar doesn't display the align and distribute buttons, you can still align and distribute by choosing Layer > Align or Layer > Distribute and then choosing a command from the Align submenu.

DIALOG TIPS

Dialogs seem like simple things, but since you probably spend a good chunk of your time in Photoshop looking at them, wouldn't it be great to be more efficient while you're there? Here are a bunch of tips that will let you fly through those pesky beasts.

Not-So-Modal Dialogs. In Photoshop, just because a dialog is open doesn't mean you can't do anything else. For instance, when the Smart Sharpen dialog is open you can still scroll and zoom the document. You can also use any command that isn't dimmed, particularly commands on the

Window menu. The panel we end up opening most often from inside dialogs is the Info panel, because it gives us readouts of color values.

Scrub-a-Dub-Dub. You can edit values in dialogs by *scrubbing*, or dragging horizontally over a value. For example, if you're in the Image Size dialog, hold down Command (Mac) or Ctrl (Windows) as you position the mouse over any number field. When the cursor appears as a finger with a two-headed horizontal arrow, you can drag left to lower the value, or drag right to raise the value (see **Figure 6-17**). This also works in panels that have number fields, including the Options bar. For faster scrubbing, hold down the Shift key, which multiplies the normal adjustment by ten.

Figure 6-17 Scrubbing a value

Command/Ctrl-drag over most number fields to increase or decrease the value.

Save Your Settings. Many dialogs have Save and Load buttons that let you save to disk all the settings that you've made in a dialog. They're particularly useful when you want to use the same dialog settings on many images.

TIP: In panels, such as the Adjustments panel, you might not see Load and Save buttons. In those cases look for Load Preset and Save Preset commands in the panel menu.

For instance, let's say you're adjusting an image with Shadows/Highlights. You increase this and decrease that, and after you click OK you realize that you'd like to apply the same settings to 50 other images shot under the same conditions. Instead of laboriously entering the same settings 50 times, just click the Save button in the Shadows/Highlights dialog to save the settings as a file. Now you can open the Shadows/Highlights dialog in any other image, click the Load button, and select the settings file you saved. This is useful when you build actions that automate your workflow, because you can have an action load a settings file. You can also send settings files to your colleagues so they can load them.

Instant Replay. There's one other way to undo and still save any tonal-adjustment settings you've made. If you hold down Option (Mac) or Alt (Windows) while selecting a command from the Image > Adjust submenu, the dialog opens with the last-used settings. Similarly, you can add the Option/Alt key to the adjustment's keyboard shortcut. For instance, in Mac OS X, Command-L is the shortcut for Levels, so Command-Option-L opens the Levels dialog with the same settings you last used. This is a great way to specify the same Levels or Curves (or Hue/Saturation, or any other adjustment) for several different images.

Previewing Tips

Most of the tonal- and color-correction features and many filters offer a Preview check box in their dialogs. Plus, most filters that have a dialog include a proxy window that shows the effect applied to a small section of the image (some dialogs have both). If you're working on a very large file on a relatively slow machine, and the filter you're using has a proxy window, you might want to turn off the Preview check box so that Photoshop doesn't slow down by drawing the screen while you're making adjustments. Thanks to today's powerful hardware, we now tend to leave the Preview feature on.

We use the Preview check box to do before-and-after comparisons of our images without leaving the dialog. You can press the P key shortcut to toggle the Preview check box in most dialogs.

Most of the tips that follow usually don't apply to the dialogs for creative filters such as Dry Brush and Plastic Wrap. They use a different dialog that provides a large preview image inside the dialog but not in the main window. We don't really cover those filters because they're more about special effects, and we're more about image correction.

Proxies. The proxy in dialogs shows only a small part of the image, but it updates almost instantly. Previewing time-consuming filters such as Smart Sharpen or Reduce Noise on a large file can take a long time. Some very time-consuming filters such as the Distort filters offer a large proxy instead.

Before and After in Proxies. In most proxies you can see a before-and-after comparison by clicking in the proxy. Hold down the mouse button inside the proxy window to see the image before the filter is applied, and release it to see the image after the filter is applied. This is obviously quicker than redrawing the whole window with the Preview check box.

NOTE A proxy shows only the layer you're working on at any one time, because a dialog affects only the current layer.

Change the Proxy View. To see a different part of the image, click and drag in the proxy (no modifier keys are necessary). Alternatively, you can click in the document itself. The cursor changes to a small rectangle, and wherever you click shows up in the Preview window.

Similarly, you can zoom the proxy in and out. The *slow* way is to click on the little (+) and (-) buttons. Much faster is to click the proxy while pressing the Command (Mac) or Ctrl (Windows) key to zoom in, or the Option (Mac) or Alt (Windows) key to zoom out. However, we rarely zoom in and out, because you see the true effect of a filter only at 100 percent view.

Keyboard Shortcuts in Dialogs

We love keyboard shortcuts. They make everything go much faster, or at least they make it *feel* as though we're working faster. Here are a few shortcuts that we use all the time inside dialogs.

Option/Alt. Hold down the Option (Mac) or Alt (Windows) key in a dialog to change the Cancel button to a Reset button, letting you reset the dialog to its original state (the way it was when you first opened it).

Command-Z/Ctrl-Z. You already know the shortcut Command-Z (Mac) or Ctrl-Z (Windows) because it's gotten you out of more jams than you care to think about. You can use the same shortcut to undo within most dialogs, too. Inside dialogs, you get only one undo step.

TIP: Camera Raw is a dialog that allows more than one step of undo if you also press Option/Alt, or more than one step of redo if you also press Shift.

Arrow Keys. When a dialog contains a number field, you can change those numbers by pressing the up or down arrow key. Press once, and the number increases or decreases by 1. If you hold down the Shift key while pressing the arrow key, the number changes by 10. (Note that some dialog values change by a tenth or even a hundredth; when you hold down Shift, they change by 10 times as much.) This is a great way to fine-tune adjustments without cramping your mouse hand.

A few dialogs use the arrow keys in a different way. In the Lens Flare filter, for instance, they move the position of the effect.

Tab Key. As in most Mac and Windows applications, the Tab key selects the next text field in dialogs with multiple text fields. Press Shift-Tab to move to the previous field instead.

P for Preview. As we mentioned a little earlier, press P to toggle the Preview check box in any dialog that has one.

NEW DOCUMENT TIPS

Before we move on to essential tips about tools, let's take a quick look at the New dialog. For instance, note that the New dialog has an Advanced button; when you click this, you're offered two additional settings: Color Profile and Pixel Aspect Ratio. Color Profile lets you specify a profile other than the working space for your image. (You can choose the default working space too, but since that's what you'd get anyway, it's a bit pointless to choose it here.) Note that we cover working spaces in Chapter 4, "Color Settings." Pixel Aspect Ratio lets you use nonsquare pixels in case your image is destined for video editing.

Preset Document Sizes. The Preset pop-up menu in the New dialog lets you pick from among common document sizes. You may not see very many choices if you click the Preset pop-up menu, but that's because it's a two-stage process: First choose a category from the Preset pop-up menu, and then choose a size from the Size pop-up menu. If you need a preset other than the ones on the list, just set the New dialog the way you want it, then click the Save Preset button (see **Figure 6-18**). You can delete user-created presets with the Delete Preset button, but the built-in ones that ship with Photoshop are there to stay.

TIP: Want the Height and Width to use different measurement units? No problem—hold down the Shift key while selecting a unit of measure.

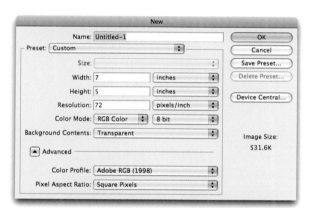

Figure 6-18 The New dialog

When you save a document preset, you can use the check boxes to choose which settings to remember. For example, if you turn off the Profile check box, when you later choose your preset from the Preset pop-up menu, Photoshop will not override the current working space.

Note that some built-in presets (those having to do with video) can also automatically add guides to the document. Unfortunately, there's currently no way to save presets with guides yourself.

Clairvoyant Image Size. The New dialog tries to read your mind. If you have something copied to the Clipboard when you create a new document, Photoshop automatically selects Clipboard from the Preset pop-up menu and plugs the pixel dimensions, resolution, and color model of that copied piece into the proper places of the dialog for you. If you'd rather use the values from the last new image you created, hold down Option (Mac) or Alt (Windows) while selecting File > New, or press Command-Option-N (Mac) or Ctrl-Alt-N (Windows).

Copying Sizes from Other Documents. In the New dialog, notice that all open documents are listed at the bottom of the Preset pop-up menu. If you want your new document to match an open document, simply choose the name of that document in this menu.

KEYBOARD SHORTCUT TIPS

You can change keyboard shortcuts you don't like, and you can add short-cuts and save them as part of a workspace that also includes your favorite panel arrangement and menu customizations. If you share the machine and don't want to confuse others, you can save your keyboard shortcut sets.

TIP: To export a list of every feature and its shortcut, click the Summarize button in the Keyboard Shortcuts and Menus dialog. This file is saved in HTML format, so you can open it in any Web browser and print it from there if you want.

Use Your Own Set. To edit or add a keyboard shortcut, choose Edit > Keyboard Shortcuts or press Command-Option-Shift-K (Mac) or Ctrl-Alt-Shift-K (Windows). If you edit the default set, it's saved as "Photoshop Default (modified)" so that you can revert to the default (just choose Photoshop Defaults from the Set menu). We recommend giving sets useful names; otherwise they can be lost when you choose another set or if you need to reset your preferences while troubleshooting a problem. To save a new set, click the New Set button (see **Figure 6-19**); by default, Photoshop saves the set in the proper location on your hard drive (inside your Photoshop application folder, in Presets > Keyboard Shortcuts).

Figure 6-19 The Keyboard Shortcuts and Menus dialog, showing the Keyboard Shortcuts tab

Click the New Set button to save the current set as a new one.

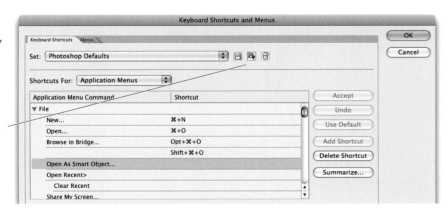

To customize keyboard shortcuts, follow these steps:

1. Pick Application Menus, Panel Menus, or Tools from the Shortcuts For pop-up menu.

2. Click an expansion triangle to reveal menu commands, and then select a command or tool from the list.

3. When the field in the Shortcut column is highlighted, you can type the keyboard shortcut you want to apply to this feature. If the shortcut is already in use, Photoshop alerts you and gives you choices.

4. To create another shortcut for the same feature (the flexibility is nice sometimes), click the Add Shortcut button. If you're done with this feature and want to change another, click the Accept button. When you're done applying shortcuts, click OK.

Note that you can edit or add keyboard shortcuts for panel menus and tools in addition to regular menu commands. You can even save shortcuts for commands added by third-party features, such as plug-ins added to the File > Import and File > Automate submenus, filters, and scripts.

Resolve Conflicts with Mac OS X Shortcut Keys. When Apple introduced Mac OS X, they started using some keyboard shortcuts that conflicted with several long-established Photoshop shortcuts. For example, Command-H (Hide Selection) was used for Hide Application by Mac OS X, Command-M (Curves dialog) was used for Minimize Application, and Command-~ (tilde) was used for cycling application windows. This tripped up Mac users and Photoshop veterans switching among Mac programs.

By default the Photoshop keyboard shortcuts always win, although you can also customize your shortcuts in Photoshop so that they don't conflict with Mac OS X. If you don't do that, you can still use the Hide Application and Minimize Window shortcuts by adding the Control key to the Mac OS X shortcut (press Command-Control-H for Hide Application, for example).

In Photoshop CS4, Adobe decided to take another swing at resolving these shortcut conflicts. Command-~ now cycles through windows, to be consistent with Mac OS X (on both platforms Ctrl-Tab still matches the Windows convention). This change caused channel viewing shortcuts to change on both platforms (more about this in Chapter 9, "Making Selections").

TIP: If you don't want to apply a new keyboard shortcut and the Shortcut field is still highlighted, press Cancel to back out of the change. Be careful. If you press Cancel a second time, you'll close the dialog without saving changes.

Menu Customization Tips

If you have trouble remembering which commands apply to your workflow, you can customize Photoshop menus by colorizing or hiding them. We think menu customization works best when you spend most of your time using Photoshop in a very specialized way, or when you're trying to train yourself or others in a specific workflow.

To edit menu commands, choose Edit > Menus or press Command-Option-Shift-M (Mac) or Ctrl-Alt-Shift-M (Windows) to open the Keyboard Shortcuts and Menus dialog. It's the same dialog used for customizing keyboard shortcuts, but when opened with the Menus command, it opens showing the Menus tab (see **Figure 6-20**). As with keyboard shortcuts, you can save your menus as a set. Note that you can't hide the Quit or Close commands in Photoshop.

Figure 6-20 The Menus tab of the Keyboard Shortcuts and Menus dialog

Click the New Set button to save the current set as a new one.

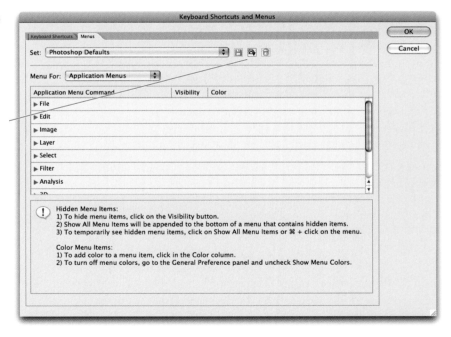

Tips for Tools

While we think it's best to talk about a tool in the chapter where it applies the most (for example, we take a good close look at the Selection tool in Chapter 9, "Making Selections") some tools can be used in more than one area, and those are the tools we'll look at here.

Single-Key Tool Shortcuts. The most important productivity tip we've found in Photoshop is being able to select any tool by pressing one key—no need to press Command or Ctrl. **Figure 6-21** shows the tool shortcuts.

Some tools in the Tools panel keep multiple related tools undercover. For instance, the Dodge tool expands to reveal the Burn and Sponge tools. The slow way to access the different modes is to hold down the mouse on the Tools panel icon to reveal the additional modes. A faster method is to press the tool's keyboard shortcut once to select it, and then press it again with the Shift key to cycle through the choices. Press M once, and you jump to the Rectangular Marquee tool; then press Shift-M, and it switches to the Elliptical Marquee tool; press Shift-M once more, and it switches back to the Rectangular Marquee tool. (Note that this shortcut doesn't cycle through the infrequently used Single Row marquee or Single Column marquee tools.)

Photoshop lets you change this behavior: If you turn off the Use Shift Key for Tool Switch check box in the General pane of the Preferences dialog, you don't have to hold down the Shift key to rotate through the tools; each time you press M, you'll get a different tool. Conrad prefers to use Shift to cycle through tools, because it ensures that pressing a letter key selects the last tool you used in a tool group. If you cycle without Shift and the Tools panel is hidden (as in Full Screen mode), pressing a letter could cycle to another tool in the group that isn't the tool you thought you were using.

Spring-Loaded Keys. New in Photoshop CS4 is the ability to switch to another tool temporarily, by holding down a shortcut key instead of simply pressing and releasing it. For example, in previous versions of Photoshop if you wanted to select an area and move it, you would have had to press L to switch to the Lasso tool and then press V to move the pixels. In Photoshop CS4, if you're already using the Move tool, just hold down L and make the selection, and when you release L you're back to the Move tool. We've found that the spring-loaded feature activates after you hold down a tool for a little more than one second.

TIP: A very efficient way to use Photoshop (or any Adobe Creative Suite software) is the two-handed method: Keep one hand on the mouse or stylus and the other hand over the keyboard, ready to press single-key tool shortcuts. By switching tools using your nonmouse hand on the keyboard, you can keep the mouse over the area you're editing instead of repeatedly pulling the mouse or stylus over to the Tools panel.

Figure 6-21 Tools panel keyboard shortcuts and tool groupings

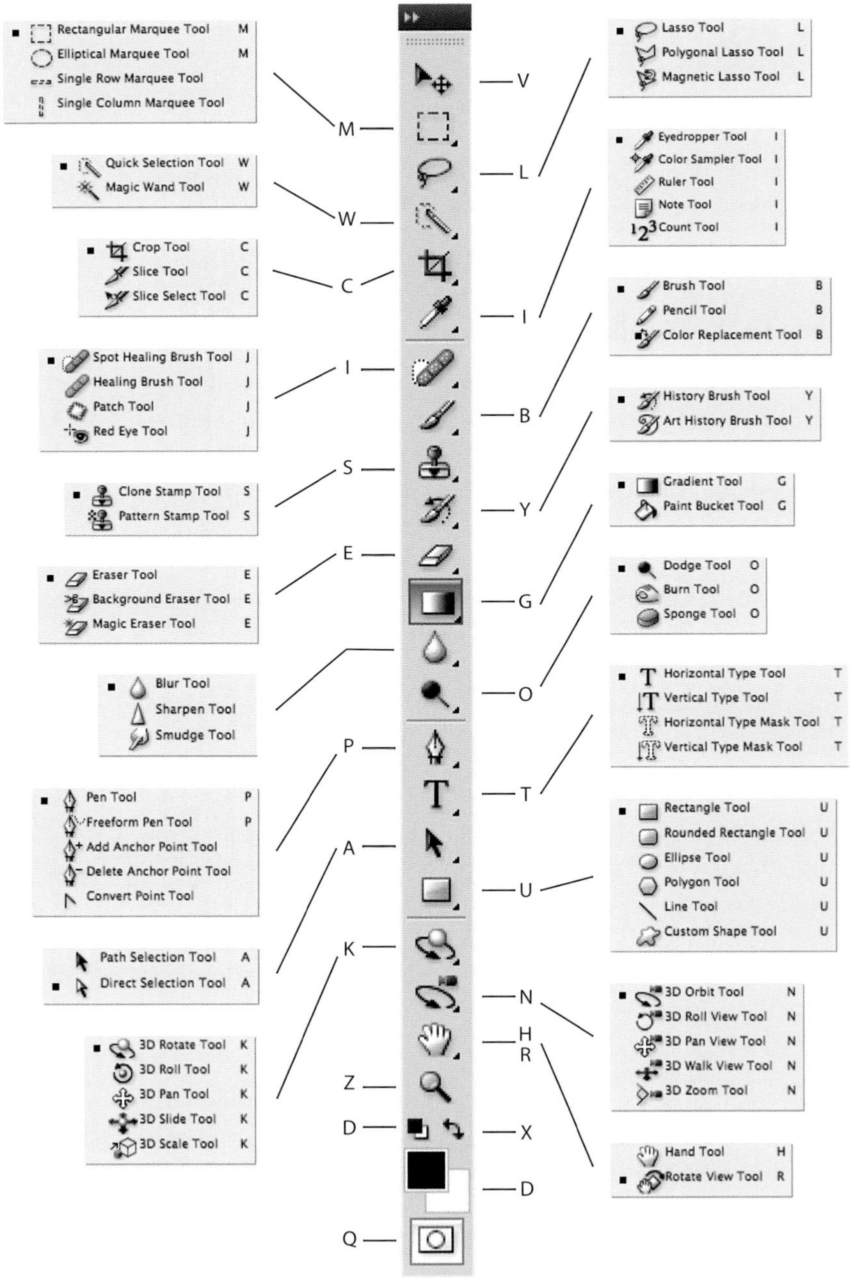

Of course, these shortcuts are just the defaults; you can edit the shortcuts by selecting Keyboard Shortcuts in the Edit menu.

Rectangular Marquee Tool   M
Elliptical Marquee Tool   M
Single Row Marquee Tool
Single Column Marquee Tool

Quick Selection Tool   W
Magic Wand Tool   W

Crop Tool   C
Slice Tool   C
Slice Select Tool   C

Spot Healing Brush Tool   J
Healing Brush Tool   J
Patch Tool   J
Red Eye Tool   J

Clone Stamp Tool   S
Pattern Stamp Tool   S

Eraser Tool   E
Background Eraser Tool   E
Magic Eraser Tool   E

Blur Tool
Sharpen Tool
Smudge Tool

Pen Tool   P
Freeform Pen Tool   P
Add Anchor Point Tool
Delete Anchor Point Tool
Convert Point Tool

Path Selection Tool   A
Direct Selection Tool   A

3D Rotate Tool   K
3D Roll Tool   K
3D Pan Tool   K
3D Slide Tool   K
3D Scale Tool   K

Lasso Tool   L
Polygonal Lasso Tool   L
Magnetic Lasso Tool   L

Eyedropper Tool   I
Color Sampler Tool   I
Ruler Tool   I
Note Tool   I
Count Tool   I

Brush Tool   B
Pencil Tool   B
Color Replacement Tool   B

History Brush Tool   Y
Art History Brush Tool   Y

Gradient Tool   G
Paint Bucket Tool   G

Dodge Tool   O
Burn Tool   O
Sponge Tool   O

Horizontal Type Tool   T
Vertical Type Tool   T
Horizontal Type Mask Tool   T
Vertical Type Mask Tool   T

Rectangle Tool   U
Rounded Rectangle Tool   U
Ellipse Tool   U
Polygon Tool   U
Line Tool   U
Custom Shape Tool   U

3D Orbit Tool   N
3D Roll View Tool   N
3D Pan View Tool   N
3D Walk View Tool   N
3D Zoom Tool   N

Hand Tool   H
Rotate View Tool   R

Activate the Opposite Tool. Some tools have an opposite, kind of like an evil twin, except that the opposite tool isn't evil (perhaps just misunderstood). When you're using one of these tools, you can switch to its opposite by pressing Option (Mac) or Alt (Windows). For example, if you're using the Blur tool, pressing Option/Alt temporarily changes it into the Sharpen tool. The same thing happens with the Dodge and Burn tools.

Change a Tool's Blending Mode. You can change blending modes (Normal, Screen, Multiply, and so on) by pressing Shift-– (minus sign) and Shift-+ (plus sign). If a painting tool is selected (such as the Brush tool), this changes the mode of the selected tool. If the selected tool doesn't use blending modes, the shortcut escalates to change the mode of the current layer.

Belly Up to the Options Bar. To enter a value in the Options bar, there's no need to move the mouse up there. Select a tool, press Return or Enter, and the first number field in the Options bar becomes selected and ready for you to enter a value. If the Options bar was hidden, press Return or Enter twice: once to display the Options bar, and again to activate a value.

TIP: As in any panel or dialog, in the Options bar you can move among fields by pressing Tab and Shift-Tab. Press Return or Enter to return to the image.

Brush Tips

Use the Brushes panel to customize Photoshop brushes (see **Figure 6-22**). Brush presets aren't only for the Brush tool—they also work with any tool that paints, such as the Clone Stamp tool and the History Brush tool. The wide range of options is valuable for detailed retouching tasks.

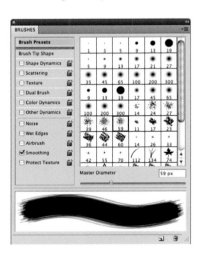

Figure 6-22 The Brushes panel, with brush presets on the right and a brush preview on the bottom

Brush Shortcuts. We've listed brush shortcuts in **Table 6-2**. Note that the Resize Brush and Change Brush Hardness shortcuts include ways to edit brush size and hardness by dragging the brush with modifier keys pressed; these are new in Photoshop CS4.

Opacity By the Numbers. Table 6-2 includes shortcuts for brush opacity, but note that if the Airbrush feature in the Options bar is turned on, typing numbers affects the Flow percentage rather than the Opacity setting.

Table 6-2 Brush shortcuts.

To do this . . .	. . . do this:
Resize brush	Press [to reduce and] to increase, or Ctrl-Option-drag (Mac OS X) or Alt-drag (Windows)
Change brush hardness	Press Shift- [to reduce and Shift-] to increase, or Ctrl-Command-Option-drag (Mac OS X) or Alt-Shift-drag (Windows)
Change brush opacity	To set 10 percent through 90 percent, type 1 through 9 To set 100 percent, type 0 To set any other number, type two numbers quickly
Select brush presets	Press comma key for previous preset Press period key for next preset

Fast Brush Preset Selection. With a brush tool selected, right-click or Ctrl-click (Mac OS X) the document to bring up a mini-Brushes panel right under the mouse, then double-click the size preset you want and the panel closes. Otherwise press Esc, Return, or Enter to close the panel.

Sample Exactly the Right Layers. If you're working on a multilayer image, you may find yourself frustrated with tools like Smudge, Blur, Magic Wand, or Clone Stamp, when you want to affect more source layers than just the one you're working on. To solve this, use the Sample pop-up menu on the Options bar. (Note that before Photoshop CS3, this was a check box called Use All Layers or Sample Merged.)

TIP: If you need to do a lot of cloning and retouching, the Clone Source panel is indispensable. We cover it in Chapter 11, "Essential Image Techniques."

When Sample is set to Current Layer, the tool acts as though the other layers weren't even there. If you choose All Layers, Photoshop samples from the other visible layers (both above and below it) and acts as though they were merged together. A third option, Current & Below, does what it says.

So what good are these new options? One common use is when you want to patch or clone onto a new empty layer, leaving the original layers intact.

If you're unhappy with the results, you can simply erase the patches on the new layer and try again. Without the Sample menu options, you would be able to paint only on the layer you're sampling. With the Sample pop-up menu, you can choose Current & Below or All Layers to paint on a blank layer while sampling from other layers that remain intact (see **Figure 6-23**).

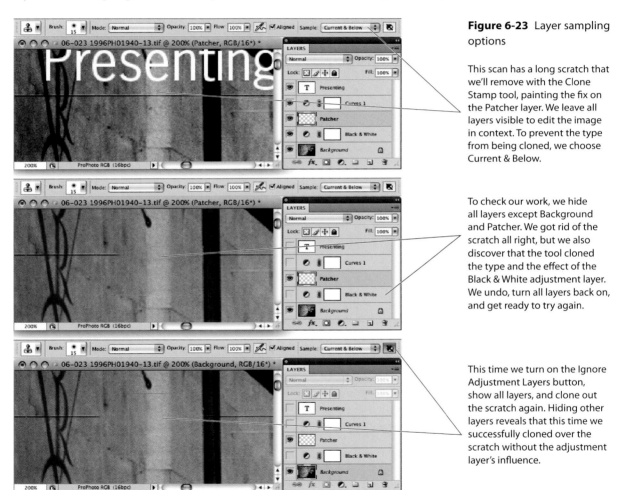

Figure 6-23 Layer sampling options

This scan has a long scratch that we'll remove with the Clone Stamp tool, painting the fix on the Patcher layer. We leave all layers visible to edit the image in context. To prevent the type from being cloned, we choose Current & Below.

To check our work, we hide all layers except Background and Patcher. We got rid of the scratch all right, but we also discover that the tool cloned the type and the effect of the Black & White adjustment layer. We undo, turn all layers back on, and get ready to try again.

This time we turn on the Ignore Adjustment Layers button, show all layers, and clone out the scratch again. Hiding other layers reveals that this time we successfully cloned over the scratch without the adjustment layer's influence.

The button next to the Sample pop-up menu is the Ignore Adjustment Layers button. Before Photoshop CS3, if you cloned or healed in a document that included adjustment layers and you sampled multiple layers, the sample would include the effect of the adjustment layers. This was frustrating, because the sample would not match the rest of the layer, and the adjustment layer would be applied again to the merged sample. We had to remember to turn off adjustment layers before sampling multiple layers and then turn them back on—very frustrating. Ignore Adjustment Layers means that we can leave adjustment layers on and sample multiple layers perfectly. If you want your samples or selections to use only one layer as the source, select the layer and choose Current Layer from the Sample pop-up menu.

Cropping Tips

The nice thing about the Crop tool (as opposed to the Crop feature on the Image menu) is that you can make fine adjustments before committing. Just drag one of the corners or side handles. But you can do a lot more than that.

See What Gets Cropped. By default, Photoshop darkens the area outside the cropping rectangle so that you can see what's going to get cropped out before you press Enter. To adjust this shading, click the color swatch in the Options bar (when the Crop tool is selected) and pick a different color from the Color Picker. There's an Opacity option too. David likes to ghost the cropped-out pixels to near-white, while Conrad likes cropped-out pixels to match the full-screen background color around the image.

Rotate and Move While Cropping. You can crop and rotate at the same time with the Crop tool: After dragging out the cropping rectangle with the Crop tool, just place the cursor outside the cropping rectangle and drag to rotate the rectangle. When you press Return or Enter, Photoshop crops and rotates the image to straighten the rectangle. It can be tricky to get exactly the right angle by eye—keep an eye on the Info panel. Also, if the cropping rectangle isn't in the right place, you can always move it—just place the cursor inside the cropping rectangle and drag.

Retain Cropped Areas. When you crop, you don't have to lose what's beyond the newly cropped edges of the document. After you drag a crop rectangle, click the Hide button on the Options bar; after you commit to the crop, the cropped-out pixels will be remembered as *big data*—material that hangs outside the actual visible image rectangle. Then, if you didn't get the crop just right, you can either move the image around with the Move tool or recrop using a different rectangle (see "Expand the Canvas by Cropping," later in this section). This works only on layers other than the Background layer; to use the Hide feature on the Background layer, double-click it to convert it to a transparency-capable layer.

Cropping May Change Resolution and Resample. The Height, Width, and Resolution fields in the Options bar for the Crop tool save you the step of using the Image Size dialog after cropping, but beware! If you enter a Height and Width into the Options bar for the Crop tool, the resolution of your image will change, as we show in **Table 6-3**. And in some cases the image will also be resampled.

NOTE: You can set the Height, Width, and Resolution values only before you start cropping. Once you draw a cropping rectangle, the Options bar changes to present different options.

Table 6-3 How Crop tool options affect resolution and resampling.

Values entered before crop	Does resolution change?	Is the image resampled?
None	No	No
Height and Width	Yes	No
Height and Width in pixels	Yes	Yes
Resolution	Yes	Yes

What's going on here? Simple math. Because resolution is the ratio of the image's pixel dimensions to its physical dimensions (see Chapter 2), when you alter either variable the resolution must change. That's why the only time resolution doesn't change is when Height, Width, and Resolution are blank, so that dragging a crop rectangle applies no scaling and no resolution change—all it does is chop away a side or two of the image.

The reason resolution must change when you enter pixel dimensions is that Photoshop is forced to take the pixels that make up the crop area and resample them to the pixel dimensions you specifically asked for. There's no mathematical way around that.

To completely eliminate the possibility of resampling when you crop, read on about cropping with the Marquee tool instead of the Crop tool.

TIP: To empty the Width, Height, and Resolution fields in the Options bar, click the Clear button.

Crop to an Aspect Ratio. Let's say you want to crop your image to a 4-by-6 aspect ratio (height to width, or vice versa), but you don't want to resample the image (which adds or removes pixels, causing blurring) or change the image resolution. This is a common requirement in Web design, where pixel-perfect graphics would be ruined by resampling. The Crop tool can't do this without resampling, so you'll need a different technique. Select the Rectangular Marquee tool and choose Fixed Aspect Ratio from the Style pop-up menu in the Options bar. Then enter values in the Height and Width fields (here you'd type *4* and *6*) in the Options bar. Select the area you want cropped, and then select Image > Crop.

Expand the Canvas by Cropping. Once you've created a cropping rectangle with the Crop tool, you can actually expand the crop past the boundaries of the image (assuming you zoom back until you see the gray area around the image in the document window). Then, after you press Enter, the canvas size actually expands to the edge of the cropping rectangle. This is David's favorite way to enlarge the canvas.

TIP: To toggle all snap-to options on or off, choose View > Snap. The shortcut is Command-Shift-; (Mac) or Ctrl-Shift-; (Windows).

Crop Near the Border. If you're trying to shave just a sliver of pixels off one side of an image, you'll find it incredibly annoying that Photoshop snaps the cropping rectangle to the edge of the image whenever you drag close to it. Fortunately, you can turn this behavior off temporarily by unchecking the command View > Snap > Document Bounds. Or you can hold down the Control key to disable snapping temporarily.

Correct Keystone Distortion. The Crop tool offers a cool option: adjusting for perspective. The key is to turn on the Perspective check box in the Options bar after drawing the cropping rectangle; this lets you grab the corner points and move them where you will (see **Figure 6-24**).

Figure 6-24 Correcting keystone distortion with the Crop tool

This sign is distorted because it was shot at an angle. We drag the Crop tool around it, turn on Perspective in the Options bar, and then drag each corner of the cropping rectangle to fit the photo's distorted shape.

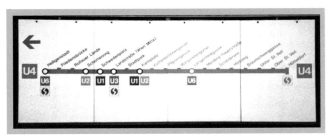

When we press Return/Enter, the Crop tool converts our perspective polygon into a rectangle, correcting the keystone distortion. There is still some barrel distortion, which means we might want to run this image through the Lens Correction filter (Chapter 11).

Positioning the corner points of the crop can be tricky. First find something in the image that is supposed to be a rectangle, and set the corner points on the corners of that shape. For a building, you might choose a wall. Hold down the Option and Shift keys (Mac) or Alt and Shift keys (Windows) while dragging one of the corner handles; this expands the crop but retains its shape. When the crop is the size you want, drag the center point icon to where the camera was pointing (or where you imagine the center of the focus should be). Then press Enter or Return.

Eraser Tool Tips

The Eraser tool has gotten a bad rap because people assume you have to use a big, blocky eraser. No, you can erase using any brush in the Brushes panel—one that's soft, or hard like an airbrush, or even textured. And what's more, you can control the opacity of the Eraser (don't forget that you can just type a number on the keyboard to change the tool's opacity). This makes the eraser fully usable, in our opinion. However, just because a tool is usable doesn't mean you have to use it. Whenever possible, we much prefer masking to erasing. The difference? Masks (which we cover in Chapter 8) can "erase" pixels without actually deleting them. They just hide the data, and you can always recover it later. Nevertheless, the Eraser tool can, on occasion, get you out of a jam. Here are a few tips:

Erase to History. The Erase to History feature (it's a check box on the Options bar when you have the Eraser tool selected) lets you use the Eraser tool to replace pixels from an earlier state of the image (see "When Things Go Wrong," later in this chapter, for more on the History feature). Erase to History more or less turns the Eraser into the History Brush tool. For instance, you can open a file, mess with it until it's a mess, then revert *parts of it* to the original using the Eraser tool with Erase to History turned on.

Watch Preserve Transparency When Erasing. Note that the Eraser tool (or any other tool, for that matter) won't change a layer's transparency when you have the Preserve Transparency check box turned on in the Layers panel. That means it won't erase pixels away to transparency; rather it just paints in the background color. Don't forget that you can turn Preserve Transparency on and off by pressing / (forward slash).

Erase to Transparency. When you use a soft-edged brush to erase pixels from a layer (rather than the Background layer), the pixels that are partially erased—that is, they're still somewhat visible, but they have some transparency in them—cannot be brought back to full opacity. For example, if you set the Eraser to 50 percent opacity and erase pixels from a layer, there's no

TIP: When using the Eraser tool, you can temporarily switch to Erase to History by holding down the Option (Mac) or Alt (Windows) key.

way to get them back to 100 percent again. The reason: You're not changing the pixel's color, only the layer's transparency mask. This isn't really a tip; it's just a warning. What you erase sometimes doesn't really go away.

Gradient Tips

The Gradient tool (press G) is a quick way to create a transition between any two colors, or between color and transparency. A Gradient adjustment layer is an even more flexible way to use an entire layer as a gradient.

Gradient Presets. Some people make hard work of creating a blend that fades away into transparency. They go through endless convolutions of layer masks and channel options, or they spend hours building custom gradients. It doesn't have to be that hard. The Options bar for the Gradient tool offers a pop-up menu with various gradient presets in it (see **Figure 6-25**). By default, these presets include gradients that use transparency. You can create or edit a gradient preset by clicking once on the gradient swatch in the Options bar. You can also select a different set of gradient presets from the pop-up menu to the right of the swatch.

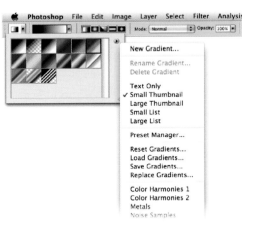

Figure 6-25 Gradient presets and their pop-up menu

Maybe You Don't Need to Use the Gradient Tool. If you've got a layer with nothing on it except a gradient, and you harbor even the slightest suspicion that you might need to edit that gradient later, consider creating it as a gradient layer. It's a kind of adjustment layer that you can edit at any time. To create a gradient layer, choose Layer > New Fill Layer > Gradient, or click the Create New Fill or Adjustment Layer button at the bottom of the

Layers panel and choose Gradient Layer. You can edit its settings by double-clicking it in the Layers panel—much faster and easier than painting it all over again with the Gradient tool! However, if you're creating a gradient on a mask, you'll need to use the Gradient tool.

Avoid Banding in Gradients. On output, a blend in Photoshop can sometimes display banding—tonal or color breaks instead of a smooth transition. This is often a limitation of the specific type of output. A common remedy is to add noise to the blend, which Photoshop does using the Dither check box on the Options bar. Dither is on by default and in most cases should be left on. You can turn it off for uses such as scientific imaging or printing to a very high-quality output device that won't cause banding.

If you still see banding even with Dither turned on, you could apply the Add Noise filter. But instead of applying noise to the entire gradient, try adding it in only a channel or two. View each channel separately (see Chapter 9, "Making Selections") to see where the banding is more prevalent. Then add some noise just to the blend area in that channel.

Better CMYK Blends. If you're going to make blends in images that will end up in CMYK mode, create them in CMYK mode. Sometimes changing modes from RGB to CMYK can give you significant color shifts in blends.

Many custom CMYK profiles produce strange results when you make a blend. In particular, blues tend to have a saturation "hole" and become less saturated when you expect them to become more so. You can often get better results by creating the blend in one of the CMYK working spaces that ship with Photoshop, then assigning your custom profile to the result. The CMYK profiles that come with Photoshop may not represent your exact printing conditions, but they tend to offer much smoother gradients than third-party profiles built with any of the common profiling tools. This is a mildly perverse use of color management, but it works—see Chapter 4, "Color Settings," for more about assigning profiles.

Notes Tips

You can leave notes in a Photoshop document to communicate anything that shouldn't be output or printed with the image. For example, you can leave a note that includes processing guidance for the person on your team who'll edit the image next, or include explanations for students or clients.

The Tools panel in Photoshop CS4 includes a Note tool grouped with the Eyedropper tool (see Figure 6-21). To create a new note, click the Note tool on the document; the Notes panel opens so you can enter text. Select a note to see its text in the Notes panel; if the Notes panel isn't already open, double-click a note. If multiple notes exist in a document, you can use the arrow buttons in the Notes panel to see the previous and next notes.

To delete a note, select it and press the Delete key. To delete every note from a document, right-click or Control-click (Mac OS X) a note and choose Delete All Notes from the context menu.

Changes from Previous Versions. If you've used notes in previous versions of Photoshop, you'll notice that note text now appears in the Notes panel instead of with each note. The Photoshop team also decided to bid adieu to the Audio Annotations tool (we're wondering who's going to notice that one). Also, the former single-key N shortcut for the Note tool now belongs to the 3D viewing tools in Photoshop Extended, so if you use notes enough to want a shortcut for the Note tool, you can define it yourself using the Keyboard Shortcuts and Menus dialog.

Display Note Icons. We usually drag a note icon off to the side so that it doesn't obstruct the view of the image. Conrad likes to keep notes just visible in the corner of an image, because in the past he's missed ones that were outside the image area. To hide notes, press Command-H (Mac) or Ctrl-H (Windows), which toggles the View > Extras command. If you can't see note icons in a Photoshop file but you suspect they're there, make sure the Notes command is selected in the View > Show submenu.

Not Just for Photoshop. If you want to send a Photoshop image with annotations to someone who doesn't have Photoshop, relax. Choose File > Save As to save the image in Photoshop PDF format. In that format, notes can be read using Adobe Acrobat or the free Adobe Reader (in Mac OS X, you can also use Preview), and you can still edit the file using Photoshop.

You can load notes from a PDF document into a Photoshop document. To do this, in Photoshop choose the Note tool, right-click (or Control-click in Mac OS X) on the document, choose Import Notes from the context menu, select the PDF document, and click Load.

Tool Preset Tips

Each tool in the Tools panel offers options, such as the size of a brush's diameter, or whether a selection is feathered, or what mode a tool will paint in (Multiply, Screen, and so on). It's a hassle to remember to set all the tool options, especially if you need to change them frequently. Fortunately, the Tool Presets feature remembers multiple tool settings for you.

Tool presets live in two places: at the far left side of the Options bar and in the Tool Presets panel (see **Figure 6-26**) Choose Window > Tool Presets to open it. The panel is most useful for fine artists who switch among various tool presets, often within the same image. Production folks like us tend to keep the panel closed and select tools from the Tool Presets pop-up menu in the Options bar. One reason that tool presets live on the Options bar is that a tool preset includes the settings you've made in the Options bar.

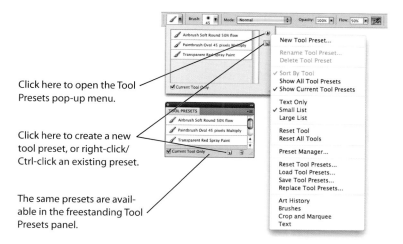

Click here to open the Tool Presets pop-up menu.

Click here to create a new tool preset, or right-click/Ctrl-click an existing preset.

The same presets are available in the freestanding Tool Presets panel.

Figure 6-26 Tool presets their pop-up menu, and the Tool Presets panel

To create a new tool preset, select any tool in the Tools panel, change the Options bar to the way you want it, click the Tool Presets icon in the Options bar, then click the New Tool Preset button. Or even faster, Option-click (Mac) or Alt-click (Windows) the Tool Presets icon in the Options bar. When Photoshop asks you for a name, avoid confusion by giving the tool preset a descriptive name such as "Shape Tool Circle 50c20m."

Photoshop comes with several premade collections of tool presets, such as Art History and Brushes. The trick to finding these (and to doing all sorts of other things with tool presets, like saving your own sets), is to open the

Preset Manager dialog (see **Figure 6-27**) by choosing Preset Manager from the Tools panel menu; the same menu is available in the top right corner of the Tool Presets pop-up menu from the Options bar.

Figure 6-27 The Preset Manager dialog with Brushes presets displayed

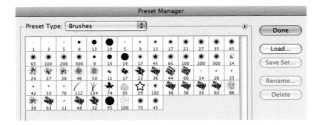

Unfortunately, there's no way to edit a tool preset once you make it—you can only create a new one and delete the old one by choosing Delete Tool Preset from the Tool Preset menu. To reset tool options for either a single tool or for all the tools, Control-click (Mac) or right-click (Windows) on the Tool Presets icon on the Options bar.

Panels and Workspaces

Panels are both incredibly useful when you need them and incredibly annoying when they're in your way, so it pays to get to know them. In this section we talk about panels and workspaces in general, and then we discuss tips for individual Photoshop panels.

Panel Tips

Photoshop uses the same turbocharged workspaces that appear in the rest of the Adobe Creative Suite applications: You can group panels, dock them to the edge of the screen, or move panel groups to other monitors; collapse panels to save space, and collapse panel stacks to maximize screen space.

Save Space. Collapse or expand a panel by double-clicking the tab.

Panel Menus. Most panels have a pop-up menu at the top right corner of the panel. To see it, click the icon that looks like a tiny menu (see **Figure 6-28**). Get to know the panel menus—sometimes it seems as though half of the power of Photoshop is inside the panel menus, which are easy to miss.

Scrubby Sliders. We talked about adjusting number fields by scrubbing them—Command-dragging (Mac) or Ctrl-dragging (Windows) over a number field (see "Dialog Tips" earlier in this chapter). You can do the same thing over number fields in most panels.

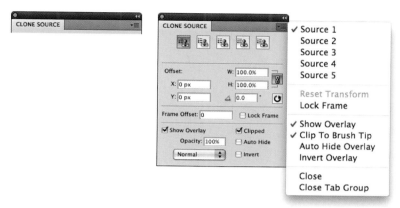

Figure 6-28 Panel features

Panel collapsed by double-clicking its tab

Panel expanded and displaying its panel menu

Rename Panel Items. To rename an item you created in a panel list, such as a layer name, double-click the panel item and type the new name. Text layers are special—they name themselves after the text you've typed and rename themselves if you edit the text. But if you manually rename a text layer, it will no longer update when you edit that layer's text.

Keep Your Options Open. When entering a value in a panel, if you might change your mind, press Shift-Return on Mac OS X or Shift-Enter on Windows. This keeps the field selected so you can enter a different value.

Workspace Tips

Workspaces are extremely useful because there is no one right way to arrange things. When Conrad connects his laptop to a color-calibrated desktop monitor, he likes to use the higher-quality desktop monitor as the main image viewing area and place as many panels as possible on the laptop monitor. When he uses the laptop by itself, there isn't nearly enough room to replicate the two-monitor desktop arrangement so he becomes picky about which panels are visible. To switch instantly between the two panel arrangements, Conrad saved each arrangement as its own workspace.

TIP: If there's anything you want to change about how panels behave, check the Panels & Documents section of the Interface pane in the Preferences dialog. Your wish might already be granted.

TIP: A collapsed stack can be as narrow as a stack of unlabeled icons. If you're still learning what the icons represent, widen a collapsed stack to reveal the labels; or to free up maximum screen space, collapse panels down to icons and use tool tips to see icon names.

Ways to Combine. You can do so much more than just push panels around the screen. **Table 6-4** describes how to get exactly the workspace you want; **Figures 6-29** and **6-30** show you some of the many possibilities.

Table 6-4 Working with panels.

To do this . . .	. . . do this:
Combine panels into one tabbed panel	Drag a tab to the top of another panel
Combine panels into a group	Drag a tab to the sides or bottom of another panel
Collapse or expand one panel	Double-click its tab
Collapse or expand a stack to or from labeled icons	Double-click a stack's top bar or click the double-arrow button
Switch between labeled and unlabeled icons	Drag the left or right edge of a stack
Dock panels to the side of the monitor	Drag a tab or a stack's top bar to the side of the monitor
Hide or show all panels	Press Tab
Temporarily reveal hidden docked panels	Move the mouse to a side edge of the screen until a thick gray line appears
Separate a panel from a stack or group	Drag its tab to an empty area

Figure 6-29 Workspace arrangements

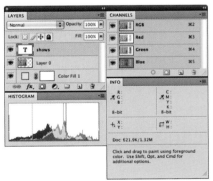

Panels grouped into tabs

Panels stacked vertically

Four panels grouped horizontally and vertically; drag the top bar to move the entire group

Change Tab Order. It's a minor thing, but when panels are in a tabbed group you can drag to change the tab order.

Workspaces are definitely personal. David always keeps his Layers, Channels, and Paths panels together in one tabbed group. When he wants to work with one of these he clicks that panel's tab heading or, better yet, uses a shortcut he defined for the panel. Conrad always keeps his Layers and Channels panels separate because he likes to see multiple views of a document's structure simultaneously. Neither of us ever mixes the Info panel with another panel because we want it to be visible all the time.

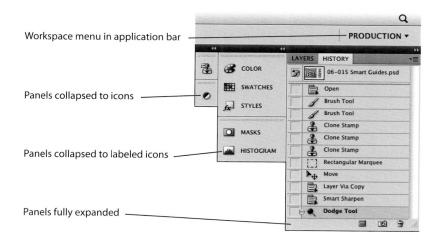

Workspace menu in application bar

Panels collapsed to icons

Panels collapsed to labeled icons

Panels fully expanded

Figure 6-30 Display options for panels docked to one side of the monitor, and the Workspace pop-up menu

The Thin Blue Line. When dragging panels or document windows to combine them, always watch for the blue line at the edge of the destination panel or window (see **Figure 6-31**). It tells you when releasing the mouse will attach a panel to another one. If you see a blue rectangle, that means the panel you're dragging will become a tab within the panel you're dragging to. Figure 6-30 shows you what this looks like.

Save Workspaces. To save a workspace, set up the panels the way you want them, optionally load any custom keyboard shortcut and menu sets, and choose Window > Workspace > Save Workspace. Saved workspaces appear on a workspace pop-up menu at the right edge of the Application bar as well as at the top of the Window > Workspace submenu. For even easier recall, use the Keyboard Shortcuts and Menus dialog to assign keyboard shortcuts to your favorite workspaces.

Workspaces and Monitors. You can dock only to the sides of your main monitor, not to the top or bottom. You can't dock stacks at all on any other connected monitor. However, the new ability to group panels both horizontally and vertically in Photoshop CS4 means you can create "flotillas" of grouped panels and drag the whole lot around on any connected monitor.

TIP: The fastest way to get to a workspace with the mouse is to click the workspace pop-up menu at the right edge of the application bar.

TIP: If you collapse panels to icons and don't like expanded panels to stay open, open the Preferences dialog, click the Interface pane, and turn on Auto-Collapse Iconic Panels.

Figure 6-31 The blue line indicates that panels are about to group or dock.

The rectangular blue line means panels will combine into a single tabbed panel.

A blue line along the side or bottom of a panel means the dragged panel will dock to that edge.

The blue and gray lines along the entire side of a monitor indicate that the panel group will dock to that edge of the monitor.

Layers Panel Tips

We wouldn't give up the flexibility of layers for anything—it's hard to conceive of a time when images were edited using no other layers. We'll be talking about layers a lot, so here we'll present an overview of the Layers panel (see **Figure 6-32**).

Figure 6-32 The Layers panel

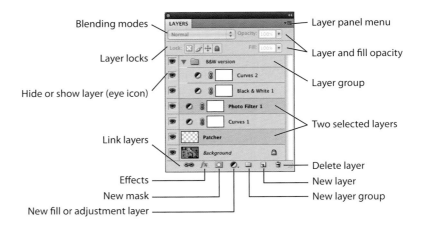

Display and Hide Layers. If you're clicking the eye icons one layer at a time, there's a faster way. Just click and drag through the column for all the layers you want to make visible. When you Option-click (Mac) or Alt-click (Windows) an eyeball in the Layers panel, Photoshop toggles the visibility of all the layers except the one you clicked on, which stays visible.

Create a New Layer. The fast way to create a new layer is to press Command-Shift-N (Mac) or Ctrl-Shift-N (Windows). If you want to bypass the New Layer dialog, press Command-Option-Shift-N (Mac) or Ctrl-Alt-Shift-N (Windows).

Duplicate Layers. Duplicating a layer is a part of our everyday workflow, so it's a good thing there are various ways to do it.

- Drag the layer's thumbnail on top of the New Layer button.

- Option-drag (Mac) or Alt-drag (Windows) the layer's thumbnail to a new position in the Layers panel.

- Press Command-J (Mac) or Ctrl-J (Windows). If some pixels are selected, only those pixels will be duplicated to a new layer.

- Choose the Duplicate Layer command. This command is on the Layer menu, the Layers panel menu, and in the context menu when you right-click or Control-click (Mac OS X) a layer in the Layers panel.

- In the document window (not the Layers panel), Control-click (Mac) or right-click (Windows) a layer with a marquee, lasso, or Crop tool and choose Duplicate Layer from the context menu.

The method you use at any given time should be determined by where your hands are. (Keyboard? Mouse? Coffee mug?)

Select Layers. You can select layers using keyboard shortcuts. To select the next visible layer behind or in front of the current layer, press Option-[or Option-] (Mac) or Alt-[or Alt-] (Windows). To extend the selection to multiple layers, add the Shift key. To select the top or bottom layer, respectively, press Option-. (period) or Option-, (comma) in Mac OS X, or press Alt-. (period) or Alt-, (comma) in Windows.

Automatic Layer Selection. Perhaps the fastest way to select a layer is to click it with the Move tool, but this doesn't happen by default. To set this up, select the Move tool, turn on the Auto-Select check box in the Options bar, and then choose Layer from the Auto-Select pop-up menu. If it isn't active when you want to select a different layer, activate the Move tool temporarily by pressing Command (Mac) or Ctrl (Windows) as you click.

TIP: In Photoshop CS4 you can now delete multiple layers at once. Just select multiple layers in the Layers panel and press the Delete key.

A variation on Auto-Select is to click layer content while pressing modifier keys, skipping the context menu entirely. Using any tool, Command-Option-Control-click (Mac) or Ctrl-Alt-right-click (Windows).

On the other hand, we sometimes find Auto-Select somewhat irritating because it's too easy to select the wrong layer. When that happens, we right-click or Control-click (Mac) layer content and choose the layer we want to select from the context menu that appears.

These techniques typically work only when you click on a pixel that has an opacity greater than 50 percent. (We say "typically" because it sometimes *does* work if the total visible opacity is less than 50 percent. See "Info Panel Tips," later in this chapter.) In general, if you make sure you click on reasonably opaque areas of layers, these techniques should work fine.

Move and Duplicate Layer Masks. In the Layers panel, simply drag a layer mask's thumbnail to a new layer. To duplicate a layer mask, Option-drag (Mac) or Alt-drag (Windows) a layer mask thumbnail.

TIP: If only one layer is visible when you press the layer arrangement shortcuts, Photoshop hides that layer and shows the next layer. This is great for cycling through a number of layers, though it doesn't always work when you have layer groups.

Rearrange Layers. To move the selected layer down or up in the Layers panel with the keyboard, press Command-[or Command-] (Mac) or Ctrl-[or Ctrl-] (Windows). To move the selected layer to the bottom or top of the layer stack, add the Shift key to either shortcut.

Create Layer Groups. The more layers you have in your document, the more difficult it is to manage them. Fortunately, Photoshop offers *layer groups* in which you can work with adjacent layers as a unit. Layer groups work much like the folders on your desktop. Here are the basics:

• Layer groups act like a single layer. When you show, hide, move, or add a mask to the group, it affects all the layers in that group.

• To create a layer group, select the layers you want to group and then press Command-G (Mac) or Ctrl-G (Windows), which is the keyboard shortcut for Layer > Group Layers. You can also click the New Layer Group button in the Layers panel (see Figure 6-32), but then you have to drag layers into the group yourself.

• To add a layer to a group, just drag it on top of the group. Or to create a new layer inside the group automatically, select the group or any layer within the group (in the Layers panel) and click the New Layer button. You can remove a layer from a group simply by dragging it out.

- You can drag a layer group (with all of its layers) to another document.

- You can nest one layer group inside another, up to five levels deep.

Unfortunately, you can't apply a layer effect to a layer group or use a layer group as a clipping mask (see Chapter 8).

Layer Groups and Blending Modes. By default, a layer group's blending mode is set to Pass Through, which means, "let each layer's blending mode speak for itself." In this mode, layers inside the group look the same as they would if they were outside the group. However, if you change the group's blending mode, a curious thing happens: Photoshop first composites the layers in the group as though they were a single layer (following the blending modes you've specified for each layer), and then it composites that "single layer" with the rest of your image using the layer group's blending mode. In this case, layers may appear very differently depending on whether they're inside or outside that group.

Similarly, when you change the opacity of the group, Photoshop first composites the layers in the group (using their individual opacity settings) and then applies this global opacity setting to the result.

Layer Comps Panel Tips

The Layer Comps panel is one of David's favorite features in Photoshop. David loves keeping his options open, and is forever trying to decide among various possibilities. For instance, he'll picture in his mind's eye five different ways to drive to the grocery store before committing to one. The Layer Comps panel won't help him with his driving choices, but it's an awesome help when making decisions about how to edit an image in Photoshop.

The Layer Comps panel is like a clever combination of the Layers panel and the History panel: It lets you save the state of your document's layers so you can return to it later. It might seem that the Layer Comps feature should be part of the Layers panel, but perhaps Adobe figured that the Layers panel was already complex enough. Although the snapshots feature of the History panel can perform most of the same tasks as the Layer Comps panel, the History panel is significantly more memory intensive and—this is important—layer comps can be saved with the document, while snapshots disappear when you close the file. Saving a layer comp makes almost no difference to your file size (each comp is only a few kilobytes on disk).

TIP: To select groups more easily using the Move tool, choose Groups from the Auto-Select pop-up menu on the Options bar for the Move tool.

To create a layer comp, click the New Layer Comp button in the Layer Comps panel (see **Figure 6-33**). Photoshop displays the New Layer Comp dialog, which lets you name the layer comp (it's easy to lose track of what each layer comp represents), specify which settings Photoshop should remember, and insert a comment about the comp.

Figure 6-33 Layer comps

Enabling a different layer comp applies a different saved set of layer visibility, appearance, and position attributes.

To create a new layer comp, click this button.

To cycle through and compare layer comps, click these buttons.

To update a selected layer comp with recent layer changes, click this button.

Photoshop can remember three kinds of information about your layer comps: visibility, position, and appearance.

- By default, layer comps just remember the *visibility* of each layer—that is, which layers and layer groups are visible and which are hidden.

- When you turn on the Position check box, the layer comp remembers the position of the layer content. For example, suppose that you save a layer comp with Position turned on and then reposition the image or text on that layer. When you return to the saved layer comp, the image or text reverts back to where it was when you saved the comp.

- The Appearance option remembers any layer effects and blending modes that you've applied to your layers. For example, let's say you save a layer comp with Appearance turned *off*, then you change the blending mode of one or more layers in the Layers panel. When you return to the saved layer comp, the blending-mode changes remain because you hadn't told the layer comp to retain the appearance of the layers.

To create a layer comp with a default name that uses the settings of the last layer comp you made (by default, just the Visibility option), hold down the Option/Alt key while clicking the New Layer Comp button.

View Layer Comps Quickly. You can apply a layer comp by clicking in the column to the left of the layer comp's name. You can also click the left and right arrow icons at the bottom of the Layer Comps panel. Better yet, if you have ten comps but want to cycle through only three of them, select those three (Command- or Ctrl-click on the comps to select more than one) and then use the arrow buttons in the panel. If you use layer comps much, we strongly suggest that you use the Keyboard Shortcuts feature (in the Edit menu) to apply keyboard shortcuts to the Next Layer Comp and Previous Layer Comp features so you don't have to keep clicking buttons.

TIP: To open the Layer Comp Options dialog, double-click a layer comp thumbnail.

You'll see a layer comp called Last Document State in the Layer Comps panel. This is the state of your document before you chose a layer comp. For example, let's say you display a layer comp, hide some layers, and move some text around. Now if you select any layer comp, your changes disappear—but if you click on the Last Document State comp, the changes return.

Update Comps. Need to change a layer comp? You don't have to delete it and start over. Make your changes, then select the comp name in the panel (don't click the left column!) and click the Update Layer Comp button—the one that looks like two rotating arrows.

Send Comps to Clients. The fact that Photoshop saves layer comps with your files, including notes, is pretty cool. You can save a document as a PSD, TIFF, or PDF file, and someone else can open the file in Photoshop and browse the Layer Comp panel. Also interesting are the Layer Comp scripts in the File > Scripts submenu: Layer Comps to Files and Layer Comps to WPG. They're intended to save all (or the currently selected) layer comps to one or more flattened files on disk. Unfortunately, Layer Comps to Files is the only one that still works in Photoshop CS4; if you choose Layer

Comps to WPG you get a message that you should try the Output module in Bridge.

Clear Comp Warnings. If, after making one or more layer comps, you delete or merge a layer, you'll notice that small warning icons appear in the Layer Comps panel. These tell you that Photoshop can no longer return to the layer comp as saved because you removed or permanently changed some content that the comp depends on. If you click such a comp, Photoshop will still display what it can, but if you don't want to see the warning icons anymore right-click (Control-click in Mac OS X) on an alert icon and choose Clear All Layer Comp Warnings from the context menu.

Info Panel Tips

The Info panel (see **Figure 6-34**) isn't flashy or colorful, but we can't live without it, because it constantly displays critical information about the current Photoshop document. We almost never close it.

Figure 6-34 The Info panel and its pop-up menus that change display options

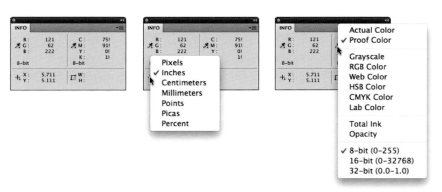

Color values and mouse position in Info panel

The units pop-up menu

The second color readout pop-up menu

You'll often encounter the Info panel working as a densitometer, where it shows the color values of the pixels under the mouse. You can use the color readout pop-up menus (click the eyedroppers) to set both color readouts to whatever color modes you like, but they are most useful when the first is set to Actual Color (the document's current color mode) and the second is set to the color mode of the output you're concerned with. When working in Levels or Curves, it displays before-and-after values (see Chapter 7, "Image Adjustment Fundamentals"). Especially note the Proof Color option, which shows the numbers that would result from the conversion you've specified in Proof Setup. This conversion may be different from the one you've specified in Color Settings (see Chapter 4, "Color Settings"). The Proof Color numbers appear in italics—a clue that you're looking at a different set of numbers than the ones you'd get from a mode change. If you're preparing photos for CMYK printing, the Info panel alerts you when the mouse is over a color that is out of the printer's gamut, by displaying an exclamation point after the color value. When you rotate a selection, the Info panel displays the angle. And when you scale, it shows percentages.

Find Opacity. When you have transparency showing (for example, on layers that have transparency when no background is showing), the Info panel can give you an opacity (Op) reading. To see this, click one of the little black eyedroppers in the Info panel and select Opacity (see Figure 6-34).

Switch Units. Although we typically work in pixel measurements, we do, on occasion, need to see physical measurements such as inches or centimeters. Instead of going into the Units pane of the Preferences dialog, we find it's often faster to do it from the units pop-up menu in the Info panel; just click on the tiny coordinates icon (see Figure 6-34).

Customize and Expand the Display. To display a wealth of data in the Info panel, choose Panel Options from the Info panel menu (see **Figure 6-35**), set the options the way you want them, and click OK. Conrad's favorite options are Document Profile (for color profile awareness), Document Dimensions (as a reality check on size and resolution), and Efficiency (as an indicator of Photoshop performance as described in Chapter 1).

TIP: Another shortcut for switching units is to right-click or Control-click (Mac) either ruler. If the rulers aren't visible, press Command-R (Mac) or Ctrl-R (Windows).

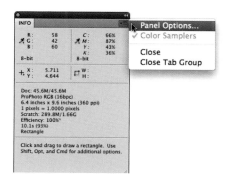

An expanded Info panel and its panel menu

The Info panel options that created the expanded panel

Figure 6-35 Customizing the Info panel

Color and Swatches Panel Tips

The Color and Swatches panels (see **Figure 6-36**) are closely related, so we almost always group them into one panel.

Figure 6-36 The Color and Swatches panels

 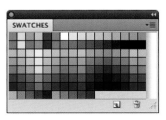

TIP: You can also cycle through the spectrums by Shift-clicking the spectrum bar. Each successive Shift-click progresses through the spectra in this order: CMYK, Grayscale, foreground color to background color, and then back to RGB.

Switch Color Models. Are the fields labeled RGB when you want to enter a value as CMYK or something else? Just choose a different mode from the Color panel menu. To choose colors visually rather than numerically, click the color spectrum at the bottom of the panel.

To switch to another color model's spectrum, right-click (or Control-click in Mac OS X) the spectrum and choose one. Changing the color spectrum changes only the way you specify the color, because the color has to be stored in the color space of the document itself. For example, if you're working in an RGB document and you specify a color in CMYK, the color must be translated into and stored as RGB.

Edit Color Swatches. You can add, delete, and edit the color swatches on the Swatches panel. **Table 6-5** shows you how. Don't ignore the panel menu . . . explore! On the panel menu are commands for managing swatches, and you can bring in swatches from a long list of color systems, such as Focoltone, PANTONE, TOYO, and TRUMATCH.

You can't actually edit a color swatch, so instead click the swatch to make it the current foreground color, edit the foreground color, then Shift-click the swatch to replace it with the current foreground color.

Table 6-5 Editing the Swatches panel.

To do this . . .	. . . do this:
Add the current foreground color	Click any empty area
Delete a swatch	Command/Alt-click the swatch
Replace a color with the foreground color	Shift-click (Mac only)

History Panel Tips

The History panel remembers what you've done to your file and lets you either retrace your steps or revert back to any earlier version of the image. Every time you do something to your image—paint a brushstroke, run a filter, make a selection, and so on—Photoshop saves this change as a *state* in the History panel (see **Figure 6-37**). At any time, you can revert the entire image to any previous state, or—using the History Brush tool or the Fill command, which we'll discuss in a moment—selectively paint back in time.

The History panel has two sections: snapshots on top and states on the bottom. The History panel stores each state until it hits the History States limit in the Performance pane in the Preferences dialog. The default is 20 states, so when you create state 21, the oldest state is deleted. Adobe set the 20-state default as a balance between performance and flexibility; increasing it is fine if you have many gigabytes of scratch disk space available.

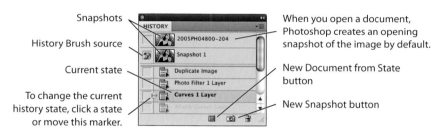

Snapshots

History Brush source

Current state

To change the current history state, click a state or move this marker.

When you open a document, Photoshop creates an opening snapshot of the image by default.

New Document from State button

New Snapshot button

Figure 6-37 The History panel

Snapshots. If you don't want a particular state to be deleted when it becomes the oldest state, turn it into a snapshot. Snapshots aren't deleted until you exit Photoshop. The other difference between a snapshot and a state is that states are created with every edit you perform, while a snapshot is created only when the document is first opened and when you manually create one yourself. To create a snapshot, click the New Snapshot button or choose New Snapshot from the History panel menu.

What's in the Snapshot? When you create a snapshot, Photoshop saves the whole document, including layers. A large document can consume a lot of scratch disk space, so Photoshop offers two other less-storage-intensive snapshot choices: a version of the image with merged layers, or just the currently selected layer. If you want to conserve scratch disk space, you can limit the layers the new history state will include—Option-click (Mac) or Alt-click (Windows) the New Snapshot button to see these choices.

Change History Panel Behavior. To change how the History panel generates states, choose History Options from the History panel menu (see **Figure 6-38**). You'll find options that let you alter some of the default behavior we talk about in this section. The first two options create snapshots automatically, so they consume more scratch disk space. The third and fifth options can potentially add a lot more states to the History panel, so you'll reach your limit sooner. Most are off by default to save disk space and to avoid generating an overwhelming number of states, but Automatically Create First Snapshot is on by default, as a safety net.

Figure 6-38 The History panel menu and History Options dialog

Step Through States. There are three ways to move among the states in the History panel:

• Click on any state's thumbnail in the History panel.

• Move the active state marker to a different state on the History panel.

• To step back to the last state, press Command-Z (Mac) or Ctrl-Z (Windows), which works like a standard undo. To move backward one state at a time, press Command-Option-Z (Mac) or Ctrl-Alt-Z (Windows), or to move forward one state at a time press Command-Shift-Z (Mac) or Ctrl-Shift-Z (Windows).

When you move to an earlier state, Photoshop dims every subsequent state on the History panel, indicating that whatever you do next will erase all of the subsequent dimmed steps. This is like going back to a fork in the road and choosing the other path. Photoshop offers another option: If you turn on the Allow Non-Linear History check box in the History Options dialog, Photoshop doesn't gray out or remove subsequent states when you move back in time (though it still deletes old states when you hit the maximum number of states).

Using Non-Linear History is like returning to the fork in the road, taking the other path, and then having the option to return to any state from the first path. For example, you could run a Gaussian Blur filter on your image using three different amounts—returning the image to the preblurred state in the History panel each time—and then switch among the three states to decide which one you want to use. Just make sure you're more intrigued by this option than you'll be confused by all of the branches.

The History Brush. The History Brush (press Y) lets you paint specific areas of one history state into another. To use the History Brush, set the History Brush source and the current state (see **Figure 6-37**), and paint over the area you want to restore. The pixels you paint will come from the History Brush source. For instance, let's say you sharpen a picture of a face and find that the lips are now too sharp. You can select the History Brush, set the source state to the presharpened state, and brush around the lips to bring back the less sharpened state only in that area. (You'd usually lower the brush Opacity value so that you can gradually paint out the sharpening.)

Fill with History. One last nifty technique that can rescue you from a catastrophic "oops" is the Fill command on the Edit menu (press Shift-F5). This lets you fill any selection (or the entire image, if nothing is selected) with the pixels from the current source state on the History panel. We prefer this to the History Brush or Eraser tools when the area to be reverted is easily selectable. Sometimes we miss some pixels when we paint with those tools, but the Fill command always covers it all.

To fill the layer or selection with the current history source state, press Command-Option-Delete (Mac) or Ctrl-Alt-Backspace (Windows). To fill with Preserve Transparency turned on, add the Shift key.

Copy States. Although Photoshop lets you copy states from one document to another simply by dragging them from the History panel onto the other document's window, we can't think of many good reasons to do this. The copied state completely replaces the image that you've dragged it over.

When History Stops Working. When you change your image's pixel dimensions, bit depth, or color mode, some history features can't be used with history states before that point because the pixels no longer line up or are fundamentally incompatible between the states. You'll see this with the History Brush or the Fill from History command. Avoid interrupting a series of history-based edits with changes to basic document properties.

TIP: The History Brush tool is very similar to the Eraser tool when the Erase to History check box is turned on in the Options bar, but the History Brush lets you paint with blending modes such as Multiply and Screen.

TIP: If you're low on disk space or just want to avoid the History feature's heavy scratch disk overhead, you can reduce the number of history states to just one. You won't need more than one history state if you're executing basic production steps or running batch actions, but we don't recommend this if you're in the middle of trial-and-error image editing,

Purge States. As we've said, history states consume a lot of scratch disk space until you close Photoshop. If you find yourself running out of room on your hard disk, try clearing out the history states by either selecting Clear History from the History panel menu or choosing Edit > Purge > Histories. The former can be undone in a pinch; the latter cannot. Curiously, neither of these removes your snapshots, so you have to delete those manually if you want to save even more space. Closing your document and reopening it will also remove all snapshots and history states.

History Log. Although there's no way to keep history states and snapshots after you close a document, you can keep a record of what you did, and it's called the History Log. The History Log is text that records your edits, but you can only read it—you can't play it back or reload it. You can use the History Log to track your edits down to the settings you used in dialogs, and you can use that data to manually reproduce the edits made to the file.

If you want to keep a History Log, turn on the History Log check box in the General pane of the Preferences dialog (see **Figure 6-39**). You can choose whether you want to save a log with each file (select Metadata) or maintain a central log for all files (Text File). You can also use the Edit Log Items pop-up menu to set the level of detail for the log.

This all seems simple enough, but there are privacy issues you might want to think about. If you increase the History Log's level of detail, the History Log can record minutiae like the folder paths and names of files you open and the text you enter on text layers. If you choose to store the History Log in metadata, it travels wherever the image travels. For example, if you type "My Stupid Boss" on a text layer because you're just playing around, and you later delete the text, the original text entry is still in the log. If you store the log in the image metadata and your boss views the file in Adobe Bridge, which can display the metadata, your boss may come across the log entry containing that text. If you or your organization has an interest in restricting certain information, you may not want detailed editing records to travel with the file. In such cases, you might limit the level of detail or choose not to store the log in file metadata.

If you set up the History Log in a way that's appropriate for your work, it can be a valuable tool in analyzing your processes and techniques.

Setting Preferences

There's a scene in Monty Python's *Life of Brian* in which Brian is trying to persuade his followers to think for themselves. He shouts, "Every one of you is different! You're all individuals!" One person raises his hand and replies, "I'm not."

This is the situation we often find with Photoshop users. Even though each person uses the program differently, they think they need to use it just like everyone else does. Not true. You can customize Photoshop in a number of ways through its Preferences submenu (on the Photoshop menu in Mac OS X, and on the Edit menu in Windows).

We're not going to discuss every preference here—we're just going to take a look at some of the key items. We think it's better to discuss individual preferences in the topics where they actually apply.

Return of Preferences. If you make a change in one of the many Preferences dialogs, and then after closing the dialog you realize you want to change some other preference, you can return to the last Preferences pane you saw by pressing Command-Option-K (Mac) or Ctrl-Alt-K (Windows).

Navigate Preferences. The Preferences dialog contains several panes (see **Figure 6-39**). Sure, you can select each one from the pop-up menu at the top of the dialog, or by clicking the Next and Prev buttons. But the fastest way to jump to any of the first nine panes while in the Preferences dialog is to press a number key along with Command (Mac) or Ctrl (Windows). For example, if you want to switch to the fourth Preferences pane (Performance) on a Mac, press Command-4. Instead of clicking Next, you can press Command-N (Mac) or Ctrl-N (Windows); instead of clicking Prev, press Command-P (Mac) or Ctrl-P (Windows).

Propagate Your Preferences. Any time you make a change to one of the Preferences dialogs, Photoshop remembers your alteration and, when you quit, saves it in the file Adobe Photoshop CS4 Prefs.psp. In Mac OS X, it's in Users\(username)\Library\Preferences\Adobe Photoshop CS4 Settings. In Windows XP, it's in Documents and Settings\(username)\Application Data\Adobe\Adobe Photoshop CS4\Adobe Photoshop CS4 Settings. In Windows Vista, it's in Users\(username)\AppData\Roaming\Adobe\Adobe Photoshop CS4\Adobe Photoshop CS4 Settings.

TIP: In Windows, the Preferences folder may be hidden by default. To see it in Windows XP, in a folder window choose Tools > Folder Options, and in the Folder Options dialog, select Show Hidden Files and Folders. To see it in Windows Vista, in a folder window choose Organize > Folder and Search Options, click the View tab, and then select Show Hidden Files and Folders in the Advanced Settings list.

Figure 6-39 The General
preferences

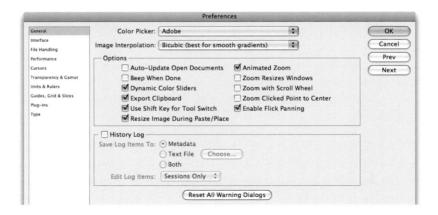

If anything happens to the Adobe Photoshop CS4 Prefs.psp file, all your hard-won preference settings are gone. Because of this, on the Mac, we recommend keeping a backup of that file, or even of the whole settings directory (people often back up their images without realizing they should back up this sort of data file, too). Note that Photoshop doesn't save changes to the preferences until you exit the program; if Photoshop crashes, preference changes don't get saved.

Certain kinds of crashes can corrupt the Photoshop Preferences file. If Photoshop starts acting strange on us, our first step is always to replace the Preferences file with a clean copy (if no copy of the Preferences file is available, Photoshop will build a new one for you). To reset the Preferences to Photoshop defaults, hold down the Command, Option, and Shift keys (Ctrl, Alt, and Shift keys in Windows) immediately after launching the program—Photoshop will ask if you really want to reset all the preferences.

TIP: In Mac OS X 10.5 or later, you create a Zip archive by choosing File > Compress [filename]. In Windows, it's File > Send To > Compressed (Zipped) Folder.

Conrad doesn't like going all the way back to the default preferences because there are so many performance-altering settings to remember (scratch disks and so on). He prefers to use the built-in ability of both Mac OS X and Windows to create a Zip archive of the Preferences file in the same folder as the original, so that when something goes wrong, he can trash the bad file and unzip the known good one.

If you administer a number of different computers that are running Photoshop, you may want to standardize the preferences on all machines. This is possible by copying the Photoshop Preferences file to each computer, but keep an eye out for machine-specific preferences that may not be preserved across machines, such as file paths.

UI Font Size. If you have a high-resolution monitor, you may want to increase the UI Font Size setting to keep text in the Photoshop user interface from becoming too small to read.

Export Clipboard. When the Export Clipboard check box is on, Photoshop converts whatever is on the Clipboard into your operating system's clipboard format when you switch out of Photoshop. This is helpful—indeed, necessary—if you want to paste a selection into some other program. But if you've got 10 MB on the Clipboard, that conversion is going to take some time. In situations when you're running low on RAM, the operating system may slow down. Since the Clipboard is probably the least reliable mechanism for getting images from Photoshop into some other application, we recommend leaving Export Clipboard off until you really need it.

Resize Image During Paste/Place. When this option is off, if you place or paste a graphic into a Photoshop document and the Photoshop document is much smaller than the incoming graphic, you'll see only the center of the incoming graphic, and you won't be able to grab its handles unless you zoom out. Turning on this option always scales down an incoming graphic to fit it within the current document. That sounds convenient, so why would you want to turn it off? If you regularly place graphics that need to maintain their original size, you don't want Photoshop to scale them at all—in that case, you should keep this option off.

Use Grayscale Toolbar Icon. By default, the Photoshop icon at the top of the toolbar is blue. If you would rather that your user interface be a neutral gray (a better background for color correction), you'll want to turn on this option in the Interface preferences (see **Figure 6-40**), in addition to choosing a neutral gray user interface color in your operating system preferences. The screen shots in this book use this preference, combined with the nice, neutral Graphite color scheme in the Appearance system preference in Mac OS X.

Show Menu Colors. This preference makes a difference only if you've used the Edit > Keyboard Shortcuts command to colorize menu commands. For example, if you choose Window > Workspace > What's New in CS4 and you can't figure out why the new commands aren't appearing in blue, as they're supposed to, it's because this preference is turned off.

Figure 6-40 The Interface preferences

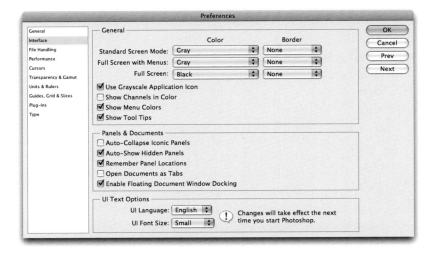

Remember Panel Locations. This remembers which panels were open, which were closed, and where they were located on the screen the last time you quit. We leave this turned on, but we tend to rely on the Save Workspace feature to manage our panels instead. Note that if you change your monitor resolution, the panels return to their default locations anyway.

Image Previews. When you save a document in Photoshop, the program can save little thumbnails of your image as file icons. Image previews increase the file size by a small amount, so if you need the smallest possible files, you might set this option (see **Figure 6-41**) to Never Save or Ask When Saving. We always set Image Previews to Ask When Saving, so we can control it on a file-by-file basis.

Figure 6-41 The File Handling preferences

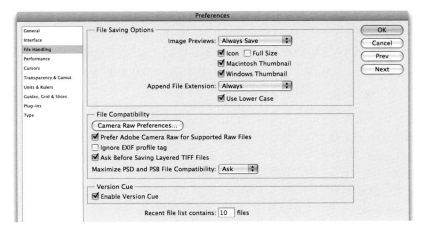

Ask Before Saving Layered TIFF Files. Many benighted souls still don't realize that TIFF files are first-class citizens that can store anything a Photoshop (PSD) file can, including Photoshop layers. We discuss this in detail in Chapter 12, but we should point out one thing here: When the Ask Before Saving Layered TIFF Files option is turned on in Preferences (as is by default), Photoshop will always alert you when you try to save a file that was a flat (nonlayered) TIFF but now has layers. For example, if you open a TIFF image and add some type, the text shows up on a type layer. Now if you press Command-S (Mac) or Ctrl-S (Windows) to save the file, Photoshop displays the TIFF Options dialog, in which you can either flatten the layers or keep them.

If you find yourself staring at this dialog too much and you keep thinking to yourself, "If I wanted to flatten the image, I would have done it myself," turn this option off in the Preferences dialog. Then Photoshop won't bother you anymore, and layered TIFF files will always save with their layers.

Ignore EXIF Profile Tag. This option exists because some early digital cameras embedded the wrong profile into their images, and turning on this option decreased the chance that Photoshop would misinterpret such an image's color. If you use a recent camera or shoot in raw format, keep this option turned off.

Maximize PSD and PSB File Compatibility. People have strong opinions about this feature, which was known in earlier versions as Maximize Backwards Compatibility in Photoshop Format, Include Composited Image with Layered Files, or 2.5 Format Compatibility. Many users dislike the fact that turning on this option can greatly increase file size because Photoshop saves a flattened version of your layered image along with the layered version. Because Photoshop can open a file just as easily whether this option is off or on, a lot of people choose to turn it off and save the disk space.

However, there are good reasons for this preference to exist, and those reasons are enough for us to set this option to Ask.

- Some non-Adobe programs claim to view or open layered Photoshop files, but (of course) they don't contain the entire Photoshop imaging engine. To view Photoshop files, they depend on the flattened compatibility copy that's provided by the Maximize PSD and PSB File Compatibility option. Without it, you see a placeholder (see **Figure 6-42**). For example, if you save a Photoshop document with this option turned off and you try to view the document in a non–Adobe application such as Apple Preview, you won't see the contents.

Figure 6-42 The place-holder that other programs may display when a layered Photoshop file doesn't include a composite version

- If you use Photoshop files in other Adobe Creative Suite programs such as Adobe InDesign or Adobe After Effects, you need to leave this option on, for the same reasons we just described.

- If you use a digital asset manager such as Adobe Lightroom, chances are you won't be able to view layered Photoshop files in it unless the files were saved with Maximize PSD and PSB File Compatibility turned on.

- Some programs can understand only 8-bit RGB Photoshop files, and they can't handle Photoshop files saved in other color modes or at other bit depths unless Maximize PSD and PSB File Compatibility is turned on.

- Future versions of Photoshop may interpret blending modes slightly differently than they do today due to improvements or bug fixes. If changes occur that affect the look of your file, you would at least be able to recover the flattened version, if there is one.

Conrad uses Photoshop files in other Creative Suite applications, and on top of that he uses a couple of different digital asset managers, so he prefers to leave this option set to Always.

Painting Cursors and Other Cursors. On the Cursors pane, we set our Painting Cursors (see **Figure 6-42**) to Normal Brush Tip or Full Size Brush Tip. Both display the diameter of the currently selected brush, but Normal marks only the diameter of the areas with 50 percent opacity or more based on the opacity and hardness of the current brush.

For Other Cursors, we prefer the Precise setting because it helps us position the cursor better than the default cursor icons do. If you set this option to Standard, you can temporarily display cursors in Precise mode; just press the Caps Lock key.

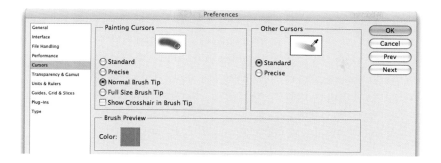

Figure 6-42 The Cursor preferences

Gamut Warning. When you turn on View > Gamut Warning (or press Command-Shift-Y on the Mac or Ctrl-Shift-Y in Windows), Photoshop displays all the out-of-gamut pixels in the color you choose here. We recommend you choose a really ugly color (on the Transparency & Gamut Preferences pane, see **Figure 6-43**) that doesn't appear anywhere in your image, such as a bright lime green. This way, when you switch on Gamut Warning, the out-of-gamut areas will be quite obvious.

Note, however, that Gamut Warning is of limited use. It tells you which colors are out of gamut, but not how they look. It's generally more informative to set up and use the View > Proof Colors command instead.

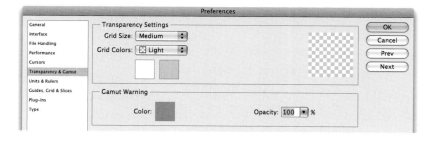

Figure 6-43 The Transparency & Gamut preferences

Transparency. Transparency is not a color—it's the absence of any color at all, even black or white. Therefore, when you see it on a layer, what should it look like? Typically, Photoshop displays transparency as a grid of white and gray boxes in a checkerboard pattern. The Preferences dialog lets you change the colors of the checkerboard and set the size of the squares. We've never found a reason to do so, but in the event you're creating a design that actually uses a gray checkerboard, you can use this preference to avoid confusing those areas with transparent areas.

WHEN THINGS GO WRONG

It's 11 PM on the night before your big deadline. You've been working on an image for 13 hours, and you're beginning to experience a bad case of "pixel vision." After making a selection, you run a filter, look carefully, and decide that you don't like the effect. But before you can reach Undo, you accidentally click on the document window, deselecting the area.

That's not so bad, is it? Not until you realize that undoing will only undo the deselection, not the filter . . . and that you haven't saved for half an hour. The mistake remains, and there's no way to get rid of it without losing the last 30 minutes of brain-draining work. Or is there? Let's find out.

Undo. The first defense against any offensive mistake is, of course, Undo. You can find this on the Edit menu, but we suggest keeping one hand conveniently on the Command and Z keys (Mac) or the Ctrl and Z keys (Windows), ready and waiting for the blunder that is sure to come sooner or later. Note that Photoshop is smart enough not to consider some things undoable. Taking a snapshot, for instance, doesn't count, so you can take a snapshot and then undo whatever you did just before the snapshot. Similarly, you can open the histogram, hide edges, change foreground or background colors, zoom, scroll, or even duplicate the file, and Photoshop still lets you go back and undo the previous action.

Revert. You'd think this command would be pretty easy to interpret. If you've really messed up something in your image, the best option is often simply to revert the entire file to the last saved version by selecting File > Revert. When you apply the Revert command, you don't lose your undo/History steps—Revert simply becomes another step you can undo. This is useful, because it means you can undo a Revert!

Note that if the only changes you've made are in the Missing Profile or Profile Mismatch dialogs that may appear while opening a file, Photoshop CS4 doesn't enable the Revert command.

History. If you get disoriented after using the Undo and Redo shortcuts too many times, or you want to see the entire list of undo steps, simply open the History panel and get oriented, then click on the history state on which you want to start over. See "History Panel Tips" earlier in this chapter.

CHAPTER SEVEN

Image Adjustment Fundamentals

Everything in image editing eventually comes down to tonal manipulation—making some tones lighter and other tones darker. Tonal manipulation is one of the most powerful and far-reaching capabilities in Photoshop, and at first it may seem like magic. But once you understand what's happening as you adjust the controls, it starts to look less like magic and more like clever technology. Your increased understanding and productivity should more than make up for any loss in your sense of wonder, however.

Tonal manipulation makes the difference between a flat image that lies lifeless on the page and one that pops, drawing you into it. But the role of tonal correction goes far beyond that. When you correct a color image, you're really manipulating the tone of the individual color channels.

In this chapter we'll concentrate on the fundamentals—the basic tonal manipulation tools and their effects on pixels. Much of this chapter is devoted to two tools—Levels and Curves—because until you've mastered these, you simply don't know Photoshop! We also cover the considerable number of other useful commands found on the Image > Adjustments submenu. In Chapter 8, "The Digital Darkroom," we'll show you some more esoteric techniques for getting great-looking images.

What Is Image Quality, Anyway?

At the most basic level, image quality comes down to a few simple things:

Optimal Contrast. We perceive images by seeing differences among tones. The more pronounced the differences (the higher the contrast), the easier it is to read an image, but only as long as you don't push contrast too far. Too much contrast reduces too much of the image to black and white, destroying smooth transitions and tonal details—essentially, you lose image data. You get the best image quality when you've found the level of contrast that brings out the tonal details all the way from dark to light and tuned for the specific way you'll output an image, whether that's for a press or a monitor.

Contrast control is important not just for an entire image, but also for specific parts of an image. While that can mean adjusting contrast in specific areas of an image (for example, using masks), it can also mean adjusting contrast within specific ranges of tones such as the shadows (for example, using Curves). Either way, manipulating contrast gives you the ability to treat specific areas that you want to clarify, emphasize, or de-emphasize.

When contrast is increased only along the edges of shapes in an image, details appear sharper; this type of contrast control is the basis for all digital sharpening. We'll explore this topic in Chapter 10.

As you move through the next few chapters, you'll find that the basic reason Photoshop has so many ways to manipulate tones is simply so that you can tailor the contrast of your image in every possible way as those situations come up. Contrast is that fundamental to image quality.

Optimal Color. Good color is balanced and believable—neutral colors appear neutral, skin tones look natural, and colors are neither too weak nor too vivid relative to how they appear in the real world. Once you've anchored image to reality, you're free to tweak image color so that it serves your creative vision. Sounds simple, but there are complications: The appearance of color is affected both by human visual perception and by how the image is output. For these reasons, while many people naturally concentrate on the tools that Photoshop provides to alter color (such as Curves), it's important to pay an equal amount of attention to the tools Photoshop provides to evaluate color objectively and in context, such as the Info panel and soft-proofing.

TIP: It's an ongoing goal (and battle) to preserve as much image quality as possible by losing as few tonal levels as possible. When Photoshop presents five ways of making a correction, very often the reason we pick a particular method is because it's the least destructive.

Optimal Detail and Sharpness. On the surface, detail and sharpness wouldn't seem to have anything to do with basic image adjustments such as contrast. You'd run a sharpening filter, right? But as we mentioned earlier, because images are formed by contrast, image details are also formed by contrast. Therefore, the decisions you make to optimize contrast contribute to how visible the details of your images will be. As a result, you'll find that sharpening works a lot better if your basic image corrections were done well in the first place.

With all that in mind, let's plunge ahead and see how the tools in Photoshop relate to what we need to do to achieve the image quality we want. We started to cover the basics of image editing back in Chapter 5, "Building a Digital Workflow," where we talked about image-editing basics strictly within the context of Adobe Camera Raw. Now we'll talk about it in terms of Photoshop in general—how you would handle any photographic image that you've opened in Photoshop.

Visualizing Tonal Values with the Histogram

Although most of the images we correct are in color, it's a lot easier to learn how tones work by leaving the color out, so we'll start with grayscale images and move on to color later. A grayscale image contains nothing but tonal information. When we talk about correcting color images later in this chapter, however, you'll find that color images consist of multiple grayscale channels—and so what you learn here about grayscale images will apply to color images as well.

You can't necessarily see the distribution of tones in your image just by looking at the image itself, so to help you out Photoshop provides the Histogram panel. A *histogram* is a simple bar chart that plots the tonal levels from 0 to 255 along the horizontal axis, and the number of pixels at each level along the vertical axis. We show you some examples of images and their histograms in **Figure 7-1**.

Typical images show a range of tones from end to end across the histogram. Don't worry about whether the histogram is even across the graph; that doesn't matter—tones group into different peaks and valleys depending on the content of each image. If an image is intentionally very dark or very light, it's fine for the histogram to be weighted to one end or the other.

Figure 7-1 Histograms for images with different tonal distributions

Histogram for an image with tones from dark to light, but mostly midtones

A high-key (light) image has more tones to the right of its histogram.

A low-key (dark) image has more tones to the left of its histogram.

There are just a few things to watch out for. If the graph reaches all the way to the top at either end, the black or white point may be clipped (detail lost). If the graph stops some distance before it reaches either end, the black or white point may be set too far out. And if the histogram displays a few spikes of tones with wide gaps between them, instead of a rather solid graph, check for posterization (also called stair-stepping or banding). However, don't judge these problems by the histogram alone. Evaluate them by also looking closely at the image and using the clipping indicators in the Levels and Curves adjustments, which we'll talk about soon. Never condemn an image solely on the basis of the histogram, because a good-looking histogram isn't necessarily the sign of a good image, and many good-looking images have ugly histograms. The histogram is just a handy way of looking at the data so that you can see how it relates to the image appearance.

TIP: Fixing the histogram doesn't mean you've fixed the image. If you want a nice-looking histogram, the Gaussian Blur filter with a 100-pixel radius will smooth out the histogram nicely, but there won't be much left of the image!

More Histogram Panel Features. The Histogram panel offers several options for viewing image tonal data in more detail (see **Figure 7-2**):

- Uncached Refresh icon. For performance reasons, the Histogram panel usually shows you values based on a cached anti-aliased screen display of the image instead of evaluating the image at full resolution. This view can hide posterization, giving you an unrealistically rosy picture of your data. Photoshop warns you of this by displaying a warning icon when the histogram is approximating your data. To see what's really going on, click this icon or the Uncached Refresh button.

- Expanded views. The Histogram panel defaults to a compact size. Choose Expanded View from the Histogram panel menu to make it bigger. Expanded View also shows color channels in color and displays statistics under the histogram; if you don't need to see these, you can turn off Show Statistics in the Histogram panel menu and choose your preferred display mode from the Channel pop-up menu above the histogram. On this pop-up menu, in addition to the color channels, you see the Luminosity option. The difference between Luminosity and the default composite view (such as RGB or CMYK) is that Luminosity displays only the luminance of each pixel, with a value of 255 meaning white. In a composite view, a value of 255 may represent a fully saturated color pixel.

- Channel displays. In Expanded View you can also display each channel in its own histogram (making the Histogram panel very tall); choose All Channels View from the Histogram panel menu. The channel histograms display in black unless you also turn on Show Channels in Color in the Histogram panel menu.

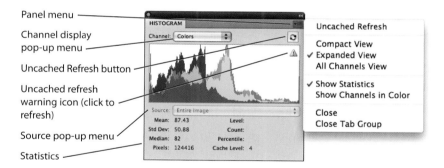

Panel menu

Channel display pop-up menu

Uncached Refresh button

Uncached refresh warning icon (click to refresh)

Source pop-up menu

Statistics

Figure 7-2 The Histogram panel

In this chapter you'll be making the bulk of your edits using the Levels and Curves adjustments. Both of them display the histogram, so you don't have to keep the Histogram panel open while you're using those features.

THE THREE BASIC TONAL ADJUSTMENTS

The first step to great image quality is setting three specific aspects of the image: the black point, the white point, and the midpoint. Doing so sets the overall *dynamic range* of the image, ensuring that the range of tones from light to dark in the image takes full advantage of the available tonal range that the file can reproduce. Dynamic range is a primary factor in image contrast, so if you get it right, the contrast adjustments you make later become easier. Another reason to optimize the dynamic range is that it gives us room to optimize contrast—and contrast is the resource we draw upon to preserve and accentuate image detail.

Here's how the three basic tonal adjustments work: In many unedited photographs, if the darkest and lightest tones are more than a few levels away from black and white, respectively, the image appears relatively flat because it has less contrast than it should (see **Figure 7-3**). Redefining the darkest available tone in the image as black and redefining the lightest tone as white expands the dynamic range of the image, adding contrast, which gives it more life. And the midpoint? That determines the overall brightness of the image by specifying where the 50 percent level really should be. For well-lit, well-exposed photographs, these three adjustments may be all you need.

Let's walk through how to make these three basic adjustments using the Levels feature in Photoshop. Later in this chapter we'll show you how to do the same thing in Curves.

Making Adjustments Using Levels

TIP: If you're working with an image freshly converted from a digital camera raw file, and the shadows and highlights are already clipping when the black and white triangles are all the way to the ends of the histogram, consider checking the image in Camera Raw to see if you can coax additional dynamic range out of the raw file by using the sliders in the Basic tab (see Chapter 5), and then reconvert the image to Photoshop.

The Levels feature is tailor-made for the three basic edits we want to make. In the Levels dialog or Levels Adjustments panel, the Input Levels sliders include black-point, white-point, and midpoint controls. There's also a histogram so that you can monitor how your changes affect the tonal distribution. To make the three basic adjustments using Levels, do the following:

1. Choose Image > Adjustments > Levels.

2. Set the black point by dragging the black triangle (under the histogram) to the right until the darkest parts of the image are as dark as you want them (see **Figure 7-4**). If you notice that details previously visible in the shadows are now gone (shadows have become solid black), you've gone too far; back off a bit by dragging the black triangle to the left until the shadow detail comes back. Watching the histogram can help you see when you're starting to clip too many of the shadow tones.

3. In the same way, set the white point by dragging the white triangle under the histogram to the left until the lightest parts of the image are as light as possible without losing detail. If you notice that details in the highlights are gone (highlights have become solid white), back off a bit by dragging the white triangle to the right until the highlight detail comes back.

4. Set the midpoint by dragging the gray triangle under the histogram. Drag to the left to lighten the image or to the right to darken it (see **Figure 7-5**).

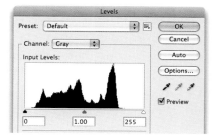

Original Levels dialog

Image before corrections

Figure 7-3 Image before a Levels adjustment lacks contrast, and the clouds are dull gray.

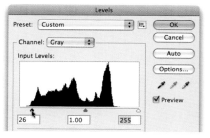

Dragging the black-point slider to the darkest tone in the image (as shown on the histogram)

Figure 7-4 Adjusting the black-point slider

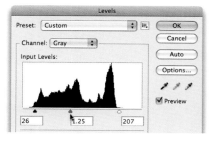

After adjusting the white point for a full range of tones and better contrast, the gray midpoint slider is dragged to adjust overall brightness.

Figure 7-5 Adjusting the white-point and midpoint sliders

5. Check your work by using the Preview check box (press P). Watch carefully what happens to details in the shadows and highlights; if you've lost detail at either end, adjust the black and white triangles. If you see an issue with overall brightness, adjust the gray triangle. For more precision, click in any of the three number fields under the sliders and press the up arrow or down arrow key to nudge the values (add the Shift key to nudge the values by 10 times the default increment).

Using the Clipping Display. When dragging the black and white sliders in Levels, we prefer to use a technique that helps us more clearly visualize where shadow details are being clipped, because looking at the image and the histogram usually doesn't tell us precisely enough. Hold down the Option (Mac OS X) or Alt (Windows) key as you drag the black slider—you should see the entire image become white. As you drag the black triangle to the right, areas of black will begin to grow (see **Figure 7-6**). The black areas are the parts of the image that would be clipped if you let go of the black triangle at that point. If a shadow area doesn't contain any detail you care about, it may be acceptable to let that area clip, if you gain contrast in the rest of the image. But if there are other shadow areas where detail is important, don't let them become black when you Option/Alt-drag the black triangle. When you drag the white triangle with Option/Alt pressed, the image appears black and clipped areas appear white. As you Option/Alt-drag the black (or white) slider toward the center, a good way to tell when to stop is when large clumps of pixels go black (or white). Small clumps are acceptable as long as they're either true black areas or specular highlights—areas that are truly devoid of detail.

TIP: If the histogram already touches the left or right end of the graph, you may not need to move the black- or white-point slider very much, or possibly not at all, because the shadows or highlights may already be clipping, or about to. On the other hand, if the histogram doesn't touch the left or right sides of the graph, you can usually assume that you'll have to pull in the sliders.

Figure 7-6 Using the black-point clipping display

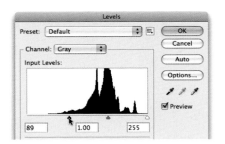 

Option/Alt-drag the black-point slider (left) to see which levels become black (right).

Let's go over what was really happening as you dragged those sliders.

TIP: The clipping display works only in the Grayscale, RGB, Duotone, and Multichannel modes.

Black- and White-Point Sliders. Moving the black and white sliders in toward the center expands, or stretches, the dynamic range of the image. When you move the black-point slider, you tell Photoshop to set all the tones at that level and darker to level 0 (black) and to set all the tones to the right of the slider to fill the entire tonal range from 0 to 255. Moving the white-point slider does the same thing to the other end of the tonal range, setting all of the tones at the white-point slider and lighter to level 255 (white), and setting the levels to the left of the slider to fill the tonal range from 0 to 255 (see **Figure 7-7**).

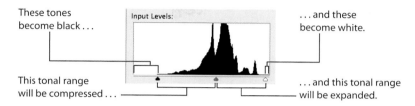

These tones become black . . .

Input Levels:

. . . and these become white.

This tonal range will be compressed . . .

. . . and this tonal range will be expanded.

Figure 7-7 How Input Levels adjustments affect an image's dynamic range

Gray Slider. The gray (middle) slider lets you alter the midtones without changing the black and white points. When you move the gray slider, you're telling Photoshop which tone should become the midtone gray value (50 percent gray, or level 128). If you move the slider to the left, the image gets lighter because you're choosing a value that's darker than 128 and making it 128. As you do so, the shadows stretch to fill up that part of the tonal range and the highlights squeeze together. Conversely, if you move the slider to the right the image gets darker because you're telling Photoshop that a lighter value should darken down to level 128, stretching the highlights and squeezing the shadow values. David likes to think of this as grabbing a rubber band on both ends and in the middle, and pulling the middle to the left or right; one side is stretched out and the other gets bunched up.

The value in the slider's number field is a *gamma* value—for you math types, that's the exponent of a power curve equation. Values greater than 1 lighten the midtone, values less than 1 darken it, and a value of 1 leaves it unchanged. If you adjust only the midtone slider, you really are applying a pure gamma correction to the image.

Reality Checks. If you set the black point and white point too far out, the image can seem flat, lacking contrast—contributing to an absence of what photographers call *pop*. If you set them too far in, you'll clip important shadow or highlight detail out of the image, causing shadows to appear solid black (plugged) and highlights to appear solid white (blown out).

If the image will be displayed onscreen, you can set the black point and white point rather tightly. But if the image will be printed, you may want to leave a little room at the ends. For example, many printers have trouble

TIP: If you want a more detailed mathematical understanding of gamma encoding and gamma correction, a good place to start is http://chriscox.org/gamma/, written by Photoshop engineer Chris Cox.

reproducing very dark shadow details that you can see on screen, so you may not want to push those details too close to black by dragging the black slider too far up. You may be working with a printing company that recommends specific Levels adjustments for their equipment; in that case you can simply apply their recommendations.

ADJUSTING LEVELS FOR COLOR IMAGES

A color image consists of multiple channels, each of which stores grayscale information. When you use Levels to correct a color image, it's similar to the grayscale corrections we just showed you, except that you're doing it for each color channel. For this reason, you can select the channel you want to edit from the Channel pop-up menu (see **Figure 7-8**). In addition, you can edit the composite view (all channels at once).

Figure 7-8 Choosing an individual channel view in Levels

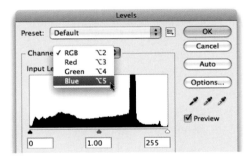

When you work in the composite (RGB, CMYK, or Lab) view, Levels works in much the same way as it does on grayscale images. It makes the same adjustment to all the color channels, so it affects only tone—in theory. In practice, it may introduce some color shifts when you make big corrections, so we tend to use Curves more than Levels on color images. But Levels is useful on color images in at least two ways:

• As an image-evaluation tool, using the histograms and clipping display

• When we have a color image that has no problems with color balance but needs a small midtone adjustment using the gray slider

Manipulating channels individually can be a chore, so to quickly make major initial corrections we manually guide the Auto Color feature in Levels and Curves (see the next section, "Controlling Auto Corrections").

How Levels and Clipping Work on Color Images. As the composite histogram implies, when you make an edit in the composite channel view, it's as if you made the same edit to each channel individually. However, since the contents of the individual channels are quite different, applying the same value changes to each channel can sometimes have unexpected results. This causes a potential problem with the black and white Input Levels sliders.

The white slider clips the highlights *in each channel* to level 255. This brightens the image overall, and neutral colors stay neutral. But it can have an undesirable effect on non-neutral colors, ranging from oversaturation to pronounced color shifts. The same applies to the black Input Levels slider, although the effects are usually less obvious. The black slider clips the values in each channel to level 0, so when you apply it to a non-neutral color, you can end up removing all trace of one primary from the color, which also increases its saturation.

Because of this behavior, we use the black and white Input Levels sliders primarily as image-evaluation tools in conjunction with the Option/Alt-key clipping display (see **Figure 7-9**). They let you see exactly where your saturated colors are in relation to your neutral highlights and shadows. If the image is free of dangerously saturated colors, you can make small moves with the black and white Input Levels sliders, but be careful of unintentional clipping, and keep a close eye on what's happening to the saturation—it's particularly easy to create out-of-gamut saturated colors in the shadows.

➡️ **TIP:** The clipping display techniques apply whether you're working in Levels or Curves as a dialog or Adjustments panel.

The Composite and Luminosity Histograms. Labeled RGB, CMYK, or Lab, depending on the image's color space, the composite histogram is the same as the default Colors histogram in the Histogram panel but different from the Histogram panel's Luminosity histogram. In the Luminosity histogram, a level of 255 represents a white pixel. In the RGB and CMYK histograms in Levels, however, a level of 255 *may* represent a white pixel, but it could also represent a fully saturated color pixel—the histogram simply shows the maximum of all the individual color channels. Fortunately, the Levels clipping display makes this clear (see Figure 7-9).

Saturation clipping isn't necessarily a problem, but it is a sign that you should check the values in the unclipped channels to make sure that things are headed in the right direction. If you're trying to clip to white and the unclipped channel is up around 250, or you're trying to clip to black and the unclipped channel is under 10, you don't really have a problem. But if the values in the unclipped channels are far away from white or black clipping, you may actually be creating very saturated colors that you didn't want.

Figure 7-9 Viewing the clipping display for a color image by Option/Alt-dragging the black-point and white-point sliders

Black point at 71: too many colors clipped

Black point at 36: much less is clipped

White point at 185: highlight detail clipped

White point at 252: only specular highlights clipped

Original image

Final image with black point at 36, white point at 252, and midtone at 1.15

As you Option/Alt-drag the black-point slider, the following colors indicate the channels you're currently clipping:

White = No channels clipping
Cyan = Red channel
Magenta = Green channel
Yellow = Blue channel
Red = Green and blue channels
Green = Red and blue channels
Blue = Red and green channels
Black = All channels

As you Option/Alt-drag the white-point slider, the following colors indicate the channels you're currently clipping:

Black = No channels clipping
Red = Red channel
Green = Green channel
Blue = Blue channel
Cyan = Green and blue channels
Magenta = Red and blue channels
Yellow = Red and green channels
White = All channels

Adjusting Each Channel Individually. In Figure 7-9 we adjusted levels by dragging just the composite sliders. But if the image needs a color tweak, you can adjust the input levels for each channel individually (see Figure 7-8) to change the color balance. You can adjust the color balance of the shadows by adjusting the black-point value in each channel, and similarly adjust the color balance of the highlights and midtones by adjusting those values in each channel. But dragging the sliders yourself is not always the best way to adjust channels individually. We recommend that you start by customizing the powerful Auto Color correction feature, which can do a great first pass at setting initial levels for individual color channels (see the next section, "Controlling Auto Corrections"), and then fine-tune the color with Curves.

Channel-Viewing Shortcut Changes. In Photoshop CS4, Adobe finally implemented long-popular feature requests to use the standard Command-` shortcut for cycling document windows in Mac OS X and the Command/Ctrl-1 shortcut for the 100 percent window magnification used by many applications in Mac OS X and Windows. As a result, the long-established Photoshop shortcuts for displaying the composite and first channels had to change. Adobe simply moved them down two keys on the top row of the keyboard (see **Table 7-1**). For example, where you used to press Command-1, 2, and 3 to respectively view the R, G, and B channels in Mac OS X, you now press Command-3, 4, and 5 in Photoshop CS4.

TIP: Changes to the keyboard shortcuts for channels can trip up long-time Photoshop users. If this affects you, train yourself to use the Option/Alt key to display channel curves, the Command/Ctrl key to display channels, and the 2 key as the new composite channel key.

In addition, making Curves available as a nonmodal panel meant that the former shortcuts for viewing curves and channels would conflict (they both used the Command/Ctrl key), so in Photoshop CS4 you view channels with the Command/Ctrl key and channel curves with the Option/Alt key.

Table 7-1 Photoshop CS4 shortcut changes for viewing image channels.

To do this . . .	. . . in Photoshop CS3 press:	. . . in Photosohop CS4 press:
View composite Levels or Curves (all channels)	Command-` (Mac OS X) Ctrl-` (Windows)	Command-2 (Mac OS X) Ctrl-2 (Windows)
View a channel in Levels/ Curves adjustment panel	(not available)	Option-3 and up (Mac) Alt-3 and up (Windows)
View a channel in Levels or Curves dialog	Command-1 and up (Mac) Ctrl-1 and up (Windows)	Command-3 and up (Mac) Ctrl-3 and up (Windows)
View a channel in document window*	Command-1 and up (Mac) Ctrl-1 and up (Windows)	Command-3 and up (Mac) Ctrl-3 and up (Windows)

*Doesn't work when the Levels or Curves dialog is open.

CONTROLLING AUTO CORRECTIONS

There's a certain amount of distrust of the automatic (Auto) color correction features in Photoshop, and it is well-founded. But if you keep a few tips in mind, the Auto commands can be useful. The worst way to use the Auto corrections is to apply them blindly, so let's start by looking at how they work.

Auto Tone. Expands the dynamic range of all image channels as much as possible. This seems fine mathematically, but visually this option stands the highest chance of wrecking an image, because it adjusts each channel separately by an arbitrary amount, without any reference to image content.

Auto Contrast. Maximizes contrast like Auto Tone, except that it tries to prevent color shifts by applying the same amount of adjustment to all channels. However, the adjustment is still arbitrary.

Auto Color. Similar to Auto Tone, except that it also tries to identify the midtone value to make it neutral so that any color cast is removed; this works correctly only if the midtone really is supposed to be neutral.

Auto Corrections Appear in Different Forms. The Auto corrections just described are also options in the Auto Color Correction Options dialog that we'll soon cover. Auto Tone is the same as Enhance Per Channel Contrast, Auto Contrast is the same as Enhance Monochromatic Contrast, and Auto Color is like Find Dark & Light Colors with Snap Neutral Midtones turned on. And in the Levels and Curves adjustments, the Auto button is an alternate way to apply Auto Tone.

Auto Color Works Best When You Take Over. You can control how the Auto corrections are applied if you use the Auto Color Correction Options dialog. If you take charge of Auto Color, it can be useful for making major initial corrections, particularly on scans of color negatives or on images that need major adjustments in color balance and contrast.

Here's how we alter Auto Color settings to get a result we actually want:

1. Open the Levels or Curves Adjustments panel and choose Auto Options from the Levels panel menu. If you're using the Levels or Curves dialog, click the Options button.

2. Turn on Find Dark & Light Colors (see **Figure 7-10**).

3. Turn on the Snap Neutral Midtones check box.

TIP: Auto corrections work best with images in which endpoint clipping hasn't already been applied.

TIP: When setting Auto Color options, stay slightly on the conservative side and leave the fine-tuning to Curves. Never over clip the ends of the tonal range.

TIP: Because the Auto button in Levels and Curves is another way of applying Auto Tone, we never click Auto unless we've customized the Auto Color Correction Options defaults and we know that they're appropriate for the image.

4. Adjust the clipping percentages from the rather high default value of 0.10 percent to a much lower value, typically in the range of 0.00 to 0.05 percent, depending on the image content.

5. When necessary (that is, more often than not), click the Midtones swatch to open the Color Picker and adjust the target value. You can do this by changing the numbers in the Color Picker or by dragging the target indicator in the color swatch. They're equally effective—use the method you find more convenient.

TIP: If nothing happens when you adjust the Midtones target color, make sure Snap Neutral Midtones is on.

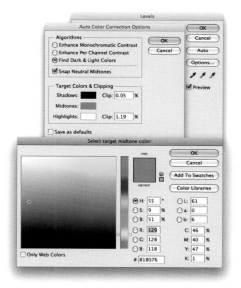

Figure 7-10 Controlling Auto Color correction

The original image was shot under tungsten light with the wrong white balance.

In Auto Color Correction Options, Shadows clipping was minimal; Highlights could be clipped further while keeping detail in the metal and salt, but the overall image is slightly bluish.

To warm the image back up a little, we adjusted the target midtone color.

Levels dialog (top), Auto Color Correction Options dialog (middle), and Select Target Midtone Color dialog (bottom)

6. Click OK to close the Midtones Color Picker, and click OK to close the Auto Color Correction Options dialog.

If you view different channels in Levels or Curves at this point, you'll find that the Input Levels sliders have been adjusted for you.

Setting Useful Auto Color Correction Defaults. If you'll be working with many images that are consistent in tonal character, come up with Auto Color Correction settings that provide a good, time-saving initial correction for them and then turn on the "Save as defaults" check box. When you create relevant default settings, the Auto commands on the Image menu and the Auto button in Levels and Curves may actually be somewhat useful to you, because they'll apply the defaults you set.

We don't aim for perfection with Auto Color. The goal is to get the image into the ballpark quickly, and fine-tune the results using the Curves dialog.

THE INFO PANEL

Like the Histogram panel, the Info panel is purely an informational display. But where the Histogram panel shows a general picture of the entire file, the Info panel lets you analyze specific pixels in the image. When you move the cursor across the image, the Info panel displays the values of the pixel under the cursor. More important, when you are using tone- or color-correction features (such as Levels or Curves), the Info panel displays the values for the pixel before and after the correction (see **Figure 7-11**).

Figure 7-11 The Info panel

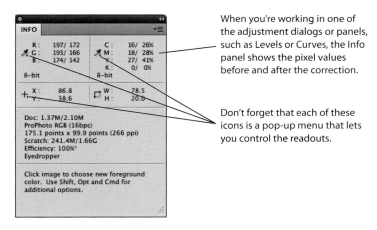

When you're working in one of the adjustment dialogs or panels, such as Levels or Curves, the Info panel shows the pixel values before and after the correction.

Don't forget that each of these icons is a pop-up menu that lets you control the readouts.

As we've said about other evaluative tools, you shouldn't use the Info panel alone. But using it together with the histogram and the clipping display on a calibrated monitor gives you a more complete picture of the corrections you need to make and the effects of pending corrections. The Info panel can show you very small differences that may be difficult to see using monitor feedback alone.

You can control the information that the Info panel displays; we showed this in "Info Panel Tips" and "Workspace Tips" in Chapter 6. Actual Color displays the color model of the image you're viewing, so if you change the color mode, the Actual Color readout follows suit. Because the Workspace feature captures Info panel settings in addition to the panel locations, we use workspaces to load different customized Info panel setups as needed.

Info Panel Setup. We use the same Info panel setup most of the time. For grayscale, duotone, or multichannel images, we generally set the first color readout to RGB Color and the second color readout to Actual Color. For color images, we set the first color readout to RGB, the second color readout to CMYK or our Proof Setup (such as a photo lab printer profile).

Setting Eyedropper Options. You can set the size of the sample area from the Sample Size pop-up menu in the Options bar, or by Ctrl-clicking (Mac) or right-clicking an image with the eyedropper. You can sample as little as a single pixel (Point Sample) or as much as 101 by 101 pixels. David chooses 3-by-3 Average unless he's working with a very high-resolution image, in which case he might increase it. If you leave the eyedropper set to Point Sample, zoom in to make sure you don't sample a noise pixel by mistake.

Precision of the CMYK Readout. If you're preparing a job for a press, the Info panel can show you the approximate CMYK values that you'll get when you do a mode change to CMYK. We say approximate because if you examine the CMYK values for an RGB file, then convert to CMYK and examine the values again, they may differ by a percentage point in one channel (which is a closer match than many production processes can consistently hold).

TIP: For more precision with high-bit images, change the Info panel units to 16-bit or 32-bit.

TIP: You can use the Info panel to hunt down hidden detail, particularly in deep shadows and bright highlights, where it can be hard to see on the monitor. If the numbers change as you move the cursor over an area of the image, tonal differences are lurking—it may be detail waiting to be exploited or it may be noise that you'll need to suppress, but something is hiding in there.

OUTPUT LEVELS

The Output Levels controls (see **Figure 7-12**) let you compress the tonal range of the image into less than the full range of levels. You can use this feature to produce the graphic design effect of ghosted background images. And on those rare occasions when we're forced to deal with old-style legacy CMYK or grayscale workflows that use a single dot-gain value, we may still use the output sliders to make sure that we don't force our highlight or shadow dots into a range that the output process can't print.

Black Output Levels. When this slider is at its default setting of 0, pixels in the image at level 0 will remain at level 0. As you move the slider to the right, it limits the darkest pixels in the image to the level at which it's set, compressing the entire tonal range.

White Output Levels. This control behaves like the black Output Levels slider, except that it limits the lightest pixels in the image rather than the darkest ones. For example, setting this slider to level 245 will put all the pixels that were at level 255 at 245 (see Figure 7-12).

Figure 7-12 Adjusting the Output Levels sliders for the image from Figure 7-5

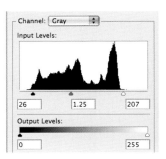

Before adjusting the Output Levels, the original tonal range was expanded to levels 0–255.

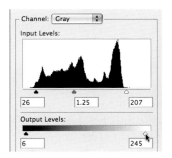

After adjusting the Output Levels, the tonal range is compressed to levels 6–245. This makes the darkest shadow detail more visible but reduces contrast (unavoidable if the Output Levels accurately represent the tonal range of the final output device).

Output Levels for Non-Color-Managed Grayscale Output. Even though grayscale is a first-class citizen in good color-management standing in Photoshop, very few other applications recognize grayscale profiles. When using grayscale images in a non-color-managed workflow, Output Levels can be used to make sure that highlights don't blow out and shadows don't plug up on press—the sliders let you limit black to a value higher than 0 and white to a value lower than 255. Good ICC profiles tend to make this practice unnecessary, since they take the minimum and maximum printable dot into account. When we have grayscale images with no specular highlights (the very bright reflections one sees on polished metal or water), we still use the output sliders in Levels to limit our highlight dot and—in images with very critical shadow detail—our shadow dot. To avoid making specular highlights gray in images that contain them, we use Curves instead.

Leave Room When Setting Limits. Always leave yourself some room to move when you set input and output limits, particularly in the highlights. If you move the white input slider so that your highlight detail starts at level 254, with your specular highlights at level 255, you run into two problems:

- When you compress the tonal range for final optimization, your specular highlights go gray.

- When you sharpen, some of the highlight detail blows out to white.

To avoid these problems, try to keep your significant highlight detail below level 250. Shadow clipping is less critical, but keeping the unoptimized shadow detail in the 5 to 10 range is a safe way to go.

Likewise, unless your image has no true whites or blacks, leave some headroom when you set the output limits. For example, if your press can't hold a dot smaller than 10 percent, don't set the output limit to level 230. If you're optimizing with the output sliders in Levels, set it to 232 or 233 so you get true whites in the printed piece. If you'll be optimizing later with the eyedroppers or Curves, set it somewhere around 237 or 240. This lets you fine-tune specular highlights using the eyedroppers or Curves, but it also brings the image's tonal range into the range that the press can handle.

EYEDROPPERS IN LEVELS AND CURVES

When using Levels and Curves, you'll find black, white, and gray eyedropper tools. They're basically another way to set your input and output levels. Instead of dragging sliders in a dialog or panel, you work visually, clicking parts of the image that you'd like to take on your desired shadow, highlight, or midtone values. For example, if you select the white eyedropper and click a light pixel, that pixel becomes the target value you set (pure white by default) and the rest of the tonal range shifts accordingly. We haven't talked about the Levels/Curves eyedroppers until now because customizing the Auto Color Correction values (which we covered earlier) is a newer, faster way to set input levels, and ICC profiles are a newer, faster, and more accurate way to set output levels. But that doesn't mean the Levels/Curves eyedroppers are useless. We sometimes still use them for:

- Grayscale images

- Non-color-managed CMYK workflows with single dot-gain values instead of dot-gain curves

- RGB for non-color-managed, standard-definition television display (we set highlights to 235 and shadows to 15)

The rest of the time, we let the profile handle the minimum dot (though when highlight detail is critical, we check the Info panel numbers).

Setting the Black Point and White Point. There are a couple of ways to use the eyedroppers to set tonal endpoints, and the distinction is important. If you simply select each eyedropper and click it without customizing its target value, it's like dragging the Input Levels sliders. Because it affects only the input levels, it's an alternative to dragging sliders manually or customizing the Auto Color Correction settings.

The other method is to first double-click the black or white Levels/Curves eyedropper and set its target value before clicking the image. Setting a target value also changes the Output Levels sliders, and that's why it's now useful primarily within a non-color-managed prepress workflow.

Killing Color Casts. We sometimes use the eyedroppers to eliminate color casts quickly (see **Figure 7-13**). If a shadow is blue and you click it with the black eyedropper set to a neutral target value, the shadow becomes neutral.

However, this behavior can cause some confusion. While the eyedroppers appear in two nonlinear editing tools—Levels and Curves—their effect is a linear adjustment. So if you labor mightily in Levels or Curves and then apply the black or white eyedroppers to the image, they promptly wipe out any adjustments you'd already made. This behavior leads us to use the eyedroppers only when there's a heavy cast near the shadows or highlights and we haven't applied any fine-tuning corrections yet.

The Gray Eyedropper. The gray eyedropper behaves quite differently from the black and white ones. It forces the clicked pixel to the target hue while attempting to preserve brightness. By default, the target is set to RGB 128 gray, because the tool was designed for gray balancing. Unlike its black

TIP: What can make the eyedroppers frustrating to use is that if you aim for a color and you happen to click a pixel of a slightly different color, the image may not be corrected as you were expecting. Try right-clicking the image with an eyedropper to enlarge the sample size, or instead try using the Auto Color Correction Options dialog, as described earlier in this chapter.

and white counterparts, it doesn't undo other edits you've made in Levels or Curves, though it may change their effects. We use the gray eyedropper occasionally for gray-balancing, but these days we find that the Midtones swatch in the Auto Color Correction Options dialog is more predictable.

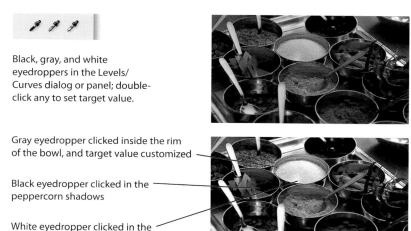

Black, gray, and white eyedroppers in the Levels/Curves dialog or panel; double-click any to set target value.

Gray eyedropper clicked inside the rim of the bowl, and target value customized

Black eyedropper clicked in the peppercorn shadows

White eyedropper clicked in the brightest salt details

Figure 7-13 Using the Levels/Curves eyedroppers

At the top of Figure 7-13 is the same starting image as in Figure 7-10, so that you can compare the process to customizing the Auto Color Correction settings. In Levels, we set the black and white points by clicking the black eyedropper on the shadows of the black peppercorns, and clicked the white eyedropper in the lightest area of the salt. We did not alter the default target values of those eyedroppers. We clicked the gray eyedropper inside the rim of the salt bowl, but the result was too cool, so we double-clicked the gray eyedropper to warm its target value and clicked again. This took more time than Auto Color because we had to click each eyedropper more than once to identify the most representative black, white, and neutral pixels.

Setting Minimum and Maximum Dots. Unlike the Output Levels sliders in Levels, which simply compress the entire tonal range to minimum and maximum values, the eyedroppers let us set a specific value for minimum highlight and maximum shadow dots. To preserve specular highlights, set the white eyedropper to the minimum printable dot value, then click on a diffuse highlight. This pins the diffuse highlight to the minimum dot while allowing the brighter specular highlights to blow out to paper white. As you might guess, when you click a pixel with the black eyedropper, the clicked pixel is set to the target value and all darker pixels clip to solid black.

PRESERVING QUALITY AS YOU EDIT

As with most things in digital imaging, editing tone and color involves trade-offs. As you stretch and squeeze various parts of a image's tonal range, every edit you apply causes some loss of image data . . . sometimes a little, sometimes a lot. The ideal image correction is one where you get it done in as few moves as possible, which is why Conrad calls this process *image golf*. The fewer attempts it takes for you to finish, the better you do; in golf this results in a better score, while in Photoshop this results in the least amount of data loss, preserving image quality—a major goal of this book.

The Details Are in the Differences

Why is it important to preserve image data? To preserve detail. Image detail is formed by adjacent pixels with different tone or color values. When you bring out the details in an image, whether through tonal adjustments or a sharpening filter, what you're really doing at a basic level is accentuating those differences in tonal levels between adjacent pixels.

For instance, when you stretch the shadow values apart to bring out shadow detail, highlight values are squeezed together, as we showed in Figure 7-7. Once you merge two different pixel values into one, as in the highlights we just talked about, you can't re-create the original difference later—that detail is gone forever. That's what we mean when we say that information is lost.

Complicating matters somewhat is that some differences don't represent image detail. They're differences that aren't supposed to be there, and they obscure the details you want. Here are two kinds of unwanted differences:

Noise. Low-cost scanners and high ISO ratings on digital cameras introduce random signals that create differences between pixels that don't represent any image detail in the image. That's *noise*, a well-known enemy of detail. Good tonal and color corrections accentuate detail while minimizing noise. When an image contains a noticeable amount of noise, it's often a good idea to apply noise reduction (see Chapter 10) before making further edits, so that your edits can emphasize image detail more than noise.

Posterization. When you see stair-stepping of tonal or color levels in distinct, visible jumps or bands rather than smooth gradations, you've got *posterization*. Posterization manifests in two ways. When you start making dark

TIP: Details may exist in image data even if they're hard to see, which is why we don't evaluate images only by looking at them. We also use the histogram and the Info panel to observe pixel value differences that are too slight to see.

pixels more different, you eventually make them so different that the image looks splotchy—covered with patches of distinctly different pixels rather than smooth transitions. In addition to wiping out detail, posterization can turn smooth gradations into flat blobs.

How Editing Can Lose Image Data

Let's try an experiment with an image that's technically similar to those edited thousands of times a day in Photoshop. It's made up of an 8-bit channel in which each pixel is represented by a value from 0 (black) to 255 (white). Eight-bit grayscale images have one such channel, while 8-bit color images have three (RGB or Lab) or four (CMYK).

Although you might be working with higher-quality images, here we're acknowledging that the majority of images edited in Photoshop are 8 bits per channel, such as scans or digital camera images shot in JPEG mode. Image edits drop more information from 8-bit/channel files than in files using more bits per channel, simply because you have much less data to start with. Here's a worst-case scenario that you can try yourself (see **Figure 7-14**).

1. In Photoshop, choose File > New, and choose Default Photoshop Size from the Preset menu. Choose Grayscale from the Color Mode pop-up menu, and click OK.

2. Press D to set the default black foreground and white background colors. Using the Gradient tool (press G to select it), Shift-drag to create a horizontal gradient across the entire width of the image.

3. Choose Image > Adjust > Levels (press Command-L in Mac OS X and Ctrl-L in Windows), change the gray (middle) Input Levels slider to 3.00, and click OK. In addition to the midtones becoming lighter, you may already be able to see some banding in the shadows.

TIP: Do not use adjustment layers for this exercise.

4. Open the Levels dialog again, and change the gray slider value to 0.325. The midtones are back almost to where you started, but you should be able to see that, instead of a smooth gradation, you have distinct bands, or posterization, in the gradient.

What happened? With the first midtone adjustment, you lightened the midtones—stretching the shadows and compressing the highlights. With the second midtone adjustment, you darkened the midtones—stretching the highlights and compressing the shadows.

With just two moves, many tonal levels were lost. Instead of a smooth blend with pixels using every value from 0 to 255, the histogram shows that some of those levels became unpopulated as the tones stretched out again.

Figure 7-14 Data loss with just two tonal edits

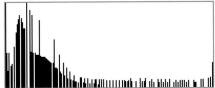

Original 8-bit image, straight from a raw file, shows a solid histogram—values present at all levels for smooth rendering of colors and tones.

After moving just one Levels slider twice, the images appear identical, but there's evidence that tonal data is already lost. The gradient is starting to posterize into bands, and the image histogram shows many new gaps in the tonal range. More edits will visibly degrade the image.

If you repeat the pair of midtone adjustments, you'll see that each time you make an adjustment, the banding becomes more obvious as you lose more and more tonal information. Repeating the midtone adjustments half a dozen times produces a file that contains only 55 gray levels instead of 256. And once you've lost that information, there's no way to bring it back.

But don't get too alarmed about image data loss just yet.

Repeat the experiment, but this time, in the New dialog choose "16 bit" from the menu to the right of the Color Mode pop-up menu. The two moves should not visibly change the image or the gradient, and the histogram should retain most of its integrity. You *are* losing levels, but because a 16-bit channel contains thousands of levels compared to the 256 levels in an 8-bit channel, you can lose many more levels in a 16 bit/channel image before your image visibly degrades. That's a primary advantage of working with high-bit files. And we've got more ways for you to avoid image data loss.

Guidelines for Preserving Image Quality

Given what we've learned so far, here are some guidelines you can employ to minimize the tones and colors that you lose when editing images.

Get Good Data to Begin With. When you shoot digital camera images or scan images, fit the entire tonal range into the histogram when possible. When that isn't possible, decide whether you're going to preserve highlight or shadow detail and expose for that. Avoid exposure-related problems that can't be reversed after you create the image file, such as the following:

- Clipped highlights. If an image contains important highlight detail and you overexpose it with your digital camera or scanner, the highlights become completely white—they contain no detail. It's especially important to avoid overexposing the tones and colors of skin in portraits, because it just looks ugly.

- Underexposed images. When you severely underexpose an image, too much detail gets pushed into the shadows. Due to the linear nature of digital image sensors, most of the available digital levels are used to record the brightest f-stop of data, and very few levels are available to record the darkest. When you underexpose an image, tones are pushed down where fewer levels record them, so that future edits run a higher risk of creating posterization and making noise more visible. With digital camera images, making a dark image lighter always looks worse than making a light image darker, as long as highlights weren't clipped.

Capture High-Bit Data When Possible. Most digital cameras and scanners sold today can capture at least 12 bits per channel. When you shoot in raw mode, a digital camera saves all of the bits it shot, but in JPEG mode a camera must convert images to 8-bit files before saving them on the card.

When you set your digital camera or scanner to its highest bit depth, you are, in effect, telling your capture device to "just give me all the data you can capture" so that you can have the most flexibility in Photoshop. In the 16-bit/channel space, you have much more editing headroom before you run into posterization. Photoshop opens a file of any bit depth between 8 and 16 bits as a 16-bit image.

Don't Overdo It. There are two ways to overdo tonal changes: big moves and repeated moves. Fewer, smaller tonal moves preserve image quality the most. The more you want to change an image, the more compromises you'll

NOTE: You gain nothing by capturing at a lower bit depth and converting to a higher one, such as capturing in 8-bit mode and editing in 16-bit mode. Converting to a higher bit depth just takes up more disk space and processing power.

have to make to avoid obvious posterization, artifacts due to noise, and loss of highlight and shadow detail. When you properly expose an image in the camera, your risk of data loss is lower once you get to Photoshop, and you can spend less time on tonal edits.

Repeated moves are bad because data loss is cumulative. If you go back to our exercise at the beginning of the previous section and repeat steps 3 and 4 ten times, the gradient will be thoroughly trashed. If you're trying to decide between one correction or another, never do a before-and-after comparison by repeatedly applying one correction and then another that counteracts it. Instead, perform comparisons by taking advantage of Undo/Redo, History panel states, layer visibility, and layer comps.

TIP: With an adjustment layer you can make any number of successive edits to an image, and the net amount of data loss will be as if you made just one edit. If you add an adjustment layer and later remove it, there is no data loss at all.

Use Adjustment Layers. You can avoid most of the penalties incurred by successive corrections by using an adjustment layer instead of applying the changes directly to the image. Adjustment layers use more RAM and create bigger files, but the increased flexibility makes the trade-off worthwhile—especially when you find yourself needing to back off from previous edits. But since the various tools offered in adjustment layers operate identically to the way they work on flat files, we started this chapter by discussing how the features (Curves, Levels, Hue/Saturation, and so on) work as dialogs. In Photoshop CS4, another major reason to use adjustment layers is that Adobe has significantly streamlined the adjustment layer workflow. For a detailed discussion of adjustment layers, see Chapter 8, "The Digital Darkroom."

Cover Yourself. Since the data you lose is irretrievable, leave yourself a way out by working on a copy of the file, by saving your tonal adjustments in progress separately (via adjustment layers), or by using any combination of the above. Or you can use the History panel to leave yourself an escape route—just remember that History remembers only as many states as you specify in the Preferences dialog, it's only retained until you close the file, and it can consume mind-boggling amounts of scratch disk space.

Data Loss in Perspective

Even before the digital age, photography was about throwing away everything that couldn't be reproduced in the photograph. We start with all the tone and color of the real world, with scene contrast ratios that are easily in the 100,000:1 range. We reduce that to the contrast ratio we can capture on film or silicon, which—if we're exceptionally lucky—may approach 10,000:1. By the time we get to reproducing the image in print, we have perhaps a 500:1 contrast ratio to play with. This means you have to throw out some data just to get your job done. It's only a matter of degree—the important thing to remember is that the goal isn't to eliminate data loss, since that's impossible, but to make sure that you did your best to keep the most important image data and throw out the least important data. Once good image editing habits become ingrained, you can worry less about data loss and concentrate more on enhancing image quality.

It Ain't Necessarily So

For many years, everyone who taught or wrote about Photoshop passed along several pieces of advice that were, at the time, correctly intended to avoid image data loss. As Adobe has refined version after version of Photoshop, however, some of the old assumptions are no longer true.

Never Use Brightness/Contrast? In Photoshop CS2 and earlier, the Image > Brightness/Contrast command could clip highlight and shadow detail. The default behavior changed starting with Photoshop CS3. Brightness now works like the midtone slider in the Levels dialog, and Contrast now works as if you created an S-curve in the Curves dialog—they don't clip by default. If you want Brightness/Contrast to work in the more destructive manner of Photoshop CS2 and earlier (which is actually sometimes useful when editing masks), turn on the Use Legacy check box in the Brightness/Contrast dialog. Brightness/Contrast is still less precise than Levels or Curves, but at least it is no longer such a blunt instrument. We still prefer to perform brightness and contrast adjustments in Curves.

Note that the Brightness and Contrast adjustments in Camera Raw work differently and do not clip highlights or shadows.

Never Use Auto Corrections? While it's true that if you simply apply Auto corrections you'll probably wreck images, they can be turned to your advantage if you take control over the Auto Color Correction settings. We discuss this in "Controlling Auto Corrections" earlier in this chapter.

Never Use Dodge/Burn? It used to be that the Dodge and Burn tools were hard to control; it was too easy to oversaturate skin or clip values. In Photoshop CS4, new Protect Tones and Vibrance options make these tools more acceptable to use, though we still prefer dodging and burning with adjustment layers (see Chapter 8, "The Digital Darkroom").

Making Adjustments Using Curves

TIP: If you're trying to make the transition from the Curves features of Photoshop CS3 or earlier to Photoshop CS4, you can get oriented by using Figures 7-15 and 7-16 together with Table 7-1 and 7-2.

The Curves feature displays a graph that plots the relationship between input (unaltered) level and output (altered) level. Input levels run along the bottom, and output values run along the side. When you first choose the Curves command, the graph displays a straight 45-degree line (or baseline), meaning that for each input level, the output level is unchanged (see **Figure 7-15**). As you add points to alter the Output levels, a curve forms. We think of Levels as like an automatic transmission (easy and effective), and Curves as a manual transmission (more effort to master, but much more control).

You can perform the three basic input levels adjustments in Curves, letting you skip Levels if you want. It might be overkill to use Curves to make only those three adjustments, but the point is that if you were trained (using earlier versions of Photoshop) to set Levels before fine-tuning in Curves, you can now do it all using Curves alone. Once you make the three basic adjustments, you can stay in Curves to execute finer contrast control over different tonal ranges within the image—more than you could ever do in Levels.

TIP: As in other panels and dialogs, you can apply presets using the Preset pop-up menu at the top and you can load and save your own custom presets using the button menu to the right of the Preset pop-up menu. It's worth taking a look in the Preset menu to see if any of the built-in presets are useful to you.

You'll find that the black-point and white-point sliders are similar to those in Levels—they're at the bottom of the Curves graph/histogram, and you can see the clipping display by Option/Alt-dragging those sliders (or turn on the Show Clipping option). But where's the midtone slider? There isn't one; you click the exact center of the curve to add a new curve point, and then you drag that new point straight up to lighten the image or straight down to darken the image.

As you'll see in the next section, in Photoshop CS4 the Curves feature works somewhat differently as a dialog than it does in the new Adjustments panel. (Levels works pretty much the same either way.)

Customizing the Curves Display Options

In Photoshop CS4, Curves is available in both a dialog (see Figure 7-15) and in the nonmodal Adjustments panel (see **Figure 7-16**), a new and more direct front end to the adjustment layers we talk about in Chapter 8. In the Curves dialog, the display options appear in the Curve Display Options section of the dialog, while in the Adjustments panel you get to them through the Adjustments panel menu. **Figure 7-17** shows more Curves display options.

Preset pop-up menu

Channel views pop-up menu

Point and Freehand tools

Output level axis (value after correction)

Baseline

Histogram

Output value for currently selected curve point

Input level axis (existing value)

On-Image tool

Input value for currently selected curve point

Show or hide display options

Curves eyedroppers

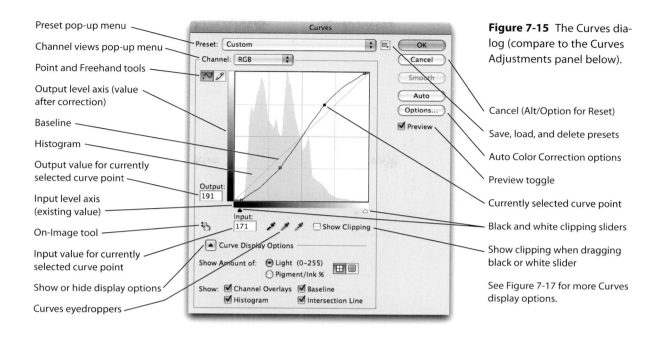

Figure 7-15 The Curves dialog (compare to the Curves Adjustments panel below).

Cancel (Alt/Option for Reset)

Save, load, and delete presets

Auto Color Correction options

Preview toggle

Currently selected curve point

Black and white clipping sliders

Show clipping when dragging black or white slider

See Figure 7-17 for more Curves display options.

Preset pop-up menu

On-Image tool

Eyedroppers

Output level axis (value after correction)

Point tool, Freehand tool, Smooth button

Output value for selected curve point

Histogram uncached refresh warning

Input value for selected curve point

Back to adjustments list

Expanded mode toggle

Make clipping mask

Toggle layer visibility

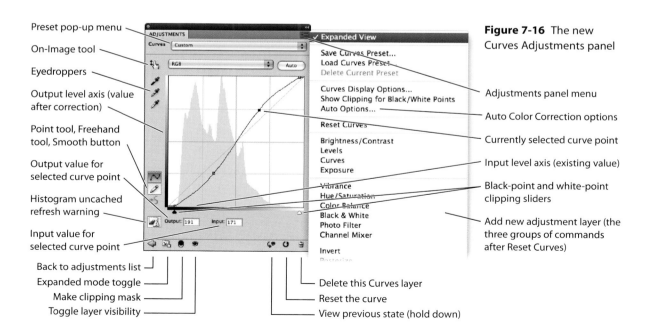

Figure 7-16 The new Curves Adjustments panel

Adjustments panel menu

Auto Color Correction options

Currently selected curve point

Input level axis (existing value)

Black-point and white-point clipping sliders

Add new adjustment layer (the three groups of commands after Reset Curves)

Delete this Curves layer

Reset the curve

View previous state (hold down)

Figure 7-17 More Curves
dialog display options

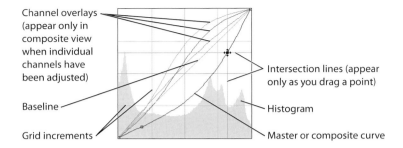

Channel overlays
(appear only in
composite view
when individual
channels have
been adjusted)

Intersection lines (appear
only as you drag a point)

Baseline

Histogram

Grid increments

Master or composite curve

TIP: We usually leave
Show Clipping off, pre-
ferring to see the temporary
clipping display shown when
you Option/Alt-drag the black-
point or white-point slider.

Show Clipping. Turn this on to see the pixels that are currently being
clipped by the black- or white-point slider at the bottom of the graph area.
Show Clipping can show either black clipping or white clipping, but not
both at the same time. The clipping you see is for the last slider you
touched, or for black if you haven't touched either slider since opening the
dialog. Show Clipping works only when Show Amount Of is set to Light.

Show Amount Of. This option sets the units and graph orientation used
to display values on the graph. Those who work with Web, video, and other
RGB-based media are used to thinking of tone in terms of levels from 0
to 255. Those accustomed to working with ink on press will want to work
with dot percentages. You can flip the graph display by selecting Light or
Pigment/Ink. When you select Light, the 0,0 shadow point is at bottom left
and the 255,255 highlight point is at top right. When you select Pigment/
Ink %, the 0,0 highlight point is at the bottom left and the 100,100 shadow
point is at the top right corner. RGB and Lab mode images default to Light;
CMYK and Grayscale mode images default to Pigment/Ink %.

TIP: Another way to
toggle the grid incre-
ments is to Option-click (Mac)
or Alt-click (Windows) the
graph area.

Change Grid Increments. The two grid icons let you change the Curves
graph gridlines. The left icon (the default) displays gridlines in 25 percent
increments, and the right icon displays them in 10 percent increments. The
25 percent grid lets prepress folks think in terms of shadow, three-quarter-
tone, midtone, quarter-tone, and highlight, while the 10 percent grid provides photographers with a reasonable simulation of the Zone System.

Show Channel Overlays. When you view the composite view (for example, choosing RGB from the Channel pop-up menu), the Curves dialog can
display the curves of each channel in that channel's color. However, you
can't edit the overlay curves—to do that, choose the name of the channel
you want to edit from the Channel pop-up menu.

Show Histogram. The histogram is as useful here as it is in the Levels dialog, so we leave this on.

Show Baseline. This diagonal gray line reminds you of the shape of the unedited state of a curve. We don't find it very useful in its current state; we'd prefer that it show you the shape of the curve at the time you opened the Curves dialog, before you started editing. Maybe in the future it will!

Show Intersection Line. This feature appears only as you drag a curve point. Intersection Line actually consists of two lines that lead from the cursor to all sides of the graph, so that you can see exactly where the curve point values cross the Input and Output axes.

Creating and Editing Curves

The great power of the Curves command comes from being able to place up to 16 curve points so that can you change the shape of the curve and the angle of curve segments (we rarely need to add all 16 points). Remember, steepness is contrast—the steeper the curve segment, the more definition you create between the values of adjacent pixels.

For example, an S-shaped curve (see **Figure 7-18**) increases contrast in the midtones without blowing out highlights or plugging up shadows, though it sacrifices highlight and shadow detail by compressing those regions. We often use a small bump on the highlight end of the curve to stretch highlights, or on the shadow end of the curve to open up extreme shadows.

TIP: Dragging curve points with the mouse is often the least efficient way to edit a curve. The fastest way is using a click-to-add shortcut and adjusting points using the arrow keys, or in Photoshop CS4 you can also use the On-Image tool.

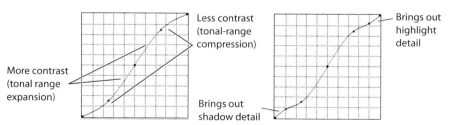

More contrast (tonal range expansion)

Less contrast (tonal-range compression)

Brings out shadow detail

Brings out highlight detail

Figure 7-18 S-curves

Photoshop CS4 Shortcut Changes. In Photoshop CS4, the introduction of the Adjustments panel changes the Curves shortcut workflow significantly, particularly for Photoshop veterans with long-ingrained shortcut habits. There are now two sets of shortcuts for editing curves—one for the Curves dialog and the other for the Curves Adjustments panel. This really should not be much of a problem, because if you typically use the

Curves Adjustments panel instead of the dialog (as we recommend), you need to know only one set: the Curves Adjustments panel shortcuts listed in **Table 7-2**. (You'll also need to switch to the new channel-viewing shortcuts we covered in Table 7-1, earlier in this chapter.) To ease your adjustment to the Photoshop CS4 shortcuts, take advantage of the On-Image tool . . .

The On-Image Tool. This tool adds a great time-saving feature to Photoshop CS4: adding and adjusting a curve point in a single intuitive, visual step. With the On-Image tool selected, position the cursor over a tone or color you want to change in the image (not in the graph) and drag (see **Figure 7-19**). Photoshop adds a point to the curve at that level in the graph; drag up to increase the Output value, and drag down to decrease it. This works in both the Curves dialog and the Adjustments panel. If you've used the Targeted Adjustment Tool in Adobe Lightroom, it's the same idea.

The On-Image tool also overcomes a major obstacle Adobe faced in its worthy quest to make Curves nonmodal in Photoshop CS4. When Curves is in a dialog, the cursor lets you sample values from the image (see "The Eyedropper Sampler" later in this section), and that's easy because the cursor can't do anything else to the image while the dialog is open. But when Curves is in the nonmodal Adjustments panel, the cursor would normally be whatever tool is selected in the Tools panel, preventing you from using the cursor to sample color values directly from the image. The On-Image tool solves this problem by forcing the cursor to serve the Adjustments panel only. When the On-Image tool is enabled, you can perform the sampling and point-editing functions that were taken for granted in the Curves dialog, as we describe in Table 7-2. For Photoshop veterans, the On-Image tool makes it possible for you to use many of the old Curves dialog shortcuts; in some cases the new shortcut is simpler than the old one.

More Ways to Add Curve Points. When you're in the Curves dialog (not the Curves Adjustments panel), you can add a new point to a curve by Command-clicking (Mac OS X) or Ctrl-clicking (Windows) in the image. Of course, you can also add a point to a curve by clicking directly on the curve itself. For example, if you place the cursor in the graph at Input 128, Output 102 and click, the curve changes its shape to pass through that point, all the pixels that were at level 128 change to level 102, and the rest of the midtones are darkened correspondingly. We summarize these shortcuts in Table 7-2, including a one-click shortcut for adding a point at a pixel's

TIP: If you're going to be working in the Adjustments panel for a while, it's worth it to turn on the On-Image tool. And if you're used to the old Curves dialog shortcuts, turning on the On-Image tool is the only way to make sense of the new Curves Adjustments panel.

TIP: If you just can't get used to the Photoshop CS4 curve-editing shortcuts, you can download a free plug-in that restores the shortcuts used in CS3 and earlier. As we write this, the link to the plug-in is http://blogs.adobe.com/jnack/files/Use_Old_Shortcuts.zip.

color value on the curves in all of the color channels of a color image—a big time-saver for removing color casts.

Selecting a Curve Point. The most obvious way to select a curve point is to click one with the mouse. You can also select a point with the keyboard; press the plus sign key (+) to cycle through the points on the curve, selecting the next one with each press, or reverse direction by pressing the minus sign key (–). This is a change from Photoshop CS3 (see Table 7-2).

Curves as a Dialog or as a Panel? In most cases you'll want to work with Curves from the Adjustments panel because it applies the changes as a non-destructive adjustment layer instead of altering pixels permanently. You may want to assign a shortcut of your choice to the Layer > New Adjustment Layer > Curves command (choose Edit > Keyboard Shortcuts). Choosing that command does the same thing as clicking the Curves icon in the Adjustments panel. The Curves dialog is still useful for certain cases when Curves is simply not available as an adjustment layer, such as when you want to use a curve to edit a mask or alpha channel.

The Eyedropper Sampler. Separate from the three eyedropper icons in Curves is an eyedropper sampler that appears when you move the cursor over the image while the Curves dialog is open, or when the Curves Adjustments panel is open and the On-Image tool is selected. A circle shows the location of that point on the curve. For sampler shortcuts, see Table 7-2.

TIP: You can customize the sample size of the eyedropper by Control-clicking (Mac) or right-clicking (Windows) it on an image, even if a dialog is open.

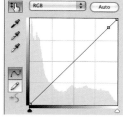

Clicking the On-Image tool in a light area of the image adds a point high on the curve.

Figure 7-19 The On-Image tool

Dragging the On-Image tool upward in a shadow adds a curve point and increases its Output value, lightening that curve segment.

Table 7-2 Shortcuts for the Curves dialog and Curves adjustments panel.

To do this . . .	. . . in Curves dialog (Photoshop CS3 and CS4):	. . . in Curves Adjustments panel (Photoshop CS4):
Add a new Curves adjustment	Choose Image > Adjustments > Curves or press Command/Ctrl-M	Click the Curves icon (the CS3 methods still work too)
Use eyedropper sampler	Drag cursor over image	Turn on On-Image tool and move cursor over image
Display Input/Output value of underlying pixel	Drag cursor over image	Turn on On-Image tool and position cursor over pixel
Add point to current curve by clicking image	Command/Ctrl-click the image	Turn on On-Image tool and click image
Add a curve point to all color image channels from composite view	On the image, Command-Shift click (Mac) Ctrl-Shift-click (Windows)	Turn on On-Image tool and Command-click (Mac) or Ctrl-click (Windows)
Select next curve point	Press plus sign key (+) or press Ctrl-Tab	Press plus sign key (+)
Select previous curve point	Press minus sign key (–) or press Ctrl-Shift-Tab	Press minus sign key (–)
Add color sampler (up to four)	Shift-click image	Turn on On-Image tool and Shift-click image
Compare view to before the current Curves session	Toggle Preview check box or press P	Hold Previous State button or hold \ (backslash) key
Undo most recent curve edit	Command-Z (Mac) Ctrl-Z (Windows)	Command-Z (Mac) Ctrl-Z (Windows)
Hide current Curves adjustment	(possible only in Layers panel)	Click Toggle Layer Visibility button in Adjustments panel
Remove all Curves edits (reset to default)	Option-click (Mac) or Alt-click (Windows) the Cancel button	Click Reset button
Clip to next layer down	(only in Layers panel)	Click Clipping Mask button

NOTE: In Windows, if you want to go to the next point on the curve and a Curves number field is active, you may need to add Shift to the plus sign shortcut.

TIP: In the Curves Adjustments panel, the Edit > Step Forward and Edit > Step Backward shortcuts work, giving you multiple undos (compared to the single undo you get in the Curves dialog).

Input/Output Level Readouts. When you move the cursor into the Curves graph, the Input and Output levels show the tonal levels on the graph (see **Figure 7-20**). You can follow the shape of the curve with the cursor and watch the readout to see exactly what's happening at each level.

The readouts become editable when you add or select a curve point. In the Curves dialog you can press Tab to highlight the Input or Output field as needed, but in the Adjustments panel you'll usually have to click a field with the mouse; because the Tab key hides all panels, it usually doesn't navigate fields in the Adjustments panel unless a panel field is already active.

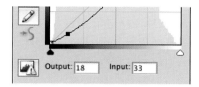

Figure 7-20 Input/Output levels become editable when you select a point or drag a slider

Input and Output level readouts for the selected point in the Curves Adjustments panel

Input and Output level readouts for the selected point in the Curves dialog

More-Accessible Curves Presets. Although adjustment presets have been part of Photoshop for a while, they've always been buried in some menu. In the new Adjustments panel, just click the triangle next to the Curves pop-up menu and click a preset name to apply one. A preset makes a great starting point for pros as well as novices, because you can fully edit the Curves adjustment layer that a preset produces. Keep in mind that every time you click a preset Photoshop adds another adjustment layer—keep an eye out for redundant layers added to the Layers panel.

Other Curves Goodies. In the bottom half of Table 7-2 are extra conveniences built into the Curves dialog and Adjustments panel, including the valuable abilities to toggle a before-and-after view of the current edit and to reset Curves to the state before the current edit. Again, veteran Curves jockeys will want to adapt to the new shortcuts for these features.

Drawing Curves with the Freehand Tool

We'd be remiss if we didn't mention the Freehand (pencil) tool in the Curves dialog, which lets you draw freehand curves rather than bending the curve by placing points. We use the Freehand tool to handle specular highlights on printing processes where the minimum highlight dot is relatively large, such as laser printer or newsprint output. For the rare times we need to do this, nothing else does the job.

Trouble in the Transition Zone. If you're dealing with newsprint or low-quality printing, the transition zone—that ambiguous area between white paper and the minimum reliable dot—can make your specular highlights messy. Some may drop out, while others may print with a visible dot. The solution is to make a curve that sets your brightest highlight detail to the minimum highlight dot value and then blows everything brighter than that directly out to white. This is a two-step process (see **Figure 7-21**).

1. Select the highlight point, then use the numeric fields to set the Input to a value corresponding to your brightest real detail, and the Output to a value corresponding to your minimum printable dot. Figure 7-21 shows a point that sets the Input value at 253 and the Output value at 231, corresponding to a 10 percent dot. This sets all the pixels with a value of 253 to 231. But it also sets pixels with values of 253 through 255 to 231, which isn't what you want. You want them to be white.

2. Select the Freehand (pencil) tool, and very carefully position it at the top edge of the curve graph until the input value reads 253 and the output value reads 255, then click the mouse button. This keeps pixels with an input value of 252 set to an output value of 231, but blows out pixels with a value of 253 through 255 to paper white. Your highlight detail will print with a reliable dot, and your specular highlights will definitely blow out. Don't click the Smooth button, because it will smooth the curve—which in this case is not what you want.

Figure 7-21 Blowing out the specular highlights

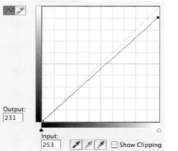

A curve point at Input 253, Output 231 compresses the image to the printable range.

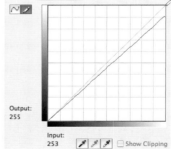

A little touch-up with the Freehand tool makes all of the white pixels white.

If this is something you have to do often, choose Save Preset from the Adjustments panel menu to save the curve. You can load the saved curve whenever you need it, or even create an action that you run as a batch to process multiple images.

Hands-On Curves

Now that you're armed with all the preceding information, let's look at some practical examples of working with Curves. We'll look at several different scenarios, because we have two different reasons for editing images, as we discuss in the upcoming sidebar, "What's Your Motivation?"

The classic order for preparing images is as follows:

- Retouching and removing spots, dust, and scratches

- Overall tonal correction (black point, white point, midtone, contrast)

- Overall color correction (remove color casts, add vibrance/saturation)

- Selective tonal and/or color correction

- Output-specific optimizations (resizing, sharpening, handling out-of-gamut colors, compressing tonal range, converting to other color spaces)

We loosely adhere to this sequence, but a great deal depends on the image and on the quality of the image capture. For instance, you often have to apply some basic tonal correction to a scanned image before you can even consider removing dust and scratches. And because changes to the color balance can affect tonal values, it can sometimes be impossible to separate tonal correction from color correction. When that happens, you may need to go back and forth between tonal and color corrections.

Evaluating Images for Correction

Before we edit an image, we spend a few moments evaluating it to see what needs to be done and to spot potential pitfalls. We check the Histogram panel to get a sense of the image's dynamic range: If shadows or highlights are clipped, we can't bring back any detail, but we may still be able to make the image look good. If all the data is clumped in the middle, with no true blacks or whites, we'll probably want to expand the tonal range.

We also check the values in the bright highlights and dark shadows on the Info panel, in case there's detail lurking there that we can exploit. We're pretty good at identifying color casts by eye on a calibrated monitor, but we still check the Info panel—a magenta cast and a red cast, for example, appear fairly similar, but the prescription for fixing each is quite different.

If we're working with a scan of film or a print, the first thing we do is zoom to 100 percent (Actual Pixels) or higher and look at every pixel using the Home, Page Up, Page Down, and End keys. (To scroll sideways, press Page Up or Page Down, along with the Command key in Mac OS X or the Ctrl key in Windows.) We check for dust, scratches, noise (especially in the blue channel), the strengths and weaknesses visible in each channel, and the tonal range in the histogram. A few minutes spent critically evaluating the image early on can save hours later.

Fix the Biggest Problem First. The guideline we've developed over the years is simple: Fix the biggest problem first. You often have to fix the biggest problem before you can even see what the other problems are. But it's usually also the most effective approach, requiring the least work and degrading the image the least.

TIP: Take advantage of the Image > Duplicate command when you want to experiment with potential solutions without accidentally saving unwanted changes to the original file.

Leave Yourself an Escape Route. The great Scot poet Robert Burns pointed out that "the best-laid schemes o' mice and men gang aft agley." He didn't have the benefit of the History panel or the Undo and Revert commands, but you do. History is a great feature, but it eventually it starts dropping the oldest history states, so don't consume them unnecessarily. If a particular move doesn't work, just undo (Command-Z in Mac OS X, or Ctrl-Z in Windows). You can reapply any of the Image > Adjustments submenu commands with their last-used settings by holding down the Option key (Mac) or Alt key (Windows) while selecting them, either from the menu or with a keyboard shortcut. If a whole train of moves has led you down a blind alley, back up in the History panel or revert to the original version.

Before you apply a move using Levels, Curves, or Hue/Saturation, save the image first. That way, you can always retrace your steps up to the point where things started to go wrong.

Adjustment layers let you avoid many of the pitfalls we've just discussed. You don't need to get your edits right the first time, because you can go back and change them at will without damaging the underlying pixels. You automatically leave yourself an escape route because your edits float above the original image rather than being burned into it. For a much deeper discussion of adjustment layers, see Chapter 8, "The Digital Darkroom."

Evaluation Examples

We show two unedited images in **Figures 7-22** and **7-23** and discuss the conclusions we draw as to what we need to do to them. We'll execute the edits a little later. The evaluation process takes only a few seconds, and it's time well spent. In the following examples, we'll apply the edits directly to the image, but later you can perform the same edits with adjustment layers. So now that you're armed with a plan, let's proceed to the edits.

Earlier in this chapter, we showed you Levels and Curves as dialogs, for simplicity as we introduced them. From now on, however, we're going to stick with the new Adjustments panel. This is not only because using adjustment layers has always been the recommended workflow in terms of preserving image quality, but also because Adobe worked hard to make the Adjustments panel the front-line image correction workflow in Photoshop CS4.

Tonal Refinements. Figure 7-22 shows an image scanned from black-and-white negative film using a film scanner. We deliberately scan with the black point and white point set with a few unused tones at the ends, because we know we can set the endpoints more accurately in Photoshop than in the scanning software. To minimize image degradation during editing, we scanned the image as a 16-bit/channel grayscale TIFF file. We also chose Image > Invert to make it a positive image. Because it was old film, we removed dust and scratches (see Chapter 11, "Essential Image Techniques"). After that was done, we evaluated the image in terms of tonal quality.

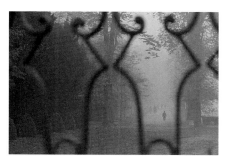

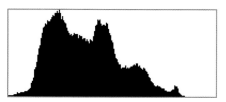

Figure 7-22 A scanned negative that just needs a good tone curve

Details are hard to see due to low contrast. Our goal is to use a curve to separate the tones more clearly without losing the subtle tonal atmosphere of the fog.

The histogram shows no clipping at either end, but one reason the image looks flat is that there are clearly levels in the highlights that aren't being used.

A Shot Through a Car Window. Figure 7-23 was shot using a digital SLR, and it poses several challenges. It was shot in traffic through a car windshield, which added glare and reflections and also a color cast. It was also a sunny day, so the image involves a much wider dynamic range than the previous image—we'll have to make harder choices.

Figure 7-23 An image shot under challenging conditions

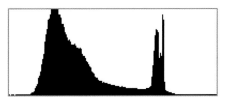

This image is washed out due to sun glare and the contrast-reducing effect of the car windshield through which the image was shot. In addition, there appears to be a color cast that needs to be neutralized.

In the histogram it looks as though we have the tones we need; they're just not in the right place. Most of the tones are at the extremes, so our curve may have to work extra hard to manage them effectively.

Correcting the Black-and-White Image

In the Adjustments panel we click the Curves button (see **Figure 7-24**) so that we've got a new Curves adjustment layer to work with.

Figure 7-24 Adding a new Curves adjustment layer

Clicking the Curves button in the Adjustments panel adds a new Curves adjustment layer in the Layers panel. This also causes the Curves controls to appear in the Adjustments panel (see Figure 7-25).

Our first task with the image is to refine the black point and white point. We want to use the interactive clipping display, as we did in Levels, so under the Curves graph we Option-drag (Mac OS X) or Alt-drag (Windows) the black-point slider and then the white-point slider (see **Figure 7-25**). For the black point we let a few of the pixels in the iron gate go black; for the white point we don't clip any pixels because we want to preserve the fog as well as leave a little headroom for sharpening (since sharpening adds contrast along edges, driving some of those pixels toward levels 255 and 0).

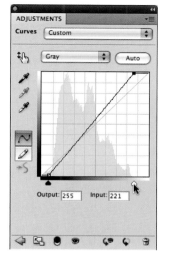
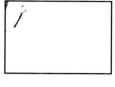

Option/Alt-dragging the white-point slider

Black-point (top left) and white-point (top right) clipping displays, and full tonal range achieved after setting the black-point and white-point sliders (bottom)

Figure 7-25 Using Curves to set the black point and white point

After setting the endpoints, it's already easier to see the row of hedges at the left and the people in the distance on the right. Now we just need to set any necessary points in between. However, we do notice one thing: There's posterization, but in just some of the parts of the tonal range. We've learned that when the tonal distribution is inconsistent, it's a clue that the tonal range hasn't been made linear. This makes sense, because we've made no changes to the tone curve since scanning the negative—we've set only the endpoints. Because the posterization is most visible in the shadows, we place our first curve point there and adjust it until the tones even out (see **Figure 7-26**). The result is probably closer to how the image would have printed in a darkroom enlarger. It also reminds us that you can stretch tones only so far before they break apart and posterize, and that posterization will happen faster in images like this high-speed film negative, where there may not be that many tones to work with in the first place.

We don't think we need a second major linearization adjustment, so the rest of the curve points we add are for a different purpose: to emphasize individual areas of interest. The dark and light areas are distinctive enough,

TIP: If the black- and white-point sliders do nothing, try deselecting all curve points; press Command-D (Mac OS X) or Ctrl-D (Windows).

but it would be nice to separate the midtones a little more, so we grab the On-Image Tool and drag a midtone in the image up and down until we like the result. We end up adding another curve point at a near-highlight value, trying to separate tones without killing the fog effect. It's always a balancing act, because increasing contrast in one part of the tonal range inevitably decreases it somewhere else. The only way around that is to make corrections that you limit to specific areas; we cover that in Chapter 8.

Figure 7-26 Our first curve point tries to restore the tonal curve of the film

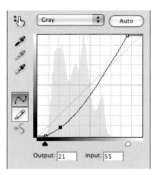

We notice that film grain is more visible in the shadows than in the midtones and highlights (top), a clue that there's posterization in the shadows. We turn on the On-Image tool, position it over a darker shadow tone, and drag down; this adds a curve point in the Adjustments panel and reduces the point's Output value (left). By compressing shadow values more than midtones and highlights, we smooth the tonal distribution from dark to light (middle).

TIP: By default, the gray curve displays from white (0% ink) on the left to black (100% ink) on the right. Conrad's gotten used to a dark-to-light display, so for these examples he chose Curves Display Options from the Adjustments panel menu and selected Light (0-255) to flip the Curves graph.

Due to that balancing act, we're always keeping an eye on both the Curves graph and all of the tones in the image to make sure nothing we care about is getting trashed by one of our other moves. Also, we constantly fine-tune curve points we've already laid down. The On-Image tool is sometimes a little coarse for tiny adjustments; we often prefer to ride up and down the curve from point to point using the plus sign key (+) and minus sign (–) key until we select a point we want to adjust, and then we press any of the arrow keys to nudge the selected point until we get what we want.

If we're not sure whether we've improved the image, we do a before-and-after comparison by holding down the backslash key (\). Holding down this key displays the image without the changes you made since displaying Curves in the Adjustments panel. It's actually a shortcut for holding down the View Previous State button (see Figure 7-16). For Photoshop veterans, this replaces the old Curves method of pressing P or toggling the Preview check box.

Our final curve is shown in **Figure 7-27**. It linearizes the tones, adds depth, and makes it easier to distinguish the different trees and the foliage as they fade into the fog in the distance.

TIP: When you use the backslash key for a before-and-after view, don't tap the key, hold it down. Tapping displays a layer mask instead.

Figure 7-27 Our final curve and image

Our final curve. The single curve includes endpoint, midtone, and creative adjustments.

Our final image. Compared to Figure 7-22, it has more dynamic range, and the gray tree in the middle, the leaves on the ground, and the figures in the distance are more distinct.

Correcting the Color Image

Again, we start by using the Adjustments panel to add a Curves adjustment layer to the image, and we check and set the endpoints in the same way we did in Figures 7-9 and 7-25. For the black point, we stop as soon as channels start clipping, We make a decision to let the white point clip part of the brightest part of the paper that the man is holding, in order to give more levels to other parts of the image. We do not allow the sky to clip. See **Figure 7-28** for our endpoints and the image so far.

Now on to the curve itself. Our evaluation noticed low contrast, which was partially addressed by the endpoints but still needs work with a curve. We'll also try to lighten the front of the backlit man, and we'll need to identify an odd color cast and remove it, all with Curves.

TIP: If you come up with a successful curve and you're going to process many more similar images (like a big batch of scans from the same film), save your curve as a preset so you can quickly apply it to any other image from the Curves panel.

Figure 7-28 Setting endpoints for the color image

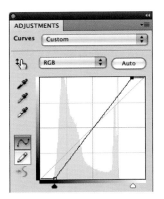

We select the On-Image tool, position it over the man's face, and drag up. This brightens the entire image, starting from the man's face, which helps to overcome the backlighting (see **Figure 7-29**).

Figure 7-29 Lightening the dark foreground

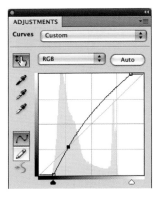

This weakens the shadows a bit too much, so we position the On-Image tool inside the cuff of the pant leg on the man's right and drag down, which adds a point near the bottom of the curve. By now the formerly blue sky has gone almost white, so we drag the On-Image tool downward in the sky to give it some density again. Originally we pulled down the sky quite a bit, but that amount killed the highlights in the rest of the image, so we backed off. We then decided to click the curve graph itself to add two more points on either side of the point added by the On-Image tool, so we could more precisely manage the contrast from the midtones to the sky. The curve and image so far are shown in **Figure 7-30**. The point selected on the curve is the sky point we added with the On-Image tool; the two points above and below that were added by clicking directly on the curve.

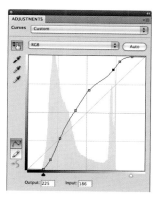

Figure 7-30 Fine-tuning the curve

Through our management of contrast with the curve we have largely overcome the glare from the sun and the windshield. The last item on our to-do list is the color cast. We're not sure exactly what the cast is, but there's a way to find out if we can identify something in the image that should be a neutral color. We decide that the utility pole on the right is a good candidate.

We need to get a color value sample from the pole. When the On-Image tool is selected, it functions as a color sampler, so we position it over the utility pole and look at the Info panel. It reads highest in red and lowest in blue. We decide to see what happens if we neutralize that. But first, so that we can continue monitoring the Info panel, we Shift-click the On-Image tool on the utility pole to leave behind a color sampler, which adds its own persistent readout to the Info panel (see **Figure 7-31**).

TIP: Remember, the Curves shortcuts we talk about in this section—and many more—are summarized in Table 7-2.

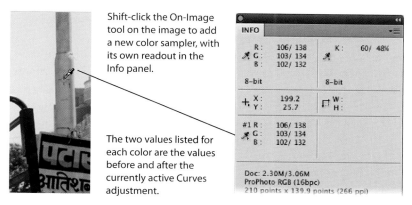

Shift-click the On-Image tool on the image to add a new color sampler, with its own readout in the Info panel.

The two values listed for each color are the values before and after the currently active Curves adjustment.

Figure 7-31 Dropping a color sampler

With the sampler in place, we're ready to neutralize the cast. We suspect that it will take a correction in more than one channel, so we want to add points to the red, green, and blue channels. We can add a point to all channels at once using a shortcut. With the On-Image tool selected, we Command-Shift-click (Mac OS X) or Ctrl-Shift-click (Windows) the utility pole where we dropped the color sampler. This works as long as you're viewing the composite curves, and it saves you the time and trouble of figuring out where to add points in each channel to correct a color in the image.

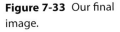 **TIP:** If you still see a color cast in another tonal range, such as the highlights or shadows, just add another set of points to all channels and edit those.

Now it's just a matter of adjusting the points until the color sampler reads neutral in the Info panel. We use the middle value (green channel) as the baseline, so we view the red channel in the Curves panel, select the point we added with the shortcut, and nudge it down until its value matches the green channel in the Info panel (see **Figure 7-32**). We then switch to the blue channel and do the same thing. We use keyboard shortcuts to view the red, green, and blue channels, respectively: Option-3, Option-4, and Option 5 (Mac OS X) or Alt-3, Alt-4, and Alt-5 (Windows).

Figure 7-32 Points added to all channels at once and then edited individually; the Info panel shows color neutralized in the post-correction value.

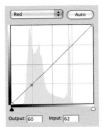   

We think the last correction was the right decision (see **Figure 7-33**)—the previous version now seems too warm. We controlled contrast and removed a color cast by editing several channel curves in one Curves adjustment.

Figure 7-33 Our final image.

Using Color Samplers

You can use the Eyedropper tool in the Tools panel to check pixel values in the Info panel. But when you're comparing or tracking the pixel values of two or more areas in an image, you don't want to try to keep moving the mouse back to the exact same position every time. Fortunately, you can drop up to four color samplers on the image. Each sampler stays in place and continuously reports the underlying color values in the Info panel, as we did back in Figure 7-31.

You can select the Color Sampler tool in the Tools panel, but you may not have to. If you're using the Eyedropper tool, temporarily enable the Color Sampler tool by holding down Shift; for example, Shift-clicking adds a color sampler. If you're using a painting tool you can temporarily enable the Color Sampler by pressing Option-Shift (Mac) or Alt-Shift (Windows).

You can't get to the Color Sampler tool in the Tools panel when an adjustment dialog is open (such as Levels or Curves), but, as you saw in the color example, the eyedropper appears when the On-Image tool is enabled in the Curves Adjustments panel (or when you're in a Levels or Curves dialog) and you move the mouse outside an open adjustment dialog. **Table 7-3** summarizes the ways you can use the Color Sampler tool.

TIP: When the Color Sampler tool is selected, the Options bar lets you customize the size of the area the tool samples, and also provides a Clear button to remove all color samplers.

Table 7-3 Using color samplers.

To do the following when the Color Sampler tool is active . . .	. . . do this:
Add a new color sampler	Shift-click the image
Move a color sampler	Drag the color sampler
Delete a color sampler	Option-click an existing color sampler (Mac OS X) Alt-click an existing color sampler (Windows)

To use one of the above Color Sampler shortcuts in the following mode. . .	. . . combine the shortcuts above with the following:
When the Eyedropper tool is active	Press Shift
Inside an adjustment dialog	Press Shift
When an Adjustments panel is active	Turn on the On-Image tool
When a painting tool is active	Press Option-Shift (Mac OS X) Press Alt-Shift (Windows)

You can click an eyedropper on any open Photoshop document, not just the one you're working on. When a dialog is open and you see the eyedropper when you position the cursor outside the dialog, that means you can sample that color (from the Swatches panel, for example). To sample a color from another application, start dragging the eyedropper from inside a Photoshop document window and release the mouse button over the color you want to sample outside Photoshop.

Using Shadows and Highlights

TIP: In Adobe Camera Raw, the Recovery and Fill Light commands are similar to the Shadows/Highlights feature in Photoshop. But because Recovery and Fill Light have access to the raw camera sensor data, they can potentially do more to save an image than Shadows/Highlights.

The Shadows/Highlights command is unlike all the other commands on the Image > Adjust submenu. They compare a pixel on the adjustment layer to the corresponding pixel on underlying layers, while Shadows/Highlights evaluates and adjusts each pixel differently depending on the values of neighboring pixels on the same layer. Shadows/Highlights lets you recover detail from nearly blown-out highlights and nearly plugged shadows in a way that Curves and Levels can't. Where Levels and Curves shift the value of all layer pixels uniformly, Shadows/Highlights can vary the amount of adjustment to achieve the local contrast settings you've established. That's a lot of what Shadows/Highlights is about: local contrast.

In its default form, the Shadows/Highlights dialog is very simple—frankly, too simple to be of real use. Turn on the More Options check box to reveal the full capabilities of this command (see **Figure 7-34**).

When expanded, Shadows/Highlights offers Amount, Tonal Width, and Radius sliders for Shadows and for Highlights; a Color Correction slider (on grayscale images, it's replaced by a Brightness slider); a Midtone Contrast slider; and clipping percentage fields for black and white. The interactions between the controls are fairly complex, so let's look at them in turn.

Figure 7-34 shows a Shadows/Highlights correction of an image with a long tonal scale, compared with a correction attempt in Curves. The Shadows/Highlights version cannot be achieved through Curves except by applying multiple curves to different areas masked by hand.

Amount. These options control the strength of the correction—they're the volume knobs. Be careful; as you approach and pass 50 percent, keep an eye on the entire image for unintended consequences.

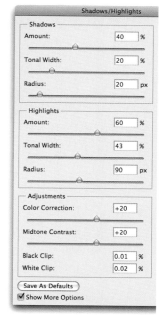

Figure 7-34 Comparing Shadows/Highlights to Curves. Our Shadows/Highlights settings are below.

In the original image, the trees are too dark and the mountain and sky are flat.

Curves: We improve the mountain but the meadow midtones go flat. Lightening shadows flattened the midtones even further, so we backed off.

Shadows/Highlights: We take the dark trees out of the shadows and give the mountain more presence, while preserving midtone contrast in the meadow.

Tonal Width. These sliders dictate how far up the tonal range from black the Shadow correction applies, and how far down the tonal range from white the Highlight correction applies. They let you constrain the correction to the tonal range that needs it.

Radius. This slider sets how far out Shadows/Highlights looks around each pixel to analyze and then alter local contrast. Tune the Radius value for the size of the features you're trying to emphasize. If the Radius value is too large or too small, you may lose detail instead of emphasizing it.

Color Correction. This is a saturation control that operates only on the corrected colors, not on colors that are unchanged by the correction, to compensate in case your Shadows/Highlights settings reduce color saturation as a side effect. We generally find that the default value of +20 is about right, but don't be afraid to experiment.

Brightness. On grayscale images, the Brightness slider replaces the Color Correction slider. It lightens or darkens the image, and unlike the Color Correction slider, it affects the entire image, not just the pixels that are affected by the Shadow and Highlight adjustments.

Midtone Contrast. The Midtone Contrast slider adjusts contrast— negative values decrease contrast and positive ones increase it. While its

TIP: Use care when using the Shadows Amount slider with underexposed or noisy images. Such images withstand less of a shadow boost before noise emerges from the shadows.

effect is most pronounced on the midtones, it applies to the entire image, so use it carefully. If you push it too far, you might just end up undoing the effects of your Shadow and Highlight adjustments.

Black Clip/White Clip. The clipping percentages dictate how many of the corrected pixels are mapped to black (0) and white (255), so these controls let you adjust the contrast of the pixels that are close to black and white. Note that unlike the clipping percentage fields in Levels, these use three decimal places. Use them to fine-tune the contrast near the endpoints—when they're set too low, the image can turn muddy.

Shadows/Highlights isn't available as an adjustment layer. It has to calculate the value for each pixel based on surrounding pixels on the same layer, while adjustment layers compare a pixel only with the same pixel on layers behind it. The additional calculations required by Shadows/Highlights would make it agonizingly slower as an adjustment layer. In Photoshop CS3 and later, you *can* use Shadows/Highlights as a Smart Filter, where you have control over when the lengthy recalculations take place.

Hue, Saturation, and Lightness

When we see people trying to make skin tones less red or skies less purple with Curves, we have to roll our eyes and bite our tongues, which is uncomfortable to say the least! The best tool for addressing issues with hue and saturation is, believe it or not, the Hue/Saturation feature.

Hue/Saturation is best used for specific color adjustments instead of overall adjustments. But Hue/Saturation isn't hard to master, and once you've done so, you'll find it's indispensable.

TIP: Colorize is great for CMYK or RGB output, but if you're trying to make a true multitone image and not simply an RGB or process-color simulation of one, choose Image > Duotone instead of applying Colorize.

Colorize. This check box can be used for simple simulations of sepia tones, cyanotypes, selenotypes, bromide prints, and such. Hue/Saturation presets for these effects are in the Adjustments panel. When Colorize is turned on, the Hue slider sets the dominant hue (the number is the hue angle, the same as the Hue field in the Color Picker); the Saturation slider sets the saturation on a scale from 0 to 100, with 0 being grayscale (completely unsaturated) and 100 being fully saturated; and the Lightness slider lets you darken or lighten the image on a scale of –100 to 100, with the default center point at 0. If you experiment, you'll find that the same settings produce different results depending on both the color mode (RGB, CMYK, or Lab), and the specific RGB or CMYK color space.

Master Pane Controls

In the default Hue/Saturation view, changing a value changes the entire image, so we call it the Master pane.

Hue. The Hue slider shifts all the colors in the image by the specified hue angle. The top color bar shows the original color, and the bottom color bar shifts to show the resulting color. Small shifts are sometimes useful, but shifting hue by more than 5 degrees or so usually produces effects that can charitably be described as creative (see **Figure 7-35**). For this reason we rarely use the Master Hue slider—instead, we adjust the hue of specific color ranges (see the next section, "Color Pane Controls").

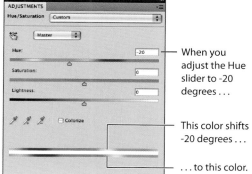

When you adjust the Hue slider to -20 degrees ...

This color shifts -20 degrees ...

... to this color.

Figure 7-35 The Master Hue slider

Saturation. Like the Master Hue slider, the Master Saturation slider is more chainsaw than scalpel. Boosting the Master Saturation value in small doses can work, but it's easy to drive your color into cheap-postcard territory (which is fine if you're in the cheap-postcard business).

TIP: As you saw with the Curves Adjustments panel, the shortcuts for individual colors in the Hue/ Saturation Adjustments panel have shifted from Command/ Ctrl-1 and up in Photoshop CS3 to Option/Alt-2 and up in Photoshop CS4.

We tend to adjust the hue and saturation of individual color ranges separately, because with the Master pane sliders, when we get one color right, we've typically pushed another too far, and yet another not far enough. In Photoshop CS4 we're even less likely to use the Saturation slider because we prefer the Vibrance adjustment, which we talk about later in this chapter.

Lightness. We never use the Master pane's Lightness slider for corrections. It simply shifts all the values, usually clipping either highlights or shadows—better to use Curves or Levels. We do use the Lightness slider for individual colors, as we describe next.

Color Pane Controls

The power of Hue/Saturation is in the individual color views. There's a pop-up menu from which you can choose Reds, Yellows, Greens, Cyans, Blues, or Magentas. At first glance, the controls offered in the individual color panes may seem identical to those in the Master pane—there's a Hue slider, a Saturation slider, and a Lightness slider. The difference? They affect only the color selected in the pop-up menu. What's less obvious is that the named color ranges are simply starting points that you can adjust to affect exactly the color range you want. For example, you can affect a specific red or a wide range of them.

TIP: Like the Curves shortcuts, the Color selection shortcuts have been updated in Photoshop CS4: Option-2 (Mac) or Alt-2 (Windows) for the Master view, and Option-3 and up (Mac) and Alt-3 and up (Windows) for other colors.

Between the two color bars at the bottom of the pane are two inner vertical sliders and two outer triangular sliders. These define the range of color affected by the sliders (see **Figure 7-36**). For additional feedback, the numbers above the color bar show you the hue angles of the four slider positions. You can adjust the color that will be fully affected by dragging the dark gray bar between the inner sliders, or by adjusting the inner sliders individually, and you can adjust the feather—the range of colors that will be partially affected—by dragging the outer sliders.

You can also adjust the range by selecting the three eyedropper tools located above the color bars and clicking them in the image. The left eyedropper centers the range of fully affected colors on the hue of the pixel on which you click; the center eyedropper (with the plus sign) extends the range of fully selected colors to include the hue of the pixel on which you clicked; and the right eyedropper (with the minus sign) excludes the hue of the pixel on which you clicked from the fully affected range of colors. The size of the feather doesn't change with the eyedroppers, but it moves as the fully affected color range expands and contracts. Essentially, the controls provide a color-range selection with a controllable feather.

Choose a color to edit from the pop-up menu ...

... or use the On-Image tool to edit a color range by dragging in the image.

The range of color between the inner and outer sliders is partially affected.

Inner slider

Outer slider

This range of color is fully affected by the sliders.

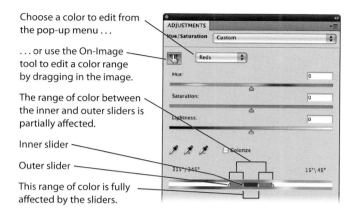

Figure 7-36 Color-range controls in the color panels

The preset color ranges are simply arbitrary labels. There's nothing to prevent you from tweaking six different ranges of reds, greens, or yellows, though we rarely need more than three ranges.

On-Image Tool. Like Curves, Hue/Saturation includes an On-Image tool in Photoshop CS4. It's an intuitive way to select and edit a color range in one step. Position it over the color you want to edit, and drag horizontally. By default it adjusts saturation; to adjust hue, Command-drag (Mac OS X) or Ctrl-drag (Windows) the tool.

Skin Tone Adjustments. Hue/Saturation is invaluable for adjusting skin tones. It's a great deal easier to adjust the red-yellow balance of Caucasian skin with the Hue slider than it is to do so with Curves—in Curves you usually have to adjust all three color curves to obtain the correct hue, whereas as the Hue slider lets you get it right in a single move.

Figure 7-37 shows an image of our friend and colleague Bruce Fraser, shot by Jeff Schewe. As with many digital captures, the skin tones are a bit too red. We'll use Hue/Saturation to make his complexion a little less florid.

Making these kinds of adjustments with Curves is akin to medieval torture! In RGB, you'd have to manipulate at least two curves, but more likely all three color curves plus the composite, and you'd probably have to bounce back and forth between the individual curves several times, since each move affects the others. In CMYK, a curve edit is even more complex, since you have four color channels plus the composite rather than three.

TIP: The color-range controls don't provide additional visual feedback as to which colors are affected, which can make subtle changes hard to follow. Here's a simple trick: Move the Hue slider all the way to the right or left before you start adjusting the color-range sliders, then set it back to 0 once you've adjusted the range. You'll see us do this a couple of times in Figure 7-37.

Figure 7-37 Using Hue/
Saturation to fix skin tones

The skin tones are much too red.

This is the finished image.

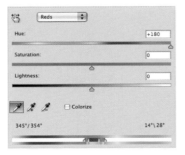

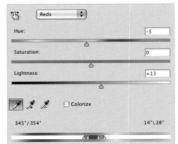

We start by targeting the very
red areas, using the Hue slider to
make the selected range obvious.

We tame the screaming reds
by shifting the hue slightly and
lightening them.

We'll need a separate adjustment for the next move, so at this point
we choose a different color from the pop-up menu and drag the
center slider into the reds. This causes the pop-up menu to say "Reds
2"—a second range of reds that we're editing.

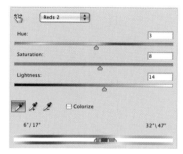

We set up the next adjustment (a general tweak to all the skin tones), but first we make sure that we exclude the yellow stars on the vest from the color range.

A smaller hue shift with further lightening, accompanied by a saturation boost to counteract the lightening, produces the result shown above.

Hue/Saturation is useful in both RGB and CMYK, but it lends itself to much finer adjustments in CMYK than in RGB. In RGB, it manipulates light, while in CMYK it manipulates ink percentages. If you have sharp eyes, you will have noticed that we made the edits to this image in RGB with CMYK soft-proofing turned on.

When we're preparing images for a CMYK destination we always try to get as close as possible to the desired result in RGB with the help of soft-proofing, especially on Hue/Saturation adjustments. But even with good output profiles and a well-calibrated display, we're likely to make small adjustments after conversion to CMYK.

Matching Hues. Another common task for which Hue/Saturation is well suited is matching hues across images. The light may change during an event, or you may simply have to force two disparate images to match. Although Photoshop does offer an Image > Adjustment > Match Colors command, it often doesn't work well. Hue/Saturation is quick and controllable.

What's Your Motivation?

Your motivation for editing drives the editing choices you make, and we've found that editing is driven fundamentally by the need to create one of two types of images:

Output-Neutral. We edit an image to make it look as good as we can without regard to a specific output process, creating an output-neutral master image.

Output-Specific. We edit to so that an image is rendered in the best possible way, given the limitations imposed by the output process.

If you're a photographer, you may anticipate multiple uses for an image and produce a master version not optimized for any specific type of output. Once you create the master, you can duplicate it and then optimize the duplicate for a specific output process such as the Web, HDTV, or a particular press.

The reason a master image should be output-neutral has to do with the flip size of optimization: When you optimize an image to get the most out of a specific medium, those optimizations can work against optimal reproduction in another medium. For example, converting an image to CMYK for press reproduction removes huge parts of the color gamut that could have been reproduced by a computer display or a high-quality desktop printer.

We edit output-neutral color images in an RGB working space designed as an ideal environment for editing. CMYK is inherently output-specific, so we avoid working in CMYK except to make final optimizations for known output.

When we optimize color images for specific output, we still prefer to do as much of the work as possible in RGB, but viewed through Proof Setup configured to represent the final output space (see "Customize Proof Condition Dialog" in Chapter 4, "Color Settings"). For RGB output, we've never seen any advantage to working directly in the output space—RGB output spaces are generally nonlinear with poor gray balance, so it's hard to edit in them.

For CMYK output, some fine-tuning is best done after conversion to CMYK.

For grayscale output-neutral edits, we use the Gray Gamma 2.2 working space, because it's close to being perceptually uniform. When optimizing grayscale images for press, we use a measured dot-gain curve where possible or, failing that, a single dot-gain value.

You may find it useful to change one of the Info panel color readouts to Lab Color, especially if you are matching documents in different color spaces, because you can use Lab values as a universal translator across color spaces.

Gamut Mapping. One further task for which we rely on Hue/Saturation is gamut mapping—controlling the rendering of colors present in the source image that are outside the gamut of the output process. In theory, perceptual rendering is supposed to take care of this for you; in practice it sometimes fails. All profile-creation tools make assumptions, almost invariably undocumented, about the source space they attempt to map into the gamut of the device being profiled, and when the source space doesn't match the undocumented assumption, you can wind up with solid blobs of saturated color.

Sometimes the fix is as simple as just desaturating the color while looking at a soft-proofed version of the image. In other cases, you may be able to improve the rendering by adjusting hue and/or lightness too. You have to make the fix before converting to the output space, because after the conversion is done, all you can do is make the blobs more or less saturated—you can't recover the differences that represented detail.

The Color Picker's Gamut Warning. The View > Gamut Warning command (press Command-Shift-Y in Mac OS X or Ctrl-Shift-Y in Windows) isn't something we find terribly useful on images. It shows us which RGB or Lab colors are outside the gamut of our CMYK working space, but it doesn't show how far out of gamut they are, nor does it show the nearest in-gamut colors. However, if you turn on the Gamut Warning command while you're in the Color Picker, you can see exactly where the gamut boundary lies at different hue angles and lightness—see **Figure 7-38**.

TIP: Converting RGB blues into CMYK can be a challenge because of the very limited range of blues in CMYK. If blues are giving you a problem during such a conversion, first try using Hue/Saturation to desaturate the blue, but if the result isn't pleasing, a lightness shift can save the day.

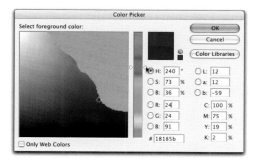

When you turn on the Gamut Warning in the Color Picker, it shows you the gamut boundary for all lightness levels at a single hue angle. To change the hue, click or drag along the vertical spectrum.

Figure 7-38 The Gamut Warning in the Color Picker

Vibrance

Vibrance is now available in the Adjustments panel in Photoshop CS4, which means you can now take advantage of Vibrance in any image Photoshop can open, not just the file types you can open in Camera Raw. The value of Vibrance is that it's carefully engineered to boost dull colors the most while limiting saturation increases for flesh tones and colors that are already highly saturated. Because Vibrance debuted in the Basic tab in Adobe Camera Raw 5, we showed an example of it in Chapter 5. In the Adjustments panel, Vibrance conveniently includes a Saturation slider for those occasional times when a uniform color boost is warranted. When we want more vivid color and we don't need to make the finer adjustments we just showed you, we usually try Vibrance before Saturation.

Choosing a Color Mode for Editing

RGB is the color mode in which most images start (when scanned or created with a digital camera) and end (when displayed on the Web, included in an onscreen presentation, used in a digital video project, or sent to an inkjet printer or photo-printing service). It might not even occur to you to work in a color mode other than RGB.

But those other color modes on the Image > Mode menu exist for a reason, and features like Curves and Levels work in more than one of those modes. In particular, CMYK is a natural choice when you are preparing images for press output, and some professionals who spend all day perfecting images for a press may not recommend anything but CMYK. But don't change modes on a whim; each change involves some data loss (as we discussed in Chapter 3, "Color Essentials"), although the amount depends on the quality and bit depth of the image.

Another penalty for changing modes is that some layer features can't be carried across modes. For example, if you create curves in an RGB adjustment layer and then convert to Lab mode, the RGB curves can't be translated channel to channel and still look the same, because the channels are completely different. Blending modes work similarly. This is why, when you switch color modes, Photoshop asks you if you want to flatten a document.

Our simple rule: Don't change color modes unless or until you have to, and do as much of your correction as possible in the image's original color mode. The ideal number of color-mode conversions is none, but in the real world one mode change is quite acceptable as long as it's done properly.

When to Edit in RGB

If your image comes from an RGB source, such as a desktop scanner or a digital camera, you should do as much of your work as possible in RGB. You'll have the entire tonal range and color gamut of the original at your disposal, particularly if you're working with the raw camera data, allowing you to take full advantage of the small differences between pixels that you want to emphasize in the image. Compared to CMYK, RGB images are also much easier to repurpose for different kinds of output, and using three channels instead of four keeps file sizes down. RGB has less-obvious advantages as well. A number of Photoshop features, such as the clipping display in Levels, are available only in RGB, not in CMYK or Lab. It's likely that a photographer will stay in RGB mode for the entire workflow.

When to Edit in CMYK

If you received your images in CMYK form (such as images from a traditional drum scanner or from an older edition of that job), it makes no sense to convert them to RGB for correction if they are going to press—instead, stay in CMYK. If you find that you have to make major corrections, though, you'll almost certainly get better results by rescanning the image as RGB instead of fixing it in Photoshop. In high-end prepress shops, it's not unusual to scan an image three times before the client signs off on it.

Certain kinds of fine-tuning, such as black-plate editing, can *only* be done on the separated CMYK file. But if you're a photographer, you'll never do that—it's the job of a prepress technician. If you find you need to make large Hue/Saturation edits in CMYK after a mode change, it's time to look at your CMYK settings in Color Settings, because the problem probably lies there—a wrong profile, incorrect settings in Custom CMYK, or color management policies that weren't set the way you thought they were (see Chapter 4, "Color Settings"). In that case, go back to the RGB original and reseparate it using new settings that get you closer to the desired result.

CMYK and Inkjet Printers. There's a myth that because inkjet printers use CMYK inks, jobs sent to them should be converted to CMYK. There are two problems with that: First, the inks used in inkjets are not the same as press CMYK inks, and many of today's inkjet printers use more than four inks anyway. Second, inkjet driver software typically expects to receive

TIP: If you order a scan from a color house and you plan to manipulate the image yourself in Photoshop or use the image for different kinds of output, ask the shop to save the image in RGB format. Of course, if your job will ultimately require converting the image to CMYK, you'll be responsible for performing the final conversion.

RGB data and convert it to the specific formulation of inks used by the ink-jet printer. If you're printing fine-art photographs on a large-format inkjet, staying in RGB mode should result in optimal quality. On the other hand, if you're working with a job already edited in CMYK for press output and you're using an inkjet to proof it, don't convert that job to RGB.

Don't Convert to CMYK Too Early

TIP: One of the great advantages to doing major corrections in RGB for prepress is that you have a built-in safeguard: It's impossible to violate the ink limits specified by your CMYK profile or Custom CMYK settings, because they'll always be imposed at the time you convert to CMYK.

You may encounter people who maintain that if your work is destined for a press, you should work exclusively in CMYK. These people may have excellent traditional prepress skills and a deep understanding of process-color printing, but they probably are not comfortable working in RGB, and they may not realize how much image information Photoshop loses during the conversion from RGB to CMYK. When you prematurely convert to CMYK, you restrict yourself in several ways:

- You lose a great deal of image information, making quality tonal and color correction much more difficult.

- You lock the image into a particular set of press conditions (paper, press, inks, and so on). If press conditions change, or you just want to print under different conditions, you're in a hole that's hard to climb out of.

- You increase file size by one-third, which slows down operations.

- You lose the valuable Photoshop features that work only in RGB.

It's best to work in RGB for as long as possible and convert your image to CMYK only after you're finished with your other corrections and you know the printing conditions. It's useful to keep an eye on the CMYK dot percentages while you work, but you don't need to work in CMYK mode to do that, since the Info panel can display CMYK values for an image in any color mode. Using the View > Proof Setup > Custom command (see Chapter 8, "The Digital Darkroom") with your CMYK output profile can also help you visually preview the CMYK results of your RGB edits.

Converting CMYK to RGB

In general, you should treat RGB to CMYK as a one-way trip. However, we can think of reasons to convert a CMYK image to RGB: You need an image for the Web or multimedia and a CMYK version is all you have, or you need to repurpose a CMYK image for a larger-gamut output process. In either case, you need to expand the tonal range and color gamut. If you just do a mode change from CMYK to RGB, you'll get a flat, lifeless image with washed-out color because the tonal range and color gamut of the original were compressed in the initial RGB-to-CMYK conversion. Instead, use the Convert to Profile command, using Perceptual intent and with Black Point Compensation and Dither turned on. Then open Levels and click Auto. If this makes the image too saturated, back off the black- and white-point sliders a few levels. This works surprisingly well but is definitely a last resort. Work on a copy of the file, and watch for color shifts and posterization.

When to Edit in Lab

The somewhat obscure Lab color mode is used far less often than RGB or CMYK, but many prefer to edit in Lab mode due to the special advantages it offers. Lab mode separates luminance (its L channel) from color (its A and B channels), making it far easier to apply tonal corrections and filters (such as sharpening) without introducing hue shifts. This concept appeals to those who tweak the black plate in CMYK. The way that Lab mode puts opposing colors on its two A and B axes also makes it easy to remove color casts or enhance color contrast without wrecking the image or its tonality.

Going to Lab mode always adds a conversion step (since original image files are either RGB or CMYK), and we like to keep those conversions to a minimum. Also, Lab mode encompasses such a wide color gamut that editing in Lab is usually best with images having at least 16 bits per channel, to keep posterization at bay. Changing color modes often flattens adjustment layers and blending modes, and some Photoshop features that are available in RGB mode do not work in Lab mode. If you're able to perform most of your layered editing in Lab mode, and you don't need to convert your layered working file to another mode, only saving flattened RGB and CMYK copies for final output, mode conversion issues may not come up at all.

Because Lab can be so helpful in situations such as rescuing difficult images, there are times when it is certainly worth the side trip. If you want to explore the challenging yet powerful world of Lab, look for books by Dan Margulis—a good place to start is *Photoshop Lab Color* (Peachpit Press). Dan's eye-opening techniques have transformed Lab mode from a color scientist's exercise into a surprisingly valuable color-correction tool.

QUICK LAB MODE FIXES

The color tools have improved so much in Photoshop CS4 and Camera Raw 5 that you can fix more kinds of problems that used to require a trip into Lab mode. But converting to Lab mode can still enable a more direct way to make certain types of corrections:

- You want to make major changes in tonality without introducing a color cast or any changes to the color relationships. In this case you can edit just the L channel. (However, you can achieve similar results in RGB mode by editing the master curve or a Curves adjustment layer and applying the Luminosity blending mode to it).

- You're having trouble getting rid of a color cast in RGB using the Auto Color Correction settings or Curves.

- You want to create more contrast between magenta and green, or between blue and yellow.

In **Figure 7-39**, we have a sample image that can benefit from a Lab tweak. It's a 16-bit image of a trees along a lake, and we'd like to boost the contrast a bit. The trees are one mass of similar color, but we think we can create more color contrast there by using Lab mode to enhance the complementary colors in the image.

We also think the sky might be too red, and the Info panel confirms this. We Shift-click a color sampler on the sky so we can track its values later.

Editing the L Channel. After clicking the Curves button in the Adjustments panel, our first move is to edit the L (luminosity) channel, which in Lab mode contains all tonal information. Changes you make to the other two channels don't affect tones at all. Edit the L curve as you would the RGB composite curve (or the K curve when editing in CMYK). Our change boosts tonal contrast, but the colors are still a bit weak.

Editing the A Channel. When we open the A channel curve, the first thing we do is add a point and set it to Input 0, Output 0. This locks the color balance in that channel, because (as we mentioned in Chapter 2, "Image Essentials") the A channel of Lab mode has magenta on one end and green on the other end. At the center—Input 0, Output 0—the A channel is neutral.

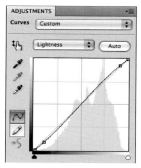

The L channel edited
for tone only.

Color cast

Cast
neutralized

After adjusting tonal contrast
using the L curve, the first
color problem to fix is the
red cast indicated in the sky
by the color sampler, which
shows that the A channel
is not neutral. Setting the A
channel to 0 fixes the cast.

The A channel edited.

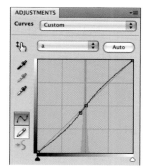

In the A channel we add a
center point. We add a point
on the red side and move it
down to steepen the A curve,
increasing the magenta/
green color contrast.

Unfortunately, Curves
doesn't show you which
areas control which colors,
so for clarity we added color
gradients to our A and B
channel screen shots.

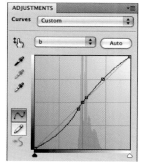

The B channel edited with different
adjustments for blue and yellow.

In the B channel, a center
point is added, and points
are added on both sides of
the center point to boost
blue and yellow by different
amounts.

➜ **TIP:** If you need an eyedropper sample bigger than 5 by 5 pixels, make a marquee selection of the required size, choose Filter > Blur > Average, and read the result from the Info panel. Just don't forget to undo the filter once you've read the values! (Or use a Smart Filter.)

The Info readout for the color sampler says L 93, A 3, B 0. We aren't concerned with L (luminosity); we're focused on the A and B numbers: A is slightly red and B is neutral. We press the plus sign key to select the 0,0 midpoint we added, and keeping an eye on the Info panel, we press the right arrow key to nudge the point until the A channel "after" readout (after the slash) reads 0. Now that the Info panel reads 0 for both the A and B channels, we know that point is perfectly neutral.

Now we'll do what we came here for: bump up the color contrast. In Curves we use the On-Image tool to click a green area of a tree to add a curve point and then press the down arrow and right arrow keys to nudge the point away from the center, making the curve steeper (pivoting it around the neutral center point) and boosting the contrast between green and magenta. Not only does this create more variation in the foliage, it boosts magenta in the wooden pier, setting it off against the green.

It's normal for the A and B channel histograms to be narrow and centered—most of the action happens close to the center in Lab, where moderately saturated colors live in the real world. The gamut of Lab mode is so wide that you don't have to get very far from the center to oversaturate your colors. Don't steepen the curve so far that your colors go neon on you. (In the A and B channels, drawing a flat horizontal line across the center would desaturate the colors completely.)

Editing the B Channel. Next we perform the same procedure on the B channel: We add a center pivot point and steepen the curve. However, we also add a point on the yellow side for more control. When we steepen the curve to boost the blue in the water, the yellow in the trees becomes too vivid, so we use the curve point on the yellow side to pull that side of the curve back in, closer to the baseline.

Lab is worth a try when you need to make large moves, quickly correct a color cast, or set complementary colors against each other, but you may find it easier to make subtle color changes in RGB mode (or for a raw file, use the HSL tab in Camera Raw to isolate a color).

Photo Filter

The Photo Filter command (choose Image > Adjustments > Photo Filter) is designed to simulate traditional over-the-lens warming and cooling filters (see **Figure 7-40**), though it actually lets you choose custom colors in addition to the presets. Its effect is similar to a solid color layer set to Color Blend mode. We find that the default 25 percent intensity is usually about twice what we need, and we often disable the Preserve Luminosity check box because it tends to exaggerate the effect in the highlights.

Figure 7-40 Photo Filter simulates traditional lens filters

Photo Filter is particularly effective at low intensity settings. We typically use intensities in the 3 to 12 percent range, but we set our examples here a little higher to make the effect obvious in print.

You can also achieve many different creative effects by either using the stronger preset colors or creating your own filter color—just double-click on the color swatch to open the Color Picker.

REPLACE COLOR

Replace Color (choose Image > Adjustments > Replace Color) is really a shortcut for making a color range selection (see "Color Range" in Chapter 9, "Making Selections") and then performing a Hue/Saturation tweak.

Replace Color doesn't let you do anything you couldn't do with Hue/Saturation, but if you need to adjust only a single color, it's sometimes more convenient.

SELECTIVE COLOR

Selective Color (choose Image > Adjustments > Selective Color) mimics the *system color* or *color-in-color* controls found in most traditional prepress drum scanners. We use Selective Color as a fine-tuning tool on images that have already been converted to CMYK. For RGB images there really isn't any advantage over using Hue/Saturation. Selective Color lets you increase or decrease the percentage of Cyan, Magenta, Yellow, and Black in the nine preset color ranges that appear on the Colors menu (see **Figure 7-41**). These color ranges are hard-wired—you can't change them.

Figure 7-41 Selective Color is useful only on CMYK images.

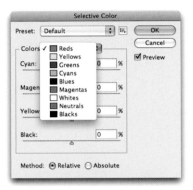

Absolute and Relative Methods. If you're using a well-tuned color management system and are creating direct-to-plate output, stick with Relative. (Absolute was more useful in non-color-managed prepress workflows, when we burned film to make plates.) With Relative selected, Selective Color looks at how much of the specified ink is present in each pixel in the color range, how close it is to the center of the named color range, and how saturated the color is, so the effect is gentler than Absolute on everything except the fully saturated colors corresponding to the named color ranges.

When you select Absolute, Selective Color adds or subtracts the specified percentages of each ink from colors in the center of the color range. For example, if you ask for –20 percent magenta from reds, a 100M 100Y red becomes an 80M 100Y red and an 80M 80 Y red becomes 64M 80Y. As you move away from the pure-red axis, the percentage by which magenta is reduced lessens in proportion to how far off the red axis the color lies.

Channel Mixer

The Channel Mixer (choose Image > Adjustments > Channel Mixer) does what it says—you can mix the channels, combining content from one or more channels and feeding it into another. For maximum flexibility, the Channel Mixer is typically applied as an adjustment layer. It's a useful color-correction tool, but we don't use it as a global correction tool on

RGB images. We sometimes use it to make local corrections, typically to bring out highlight or shadow detail that's present in only one channel. On CMYK files, it's useful for tweaking the black plate in specific color ranges, as we show in **Figure 7-42**.

Figure 7-42 Using the Channel Mixer to remove black from skin tones in CMYK

The image at left has black in the skin tones. We subtracted some yellow and a smaller amount of magenta (the pink background relies on magenta) and boosted the black slightly to produce the result at right.

In Figure 7-42, the original separation setup added black into the skin tones, making them muddy. We'd rather fix this by going back to the RGB original and reseparating the image, but that's not always possible. Lightening the black plate in Levels or Curves would destroy the contrast—we want to change only the skin tones. The Channel Mixer provides an easy means of doing this, with better feedback and finer control than Selective Color. We set the Output Channel to black, subtracted some of the magenta and yellow channels from the black, and boosted the black to preserve the black values in the shadows.

TIP: The Channel Mixer has been a popular way to convert color images to black-and-white images, but starting in Photoshop CS3 it's much better and easier to use the new Black & White adjustment (see "The Color of Grayscale" in Chapter 11, "Essential Image Techniques").

Tools We Don't Use

We've covered most of the tools on the Adjustments submenu, but we left out a few of them because we never use them for corrections, though they can be useful for creative effects. Don't take our word as gospel; if one of these features solves a problem for you then it's justified its existence. That said, here are the tools we don't use and our reasons for avoiding them.

Color Balance. The Color Balance command lets you make separate adjustments for red/cyan, green/magenta, and blue/yellow to three arbitrary tonal ranges labelled Highlights, Midtones, and Shadows. The problem is that these ranges overlap and are never quite where we need them. When there are color balance problems that Auto Color can't fix, the required corrections are usually selective rather than global. We find that it's easier to tweak the color balance of different tonal ranges using Curves.

Brightness/Contrast. While Brightness/Contrast performs acceptably now that Adobe has updated the feature to avoid highlight and shadow clipping by default, it's still kind of a blunt instrument compared to Levels or Curves, which do the same thing as Brightness/Contrast but with more control. If you actually have a reason to make adjustments that push levels off either end of the histogram, you can use Brightness/Contrast with the Use Legacy check box turned on.

Match Color. Matching one image's color to another sounds like a great idea, but we never gotten it to work reliably. We find that we can match colors more quickly by using either Hue/Saturation or Replace Color.

Gradient Map. This is useful for making custom grayscale conversions and for creating truly wacky color effects. It's low on our list of grayscale conversion methods because it takes a lot of work—you have to edit the gradient to get the results you want, then use Gradient Map to actually get them.

Exposure. The Exposure command is really designed for working with HDR (High Dynamic Range) images. On those, it's pretty useful—see "HDR Imaging" in Chapter 11, "Essential Image Techniques"—but on 8-bit or 16-bit/channel images, it doesn't do anything useful that you can't do just as easily with the gray input slider in Levels. The Exposure and Offset sliders basically replicate the behavior of the Brightness slider in Brightness/Contrast (when Use Legacy is on).

TIP: Threshold can be a useful way to inspect what pixels exist at any tonal level in the image.

Equalize, Threshold, and Posterize. These commands are more useful for image analysis or special effects than they are for straight image editing. Equalize redistributes tonal values so that the brightest pixels are white, the darkest pixels are black, and intermediate values are evenly distributed across the tonal range. Threshold is useful for turning images into 1-bit black-and-white bitmaps. Posterize does something we struggle to avoid!

Variations. This is a nice tool for learning to distinguish color casts, but it's a very blunt instrument indeed for correcting them, and it's limited to 8-bit/channel images. It doesn't do anything that can't be done with a great deal more control and precision using Hue/Saturation.

CHAPTER EIGHT

The Digital Darkroom

What would you say if we told you that you could perform color correction, use dodging and burning, build up density in overexposed areas, open up underexposed areas, and more—all with a minimum of image degradation and with an unlimited number of undos? You might just laugh at us. But in this chapter, we'll show you how to do all of these things.

In the previous chapter we introduced the difference between using Levels or Curves in the traditional dialog versus the Adjustments panel that's new in Adobe Photoshop CS4. The Adjustments panel is a more streamlined way to use Photoshop adjustment layers. With adjustment layers you can go much further, and with more freedom to experiment, rather than permanently altering the actual image pixels. You can change your adjustment settings at any time, and vary their overall strength by changing the adjustment layer's opacity. Even better, you can restrict corrections to specific areas by painting on the layer mask that every adjustment layer has. In effect, you have not just unlimited undo, but also selective, partial undo.

The techniques in this chapter can help you get a better image with little or no degradation and unprecedented control. But just as importantly, they're designed to give you maximum flexibility so that you can experiment and play with your images while still having an escape route back to safe territory if you push things too far. Making mistakes is one of the surest ways to learn lessons—and we're living proof—so an environment where you can make mistakes safely is a great learning tool.

Adjustment Layer Basics

An *adjustment layer* is a tone or color edit stored in a Photoshop or TIFF document, on a layer apart from the image pixels themselves. It's much easier to understand adjustment layers if you think of them as copies of the base image, particularly when you start using adjustment layers in conjunction with blending modes. Fortunately, using an adjustment layer takes less RAM and disk space than actually copying the base image.

You can't do much harm to your image with adjustment layers, because your original image layer stays intact until you flatten the file. However, there's no free lunch. When you flatten the image, the adjustment layers are calculated by their stacking order, so you should still avoid successive edits that go in the opposite direction from one another—avoid adding one Curves layer that darkens the image and another that lightens it, for example.

Why Use Adjustment Layers?

Whenever you apply a Curves or Levels tweak (or even a Hue/Saturation adjustment) to an image, you're degrading it a little by throwing away some image data, as we showed in Chapter 7. Once that data is gone, you can't get it back. This degradation can be avoided when you can make edits to adjustment layers rather than editing the image pixels directly. It's somewhat analogous to working with raw camera files, where the changes you make are stored alongside the original file and take effect only when you export or print a new version of the image. For example, you can apply a Curves adjustment layer, which you can turn off to see the unadjusted, original image.

There are several other reasons we love working in the digital darkroom of Photoshop.

- Changing your mind. With adjustment layers, you can change an edit at any time without increasing cumulative degradation. This gives you endless freedom to experiment. Because you can fine-tune your edits with no penalty, you're more likely to get the results you want.

- Instant before-and-after. You can always tell exactly what you're doing when you use adjustment layers. Because all your edits are on layers, you can easily see before-and-after views by hiding the adjustment layer you're editing and then turning it back on again (by clicking on the eye-ball icon in the left column of the Layers panel).

- Variable-strength edits. The Opacity slider in the Layers panel acts as a volume control for your edits.

- Applying the same edits to multiple images. You can drag an adjustment layer to other images, and even script the layer with actions to batch-apply the adjustment layer to a folder full of images.

- Brushable edits. By using a mask, you can make selective, local edits to a particular area of an adjustment layer. This means you have not only essentially unlimited undo, but also selective and partial undo.

- Storing alternative edits in the same file. Because you can hide an adjustment layer, you can create multiple versions of the same adjustment layer edit and display only the edit you want to use at any particular time. For example, you can store two different Curves adjustment layers that store curves for two different printers, and display only the adjustment layer for the printer you're using at the moment.

- Doing the impossible. You can use adjustment layers in conjunction with blending modes to do things that are usually extremely difficult, if not impossible—such as building density in highlights or opening up shadows without posterizing the image.

Why Not Use Adjustment Layers?

With all these advantages, why not use adjustment layers for all your edits? Two reasons: file size and file complexity.

Adjustment Layers Increase File Size. An adjustment layer is an additional component stored with an image, so it uses more RAM and hard drive space, both for scratch space and storage, than simply saving an edit directly into an image without layers.

Adjustment layers don't enlarge file size as much as you'd think, though. Yes, the first adjustment layer you add to a file may double the file size. But don't be alarmed—any adjustment layers you add after the first one add relatively little to the file size. The file size impact of an individual adjustment layer is much higher when you paint on its layer mask, because then you're adding pixels to the document.

TIP: You can minimize the file-size increase caused by adjustment layers by turning off the Maximize Compatibility option (see "Setting Preferences" in Chapter 6, "Essential Photoshop Tips and Tricks"). However, this reduces compatibility with other software you may be using with Photoshop files, such as Adobe InDesign or Adobe Lightroom.

Adjustment Layers Add Complexity. If you open a file you made a year ago, and it contains 20 layers with names like Curves 13 and Hue/Saturation 5, you may have to spend quite a bit of time remembering what all those layers do! Naming your layers and organizing them into (informatively named) layer groups helps a lot.

Computers have become loaded with much more RAM and disk space since adjustment layers were introduced, and the advantages of adjustment layers now far outweigh the disadvantages. We can't live without them.

CHANGES TO ADJUSTMENT LAYERS IN PHOTOSHOP CS4

In Photoshop CS4, Adobe has streamlined the image adjustment workflow, most notably the way Levels and Curves work. Photoshop CS4 may make Photoshop veterans feel like newbies again, because they'll have to relearn much of how adjustment layers work, but it's worth it. The renovation involved a few simple principles:

Eliminate Modal Dialogs. In Photoshop CS4 you can apply adjustments such as Levels and Curves with fewer dialogs.

Make Simple Adjustments Easier and Faster. Adobe made presets for common corrections more accessible (see **Figure 8-1**), so if you're new to adjustment layers you can click a preset first and edit it later.

Don't Throw Out the Good Stuff. Due to the nonmodal nature of the Adjustments panel, some old techniques and shortcuts don't work the same way. However, Adobe translated as many as it could into a nonmodal context. If you start working in the Adjustments panel and wonder what happened to your favorite adjustment shortcuts from earlier versions of Photoshop, see Tables 7-1 and 7-2 in Chapter 7.

Make Convenient Features More Visible. In Photoshop CS4, Adobe collected various features that were useful for adjustment layers and added them to the Adjustments panel, so that you can use them directly without memorizing shortcuts and constantly running off to other panels. There's a clipping mask button so that you don't have to remember the old shortcut, a layer visibility button so that you don't have to open the Layers panel just to hide and show layers, and a button that expands the Adjustments panel to a larger size. We show you these features in **Figure 8-2**, and a clipping mask example is coming up later in this chapter.

CREATING ADJUSTMENT LAYERS

Photoshop offers three ways to create an adjustment layer:

- The Adjustments panel. Click the icon for the type of adjustment you want (see Figure 8-1), or click a preset from the list under the icons.

- The Layers panel icon. Click the New Content Layer icon in the Layers panel and choose the adjustment from the pop-up menu that appears. This pop-up menu also lets you add any of the fill layers—Solid Color, Gradient, and Pattern.

- The Layer menu. Choose an adjustment layer command from the Layer > New Adjustment Layer submenu.

When you use any of these methods, a new adjustment layer is added to the document, even if it already contains an adjustment layer of the same type. If you want to edit an existing adjustment layer, you must select it in the Layers panel; the controls and current settings for that adjustment layer then appear in the Adjustments panel.

TIP: The Layer menu may be the long way to add an adjustment layer, but it's an important technique to know. When you're editing keyboard shortcuts or creating an action, the Layer menu is how you give those features access to adjustment layers.

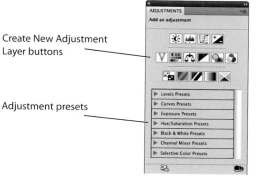

Create New Adjustment Layer buttons

Adjustment presets

Figure 8-1 Two ways to create an adjustment layer

Click a button or preset in the Adjustments panel.   Click the adjustment layer pop-up menu in the Layers panel.

CONTROLLING ADJUSTMENT LAYERS

The critical difference between using adjustment layers and editing a *flat* (nonlayered) file is that adjustment layers give you reversible ways to control and refine your edits. We'll introduce the basic techniques for doing this here and go into more detail and give examples a little later.

Click an Adjustment Layer to Edit It. When you click an adjustment layer in the Layers panel, its settings appear in the Adjustments panel (see **Figure 8-2**). This is a shortcut for choosing Layer > Layer Content Options. To get back to the buttons and presets in the Adjustments panel, click the arrow at the bottom left of the Adjustments panel.

Figure 8-2 Editing an adjustment layer

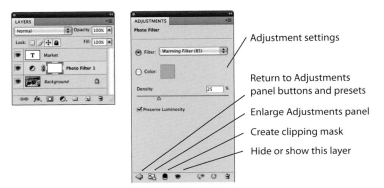

Adjustment settings

Return to Adjustments panel buttons and presets

Enlarge Adjustments panel

Create clipping mask

Hide or show this layer

Click an adjustment layer . . .

. . . to see its settings in the Adjustments panel.

TIP: Use the Edit > Keyboard Shortcuts command for better keyboard access to your favorite types of adjustment layers. For example, you can reassign the keyboard shortcut for Image > Adjust > Curves to Layer > New Adjustment Layer > Curves.

Use Opacity to Vary Strength. Control the opacity of the adjustment layer by changing the Opacity slider in the Layers panel. This lets you change the intensity of the overall adjustment. We often make edits that are slightly more extreme than we really want, then back off the opacity of the editing layer to reduce the effect to just where we want it. This can be faster than trying to fine-tune settings in the Adjustments panel.

Isolate Edits Using Multiple Adjustment Layers. You can use as many adjustment layers as you want, each stacked on top of the next, to make successive edits. This technique is particularly useful when you want one curve to correct the image globally while another curve edits the image in selective places. However, if one adjustment counteracts another, the image will suffer some loss of quality, though not quite as much as if you applied the edits successively to a flat file. To restrict the effect of an adjustment layer to specific areas, paint in an adjustment layer's mask; see the next section, "Selections, Masks, and Channels."

Adjustment layers apply to all visible layers beneath them. The stacking order makes a difference, because each layer's result depends on the layers underneath it, although the actual amount of the difference can vary.

Isolate Areas Using Masks. Although the Opacity slider applies to an entire adjustment layer, you can vary the opacity of the layer locally by painting on the adjustment layer's layer mask (see the next section, "Selections, Masks, and Channels"). To paint on the layer mask, click an adjustment layer thumbnail in the Layers panel and paint; the paint automatically goes on the layer mask. Black paint hides the effect of an adjustment layer; white paint reveals it; gray paint applies the effect partially (25 percent black ink applies 75 percent of an adjustment layer's effect). By varying the brush opacity (in the Options bar or using shortcuts), you can achieve precise control over an adjustment layer's opacity in specific areas.

Save Adjustment Layers. You can save an adjustment layer separately from an image. We find this most useful when we want to apply the same color- and tonal-correction edits to multiple images.

To save an adjustment layer into either a new or a different document, select an adjustment layer, and then choose Layer > Duplicate Layer. For Destination, you can either choose an open document or enter a name if you want Photoshop to create a new document containing the adjustment layer. When you're done, click OK. If you duplicate the adjustment layer as a new document, it will have the same document specifications as the original—potentially a disk-space issue if it's very large. You can use the Image > Image Size command to reduce the dimensions of the document you're using to store the adjustment layer. If an adjustment layer's mask is empty, the adjustment layer is resolution-independent.

The ability to copy adjustment layers also opens up additional workflow possibilities. Without adjustment layers, you'd want to take care of retouching (dust and scratches and so on) before editing for tone or color. However, with adjustment layers, the order of these tasks doesn't matter as much. Two people can even work on the same image at the same time—one doing the retouching while the other edits tone and color—and then apply the adjustment layer(s) to the retouched image later.

TIP: When you select an adjustment layer in the Layers panel, an additional channel automatically appears in the Channels panel. That's the channel for the layer mask.

TIP: Another way to copy an adjustment layer between two existing documents is simply to drag it from the Layers panel in one document to another document window. To center a layer or mask precisely when you release the mouse, Shift-drag the layer or mask.

Selections, Masks, and Channels

The ability to restrict the effect of an adjustment layer to specific areas using its layer mask means that it's important to understand how selections, masks, and channels work in Photoshop. We give this subject the full treatment in Chapter 9, "Making Selections," but you'll want to get the basics here, since we'll be referring to masks shortly.

If you've ever carefully painted around a window in your home, you've probably used masking tape to mask out the areas you didn't want to paint. If you apply the masking tape to the window, you can paint right over it, knowing that the window remains untouched. Selections, masks, and channels are like electronic masking tape.

The key to understanding the relationship among selections, masks, and channels is to realize that deep down, they're different forms of the same thing. No matter what kind of selection you make—whether you drag a rectangular marquee, draw a path with the Lasso, or use the Quick Selection tool to select a colored area—Photoshop sees the selection as a grayscale channel. In this selection channel, the areas that you selected (the parts with no masking tape over them) are white, and the unselected areas (the parts with masking tape over them) are black. This has led to a popular saying: Black conceals, white reveals. Photoshop offers three ways to interact with selection channel information:

- You can use the selection tools—Marquee, Lasso, Magic Wand, Color Range, and so on—to create a selection.

- When you save a selection, Photoshop saves it as an *alpha channel*— a regular grayscale channel stored alongside the color channels. *Alpha channel* is a fancy term for a very simple concept: It's just a saved selection.

- To apply selection information nondestructively to a layer (meaning that you can change or remove the selection), you use it as a layer mask— in other words, you're attaching the masking tape to just that layer.

We'll start with a simple example, a rectangular marquee (see **Figure 8-3**). The marquee is a very simple bi-level selection—each pixel is either selected or unselected, and the channel that results when the selection is saved contains only black and white pixels. It works like real masking tape—the black pixels in the selection are the masking tape, protecting whatever's underneath, and the white pixels represent the area without masking tape, letting the paint (that is, the adjustment) pass through.

Rectangular selection marquee

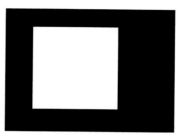

The selection as Photoshop sees it

Figure 8-3 How Photoshop thinks of selections

We'll show you how to bounce the information back and forth among selections, channels, and masks as we progress through this chapter.

Feathered and Semitransparent Selections

There's reality, and there's Photoshop. In real life, light never forms solid edges; there's always some transparency where light meets shadow. The ability to create *feathered* (soft-edged) selections and masks is key to making localized corrections blend into the image in a way that seems natural—and it makes Photoshop selections a lot more useful than hard-edged, solid, real-world masking tape.

Figure 8-4 shows a soft-edged selection. We created it by clicking the Refine Edge button in the Options bar while the selection was active, and then applying a 50-pixel Feather. Behind the scenes, rather than creating a simple bi-level channel, the feathered selection creates a channel that contains intermediate grays as well as black and white, which you can see if you click the rightmost button at the bottom of the Refine Edge dialog. The gray pixels are partially selected—lighter grays are more selected than darker ones—so any effect applied through the selection affects the fully selected pixels completely and the partially selected pixels in direct proportion to how selected they are, and it doesn't affect the unselected pixels at all.

The ability to partially select pixels is insanely useful in all sorts of situations, many of which we cover in Chapter 9, "Making Selections." For the purposes of this chapter, we'll focus on the role of partially selected pixels in layer masks.

Figure 8-4 A selection with an edge feathered using Refine Edge

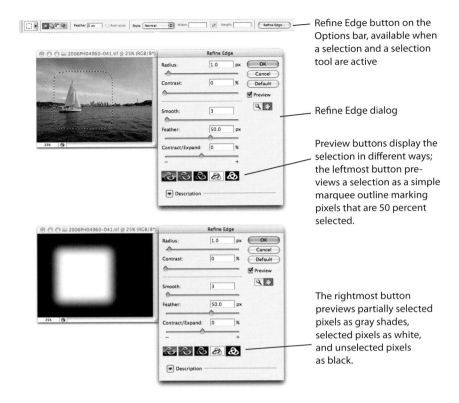

Refine Edge button on the Options bar, available when a selection and a selection tool are active

Refine Edge dialog

Preview buttons display the selection in different ways; the leftmost button previews a selection as a simple marquee outline marking pixels that are 50 percent selected.

The rightmost button previews partially selected pixels as gray shades, selected pixels as white, and unselected pixels as black.

Saving, Reusing, and Converting Selections

Another huge advantage of digital masking tape is that, unlike its real-world equivalent, you can easily copy it, move it, tweak it, or reuse it a year later. When you save a selection as a channel, you can recall it easily and either reuse it as a selection or apply it as a mask to a layer. Basically, the difference between a mask and a channel is that a mask currently affects its layer, while a channel is stored in the Channels panel without affecting the image in any visible way until you convert it to a selection or mask.

The flexibility with which you can turn a selection into a channel or mask is one of the major reasons for getting into the habit of always saving any selection that's even slightly complex. Loading a saved selection from a channel is certainly much faster than having to rebuild it all over again.

Saving Selections as Channels. To convert a selection to a channel, click the Save Selection as Channel button at the bottom of the Channels panel (see **Figure 8-5**). The selection appears as a new channel in the Channels panel. That's a shortcut for choosing the Select > Save Selection command and filling out the dialog, although the dialog gives you more options.

Channels panel

Selection

Save Selection as
Channel button

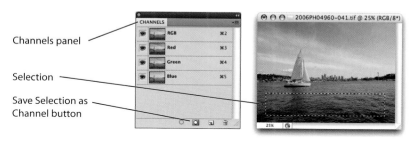

Figure 8-5 Saving a selection as a channel

Selection converted to
a channel, where white
pixels are selected
and black pixels are
unselected

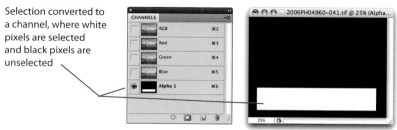

Converting Channels to Selections. To turn a channel into a selection, Command-click (Mac) or Ctrl-click (Windows) the channel in the Channels panel (see **Figure 8-6**). That's a shortcut for selecting the channel and then clicking the Load Channel as Selection button in the Channels panel, or choosing Select > Load Selection.

Command/Ctrl-clicking
a channel

Resulting selection

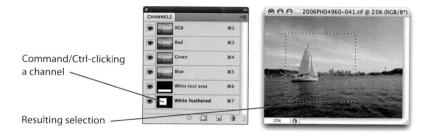

Figure 8-6 Converting a channel to a selection

Converting Selections to Masks. Photoshop always adds a layer mask when you create an adjustment layer. Even better, if you have a selection active when you add an adjustment layer, that selection automatically becomes the layer mask for that adjustment layer.

For other types of layers, select a layer and click the Add Layer Mask button at the bottom of the Layers panel (see **Figure 8-7**). If you're in the Masks panel, click the Add Pixel Mask button. The long way to do this is to choose a command from the Layer > Layer Mask submenu (the menu also provides more options).

Figure 8-7 Converting a selection to a layer mask

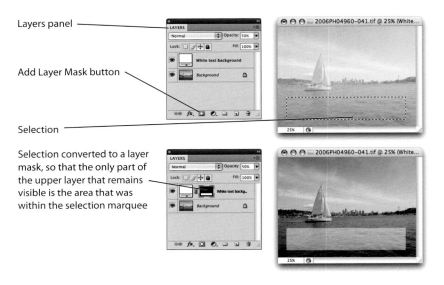

Layers panel

Add Layer Mask button

Selection

Selection converted to a layer mask, so that the only part of the upper layer that remains visible is the area that was within the selection marquee

Adding a Selection to a Mask. Sometimes we add an adjustment layer without remembering first to load the selection we want to use as a mask. In this case, the procedure is a little trickier.

TIP: To quickly disable or enable a layer mask, Shift-click on the layer mask thumbnail in the Layers panel. When the mask is disabled, it shows a red X. This is a shortcut for choosing Layer > Layer Mask > Disable.

If the selection is saved as an alpha channel, you can copy it into the mask channel. The trick is that you *must* make the channel visible before copying and make the mask visible before pasting. Otherwise, you'll get a new layer instead of the mask you wanted (this still trips us up). Click the alpha channel's thumbnail in the Channels panel to make it visible, choose Edit > Select All, then choose Edit > Copy. Click the layer mask thumbnail in the Channels panel, click the eyeball to make it visible, and choose Edit > Paste (see **Figure 8-8**). Of course, it all goes much faster if you've memorized the keyboard shortcuts for those Edit menu commands: Command-A for Select All, Command-C for Copy, and Command-V for Paste (Mac) or, respectively, Ctrl-A, Ctrl-C, and Ctrl-V (Windows).

Figure 8-8 Copying a channel to a layer mask

Alpha channel
selected

Layer mask channel
selected and visible

Alpha channel contents
pasted into layer mask

If a selection is already active, you can use the following method instead. Target the mask channel, either by clicking its thumbnail in the Layers panel or by clicking its thumbnail in the Channels panel. Make sure that black is the background color (press D to set black and white as foreground and background, respectively, then press X to switch them), and press Delete to fill the selection with the foreground color (black) on the layer mask. This gives you the opposite selection from the one you want. To fix it, deselect the current selection (Command-D on Mac, Ctrl-D in Windows), and then invert the layer mask (Command-I on Mac, Ctrl-I in Windows). It's a little fiddly, but it takes less time to do than to explain.

Painting the Layer Mask. To restrict the effect of an adjustment layer to specific areas, we first create an adjustment layer at the settings for the areas where we'd like to apply it at full strength. For the local corrections, we then edit the layer mask, painting white where we want the adjustment layer to apply completely, black where we don't want to see the effects of the adjustment layer at all, and gray for a partially visible adjustment. Quite often we'll use a gradient fill to apply a graduated change across the image, and sometimes we'll even resort to using the selection tools. (Again, see Chapter 9, "Making Selections," for more on selections and masking.)

In some cases, using selection tools to create a selection and filling it with black or white may be faster than painting the mask with the Brush tool.

USING THE MASKS PANEL

If you spend any significant amount of time working with masks, get to know the Masks panel in Photoshop CS4 (see **Figure 8-9**). Editing masks

TIP: The Option (Mac) and Alt (Windows) key reverses the selected and unselected areas when you click the Add Layer Mask button in the Layers panel or the Save Selection as Channel or Load Channel as Selection buttons in the Channels panel.

TIP: If you want an adjustment layer to affect a small area, fill its mask with black and paint in the adjustment with white. Press D to set the default mask colors (white foreground and black background). Press Command-Delete (Mac) or Ctrl-Delete (Windows) to fill the layer with the background color (black). You're ready to brush in the adjustment with white. If needed, press X to switch between foreground and background colors.

to get them just right has traditionally involved various power-user techniques. Like the Refine Edge dialog (which we discussed earlier in this chapter) and the Adjustments panel, the Masks panel is another example of how related features in Photoshop have been simplified and consolidated from a task-oriented point of view. For example, instead of having to control mask density by using the Output Levels sliders in the Levels dialog, all you have to do now is yank the Density slider in the Masks panel.

Figure 8-9 The Masks panel

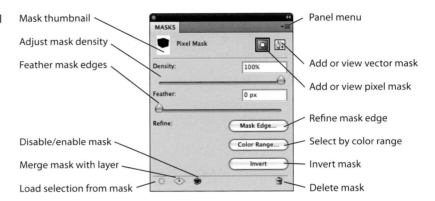

Mask thumbnail
Adjust mask density
Feather mask edges
Disable/enable mask
Merge mask with layer
Load selection from mask

Panel menu
Add or view vector mask
Add or view pixel mask
Refine mask edge
Select by color range
Invert mask
Delete mask

Up to this point we've been talking about *pixel masks* that are made up of pixels, but the Masks panel also accommodates *vector masks* made up of paths (see **Figure 8-10**). When you click the Pixel Mask or Vector Mask button in the Masks panel, the current layer gets a new mask of that type if it doesn't already exist for that layer.

TIP: Clicking the Pixel Mask button is the same as clicking the New Layer Mask button in the Layers panel.

Pixel Masks. When you click the Pixel Mask button in the Masks panel, a new pixel mask is added to the current layer, if it doesn't already have one. Use any painting tool to create black (transparent), white (opaque), and gray (semitransparent) areas in a pixel mask. The Masks panel provides these controls for a pixel mask:

- Density. Use this option to change the opacity of the mask so that you can control it independently of the layer opacity. Sure, you were able to do this in Photoshop CS3 and earlier by applying an image adjustment such as Levels to the mask, but repeated adjustments would degrade the mask. The Density slider is better because it's nondestructive—you can easily dial it back at any time.

- Feather. This option controls the softness of the mask edges. This non-destructive option lets you freely adjust edge blur without having to apply a blur filter.

- Mask Edge. This button is the same as the Refine Edge feature we discussed earlier in this chapter; it fine-tunes the edge of a selection. Because selections and masks are two forms of the same thing, it's as helpful to have Refine Edge in the Masks panel as it is to have it in the Options bar for selections.

- Color Range. This option is good for creating a mask if you just added one and you need to isolate an area by color. We discuss Color Range in Chapter 9, "Making Selections."

- Invert. This option exchanges the opaque and transparent parts of a mask so that you can choose to paint the masked area with black or white and just swap those colors later. It's yet another shortcut to the Image > Invert command, which we've used for years by pressing Command-I (Mac OS X) or Ctrl-I (Windows).

Vector Masks. This type of mask is defined by paths you draw and edit using the Pen tool and shape tools (see Chapter 11, "Essential Image Techniques"). Areas outside the path are transparent, and areas inside it are opaque. Although a vector path is hard-edged by nature, Photoshop CS4 lets you use the Feather slider to apply a nondestructive feathered edge to a vector mask—this was not possible in earlier versions. The only other option for vector masks is Density. To make any other kind of change to a vector mask, you must either edit its path using the Pen tool group or convert its path to a selection or channel so that you can edit it as a selection or as pixels, respectively.

TIP: The controls in the Masks panel work best on mask edges that already fit the content well. When they don't, you may still have to edit the mask by hand, using the painting, selection, and retouching tools.

TIP: Vector masks work best for geometric shapes and smooth curves. Pixel masks work best when you anticipate painting irregular, soft-edged details in the mask or when you want mask areas of varying opacity.

Image

Pixel mask

Vector mask

Figure 8-10 Pixel and vector masks

Clipping Masks. A clipping mask lets a layer act as a mask (see **Figure 8-11**). In the Layers panel, select one or more layers directly above the layer you want to use as a mask, and press Command-Option-G (Mac) or Ctrl-Alt-G (Windows), the keyboard shortcut for choosing Layer > Create Clipping Mask. You can also Option-click (Mac) or Alt-click (Windows) the dividing line between the base layer and the higher layers you want it to clip.

Figure 8-11 Using a layer as a clipping mask

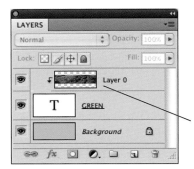

In this clipping mask, Layer 0 uses the underlying type layer as a mask so that the grass shows through the type. Layer 0 becomes indented in the Layers panel, indicating that it's using a clipping mask.

TIP: A common use for clipping masks is to make an adjustment layer apply only to the next layer down in the Layers panel, instead of to every layer below it.

The Adjustments panel offers a clipping mask button, which can be confusing because it appears in two different ways. When no adjustment layer is applied, the button controls whether new adjustment layers are added as clipping masks. When an adjustment layer is selected (you see its controls in the Adjustments panel), the button appears near the middle and controls whether that specific layer acts as a clipping mask (see **Figure 8-12**).

Figure 8-12 The clipping mask buttons in the Adjustments panel

The Clip New Adjustment Layers button appears when no adjustment layer is selected.

The Clip to Layer button (when an adjustment layer is selected) controls the clipping mask behavior of the selected layer.

TIP: Because a mask is simply a grayscale channel, you can edit it using any of the painting, selection, and editing tools.

Viewing Masks. If you want to see *only* the layer mask (see **Figure 8-13**), Option-click (Mac) or Alt-click (Windows) on the layer mask's thumbnail in the Layers panel. This is most helpful when touching up areas of the layer mask (it's sometimes hard to see the details in the mask when a background image is visible). You can disable (hide) a mask by Shift-clicking a mask thumbnail or clicking the Disable Mask button in the Masks panel (see Figure 8-9); when you do this a red X appears in the mask thumbnail in the Masks and Layers panels.

If you want to see the mask as a transparent overlay over the image, press the backslash key (\). If you're editing an adjustment layer, make sure you only tap the backslash key, since holding down that key displays the state of the image before the current adjustment (a before-and-after comparison).

Masked image only   Pixel mask only   Mask and image

Figure 8-13 Mask views of the image shown in Figure 8-10

Copying Layer Masks. To copy a layer mask, in the Layers panel Option-drag (Mac) or Alt-drag (Windows) the layer mask thumbnail to the layer where you want to apply the mask.

TIP: A checkerboard pattern behind an image represents a completely transparent area. You can customize the checkerboard in the Transparency & Gamut pane in Preferences.

ADJUSTING IMAGES USING BLENDING MODES

Applying Levels, Curves, Hue/Saturation, and the other adjustments as adjustment layers offers tremendous flexibility and power, but they aren't always the quickest or easiest ways to fix your images. In some cases, you may find it easier and faster to do the heavy lifting with blending modes, and save Curves for fine-tuning.

Using Layer-Blending Modes

A blending mode takes the color values of two layers and combines them using a formula, so it's more sophisticated than just changing opacity. Some blending modes happen to have effects that conveniently help you with basic tone and color edits, and all you have to do is copy a layer on top of the original and apply a blending mode to the copy. You can achieve the same result by adding an adjustment layer and then change only its blending mode. That's faster and easier than making a duplicate of an image layer, and it saves disk space. If the result of the blending mode isn't quite perfect, just edit the adjustment layer (we typically use Curves) to cover the rest of the distance. When blending modes and adjustment layers join forces, their powers multiply many times over. If the following blending mode descriptions make your eyes glaze over, hang on—examples are coming up.

How Blending Modes Think. The biggest question anyone has when using blending modes is, "How do I know which blending mode will do what I want?" To find out, ask yourself the following questions:

- Do I want to alter the light areas of the underlying layers, the dark areas, or both? Many blending modes have a *neutral color* that doesn't change the layers under it. For example, for the Lighten, Screen, Color Dodge, and Linear Dodge blending modes, black pixels on the applied layer don't alter the same pixels on the underlying layer, and the farther an applied pixel is from black (that is, the lighter it is), the more it affects the underlying layer.

- For other blending modes, white or 50 percent gray is the neutral color. When 50 percent gray is the neutral color, that means 50 percent gray pixels on the applied layer don't affect underlying pixels at all, and the farther an applied pixel is from 50 percent gray (that is, the closer it is to black or white), the more it affects the underlying layer.

- How much additional contrast do I want? Part of the reason there are so many blending modes is that quite a few of them are merely variations of other blending modes that produce more or less contrast. For example, Hard Light is a higher-contrast version of Soft Light. Certain blending modes, such as Difference, take contrast to the extreme, inverting (creating the negative of) the original layer color. The blending modes that produce lower contrast tend to compare an applied pixel to an underlying pixel and simply keep one or the other, while the blending modes that produce higher contrast tend to mathematically amplify the differences between the applied and underlying layers.

- What do I want to change? Most blending modes affect any underlying pixel (other than those in the blending mode's neutral color, if it has one), while some blending modes affect only color or tone.

The blending modes are arranged in logical groups, according to the way they answer those three questions.

TIP: When you're happy with your adjustment layer edits, you can lower memory requirements by flattening the document (choose Layer > Flatten Image). Just remember that flattening is a one-way trip— once you save and close a flattened file, you can never get the layers back. Instead of flattening everything, you can select a few layers and choose Layer > Merge Layers.

TIP: You can, of course, use a layer's Opacity value to reduce the effect of a blending mode.

The Independent Modes. Normal and Dissolve both replace the underlying pixels with the pixels of the applied layer when the layer is at 100 percent opacity. At lower opacities, Normal blends the overlying pixels with the underlying ones according to the layer Opacity value, while Dissolve replaces pixels randomly (see **Figure 8-14**).

At right are the layers used in the examples that follow. Watch what happens to white, black, 50 percent gray, color, and the semitransparent circle in the lower right corner of the top layer.

Overlying (applied) layer

Underlying (base) layer

Independent modes

Normal   Dissolve

Figure 8-14 Blending mode examples

The Darken Modes. The neutral color for the Darken modes is white. White pixels on a layer set to a Darken mode leave the underlying pixels unchanged. Nonwhite pixels darken the result by varying amounts, depending on each blending mode's math and the difference in value between the applied and underlying pixels (see **Figure 8-15**).

Darken   Multiply   Color Burn   Linear Burn   Darker Color

Figure 8-15 The Darken modes

The Lighten Modes. The Lighten modes are the inverse of the Darken modes. The neutral color for the Lighten modes is black—black pixels on a layer set to a Lighten mode leave the underlying pixels unchanged. Nonblack pixels darken the result by varying amounts, depending on each blending mode's math and the difference in value between the applied and underlying pixels (see **Figure 8-16**).

Lighten   Screen   Color Dodge   Linear Dodge   Lighter Color

Figure 8-16 The Lighten modes

The Contrast Modes. These modes combine corresponding Darken and Lighten modes. The neutral color for the Contrast modes is 50 percent gray—50 percent gray pixels on a layer set to a Contrast mode leave the underlying pixels unchanged. Lighter pixels lighten the result and darker pixels darken the result; the amount depends on the blending mode and the value difference between the applied and underlying pixels (see **Figure 8-17**).

Figure 8-17 The Contrast modes

Overlay   Soft Light   Hard Light   Vivid Light   Linear Light   Pin Light

Hard Mix

The odd man out is the Hard Mix blend, which has no neutral color but doesn't fit anywhere else either. It reduces the image to eight colors—red, cyan, green, magenta, blue, yellow, white, and black—based on the mix of the underlying and blend colors, with a strength related to 50 percent gray.

The Comparative Modes. The neutral color for the Comparative modes is black. The Comparative modes look at each channel and subtract the underlying color from the overlying color or the overlying color from the underlying color, whichever returns a result with higher brightness. Blending with white inverts the underlying color values (see **Figure 8-18**).

Figure 8-18 The Comparative modes

Difference   Exclusion

The HSL Modes. Blending modes in other groups generally operate on overall tone and color values. The members of the HSL group work with hue, saturation, and luminosity (HSL) instead (see **Figure 8-19**).

• Hue. This blending mode creates a result color with the brightness and saturation of the underlying color and the hue of the overlying color.

- Saturation. This mode creates a result color with the brightness and hue of the underlying color and the saturation of the overlying color.

- Color. This mode creates a result color with the luminosity of the underlying color and the hue and saturation of the overlying color.

- Luminosity. This is the inverse of the Color blending mode. It creates a result color with the hue and saturation of the underlying color and the luminosity of the overlying color.

Hue   Saturation   Color   Luminosity

Figure 8-19 The HSL modes

Layer Blending in Practice

Despite the mind-bending variety of blending modes, for the purposes of tonal and color correction we tend to use just a few of them. We use Multiply to build density, Screen to reduce it, Soft Light and Hard Light to increase contrast, Color to change color balance without affecting luminosity, and Luminosity to sharpen images without introducing color fringes (we discuss sharpening layers in more detail in Chapter 10, "Sharpness, Detail, and Noise Reduction").

The practical example that follows doesn't pretend to exhaust the power of blending modes, but we hope it fires your imagination and gives you alternative ways of approaching problems. Blending modes are so quick and easy for basic adjustments that the image practically edits itself.

Building Density Using Multiply. Multiply mode always creates a result that's darker than both the layer you apply it to and the layer behind that. If you've worked in a darkroom, it's like sandwiching two negatives in an enlarger. Mathematically, Multiply takes two values, multiplies them by each other, and divides by 255.

If a pixel is black in the base image, the result after applying an adjustment layer with Multiply is also black. If a pixel is white in the base image, the adjustment layer has no effect (because white is the neutral color for Multiply). We use Multiply with Curves adjustment layers to build density, par-

TIP: It's important to remember that when you use an adjustment layer purely for layer blending, in many cases you don't actually need to edit that layer, other than changing the layer's blending mode.

ticularly in the highlights and midtones of washed-out images. In **Figure 8-20**, we use Multiply to knock down the near-blown-out sky highlights.

Figure 8-20 Using Multiply to rescue highlights that are almost blown out to white

The original image has little tonal subtlety and seems unusable, but we'll retrieve available highlight and shadow detail on this page and the next.

We isolate the highlights by pressing Command-Option-2 (Mac OS X) or Ctrl-Alt-2 (Windows) to load a selection based on luminosity.

TIP: You can select the luminosity of the composite channel by pressing pressing Command-Option-2 (Mac OS X) or Ctrl-Alt-2 (Windows). To select the luminosity of other channels use the same shortcut, but instead of pressing 2, press 3 and up (as with the channel viewing shortcuts). Alternatively, you can Command-click (Mac OS X) or Ctrl-click (Windows) a channel in the Channels panel.

We Option-click (Mac OS X) or Alt-click (Windows) the Curves button in the Adjustment panel to open the New Layer dialog, where we choose Multiply.

The selection becomes the mask for the new adjustment layer, keeping the effect of Multiply within the highlights, where it increases their density.

In the Masks panel, we set Feather to 3 pixels to soften the mask edges.

We edit the Curves adjustment layer to make the bright sky easier to see.

Opening Shadows Using Screen. Screen is literally the inverse of Multiply. A popular analogy is that Screen is like projecting two slides on the same screen. The result is always lighter than either of the two sources.

If a pixel is white in the base image, the result is white, and if it's black in the base image, the result is also black (black is the neutral color for Screen). Intermediate tones get lighter. We use Screen to open up dark shadows.

If you want to know the math, Photoshop inverts the two numbers (subtracts them from 255) before doing a Multiply calculation (multiplies them by each other and divides by 255); then the program subtracts the result from 255.

In **Figure 8-21** we open up the shadows of the image we just worked on. To save time, we use an inverted copy of the mask we've already made.

Figure 8-21 Using Screen to open up shadows

We create a second Curves adjustment layer. This time we set its blending mode to Screen and decide to name the layer Dodge.

We Option-drag (Mac OS X) or Alt-drag (Windows) the Burn layer's pixel mask and drop it into the new Dodge layer's mask to copy it there. We then click the Invert button in the Masks panel.

The inverted mask keeps the effect of Screen out of the highlights, since we don't want them to be any lighter.

The Screen blending mode has made more detail visible in the shadows. Together, the Screen and Multiply blending modes improved the entire image.

Adding Contrast Using Hard Light. We use Soft Light, Hard Light, and Overlay to build contrast (since the overlying and underlying pixels are identical, Hard Light and Overlay produce exactly the same result). We use Soft Light for smaller contrast boosts and Hard Light or Overlay for stronger ones. All three blending modes preserve white, black, and 50 percent gray while lightening pixels lighter than 50 percent gray and darkening those that are darker.

In **Figure 8-22** we show an example of using Hard Light. Not surprisingly, it gave us a rather extreme result. We chose to back it off by reducing the opacity of the Curves adjustment layer, but another alternative would have been to try another contrast blending mode, such as Soft Light.

Figure 8-22 Increasing contrast using Hard Light

The original image needs more contrast.

After adding a Curves adjustment layer set to Hard Light, the effect is too harsh.

We reduce the opacity to 70%.

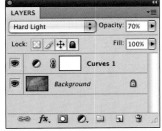

The Layers panel for the final image

Adjusting Color Balance Using Color. While we sometimes use Photo Filter adjustment layers for warming and cooling effects, we find that a Solid Color layer set to the Color blending mode and low opacity offers more control. Tweaking the color by double-clicking the layer thumbnail in the Layer panel is faster than tunneling through the Photo Filter dialog.

We start out by creating a Solid Color layer of approximately the color we want, then we reduce the opacity, typically to around 10 to 20 percent. We then fine-tune the color to get the final result, usually tweaking the Hue and Saturation fields of the Color Picker by placing the cursor in them and pressing the up and down arrows on the keyboard. It's very similar to the way we edited the target midtone value of the Auto Color Correction settings in Figure 7-10 in Chapter 7.

DODGING AND BURNING BY HAND

The powerful one-two punch of adjustment layers and blending modes also comes in handy for those times when specific areas of your image aren't successfully addressed by overall changes to curves or blending modes. You already saw forms of local corrections back when we masked adjustment layers for edits based on Curves and the Multiply and Screen blending modes. For more free-form control, you can set up a single layer that gives you reversible dodging and burning without having to draw a curve, and it's possible because of the Overlay blending mode.

If you stayed awake during the descriptions of each blending mode a few pages back, you might remember us talking about a blending mode's neutral color—the color that doesn't change the image in that blending mode. For Overlay, the neutral color is 50 percent gray. The useful side effect of a 50 percent gray neutral color is that painting tones lighter than 50 percent gray into the layer lightens an image, and painting tones darker than 50 percent gray darkens the image.

Unlike other techniques in this chapter, this one doesn't involve an adjustment layer. You create a new pixel layer, but instead of clicking the Create New Layer button in the Layers panel, Option-click (Mac OS X) or Alt-click (Windows) that button so that the New Layer dialog appears with its options (see **Figure 8-23**). Choose Overlay from the Mode pop-up menu and the "Fill with Overlay-neutral color (50% gray)" check box becomes available—turn it on and click OK. Now use the Brush tool to lighten (paint with white) or darken (paint with black) any areas of the image. Painting pure white or black on a 50 percent gray Overlay layer can produce high-contrast results, so you'll probably prefer to reduce the opacity value for the brush (in the Options bar) and build up the effect.

TIP: Remember brush shortcuts when dodging and burning: Press D to reset the foreground and background colors to black and white (the brush paints the foreground color), X to swap them, and a number key to change the opacity of the brush.

At this point you might be asking, "Why not just use the Dodge and Burn tools?" While the Dodge and Burn tools are improved in Photoshop CS4, they are still destructive—you permanently change image pixels. The only way to reverse your changes is with Undo and the History panel, both of which you lose when you close a document. With an Overlay-based dodge-and-burn layer, if you change your mind you can simply paint a different tone on the Overlay layer (or paint 50 percent gray to restore the original image), all without ever altering the pixels of the original image's layer.

Figure 8-23 Dodging and burning using Overlay

Cloud reflections in a glass elevator shaft aren't quite what we want.

We add a new layer with Overlay mode filled with 50 percent gray neutral color.

With the Brush tool we paint white to dodge and black to burn specific areas.

The Layers panel for the final image shows the Overlay layer and its contents.

TIP: Get into the habit of giving your layers descriptive names. Instead of accepting default layer names such as "Curves 78" or "Color Fill 15," use names like "Sky color cast" or "Foreground brightness."

Updated Dodge and Burn Tools in Photoshop CS4. Although we prefer to use the nondestructive Overlay layer method instead of the Dodge and Burn tools in the Tools panel, if you do decide to use these two tools it's worth mentioning that Adobe has improved them in Photoshop CS4. In previous versions, Dodge and Burn got out of control so easily that they were best used at a very low opacity value, so that you could build them up. In Photoshop CS4, those tools now have a Protect Tones check box in the Options bar that minimizes the chance of color shifts and ugly, clipped tones; we recommend that you leave Protect Tones on. In addition, the Sponge tool (in the same tool group) now has a Vibrance check box in the Options bar that helps avoid extreme saturation or desaturation.

USING HISTORY TO MIX ADJUSTMENTS

A more free-flowing, seat-of-the-pants alternative to layers is the History panel. History does a lot more than give you as many as 1000 levels of Undo. When you use the History Brush together with edits such as filters or blending modes, you can apply effects that are very similar to those you can achieve with layers and masks. It helps to be familiar with how the History panel works. For that, see "History Panel Tips" in Chapter 6, "Essential Photoshop Tips and Tricks."

You can think of History states as layers in time or frames in a sequence, instead of as a stack of structural layers in the Layers panel. Instead of painting masks to combine layers, you paint parts of one History state into another (see **Figure 8-24**). But let's look at the important ways in which History Brush painting differs from using layers and masks:

- History is available only as long as your file is open. Once you close the file, its history is gone forever, so you have to get your edits right before you close. (In General Preferences you can turn on a History log, either in the file's metadata or in a text file, but the log doesn't let you apply the logged states.)

- History is easier to use than layers when you know exactly what you're doing and can get things right on the first (or possibly second) try, but if you're less decisive than that, it quickly becomes more work than using layers to achieve the same effects. On the other hand, layers require some advance planning and organization, and if that doesn't fit your creative personality, you may find History more fluid and natural.

- With large files, history can be just as demanding on your hardware as adjustment layers. It requires plenty of scratch space and a fast disk.

Nevertheless, History is a powerful feature for making edits that are quick, but not dirty.

Applying History. You can apply History using either the History Brush tool or by choosing Edit > Fill. Fill is easier to use when you have a selection or you want to affect the entire image. The History Brush is useful for actually brushing in edits. When you use either one, you can immediately use the Fade command (on the Edit menu) to adjust the edit's opacity (and hence its strength).

Figure 8-24 Using History to combine different edits

We'd like to lighten the interior of this room without blowing out the windows.

We choose Edit > Fill, then choose History from the Use pop-up menu and Screen from the Mode pop-up menu (left). The layer fills with a Screen-mode copy of the current state (right).

We Option/Alt-click the New Snapshot button to create and name a new snapshot called "screen" (left). We use the Fill dialog again, starting from the Open state, but this time we set Mode to Multiply (right).

We create a snapshot called "multiply," make the lighter "screen" snapshot the current state, click to the left of the "multiply" snapshot to make it the History Brush source (left), and use the History Brush to paint dark detail from the Multiply state back into the windows (right).

SOFT-PROOFING AN IMAGE FOR PRINT

Thanks to the wonders of color management, the digital darkroom offers a key advantage over the traditional, analog darkroom: You can see what will happen in the print before you actually produce it.

The naïve view of color management is that it makes your prints match your monitor. If you've read this far, you've probably realized that this is an impossible goal—printers can't print the range of color that a good monitor can display. Instead, color management tries to reproduce the image as faithfully as the limitations of the output process will allow. In other words, you can't really make the print match your monitor, but you can use your monitor to tune the print for the specific printer you're using. What makes this possible is the output profile, which describes the printer, ink, and paper.

But color management knows nothing about images, only about each image's color space. No output profile, however good, does equal justice to all images. When you convert an image from a working space to the gamut and dynamic range of a composite printer, the profile treats all images identically, using the same gamut and dynamic range compression for all.

Fortunately, the soft-proofing features in Photoshop let you preview exactly how the profile will render your images, so that you can make the necessary corrections. If you want great rather than good, optimize images for different output processes, because each image requires its own compromises.

You can use layers, layer groups, or Smart Filters to optimize the same master image for printing to different printers, or to the same printer on different paper stocks. This technique uses three basic elements:

- A reference image. Duplicate the image with Edit > Proof Colors turned off to serve as a reference for the image appearance you're trying to achieve.

- A soft-proof. Use the Proof Setup command to provide a soft-proof that shows how the output profile will render the image.

- A layer group. Group each set of optimizations for a specific output condition (printer, paper, ink) into a layer set, so that you can turn them on and off conveniently when you print to different devices.

TIP: When you stare at an image, an afterimage of opposite colors builds up in your eyes that can distort your color perception. For example, if you stare at red for too long, a green afterimage builds up in your eyes. To avoid this, take regular breaks from editing.

TIP: It helps to master the tools for managing multiple document views, such as the n-up and tabbed document options we described in Chapter 6.

Make a Reference Image. Choose Image > Duplicate to create a temporary copy of the image in another window. The duplicate will serve as a reference for the appearance you're trying to achieve in the print.

You need to make a duplicate rather than simply open a new view, because you'll be editing the master image to optimize it for the print, and the edits would show up in a new view. The duplicate isn't affected by the edits you make to the master file, so it can serve as a reference—a reminder of what you want to achieve in the print.

Arrange Windows. Click the Arrange Documents button on the Application bar and then click the 2-up icon (see **Figure 8-25**). This arranges the reference and output documents side by side. If the Application bar is off, choose Window > Arrange > Tile.

Figure 8-25 Arranging the two images using 2-up view

Set Up the Soft-Proof. In the image you'll be editing, choose View > Proof Setup > Custom (see **Figure 8-26**). Load the profile for your printer and check Simulate Paper Color.

Figure 8-26 Setting up a soft-proof

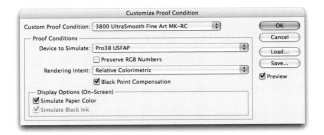

When you click Save and name the proof setup, it becomes available in the Custom Proof Condition pop-up menu and at the bottom of the View > Proof Setup submenu.

All of the soft-proof views (using the different combinations of Paper Color and Black Ink) tell us something useful, but checking Simulate Paper Color is, in theory, the most accurate because it uses Absolute Colorimetric to account for the paper color. That doesn't change the Rendering Intent you specified above that; both still apply. For example, if you create a soft-proof for a particular paper profile using the Relative Colorimetric rendering intent, Photoshop performs the following two stages of processing:

1   Figure out the printed colors. Photoshop takes the document and uses the selected Device to Simulate profile and the selected Relative Colorimetric rendering intent to calculate how the document's colors must be adjusted for the output conditions represented by the selected profile.

2   Figure out the monitor preview. Photoshop takes the print colors it just calculated, applies the Display Options (and the Absolute Colorimetric rendering used by Simulate Paper Color), and runs all of that through your monitor profile to calculate exactly how to represent the document's print appearance on your monitor.

Together, those two stages form the soft proof, and you can tell how important it is that each profile in the chain is accurate. Upon switching to the soft-proof view, you'll probably see the following:

- Simulate Paper Color makes the image appear much worse. A soft-proof typically shows washed-out shadows, compressed highlights, and an overall color shift caused by the difference between the white of your working space and the white of your paper. Don't despair—Photoshop isn't wrecking the image, it's previewing the unavoidable dynamic range compression and gamut compression that occurs when printing.

- White appears dimmer. Photoshop can show you the gamut and dynamic range compression only within the confines of your monitor color space, and it can do so only by turning things down, so white in the image is always dimmer than your monitor's white.

- Black may be slightly lighter than it will actually appear in the print, because in many monitor profiles, black has a Lightness value of 0 in Lab. But because most monitors actually have a Lightness of 3 or higher, we tend to call a Lightness value of 0 a *black hole* black point.

- Some profiles, particularly older ones, may not be built with soft-proofing in mind. They do a good job of converting the source to the output, but they don't do nearly as good a job of *round-tripping*—converting the output back to a viewing profile. A good third-party profiling tool can create custom profiles that tend to round-trip very well, as do many vendor-supplied profiles for recent professional-quality desktop printers.

TIP: The two most frequently used rendering intents are Relative Colormetric and Perceptual. The one to use depends on each individual image; it's common to view a soft-proof of each before deciding.

TIP: When you turn on the Simulate Paper Color check box, look away from the monitor. Much of the shock you feel when you see Absolute Colorimetric rendering to the monitor stems from seeing the image change. If you look away, your eyes will adapt to the new white point more easily. It's even easier if you use Full Screen mode (press F) and hide panels (press Tab). Panels don't change with the image, so they can distract you.

Problems with profiles aside, the soft-proofs offered by Photoshop are not, in our experience, any less accurate than those offered by traditional proofing systems. You simply need to acclimate to them.

Make Your Edits. Start by viewing the soft-proof and the reference image side by side. After you've edited the soft-proofed image to more closely resemble the reference image within the limitations of the soft-proof, fine-tune your edits while looking at the soft-proofed image in Full Screen view.

Figure 8-27 shows an example of an image that looked fine on the monitor, but a soft-proof indicated that we needed to bring the shadow detail up into a range where the printer could reproduce them. We can accurately show only the final results, because the printing process for this book can't show you the full tonal range of the reference image. In this example, we applied Image > Adjustments > Shadows/Highlights as a Smart Filter (see Chapter 11) so that we could later turn it off, since the adjustment was made only for a specific printing process.

Figure 8-27 Using soft-proofing to make output-specific edits

When we viewed this image as a soft-proof, dark shadows were blocked up.

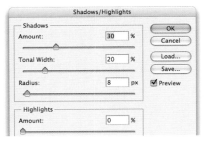

We opened Shadows/Highlights and applied only a Shadows boost.

The shadows now print better on this book's paper stock.

We applied Shadows/Highlights as a Smart Filter, turning it on only for the output we targeted in the soft-proof.

Handling Multiple Versions. It's common to make output-specific edits as adjustment layers whenever possible, to keep them separate from the full-range image. (In Figure 8-27, we applied Shadows/Highlights as a Smart Filter because it isn't available as an adjustment layer.) If there are a number of adjustment layers, we put them in a layer group named for the print process it addresses. That way, we can easily optimize the master image for different print processes by turning the layer sets on and off without having to create a new file for each print condition. Using this technique, we can keep a single RGB master file with built-in optimizations for each print condition, and let Photoshop do the conversion from RGB working space to printer space at print time. It's also valuable when preparing images for CMYK output, which often involves greater compromises. We may do a final fine-tuning on the converted CMYK image, but we make heavy use of soft-proofing to get the RGB image into the best possible state to withstand the CMYK conversion before we actually convert it. **Figure 8-28** shows a Layers panel with layer groups optimized for two types of output.

TIP: If you're not the person who will ultimately be printing the image you're preparing, or you need to make a copy for later printing from a page-layout program, turn on the correct layers for the final output and then choose Image > Duplicate so that you can save a flattened copy to send to the print service provider or to place in a layout.

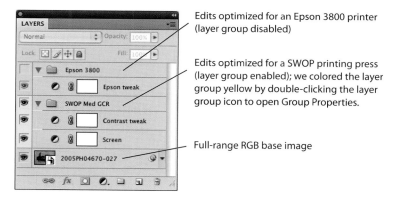

Edits optimized for an Epson 3800 printer (layer group disabled)

Edits optimized for a SWOP printing press (layer group enabled); we colored the layer group yellow by double-clicking the layer group icon to open Group Properties.

Full-range RGB base image

Figure 8-28 Using soft-proofing to make output-specific edits

Once we've edited the soft-proofed image to match the reference image, we use Full Screen view to take a final look at the soft-proofed image prior to printing. (We prefer the gray background, with the menu bar hidden—the black background makes the shadows look too light.)

When You Print. It's important to remember that the choices in the Customize Proof Condition dialog don't actually change the image—they merely simulate how it will look if you print under those conditions. Use the same profile, Rendering Intent, and Black Point Compensation settings for both the soft-proof and the final print. For example, if you made your edits viewing a soft-proof using the Relative Colorimetric intent, be sure you also choose Relative Colorimetric in the Print dialog. Don't duplicate all of the Customize Proof Condition settings in the Print dialog; the rest of the settings are for proofing only.

Also, make sure you've enabled any layers, layer groups, or Smart Filters that apply to the output you've currently targeted. If an image contains a layer group of corrections for your exhibition-quality inkjet printer and another layer group of corrections for eventual conversion to CMYK, when you print to the inkjet printer you must remember to turn on the inkjet corrections layer group and turn off the layer group with the CMYK corrections. For the rest of the details about printing, see "Printing from Photoshop" in Chapter 12, "Image Storage and Output."

CHAPTER NINE

Making Selections

You love the painting and retouching tools that Photoshop offers; you love layers; you even love all the options it gives you for saving files. But as soon as someone says alpha channel or mask, your eyes glaze over.

It doesn't have to be this way. Masks, channels, and selections are actually really easy once you get past their bad reputation. Making a good selection is obviously important when silhouetting and compositing images—two of the most common production tasks. But perhaps even more important, selections are also a key ingredient for nondestructive tonal corrections, color corrections, sharpening, and even retouching. We discussed some of these in the previous chapter, and we'll explore them further in later chapters. But before we get there, we must first make you a mask maven and a channel champion!

Reviewing the Basics

Back in Chapter 8, "The Digital Darkroom," we introduced a few concepts that are crucial to becoming a selection expert.

- Selections, channels, and masks are actually all the same thing in different forms, and you can convert one to another easily.

- A channel is a saved selection and looks like a grayscale image in which the black parts are fully deselected (masked out), the white parts are fully selected, and the gray parts indicate partially selected pixels.

- A layer mask is a selection or channel applied to a layer so that the black areas of the mask fully hide the layer and the white areas of the mask are transparent (they show the layer's pixels). If an area in a layer mask (or channel) is 25 percent gray, that area is 75 percent visible. Remember: "Black conceals, white reveals," and the lighter the gray, the more selected or visible the area.

- Smooth edge transitions between selected (white) and unselected (black) areas are incredibly important for compositing images, painting, correcting areas within an image—in fact, just about everything you'd want to do in Photoshop.

Selection Strategies

The key to using selection tools wisely is knowing what each of them is good for. The whole point of selection is to separate the areas you want to change from the areas you don't want to change, and being aware of that goal gives you a head start in choosing the right selection method. It helps if the area you want to select is visually distinct in some way, because Photoshop has ways of selecting areas based on visual differences such as tone, color, or intelligent edge detection. We'll discuss the following tools later in this chapter, except where noted.

Selecting Manually. Manual selection tools, including the marquee and lasso tools (see **Figure 9-1**), date back at least as far as Apple MacPaint on the original 1984 Mac. These classic tools are simple and effective. However, they are one hundred percent manual, so making complex selections is difficult and requires a steady hand. The Pen tool also falls into this category because you can draw a path and convert it to a selection. The advantage of the Pen tool is that paths can be much easier to edit than floating marquee selections; for this reason, storing selections as paths in the Paths panel is a useful alternative to storing selections in the Channels panel.

To cut down on the amount of manual labor, we start with one of the following methods to rough out an initial selection, and then carve out details with a manual tool.

Selecting by Edge Detection. The newest and most advanced set of selection tools in Photoshop uses intelligent edge detection. They don't find an edge using contrast alone, they're programmed to try to find edges based on content. The Magnetic Lasso is like a Lasso tool that follows a detailed edge based on your general dragging direction. The Quick Selection tool is newer and more effective because it's often capable of following complicated edges that include multiple tones and colors. Because it works more like the Magic Wand (selecting areas instead of edges), it's generally much faster than the Magnetic Lasso tool.

The bottom line: Don't just randomly reach for a selection tool. Think about the ways in which the selection you want can be isolated, and then go for the tools and techniques that will isolate it that way for you.

Selecting by Color and Tone. If the area you want to select is already plainly visible, it's worth using a tool that will just pick out that area for you. The Magic Wand tool is the traditional way to do this; click it on a pixel and it selects areas with similar tone or color values, such as a blue sky. If you want to select so many areas that using the Magic Wand would be tedious, the Select > Color Range command works similarly but using a dialog. Image > Adjustments > Selective Color (see Chapter 7) also selects color ranges, but it's specifically tuned for tuning the color of CMYK images.

Another way to select by color and tone is to look through each channel of an image. Sometimes an area that isn't distinct in the composite channel stands out in one of the image channels, or built by combining multiple channels. We walk through a great example of this in "Step-by-Step Selections and Masks" at the end of this chapter.

SELECTING AREAS MANUALLY

If the shape of the area you want to select is so simple that you can quickly draw it, reach for one of the marquee or lasso tools (except the Magnetic Lasso). Use these tools by clicking and dragging. The Polygonal Lasso tool is a bit different; click to set each straight-line segment it creates. The marquee tools select an enclosed area from the start. With the lasso tools, the area you draw automatically closes when you finish drawing. To finish drawing with the Lasso tool, release the mouse; with the Polygonal Lasso tool, double-click when you're done. Figure 9-1 shows some examples of these techniques, and **Table 9-1** is a quick reference for manual selection tool techniques.

Figure 9-1 Selection tools

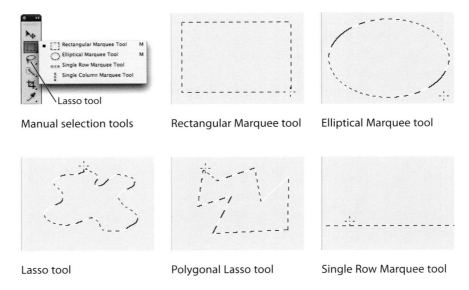

Manual selection tools

Rectangular Marquee tool

Elliptical Marquee tool

Lasso tool

Polygonal Lasso tool

Single Row Marquee tool

The Single Row Marquee and Single Column Marquee tools select a single row of pixels and don't work quite like the others. They always extend across the width or height of the image. They're useful for things like selecting individual scan lines in an interlaced television image, cleaning up screen captures, or painting a precise line for graphic design.

The last manual selection technique is to use the Pen tool and then convert the resulting path into a selection. But that technique is different enough from those in this section that we discuss the Pen tool in Chapter 11, "Essential Image Techniques."

TIP: To select an area of a specific size, choose Fixed Size from the Style pop-up menu in the Options bar, and then, after typing a value, enter the units you want ("in" for inches, "px" for pixels, and so on). Then press Return or Enter.

Table 9-1 Manual selection tool techniques.

To do this . . .	. . . do this:
Draw a square selection	Shift-drag the Rectangular Marquee tool
Draw a circular selection	Shift-drag the Elliptical Marquee tool
Draw from the center	Option/Alt-drag the Rectangular Marquee or Elliptical Marquee tool
Draw both straight and freeform segments with the Lasso or Polygonal Lasso tool	As long as you hold down Option (Mac) or Alt (Windows), dragging creates freeform segments and clicking creates straight segments
Draw straight segments at 45-degree increments	Shift-click the Polygonal Lasso tool
Close a Polygonal Lasso tool selection	Move mouse to start of selection, click when close icon appears; or double-click anywhere
Cancel the selection you're drawing	Press Esc

SELECTING WITH EDGE DETECTION TOOLS

If the area you want to select is recognizable as a distinct shape, it's worth trying the edge detection tools. They try to identify an edge using methods such as looking for contrast in all of an image's channels.

Magnetic Lasso

Where edges are distinct, you may be able to draw selections faster with the Magnetic Lasso tool than with the Lasso tool that it's grouped with in the Tools panel. The Magnetic Lasso can seem like magic, or it can seem like a complete waste of time; it all depends on three things: the image, your technique, and your attitude. Use this tool only when you're selecting something in your image that has a distinct edge. In fact, the more distinct the better, because the program is really following the contrast between pixels. The lower the contrast, the more the tool gets confused and loses the path.

To use the Magnetic Lasso tool, click once along the edge of the object you're trying to select, then move the mouse along the edge of the selection. You don't have to click or hold down the mouse button except in specific places where the tool isn't following the edge you want; in those cases click to place points manually, or drag to show the tool where to go. As you move the mouse, Photoshop snaps the selection to the object's edge (see **Figure 9-2**). When you're done, click on the first point in the selection again (or triple-click to close the path with a final straight line). **Table 9-2** is a quick reference for Magnetic Lasso tool techniques.

Figure 9-2 Edge selection tools and using the Magnetic Selection tool

Magnetic Lasso and Quick Selection tools

Drawing a path with the Magnetic Lasso

Closed Magnetic Lasso path becomes a selection

Table 9-2 Magnetic Lasso tool techniques.

To do this . . .	. . . do this:
Let tool find edges	Move mouse with mouse button released
Show tool where edges are	Drag the tool along an edge
Add an anchor point manually	Click the tool
Remove last anchor point	Release mouse button and press Delete
Draw straight segment	Option/Alt-click beginning and end of segment
Adjust lasso width	Press [to decrease or] to increase, press Shift-[or Shift-] to set minimum or maximum width
Commit to the selection	Move mouse to start of selection, click when close icon appears; or double-click anywhere
Cancel the selection you're drawing	Press Esc

The Magnetic Lasso tool has some key settings on the Options bar that can significantly influence how well it works for you.

Vary the Lasso Width as You Go. The Lasso Width option (in the Options bar; see **Figure 9-3**) determines how close to an edge the Magnetic Lasso tool must be to select it. In some respects it determines how sloppy you can be while dragging the tool, but it becomes very important when selecting within tight spots, such as the middle of a V shape. In general, use a large width for smooth areas and a small width for more detailed areas.

TIP: To see the actual size of the Lasso Width and other brush and tool sizes, open the Cursors pane of the Preferences dialog and set Other Cursors to Precise.

Fortunately, you can increase or decrease this setting while you move the mouse by using the lasso width adjustment shortcuts in Table 9-2. If you use a pressure-sensitive tablet, select the Stylus Pressure button on the Options bar; the pressure then relates directly to the Lasso Width.

Figure 9-3 The Options bar for the Magnetic Lasso tool

Stylus Pressure

Tuning Frequency and Contrast. These settings (on the Options bar) control how often Photoshop drops an anchor point and how much contrast between pixels it's looking for along the edge. In theory, a more detailed edge requires more anchor points (a higher frequency setting), and selecting an object in a low-contrast image requires a lower contrast threshold. To be honest, we're much more likely to switch to a different selection tool or technique before messing with these settings.

Don't work too hard to get a perfect selection with the Magnetic Lasso tool; it isn't designed to make a perfect selection. It's designed to create a great starting point that you can edit with other tools.

Quick Selection

If you're more comfortable painting a selection area than with drawing an outline around a selection area, you may want to try the Quick Selection tool. You drag this tool as though you were painting a mask, but instead of getting painted bits back, you get a selection outline similar to a lasso selection. In other words, the Quick Selection tool lets you paint a selection (as if you were working with masks or channels) but see a marquee outline (as if you were dragging a lasso or marquee tool). Another way to look at this tool is that it lets you select while painting, saving you the step of converting a mask or channel into a selection.

Use the Quick Selection tool as you would a brush. Drag it through the area you want to select (see **Figure 9-4**). Any additional areas you drag over with the Quick Selection tool are automatically added to the existing selection—no need to hold Shift to do that. For this reason alone, Magic Wand fans may want give the Quick Selection tool a try.

TIP: When using the Quick Selection tool, keep your left hand camped out by the bottom left corner of the keyboard. When it's there, you're always ready to press Command-Z/Ctrl-Z to undo, or Option/Alt to remove areas from the selection.

Figure 9-4 Using the Quick Selection tool

In this example, we want to select a car and its shadow, but the similar colors inside and outside our desired selection confuse most color-based selection tools. With the Quick Selection tool, we can indicate where our desired edges really are.

First we try the Magic Wand tool, but one click selects too many similar colors all over the image. The car color is too close to the pavement color, and the Magic Wand can't tell the difference between the car's shadow and all of the other shadows.

We do better by dragging the Quick Selection tool, which easily includes the colors of the red taillight and orange turn lamps in the selection, yet without including the unwanted areas outside the car and its shadow.

We accidentally overshoot the car outline with the brush edge, so the tool picks up some unwanted background.

Option-dragging (Mac) or Alt-dragging (Windows) the Quick Selection tool over unwanted areas excludes them.

It's important to realize that the Quick Selection tool remembers which colors you've included and excluded until you switch tools or switch to Quick Mask mode. For this reason, if you drag any part of the brush over a color you don't intend to select, press Command-Z (Mac) or Ctrl-Z (Windows) to immediately undo, so that the tool doesn't start thinking those are examples of areas to include. If you don't do this, large unwanted areas may be added to the selection, which will make the tool much less effective.

To remove an area selectively, Option-drag (Mac) or Alt-drag (Windows) the tool. We recommend that after you make your initial drag-selection, your second step be to Option-drag/Alt-drag color outside your intended selection area to teach the tool about areas that should *not* be included in the selection. This marks those colors off limits, so that as you continue using the Quick Selection tool on the current image it can be much smarter about which areas it considers to be inside and outside.

Size and Pressure. If the tool consistently selects too much area, go to the Options bar and make the brush harder and its size smaller. If you're using a pressure-sensitive stylus, apply less pressure for a smaller brush tip, or just turn off Pen Pressure in the Brush pop-up menu and use a small brush size.

Auto-Enhance. In the Options bar, the Auto-Enhance option tries to guess at making a better selection. If you think it's guessing wrong, turn off Auto-Enhance and fine-tune the edge yourself by clicking Refine Edge. We cover the Refine Edge dialog later in this chapter.

Although the Quick Selection tool has gotten a lot of press as a miraculous selection tool, it's really just another weapon in your selection arsenal. As with the Magnetic Lasso, the effectiveness of the Quick Selection tool depends in large part on the amount of contrast along the edges of the area you want to isolate. There are still many situations in which another selection method may be faster or easier.

TIPS FOR USING SELECTION TOOLS

The important thing to remember about the selection tools (and, in fact, about every selection technique in Photoshop) is that you can freely switch among them as you work. Don't get too hung up on getting one tool to work just the way you want it to; you can always modify the selection using a different technique. This idea of modifying selections is very important, and we'll touch on it throughout the chapter. Here are more pointers that can help you use the selection tools most efficiently:

Move a Selection Marquee as You Draw It. If you start drawing a new selection with the Lasso tool or a marquee tool and realize the selection is not in position, keep the mouse button held down, hold down the spacebar, drag to reposition the selection, and release the spacebar.

Move a Selection Marquee After You Draw It. As long as you see the animated selection marquee, you can move the marquee without moving pixels, as long as you drag it using the Lasso tool or a marquee tool.

Scroll the Window While Selecting. It's natural to zoom in close when you're dragging a selection tool—nothing wrong with that. But unless you have an obscenely large monitor, you won't be able to see the whole of the object you're selecting. No problem; the grabber hand works just fine while

TIP: There's a fair chance that Photoshop will forget the last selection after you've made a few other types of edits, so if you have the slightest suspicion that you might need a selection again, choose Select > Save Selection to store it in the Channels panel.

you're selecting—just hold down the spacebar and drag the image around. You can also press the + and - (plus and minus) keys to zoom in and out while you make the selection.

Add To and Subtract From Selections. You can add to the current selection by holding down the Shift key as you drag a selection tool outside the current selection area. Conversely, you can subtract from the current selection by holding down the Option key (Mac) or Alt key (Windows). Or if you want the intersection of two selections, hold down the Option/Alt and Shift keys while selecting (see **Figure 9-5**). If you don't feel like remembering these keyboard modifiers, you can click on the Add, Subtract, and Intersect buttons on the far left side of the Options bar instead.

Figure 9-5 Adding to and subtracting from selections

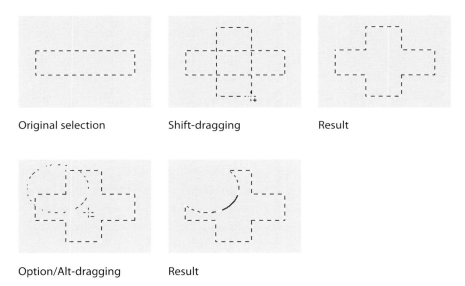

Original selection   Shift-dragging   Result

Option/Alt-dragging   Result

TIP: You can often combine selection tool keyboard shortcuts. For example, to draw a circle outward from the center using the Elliptical Marquee tool, combine the shortcut for drawing from the center (Option/Alt) with the shortcut for drawing a circle (Shift): Option-Shift-drag (Mac OS X) or Alt-Shift-drag (Windows) the tool.

Inverse Selecting. One simple but nonobvious method that we often use to select an area is to select a larger area with the Lasso or a marquee tool and then subtract the parts we don't want, like sculpting marble.

Select It Again. It's common to charge ahead with edits after selecting an area and later realize you need that last selection back. You can often recall it by pressing Command-Shift-D (Mac) or Ctrl-Shift-D (Windows), the shortcut for Select > Reselect).

Transform Selections, Not Contents. When you choose Select > Transform Selection (**Figure 9-6**), Photoshop places the Free Transform handles around your selection and lets you rotate, resize, skew, move, or distort the selection as needed. When you're done, press Return or Enter or click the check mark button (which appears only during a transformation) in the Options bar.

Original elliptical selection doesn't match subject

After using Transform Selection

Selection is now at the correct size and angle

Figure 9-6 Using the Transform Selection command

After you choose Transform Selection, you can pick options from the Edit > Transform submenu, or type transform values into the fields in the Options bar. For example, if you want to mirror your selection, turn on Transform Selection, drag the center point of the transformation rectangle to the place around which you want the selection to flip, then choose Flip Vertical or Flip Horizontal from the Edit > Transform submenu.

Don't Forget About the Options Bar. Each tool has additional settings in the Options bar that may come in handy. The most useful is probably the Refine Edge button, which opens the Refine Edge dialog, which we'll cover later. For the marquee tools, the Style pop-up menu lets you specify a size or aspect ratio for the selection, making it easy to precisely select areas to fit the space set aside for an image in a Web page or page-layout program.

Figure 9-7 The Options bar for the Rectangular Marquee tool, showing the Style pop-up menu

Selecting by Tone or Color

The selection tools we've discussed so far isolate a selection spatially (in terms of space)—either you're drawing an edge or a Photoshop tool is looking for an edge. But there's more than one way to look at an image. When the selection you want is easy to isolate by tone or color value, you can use this next set of Photoshop selection tools and tricks.

An important feature of the tone and color selection tools is the idea of *tolerance*—how similar a tone or color value should be to the value you've clicked before it's considered part of a selection. For example, a blue sky is normally many shades of blue, so if you want to select it by color you'd typically set the Tolerance range wide enough to include all of the sky's blues, without admitting nearby colors that aren't part of the sky.

Magic Wand

The Magic Wand is named more for its icon than for its prestidigitation. When you click on an image with the Magic Wand (dragging has no effect), Photoshop selects every neighboring pixel with the same or similar gray level or color. *Neighboring* means that the pixels must be touching on at least one side (see **Figure 9-8**). If you want to select all the similar-toned pixels in the image, whether they're touching or not, turn off the Contiguous check box in the Options bar before clicking.

You can set the Tolerance value on the Options bar from 0 to 255. In a grayscale image, this tolerance value refers to the number of gray levels from the sample point's gray level. If you click on a pixel with a gray level of 120 and your Tolerance is set to 10, you get any and all neighboring pixels that have values between 110 and 130.

In RGB and CMYK images, the Tolerance value is applied to the value in every channel value, not just the gray level. For instance, let's say your Tolerance is set to 10 and you click on a pixel with a value of 60R 100G 200B. Photoshop selects all neighboring pixels that have red values from 50 to 70, green values from 90 to 110, and blue values from 190 to 210. All three conditions must be met, or the pixel isn't included in the selection (see the next section, "Grow and Similar").

The Magic Wand will probably be used less frequently now that Photoshop has the Quick Selection tool. This is no doubt because the Magic Wand involves a lot of careful trial-and-error clicking, which may be why some have dubbed this tool the Tragic Wand. The following techniques can increase your chances of success.

Figure 9-8 Using the Magic Wand tool

The consistent window color is mostly easy for the Magic Wand, but a small corner is not selected.

Increasing the Tolerance to 100 includes the blue window but extends into the green clock.

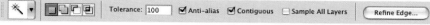

Options bar for the Magic Wand tool

Try Selecting from a Channel. It's often difficult to predict how the Magic Wand tool is going to work in a color image. We find it's easier to make selections using a single channel of the image. The Magic Wand is more intuitive on this grayscale image, and when you switch back to the composite channel, the selection's flashing marquee is still there.

Sample Small, Sample Often. The Magic Wand tool can be frustrating when it doesn't select everything you want it to. When this happens, novice users often set the Tolerance value higher and try again. Instead, try keeping the Tolerance low (between 12 and 32) and Shift-click to add more parts, or Option-click (Mac) or Alt-click (Windows) to take parts away.

Sample Points in the Magic Wand. When you select a pixel with the Magic Wand, you may not get the pixel value you expect. It all depends on the Sample Size pop-up menu on the Options bar (when you have the Eyedropper tool selected). If you select 3 by 3 Average or 5 by 5 Average in that pop-up menu, Photoshop averages the pixels around the one you click on with the Magic Wand. On the other hand, if you select Point Sample, Photoshop uses exactly the one you click.

Select in Reverse. Sometimes it's easier to first select a large area using a marquee or lasso tool, then subtract the areas you want selected by Option-clicking (Mac OS X) or Alt-clicking (Windows) unwanted areas.

Grow and Similar

The Select > Grow command can be useful when you have an active selection and you wish it was extended just a bit in terms of tone or color. Grow adds to an active selection according to the following criteria:

1. It finds the highest and lowest gray values of every channel of every pixel selected—the highest red, green, and blue, and the lowest red, green, and blue of the bunch of already-selected pixels (or the highest cyan, magenta, yellow, and black, and so on).

2. It adds the Tolerance value to the highest values and subtracts it from the lowest values in each channel. Therefore, the highest values get a little higher and the lowest values get a little lower (of course, it never goes above 255 or below 0).

3. Finally, Photoshop selects every adjacent pixel that falls between all those values (see **Figure 9-9**).

Figure 9-9 The Grow and Similar commands

  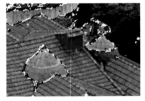

Original selection made with the Magic Wand tool

Grow selects more of the same color, contiguously.

Similar does the same but includes other areas.

TIP: You may find Grow easier to control if you use it within a single channel—the results are much easier to predict.

In other words, Photoshop spreads the selection in all directions, but only in similar colors. It doesn't always work the way you want, however. For instance, if you select a pure red area (RGB values 255, 0, 0) and a pure green area (RGB values 0, 255, 0), then choose Grow, Photoshop selects every adjacent pixel that has any red or green in it as long as the blue channel is not outside the Tolerance range. That means it'll select dark browns, lime greens, oranges, and so on—even if you set a very small tolerance level.

The Similar Command. The Grow command selects only contiguous areas of your image. If you're trying to select the same color throughout an image, using the Magic Wand and Grow may become quite tedious. Choosing Select > Similar does the same thing as choosing Select > Grow, but it chooses pixels from throughout the entire image (see Figure 9-9).

Color Range

Choosing Select > Color Range opens a dialog where you can set up a selection based on color. It has a couple of advantages over the Magic Wand tool: It can preview which pixels will be selected, and it can partially select far more pixels than the simple anti-aliasing of the Magic Wand tool. This can be incredibly helpful when you're trying to tease a good selection mask out of the contents of an image. There's quite a bit going on in the Color Range dialog, so let's take a look. **Figure 9-10** shows Color Range in action.

Adding and Deleting Colors. When you open Color Range, Photoshop creates a selection based on your foreground color. You can use the eyedroppers in the Color Range dialog to add or delete colors image colors from the selection or, better yet, hold down the Shift key to get the Add Color to Mask eyedropper, or Option/Alt to get the Remove Color from Mask eyedropper. You can sample colors from any other open image.

Fuzziness. Color Range uses the Fuzziness value to determine not only whether a pixel should be included but also how selected it should be. It's similar to an alpha channel, in which a pixel can be any value from 0 to 255 on the scale between black and white; lighter values are more selected.

Fuzziness is *not* the same as the Tolerance field on the Magic Wand Options bar. With Tolerance, the only partially selected pixels occur along the selection border. With Fuzziness, a partially selected pixel can be anywhere in the image because it's based on color, not area.

Localized Color Clusters. One of the problems with Color Range is that because the default settings are purely color based, areas you don't want may be added to the selection only because they're too similar in color to the areas you do want. Reducing Fuzziness is often not the answer if doing so excludes areas you want. In Photoshop CS4, the Localized Color Clusters option largely solves this problem. It does this by adding spatial selection to a dialog that up until now selected areas only by color.

When you turn on Localized Color Clusters, Color Range fully selects the pixels that are closest both in color and location to the spot where you clicked with the eyedropper. Pixels having the same color values are less selected farther from where you clicked, so that unwanted areas of the same color are excluded. If too much or too little is selected, use the Range slider to determine the distance used for the selection.

TIP: To open the Color Range dialog with exactly the same settings you last used, hold down the Option key (Mac) or the Alt key (Windows) when choosing Select > Color Range.

TIP: Color Range is always in Sample Merged mode. It sees your image as though all the visible layers were one. To exclude a layer from the selection mask, hide that layer before opening Color Range.

TIP: Fuzziness controls the selected color range by color, while Range controls the selected color range by the distance from where you click the sampler.

Figure 9-10 Using Color Range

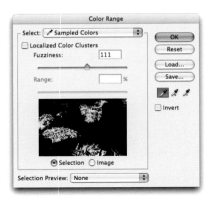

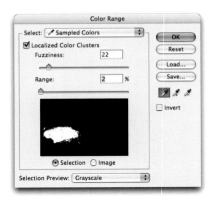

We want to select only the green beans, but other green vegetables prevent Fuzziness from isolating only the desired areas.

We turn on Localized Color Clusters, Option/Alt-click green areas we don't want, adjust Range and Fuzziness, and Shift-click green areas we do want.

The original image

The selection after closing Color Range (shown as a Quick Mask for clarity)

TIP: Color Range is one of those dialogs that allows you to continue to navigate in the document window while the dialog is open.

Preset Colors. The fastest way to select colors that are primary in RGB or CMYK, such as all the blues or all the greens, is to choose a color preset from the Select pop-up menu at the top of the Color Range dialog. The greater the difference between the color you choose and the other primaries, the more the pixel is selected. (To get really tweaky for a moment, the percentage the pixel is selected is the percentage difference between the color you choose and the primary color with the next highest value.)

You can also choose Highlights, Midtones, or Shadows; we tend to use these more than the preset colors. When you choose one of these, Photoshop decides whether to select a pixel (and how much) based on its Lab mode luminance value. We find selecting Highlights, Midtones, and Shadows most useful when selecting a subset of a color we've already selected.

Selection Preview. When you select anything other than None (the default) from this menu, Photoshop previews the Color Range selection mask in different ways.

The first choice, Grayscale, shows you what the selection mask would look like if you saved it as a separate channel. The second and third choices, Black Matte and White Matte, are the equivalent of copying the selected pixels and pasting them on a black or white background. This is great for seeing how well you're capturing edge pixels. The last choice, Quick Mask, is the same thing as clicking OK and immediately switching into Quick Mask mode. Selection Preview can be really helpful in making sure you're selecting exactly you want (no more and no less), but on older or slower machines you may find that it slows you down.

ANTI-ALIASING AND FEATHERING

You can partially select pixels in Photoshop. How is this possible? Remember that Photoshop internally handles a selection as a grayscale channel, so it's a simple matter to store a partially selected pixel as a shade of gray in that channel. One of the most common partial selections is along the edges of a selection. The two most common ways of partially selecting the edges are anti-aliasing and feathering (see **Figure 9-11**).

Anti-Aliasing. If you use the Rectangular Marquee tool, the edges of the selection are nice and crisp, which is probably how you want them. Crisp edges around an oval or irregular shape, however, are rarely a desired effect. That's because of the stair-stepping required to make a diagonal or curved line out of square pixels. What you usually want are partially selected pixels in the notches between the fully selected pixels. This technique is called *anti-aliasing*.

Every selection in Photoshop is automatically anti-aliased for you, unless you turn this feature off in the selection tool's Options bar. Unfortunately, you can't see the anti-aliased nature of the selection unless you're in Quick Mask mode, because anti-aliased (partially selected) pixels are often less than 50 percent selected. Once you've made a selection with Anti-alias turned off in the Options bar, you can't anti-alias it—though there are ways to fake it, as we describe next.

TIP: Instead of using the Image and Selection radio buttons, press the Command or Ctrl key (either one works on the Mac). This toggles between the Selection preview and Image preview much faster than by clicking buttons.

TIP: You can change your Quick Mask options settings while the Color Range dialog is open. Hold down the Option key (Mac) or Alt key (Windows) while selecting Quick Mask from the Selection Preview pop-up menu.

Figure 9-11 Magnified views of anti-aliasing and feathering

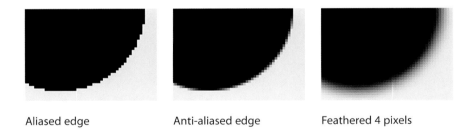

Aliased edge   Anti-aliased edge   Feathered 4 pixels

TIP: In Mac OS X, the traditional Photoshop keyboard shortcut for Feather is Command-Option-D. Mac OS X took over this shortcut for hiding and showing the Dock. If you want the Feather shortcut to work, either redefine it by choosing Edit > Keyboard Shortcuts in Photoshop, or open the Keyboard Shortcuts tab in Mac OS X System Preferences to redefine or disable the hide/show Dock shortcut.

Feathering. Anti-aliasing simply smooths out the edges of a selection, adjusting the amounts that the edge pixels are selected in order to appear smooth. But it's often (too often) the case that you need a larger transition area between what is and isn't selected. That's where feathering comes in. *Feathering* is a way to expand the border around the edges of a selection. The border isn't just extended out; it's also extended in.

To understand what feathering does, it's important to understand the concept of the selection channel that we talked about earlier in the chapter. That is, when you make a selection, Photoshop is really seeing the selection as a grayscale channel behind the scenes. The black areas are totally unselected, the white areas are fully selected, and the gray areas are partially selected.

When you feather a selection, Photoshop is essentially applying a Gaussian Blur to the grayscale selection channel. (We say "essentially" because in some circumstances—such as when you set a feather radius of more than 120 pixels—you get a slightly different effect; however, there's usually so little difference that it's not worth bothering with. For those technoids out there who really care, Adobe tells us that a Gaussian Blur of the Quick Mask channel is a tiny bit more accurate and true than a feather.)

There are several ways to feather a selection:

* Before selecting, specify a Feather amount in the Options bar.

* After selecting, click Refine Edge in the Options bar and adjust the Feather option.

* After selecting, choose Select > Modify > Feather.

* Apply the Gaussian Blur filter to the selection's Quick Mask.

If you use the Refine Edge dialog, your entire selection is feathered. Sometimes, however, you want to feather only a portion of the selection. Maybe you want a hard edge on one half of the selection and a soft edge on the other. You can do this by switching to Quick Mask mode, selecting what you want feathered with any of the selection tools, and applying a Gaussian Blur to it. When you flip out of Quick Mask mode, the feathering is included in the selection.

REFINING A SELECTION

Some features come about because someone sees an opportunity to streamline a multistep manual chore. The Refine Edge dialog represents this type of new feature. In previous versions of Photoshop, if you applied the Select > Feather command, the only way to actually see the size of the feather was to view the selection as a Quick Mask or channel. And we have often mentioned that you can tweak a selection edge by converting the selection to a Quick Mask or a channel and then using image-editing commands (such as Levels and Gaussian Blur) to alter contrast along the edges of the selection channel. Of course, that meant you had to know which series of operations would get you the result you wanted.

The Refine Edge dialog takes away much of that brainwork. Now you can simply tell Refine Edge how you want to tune the selection edge, and it's done. Behind the scenes, Refine Edge works with a selection as a channel, so that you don't have to go through those steps yourself. You can even use Refine Edge on a mask or channel.

To use Refine Edge, click the Refine Edge button in the Options bar while a selection tool and a selection are both active (see **Figure 9-12**). You'll see five sliders divided by a line. The Radius and Contrast options above the line set the initial edge (see **Figure 9-13**), and the three options below the line take it from there. The best way to use the controls is as they're laid out, in order from top to bottom.

Radius. Starting from the initial edge you created, the Radius value determines how far out Refine Edge extends the feathered transition between selected and unselected pixels. A higher Radius value can help when the exact edge is harder to identify, such as the edge of a soft shadow or hair.

Radius is more sophisticated than a standard feather or edge blur, in that it protects existing hues and creates a less artificial-looking transition. For a traditional feather, leave Radius at 0 and use the Feather slider instead.

TIP: Refine Edge isn't just an Options bar button. It's also a command (Select > Refine Edge), so you can open the dialog by pressing its keyboard shortcut—Command-Option-R (Mac) or Ctrl-Alt-R (Windows).

TIP: Refine Edge should usually be your next step after using tools such as the Quick Selection or Magnetic Lasso. Those tools usually produce an edge that needs to be cleaned up.

Figure 9-12 The Refine
Edge dialog

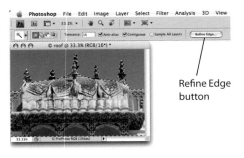

Refine Edge
button

To open the Refine Edge dialog, click the Refine
Edge button while a selection tool and a selection
are both active.

Figure 9-13 Using Radius
and Contrast

Original selection before
using Refine Edge

Selection viewed at
default settings in
Refine Edge

Radius widened to
include more variations
in the hair edge

Contrast increased to
sharpen hair details

Contrast. This option determines the sharpness of the feathered transition across the radius you set. A higher value creates a sharper edge.

Smooth. The Smooth slider evens out bumps along the selection edge to help compensate for sloppy selections. However, if your edge follows details like hair, a high Smooth value can obliterate them. If you have to set such a high Smooth value that you lose details, you may need to click Cancel and improve the precision of your initial selection.

Feather. The Feather slider is essentially the traditional Feather command in Photoshop (which is still available at Select > Feather). It simply blurs the edge resulting from your Radius, Contrast, and Smooth settings.

Contract/Expand. If your selection is a little bit inside or outside of the area you wanted to select, use Contract/Expand to compensate. As the last option in the second group of options, it acts on the results of the four options above it, so if no Contract/Expand value gets you what you want, try adjusting the other sliders (see **Figure 9-14**).

TIP: To toggle the Refine Edge selection view off and on, press the X key. Of course, as in other dialogs, the P key toggles the Preview check box.

Lowering the Contract/Expand value pulls the selection in from its original edge. Increasing the value would have pushed it outside the original edge.

Figure 9-14 Using Contract/Expand

Selection View Icons. The five icons along the bottom of the Refine Edge dialog are simply different ways of previewing the selection. They follow the basic principle we set forth earlier in the chapter: A selection can be represented as a marching-ants border, a Quick Mask, or a grayscale image channel. Click an icon to set the view your way, or just press F to toggle through the viewing modes with the keyboard.

Advanced Edge Editing. When tuning the edge of a selection, your first stop should be the Refine Edge dialog, which is accessible by clicking a button on the Options bar when a selection is active. If Refine Edge doesn't get you what you want, go back to the idea that a selection is a grayscale channel. This means you can either switch to Quick Mask mode or save the selection as a channel, and either way you can then use any image-editing tool in Photoshop to edit the selection. For example, you can adjust the hardness of a feathered selection by applying Levels or Curves to the selection channel. You can even use selection tools in a selection channel.

THE MODIFY SUBMENU

When you think of the most important part of a selection, what comes to mind? If you answer, "what's selected," you're wrong. No matter what you have selected in your image, the most important part of the selection is the boundary or edge. This is where the rubber hits the road, where the money slaps the table, where the invoice smacks the client. No matter what you do with the selection—whether you copy and paste it, paint within it, or whatever—the quality of your edge determines how effective your effect will be.

When making a precise selection, you often need to make subtle adjustments to the selection boundaries. The four menu items on the Modify submenu under the Select menu—Border, Smooth, Expand, and Contract—focus entirely on this task.

Border. There's a faster way to get a doughnut than driving down to the local Krispy Kreme. Draw a circle using the Elliptical Marquee tool, then choose Select > Modify > Border. You can even specify how thick you want your doughnut (in pixels, of course). Border transforms the single line (the circle) into two lines (see **Figure 9-15**).

The problem with Border is that it creates only soft-edged borders. If you draw a square and give it a border, you get a soft-edged shape that looks more like an octagon than a square. To get a harder edge out of the Border command, click Refine Edge on the Options bar and turn up the Contrast.

Smooth. The problem with making selections with the Lasso tool is that you often get very jagged selection lines; the corners are too sharp, the curves are too bumpy. You can smooth these out by choosing Select > Modify > Smooth. Like most selection operations in Photoshop, this actually runs a convolution filter over the selection mask—in this case, the Median filter. That is, selecting Smooth is exactly the same thing as switching to Quick Mask mode and choosing the Median filter.

Smooth has little or no effect on straight lines or smooth curves. But it has a drastic effect on corners and jagged lines (see Figure 9-15). Smooth looks at each pixel in your selection, then looks at the pixels surrounding it (the number of pixels it looks at depends on the Radius value you choose in the Smooth dialog). If more than half the pixels around it are selected, the pixel remains selected. If fewer than half are selected, the pixel is deselected.

If you enter a small Radius value, only corner tips and other sharp edges are rounded out. Larger values make sweeping changes. It's rare that we use a radius higher than 5 or 6, but it depends entirely on what you're doing (and how smooth your hand is!).

Figure 9-15 Border

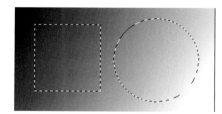

Original selection

Mask of original selection

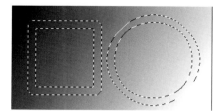

After Border (20 pixels)

Mask of post-Border selection

Expand and Contract. The Expand and Contract features are two of the most useful selection modifiers. They let you enlarge or reduce the size of the selection. They work the same way as the Expand/Contract option in the Refine Edge dialog.

Once again, these modifiers simply apply filters to the black-and-white mask equivalent of your selection. Choosing Expand is the same as applying the

TIP: Expand and Contract adjust a selection spatially, while the Grow and Similar commands we discussed earlier adjust a selection by tone and color.

Maximum filter to the mask; choosing Contract is the same as applying the Minimum filter. While we frequently find these older selection modifiers useful, they aren't very precise. You can specify the radius only in 1-pixel increments. For a lot more control, use the Refine Edge dialog instead.

FLOATING SELECTIONS

TIP: If you enter 5 as the Radius value in the Expand or Contract dialog (or in the Maximum or Minimum dialog), it's exactly the same as running the filter or selection modifier five times. The Radius value here is more of an iteration value: How many times do you want to apply the filter at a 1-pixel radius?

We need to take a quick detour off the road of making selections and delve into the world of what happens when you select pixels and then move them: They turn into a *floating selection*, a temporary layer just above the current layer. As soon as you deselect the floating selection, it merges down into the current layer, replacing whatever pixels were below it. Although these floating selections act like layers, they don't show up in the Layers panel and will merge down if you lose the selection. We prefer to avoid floating selections and instead move pixels to a real layer for accurate positioning: Right after making a selection of pixels that we're about to move, we usually press Command-J (Mac OS X) or Ctrl-J (Windows) to make a new layer out of the selection—that's the shortcut for Layer > New > Layer from Selection (see **Figure 9-16**). After we move the new layer, we drop it back into the underlying layer by pressing Command-E (Mac OS X) or Ctrl-E (Windows), the shortcut for Layer > Merge Layers (unless we want to keep it as its own layer).

You can manipulate a floating selection as you do a layer. You can change its blending mode by choosing Edit > Fade. (Unintuitive, but true.) However, as soon as you try to paint on it, or run a filter, or do almost anything else interesting to the floating selection, Photoshop deselects it and drops it back down to the layer below it. That's one reason we would rather just place pixels onto a real layer before messing with them.

Figure 9-16 Floating selections and layers

A floating selection . . .

. . . does not appear in the Layers panel . . .

. . . unless you create a new layer from the selection (Command/Ctrl-J).

QUICK MASKS

If Photoshop handles a selection as a grayscale channel, why can't you work with it that way? You can if you switch to Quick Mask mode; select the Quick Mask icon in the Tools panel or press Q. A red overlay indicates the Quick Mask. Solid areas of the mask are 50 percent opaque red, and the white (selected) areas are even more transparent than that (see **Figure 9-17**). The red is supposed to remind you of Rubylith, if you remember the amber-colored acetate that was once cut up to create masks for film. One of the advantages of Quick Mask mode is that if you're finding it a challenge to edit a selection with the marquee and lasso tools, in Quick Mask mode you can sculpt your selection using the brush and retouching tools.

Another advantage of Quick Mask mode is that you can actually see partially transparent pixels. In a typical selection, the selection marquee (also popularly called the marching ants) outlines the boundary of pixels that are selected 50 percent or more. There are often loads of other pixels that are selected 49 percent or less that you can't see at all from the marching ants display. Quick Mask mode shows you exactly which pixels are selected and by how much.

A disadvantage of Quick Mask mode is that, like a marquee selection, it isn't permanent. The Quick Mask goes away when you deselect, and it isn't saved with the document. Choose Save > Save Selection to save it for later.

While you're in Quick Mask mode, a temporary Quick Mask channel appears in the Channels panel.

Customizing How a Quick Mask Appears. If you don't like the red color that indicates a Quick Mask, double-click the Quick Mask icon in the Tools panel. You can change both the color and the transparency of the Quick Mask. We almost always increase the opacity of the color to about 75 percent so it displays more prominently against the background image.

TIP: Select > Inverse won't work on a Quick Mask because it's pixels, not a selection. To swap selected and unselected areas in Quick Mask mode, choose Image > Adjustments > Invert instead.

TIP: For special effects ideas, experiment with running filters on the Quick Mask. When you exit Quick Mask, you can fill, paint, or adjust the altered selection, and your edit will affect only the filtered selection.

Original selection

Quick Mask view

Figure 9-17 Quick Mask view of a selection

Channels

Back in "Reviewing the Basics," we said that selections, masks, and channels are all the same thing down deep: grayscale images. This is not intuitive, nor is it easy to grasp at first. But once you really understand this point, you've taken the first step toward really surfing the Photoshop big waves.

A *channel* is an independent grayscale image. You can have up to 56 channels in a document—and that includes the three in an RGB image or four in a CMYK image. (Actually, there are two exceptions: Images in Bitmap mode can only contain a single 1-bit channel; second, Photoshop allows one additional channel per layer to accommodate layer masks, which we'll talk about later in this chapter.)

Color Channels

When a color image is in RGB mode (under the Mode menu), the image is made up of three channels: red, green, and blue. You can make any single color channel visible or invisible, but you can't delete or add a color channel without first changing the image mode, because the channels are integral to the color mode (you can't have an RGB image without a red channel).

The first thumbnail in the Channels panel (see **Figure 9-18**) is the composite channel. Actually, this isn't really a channel at all. Rather, it is the full-color representation of all the individual color channels mixed together. The composite channel gives you a convenient way to select or deselect all the color channels at once, and also lets you view the composite color image, even while you're editing a single channel.

Figure 9-18 The Channels panel

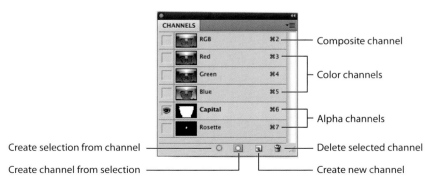

Composite channel

Color channels

Alpha channels

Create selection from channel

Create channel from selection

Delete selected channel

Create new channel

Viewing and Selecting Channels. The tricky thing about working with channels is figuring out which channel(s) you're editing and which channel(s) you're seeing on the screen. They're not always the same!

The Channels panel looks a lot like the Layers panel, with the same eyeball icons that you can turn on and off to show or hide individual channels. Clicking a thumbnail or channel name displays that channel and makes it active for editing.

As with layers, you can select more than one channel at a time by Shift-clicking channel thumbnails. When you display more than one channel at a time, the alpha channels automatically switch from their standard black and white to their channel color (you can specify what color each channel uses in Channel Options by double-clicking the channel thumbnail).

Table 9-3 lists keyboard shortcuts that are useful with channels.

Table 9-3 Channel shortcuts.

To do this . . .	. . . do this:
View the composite channel	Press Command-2 (Mac OS X) or Ctrl-2 (Windows)
View other channels	Press Command/Ctrl-3 through Command/Ctrl-9
Load a channel as a selection	Add the Option (Mac OS X) or Alt (Windows) key to the above shortcuts

Alpha Channels

People get nervous when they hear the term "alpha channel," because they figure that with such an exotic name, it has to be a complex feature. Not so. An *alpha channel* is really just another grayscale channel. The reason it needs its own name is that it isn't one of the channels that make up the visible image. For example, although a typical RGB image has three channels—red, green, and blue—an RGB image with one alpha channel has four channels in all.

Alpha channels aren't just another way of storing a selection marquee. They're also used by various Photoshop features as a way of marking areas you want to alter or protect. For example, the Lens Blur filter can simulate depth of field by using gradients in an alpha channel as a depth map, and the Content-Aware Scale command can use an alpha channel to protect specific areas from being scaled.

Saving Selections. We've mentioned before that you can choose Select > Save Selection to store a selection with an image as an alpha channel. If the Channels panel is visible, it's faster to click the Save Selection icon in the Channels panel. Or if you want to see the Channel Options dialog first (for instance, if you want to name the channel), Option-click (Mac) or Alt-click (Windows) the icon (see **Figure 9-19**).

Figure 9-19 The Save Selection and Load Selection dialogs

Loading Selections. Saving a selection as an alpha channel doesn't do you much good unless you can retrieve it. In the Channels panel, Command-click (Mac) or Ctrl-click (Windows) on the channel that you want to turn into a selection (the shortcut for choosing Select > Load Selection). Even better, press the Command and Option (Mac) or Ctrl and Alt (Windows) keys along with the number key of the channel you want (the numbers are listed along the right side of the Channels panel). For instance, if you want to load channel 6 as a selection on a Mac, press Command-Option-6.

Channels in TIFF Files. If you're saving a mess of channels along with the image you're working on, and you want to save the file as a TIFF, you should probably turn on LZW compression in the Save as TIFF dialog. Zip compression is even better if the destination program supports it (Adobe InDesign does). Whatever the case, use some kind of compression—otherwise, the TIFF will be enormous. Of course, you could save in the native Photoshop format, but we find that a Zip-compressed TIFF is almost always smaller on disk.

Adding, Subtracting, and Intersecting Selections. Let's say you have an image with three elements in it. You've spent an hour carefully selecting each of the elements, and you've saved each one in its own channel (see **Figure 9-20**). Now you want to combine the three selections. After you load one channel as a selection, choose Select > Load Selection to add another channel to the current selection, subtract another channel, or find the intersection between the two selections. Even easier, use the key-click combinations in **Table 9-4**. Confused? Don't forget to watch the cursor icons; as you hold down the various key combinations, Photoshop indicates what will happen when you click.

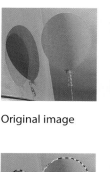

Original image

Channel A

Channel B

Channel C

Figure 9-20 Combining channels

All three channels loaded by using the Add shortcut

Middle channel removed using the Subtract shortcut

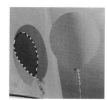

Channels A and B loaded using the Intersect shortcut

Table 9-4 Using the Channels panel to combine selections.

To get this . . .	**. . . press this:**
Add channel to current selection	Command-Shift-click (Mac) Ctrl-Shift-click (Windows)
Subtract channel from selection	Command-Option-click (Mac) Ctrl-Alt-click (Windows)
Intersect current selection and channel	Command-Shift-Option-click (Mac) Ctrl-Shift-Alt-click (Windows)

Moving Selections Between Documents

It's easy to move selections between documents. You have more options if both documents have exactly the same pixel dimensions.

Drag and Drop. You can use one of the selection tools to drag an active selection to another document. Normally the selection drops wherever you release the mouse; to drop the selection in exactly the same position in the destination document, hold down the Shift key just after you start dragging the selection from the original document. If the images don't have the same pixel dimensions, the Shift key drops the selection at the center of the destination document.

You can also drag an entire channel from the Channels panel and drop it onto another open document of the same pixel dimensions.

Save Selection, Load Selection, and Duplicate Channel. If you choose Save > Save Selection or Duplicate Channel from the Channels panel menu, you'll find a Document pop-up menu that let you save a selection to the Channels panel of another document. If you choose Select > Load Selection, the Document pop-up menu in that resulting dialog lets you import a channel from another document. In all three cases, you'll see other documents in that pop-up menu only if they're currently also open and they have the same pixel dimensions as the document that was in the foreground where you chose the command.

Selections, Layers, and Masks

By default, a Photoshop layer is transparent until you fill it with something. (The exception is the layer named Background that appears in italics in the Layers panel, which is always opaque). All layer masks go away when you merge or flatten layers.

Layer Transparency and Layer Masks. When a layer contains pixels, those pixels can be made transparent using either layer transparency or a layer mask. Here's the difference: When you create transparency by deleting areas of a layer, the deleted pixels are gone forever. When you create transparency using a layer mask, the mask carries transparency information independently of a layer while leaving the complete original layer intact. For this reason, layer masks are preferred because they're nondestructive (see **Figure 9-21**).

You can create layer transparency simply by selecting areas of a non-background layer and pressing Delete, or using any of the tools in the Eraser tool group in the Tools panel. You create transparency in a layer mask by adding one (using the Masks panel or Layers panel) and painting black onto it.

Original layer over gradient

After creating transparency

Using layer transparency

Using a layer mask

Figure 9-21 Comparing layer transparency and layer masks; both achieve the same look, but a layer mask allows transparent areas to be restored later if needed.

Selections and Masks. You can translate between selections and layer masks about as easily as you can translate between selections and channels, since like a channel, a layer mask is simply a grayscale image. Many channel concepts and techniques carry over to layer masks, such as making and refining a selection and filling it with black or white. We discussed converting between selections, channels, and layer masks in "Selections, Masks, and Channels" in Chapter 8, "The Digital Darkroom."

More Layer Mask Tips. Here are some techniques we didn't mention in Chapter 8:

- The Add a Pixel Mask button in the Masks panel, Add Layer Mask button in the Layers panel, and Layer > Layer Mask > Reveal All command all do the same thing.

- By default, a new layer mask is filled with white (the entire layer is opaque). If you Option-click (Mac) or Alt-click (Windows) the Add a Pixel Mask button in the Masks panel or the Add Layer Mask button in the Layers panel, Photoshop inverts the layer mask (the entire layer becomes transparent).

- If a selection exists when you create a layer mask, everything outside the selection becomes transparent (filled with black) in the new mask. The Option/Alt key inverts this behavior too.

- When you're editing a mask, its Layers panel thumbnail has a dashed border around it and the words "Layer Mask" appear in the document title bar. We've accidentally painted on the image instead of the mask enough times that we recommend always confirming what's selected.

- A layer group can have a mask, and that's handy for creating nested masks. Select the layers, group them by pressing Command-G (Mac) or Ctrl-G (Windows), which is the shortcut for choosing Layer > Group Layers, and then add a mask to that layer group (see **Figure 9-22**).

TIP: By default, moving a layer also moves its layer mask. To move them independently, turn off the Link icon (click between the layer and layer mask previews in the Layers panel).

Figure 9-22 Masking a group

The hand shadow stone and the gradient are grouped; one group mask reveals the background.

The Group 1 mask affects all of the layers inside that group.

Paint It In Using Masks. Layer masks let you paint in any kind of effect you want. For example, duplicate the Background layer of an image in the Layers panel, apply a filter to the new layer (such as Unsharp Mask), then Option/Alt-click on the Add Layer Mask icon to mask out the entire effect. Now you can paint the effect back in using the Brush tool and non-black pixels. If you change your mind, you can paint away the effect with black pixels. This flexibility is addictive, and you'll soon find yourself using this technique over and over, whether it's painting in texture, sharpening or blurring, or whatever.

Table 9-5 lists more helpful shortcuts for viewing and editing layers.

Table 9-5 Layer mask shortcuts.

To do this . . .	. . . do this:
Switch from layer to layer mask	Command-\ (Mac OS X) or Ctrl-\ (Windows)
Display layer mask only	Option-click (Mac OS X) or Alt-click layer mask thumbnail
Switch painting focus back to layer	Press Command-2 (Mac OS X) or Ctrl-2 (Windows) (the composite channel view shortcut)
Display both a layer and its mask	Option-Shift-click (Mac OS X) or Alt-Shift-click (Windows) layer mask thumbnail, or press \
Disable layer mask	Shift-click layer mask icon
Customize mask preview	Double-click layer mask icon

Getting Rid of the Mask. As soon as you start editing layer masks, you're going to find that you want to turn the mask on and off to get before-and-after views of your work. You can make the mask disappear temporarily by choosing Layer > Layer Mask > Disable. Or do it the fast way: Shift-click a layer mask icon.

If you want to delete a mask forever, choose Layer > Layer Mask > Delete (or, faster, drag the Layer Mask icon to the Trash icon). Photoshop gives you a last chance to apply the mask to the layer. Note that if you do apply the mask, the masked (hidden) portions of the layer are actually deleted.

STEP-BY-STEP SELECTIONS AND MASKS

If there's one thing that makes silhouettes difficult, it's the edge detail. In most cases (especially when you're trying to select fine details), some of the color from the image background spills over into the image you want, which causes an obvious fringe when you drop the silhouetted image onto a different background (even white). While the addition of Refine Edge goes a long way toward automating these processes, we sometimes find it more effective to use the old-school manual methods of massaging selections with the full range of image-processing capabilities in Photoshop.

Why would you go through all the trouble of selecting areas if the selection was already made for you? More often than not, the selection you want is already hidden within the image; you only have to look at the color channels that make up the image (see "Color Channels," earlier in this chapter).

Here's a technique that people ask us about all the time: masking out hair. It involves selection techniques and translating freely among channels, selections, and masks, so it's a great summary of the topics in this chapter. We've adapted this procedure from techniques developed by Russell Brown, Katrin Eismann, and others. For our example, we intentionally picked a casually shot outdoor portrait to show how this technique handles the unhelpful combination of background tone variations and wispy hair. We'll replace the messy green background with a background gradient.

First Pass: Roughing it Out. We just want to find the channel combination that gives us a good rough draft for the mask.

1. We add a Channel Mixer adjustment layer above the subject layer (see **Figure 9-23**). We turn on the Monochrome check box and adjust the sliders to values that make the edge of the subject stand out most clearly without losing details like fine hairs; we'll handle those later. We concentrate on the silhouette edge. The photographic appearance of this step isn't important; it just creates a starting point for the mask.

2. We choose Select > All and then choose Edit > Copy Merged, then we hide the Channel Mixer adjustment layer.

3. In the Layers panel, we select the subject layer and click the Add Layer Mask button. We Option-click (Mac OS X) or Alt-click (Windows) the new layer mask and then choose Edit > Paste, then we choose Select > Deselect. Now we have a mask based on our Channel Mixer results.

4. We check to make sure the background is darker than the subject. If it isn't, we click the Invert button in the Masks panel or press Command-Shift-I (Mac OS X) or Ctrl-Shift-I (Windows) to invert the mask.

Figure 9-23 Creating the initial layer mask

Original image

Using Channel Mixer to define edge contrast

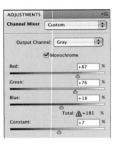

Channel Mixer settings for the edges

Inverted mask image

Layers panel after step 4

Second Pass: Increase Mask Contrast. We force to black or white everything except the transitions along the mask edge:

1. Use the Lasso tool to roughly select the interior of the subject, approaching but never touching the transition areas along the edge where you need to preserve details. In the Tools or Color panel, set the foreground color to white and then press Alt-Backspace to fill the selection with the white foreground color (see **Figure 9-24**).

2. Choose Select > Deselect.

3. With the mask still visible, choose Image > Adjustments > Curves (or Levels). (You can't use an adjustment layer here because it's a mask.) Adjust the black point to push near-black areas closer to black, and adjust the white point to push near-white areas closer to white. You may not be able to push the mask to complete black or white if doing so wipes out the details along the edges and transition areas; keep an eye on those and you'll take care of them in the next step.

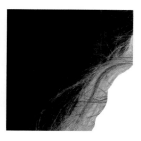

The goal of using Levels or Curves on the mask is to make the subject white and the empty background black, preserving fine details in the transitions.

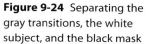

Figure 9-24 Separating the gray transitions, the white subject, and the black mask

Subject filled with white

Detail before setting black and white points

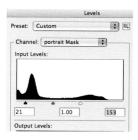

Using Levels

Detail after using Levels

Third Pass: Fine-Tune Just the Fringes. Now we concentrate only on tuning the transitions along the edges.

1. Select the Burn tool, and in the Options bar set Range to Shadows and Exposure to 50 percent or so. Paint in the large nondetailed areas of the black mask to force the remaining near-black areas to black (see **Figure 9-25**). For the transition areas containing details, reduce Exposure to 10 percent or below and reduce the brush size so that you can darken more gently and preserve details more easily. When you're done, repeat for

the near-white subject and transition areas using the Dodge tool with its Range set to Highlights. This should complete the mask itself.

2. If there are still some edges that didn't work out, you may have to create additional Channel Mixer-based masks to isolate them, and then paste specific corrected areas into the subject layer's mask.

3. Option-click (Mac OS X) or Alt-click (Windows) the subject layer's mask once in a while to see how the subject looks against the new background, which should now be revealed behind the subject layer.

Figure 9-25 Separating the gray transitions, the white subject, and the black mask

Our Burn tool settings for forcing background areas of the mask to black

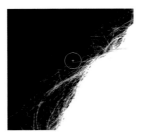  

Forcing the mask background to black with the Burn tool (compare to Figure 9-24)

After switching the view back to the main image; it looks all right so far.

Using the Dodge tool in mask transitions makes fine hairs more visible.

Getting Rid of Color Fringing. In Figure 9-25 you can see some of the original green background spilling out around the hair. Here's one way to take care of background spill and color fringing problems in a mask:

TIP: In Photoshop CS4, you can also create a clipping mask by selecting the new layer and clicking the Create Clipping Mask button in the Masks panel.

1. In the Layers panel, add a Solid Color fill layer directly above the subject layer (choose Layer > New Fill Layer > Solid Color or click the Create New Fill or Adjustment Layer button in the Layers panel).

2. In the Layers panel, Option-click (Mac OS X) or Alt-click the dividing line between the subject layer and the Solid Color layer to create a clipping mask, so that the Solid Color layer (Color Fill in the Layers panel) affects only the subject layer (see **Figure 9-26**).

3. Set the blending mode of the Solid Color layer to Color.

4. Click the mask of the Solid Color layer and fill it with black.

5. Double-click the Solid Color layer thumbnail, and with the Color Picker open, sample a good hair color in the area where the color fringing is visible. (Up to this point, you still won't see any change in the main image, so don't worry about that.)

6. Make sure the mask of the Solid Color layer is active (with the extra border around it). Select the Brush tool, set the foreground color to white, set an appropriate size for retouching the hair, and paint areas with color fringing. The color fringe should disappear, because it's replaced by the color of the Solid Color adjustment layer. If the hair color looks off, double-click the Solid Color layer thumbnail again and try to sample a better hair color.

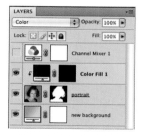

Figure 9-26 Using a Color Fill layer to remove color fringing from the original green background

Layers panel after step 3

Sampling hair color with the Color Fill Color Picker

Removing color fringes in the Color Fill mask

7. If the background color fringing involves more than one color (ours was only green), you'll need to create separate Color Fill layers with different sample colors for each area. Any additional Color Fill layers must be part of the same clipping mask (indented above the subject's layer in the Layers panel). We ended up adding a second Color Fill layer to sample a skin color we needed to paint over skin with reflected greens.

Our final image shows a mask that preserves fine details as it reveals the new background behind the subject (see **Figure 9-27**).

Figure 9-27 The entire new mask

The mostly finished image (there's still a little touch-up left to do)

Mask for the image

Final Layers panel

Plug-Ins for Complex Masks

TIP: If you used to use the Extract plug-in, it's unsupported in Photoshop CS4. You can still find it on the Photoshop installer DVD or disk image. Look in the folder /English/Goodies/Optional plug-ins/ or on the Adobe Web site. To install, drag them into the Adobe Photoshop CS4/Plug-Ins folder.

After working with the Photoshop selection tools for a while, you begin to know instinctively when you're up against a difficult task. For instance, trying to create a selection mask for a woman in a gauzy dress, with her long, wispy hair blowing in the wind, could be a nightmare. And if you have to perform 20 of these in a day . . . well . . . 'nuf said. It's time to plunk down some cash for one of the several masking programs on the market—for instance, Mask Pro from OnOne Software or KnockOut from Corel.

We're not saying that these plug-ins are perfect, but they can often get you 90 percent of the way to a great selection in 10 percent of the time it would take you with Photoshop alone.

CHAPTER TEN

Sharpness, Detail, and Noise Reduction

The human visual system depends to a great degree on recognizing edges. Our eyes pass information to our brain, where every detail is quickly broken down into whether it is or is not an edge. (Millions of years of evolution have developed our brains to ignore most of what's going on in our field of vision and instead focus immediately on moving edges that might turn out to be a hungry tiger.) An image may have great contrast and color balance, but without good edge definition, we simply see it as less lifelike.

No matter how good your camera or scanner and how crisp your original may be, you always lose some sharpness when an image is digitized. Images from scanners and digital cameras always need a considerable amount of sharpening, though high-end scanners may sharpen as part of the scanning process. Even a high-resolution digital camera back mounted on a finely focused view camera produces images that will benefit from sharpening. You *cannot* solve the problem of blurry scans by scanning at a higher resolution. It just doesn't work that way.

Your images also lose sharpness in the output process. Halftoned images (almost anything printed on a printing press) and dithered ones (such as those printed on inkjet or other desktop printers) are by far the worst offenders. But even continuous-tone devices such as film recorders and dye-sublimation printers lose a little sharpness.

What's Sharpening All About?

Sharpening encompasses a wide range of factors that affect whether you perceive an image to be sharp. The central idea behind sharpness is that you're trying to make image detail easier to see. However, there are many reasons that detail can be obscured. Sharpening is all about enhancing detail while suppressing the factors that obscure it.

Detail vs. Noise. In addition to detail, images contain *noise*—digital captures have sensor noise, and film scans have film grain that may be exacerbated by noise in the scanner sensor. We want to sharpen only the detail, not the noise. However, because it's hard for software to tell the difference between noise and detail, all noise-reduction solutions have to walk the fine line between increasing edge detail and decreasing noise.

In Photoshop itself, we generally apply noise-reduction techniques only on very noisy images—scans of color negatives and digital captures at high ISO values are prime candidates. When working with digital raw captures, we often apply the noise reduction in Adobe Camera Raw. Otherwise, we prefer to concentrate on sharpening the available detail but not the noisy areas, partly because we don't want to soften the image unnecessarily with noise reduction, and partly to avoid another workflow step.

When we do perform noise reduction—with either the Reduce Noise filter in Photoshop or a third-party plug-in such as Noise Ninja, Grain Surgery, or Neat Image—we always do so before sharpening, for the simple reason that it works better than doing so afterward (why sharpen noise?). We'll cover noise reduction further later on in this chapter.

Lens Defects. Lenses introduce their own quirks. Some lenses are simply sharper than others. (The Lens Blur mode in the Smart Sharpen filter specifically addresses lens softness.) A second lens problem, which we encounter a great deal more with digital capture than we did with film, is chromatic aberration, in which the lens fails to deliver the red, green, and blue wavelengths to the same plane of focus, producing color fringing. It's a particular problem toward the wide end of wide-angle zooms.

We suspect that we see chromatic aberration in digital capture more than in film simply because digital is much less forgiving to lenses. Film grain and interlayer scattering of the light tend to mask chromatic aberration, while digital capture reveals it quite brutally—shooting film and digital with the same lens can show this. You can correct chromatic aberration in digital raw files using the Lens Corrections tab in Camera Raw; in Photoshop the Lens Correction filter (see Chapter 11) can compensate for chromatic aberration.

We'll cover noise reduction and lens corrections in the course of this chapter, but while only some images need noise reduction or lens fixes, *every* image needs sharpening, so that's where we'll start.

Photoshop Sharpening Tools. To counteract the blurries in both the input and output stages, you need to sharpen your images. Photoshop offers several sharpening tools and filters, but the Unsharp Mask and Smart Sharpen filters are the only ones that are truly effective in a production workflow. There are also advanced techniques that combine these sharpening filters with selections, masks, and other filters to address specific issues.

WHY UNSHARP MASKING?

When we perceive an edge, we're really seeing an area of high contrast between adjacent pixels. The higher the contrast, the sharper the edges appear. To increase sharpness, you need to increase the contrast along the edges. A common technique to achieve this is *unsharp masking* (often abbreviated as USM). That may sound like the last thing you'd want to do if you're trying to make an image appear sharper, but the term actually makes some sense. It has its origins in a traditional film-based technique for enhancing photographic sharpness. Although Photoshop has several sharpening tools, unsharp masking is the basis for many of them.

Traditional Unsharp Masking

In the traditional film-based unsharp masking process, the photographic negative is sandwiched in the enlarger along with a slightly out-of-focus duplicate negative—an unsharp mask—and the exposure time for printing is approximately doubled. Because the unsharp mask is slightly out of focus and the exposure time has been increased, the light side of the edges prints lighter and the dark side of the edges prints darker, creating a *halo* around objects in the image (see **Figure 10-1**). As you'll see throughout this chapter, this halo effect is both the secret of good sharpening and its Achilles' heel, depending on the size and intensity of the halo and where it appears in the image. Photoshop lets you control the halo very precisely, but there's no single magic setting that works for all images, so you need to know not only how the controls work, but also what you're trying to achieve in the image.

Figure 10-1 Edge transitions and sharpening

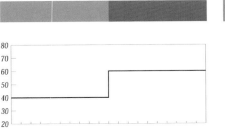

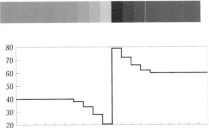

This image and graph depict an edge transition—from 40 to 60 percent. Each tick mark across the bottom of the graph represents a column of pixels.

After sharpening, the transition is accentuated—darker on the dark side, and lighter on the light side, creating a halo around the edge.

Before and after applying Unsharp Mask (slightly oversharpened for clarity)

Detail of photo showing increased pixel contrast (halo) around sharpened edges

Digital Unsharp Masking

TIP: You need to walk a fine line, sharpening only where your image needs it. Because the Unsharp Mask filter affects the entire image, we prefer running sharpening through a mask.

A digital sharpening tool such as the Unsharp Mask filter (see **Figure 10-2**) operates pixel by pixel, which explains why it can sometimes take a while to process. It compares each pixel to its neighbors, looking for a certain amount of contrast between adjacent pixels, which it assumes is an edge. It then increases the contrast between those pixels according to the parameters you set. This creates a halo that, at normal viewing distances, increases apparent sharpness.

But Photoshop can't actually detect edges—it just looks at contrast differences (zeros and ones again). So unsharp masking can also have the undesired effect of exaggerating texture in flat areas and skin tones and emphasizing any noise introduced by the scanner in the shadow areas.

Sample image (not sharpened)

The Unsharp Mask dialog with the initial settings for the examples to follow; image resolution is 266 ppi.

Figure 10-2 The Unsharp Mask filter and the image we'll use for the examples

Amount. We think of this setting as the volume control. It adjusts the intensity, or contrast, of the sharpening halo (see **Figure 10-3**). High Amount settings produce intense halos with many pixels driven to pure white or solid black; low Amount settings produce less intense ones. Amount has no effect on the width of the halos; Radius deals with that.

We almost always start out by setting Amount much higher than we'll eventually want it—between 400 and 500—just so we can clearly see the effect of the Radius option. Once we see what Radius will do to a specific image, we adjust Amount downward to a reasonable final value.

As you increase the Amount setting, the blips around big tonal shifts (edges) can be pushed all the way to white and black. At that point, increasing Amount has no effect—you can't get more white than white! Worse, the all-white halos often stand out as artifacts and just don't look good.

TIP: If your computer is on the slow side, try turning off the Preview check box to avoid the time-consuming full-screen redraw of the preview. You can still use the preview inside the Unsharp Mask dialog to check the results. Pressing and releasing the mouse button inside the dialog preview toggles between the before and after states.

Amount: 50 percent

Amount: 100 percent

Amount: 400 percent

Figure 10-3 The effect of different Amount settings

Radius. This option sets the width of the halo the filter creates around edges (see **Figure 10-4**). The wider the halo, the more obvious the sharpening effect. Choosing the correct Radius value is probably the most important choice in avoiding an unnaturally oversharpened look. There are several factors to take into account, starting with the content of the image itself, the output method, and the intended size of the reproduction (see the sidebar "Image Detail and Sharpening Radius").

TIP: Image resolution affects the Radius value you should set. The correct Radius value for a 300 ppi image will be far too strong for a Web page version of that image that's likely to be displayed at 100 ppi or less.

As you increase the Radius, the apparent sharpness also increases—often to an undesirable extent. This is where the aesthetic considerations come in. Some people like more sharpening than others. We find highly sharpened images more disturbing than slightly soft ones, but that's a matter of taste. It's up to you to decide how much sharpening you want.

Note that a Radius value of 1.0 does not result in a single-pixel radius. In fact, the halo is often between 4 and 6 pixels wide for the whole light and dark cycle—two or three pixels on each side of the tonal shift. However, it varies in width depending on the content of the image.

Figure 10-4 The effect of different Radius settings

Radius: 0.5 pixel   Radius: 1 pixel   Radius: 6 pixels

Threshold. Unsharp Mask only evaluates contrast differences: it doesn't know whether those differences represent real edges you want to sharpen or areas of texture that you don't want to sharpen. The Threshold control lets you specify how far apart two pixels' tonal values have to be (on a scale of 0 to 255) before the filter affects them (see **Figure 10-5**). For example, if Threshold is set to 3, and two adjacent pixels have values of 122 and 124 (a difference of 2), they're unaffected.

Figure 10-5 The effect of different Threshold settings (we used an Amount of 150 percent for this example)

Threshold: 0 levels   Threshold: 2 levels   Threshold: 10 levels

Low Threshold values (0 to 4) result in a sharper-looking image overall because fewer areas are excluded. High values (above 10) result in less

Image Detail and Sharpening Radius

To set the Radius value properly, look closely at the image. How big, in pixels, are the details that you want to sharpen? You need to match the size and intensity of the sharpening halo to the size of the details in the image.

High-frequency images contain a lot of detail, with sharp transitions between tonal values, while low-frequency images have smoother transitions and fewer small details. Whether a given image is high frequency or low frequency depends on the content of the image and on its pixel density. High-frequency images, in which the edges of objects are reproduced using only one or two pixels, need a smaller Radius setting than low-frequency images, in which the edges may be a dozen or so pixels wide.

An image containing fine detail, such as a photo of trees, is likely to have many more high-frequency transitions than a photo of a car, for example. But if the image has a high enough resolution, even the edges on the tiniest leaves will be several pixels wide in the scan. So it isn't just the content that dictates the sharpening, it's the relationship between content and resolution.

An excessive Radius value is the prime cause of oversharpened images. Moreover, an overly large radius can actually wipe out the detail it's supposed to be accentuating. Too small a radius can result in too little apparent sharpening. This might in turn seduce you into cranking up the Amount setting so far that you create spurious specular highlights and overemphasize textures such as skin in undesirable ways. With very extreme settings, you can change the overall image contrast, which is sometimes good and sometimes not.

A good strategy is to set the correct Radius setting first. You can then achieve the degree of sharpness you want by tweaking the Amount setting. Finally, adjust the Threshold setting to suppress noise and to avoid oversharpening patterns, film grain, and the like.

TIP: To start over after you've closed a filter dialog, press Command-Z (Mac) or Ctrl-Z (Windows) to undo, then press Command-Option-F (Mac) or Ctrl-Alt-F (Windows) to reopen the filter dialog with the filter and settings you used most recently.

sharpening but often produce unnatural-looking transitions between the sharpened and unsharpened areas. We typically start out with a zero Threshold value and then increase it only if necessary. Be careful at higher Threshold settings because dramatic, unnatural sharpening of high-contrast edges may combine with unsharpened smaller details, which can make the image appear as if something isn't quite right.

When you use Threshold, your goal is to make the filter ignore the relatively slight differences between pixels in smooth, low-contrast areas while still creating a halo around details that have high-contrast edges. You can use Threshold with portraits, to avoid sharpening every last detail of a person's skin, and to avoid sharpening noisy areas of digital images. In both cases low Threshold values are used.

TIP: If sharpening looks too strong after applying Unsharp Mask, choose Edit > Fade and lower the Opacity value (see "Filters and Effects" in Chapter 11, "Essential Image Techniques").

Everything's Relative. One of the most important concepts to understand about sharpening is that the three values you can set in the Unsharp Mask dialog are interrelated. As you increase the Radius setting, you generally need to decrease the Amount to keep the apparent sharpness constant. At higher Radius settings, you can use much higher Threshold values; this smooths out unwanted sharpening of fine texture while still applying a good deal of sharpness to well-defined edges.

A Practical Sharpening Workflow

To understand how to sharpen, we first have to understand why we're doing it at all. It turns out that there are basically three reasons why an image might need to be sharpened. Each of those reasons imposes its own demands, and sometimes these demands contradict one another. Fortunately, the reasons break down nicely into three stages that are easy to handle separately and in sequence during a production workflow: sharpening the original digital capture, sharpening image content for creative purposes, and sharpening to optimize image detail for specific output.

If you don't recognize all of the techniques and features we mention in this section, don't worry—we'll explain them all later in this chapter.

Capture Sharpening

TIP: For a deeper dive into the multi-stage sharpening workflow, pick up Bruce Fraser's book *Real World Image Sharpening in Photoshop CS2*.

When a sensor turns photons into pixels, some sharpness is always lost. No matter how high the resolution of your capture devices, they sample based on a fixed grid. Inevitably, this means that the continuous gradations of tone and color that exist in the real world turn into discrete pixels. Also, each capture device imposes its own noise characteristics on the image.

Strategy. You need to sharpen the image content to restore what was lost in the conversion to pixels, but you don't want to also sharpen—and hence emphasize—the noise and grain. The goal of capture sharpening is to take into account the source of the image, compensating only for the amount of sharpness lost to a specific digital camera or scanner sensor.

Sharper Images from the Start

If you don't think about sharpness until you're in Photoshop, you've waited too long. As with exposure and color, the sharper your photos are out of the camera, the less work you'll face after you import the images into your computer. Many different kinds of choices affect image sharpness. We think it's good to list those reasons, because while some types of blur can be fixed in Photoshop, others can't and are best addressed in camera.

Focus. We do run into people who aren't sure how to read or aim the focus points in their camera's viewfinder, or how to choose the right autofocus mode. Be sure you know how to confirm that the right part of the scene is in focus—always leaving it up to the camera may not be reliable enough, and you'll end up with more sharpening challenges in Photoshop.

Depth of Field. When the lens aperture (opening) is smaller, more near and far objects are in focus, so you have a larger margin for focusing errors. When the aperture is larger (the f-stop value is lower), the distance range that's in focus is narrower, so you've got to focus much more carefully. If you're just a little bit off, the right part of the image will end up in an out-of-focus range and the wrong part of the image will be sharp. This is difficult to correct in Photoshop.

Shutter Speed. Unsharp images can be caused by *motion blur*, which happens when the camera or the subject moves while the shutter is open. A sufficiently fast shutter speed prevents both types of motion blur by freezing it. When you can't increase the shutter speed, a lens equipped with image stabilization can help cancel out camera motion, but not subject motion. The Smart Sharpen filter in Photoshop can correct motion blur, but only in a straight line—the wavy motion blur you can get from camera shake is nearly impossible to fix.

Lens Quality. Much of the price difference between professional and consumer lenses lies in the level and quality of sharpness. If you've done all you can above and you think the images could still be sharper, test another lens.

Tonal Correction. Sharpness is really about contrast, so if you optimize the contrast of your image in Camera Raw or Photoshop it will appear sharper than if the image lacks contrast. When we say *optimize the contrast*, we mean properly setting the black and white point, then the overall contrast, the tone curve, local contrast (for example, using Clarity in Camera Raw), and finally, contrast adjustments for specific areas of the image using masks or the History brush. You'll notice that this is a progression from general to specific.

Sharpness. The sharpening controls we discuss in this chapter and in the Camera Raw discussion in Chapter 5 represent the last link in the sharpness chain. If you look at the sharpness controls in terms of contrast, you'll recognize that what they really do is manage contrast primarily along edges. In other words, sharpening in Photoshop is a specialized type of local contrast.

TIP: If noise reduction is required, we'll do it before sharpening, by running the Despeckle filter through a mask, running Reduce Noise on its own merged layer, or if it's a raw digital camera file, we may employ the noise reduction in Adobe Camera Raw or Lightroom. When extreme noise reduction is required, we'll apply a mask to the noise reduction layer to protect the edges.

This first round of sharpening must be done very gently indeed; otherwise the result is likely to be a hideously oversharpened mess. Remember, it's only the first stage of sharpening, where you essentially perfect the capture. Don't try to solve all of an image's sharpening issues at this stage, because all you need to do here is set a solid baseline of overall sharpness that you'll build on during the next two stages.

Tactics. Our first sharpening pass aims to compensate for the shortcomings of the capture in a way that's sensitive to the image content. We create a sharpening layer and apply an edge mask so that only the high-contrast edges get sharpened. We sharpen the layer with a Radius value that matches the image content, then constrain the tonal range to the midtones using the Blend If sliders in the Layer Style dialog. We use the Blend If sliders to focus the sharpening on the midtones, protecting highlights and shadows so that they don't get driven to solid black and solid white.

With grainy or noisy originals such as high-ISO digital capture or film, first try applying noise reduction using the Reduce Noise filter or a third-party noise reduction plug-in. If you're working with raw digital camera files, you can use the sharpening sliders in Adobe Camera Raw or Lightroom—those controls were specifically designed for the capture sharpening stage.

Creative Sharpening

TIP: One way to make an object appear sharper is to blur the rest of the image. You can create smoothing brushes using the same techniques as for sharpening brushes but substituting a blur for the sharpen.

The creative sharpening stage is unlike the capture and output stages in that it doesn't optimize the image for a specific device. Instead, it directs the viewer to specific areas to help clarify the intended meaning of the image. If we find ourselves wanting to apply different amounts of sharpening to various parts of an image, this is the time to do it. In other words, creative sharpening is about the content, not the devices.

After capture and creative sharpening, we end up with an idealized image—corrected and enhanced as far as possible without being shackled to one specific purpose, size, or output device.

Strategy. We apply creative sharpening after we've fine-tuned the tone and color both globally and locally, because changes to contrast and color can easily affect the perceived sharpness. When sharpening image content, you want to emphasize edges without overemphasizing textures such as skin tones and without introducing spurious texture into flat areas such as skies.

Tactics. You can build sharpening layers to paint sharpening just where you want it, such as the eyes of a portrait (see **Figure 10-6**). We'll soon discuss a technique that lets you add or remove sharpening with a brush.

If Camera Raw and Lightroom are part of your standard workflow and you're using a version that includes the new Adjustment Brush, that tool provides a nondestructive way to apply local, creative sharpening before you open a digital camera image in a Photoshop.

Capture sharpening only

Creative sharpening added to eye and eyebrow areas only

Figure 10-6 Creative sharpening

Output Sharpening

When you print, you lose sharpness again. In most cases, one pixel isn't directly translated into one dot of ink or dye, and even for those devices where it is, they're often round dots instead of square pixels. These mismatches cause a loss of sharpness.

Strategy. Because the source-specific and image-specific concerns were already addressed in the capture and creative sharpening phases, output sharpening can concentrate solely on the requirements of the output process. Effective output sharpening must take into account the output process so that the amount of output sharpening is tightly matched to the output device—not oversharpened or undersharpened. Output sharpening must be done at the final size and resolution, often as the last step before converting an RGB file to CMYK and saving the file to disk. Similarly, apply output sharpening to a copy of a master file, since it's tuned to a specific device. When you want to create output for another device, start from the master image and apply sharpening settings tuned to the other type of output.

Tactics. Unlike capture and creative sharpening, output sharpening should be applied across the entire image. We typically do this using a sharpening layer with no layer mask. For halftone and inkjet output, we often use the

TIP: If you aren't sure about the correct output sharpening settings, run some tests. If you're preparing images for a commercial press and sending out for a color proof, test sharpening by adding copies of the same image sharpened at different values.

Hard Light/High Pass sharpening technique. For monitor-based output, Smart Sharpen may be enough.

If you expect the image to be resized significantly after it leaves your hands, don't apply output sharpening. Anyone who resizes the image will probably resharpen it anyway, and if you've done a reasonably good job in the capture and creative phases, the final result will still be sharp.

Previewing Output Sharpening. Correct output sharpening values may often look downright scary on the monitor. This is normal, because you're viewing the sharpening values on a device that's very different from the final output device. Light and dark contours that are 3 pixels wide may look hideous on the monitor, but if you're printing at 300 ppi they'll translate into contours (light and dark parts of the sharpening halo) that are only $\frac{1}{100}$ inch wide and won't be obvious on the final print.

There's really no way to get an accurate onscreen representation of how a sharpened halftone output will look—the continuous-tone monitor display is simply too different from the halftone. An image sharpened for halftone output can look a little crunchy on screen. And the monitor resolution and view percentage can help or hinder your appraisal of an image's sharpness. See the sidebar "Sharpening and the Display" for more on this subject.

The onscreen appearance at Actual Pixels view varies dramatically over different display types and resolutions, but as you zoom in, the differences between display types become much less significant.

Suggested Formulas. Output sharpening is the only phase that easily lends itself to a formula, because once the image has been sized and the output process chosen, the physical size of the pixels, and hence of the sharpening halos, is a known quantity. For the capture and creative phases of the sharpening workflow, common sense, good taste, and, in the long run, experience are the best guides.

A guideline that's served us well is to aim for a sharpening halo that is approximately $\frac{1}{50}$ to $\frac{1}{100}$ inch (0.5 to 0.25 mm) wide. The idea is that at normal viewing distances, a halo this size falls below the threshold of human visual acuity, so you don't see the halo as a separate feature; you just get the illusion of sharpness that it produces. For example, at 360 ppi each pixel is only $\frac{1}{360}$ inch, so to produce a $\frac{1}{50}$-inch halo, you'd need a dark contour approximately 3.6 pixels wide ($\frac{1}{100}$ inch) and a light contour the same size.

TIP: For the Web or video, sharpness can be lost because typically, several high-resolution original pixels are merged into fewer pixels at monitor resolution.

TIP: To keep output-specific edits, such as output sharpening, from accidentally being saved with your layered master image, choose Image > Duplicate (with the Duplicate Merged Layers Only option enabled) to create a flattened duplicate document. You can then apply output-specific optimizations to the copy, such as the appropriate sharpening settings for the printer you're about to use.

Sharpening and the Display

LCD monitors are much sharper than CRTs at any given display resolution. Moreover, an image will appear quite different in terms of sharpening at a lower display resolution than it will at a higher one. So although color management lets us compensate for a huge range of different display behaviors, we have no such solution for sharpening.

What we do have is a set of very general guidelines. Use these with caution: You need to learn the relationship between what you see on your particular display at your preferred resolution and the resulting output (just as you had to do with color in the days before color management).

Zoom Percentage. It's a good idea to look at the Actual Pixels view to see what's happening to the actual image pixels, but unless your output is to a monitor, Actual Pixels view may give a fairly misleading impression of the actual sharpness on output.

For halftone output, bear in mind that each halftone dot may comprise four image pixels. Viewing at 25 percent or 50 percent view may give a truer, but still not exact, impression of halftone sharpness. For inkjet output, the key factor is the resolution you're sending to the printer. It may help to set Screen Resolution correctly in the Units and Rulers preference in the Preferences dialog so that when you choose View > Print Size, the image displays at the size it will print (we discussed this in "Navigation Tips" in Chapter 6).

How Sharp Is Sharp? For the first two passes of sharpening—capture and localized creative—our general guideline is to apply sharpening that looks good on a CRT display, or slightly oversharpened on an LCD.

For output sharpening intended for print, you can push the sharpening far beyond what looks acceptable on the monitor at Actual Pixels view, particularly when you print at higher resolutions (like 350 ppi for a 175-lpi halftone or 360 ppi for an inkjet print). This is where you need to compare how successful print sharpening settings look on screen so that you can recognize the look.

TIP: PixelGenius, a company cofounded by the late Bruce Fraser (who originally coauthored this book), publishes a sharpening plug-in called PhotoKit Sharpener. Much of what it does is based on the information and formulas in this chapter. The plug-in just does it a lot faster than you can manually. For more information, visit www.pixelgenius.com.

For output sharpening, a good starting point for the Unsharp Mask filter's Radius setting is image resolution ÷ 200. (Remember, we're talking about final image resolution, after it's been scaled to the final physical dimensions, such as 10 inches tall.) Thus, for a 300-ppi image, you'd use a Radius of 1.5 (300 ÷ 200). For a 200-ppi image, you'd use a Radius setting of 1. This is a suggested starting point, not gospel. As you gain experience, you'll find situations where the rule has to be bent. When sharpening using methods that don't involve Unsharp Mask, you'll have to look closely and adjust the math.

On very large prints, you may have to use a slightly larger sharpening halo—if the resolution is less than 100 ppi, the halo will be larger than $\frac{1}{50}$ inch because it takes at least two pixels (one light, one dark) to create the halo. But large prints are generally viewed from farther away, so the longer viewing distance tends to compensate for the larger halo.

Sharpening Techniques

We use a host of techniques in the sharpening workflow—some obvious, others less so. Some use a mask to avoid accentuating dust, scratches, noise, and film grain. Others make sharpening nondestructive and editable by applying it on a masked copy of the image.

Sharpening with Layers

We do most of our sharpening on layers, for much the same reason that we prefer using adjustment layers to burning Curves or Levels directly into an image—it's nondestructive, it's always editable, and it lets us use masking when we need to. In the first stage of the sharpening workflow, layer-based sharpening also provides an easy way to concentrate the sharpening in the midtones through the Blend If feature.

Layer-Based Sharpening. You'll apply sharpening to the duplicate (see **Figure 10-7**), so first duplicate the image layer (drag a layer to the New Layer icon in the Layers panel). It's usually a good idea to apply slightly more sharpening to the duplicate than you ultimately desire, because it gives you a wider range of sharpening to work with. Add a mask to the duplicate layer (click the Pixel Mask icon in the Masks panel). Next, fill the layer with black to hide the sharpened duplicate layer. Now paint the sharpening only where you want it: Make sure that the layer mask is targeted in the Layers panel, choose the Brush tool, set the foreground color to white, and simply brush where you want to reveal the sharpened duplicate layer. We prefer to use a brush set to substantially less than 100 percent opacity because it gives you some headroom to increase sharpening by increasing opacity. We also like to apply the Luminosity blending mode to the layer to avoid any color shifts or color fringes—it produces essentially the same result as converting the image to Lab and sharpening the Lightness channel.

TIP: Some people like to sharpen images by converting them to Lab and sharpening only the Lightness channel. You can get a nearly identical result by sharpening the RGB file, then choosing Edit > Fade, and setting the Mode to Luminosity. It's faster, and you don't lose layers through a mode change.

TIP: If you have a pressure-sensitive stylus, you can control opacity using stylus pressure. If your stylus isn't already set to do this, open the Brushes panel, click Other Dynamics, and choose Pen Pressure from the Control pop-up menu.

Figure 10-7 Using layers for creative sharpening

 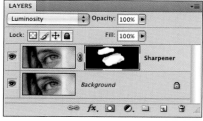

The Layers panel displays the original image (Background) and the sharpened layer copy hidden by its black mask.

Sharpening is visible only where the layer mask has been painted with white, revealing the sharpened layer.

Concentrating Sharpening on the Midtones. Because sharpening boosts contrast along edges, the severe contrast caused by high sharpening values can drive some edge pixels to pure black or white. You can address this using the Blend If sliders in the Layer Style dialog (see **Figure 10-8**). These sliders let you control which tonal values in the overlying (sharpening) layer get applied to the underlying layer (and, conversely, which tonal values in the underlying, unsharpened layers are affected by the sharpening layer). Bruce Fraser likened the overlying layer as a ton of bricks suspended over a basket of eggs (the underlying layers). The top Blend If slider controls which bricks fall, and the bottom Blend If slider dictates which eggs receive the impact. Another way to look at it is that the Blend If sliders are masks based on tonal levels, while pixel masks are based on area.

To use the Blend If sliders, double-click the thumbnail of the sharpened layer in the Layers panel. Now drag the Blend If sliders so that they mark the lowest and highest levels at which the layer's effects (in this case, sharpening) should apply.

Of course, if the layer's effects suddenly started and stopped at specific layers, the abrupt transition would be jarring. That's why you can feather the right and left sliders (meaning the lower and upper tonal limits) by splitting the sliders—to do that, Option-drag (Mac OS X) or Alt-drag half of a slider.

The feathering creates a gradual transition from complete suppression to complete application of the layer.

Figure 10-8 The Blend If sliders at the bottom of the Layer Style dialog

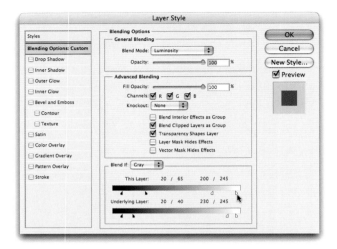

Figure 10-8 The Blend If sliders at the bottom of the Layer Style dialog

Figure 10-8 shows some typical settings for the Blend If sliders for initial midtone sharpening. The This Layer slider is set so that nothing happens between levels 0 and 20 and between levels 245 and 255, the layer is applied full strength between levels 65 and 200 and is feathered from nothing to full strength between levels 20 and 65 and levels 200 and 245. The Underlying Layer slider works similarly. The meaning of the name Blend If is that the layer's effects are blended with the underlying layer, but only if the value of the layer and the value of the underlying layer are not beyond the levels marked by the outermost sliders of both layers.

The goal of applying the Blend If sliders is to reduce the contrast of the dark and light sharpening halos, allowing headroom for subsequent creative or output sharpening. Depending on the image source (film or digital) and the amount of noise present, you may find that the shadow values need to be set higher or lower, but the basic principle is to set the bottom sliders to protect extreme highlights and shadows and to set the top sliders to apply most of the sharpening in the midtones.

Sharpening with Smart Filters

With Smart Filters, you enjoy a freedom of choice with filters that's similar to what you have with adjustment layers. Unlike Undo steps and the Fade command, the settings of a Smart Filter can be edited at any time without altering the original layer, even after you close and reopen a document.

You can apply a filter as a Smart Filter only to a Smart Object; if you're working with a file from Adobe Camera Raw that you opened as a Smart Object, you're ready to go. With any other layer, you must first select the layer and choose Filter > Convert for Smart Filters (which is actually the same as choosing Layer > Smart Object > Convert to Smart Object). As long as a layer is a Smart Object, applying any available filter from the Filter menu creates a Smart Filter, shown in the Layers panel under a Smart Filters heading indented under the layer that uses them (see **Figure 10-9**). Not all filters are available as Smart Filters, but many of our favorite production filters are, including Unsharp Mask and Smart Sharpen. To edit a Smart Filter, just double-click it in the Layers panel.

One subtle aspect of Smart Filters is how to fade them. You can't use the Layers panel blending mode or opacity controls to edit a Smart Filter independently of its layer or the layer's other Smart Filters, and the Edit > Fade command isn't available either. What do you do? Ctrl-click (Mac) or right-click the Smart Filter thumbnail and choose Edit Smart Filter Blending Options; this displays a dialog with a Mode pop-up menu, an Opacity setting, and a preview thumbnail.

TIP: When evaluating a layer with Smart Filters off, avoid hiding or showing individual Smart Filters whenever possible, because it forces Photoshop to re-render the entire filter stack. Instead, click the eye icon next to a layer's Smart Filters heading in the Layers panel, which hides and shows all Smart Filters. That's dramatically faster because then all Photoshop has to do is hide or show the cached image for the entire layer stack.

Show/hide Smart Filter stack

Smart Filter mask

Show/hide one Smart Filter

Figure 10-9 Using Unsharp Mask as a Smart Filter

In the Layers panel, all Smart Filters for a layer are listed under a single Smart Filter heading indented within that layer. To control the blending mode and opacity, Ctrl-click (Mac) or right-click the empty area of a Smart Filter and choose Edit Smart Filter Blending Options.

For Smart Filters, use the Blending Options dialog instead of the Fade command or the Layers panel blending controls.

TIP: A stack of Smart Filters can have only one mask for all of the filters in the stack. If you need to use a separate mask for each filter, you'll have to duplicate the image layer.

Trade-Offs. Given the ways that Smart Filters preserve your options indefinitely, it sure sounds like Smart Filters could be editing nirvana. Unfortunately, they aren't. Smart Filters suffer from the same gotchas that afflict Smart Objects: They place huge demands on the CPU and on disk space, slowing down operations and creating very large files. For this reason, Conrad sometimes talks about Smart Objects as "editing on credit." That is, Smart Objects give you a lot of desirable power and flexibility, but overusing them can create an ongoing burden that can cost more than you expected.

Another disadvantage is that you can't rename or group Smart Filters as you can with layers. For instance, if you apply multiple output-specific Smart Filter instances of Unsharp Mask, it won't be easy to identify them so that you can figure out which ones to turn on or off.

We ran a quick test to see whether Unsharp Mask applied to a duplicate layer would take up more or less disk space than Unsharp Mask applied to the original layer as a Smart Filter. We found that a 13.7 MB TIFF file became a 36.2 MB TIFF file after duplicating the original layer, running Unsharp Mask on the duplicate layer, and creating and painting on a layer mask for the duplicate layer. We took an unaltered copy of the original file and applied the same filter settings and mask, but this time as a Smart Filter, and ended up with a file size of 49.8 MB. The difference in RAM usage was similarly dramatic.

The trade-off is clear. If you've got the CPU, the RAM, and the disk space, Smart Filters can completely revolutionize your workflow, but on a machine with mediocre performance or limited available disk space, the old-school techniques will help preserve your sanity.

High-Pass Sharpening

Unsharp Mask is the Swiss Army knife of sharpening tools, but it's not the only way to sharpen images. Another way is to use the High Pass filter (Filter > Other > High Pass). The High Pass filter is a simple way to create an edge mask, but in this case we don't use it that way. Instead, we apply the filter directly to the duplicate layer and set the layer's blending mode to Soft Light or Hard Light. Because applying Soft Light increases local contrast, it has the side effect of sharpening details.

As with the other layer-based sharpening techniques, you can use a whole bag of tricks to refine the sharpening—like blurring noise in the mask or painting on the layer itself with 50 percent gray (the neutral color for both the Hard Light and Soft Light blending modes) to erase the sharpening in local areas. You can apply a layer mask to confine the sharpening to a specific area, and you can stack multiple sharpening layers to apply selective sharpening to different areas of the image.

The critical parameter in this technique is the Radius setting for the High Pass filter. If it's too small, you'll get little or no sharpening. If it's too big, grain and noise will appear in the image as if by some evil magic. However, for optimum output sharpening, we often need to produce a result that appears very ugly onscreen (see the sidebar "Sharpening and the Display," earlier in this chapter). You'll see an example of High Pass sharpening in the next section.

TIP: You can also use an edge mask when you apply noise reduction, to keep the noise reduction away from edges. When you do this, invert the mask we make here (make edges black and broad areas white).

On soft subjects and skin tones, Hard Light can give too strong a sharpening effect. For these types of images, or in any case where we want a more gentle sharpening effect, we often use Soft Light instead of Hard Light to avoid oversharpening skin texture. You can switch between Hard Light and Soft Light after running the High Pass filter to see which you prefer. If you need a level of sharpening between the two modes, apply High Pass and reduce that layer's Opacity value.

Edge Masking

Edge masks are a valuable tool for both sharpening and noise reduction. When sharpening, we use an edge mask to concentrate the effects of the sharpen on the edges, so that flat areas such as skies, and textured areas such as skin tones, don't get oversharpened. **Figure 10-10** shows an example of both High Pass sharpening and an edge mask built to restrict sharpening to the edges and keep it away from film grain in uniform areas of color.

TIP: You don't have to build an edge mask the way we do here, simply pasting the image into a layer's grayscale mask. You can use techniques we've shown earlier in the book, such as customizing a grayscale edge mask with the Channel MIxer.

Building a High Pass Sharpening Layer. We duplicate the original layer and apply the High Pass filter with a Radius amount that gives us acceptable halos around the edges. We then apply the Soft Light blending mode to the duplicate layer, and with that we're done with the sharpening layer.

Building the Edge Mask. In the Layers panel we select the original layer and select all the pixels (Command-A in Mac OS X or Ctrl-A in Windows).

TIP: Building an edge mask may seem to involve a lot of steps, but fortunately it isn't hard to record them as an action (we talk about that in Chapter 11). The Masking option in Camera Raw sharpening is another example of semi-automated edge masking.

We then select the duplicate layer in the Layers panel and click the Add Layer Mask button at the bottom of the Layers panel. We Option-click (Mac OS X) or Alt-click (Windows) the layer mask to display only the mask, and we paste the original image into it. We choose Filter > Stylize > Find Edges and invert the image by pressing Command-I (Mac OS X) or Ctrl-I (Windows); this gives us a mask that hides everything except the edges of the duplicate layer. Our last step is to press Command-M (Mac OS X) or Ctrl-M (Windows) to open the Curves dialog. We edit the curve to adjust mask contrast, which controls the sharpening strength at edges (white and the lighter tones) and away from edges (black and the darker tones).

Figure 10-10 Building an edge mask for a layer sharpened using the High Pass/ Soft Light method

Original image from a scanned film negative

Detail shows film grain we don't want to sharpen

Applying High Pass filter to duplicate layer

Original layer pasted into layer mask of duplicate, after running Find Edges and inverting

Contrast increased to focus sharpening on edges and away from broad grainy areas

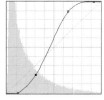
The curve used to increase contrast (choose Image > Adjust > Curves; you can't use an adjustment layer)

Final image

Final Layers panel

Duplicate of original layer, with High Pass filter applied

Edge mask containing duplicate of original layer with Find Edges filter applied, inverted, and contrast adjusted by Curves

Sharpening in Photoshop vs. Camera Raw

When we first wrote about many of the techniques in this chapter, such as High Pass sharpening and edge masks, Photoshop was pretty much the only place in town where you'd consider doing them. Today, far more images are being captured by digital cameras, and for many of them, the first stop after the camera isn't Photoshop, but intermediate processing software such as Camera Raw, Lightroom, or Apple Aperture, all of which have their own sharpening controls. Camera Raw and Lightroom go so far as to include a form of edge masking based on the concepts in this chapter and the ability to process JPEG files and TIFF files as well as raw digital camera files. (Apple Aperture is outside the scope of this book.)

As the feature sets of Camera Raw and Lightroom have expanded so dramatically, where and how do they fit into the sharpening workflow? Should you do any sharpening in those programs, or leave it to Photoshop?

Camera Raw and Lightroom are not yet ready to replace all three stages of the sharpening workflow, but they're quite effective at addressing capture sharpening. Lightroom 2 provides creative sharpening through the Adjustment Brush but offers only a very limited form of output sharpening.

The biggest benefit of using Camera Raw and Lightroom for capture sharpening is ease of use. If you feel at all intimidated by our multistep descriptions of manipulating layers, channels, masks, and blending modes, you owe it to yourself to study the Camera Raw and Lightroom sharpening controls, which automate and condense stacks of layers and channels into four simple and well-engineered sliders. (If we sound a bit enthusiastic about Camera Raw and Lightroom sharpening, it's because Bruce Fraser helped design how those controls work.) We describe Camera Raw sharpening in Chapter 5, "Building a Digital Workflow"; the controls in Lightroom operate the same way.

One of the few remaining reasons to perform capture sharpening of digital camera images in Photoshop is if you want more control over the sharpening parameters than the features in Camera Raw can provide. For example, you may want to tune the sharpening mask more than you can using the Mask slider in Camera Raw.

TIP: If you don't want to apply Camera Raw sharpening to your images as you convert them, open the Camera Raw preferences and choose Preview Images Only from the Apply Sharpening To pop-up menu.

SMART SHARPEN

The Smart Sharpen filter (Filter > Sharpen > Smart Sharpen) takes a bit longer on slower machines, both in execution and in updating the proxy image when you change settings. For high-resolution images, Smart Sharpen is most useful if you have the latest fast hardware.

If you need to make low-resolution images look good onscreen, Smart Sharpen is great. If the idea of making sharpening masks fills you with terror, Smart Sharpen does a fairly good job of differentiating edges from non-edges. It's quite useful for capture sharpening, though on the whole we prefer our tried-and-true techniques. On the other hand, it's a rather slow way to do output sharpening, especially on a large batch of images. Smart Sharpen is also more effective on digital camera images than it is with scans.

Smart Sharpen Remove Modes

Smart Sharpen is really three sharpening filters in one. You select one by choosing an option from the Remove menu (see **Figure 10-11**).

TIP: If your machine isn't fast enough to use Smart Sharpen for rapid production work, you can obtain very similar results running Unsharp Mask on masked layers set to Luminosity mode. When we automate the process with actions, it's quite a bit faster than Smart Sharpen.

Gaussian Blur. The Gaussian Blur mode is the Unsharp Mask filter with a different user interface. If you turn on the More Accurate option, the result is a good deal gentler than Unsharp Mask at the same amount and radius, but it's basically the same type of sharpening. The reason you have a choice of not using More Accurate is that it takes a lot more time to process.

Lens Blur. In Lens Blur mode, Smart Sharpen is a whole different animal than Unsharp Mask. Lens Blur uses much more sophisticated algorithms from Unsharp Mask (or Smart Sharpen in Gaussian Blur mode) to detect edges and detail, and hence typically produces better sharpening with less-obvious sharpening halos.

Motion Blur. In Motion Blur mode, Smart Sharpen tries to undo the effects of blurring caused by either camera or subject movement. If the movement is truly unidirectional, it does a surprisingly good job, but camera shake rarely happens in just one direction, and subject movement is often quite complex, so don't expect blurred subjects to be rendered razor-sharp by the filter.

Image before sharpening

Smart Sharpen applied

Figure 10-11 Using Smart Sharpen

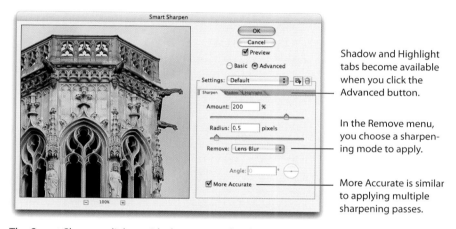

Shadow and Highlight tabs become available when you click the Advanced button.

In the Remove menu, you choose a sharpening mode to apply.

More Accurate is similar to applying multiple sharpening passes.

The Smart Sharpen dialog with the settings for the top right image

Advanced Mode

When you click the Advanced radio button, two additional tabs, labeled Shadow and Highlight, become available. They offer controls very similar to those offered by the Shadows/Highlights command found in the Adjust submenu (under the Image menu)—see "Using Shadows/Highlights" in Chapter 7, "Image Adjustment Fundamentals."

Each tab provides three sliders for Fade Amount, Tonal Width, and Radius. They let you reduce the strength of the shadow and highlight sharpening contours, allowing stronger sharpening of the midtones.

• Fade Amount controls the strength of the fade from 0 to 100 percent.

- Tonal Width controls how far up from the shadows or down from the highlights the adjustment extends into the tonal range.

- Radius controls the size of the neighborhood used to decide whether a pixel is in the shadows or the highlights. A useful guideline is to set the Radius in the Shadow and Highlight tabs to double the Radius setting in the main panel.

Our use of Smart Sharpen is confined to the Lens Blur and Motion Blur modes, and we always use the Advanced setting with the More Accurate option turned on.

Smart Sharpen in Action

The key option in Smart Sharpen is Radius. As with Unsharp Mask, for good sharpening you typically need to match the Radius to the image content, unless you're intentionally using very large Radius settings to create special contrast effects. But as you'll see, you need very different Radius settings for the Lens Blur and Motion Blur modes.

In Lens Blur mode, finding the right settings for all three tabs in Smart Sharpen is an iterative process—after adjusting the Shadow and Highlight tabs, we may go back and tweak the Amount in the main panel, then revisit the Shadow and Highlight tabs once again. Generally, though, we follow this sequence, which you'll find similar to what we do with Unsharp Mask:

TIP: To sharpen a small area of a large image more quickly than using a mask, select the small area, press Command-J (Mac) or Ctrl-J (Windows) to duplicate the selection as a new layer, and run the filter on the new small layer. This is faster than running the filter on an entire large image.

1. In Basic mode, increase Amount to 500 percent just to be able to observe the effect of the Radius values, then adjust Radius to match the frequency of the detail in the content—enough to sharpen without obliterating important fine details.

2. When you reach the correct Radius value, decrease Amount.

3. If it looks as though the shadows and highlights need lower amounts of sharpening, click the Advanced button, click the Shadow tab, and fade back the sharpening effect as needed; repeat with the Highlight tab if needed (see **Figure 10-12**). In Smart Sharpen, these tabs are the place to dial back excessive contrast in the sharpening halos.

You'll often find that you can apply a higher Amount setting than you could using the Unsharp Mask filter, thanks to the Shadow and Highlight tabs, together with the better overall sharpening in Smart Sharpen.

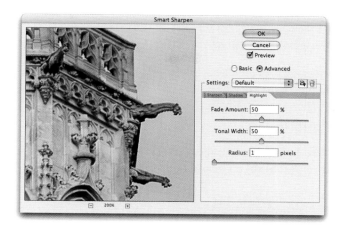

Figure 10-12 The Highlight tab of Smart Sharpen in Advanced mode

In the Highlight tab of Advanced mode, we fade the original effect to tone down the edge highlights created by the settings in the Sharpen tab.

Motion Blur. When we use Smart Sharpen to remove motion blur, the process is only slightly different. The main difference is setting the correct Angle to match the angle of the motion blur. After clicking OK, we recommend building a mask and painting the filter effect into the image where you want it. Few, if any, images benefit from applying Motion Blur mode to the entire image. And because motion blur often happens in more than one direction (think camera shake), you may have to apply multiple instances of Motion Blur at different angles. It gets tedious.

TIP: Although Smart Sharpen lets you save settings, in practice the mechanism isn't very reliable. If you load a saved setting, change it, and simply run the filter without renaming the saved setting, the new settings overwrite the old ones, so the next time you call up your carefully constructed saved setting, it doesn't contain the values you expect.

Noise Reduction

Any attempt at reducing noise will also soften the image. Despite the noise-reduction features in Photoshop, third-party sharpening plug-ins such as PictureCode Noise Ninja, ABSoft Neat Image, and Imagenomic Noise-ware remain popular because they do tend to be more effective. We've been known to use these in various situations, but here we'll describe Photoshop noise-reduction techniques that don't rely on third-party add-ons.

Until the Reduce Noise filter appeared in Photoshop CS2, we generally relied on the Despeckle filter (choose Filter > Noise > Despeckle), applied separately to individual channels multiple times through an edge mask. We wish we could say that the Reduce Noise filter renders such kludges unnecessary, but we encounter two major problems with Reduce Noise:

- The Preserve Detail feature really doesn't know the difference between detail and digital noise or film grain, so we still need to use masks.

- If you're using a machine that isn't well optimized for Photoshop (such as a notebook computer with a single-core CPU), Reduce Noise can be frustratingly slow, especially when you turn on the Preview check box to preview the entire image.

However, even with these problems, when we encounter *really* noisy images, we will use Reduce Noise rather than Despeckle.

Light Noise Reduction with Despeckle. When we just need relatively light noise reduction, the Despeckle filter works well. A typical case is noisy skies from a transparency scanner. We generally run Despeckle first on the red channel, then we run it a few more times on the green channel and even more times on the blue channel, which tends to be the noisiest.

The Reduce Noise Filter

We don't mean to suggest that Reduce Noise is useless—far from it. But you *do* have to be careful, tune the subsequent sharpening to the noise reduction to avoid exaggerating the characteristic artifacts that Reduce Noise produces, and (in some cases) mask edges and important textural detail so that Reduce Noise doesn't destroy them.

In Basic mode, Reduce Noise (see **Figure 10-13**) offers four slider controls and a check box for reducing JPEG artifacts:

Strength. The Strength slider controls the strength of luminance noise reduction only—it's not an overall strength control. When the value is zero, you can still apply color noise reduction or use the Advanced options on the individual channels.

Preserve Details. The Preserve Details slider attempts to do what it says—preserve details. Unfortunately, on anything except very low-resolution files, it also seems to preserve the noise you're presumably trying to eliminate. We find that the useful range is between 1 and 5—beyond that, it's difficult to get rid of the noise (see Figure 10-13).

TIP: A small Reduce Color Noise value can noticeably improve digital camera photos shot at a high ISO speed, and can also effectively reduce the appearance of color grain in scans of color negative film.

Figure 10-13 Using the Reduce Noise filter

In the original low-light, ISO 1600 image there's visible color noise, especially in the blue cowling.

Setting Reduce Color Noise to 75 eliminates all color noise but also dulls some colors—it's set too high.

With Preserve Details set to zero, noise reduction smears out details.

Setting Preserve Details at 5 balances noise reduction and detail preservation.

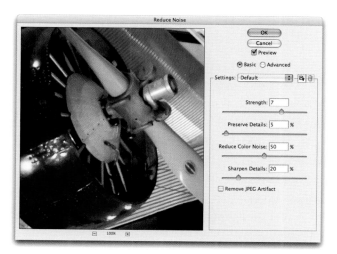

The Reduce Noise dialog with the final settings

The Preserve Details and Sharpen Details controls seem designed to sharpen and reduce noise in one fell swoop. On Web-resolution images, this works reasonably well. But if you plan on sharpening later, you need to keep the Preserve Details slider at or near zero.

Reduce Color Noise. The Reduce Color Noise slider reduces color noise independently of luminance noise. At very high settings, Reduce Color Noise can lose saturation, but settings of 35 to 50 percent work well, as we show in Figure 10-13.

In many cases, images from a digital camera will not need color noise reduction in Photoshop. This is because noise reduction is typically applied by the camera for JPEG images, and for raw images you should be applying noise reduction in the raw converter. For film, transparency film has little or no color noise, while negative film typically has more.

Sharpen Details. Although the Sharpen Details slider works independently of Preserve Details, its effect depends very much on that slider's value (whose effect depends—as we said just above—on the image resolution). Feel free to try reducing noise *and* sharpening with Reduce Noise, but we suggest that you attempt to do so only on low-resolution images—the significant lack of speed with which the filter updates the proxy on higher-resolution images doesn't really invite experimentation!

If you plan on sharpening the image after running Reduce Noise, we recommend leaving Sharpen Details at zero. Otherwise, you'll wind up with artifacts that are almost impossible to deal with.

TIP: When you're in the Advanced mode of the Reduce Noise dialog, you can use the same channel display shortcuts available in the Channels panel. For example, press Command-2 (Mac) or Ctrl-2 (Windows) to display only the green channel.

Remove JPEG Artifact. This option attempts to remove the characteristic 8-by-8-pixel artifacts caused by heavy JPEG compression. Sadly, we haven't enjoyed much success with it.

Advanced Mode. In Advanced mode, Reduce Noise lets you set values for Strength and Preserve Details for each channel individually. You can use this to apply noise reduction only to the noisiest channel, which is usually blue. Advanced Mode settings apply in addition to the settings you make in the main panel of the dialog. Piling all of these settings on top of each other can take a while to render, so on a slower or older machine, you may be better off running the Despeckle filter through a mask.

More Techniques. We use Reduce Noise on very noisy images as a precursor to sharpening. But we prefer to run it on a layer made by merging the visible layers, usually through a light edge mask (that is, a mask with no solid blacks, that deemphasizes rather than fully protects the edges). Since we use Reduce Noise only on extremely noisy images, we tend toward extreme settings.

Another way to reduce noise is to downsample. For example, if an image has noise from a digital camera or scanner, instead of editing the image from the beginning at its final size we may perform noise reduction and sharpening at the device's maximum resolution and then downsample later to create a smaller but cleaner master image.

Reducing Noise with Image Stacks

The image stack feature in Adobe Photoshop CS4 Extended is designed primarily as a tool for scientific image analysis, but it turns out to be useful for noise reduction. Don't confuse image stacks with the stack feature in Adobe Bridge—this is completely different. In Photoshop Extended, you process image stacks using the Stack Mode commands on the Layer > Smart Objects submenu. You can apply Stack Mode commands only to a Smart Object containing multiple images.

In our example (see **Figure 10-14**), we shot six handheld images under a fluorescent lamp using a Canon PowerShot S60 point-and-shoot camera in Raw mode. To achieve a decent shutter speed in such low indoor light, we set the camera to ISO 200, which happens to be a recipe for noise on that particular pocket camera. We applied no noise reduction while processing the images using Adobe Camera Raw.

In Photoshop, we choose File > Scripts > Load Files into Stack, click Browse, and select our six images. We turn on the two check boxes at the bottom of the dialog, Attempt to Automatically Align Source Images (because our handheld shots are not perfectly lined up) and Create Smart Object After Loading Layers (required to create an image stack). Finally, we click OK and stand back as Photoshop aligns the images and gathers them into a Smart Object. In the finished Smart Object, it's obvious how much noise is in this low-light scene, but we're about to take care of that.

We select the Smart Object in the Layers panel, and then choose Layer > Smart Objects > Stack Mode > Mean. As you may remember from math class, mean means average—and the Mean command averages the color

TIP: For best results with noise reduction using image stacks, try to shoot five or more images of the subject. The optimal number of frames depends on the anticipated level of noise, so it's always a bit of a guess.

values of each pixel across the six images. This smooths out the noise in the image, as you can see in Figure 10-14.

This technique may seem like a godsend for high-noise, low-light situations, and sometimes it is. But keep in mind that you can use it only when you're able to take several frames of a still subject. If the subject moves at all it may not be sharp after the frames are averaged, so this technique won't work for sports or theater. You also can't cheat by duplicating a single image—the noise won't average out, because it will be in the same place in all the duplicates. Where this technique doesn't work, you must fall back on the Reduce Noise or Despeckle filter.

Figure 10-14 Reducing noise with image stacks

The six original images

The Load Layers dialog with images loaded

The Stack Mode icon indicates that a Stack Mode command is applied.

The Smart Object containing the six images as an image stack

Noisy detail before applying the Mean command

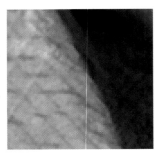

After applying the Mean command to the image stack

CHAPTER ELEVEN

Essential Image Techniques

The vast majority of Adobe Photoshop users stare at the program many hours a day, doing the same sort of image manipulation over and over again. Retouch the background of this photo, convert this color image to grayscale, put a new background behind this amazing kitchen appliance, make a panorama out of these seven images.

In this chapter we offer a whole mess of techniques to make your images fly a little faster, and perhaps even make them a little more fun to manipulate. The chapter is split up into a hodgepodge of common Photoshop issues: retouching, grayscale conversions, working with vector graphics and text, and so on. Read 'em and reap!

The Color of Grayscale

TIP: Clicking Auto is a good first step in Black & White. It adapts to the colors in an image, giving you a good starting point.

Many digital cameras and scanners let you capture images in grayscale. However, you can often get better results by starting from a color image and converting to grayscale in Photoshop. This is because some hues are darker than others at the same level of saturation (for example, the most saturated yellow is much lighter than the most saturated red). Whenever you have an image in which color helps define the subject, try one of the techniques that let you customize the conversion to grayscale, so that the existing color relationship is translated into a similar tonal relationship.

Using Black & White

The Black & White feature lets you control how colors translate into tones in a way similar to how film photographers place colored filters in front of their lenses to control contrast in the resulting black-and-white image.

TIP: If you use Black & White as an adjustment layer, you can keep both color and black-and-white versions in the same document. When the layer is on, it's your tuned black-and-white conversion. When the layer is off, you see the original full-color image.

Black & White is available as a dialog (Image > Adjustments > Black & White), but it's best to use it as an adjustment layer (through the Adjustments panel). You can open the Adjustments panel and click the Black & White button, or use any of the other methods that you've used to add an adjustment layer. In Black & White (**Figure 11-1**), each of the color sliders determines how dark each color appears in the grayscale image. For example, to deepen a blue sky, drag the Blues slider to the left to darken the blues in the grayscale image. By altering the relationships of colors to tones in Black & White, you can often arrive at more satisfying grayscale conversions in less time than if you had simply converted to grayscale and adjusted tones using curves, masks, and blending modes. You may still need to use those tools, but probably just for fine-tuning and special cases. If you are after a certain look, try the Black & White presets in the Adjustments panel—they include settings that emulate effects traditionally produced using color filters with black-and-white film, along with a simulation of infrared rendering. Use the Tint sliders to apply color effects such as sepia tones.

If you're working with a raw digital camera file, you may prefer to perform the grayscale conversion using the HSL/Grayscale tab in Adobe Camera Raw (see Chapter 5, "Building a Digital Workflow"), because it's earlier in the workflow and doesn't require saving a much larger Photoshop file and adjustment layer. On the other hand, if you want the original raw file to maintain its color conversion settings, or if the image needs additional edits that can't be done in Camera Raw, it makes sense to use Black & White in Photoshop. The controls are similar in both places.

Black & White includes the On-Image tool we discussed in Chapter 7, and it's stupendously intuitive here. When it's selected, you don't even have to use the sliders. Position the On-Image tool over the tone of the image you want to darken or lighten, drag right to lighten or left to darken, and Black & White automatically changes the color value for the tone you drag.

Figure 11-1 The Black & White adjustment

Original image

On-Image tool

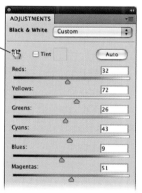

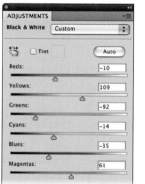

Storing alternate conversions in the Layers panel

After clicking Auto

After adjusting the dialog sliders to darken the blue sky and maintain contrast in the grass

TIP: Remember that a complete overview of all Adjustments panel controls is in Chapter 7, "Image Adjustment Fundamentals."

Instant Grayscale Images

The following techniques can be useful when you just want a quick grayscale and don't want to face a dialog full of sliders. On the other hand, you have to take what you get, since they aren't customizable.

Use the Grayscale Command. As we mentioned earlier, you can simply choose Image > Mode > Grayscale. When you do so, Photoshop weights the red, green, and blue channels differently, using a standard formula that purports to account for the varying sensitivity of the eye to different colors.

Desaturate. The Image > Adjustment > Desaturate command produces the same result as reducing the Saturation setting in the Hue/Saturation dialog to zero, producing a different result than the Grayscale command. Note that the Desaturate command affects only the selected layer, so it can be useful when you want to convert just one layer to grayscale while leaving the rest of the document in color.

Load the Image Luminance. One of David's favorite methods for squeezing a grayscale image out of a color photograph is to Command-click (Mac OS X) or Ctrl-click (Windows) on the composite color channel (the RGB or the CMYK thumbnail in the Channels panel), which loads the file's luminance map. You can then choose Select > Save Selection to save the selection to a new document. This produces a different result than the previous techniques and also usually looks better than choosing the Grayscale command.

TIP: The Channel Mixer adjustment is a way to build a grayscale image from channels. Turn on the Monochrome check box and make sure the channel percentages add up to 100 percent.

Harvest a Channel. Each image channel typically looks different from the other channels, so if you're trying to get a grayscale image out of a color image, just looking at each channel gives you a nice head start. You can get an idea of which sliders to adjust in Black & White or, if one of the channels already looks like the black-and-white image you're after, copy it. For Lab images you can try taking just the L channel, which carries all luminance information. For CMYK images, the K channel is the one you want.

HDR Imaging

If 16 bits per channel just isn't enough, Photoshop supports HDR (High Dynamic Range) imaging, which uses 32 bit/channel floating-point data to record unlimited dynamic range. Photoshop supports established HDR formats such as Industrial Light and Magic's OpenEXR and the Radiance format used by the open-source Radiance ray-tracing and rendering engine, in addition to Portable Bitmap Format (PBM), Large Document Format (PSB), Photoshop (PSD), and TIFF. The last three formats allow profile embedding, but be aware that color-managing HDR data is uncertain at best.

For photographers, an interesting aspect of Photoshop HDR support is that it allows you to create HDR images from bracketed exposures shot with normal cameras. But HDR is challenging because we lack any output methods that can display the full dynamic range—not even our monitors can do that. An HDR image can be more useful as a source image from which to create other images derived from subsets of the dynamic range.

Merge to HDR

You can create HDR documents using Merge to HDR with bracketed exposures shot as raw or JPEG files. Merge to HDR uses the EXIF metadata to determine the exposures and blend them accordingly, and it needs them to be unretouched images. If you've edited raw camera files, those metadata edits are simply ignored by Merge to HDR. If you apply edits to any other formats you feed into Merge to HDR, you'll get really nasty results.

Shooting for HDR. We find that we get the best results when we bracket by one-third of a stop, though this may be overkill. Bracketing by one stop, using enough exposures to cover the entire dynamic range you're trying to capture, often works well. A heavy tripod, mirror lockup, and static scene all help. Any objects in the scene that move will result in ghost fragments of the moving objects as they vary across frames, and such objects can be as seemingly innocuous as fluttering leaves. Some third-party HDR plug-ins handle moving objects better than Photoshop does.

TIP: It may occur to you to use your camera's auto-bracketing feature to bracket for HDR. Check your camera specs first, though—many cameras can't bracket in the wide increments (one stop or greater) that are more appropriate for HDR work. You may have to bracket manually.

Using Merge to HDR. Start by shooting a series of bracketed exposures that cover the dynamic range you're trying to capture. (Don't vary the aperture; that will give you inconsistent depth of field.) The easiest way to merge the images to an HDR document is to select them in Adobe Bridge, then choose Tools > Photoshop > Merge to HDR. Or, if you want to do things the hard way, you can start from Photoshop, choose File > Automate > Merge to HDR, click Browse and navigate to the source images, and select Attempt to Automatically Align Source Images before finally clicking OK.

TIP: Remember, highlights and shadows in a 32-bit image aren't necessarily clipped just because they look that way onscreen. Always drag the 32-bit preview slider to check the results of your edits on tonal levels that are darker or lighter than your monitor can show at any moment. The 32-bit preview slider works when a dialog is open; take advantage of that.

When you start Merge to HDR from Bridge, or when you click OK in the Merge to HDR dialog, you get the dialog shown in **Figure 11-2** (also, somewhat confusingly, named Merge to HDR). You're not done yet—the purpose of this dialog is to double-check the shots you're bringing into the merged HDR document (displayed in the filmstrip along the left side) and to preview the image that would result from the files you've selected in the filmstrip. To exclude an image from the merge, turn off its check box.

Because an HDR image has far more dynamic range than a monitor can display, you can set a white point for the image preview by dragging the slider under the histogram. The preview slider affects only the 8 bit/channel preview on screen. The preview has no effect on the data in the HDR document itself—don't worry, it's all still there. When you click OK, Photoshop closes the dialog and produces the merged HDR document.

Figure 11-2 The Merge to HDR preview dialog

Click a check box to include or exclude an image from the conversion.

The histogram represents only the images included at left. Drag the preview slider to shift the 8-bit preview to the higher and lower tonal ranges of the 32-bit image.

Editing the Merged HDR Document. Not all Photoshop features are available for a 32-bit HDR document. The available features are focused on basic image correction, such as Levels, Photo Filter, Smart Sharpen, Unsharp Mask, and the healing and cloning tools. In Photoshop Extended, painting and layers are also available. Don't try to do everything here—your goal is simply to create a great 32-bit source file that you'll downsample later. We find we get significantly better results sharpening the HDR image than we do sharpening after we've downsampled to 16 or 8 bits per channel.

In the 32-bit merged HDR document, the preview slider you saw in the Merge to HDR preview dialog now appears in the status bar at the bottom of the document window. When you make an adjustment that affects the entire image, drag this slider to see how the adjustment affects different parts of the tonal range (see **Figure 11-3**). Again, the preview slider shifts only the preview's tonal range—it doesn't alter the image itself. If you actually do want to alter the tones in a 32-bit image, use one of the available adjustment commands, such as Exposure or Levels.

 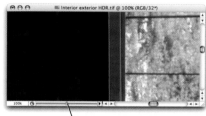

Figure 11-3 Previewing an HDR edit

This image was just sharpened. We first drag the 32-bit preview slider at the bottom of the image to check sharpening in a darker area of the image . . .

. . . and then we drag the slider to the left to check a lighter area of the image. The image isn't actually lightened or darkened; we're just previewing the entire tonal range.

We haven't mentioned the Exposure command until this point in the book because it's primarily intended for use with 32-bit images. It's similar to Levels in that you can use its controls to adjust highlights, midtones, and shadows, but it operates in a gamma 1.0 (linear) color space. (All other adjustments in Photoshop operate using the gamma correction of the document's color space.) There are only three sliders in the Exposure dialog: Exposure controls highlights, Offset sets the shadow level, and Gamma Correction sets the midtones (see **Figure 11-4**).

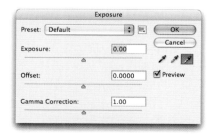

Figure 11-4 The Exposure dialog

Downsampling HDR Images

TIP: The wider the dynamic range you want to retain, the more difficult it will be to keep all of the detail when downsampling, since monitors and printers often can't reproduce it all. The more tonal range you want to convert, the better the Local Adaptation conversion option will probably work for you, as opposed to the other three options. When using the toning curve, remember: To gain contrast in one area, you must lose it in another, so know which ranges are expendable.

To do just about anything else with an HDR image, including print it, you need to downsample by choosing either 16 Bits/Channel or 8 Bits/Channel from the Image > Mode submenu. If you are working with a layered file and you want to have control over how the 32-bit tones map to the lower bit depth, first choose Layer > Flatten Image, so that when you choose Image > Mode > 8-Bits/Channel or 16-Bits/Channel, the HDR Conversion dialog appears (see **Figure 11-5**). It offers four ways to convert to a lower bit depth. Note that while you can display the toning curve and histogram at the bottom of the dialog in all four methods, the controls are enabled only when you choose Local Adaptation.

Exposure and Gamma. This option offers two slider controls. Exposure sets the white point, so drag it until you like where the highlights clip. Gamma sets the midtone, so drag Gamma after setting Exposure.

Highlight Compression. There are no options for Highlight Compression—it simply does what it says. The biggest change to the image is that the highlight end of the tonal range is compressed to fit the luminance values into the 16-bit or 8-bit version.

Equalize Histogram. As with Highlight Compression, there are no options for Equalize Histogram.

TIP: If you want to do HDR right, you'll probably have better luck with specialized HDR utilities such as Photomatix or the command-line tool Enfuse. Some developers have written easy-to-use interfaces for Enfuse. One of these is Bracketeer; if you use Lightroom there is also the LR/Enfuse plug-in.

Local Adaptation. Local Adaptation offers the most control, but at default settings, it often produces the least encouraging results. Nevertheless, persistence is rewarded. Local Adaptation is similar to the Shadows/Highlights command. The Radius setting adjusts the size of the neighborhood the algorithm uses to calculate the local adaptation, while the Threshold setting tells it how far apart two pixels' tonal values must be before they're no longer part of the same brightness region. The Threshold setting essentially sets the local contrast, while the Radius setting controls the size of the local pixel neighborhood to which that contrast applies. Images with finer details will generally require a smaller Radius value.

We recommend that you always preview all four conversion methods in the HDR Conversion dialog, because the best choice for one image may not work for an image with a different distribution of tones.

For further control, Local Adaptation also offers the toning curve and histogram. The toning curve differs from curves in a couple of ways. First, the red tick marks on the horizontal scale represent 1 EV (Exposure Value) increments—approximately one f-stop (remember that you're dealing with an unbounded dynamic range). The second difference is that you can place corner points on the curve (click the Corner check box to turn the selected curve point into a corner point), thereby creating a sharp tonal break. This can be useful for placing a diffuse highlight and ensuring that the specular highlights blow out.

As with the Curves dialog, click in the image to see where on the toning curve the pixels under the cursor lie. However, in the HDR Conversion dialog you can't place points by clicking the image.

The toning curve and histogram are functional only when you choose the Local Adaptation method.

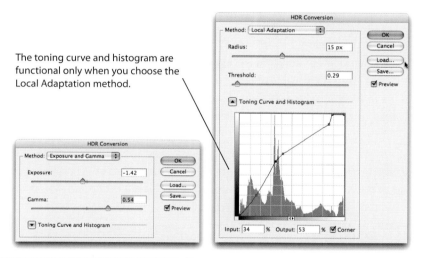

Figure 11-5 Converting a 32-bit HDR image to 16-bit

We first try the Exposure and Gamma method, but with just two sliders to cover such a wide range of tones, it's hard to avoid clipping and flat contrast.

Using the Local Adaptation method with a customized toning curve, we're better able to maintain detail all the way from the shadows to the highlights.

Retouching

It's useful to make the distinction between *dust-busting* (removing specks of dirt, dust, mold, hair, and so on) and *retouching* (actually changing the content of an image). In this section, we'll relay a few key pointers that we've learned over the years about both dust-busting and retouching images, in the hope that they'll help you work more efficiently.

Evaluating

TIP: In Photoshop CS4, the keyboard shortcut for Actual Pixels view is Command-1 (Mac OS X) or Ctrl-1 (Windows). This is a change from earlier versions of Photoshop, but it's now consistent with other programs.

Inspect the entire image at 100 percent (Actual Pixels) view or higher, so you can get a sense of what's going on in your image and check for sensor dust, skin imperfections, or film scratches in scans. You usually don't need to zoom in more than 200 percent.

When the image is larger than the screen, you can easily get around by using keyboard shortcuts. Press Home to start at the top left corner, then press Page Down to move down until you reach the bottom. Press Command-Page Down (Mac OS X) or Ctrl-Page Down (Windows) to move one screen to the right, then press Page Up to move up a screen. To move to the left, press Command-Page Up (Mac OS X) or Ctrl-Page Up (Windows). Press the End key to zip straight to the bottom right corner. When pressing Page Up or Page Down, add the Shift key to scroll a short distance instead of a whole page.

Dust-Busting

TIP: If your scanner has a hardware-based dust and scratch removal feature such as Digital ICE, which detects actual dust and scratches at scan time, it will be significantly more effective than the Dust & Scratches filter in Photoshop.

While dust tends to be a bigger problem with film scans than with digital captures, the latter are by no means immune. For digital SLRs, dust can land on the sensor when you change the lens. We usually apply noise reduction and correct overall tone and color, then dust-busting, then everything else, although that order isn't strict.

Paint Corrections on a Separate Layer. When you keep retouching edits on a separate layer, it's easy to back out of a change, and it's easy to see before-and-after views by turning the layer's visibility off and on. Conrad normally adds such a layer and names it "Patcher."

By default, a retouching tool paints on the layer you're correcting. However, when you're painting corrections on a separate layer, you need a way to tell the correction tool to base its correction on the image layer, since your retouching layer starts out blank. To achieve this, some tools, such as the Clone Stamp tool, provide a Sample pop-up menu in the Options bar, so that you can also make the tool sample from the current layer and layers below, or from all layers. Other tools, such as the Spot Healing Brush tool, provide only the option to sample all layers. We showed this in "Brush Tips" in Chapter 6, "Essential Photoshop Tips and Tricks."

The Dust & Scratches Filter. Although the Dust & Scratches filter (Filter > Noise > Dust & Scratches) promises great things ("Wow, a filter that dust-busts my image!"), you should be aware that this tool can do significant harm to the rest of your image. The Dust & Scratches filter is basically the same as the Median filter, but with a threshold feature (so you have some control over what gets Median-ized). That means it removes all of the small details in your document, including film grain and other image details that might be important. It's often better to use some of the other techniques we cover in this chapter, such as the duplicate-layer-nudging method we'll discuss a bit later.

If you're actually trying to smooth out a grainy image while dust-busting, Dust & Scratches might be just the ticket. In that case, make sure you set the Radius value as low as possible and the Threshold value as high as possible. It'll take some trial and error to get it right, so that the dust and scratches are gone but the image isn't too blurry. After that, resharpen the image with Unsharp Mask to restore some edge contrast.

TIP: If you discover that a certain dust spot occurs in exactly the same position on a number of frames, consider using the Retouch tool in Adobe Camera Raw 4. Once you retouch a spot in Camera Raw, you can use the Synchronize command to apply the same correction to any number of other raw, TIFF, or JPEG images. Another way to sync the correction is by using the Copy Camera Raw Settings and Paste Settings commands in Bridge.

The Healing Brushes and the Patch Tool

The Healing Brush (press J) is quite a marvel of modern science; you first pick a spot on your image that you want to clone. As with the Clone Stamp tool, you Option-click (Mac OS X) or Alt-click (Windows) to pick the source. You then paint in the area you want to change (see **Figure 11-6**). While the mouse button is pressed, the screen looks as though you were using the Clone Stamp tool. However, when you let go of the mouse button, Photoshop uses a complicated algorithm to blend the image of the source layer with the tone and texture of the area you're painting. The result is a clone that blends in better than the Clone Stamp tool ever could.

Figure 11-6 Painting with the Healing Brush

Option/Alt-click to set the Source point.

Paint over the blemish.

Infants often have splotches and scratches that pass in a day or two.

Here the red marks and other distractions were removed with the Healing Brush.

The more automatic Spot Healing Brush (see **Figure 11-7**) does away with the pesky requirement to choose a source point; instead, it automatically samples the surrounding area. Use a small brush just big enough to cover the spot. For long scratches you can paint in a straight line if you hold down the Shift key the whole time as you click the Spot Healing Brush at one end of the scratch and click again at the other end of the scratch.

Figure 11-7 Using the Spot Healing Brush

This scanned film has both spots and scratches.

Click with the Spot Healing Brush . . .

. . . and no more spot. Next, remove the scratch.

Shift-click one end, don't let go of Shift . . .

. . . and Shift-click at the other end of the scratch.

The scratch is now gone.

The Patch tool is like a combination of the Healing Brush and the Lasso tool. The way it works depends on whether you select Source or Destination in the Options bar for the tool. If it's set to Source, drag the Patch tool around an area you want to fix, just as you would to make a selection with the Lasso tool. Then click inside this selection and drag it to the part of your image that you want to copy from. When you let go of the mouse button, Photoshop clones the destination of your drag area over the area you first selected and then performs its healing algorithm to properly blend the destination into the source (see **Figure 11-8**).

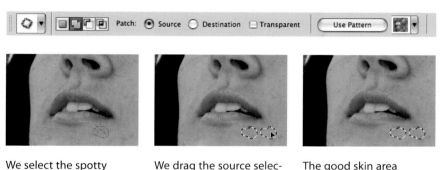

Figure 11-8 The Patch tool and its Options bar

We select the spotty source we want to patch.

We drag the source selection to a good skin area.

The good skin area patches the source.

If you select Destination in the Options bar, the only difference is that you select the good area first and drag it to the destination you want to patch.

Myriad Small Spots. With scanned film, mildew, dust, bugs, corrosives, abrasive surfaces, or even a mediocre scanner can cause hundreds or thousands of tiny white or black spots. After sharpening, these spots pop out at you like stars on the new moon. If you're like us, you're already cringing at the thought of spot-healing all those dots out.

Here's a technique that can stamp out thousands of dust spots in a single move. You still may have to use the Healing Brush tool to get rid of a few artifacts and some of the larger spots, but most of your work will already be done (see **Figure 11-9**).

1. Select the area with the spots, and feather the selection.

2. Copy the selection to a new layer by pressing Command-J (Mac OS X) or Ctrl-J (Windows).

3. If you're trying to remove white spots, set the blending mode in the Layers panel to Darken. For black spots, set the mode to Lighten.

TIP: Although the Healing Brush and the Patch tool are designed to maintain the original texture of the image (such as film grain), the other retouching tools tend to destroy texture and hence make the result appear unnatural. You can sometimes simulate lost texture by running the Add Noise or Grain filter on the affected area at a low setting, but it's generally better to keep a close eye on what's happening to your texture as you retouch.

4. With the Move tool selected, press the arrow keys to move the new layer left, right, up, or down by a few pixels—just enough to make the spots disappear; a one- or two-pixel move often does the trick.

Figure 11-9 Dust-busting in bulk

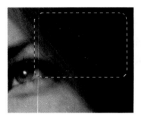  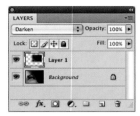

Feathered selection before making new layer

New layer nudged; spots are gone

The Layers panel for this correction

5. You can see a before-and-after difference by turning the visibility of the new layer on and off.

6. If you want, you can merge the new layer back into the original. However, we often leave these as separate layers, so that we don't damage the original image before we have to.

The Clone Stamp Tool

The Clone Stamp tool lets you copy pixels from anyplace in your image (or even another image) and then paint them somewhere else. It works much like the Healing Brush we covered earlier: Option-click (Mac OS X) or Alt-click (Windows) to pick up a source point, and then paint away elsewhere to copy those pixels. The difference is that while the Healing Brush automatically tries to blend the source and destinations, the Clone Stamp just paints the source literally. This requires more manual touch-up—which is why the newer Healing Brush is often better for this kind of work.

Keep Jumping Around. The single biggest mistake people make with the Clone Stamp tool is dragging the mouse in a painting fashion. That tends to create repeating patterns, making the retouch more obvious (see **Figure 11-10**). Instead, dab here and there with a number of clicks.

One exception to this rule is when the area you're cloning is relatively flat and has little texture or detail (such as the blurry background behind a portrait). The second exception we make is when we're using the Clone Stamp

TIP: When you're retouching a selected or masked area of an image, feathering the selection or mask by a pixel or two can help blend the correction with the background. If retouching causes texture to be lost, undo and try again using a lower feather amount.

TIP: Remember that you can control the opacity and blending mode of the tool using the Options bar or with keystrokes (see Chapter 6, "Essential Photoshop Tips and Tricks").

tool with a blending mode such as Darken, Lighten, or Soft Light—and then only when the effect is subtle and doesn't create an obvious clone.

A second mistake people make is continuing to clone from the same area. Keep changing the source point that you're cloning (the point on which you Option/Alt-click). For example, if you're erasing some specks of dust on someone's face, don't just clone from one side of the specks. Erase one speck from pixel information to the left; erase the second speck from the right, and so on.

Figure 11-10 Avoid repeating patterns by changing the source point.

In the original image, branches block the view.

Sloppy cloning creates visible repeating patterns.

Varying the source points results in seamless edits.

There are times, of course, when both of these pieces of advice should be chucked out the window. For example, if you're rebuilding a straight line by cloning another parallel line in the image, you'd be hard-pressed to clone it by any other method than painting in the whole line. The following tip provides a way to do so relatively painlessly.

Stroking Paths. Back in Figure 11-7 we showed how to get rid of straight scratches by Shift-clicking with the Spot Healing Brush. But what if you want to remove a line that isn't straight, such as power lines, which are always more noticeable in a photograph than they were in reality? For that, you can use the Pen tool to draw a path, then use the Clone Stamp tool to stroke the path, obliterating the offending pixels in one fell swoop (see **Figure 11-11**).

1. Draw the path using the Pen tool, keeping it as close to the center of the power line (or other defect) as possible. It's a good idea to save the path (double-click on Work Path in the Paths panel and name it).

2. Select the Clone Stamp tool and click the Aligned button in the Options bar. To remove a light-colored scratch, set the mode to Darken; to remove a dark power line, set the mode to Lighten.

3. Choose a soft brush a little wider than the widest point of the scratch.

TIP: Don't let the boundaries of your image's window restrict you. If you want to clone from another open document, go right ahead and do it. You don't even have to switch documents, as long as you have a large enough monitor.

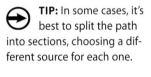

TIP: Having trouble precisely aligning the source point? Try using the preview overlay in the Clone Source panel, which we talk about next.

4. Option-click (Mac OS X) or Alt-click (Windows) beside the start of the path to set the source point for the cloning operation, just as you would if you were going to clone-stamp the scratch by hand.

5. Shift-click on the path in the Paths panel to hide it, then drag the path over the Stroke Path with Brush button at the bottom of the panel (see Figure 11-11). The power line is gone! It works because stroking a path always uses the current tool as the brush (in this case, the Clone Stamp).

Figure 11-11 Removing power lines with a path and the Clone Stamp tool

Getting rid of the power lines by hand would take forever.

But we actually completed this retouch in record time.

TIP: In some cases, it's best to split the path into sections, choosing a different source for each one.

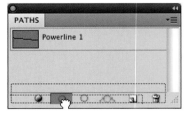

Here's how: We drew a path along the power line. Then, with the Clone Stamp tool set to a small, soft-edged brush, we carefully clicked a source point slightly offset from one end of the path.

We Shift-clicked on the path in the Paths panel to hide the path, then dragged the path over the Stroke Path with Brush button at the bottom of the Paths panel.

Using the Clone Source Panel

If you often wish you had a little help picking perfectly aligned source points with the Clone Stamp or Healing Brush tool, that help is available in the form of the Clone Source panel (see **Figure 11-12**). It helps you position and angle the source point precisely, before you start cloning. On top of that, the Clone Source panel can remember up to five source points, so that if you have to go back and redo or refine a previous area, you don't have to tediously reestablish where it was. These features save so much time that you'll never want to clone without the Clone Source panel by your side.

Open the Clone Source panel by choosing Window > Clone Source, or click the Clone Source icon in the dock, if it's visible.

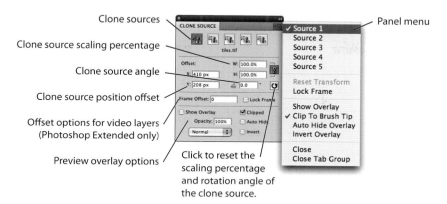

Clone sources

Clone source scaling percentage

Clone source angle

Clone source position offset

Offset options for video layers (Photoshop Extended only)

Preview overlay options

Click to reset the scaling percentage and rotation angle of the clone source.

Panel menu

Figure 11-12 The Clone Source panel

Setting Multiple Clone Sources. The five icons across the top of the Clone Source panel represent the five source points you can save. The selected Clone Source button is the one that remembers where you've Option-clicked/Alt-clicked, so if you want the Clone Source panel to remember a different source point, select a different Clone Source button first. Of course, all you have to do to switch to a different clone source is to click the Clone Source button you used to save it—kind of like saving and recalling radio stations using the radio buttons on a car stereo. Keep in mind that a clone source can be in a different open document, so your five saved clone sources can come from various open documents.

Setting the Clone Source Offset. Use the Offset section of the Clone Source panel to make the clone source do your bidding. The X and Y fields report the current distance of the cursor from where you Option-clicked/Alt-clicked the clone source; you can enter values here (to change the unit of measure, right-click, or Control-click in Mac OS X). The W and H fields control the scaling percentage of the width and height of the clone source, respectively, and the angle field lets you rotate the clone source in degrees.

Using the Preview Overlay. The very useful preview overlay shows you where the cloned pixels will land when you click or drag. To show it, turn on the Show Overlay check box in the Clone Source panel. When you do

TIP: Not sure if you're about to wipe out a Clone Source button you're already using? Hold the mouse over the Clone Source button to see its tool tip. If it's in use, the tool tip displays the clone source's document. If it isn't in use, the tool tip says "Clone source: not in use."

TIP: You can nudge the position, scale, or angle of the Clone Source overlay using the usual arrow key shortcuts in the Clone Source panel fields. Click in a field and press the up arrow or down arrow key, and optionally add the Shift key for larger nudge increments.

this, you'll see a semitransparent copy of the image that moves with the cursor (see **Figure 11-13**), telling you where you'll be painting the cloned source pixels when you click or drag. As soon as you click or drag, the overlay goes away, because you've positioned it. (If the Auto-Hide check box is on, the overlay remains visible as you paint.) If you Option-click/Alt-click a new source point, the overlay appears again until you click or drag to set the new source. If you chose to leave Show Overlay off, you can press Option-Shift (Mac OS X) or Alt-Shift (Windows) to display the overlay.

By default, the preview overlay is the size of the brush tip. If you're using a small brush tip, the overlay might be difficult to see. To make an overlay as large as the layer, turn off the Clipped check box in the Clone Source panel; if you used Photoshop CS3 you'll recognize that the layer-sized preview overlay is the way it worked by default in CS3. The Clipped check box in the Clone Source panel is called Clip to Brush tip in the panel menu.

Figure 11-13 The clone source preview overlay with the Clipped check box off

In the original image, we Option/Alt-click the clone source point where these four tiles meet.

We drag the overlay to another tile intersection to preview the alignment of the clone to the original.

Thanks to the preview overlay, the cloned pixels align perfectly when we brush them in.

NOTE: In Photoshop Extended, the Clone Source panel includes the Frame Offset and Lock Frame options, which are used when cloning between video frames. (Photoshop video layers are outside the scope of this book.)

If you don't quite manage to align the overlay correctly the first time, there's no need to start over. Just Option-Shift-drag (Mac OS X) or Alt-Shift-drag (Windows) to reposition the overlay; the overlay will be visible only when you drag. To numerically position, scale, or rotate the overlay, enter values into the Offset section of the Clone Source panel. To reflect the clone you're painting, click the link icon to turn it off, and enter a negative value into the W or H field. An undistorted reflection is represented by −100 percent.

Removing Red-Eye

A common retouching task is removing red-eye—that devilish effect that appears when a camera flash reflects off the retina. Ideally, you'll avoid red-eye by using off-camera flash, but if your (or someone else's) photograph already has red-eye, you'll have to remove the red. The Red-Eye tool (sharing a slot on the Tools panel with the healing brushes and the Patch tool) is by far the easiest way of doing so, but sometimes it removes the eye color too, so we still resort to the following techniques when necessary.

Hue/Saturation. Select the offending pupils with an oval marquee, feather the selection by a few pixels, copy the selection to a new layer (Command-J in Mac OS X, Ctrl-J in Windows), and then use Hue/Saturation to shift the color, brightness, and saturation. Every image requires different values, but we usually start with Hue at +40 (for brown eyes) or –120 (for blue eyes), Saturation at –75, and a Lightness value of –50. The key is to remove the glaring color while still maintaining the specular highlights and color that make the eye look alive.

Color Replacement Tool. The Color Replacement tool lets you change the color of pixels to the foreground color but leave the pixels' saturation and brightness alone. In other words, it changes the color but retains the detail. We haven't found it useful for large areas, but it's quite good at fixing things like red-eye. Hold down the Option key (Mac OS X) or Alt key (Windows) and click on the darkest part of the eye (or some other dark area nearby), then let go of the Option/Alt key, adjust the brush size to slightly smaller than the pupil, and draw over the red portions. You may need to increase the Tolerance level in the Options bar to 35 or 40 percent.

Perspective Retouching

The Vanishing Point filter makes editing in perspective orders of magnitude easier than it used to be. Vanishing Point is a very deep plug-in, and if you plan to use it a lot, we strongly recommend reading about the filter in the online Photoshop Help file and mastering the considerable number of options and keyboard shortcuts.

Defining the Planes. To open Vanishing Point, choose Filter > Vanishing Point, or press Command-Option-V (Mac OS X) or Ctrl-Alt-V (Windows). The first step in using Vanishing Point is to define a perspective plane by clicking on four points, and then to enlarge the plane to cover the area you want to affect (see **Figure 11-14**). Watch the color and size of the grid when dragging its corners or sides: Red means the grid is not valid perspective, yellow is pretty close, and blue is good. In general, it's better to see a grid of

TIP: You can also use the Red-Eye Removal tool in Camera Raw if you're retouching a camera raw, TIFF, or JPEG image.

TIP: Take care of lens distortions first. Vanishing Point calculates mathematically perfect planes, so if your lens shows any barrel or pincushion distortion, the cloned results may be a little off. We recommend running the Lens Correction filter (see the next section) before using Vanishing Point.

bigger squares than smaller rectangles. Sometimes moving the grid corners by a pixel or two will make a big difference in the quality of the perspective.

Figure 11-14 Cloning in perspective in the Vanishing Point filter

The Create Plane tool lets you click to define the corners of a perspective plane.

We zoom out and drag the outer handles to extend the perspective plane over the area with the missing building.

After using the Marquee tool to select the tall building in the back, we Option/Alt-drag the selection to create a duplicate in perspective.

Performing the Cloning. Once you've defined the plane, you can use the Marquee or Clone Stamp tool to clone regions in the image or paste elements from other images. In Vanishing Point, a selection you drag using the marquee automatically conforms to the perspective plane. In this simple example, we used the marquee to select a building that was still standing, then Option/Alt-dragged it to duplicate it, replacing a demolished building.

In this simple example, we used a single perspective plane. Once you've defined the basic plane, you can create additional hinged planes by Command-dragging (Mac OS X) or Ctrl-dragging (Windows) a side (not corner) handle on the edge of a plane. You can adjust a hinged plane's angle by Option-dragging (Mac OS X) or Alt-dragging (Windows) one of its side handles or by editing the Angle field at the top of the Vanishing Point dialog. And while we generally find that it's easier to fine-tune the result on a layer after we've run Vanishing Point, the Transform tool in Vanishing Point lets you transform floating selections.

For more complex cloning operations, we use Vanishing Point's Stamp tool, which works just like the Clone Stamp tool. We could have achieved the result shown in Figure 11-14 by using the Clone Stamp tool instead of the technique demonstrated in the figure.

> **TIP:** Whenever possible, clone from the foreground to the background. Our example in Figure 11-14 is actually not ideal because our clone scales up a background area into the larger foreground. That results in upsampling, which can visibly lower the clone's sharpness if the increase in size is significant.

LENS CORRECTION

The Lens Correction filter (choose Filter > Distort > Lens Correction) lets you address barrel and pincushion distortion, chromatic aberration, vignetting, and perspective errors.

Lens Filter Controls

The Lens Filter controls are arranged in five groups: the tool panel, the zoom controls, the grid controls, the main control buttons and Settings menu, and the actual filter adjustment controls.

Tool Panel. The Tool panel, at the top left corner of the Lens Correction dialog, contains five tools. The Remove Distortion tool is a rather blunt instrument—we can make much finer adjustments using the slider control—but we use the Straighten tool to set horizontals or verticals to rotate and straighten the image because it's often easier than typing in an angle. The Move Grid tool lets us adjust the position of the alignment grid, which is useful when adjusting distortion or perspective. We never choose the

Zoom and Hand tools from the panel, preferring to use the usual keyboard shortcuts—Option (Mac OS X) or Alt (Windows) to zoom out, Command (Mac OS X) or Ctrl (Windows) to zoom in, and the spacebar to scroll.

Grid Controls. The grid controls let you show and hide the grid and control its size and color. Also in this cluster is the Preview check box, which lets you toggle between previewing the adjusted and unadjusted image.

Remove Distortion. The Remove Distortion slider lets you remove pincushion or barrel distortions, which bow straight lines inward and outward, respectively. **Figure 11-15** shows an image before and after correction for moderate barrel distortion. The grid is useful for checking barrel distortion.

You can drag the Remove Distortion tool toward or away from the center of the image to correct barrel and pincushion distortion, respectively, but we find it's easier to use the slider. The up and down arrow keys change the value by increments of 0.1; add Shift to change it in increments of 1.

Chromatic Aberration. The Chromatic Aberration sliders work by changing the size of the red (for red/cyan fringing) and blue (for blue/yellow fringing) channel relative to the green channel. We showed an example of chromatic aberration when we discussed the Camera Raw corrections for it in Chapter 5. You can sometimes go crazy trying to eliminate chromatic aberration entirely, but if you can render it unobjectionable at 200 percent magnification, it's unlikely to be noticeable it in the final image.

With digital raw images, we prefer to fix chromatic aberration in Camera Raw because it's earlier in the workflow. However, if you need to make different corrections for chromatic aberration in different parts of the image, you might want to make this correction in Photoshop instead—simply copy the layer, run Lens Distortion with different chromatic aberration settings on each, and use masks to reveal the appropriate corrections for each part of the image.

Vignette. Vignetting, in which the lens illuminates the sensor or film plane unevenly, causing darkening in the corners, is most commonly seen when shooting at wide apertures. The Vignette Amount slider controls the amount of lightening or darkening, while the Vignette Midpoint slider controls how far from the corners the correction extends; lower values affect more of the image, higher ones confine the correction closer to the corners.

TIP: Run Lens Correction before performing creative or output sharpening. You definitely don't want to sharpen the color fringes caused by chromatic aberration, but even seemingly harmless perspective and distortion corrections are better performed before sharpening than afterward.

Figure 11-15 Removing distortion with the Lens Correction dialog

This wide-angle shot exhibits obvious barrel distortion.

We eliminate the barrel distortion by adjusting the Remove Distortion value until the bowed lines become straight.

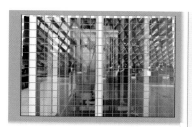

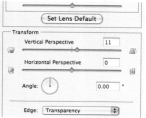

To make vertical lines parallel, we adjust the Vertical Perspective value.

After clicking OK, we crop the edges that were distorted after the lens corrections. We could have used the Scale slider in the Lens Correction dialog, but we feel we have more control using the standard Crop tool.

NOTE: Lens defaults apply automatically only to digital camera photos containing EXIF metadata—that's how Photoshop can detect how the shot was taken. For images that don't include EXIF metadata, you can manually save and apply presets using the preset menu to the right of the Settings pop-up menu.

Setting Lens Defaults. You can save the Remove Distortion, Chromatic Aberration, and Vignette corrections as defaults for a specific camera, lens, and focal length by clicking the Set Lens Default button. Then, when the filter detects other images shot with the same camera, lens, and focal length by reading the image metadata, the setting you've saved becomes available in the Settings menu, and choosing it applies those settings. When you save lens defaults, test the settings on more than one image—even then, you'll probably have to fine-tune the results for each image.

The Transform Controls. The Transform controls are image specific. They can reduce the perspective errors caused by tilting the camera, and while they do an impressive job, they don't turn an SLR into a view camera. But they do provide a reasonable substitute for 35 mm tilt/shift lenses. Figure 11-15 shows an image before and after a perspective correction.

NOTE: The Transform settings can't be saved as part of the lens default because they depend on the angle between the camera and subject, and hence are image-dependent.

Edge. When you make distortion and perspective corrections, you lose some of the image. The Edge menu lets you deal with the corrected edges, but the Edge Extension option rarely does anything useful, so we usually stick with Transparency. If we need to preserve the aspect ratio, we use the Scale slider to fill the image area, eliminating any empty areas resulting from the lens correction. When we want to keep as much of the image as possible, we crop in Photoshop instead.

BLENDING IMAGES AUTOMATICALLY

In Chapters 8 and 9 we discussed masks and selections, which are manual ways to composite images by cutting through a layer to reveal the layers underneath it. However, there are some less manual ways of doing this.

Blending images can also mean assembling multiple images along their common areas or edges, such as building a panorama. For this, Photoshop offers Auto-Align Layers, Auto-Blend Layers, and Photomerge.

Auto-Align Layers and Auto-Blend Layers

We think Auto-Align Layers and Auto-Blend Layers are two of the coolest features in Photoshop. They not only automate the onerous task of aligning images, but they do it quickly and well.

Auto-Align Layers. This feature aligns selected layers intelligently and reliably by looking for common areas in an image. Auto-Align Layers comes in handy any time you need to perfectly register two images, especially when you want to combine them. For example, you may have two or three nearly identical handheld photos of a group, with a different person blinking in each photo. Just apply Auto-Align Layers and paint in some masks, and you can easily produce a photo in which everyone's eyes are open. Because that example is widely demonstrated, we have another example: three photos with common overlapping sides.

If the layers aren't already in Photoshop, we select them in Bridge and choose Tools > Photoshop > Load Files into Photoshop Layers. We select the layers in the Layers panel and choose Edit > Auto-Align Layers. In the Auto-Align Layers dialog, we choose a Projection option (see **Figure 11-16**) and click OK. The Auto option just picks a projection based on the selected images. In the end we prefer the straight verticals produced by Cylindrical, and we settle on that one. There are visible seams due to exposure and contrast differences, which you can eliminate by applying Auto-Blend Layers. You can use as many images as you want, but more images take longer to analyze and process.

Photoshop CS4 adds two options to the Auto-Align Layers dialog: Vignette Removal and Geometric Distortion Correction. Both options can result in a more uniform tone and perspective across the completed panorama, and can save on manual touch-up. However, they can't perform miracles. Both features work best with images that have enough lens information in the EXIF metadata to calculate the degree of correction for vignetting and distortion. That means these options are most effective with digital camera images.

After auto-aligning layers, the layers are still separate, along with new layer masks added by Photoshop. You can edit the layer masks.

Auto-Blend Layers. Often, getting layers aligned is only half the battle. Exposure differences and lens vignetting can leave visible seams across images that are time-consuming to remove by hand (using masks, curves, and cloning tools). Auto-Blend Layers automates seam removal. Select the layers in the Layers panel, and choose Edit > Auto Blend Layers (see **Figure 11-17**). The Panorama option attempts to blend images at their edges, while Stack Images assumes the images are stacked on top of one another. Photoshop CS4 adds a new depth of field capability to Auto-Blend Layers; we'll discuss that option after looking at Photomerge.

NOTE: Auto-Align Layers works only with raster layers; you'll need to rasterize other types of layers before applying Auto-Align Layers. For example, if an image is a Smart Object, select it and choose Layer > Smart Objects > Rasterize.

TIP: You'll maximize your chance of a successful panorama if you capture each frame using the same exposure settings and the same lighting, using a tripod to keep the camera level.

Figure 11-16 Auto-Align Layers projections

Our three source images, shot handheld

Cylindrical. This is often the best choice for horizontal-only panoramas.

Perspective. Our first source image is not visible here, and the result is not acceptable. We think Auto-Align Layers couldn't work out the linear perspective continuity between the left and middle images. That happens sometimes.

Spherical. Spherical is good for aligning images shot both horizontally and vertically.

Collage aligns and rotates images as needed, with no additional alterations.

Reposition Only aligns edges with no other changes—not even rotation.

Figure 11-17 The Auto-Blend Layers dialog

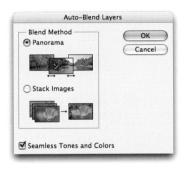

Making Panoramas with Photomerge

You might have noticed that the example we used for Auto-Align Layers is a three-image panorama. If you really are trying to build a panorama, however, it's faster to use the Photomerge feature because it applies both Auto-Align Layers and Auto-Blend Layers. As usual, the easiest way to run Photomerge is to select images in Bridge and choose Tools > Photoshop > Photomerge. If you're starting from Photoshop, choose File > Automate > Photomerge and select files using the Source Files options in the Photomerge dialog (see **Figure 11-18**).

In Bridge, we select four scans of sloppily photographed color negatives and choose Tools > Photoshop > Photomerge.

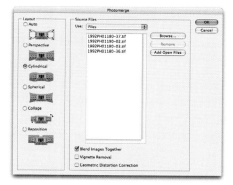

Figure 11-18 Using Photomerge

The Photomerge dialog combines the Auto-Align Layers dialog with a file selector.

The odd shape was interesting, but we decide to crop the corrected and sharpened final image.

Thanks to Auto-Align Layers, Photomerge can detect any common edges—one of the images is vertical, attached to the others by all edges except its bottom. Also, the first photo selected in Bridge is not actually part of this scene, and Photomerge correctly omits it from the panorama.

TIP: When you must align layers completely by hand, let opacity or a blending mode help you. Lowering the opacity lets you see if you're aligning to underlying layers. Changing the blending mode to Difference, Darken, or Lighten helps emphasize overlapping layers that are in register.

Because Photomerge is essentially a combination of Auto-Align Layers and Auto-Blend Layers, we've already discussed the options in the Photomerge dialog. The Layout options are the same as the ones in the Auto-Align Layers dialog, and the Blend Images Together check box applies Auto-Blend Layers. Unlike the Auto-Align Layers command, Photomerge converts the source files into a single layered file for you.

Auto-Align Layers (and, by extension, Photomerge) doesn't just align variations of a single scene or frames of a horizontal panorama. It's intelligent enough to find common edges along any sides of the selected images. For example, you can shoot a scene as a set of tiled images, eight across and eight down, and Photomerge can snap it all together, even if the images aren't perfectly straight. In Photoshop CS4 you can now assemble a 360-degree panorama. If you have Photoshop CS4 Extended, you can build a spherical panorama that you view from the inside, and after it's assembled you can use the 3D painting tools to retouch it.

Depth of Field Effects

Depth of field measures how much of an image is in focus, starting at the focus point and extending toward you and away from you. Smaller apertures and wide-angle views produce more depth of field. Larger apertures and telephoto views produce less depth of field, throwing foreground and background objects out of focus. When you need more depth of field than the lens produces, Photoshop can emulate extended depth of field.

TIP: If you see seams after resizing a document on which you ran Auto-Blend Layers, undo and choose Layer > Flatten Image before resizing.

Extending Depth of Field. In Photoshop CS4, you can use Auto-Blend Layers to extend the depth of field in an image (see **Figure 11-19**). This feature is sure to be a hit with macro photographers, who regularly battle narrow depth of field.

Start by taking photographs of the same subject that are identical except for the focusing distance; be sure your set of images covers the entire distance range you want in focus. Load each image into Photoshop as a separate layer, and apply Auto-Align Layers. Then choose Edit > Auto-Blend Layers, select both Stack Images and Seamless Tones and Colors (see Figure 11-17), and click OK. Photoshop automatically blends the parts of each layer that are in focus. After Photoshop generates the blended layers, if you have no further need for the images as separate layers you can save disk space by choosing Layer > Flatten Image.

Layer 1: Left bottle in focus

Layer 2: Right bottle in focus

Figure 11-19 Extending depth of field with Auto-Blend Layers

Layer 3: Center bottle in focus

All bottles in focus after applying Auto-Blend Layers

Restricting Depth of Field. The Lens Blur filter simulates narrow depth of field through selective blurring. You tell the filter how to narrow the depth of field using a *depth map*—a gradient, in an alpha channel or a mask (see **Figure 11-20**). This feature can simulate the effect of a tilt/shift lens.

1. In the layer mask or alpha channel where you want to store the depth map, use the Gradient tool to create a gradient, using black to mark the distance in focus and white to mark the distance you want completely out of focus.

2. In the Channels panel select the composite channel. Choose Filter > Blur > Lens Blur, and in the Depth Map section of the Lens Blur dialog, choose an alpha channel or layer mask from the Source pop-up menu.

3. Click the crosshairs to mark the point you want to be in focus. You can tune this by changing the Blur Focal Distance value.

4. If you'd like to increase the amount of blur in the out-of-focus areas, increase the Radius value in the Iris section.

5. Zoom in and compare the noisiness of the original image to the blurred areas. If the blur is too smooth, increase the Noise Amount value to try

TIP: If you don't need a graduated effect, just create a simple silhouette mask with white for the subject and choose that from the Source pop-up menu in the Lens Blur filter. Lens Blur will apply your blur settings to the black part of the mask.

to match the original image texture. If there's more color in the noise than in the original image, turn on the Monochromatic check box.

Figure 11-20 Restricting depth of field with the Lens Blur filter

The original image

Alpha channel for the blur effect

Alpha channel selected in the Lens Blur dialog and Radius set to increase blur

In the Iris section you model the lens characteristics you want to emulate—this is what visually distinguishes lens blur from the other synthetic blur effects such as Gaussian Blur. The quality of lens blur is affected by the Shape, Blade Curvature, and Rotation angle of the lens iris, and that's why those choices area available. If you don't know how to set these, leave them at the default settings.

The Specular Highlights section controls how bright a pixel is before it's treated as a specular highlight. The Brightness slider affects all levels above the level you set using the Threshold slider.

CONTENT-AWARE SCALING

If you've ever had to fit a photo into a layout that the photo wasn't composed for when it was shot, you've probably spent time trying various crops and maybe even some retouching tricks to get the content to fit. A new feature in Photoshop CS4 aims to solve that problem: content-aware scaling. Drawing from a recent breakthrough in imaging technology called *seam carving*, content-aware scaling attempts to distinguish unimportant background elements that can be spatially compressed from important content that should not be distorted. All you have to do is tell Photoshop how much to scale, and content-aware scaling does the rest.

To use content-aware scaling, start by selecting a pixel layer (to use layer groups, type layers, shape layers, or Smart Objects, you'll have to rasterize and merge them into one layer first). Choose Edit > Content-Aware Scale (Command-Option-Shift-C in Mac OS X or Ctrl-Alt-Shift-C in Windows) and drag any of the handles that appear (see **Figure 11-21**), or edit the scaling values in the Options bar. When you're done, press Return or Enter.

Content-aware scaling doesn't always correctly determine which parts should be preserved; if areas you want preserved become distorted, there are ways to protect them. If people are being distorted, try selecting the Protect Skin Tones button in the Options bar. Naturally, because that feature looks for flesh tones, the more skin there is visible the better it works. If you're trying to protect the proportions of fully clothed people or objects that aren't people at all, you have a second option: Before you apply content-aware scaling, isolate your content using an alpha channel, and then choose that alpha channel from the Protect pop-up menu in the Options bar.

If you use content-aware scaling, we recommend that you choose a high-resolution image and inspect the results closely. Although it does an amazing job, you may find that geometric shapes and patterns exhibit artifacts. It seems to work best when the background is more organic and slightly out of focus to help hide any artifacts.

TIP: As with the other transform commands, you can use content-aware scaling only on a layer that isn't a default Background layer. If you want to edit a Background layer, Option/Alt-double-click it to convert it to a regular layer. (Leave out the Option/Alt key to name the layer as you convert it.)

Figure 11-21 Content-aware scaling

It's impossible to use this image on a square CD case by cropping it. Content-aware scaling to the rescue!

With content-aware scaling enabled, resizing to a square scales the sky and grassy hill, but not the kite and people.

The Protect Skin Tones button at the right end of the Content-Aware Scale Options bar won't distort areas containing flesh tones. Of course, it works best with faces and when skin isn't totally hidden by clothing.

To ensure that the people aren't distorted during a particularly radical resize, we create an alpha channel for the critical content (below left) and choose the name of the alpha channel from the Options bar.

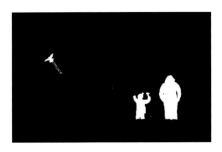 

This alpha channel isolates the content that we want to protect from distortion.

The alpha channel keeps the kite and people from being squished even as we scale down the image to almost half its original height.

VECTORS VS. PIXELS

So far, we've talked about pixel editing, because that's the reason Photoshop exists. But you can also create and edit vector-based paths, as you can in a drawing program like Adobe Illustrator CS4.

What good are vector paths and drawing tools in Photoshop? Vectors are infinitely modifiable, resolution independent, and can be converted to bit-mapped images at the drop of a hat. You can easily convert between paths and selections or use a path as a vector mask for a layer. If you're asked to silhouette an image using a clipping path, you have to use the path tools.

Strengths and Weaknesses. Curiously, both the primary strength and primary weakness of paths stem from the same attribute: Paths have no connection to the pixels below them; they live on a separate mathematical plane in Photoshop, forever floating above those bitmapped layers.

TIP: If you think you'll be drawing paths often, the best way to train is to use any of the many drawing tutorials designed for Adobe Illustrator. We can suggest *Real World Illustrator CS4* by Mordy Golding, and the *Adobe Illustrator CS4 Wow! Book* by Sharon Steuer, both from Peachpit Press.

The strength of this characteristic is that you can create, edit, and save paths without regard for the resolution of the image or even for the image itself. You can create a path in the shape of a logo (or better yet, import the path from Illustrator) and drop it into any image. You can then resize, rotate, scale, and reshape the path and it won't lose resolution. It will be locked into a resolution only when you *rasterize* it (convert it to pixels), print it, or export it to a pixel-only format.

The weakness of paths used as selections or masks is that they can't capture the subtlety and nuance found in most bitmapped images. A path can't, for instance, have any partially selected pixels or blurry parts; you can achieve only hard-edged selections (see **Figure 11-22**).

Figure 11-22 Paths vs. channels

The original image

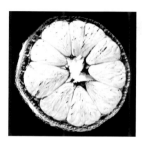

Selection masks can partially select pixels (here selecting only orange).

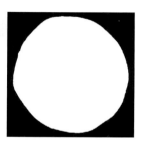

Paths are good at clean, sharp outlines, but they can't select image detail.

Creating and Editing Paths

TIP: To temporarily switch to the Direct Selection tool while using any pen tool or the Path Selection tool, hold down the Command (Mac OS X) or Ctrl (Windows) key.

If you've used an advanced drawing program such as Adobe Illustrator, you may be familiar with drawing and editing paths using the pen or shape tools; in Photoshop you find these in the Tools panel (see **Figure 11-23**). We tend to use only two or three of the pen tools, using modifier keys to get to the rest. The Paths panel (see **Figure 11-24**) displays all the paths in your document, along with tools for managing them.

In the same way that a channel has no visible effect on a document until you apply it as a selection or mask, a path doesn't necessarily have a visible effect on a document, though you may be able to see it. When you select a path in the Paths panel, you can see it in the document, but the path can't visibly change the document until you convert it to a selection, vector mask, or clipping path. Shapes and vector masks are paths that have a visible effect because they act as masks on a layer.

Figure 11-23 The pen tool group in the Tools panel

Pen Tool. The Pen tool (press P) is our primary tool for drawing paths, because it's the most precise. Draw straight-line paths by clicking (creating corner points) or curved paths by clicking and dragging (creating curve points). You can also easily access any of the other tools in the pen tool group. For instance, if you move the Pen tool over a point on a line, it automatically changes to the Delete Anchor Point tool. If you move it over a segment, it lets you add a point (click or click and drag). If you're forever adding or deleting points when you don't mean to, just turn off the Auto Add/Delete check box on the Options bar.

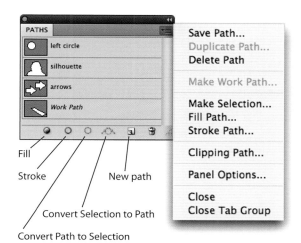

Figure 11-24 Paths panel buttons and panel menu

Fill

Stroke   New path

Convert Selection to Path

Convert Path to Selection

Freeform Pen tool. If you've got a steady hand and a sure heart—and a graphics tablet wouldn't hurt, either—you might prefer to draw paths with the Freeform Pen tool. When you release the mouse button, Photoshop converts your loose path to a smooth path full of corner, curve, and cusp points. (Exactly how closely Photoshop follows your lead is up to the Curve Fit setting on the Options bar.)

Selection Tools for Paths and Points. As in Illustrator and Adobe InDesign, Photoshop has both a Path Selection tool and a Direct Selection tool. You can press A (for *arrow*) to jump to the selection tool currently shown in the Tools panel, and then press Shift-A if you want the other selection tool. For example, you can select points on a curve with the Direct Selection tool by clicking on them or by dragging a marquee around them. To select all the points on a curve, click the curve with the Path Selection tool or Option-click (Mac OS X) or Alt-click (Windows) the path with the Direct Selection tool; you can also Command-Option-click (Mac OS X) or Ctrl-Alt-click (Windows) the Pen tool on a curve.

Once you've selected a point or a path, you can move it. As in most other programs, if you hold down the Shift key, Photoshop lets you move the points only in 90- or 45-degree angles. If you hold down the Option/Alt key when you click and drag, Photoshop moves a copy of the entire path.

Convert Point Tool. When you're working with the Pen tool, you can create a sharp corner by clicking or a rounded corner by dragging. When you have two round corners on either side of a corner point, that corner point

TIP: Like the Lasso tool, you can draw a straight line with the Free-form Pen tool by holding down the Option key (Mac OS X) or Alt key (Window) and lifting the mouse button. Then you can either click to connect the dots or release the Option/Alt key to return to free-form drawing.

is called a *cusp* point (see **Figure 11-25**). But what if you change your mind and want to make a corner into a curve, or a curve into a cusp?

Figure 11-25 Point types on a path

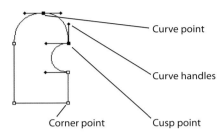

Curve point

Curve handles

Corner point

Cusp point

TIP: You can move selected paths or points one pixel at a time using the arrow keys—but only when the Pen or one of the selection tools is selected in the Tools panel. If you hold down the Shift key, the arrow keys move the path ten image pixels (not screen pixels). At 100 percent view, image pixels and screen pixels are the same thing, of course.

The Convert Point tool lets you add or remove curve *handles* (those levers that stick out from the sides of curve or cusp points). If you click once on a point that has curve handles, the curve handles disappear (they get sucked all the way into the point), and the point becomes a corner. If you click and drag with the Convert Point tool, you can pull those handles out of the point, making the corner a curve.

Similarly, you can make a cusp by clicking and dragging on one of the control handles on either side of the point. If you select the Pen tool, you can get the Convert Point tool by holding down the Option/Alt key.

Cusp Points. Many folks tell us that they make all points cusp points while drawing paths. Here's how: To create the first point of the path, just click and drag to set the angle of the first curve. All subsequent points on the path are created by clicking, dragging to set the angle of the previous curve, and then Option-dragging (Mac OS X) or Alt-dragging (Windows) from the point to set the launch angle of the next curve. Finally, to close the path (if you want it closed), Option/Alt-click if you want the final segment to be a straight line. If you want the final segment to be a curve, Option-drag (Mac OS X) or Alt-drag (Windows) the first point of the path. While it takes some getting used to and is a bit more work, this technique gives you much more control over the angle and curve of each segment in the path because each point is independent of the ones on either side.

TIP: As in Illustrator, you can drag a path segment with the Selection tool; you don't first have to select the points on the ends of the segment. If it's a curved segment, Photoshop adjusts the curve handles on either side of it automatically. If it's a straight-line segment (hence with no curve handles to adjust), Photoshop moves the points on either side of the segment.

Magnetic Pen Tool. Once the engineers at Adobe figured out how to make the Magnetic Lasso tool, it was a snap for them to add the functionality to the Pen tool as well. Thus, the Magnetic Pen tool was born. (Well, it's not really a separate tool; you get it by turning on the check box labeled Magnetic on the Options bar.) The Magnetic Lasso and the Magnetic Pen work so similarly that it's hardly worth discussing twice; instead go read that section in Chapter 9, "Making Selections." Their similarity extends to producing a result that you will almost certainly have to finesse; the magnetic tools are not known for their precision.

Paths vs. Shapes vs. Pixels. When you use the pen tools, you need to specify in the Options bar whether you want them to create a path or a vector shape. When you select one of the shape tools, you can choose path, vectors, or pixels (see **Figure 11-26**).

Connecting Paths. Use the Path Selection tool to select one of the path's endpoints, and switch to the Pen tool. If you want that point to be a cusp, Option-drag (Mac OS X) or Alt-drag (Windows) a handle out of the point. Finally, click and drag on the other path's endpoint. Alternatively, Option-drag (Mac OS X) or Alt-drag (Windows) to make it a cusp point.

TIP: To invert a vector mask or path, select the path by Command/Ctrl-clicking it with a shape tool or Option/Alt-clicking it with the Path Selection tool, then click on either the Add or Subtract button in the Options bar (if one doesn't invert the path, the other will).

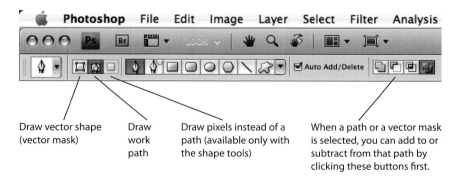

Draw vector shape (vector mask)

Draw work path

Draw pixels instead of a path (available only with the shape tools)

When a path or a vector mask is selected, you can add to or subtract from that path by clicking these buttons first.

Figure 11-26 The Options bar for the path and shape tools

Paths to Selections

Once you have a path, you can convert it into a selection, rasterize it (turn it into pixels), or fill it with a color or adjustment. Let's look at converting to a selection first. When a path is selected in the Paths panel, you can convert it into a selection in one of four ways:

- Select Make Selection from the Paths panel menu (or drag the path's thumbnail on top of this button).

- Click the Convert Path to Selection button (see Figure 11-24).

- Command-click (Mac OS X) or Ctrl-click (Windows) on the path's thumbnail in the Paths panel.

TIP: When a painting tool is selected in the Tools panel and a path is selected, pressing Enter strokes the path with that tool, using the current brush size and blending mode.

TIP: When a path is selected in the Paths panel or a vector mask is selected in the Layers panel, Photoshop displays the path as a gray line. When you have a nonpainting tool selected in the Tools panel (such as a selection tool or the Move tool), you can deselect and hide the path by pressing the Enter key.

- Press Command-Enter (Mac OS X) or Ctrl-Enter (Windows).

If you hold down the Option key (Mac OS X) or Alt key (Windows) while dragging a path on top of, or clicking on, the Convert Path to Selection button, Photoshop displays the Make Selection dialog. This dialog lets you add, subtract, or intersect selections with selections you've already made (if there is no selection, these options are grayed out). It also lets you feather and anti-alias the selections. The default for selections (if you don't go in and change this dialog) is to include anti-aliasing but not feathering.

Alternatively, you can use these keyboard shortcuts instead of the Make Selection dialog to add, subtract, or intersect paths:

- Command-Shift-Enter (Mac OS X) or Ctrl-Shift-Enter (Windows) adds the path's selection to the current selection (if there is one).

- Command-Option-Enter (Mac OS X or Ctrl-Alt-Enter (Windows) subtracts the selection.

- Command-Shift-Option-Enter (Mac OS X) or Ctrl-Shift-Alt-Enter (Windows) intersects the two selections.

Each of these works when clicking on the Make Selection icon or dragging the thumbnail over the icon, too, but the Enter key is faster.

Selections to Paths

TIP: When you're drawing paths around objects to silhouette them in Photoshop, make sure you draw the path very slightly inside the object's border—perhaps one or two pixels inside the edge. This usually avoids most of the spillover from the background color. If spillover is a significant problem with an image, you should be thinking about building a Photoshop composite instead of using a clipping path.

To turn a selection into a path, choose Make Work Path from the Paths panel menu. When you ask Photoshop to do this, you're basically asking it to turn a soft-edged selection into a hard-edged one. Therefore, the program has to make some decisions about where the edges of the selection are.

Fortunately, you can help Photoshop with this, using the Tolerance field in the Make Work Path dialog. The higher the value you enter, the shabbier the path's representation of the original selection. Values above 2 or 3 typically make nice abstract designs but aren't otherwise very useful.

There's one more way to convert a selection into a new path: Click on the New Path icon in the Paths panel. Note that this uses whatever Tolerance value you last specified in the Make Work Path dialog, unless you hold down the Option (Mac OS X) or Alt (Windows) key while clicking on the icon, in which case it brings up the dialog.

Rasterizing Paths

As we said earlier, rasterizing is the process of turning a vector object into pixels. Photoshop lets you rasterize paths in two ways: You can fill the path area and you can stroke the path.

Filling. To fill the path area with the foreground color, drag the path's thumbnail to the Fill Path icon or click on the Fill Path icon in the Paths panel. Better yet, Option-click (Mac OS X) or Alt-click (Windows) the icon, and the Fill Path dialog appears (this is the same dialog you get if you choose Fill Path from the Paths panel menu). The dialog gives you options for fill color, opacity, mode, and so on.

Stroking. Stroking the path works just the same as filling: You can drag the path's thumbnail to the Stroke Path button or click on the Stroke Path button in the Paths panel. You can change the tool it uses to stroke by Option-clicking (Mac OS X) or Alt-clicking (Windows) the Stroke Path icon, or select Stroke Path from the Paths panel menu.

TIP: If you make a selection before filling or stroking a path, Photoshop fills or strokes only within that selection. This trips up more than one advanced user, but if you're aware of the feature, it can really come in handy.

Making a Clipping Path

When you need to separate a subject from a background so that the background is invisible in InDesign or QuarkXPress, using layer transparency or alpha channels is preferred because they can be soft-edged, so that drop shadows and hair can blend smoothly into the background. However, if you're asked to do this using the old method, a clipping path (see **Figure 11-27**), here's how you'd do that.

First, draw a path around the subject; use any vector tool or create a selection and convert it to a path. Next you'll use the Paths panel to set up any path in the document as a clipping path.

Figure 11-27 The effect of a clipping path

1. Choose Clipping Path from the Paths panel menu.

2. Select the path that you want as a clipping path (see **Figure 11-28**).

3. If needed, enter a flatness value (see the tip at left).

4. Click OK. The name of the path (in the Paths panel) should now be in outline style, indicating that it's a clipping path.

5. Save the image as a TIFF or EPS file, and then import it into your page-layout program of choice.

Figure 11-28 Setting up a clipping path

Setting a flatness value for the clipping path

In the Paths panel, the designated clipping path appears in outline type.

TIP: If a clipping path prints slowly or causes a PostScript "limitcheck" printing error, raise the PostScript flatness value in the Clipping Path dialog. Try a value between 3 and 5; at higher values curves may start to look like corners.

Remember that clipping paths don't really delete the data they hide; the entire image gets sent to the printer, along with the instructions for clipping it down.

If you save more than one path in the file, InDesign and XPress can use these alternate paths. You can control the clipping path behavior of TIFFs in QuarkXPress on the Clipping tab of the Modify dialog. In InDesign, select Object > Clipping Path. This gives you the flexibility of saving one image with different paths for different subjects; in the page-layout program you simply copy the image and pick different clipping paths.

Working with Paths

The shape tools are just a way to create a vector mask quickly. Drawing something with a shape tool is the same thing as creating a Solid Color adjustment layer, adding a vector mask, and drawing on it. What we say about vector masks also applies to shapes.

Blending Vector Graphics and a Layout. How do those folks at *Sports Illustrated* do those covers anyway? You know the ones: a photo of some sports star partially over and partially under the title of the magazine, where the pixels have to anti-alias into the text. In Photoshop, you can put the text on one layer over the image layer. Then select the portion of the image that you want to appear over the type, make it a new layer (press Command-J on a Mac or Ctrl-J in Windows) and move it in above the type layer in the Layers panel (see **Figure 11-29**).

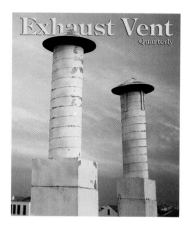

This is our goal: Vector text behind the tower, but in front of the sky.

We select the area that we want in front of the type, and press Command/Ctrl-J to convert the selection into its own layer. (All other layers are hidden here.)

In the Layers panel, we drag the new layer (Layer 1) in front of everything else, and we also add a layer mask to it.

Finally, we paint white and black in the new layer's mask to hide or reveal areas as needed.

Figure 11-29 Weaving vector and pixel graphics

Vector Masks. We discussed these in Chapter 8, "The Digital Darkroom." In Photoshop CS4, the Masks panel provides additional access to vector masks. As soon as you click the Vector Mask button in the Masks panel, the next path you draw becomes a vector mask revealing underlying layers.

➡ **TIP:** There are two different ways to import vector files into Photoshop, and they give you different options. If you use the File > Open command, you can specify the file's resolution and dimensions and Photoshop rasterizes it upon import. If you use the File > Place command, you can scale and rotate the image using handles, then press Return or Enter to rasterize it.

Adding and Subtracting Paths. If you use a shape tool while a vector mask is selected in the Paths panel (if it's visible on screen), Photoshop adds your shape to that vector mask. Before you draw the shape, you can tell the program how you want this new path to interact with the path that's already there by clicking on the Add, Subtract, Intersect, or Exclude Intersection button in the Options bar (see Figure 11-26). If you forget to select one, don't fret: Command-click (Mac OS X) or Ctrl-Click (Windows) with the shape tool on the shape you just drew (to select all its points), and *then* click the button in the Options bar.

Maintaining Vectors in Other Programs. If you've used vector masks and you want to retain those sharp edges when you print your image from your page-layout application, you should probably save your file as either a Photoshop PDF or an EPS file. If you are using a spot color, use the DCS 2.0 format. Note that while the EPS format saves and prints the layers and clipping paths properly, when you reopen your EPS file in Photoshop, it automatically gets flattened. Very annoying. So, make sure you save the EPS as a copy, and archive your layered Photoshop file just in case you need to go back to edit it. PDF files don't have this problem.

Smart Objects

➡ **TIP:** We find it easier to use Smart Object menu items using the context menu for a Smart Object in the Layers panel, instead of hunting for them in the Layer > Smart Objects submenu. Be sure to right-click or Ctrl-click (Mac OS X) on the layer name, not the thumbnail, or you won't see all of the Smart Object commands.

Simpler graphics programs (and most earlier versions of Photoshop) always rasterized placed or pasted graphics at the resolution of the current document—they were converted to pixels. If the original image had more pixels before it was imported and you scaled up the image, you'd find that many of the original pixels were gone, never to return.

Photoshop is smarter than that. You can import a file as a *Smart Object* layer, which is a layer with special abilities. You can transform it (moving, scaling, warping, skewing, and so on) and it will maintain all of its original quality and resolution, even if you scale it down to 10 pixels tall and back up to 1000 pixels tall. The key is that a Smart Object contains the complete imported file, and doesn't actually rasterize it to a specific resolution until you output or flatten the Photoshop document. We think of this as *deferred rendering*, because rendering takes place when you commit to a specific resolution. Smart Objects are also the basis for the Smart Filters feature.

Creating a Smart Object. You can make a Smart Object in several ways:

- In Photoshop, choose File > Open as Smart Object. Do this when you want to use a file as a Smart Object without importing it into another existing document. You can also select an image in Adobe Bridge, and then choose File > Place > In Photoshop.

- In a Photoshop document, choose File > Place and select an external file—either a vector file (such as a PDF, EPS, or AI) or an image file (including TIFF, JPEG, or a raw digital camera file). Use this technique when you want to add a file as a Smart Object to the Photoshop document you're already working on.

- Paste an object from Adobe Illustrator. Photoshop offers you the option to automatically convert the vector data to a Smart Object (see **Figure 11-30**).

TIP: In addition to being resolution independent, vector masks are useful because they are so easy to edit. For example, if you use a vector shape for a button on a Web page, you can resize it at any time without worrying about unsightly scaling artifacts.

Figure 11-30 Pasting Illustrator paths

- Select one or more layers in the Layers panel, and then choose Layer > Smart Objects > Convert to Smart Object. In the Layers panel, the selected layers become one layer with a Smart Object badge. That Smart Object layer is actually a new Photoshop document containing the selected layers, embedded into the current document—you'll see this additional document when you edit the Smart Object.

Smart Object layers look and act the same as normal layers in the Layers panel, with one small difference: A small badge appears in the corner of the Smart Object layer's preview thumbnail (see **Figure 11-31**).

When you paste an Illustrator vector graphic, the layer is named Vector Smart Object.

Smart Object thumbnails have a small badge in the bottom right corner of the thumbnail.

Figure 11-31 Smart Objects in the Layers panel

TIP: If you import a raw digital camera file as a Smart Object, you can always edit the raw conversion by double-clicking the Smart Object. If you convert a raw file to a Photoshop document normally, the conversion settings are permanent and irreversible.

TIP: When you duplicate a Smart Object layer in the Layers panel or using the Layer > New Layer via Copy command, the copy actually points back to the same embedded document. If you edit the Smart Object, all instances update—great for maintaining batch layouts such as a page full of identical business cards. Note that this behavior doesn't happen if you choose the Layer > Smart Object > New Smart Object via Copy command.

Editing Smart Objects. Once you create a Smart Object layer, you can transform it as you would any other layer (use the Move tool to drag it around, use Free Transform to scale or skew it, and so on). You can also adjust its blending mode, opacity, or layer style in the Layers panel. However, if you double-click on the layer's preview thumbnail in the panel (or take the long way and choose Edit Contents from the Smart Objects submenu), Photoshop opens the Smart Object in its own window, ready for you to edit. If it was a raw image, Photoshop launches Camera Raw (see Chapter 5, "Building a Digital Workflow"). Or, if it's vector data from Illustrator, Photoshop will launch Illustrator and open the file there.

Unlike placed files in layout programs, files placed in Photoshop do not link back to the original file you placed from disk, because Photoshop embeds all imported files into the Photoshop document itself. When you edit a Smart Object, Photoshop opens a temporary, invisible file. After you make edits to the file, save it and close it. (And if necessary, switch back to Photoshop.) Like magic, you'll see the Smart Object update as Photoshop replaces the embedded Smart Object data with the new file.

Replacing Smart Objects. You can replace a Smart Object with another Smart Object by choosing Replace Contents from the Smart Objects submenu, then choosing the new file you want. For instance, you might want to switch one image with another. When you replace an image, any scaling, warping, or effects you applied to the first image are maintained.

Exporting Smart Objects. Because a Smart Object is just a file embedded in your Photoshop document, you can unembed it—saving it to disk as a separate file. To do this, select the Smart Object layer in the Layers panel, then choose Layer > Smart Objects > Export Contents. You don't have a lot of control over the format of the export: Image Smart Objects are saved as PSB files (Photoshop Large Document; yes, we know the name doesn't match the extension), and vector objects are saved as PDF files.

Rasterizing Smart Objects. When Photoshop embeds a Smart Object in your document, the file size grows accordingly. That is, if you place a Camera Raw file, your document (and the RAM it needs) grows by the size of the raw image data, plus the normal amount the file would grow when you add an additional layer. If you'll no longer need to edit the Smart Object data, you might consider converting it to a normal layer (discarding the embedded data) at its current size, resolution, and so on. To do this, choose

Layer > Smart Objects > Convert to Layer. Alternately, you can choose Layer > Rasterize > Smart Object.

THE NONDESTRUCTIVE WORKFLOW

At this point in the book, you've probably noticed that we are the kind of people who like to work nondestructively whenever possible, using tools like adjustment layers and masks to keep our options open as long as possible. With Smart Filters and the enhancements to Smart Objects, particularly when it comes to raw camera images, Photoshop makes it possible to keep a wide range of edits in a reversible state, so that you can back out of them at any time. We've alluded to bits and pieces of this workflow in various parts of the book, but we thought we should put it all together here for you. Here are all of the typical image-editing steps using the nondestructive editing features in Photoshop CS4 (see **Figure 11-32**).

Using these techniques, you can always strip away every last edit and return to the original base image, or adjust the intensity of any edit whenever you like. It's an astounding degree of flexibility, but again, pushing nondestructive editing this far can eat up your hard drive space and RAM in a hurry. To mitigate this, you can head for a middle ground by rasterizing some layers into pixels when you're happy with them.

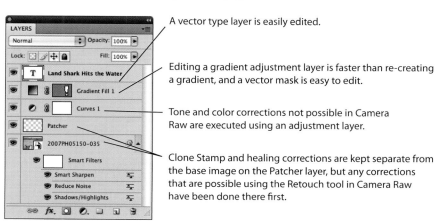

A vector type layer is easily edited.

Editing a gradient adjustment layer is faster than re-creating a gradient, and a vector mask is easy to edit.

Tone and color corrections not possible in Camera Raw are executed using an adjustment layer.

Clone Stamp and healing corrections are kept separate from the base image on the Patcher layer, but any corrections that are possible using the Retouch tool in Camera Raw have been done there first.

Figure 11-32
A Photoshop document built nondestructively

The base image is a Camera Raw Smart Object; double-click to edit the raw file's conversion settings. Shadows/Highlights, noise reduction, and sharpening are implemented as editable Smart Filters (or they can be applied in Camera Raw). All of these features can be edited at any time in the future.

Text

In Photoshop, the text tools are used far more by graphic designers than by photographers. Many photographers add text only as a watermark, such as a copyright notice or Web site URL. When you use the Horizontal Type or Vertical Type tool, the type is created on its own layer so that you can edit the text later without altering the underlying image. (Text layers are merged with other layers whenever you flatten the document, including exporting to formats that don't support layers, such as JPEG.)

If you want to add a lot of text to a document, it's usually better to bring the Photoshop document into a page-layout program such as InDesign. To save text as part of the Photoshop document, we have a few tips.

Making Text Blocks. You can add new type by clicking a type tool on an image; you can then start entering text. This is called *point type* because the text alignment is relative to the point you clicked. If you're going to type more than one line of text, the click-and-type procedure is a pain because you have to manually break lines by pressing Return or Enter. Instead of clicking, drag out a rectangular text frame with a type tool; this is called *paragraph type*. Then, when you enter text longer than a line, Photoshop automatically wraps it to fit the frame, and you can always reshape the frame by dragging its corner or edge handles, or rotate the text block by dragging outside of the frame.

You can change paragraph type to point type (and vice versa) by making sure no text or text blocks are selected (clicking on the text layer in the Layers panel will do this), then choosing Convert to Point Text or Convert to Paragraph Text from the Layer > Type submenu. You can also select these commands from the context-sensitive menu you get when right-clicking or Ctrl-clicking (Mac OS X) with a type tool.

When you're done creating or editing text, you can apply text changes and deselect the text frame by pressing Command-Return (Mac OS X) or Ctrl-Enter on the main keyboard (Windows), or press Enter on the numeric keypad. If you press Return (Mac OS X) or Enter above the Shift key (Windows), you'll type a return character instead. If you want to discard your latest text editing changes, press Esc instead.

Editing Type Layers. Once you have created some text on a type layer, there are several ways to edit it:

TIP: Keep your eye on the bottom right corner handle of a text block. When there's too much text to fit the frame, Photoshop places a little + sign there.

TIP: If you want to create a new text block near or on top of another bit of text, you might have trouble because Photoshop will think you're trying to select the existing text. No problem: Shift-click or Shift-drag with any type tool to force Photoshop to create a new text layer.

- Double-click the type layer's thumbnail icon in the Layers panel. (Double-clicking on the name lets you edit the layer name, and double-clicking outside the layer name opens the Layer Style dialog.)

- Click the text with a type tool. You know your cursor is in the right place when the tool's cursor changes to an I-beam. However, if you click in the wrong place, Photoshop will create a new type layer; in this case, press the Esc key to cancel the new layer.

- When you have both a type tool selected in the Tools panel and a type layer selected in the Layers panel, right click or Ctrl-click (Windows) and then choose Edit Type from the context menu.

TIP: Do you need a text block that is exactly 144 points wide? No problem: Just Option-click (Mac OS X) or Alt-click (Windows) with any type tool, and a dialog will appear in which you can enter an exact size.

As long as one or more type layers are selected in the Layers panel and a type tool is selected, you can use the Options bar, the Character panel, or the Paragraph panel (see **Figure 11-33**) to apply formatting to the entire text block, without having to select the text characters themselves.

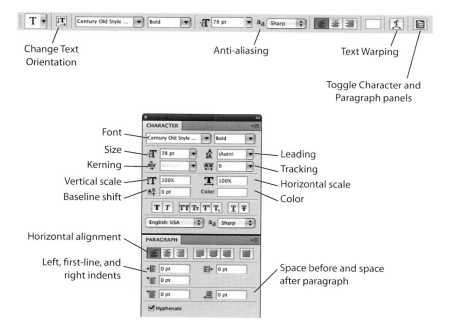

Figure 11-33
Formatting text

Text (Usually) Gets Rasterized. If you want high-resolution text, be careful about the file format you use when saving. In many cases (such as if you save as TIFF), the text gets rasterized—if you're working with a 225 ppi image, any text you add to that image in Photoshop is similarly 225 ppi.

That's high enough for most images, but it looks crummy for hard-edged type. (See Chapter 12, "Image Storage and Output," for more information about saving files with text layers.)

Using Text as a Mask. There are two tools in the Tools panel that create text masks rather than text (that is, as you type, Photoshop makes a selection in the shape of text rather than actual text). However, when it comes to making selections in the shape of text, we would rather create a normal type layer and then Command-click (Mac OS X) or Ctrl-click (Windows) on it in the Layers panel. By actually creating a type layer, we can preview it in the image before clicking OK, we can edit the text later, or we can use the type someplace else (even in another image). If we had simply used a type mask tool, we'd have nothing but an ephemeral group of marching ants.

Rendering Type Layers. Because text layers are vector-based (like shapes, you can't paint or run filters on them or do anything else that relies on pixel editing. If you need to do something like that, you have to render them (turn them into pixels) by selecting Layers > Type > Rasterize. For maximum quality, it's best to apply all the transformations (rotating, scaling, positioning, skewing) and layer effects (drop shadows and so on) that you need before rendering the type layer.

Text on a Path. Need to run text along a path? Simply draw a path with the Pen tool (see "Creating and Editing Paths," earlier in this chapter) and then click on it with a type tool. Note that a type tool's cursor changes when it's on top of a path, and when you click and then start typing, the text begins from the point you clicked. To adjust the starting and ending points for the text on the path, switch to the Path Selection tool (press A); as you hover the cursor over the start point or endpoint, the cursor changes to a vertical line with a thick black arrow. If you click and drag with this cursor, you adjust where the text begins or ends on the line.

The direction in which you draw your path determines how Photoshop draws the text. If you draw a path from left to right, the text flows on the top of the line; if you draw from right to left, the text flows from right to left—upside down. To flip the text over, use the Path Selection tool and drag the beginning or ending point to the other side of the line.

TIP: Another way to use text as a mask is to set up a clipping mask, as we demonstrated in Chapter 8.

TIP: There are two ways to scale a selected text frame. If you drag the corner handles while a text cursor is flashing inside the frame, you rewrap the text. If you drag the corner handles when a type tool is not active, you stretch the text itself.

Filters and Effects

Sure, you can paint and retouch and composite within Photoshop, but you know as well as we do that the most fun comes from playing with filters. When you're up against a deadline for a picky client, however, productivity with filters becomes more important than fun. Here are some techniques we've found to be useful.

Float Before Filtering. One's natural inclination is to make a selection, then choose a filter from one of the Filter submenus. We suggest adding a step: copy the selection to a new layer first (press Command-J in Mac OS X or Ctrl-J in Windows). Doing so gives you much more flexibility in how the filter is applied. For instance, once the filter is applied on the new layer, you can move it, change its blending mode, run an additional filter, soften the effect by lowering the layer's opacity, and so on. Best of all, you don't damage your original pixels until you're sure you've got the effect exactly right. If you don't like what you've done, you can undo, or just delete the entire layer. Similarly, if you're going to run a filter on a whole layer, consider duplicating the layer first. It's safer and much more flexible.

Filter Shortcuts. Like many other features of Photoshop, you can speed your work with keyboard shortcuts. You can tell Photoshop to run a filter again by pressing Command-F (Mac OS X) or Ctrl-F (Windows). However, this doesn't let you change the dialog settings. Pressing Command-Option-F (Mac OS X) or Ctrl-Alt-F (Windows) opens the dialog for the last filter you ran so you can change the settings.

Fading Filter Effects. Most folks figure that once they run a filter, the choice is to either move forward or select Undo. But the Fade feature (in the Edit menu) allows you to take a middle path by reducing the opacity of a filter, or even changing the blending mode, immediately after running it. (As soon as you do anything else—even make a selection—the Fade feature is no longer available.) You can get to the Fade dialog quickly by pressing Command-Shift-F (Mac OS X) or Ctrl-Shift-F (Windows).

The Fade feature works not only with filters, but also with any of the features in the Adjustments submenu (under the Image menu) and almost every brushstroke. For example, you can run Hue/Saturation on an image, then reduce the intensity of the effect with Fade. However, we use this technique much less than we used to, because adjustment layers are more powerful (see Chapter 8, "The Digital Darkroom").

TIP: Katrin Eismann taught us that running a filter on a layer mask can produce cool effects. Try running filters on a layer mask filled with white, black, or 50 percent gray.

Build Textures on Neutral Layers. Instead of burning filter effects directly into an image, you can filter a neutral-colored layer. Using filters in conjunction with neutral layers gives you much more freedom to change your mind later. When you choose Layer > New Layer or Option-click (Mac OS X) or Alt-click (Windows) the Create a New Layer button in the Layers panel, many blending modes enable the "Fill with neutral color" check box. For instance, if you set the layer to Screen mode, the check box says "Fill with Screen-neutral color (black)." The exact wording of that check box changes depending on the mode you select.

Now, when you apply a filter to that layer, the parts that get changed are no longer neutral. They change the appearance of the pixels below (see **Figure 11-34**). Of course, this primarily works with filters that add texture to an image, such as the Texturizer filter. It typically won't have any effect at all with the Distort filter or an artistic filter.

Figure 11-34 Filtering a neutral-colored layer

Original image

Texturizer filter applied to a neutral layer

Background image and neutral layer visible at the same time

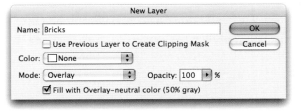

The "Fill with neutral color" check box appears for blending modes that have a neutral color.

You can now play with the filter without affecting the actual image by taking advantage of the neutral color. If you want to make a texture less prominent, paint with the neutral color on the neutral-colored layer. If the neutral color is 50 percent gray, anywhere you paint using that color will remove the texture. For example, you could paint the neutral color with a brush set to 10 percent to gradually fade a texture in some areas of a image. You can also try out different filters by running them on your neutral-colored layer, and again, the original underlying image is never disturbed. You can combine this technique with layer masks, depending on the effect you need.

Smart Filters

Smart Filters represent a powerful, nondestructive way to use filters. Like many of the newer features in Photoshop, Smart Filters help you keep your options open, because they make it possible for you to change filter settings at any time in the future, even if you close and reopen the document. Not even the History panel can do that.

We covered Smart Filters pretty extensively back in "Sharpening with Smart Filters" in Chapter 10, "Sharpness, Detail, and Noise Reduction." As we mentioned back there, because Smart Filters are based on Smart Objects, they can dramatically increase the file size and RAM requirements of a Photoshop document, and can also slow it down. Despite that, it's nice to have Smart Filters as an option when you need them.

Before you can apply a Smart Filter to a layer, the layer must be a Smart Object. If you placed or opened a graphic as a Smart Object, you've already got that covered. If you intend to apply Smart Filters before you even get a graphic into Photoshop, remember that there are now more ways to import graphics as Smart Objects, such as selecting a file and choosing File > Place > In Photoshop (when in Bridge), or clicking the Open as Object button in Camera Raw 4 (if you don't see it, press Shift).

If a layer isn't already a Smart Object, you don't have to navigate the Layer menu to turn it into one. Just choose Filter > Convert for Smart Filters, which is simply another way to convert a layer to a Smart Object.

Once a layer is a Smart Object, you'll notice that many commands on the Filter menu are not available for Smart Objects. However, choosing any command on the Filter menu that's available applies that command as a Smart Filter. There are actually a couple more important commands that you can use as Smart Filters that are not on the Filter menu: Image > Adjust > Shadows/Highlights and some of the commands on the Edit > Transform submenu. These are commands that users have wanted to be

TIP: When you transform a Smart Object using the Edit menu, it doesn't show up in the Layers panel, but the next time you choose the same transform command, you'll be able to edit the transformation settings you last applied to that layer.

able to use in a nondestructive way, but that aren't practical or possible to implement as adjustment layers. Smart Filters have given Photoshop a way to use these important commands nondestructively (see **Figure 11-35**).

You can create Smart Objects inside Smart Objects if you really need to, but nesting Smart Objects can really accelerate file bloat.

Figure 11-35 Smart Filters in the Layers panel

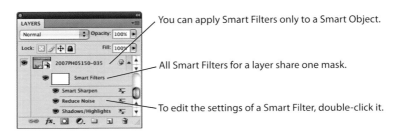

You can apply Smart Filters only to a Smart Object.

All Smart Filters for a layer share one mask.

To edit the settings of a Smart Filter, double-click it.

Actions and Scripting

The trick to being really productive and efficient with computer technology is to be lazy. Yes, it's a paradox, but it's true; the lazier you are, the more likely you are to find the really efficient ways of doing things so you can get out of work faster and go to the beach.

Photoshop offers four automation features: actions, Automate, Variables, and scripting. Actions live in the Actions panel and let you repeat a series of steps, similar to the macros you may have used in office programs. Photoshop ships with a number of premade actions, and you can easily build your own (we'll show you how). Automate refers to the built-in tools in the File > Automate submenu such as Batch and Photomerge; we've chosen to cover them where they apply. Variables provide a way to create a template image that changes depending on data imported from a spreadsheet or a database; because they're used primarily in Web design, we don't cover them in this book. Scripting automates Photoshop from behind the scenes using AppleScript, JavaScript, or Visual Basic. We'll look at aspects of actions and scripting that we haven't yet covered.

Actions

In Chapter 5, we discussed some of the basics of building actions—particularly actions that help in the processing of raw files. But Photoshop also comes with a number of premade actions that are not only useful but educational, because you can look at them to see how they produce their magic. (You can load additional sets of actions by selecting Load Actions from the Actions panel menu, or by choosing the presets that appear at the bottom the panel menu.)

The key is that you can make an action only for something you can do blindly, with no feedback from the program, and with little or no brain activity. For example, you can't record an action that says, "If the pixels in the upper left corner of the image are sort of reddish, then do such-and-such." Photoshop would have to be able to see and respond. No can do.

However, you can easily create an action that runs a particular set of Curves, adds a text layer, adds a layer effect, sharpens the background layer, and so on, because all these things are methodical.

Action Limitations. Before you get too heady with your newfound actions power, you should know that Photoshop doesn't let you record everything you might want. Although you can record blending modes, opacity, shapes, brush selections, and even pixel selections, you still cannot record brush-strokes (such those made with the Brush, Airbrush, and Clone Stamp tools), zooms, window switching, and scrolls. And there are many features that aren't necessarily recordable but that you can force into an action (see "Editing Actions," later in this chapter). Last but not least, the whole Actions mechanism has a logic unto itself. If an operation isn't recordable by keyboard shortcut, it may be recordable by choosing the menu command instead, or vice versa.

Planning Your Actions

Besides the limits of what you can and cannot record in the Actions panel, there are a few more things to keep in mind when planning actions.

Difficulty. While recording and playing simple actions (those with only two or three steps) may be easy, trying to build complicated actions can be damaging to your head (and the wall you're banging it against).

TIP: You can export all the actions visible in the Actions panel as a text file that you can open in a word processor. This is a great way to study how someone else's actions are put together. To perform the export, select any action set in the Actions panel, and then hold down Command and Option (Mac OS X) or Ctrl and Alt (Windows) as you select Save Action from the Actions panel menu.

Modularity. Rather than trying to make one big action that does everything you want, break it down into smaller steps that you can debug individually and then chain together to reuse in more complex actions.

Think It Through. You should always think the action through completely before you start recording it. You might even write down each step on paper, and then record it after you're pretty sure everything will work out the way you want.

Generic Actions. Try to make your actions as generic as possible, because there are many specifics that can trip up an action and result in an error. Actions should be able to run on any image at any time. There are a number of things to think about when making your actions generic. The following list is a good place to start:

- Never assume image mode. The image may be in RGB, CMYK, Grayscale, or even Indexed Color mode. This is very important when running filters, because some filters don't run in certain modes. You may want to add a step that converts to your intended mode.

- Don't assume the image has layers (or doesn't have layers). Also, don't assume that if the image does have layers, the Background layer is selected (or even that there is a layer called Background). If you need the lowest layer selected, press Option-Shift-[(Mac OS X) or Alt-Shift-[(Windows). You may want to add a step that flattens an image.

- Avoid using commands that pick layers by name, unless the action creates and names the layer or you are certain the files will always contain a particular name. For example, if you record clicking on a layer in the Layers panel, Photoshop records the click by layer name, not position. Instead, record pressing Option-[or Option-] (Mac OS X) or Alt-[or Alt-] (Windows) to target the next layer down or the next layer up, respectively. Command-[and Command-] (Mac OS X) or Ctrl-[and Ctrl-] (Windows) move layers up or down, respectively.

- If you're saving and loading channels, you'll almost certainly have to name the channels. Make sure you give them names that are unlikely to already be present in the image. *Do* name them, though, rather than leaving them set to the default names like "#4". If a document has two channels with the same name when you run an action, Photoshop always uses the first channel with that name.

Alternatively, you can provide the user with a message at the beginning of the action noting what kind of image is required (as well as other requirements, such as "needs text on a layer" or "must have something selected"). This is a good idea even if you're the only one using your actions, because (believe us) after you've made a bunch of actions, you'll forget which action requires what (see "Talk to Your Users," later in this section).

Cleanup. It's a good idea to make your actions clean up after themselves. In other words, if your action creates three extra channels along the way to building some other cool effect, the action should also probably delete them before ending so that they don't cause confusion or trip up another action.

TIP: When you run an action for the first time, run it on a folder of test files. There's nothing worse than ruining a folder of original images because of a glitch in an untested action. Don't run an action on production files until you've tested and debugged it.

Action Basics

Making an action is pretty straightforward:

1. Open the Actions panel (see **Figure 11-36**).

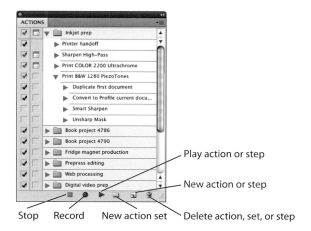

Stop Record New action set Delete action, set, or step

Play action or step

New action or step

Figure 11-36 The Actions panel

2. Click the New Action button (or select New Action from the Action panel menu). Give the action a name (and a keyboard shortcut, if you want). If you have more than one set (see "Sets," later in this section), choose which set this new action will be part of. When you click OK, Adobe Photoshop begins recording automatically.

3. Perform the steps that you want the action to do.

4. Click the Stop button in the Actions panel (or select Stop Recording from the Actions panel menu).

TIP: You can change the Actions panel into a panel full of buttons by choosing Button Mode in the panel menu. When it's in Button mode, you have to click only once on a button to run it. Switch out of Button mode to create new actions or edit existing ones.

TIP: Some steps cannot be rerecorded. For instance, a step that sets the foreground color to red should be able to change so that it sets it to blue, but it can't. Instead, you have to record a new step, then delete the original.

Then, to run the action, select the action's thumbnail in the Actions panel and click the Run button. Better yet, just Command-double-click (Mac OS X) or Ctrl-double-click (Windows) on the action. If the action is relatively simple, it may perform perfectly the first time. But in most of the actions we make, we find that something goes wrong somewhere along the line, usually due to our performing a step that Photoshop can't record into an action (see "Troubleshooting Actions," later in this section).

Save Your Work First. If you run an action and then decide that you don't like what it did, you're in trouble, because you cannot undo a full action, only the last step of an action. If the action used only a few steps, you might be able to use the History panel to return to a state before you ran the action, but this isn't always possible either, particularly if you ran the action as a batch process on multiple files. To guarantee an undo option, we're in the habit of saving a snapshot of our document in the History panel before running any action. That way, if something goes wrong or we don't like the effect, we can revert back to this snapshot. Another option is simply to save your document first, and then use the Revert command (in the File menu) to undo the action. Of course, neither of these techniques works with actions that save and close the file—we recommend always making actions that use Save As rather than saving over the original.

Sets. Photoshop lets you create sets of actions, a godsend to anyone who works with dozens of actions. Sets are pretty self-explanatory.

- To create a new action set, choose New Set from the Actions panel menu (or click the New Set button in the panel). You can delete a set by selecting it and choosing Delete from the same panel menu, or by clicking the Delete button in the panel.

- To move actions between sets, drag them.

- To rename a set, double-click its thumbnail in the Actions panel.

- To show or hide the actions within a set, click the triangle to the left of the set's name.

- You can also save sets (see "Saving Actions," later in this section).

- To play all the actions in a set (in order), select the set and click the Play button in the Actions panel.

Editing Actions. Once you've built an action, you can edit it (in fact, you'll almost certainly want to edit it unless it worked perfectly the first time). If you want to record additional steps somewhere in the middle of the action (or at the end of the action), select a step in the action and click the Record button. When you're done recording, click the Stop button. All the new actions fall after the step you first selected.

If you want to add a step that cannot be recorded for some reason (perhaps it's an item on the View menu), you can select Insert Menu Item from the Actions panel menu. This lets you choose any one feature from a menu, and then inserts it into the action (after the currently selected step).

To change the parameters of a step, double-click on it in the Actions panel. For example, if a step applies a curve to the image (using the Curves dialog), but you want to change the curve, double-click on the step and choose a different curve. Note that when you do this, you may actually change the current image; just press Command-Z (Mac OS X) or Ctrl-Z (Windows) to undo the change (to the image, not to the action).

If you want to change the action's name, its thumbnail or button color, or its keyboard shortcut, just double-click on the action's name.

Stop Where You Are. Normally, Photoshop won't display any of the usual dialogs when you run an action. For instance, if you include a numeric transform step in an action, Photoshop just performs the transform without displaying the dialog. But you can force Photoshop to display the dialog, stop, and wait for the user to enter different settings before continuing. To do so, click once in the second column of the Actions panel, next to the step. A black icon indicating a dialog appears next to the step, and a red icon appears next to the action's name.

Don't click on a red dialog icon! If you do, it turns black *and* Photoshop adds a black "stop here" icon next to every step in the action that can have one. There's no Undo here, so the only way to reset the little black icons to their original state is to turn them on or off one at a time. (You can, however, turn off *all* of them by clicking the black icon next to the action's name.)

Note that if you insert a step using the Insert Menu Item command, Photoshop always opens the appropriate dialog and doesn't even offer you the chance to turn this icon on or off (because steps inserted in this way are meant to simulate the user actually selecting the item).

TIP: if you record loading a Curves file (or a Levels or Hue/Saturation file, or any other adjustment) from disk, Photoshop records the name of the file rather than the curve itself. Instead, record loading the setting in the dialog, then change the settings just a tiny bit before clicking OK. As long as there is a difference, Photoshop records the settings in the dialog rather than the file's name. You can always go back and return the settings to the way you want them.

Talk to Your Users. You can stop the action at any point and display a dialog with a message in it. This message might be a warning like, "Make sure you have saved your image first," or instructions such as, "You should have a selection made on a layer above the background." To add a message, select Insert Stop from the Actions panel menu. Photoshop asks you what message you want to show and whether the message dialog should allow people to continue with the action (see **Figure 11-37**).

Figure 11-37 Adding a message

If your message is a warning, you should turn on the Allow Continue option, but if you're communicating instructions, you may want to leave this check box off. When Allow Continue is turned off, Photoshop stops the action entirely. After the user clicks the OK button in the message dialog, Photoshop automatically selects the next step in the Actions panel, so the user can continue running the action by clicking the Run button again (this works even if the Actions panel is in Button mode).

Saving Actions. After you've created the world's most amazing action, you may want to share it with someone else. You can get actions out of your Actions panel and onto your hard drive by selecting Save Actions from the Actions panel menu. Unfortunately, you cannot save a single action; the Save Actions feature only saves sets of actions. The work-around isn't too painful, however.

1. Create a new set (click on the New Set button at the bottom of the Actions panel) and name it something logical.

2. Either move the action you want to save by dragging it, or duplicate it by Option-dragging (Mac OS X) or Alt-dragging (Windows) it into the new action set.

3. Select the new action set and choose Save Actions from the Actions panel menu.

Of course, you can load sets of actions just as easily with the Load Actions and Replace Actions features in the Actions panel menu. Watch out for Replace Actions and its cousin, Clear Actions; these replace or clear *all* the actions in the panel, not just the selected one.

Troubleshooting Actions. As we mentioned in Chapter 5, don't immediately test an action on some mission-critical image. Rather, try it on a dummy image. Even better, try it on several dummy images, each in a different mode (RGB, CMYK, Grayscale, Indexed Color), some with layers, some without, some with selections made, others without, and so on.

Step by Step. You can force Photoshop to pause after each step and redraw the screen by selecting Step by Step in the Playback Options dialog (choose Playback Options from the Actions panel menu). This is often useful, but the best troubleshooting technique in the Actions panel (in fact, probably the only troubleshooting technique) is to select the first item in the action and click the Run button while holding down the Command key (Mac OS X) or Ctrl key (Windows). This plays only the first step. Now go check out all the relevant panels. Is the Channels panel the way you expect it? What about the Layers panel? What are the foreground and background colors? When you're convinced that all is well, Command-click (Mac OS X) or Ctrl-click (Windows) the Run button again to check the second step in the action, and so on until you've tested the entire action. If at any time you find the panels or colors set up improperly, now is the time to replace the last step or double-click on it to change its settings. If something is really messed up, you can fall back on your History snapshot, or revert.

TIP: By its nature, the History panel is a record of the steps that an action performed. You may need to increase the number of History steps so that it can hold all of the steps that a particular action executes.

Making Droplets

We're not sure why the Make Droplet feature is hiding in the File > Automate submenu instead of the Actions panel, but that's where you can find this really awesome feature. You can use Make Droplet to save any Photoshop action to disk as a file. Then, when you want to process an image (or a folder full of images) with that action, you can simply drag the image (or folder) on top of the droplet file.

If you work in both Mac OS X and Windows, you can copy droplets from one platform to the other. On the PC you simply have to make sure that the droplet has an .exe extension. When you bring a PC droplet to the Mac, you

TIP: A droplet contains action steps as they were when you saved the droplet. If you update the action that the droplet's based on, don't forget to regenerate the droplet too!

have to initialize it by dragging it on top of the Photoshop application icon, but you have to do that only once.

Scripting Photoshop

If learning about actions and variables has gotten you all excited about automating Photoshop, you're going to love scripting. Scripting is a way for one application (or your system) to talk to another application behind the scenes.

Scripting vs. Actions. There are some basic differences between actions (which are also called macros) and scripts. Actions depend on the user interface—the menus, dialogs, keyboard shortcuts, and so on. Scripts let you sneak in the back door of the program and control it from behind the scenes, like a puppeteer pulling the strings of a marionette. Scripts have *flow control*, a programming term that means you can set up decision trees and loops, like "keep doing this until that happens." Scripts can also contain variables, so you can save a value (like the color of a pixel) for later use.

Scripting also lets you control more than one program at time. For example, if you use QuarkXPress (which is also scriptable on the Mac) or InDesign (which is scriptable both on the Mac and in Windows), you could write a script that detects how you've rotated, sized, and cropped images within your picture boxes. It could then open the images in Photoshop, perform those manipulations on the original images, resave them, and reimport them into the page-layout program.

Scripting Languages. You can script Photoshop using several languages. In Mac OS X, you can use AppleScript or JavaScript. In Windows, you can use JavaScript, Visual Basic, or any other language that is COM-aware, such as VBScript, Perl, or Python. Only JavaScript scripts can be used across platforms. That would seem to make it the best option for scripting, but unfortunately, only a few other applications are JavaScript-aware—notably, Adobe applications such as InDesign and Bridge.

Guides and Examples. Of course, there are books out there about scripting, but why not start with what's already included with Photoshop? Inside the Photoshop application folder on your computer is a Scripting folder containing PDF reference guides and sample scripts. The Utilities subfolder contains the Scripting Listener plug-in, which can log what you do in Photoshop as JavaScript.

TIP: The Adobe ExtendScript Toolkit is installed with Photoshop. It's in the Adobe Utilities folder in your Utilities folder. You can use ExtendScript Toolkit to debug JavaScripts that you write for Adobe applications.

Hiring a Scripter. Even though scripting is extremely powerful, it's just a fact of life that most people don't want to learn the ins and outs of scripting. Fortunately, there are a number of scripters for hire. You can find good scripters on Adobe's scripting forum at www.adobeforums.com.

Running Scripts. Even if you never write scripts, you're missing out if you don't know how to run them. The example scripts that Adobe provides are extremely helpful. AppleScript and Visual Basic scripts must be run from outside of Photoshop, from a program such as Apple Script Editor.

JavaScript scripts are even more flexible: The easiest way to run a JavaScript from within Photoshop is to place it in the Adobe Photoshop CS4\Presets\ Scripts folder. Photoshop lists these files on the File > Scripts submenu. If your script doesn't live in that folder, you can tell Photoshop where to find it by choosing File > Scripts > Browse. Photoshop Extended includes three additional scripts: Load Files into Stack (we talked about one use for this in "Reducing Noise with Image Stacks" in Chapter 10, "Sharpness, Detail, and Noise Reduction"), Load Multiple DICOM Files (for analyzing medical images), and Statistics (for analyzing image stacks).

Running Scripts on Events. You can set up Photoshop so that it runs a script or action when certain application events occur, such as opening Photoshop, saving, or printing. To tie a script to an event, choose File > Scripts > Script Events Manager and turn on the Enable Events to Run Scripts/Actions check box (see **Figure 11-38**).

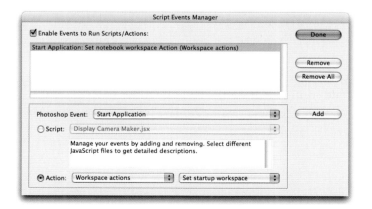

Figure 11-38 Running a script on an event

Next, choose an event from the Photoshop Event pop-up menu, such as Open Document, Save Document, or Start Application. (You can also add your own events if you understand the Photoshop scripting model well enough.) Now choose a script or action at the bottom of the dialog (the action must already be loaded into the Actions panel).

When you click Done, Photoshop starts listening for your event to take place. When the event happens, the action or script is triggered. For example, you might have a script that opens a set of files each time you launch Photoshop and an action that creates a thumbnail and saves it as a JPEG each time you open a document. In our example in Figure 11-38, Conrad uses the Start Application event to run an action that applies the workspace for his notebook computer, so that no matter how chaotic the panels become while he works, Photoshop always starts up with the panels reset to his preferred arrangement. Just remember that if you're troubleshooting a problem or letting someone else use your computer, you may want to turn off the check box at the top of the Script Events Manager dialog, in case you used it to significantly alter the behavior of Photoshop.

CHAPTER TWELVE

Image Storage and Output

We've filled the last few hundred pages with techniques for making great-looking images in Adobe Photoshop. What we haven't done very much yet is look at how to get these images *out* of Photoshop. Perhaps you'll be printing your image directly from Photoshop to a photo-quality printer. Or perhaps you're saving the file to be used in a page-layout application, such as Adobe InDesign or QuarkXPress, or on a Web page. How you save or print your image is determined by what you want to do with it next.

In this chapter we're going to explore two key subjects: how to save your images to disk and how to create printed or online output. Along the way, we'll also discuss some of the concepts you'll need to be familiar with in order to make good output decisions in Photoshop, such as file formats and how to preview output.

SAVE AS

When you choose File > Save As (see **Figure 12-1**) in just about any program, two things happen: The program writes out an entirely new copy of the document, and that new document is what you work with after you click Save. If you specify a filename that's the same as the filename of the document you're working on, you replace it with your new version.

However, the traditional Save As approach doesn't necessarily work well for Photoshop, because a Photoshop document often contains layers, while the formats you hand off to other people often don't—or shouldn't. In older versions of Photoshop, many users started with a layered file, used Save As to create a flattened version by turning off the Layers check box, and absentmindedly found themselves saving the flattened version over the layered version—a monumental loss of flexibility (and data) if you wanted to be able to keep working with those layers.

Recent versions of Photoshop try to protect you from that type of data loss through the As a Copy option. When it's on, As a Copy fundamentally changes what you'll get from the Save As dialog. Instead of saving over the original, As a Copy creates a separate, new document. After the save, you're returned to the full-featured document you were working on before you saved. If you don't realize that you're not working with the copy you just saved, you may end up very confused.

As a Copy will turn itself on if you choose Save As and then you turn off check boxes for any of the options in the Save section, because you're telling Photoshop to discard data. But As a Copy can also turn itself on if you don't touch those Save check boxes. If you simply try to save to a format that can't hold the features you've used in the document, As a Copy turns on, and you have to choose a more-capable format.

The bottom line: If As a Copy comes on, know that you're about to save a less-capable file separately from the document you've been working on. And if you don't want As a Copy to come on, don't change the state of the Save or Color check boxes, and choose a format that can preserve the checked features. Now that we've gotten that out of the way, let's look over the options in the Save As dialog.

> **TIP:** If the Save As dialog appears when you are just doing a simple Save (using the Save command), it means you've added a feature to the document that you can't store in the document's current format. This often happens if you start from a JPEG, add a layer, and then save. Go ahead and save the file in a more capable format, such as TIFF or PSD.

Figure 12-1 The Save As dialog (Mac OS X at left, and Windows at right)

Turning off a Save option check box turns on the As a Copy check box. Preview, thumbnail, and case options are enabled in the File Handling pane of the Preferences dialog.

The Format Menu

The Format pop-up menu lists all of the formats that can handle the document you're saving. You can't always see the formats you want, but when that happens there's probably a good reason. If your Photoshop document uses features like color spaces or bit depths that are pretty far from the mainstream, such as 16 bit/channel Lab color or 32 bit/channel HDR, the list of file formats will be pretty short. If formats seem to be missing from the Format pop-up menu, try choosing Image > Duplicate, and on the Image > Mode submenu choose both RGB and 8 Bits/Channel. This will enable the widest range of file formats in the Format pop-up menu.

TIP: Think the list in the Format pop-up menu is too long? In the Photoshop application folder, you'll find the Plug-Ins\File Formats folder. Move any format plug-in out of the Plug-Ins folder, and it won't show up in the menu any more. (Photoshop will still find it if it's anywhere inside the Plug-Ins folder.)

Save Options

The check boxes in the Save section are available only if you're saving a file that includes those features and you've chosen a file format that supports them. You already know about alpha channels and layers—we talked about those in earlier chapters. Notes are the text annotations you can create using the Note tool, and Spot Colors are channels that you've specifically designated for spot color inks. By the way, turning off the Spot Colors check box doesn't merge spot-color channels into an RGB or CMYK image; it just deletes those channels.

TIP: If the Notes check box is on, you might want to see what those notes are, in case they're private items that aren't intended for clients or other recipients.

Color Options

The Color options in the Save As dialog let you control whether or not you embed an ICC profile in the image, and for some file formats, these options let you make a color conversion during the save.

Use Proof Setup. This rarely used option is available only for EPS and PDF formats, and for EPS DCS when Proof Setup is set to a CMYK profile. It tells Photoshop to convert the image from its current space to the current target profile and rendering intent specified in Proof Setup (see "Soft-Proofing Other Color Spaces" in Chapter 4, "Color Settings").

Embed Color Profile. This option is on by default unless you set your Color Management Policy to Off. You'll want to leave this turned on except in the following instances:

- You might not want to include the color profile when you need to send a file to an organization that doesn't support color management. They may get nervous upon seeing an embedded profile and mess up your image in one way or another.

- If you absolutely need the smallest possible file, you might leave out the profile, but be sure that's OK within the workflow you're using. It also depends on the size of the profile. For the Web, if you've converted a file to sRGB and you leave out the profile when you save, it will display reasonably well in browsers.

- CMYK profiles are notoriously large (they may add between 700 KB and 3 MB to the file size). This book contains so many CMYK images targeting the same profile that including the profile in every single one would be redundant and consume lots of disk space unnecessarily. Instead, we brought the untagged images into InDesign and set the default *document* profile in InDesign, which works just as well. Of course, if we had to send one of these images to a friend for further editing, he or she would be lost unless we sent our color profile or at least indicated which profile to assign.

Image Preview Options

TIP: Saving an icon or thumbnail preview can considerably lengthen the time it takes to save your image (especially for very large files). But if you include at least two types of previews, saving the second type takes hardly any additional time. Saving a full-size preview takes still longer and is not very useful.

When you use Save As, Photoshop can create miniature preview images within your file if you choose Ask When Saving from the Image Previews pop-up menu in the File Handling pane of the Preferences dialog. From then on, the Save As dialog offers you Preview choices: in Windows, you get a Thumbnail check box; on the Mac, you get check boxes for saving an icon, thumbnails for Mac and Windows, and a full-size preview (see Figure 12-1). We don't bother with these, because today's operating systems and professional imaging programs like Adobe Bridge and Lightroom tend to create their own previews. But if you do want to use them, here's what they are:

Icon. This builds an icon preview that can help you recognize documents on your desktop. It doesn't seem to work reliably when viewed in Windows.

Thumbnail. The second preview, Thumbnail, is provided for the Open dialogs of QuickTime-savvy applications. We leave this off because many programs create a thumbnail on the fly, whether you save one or not.

Full Size. You only see this on Photoshop in Mac OS X when Ask When Saving is turned on in File Handling preferences. It adds a 24-bit PICT resource that is the physical output size of the image, downsampled to 72 pixels per inch. You don't need this for an EPS file, because that format can include its own full-size preview.

OPENING IMAGES

If a file doesn't open in Photoshop when you double-click it, try dragging it to the Photoshop program icon. If that doesn't work, try choosing File > Open in Photoshop and locating the file.

If you see the file in the Open dialog but can't select it, try choosing the file's format from the Enable pop-up menu. If that doesn't work, try choosing All Documents from the Enable pop-up menu. This can help if you receive an image created on a different platform that's missing the right file extension, or if you're opening a document that contains more than one format and you want to dictate how it opens.

To open multiple images, select more than one image in the Open dialog or drag multiple images from the desktop or Bridge to Photoshop. You can also select multiple images in Bridge and press the Return (Mac) or Enter key.

TIP: In Mac OS X, you'll probably see a Printer pop-up menu in the Page Setup dialog. If you see this, choose your printer here too—even if you've already chosen your printer in the Print dialog. If the wrong printer is chosen in Page Setup, the wrong paper sizes may be listed.

PRINTING FROM PHOTOSHOP

As in almost every other program, there are two dialogs tied to imaging: Page Setup and Print, usually found under the File menu. Because Mac OS X and Windows don't allow applications to add features to the Print and Page Setup dialogs, Adobe provides many of its own printing capabilities in the Print dialog (see **Figure 12-2**). If you use them correctly you can avoid a lot of wasted paper.

TIP: If clicking the Center Image check box doesn't center the image in the Print dialog preview, the margins provided by the printer driver are asymmetrical. Click the Page Setup button and choose an option or paper size that provides equal or minimum margins.

The Print Dialog

The Print dialog lets you control the position, scaling, and color management of your image on the paper, which you can preview using the proxy image superimposed on a preview of the paper size. Turning on the Match Print Colors check box applies your current Proof Setup to the proxy.

TIP: If you apply scaling in the Print dialog, leave the scaling in Page Setup at 100 percent. The Print dialog doesn't know about scaling applied in Page Setup, so if you apply scaling there, the preview and dimensions in the Print dialog may be incorrect.

Printer and Page Setup. These options are not here just as a convenience. The only way Photoshop knows how big it can print a document is from the paper sizes provided by the printer driver you've chosen. For accurate positioning and scaling, it's important for you to set the printer, paper type, and options correctly. To do this, first choose your printer from the Printer pop-up menu, which lists the printer drivers installed on your computer. Then click Page Setup and ensure that all of the options are set correctly. Note that the Page Setup options are *not* provided by Photoshop; all Page Setup options are put there by the printer driver. Photoshop simply gives you access to Page Setup because it needs that information to figure out the available margins, paper feed source, and so on. This fact causes much confusion that's hard to avoid, since printer driver and program options are typically walled off from each other in both Mac OS X and Windows.

Figure 12-2 The Print dialog and its Output options

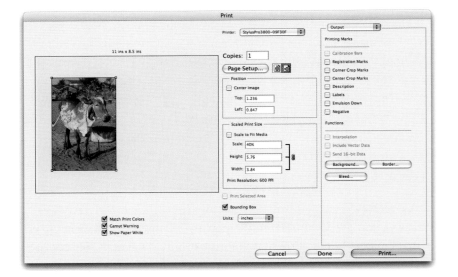

Position and Scaled Print Size. If you just want to fit the image on the paper and center it, leave Center Image and Scale to Fit Media checked. If you want to customize the image size, turn off Scale to Fit Media. If you want to customize its position, turn off Center Image. To be able to scale and position by dragging, Bounding Box must be turned on. You can't change the aspect ratio of the image in this dialog.

The initial size that's displayed when you open the Print dialog is based on the dimensions specified in the Image Size dialog. When you change the scaling, be aware that you aren't creating any new pixels—changing the scaling options is just like changing the size or resolution in Image Size with the Resample Image check box turned off.

Print Selected Area. To print just a small portion of an image, you don't have to duplicate and crop the image. Simply draw a selection marquee around the area you want to print, then turn on the Print Selected Area check box in the Print dialog. This check box is unavailable if no selection exists or if the selection is nonrectangular or feathered.

The next three options control the color-managed preview image and correspond with the Proof Setup menu commands we talked about in "Soft-Proofing an Image for Print" in Chapter 8. Match Print Colors does exactly the same thing as choosing View > Proof Colors, Gamut Warning is basically View > Gamut Warning, and Show Paper White works like the option with the same name in the Customize Proof Condition dialog.

Because these options are color-managed, the appearance of colors in the preview image is determined by the settings in the Color Management pane on the right side of the Print dialog, so you can rely on the preview only if you've set those options correctly. But the small preview limits the real usefulness of these options; for exacting checks, use the Proof Setup commands in the document window so you can zoom in.

TIP: After you click Print, you may see a warning alert that says "Some PostScript specific print settings . . . will be ignored since you are printing to a non-PostScript printer." If you're printing photographs to a desktop printer, don't worry about this—turn on the Don't Show Again check box and forget about this warning.

Output Options

The Output Options tell Photoshop how to print the document. You can see them by choosing Output from the pop-up menu at the top right corner of the Print dialog. Some of these items appear only for specific file formats or when you select a certain type of printer driver. Because many options are standard system-level features, we're going to skip them and get right to the good stuff: the Photoshop-specific items.

Printing Marks. These are printed outside the image (see **Figure 12-3**). You may find Corner Crop Marks useful if you need to cut out an image printed on a larger sheet. If you want to remember which print is which, or you want someone else to be able to identify a print, Description prints the Description metadata from the File Info dialog or the Metadata panel in Bridge. The Labels option prints the filename, but they call it Labels because if you were printing color separations the separation name would appear there. The other Printing Marks are useful primarily for prepress color separations, but most photographers will never do this themselves.

Functions. Again, many of these features are intended for prepress, but a few are of interest to photographers. Send 16-bit Data (Mac OS X only) hooks into the 16 bits/channel pipeline for certain high-end color printers. If it isn't available, you've selected a printer driver that doesn't support it. You might want to use this option if you use one of the wide-gamut printers where 16 bit/channel printing makes a visible difference compared to 8 bit/channel printing. Even then, you still have to start out with a file with 16 bits per channel or more from an excellent-quality source file, maintain the highest image quality standards while editing, and print at the printer's highest quality and resolution setting.

You can use the Background and Border options if you need to modify an image in this way while printing (they don't change the original image). The rest of the Functions options are rarely used for straight photography.

TIP: Don't downsample high-bit files before printing from Photoshop. It's both unnecessary and unwise. Photoshop is smart enough to downsample the data and convert the color space before sending it to the printer.

Figure 12-3 Printing marks

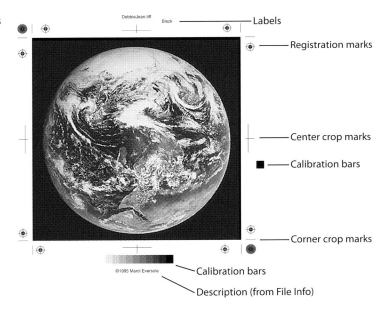

Color Management Options

We covered the Print dialog Color Management options back in "Converting Colors When You Print" in Chapter 4, "Color Settings," so that we could discuss color printing within the larger context of color management. Because all that information is back there, we won't repeat it here.

PREPARING IMAGES FOR ONLINE SERVICES

In the past, most people printed a Photoshop document from Photoshop or from a layout program. With the rise of digital photography, another world of output has emerged: the online photo service. The big difference with online photo services is that they do not represent a single, easily targeted form of output. They encompass onscreen display of images on the Web, as well as printing on photographic paper, or even on products you can order, such as mugs and T-shirts. This means that an image needs to be saved in a way that looks good onscreen and can print reliably to photographic printers (we won't worry too much about reproduction quality on mugs).

Types of Online Services. Photo services range from consumer-oriented services, where the most important feature is simplicity, to services designed for photographic professionals, fine-art photographers, and serious enthusiasts. Consumer photo services are now a commodity—your local drugstore probably offers in-store printing and free online galleries from files you upload through your Web browser. Most services expect you to upload JPEG files in the sRGB color space, even though most of their photo printers aren't actually printing in the sRGB color space. You should aim for image resolutions of 240 to 300 ppi at the dimensions of the largest print you ever want to order.

> **TIP:** Stock-photo agencies could be thought of as a type of online photo service. However, agencies can have different image requirements, which you should research and understand before you upload files to them.

Online services geared toward professionals offer more flexibility. They may support color spaces other than sRGB, such as AdobeRGB (1998) and ProPhoto RGB. To assist you in soft-proofing, they may have a custom ICC profile that represents their photo printers, and they may make it freely available for downloading. You can add such a profile to the other profiles on your system and then use it in the Proof Setup command in Photoshop, so that you can work in your color space while tuning for their printer's color space. The online gallery component of professionally oriented online services often provides more flexibility and security, such as customizable gallery appearance, private and password-protected galleries, long-term archiving, and the ability to let you take a cut of print sales.

Saving JPEG Images for Online Services. Some services may restrict uploads to JPEG format only. Because JPEG is a lossy format, there is the question of how much compression to apply. If you're determined to preserve every last bit of quality in your images, you could use maximum JPEG compression. In Photoshop, JPEG quality is represented on a scale of 1 to 12, where 12 is maximum (as in the Save As dialog) or on a scale of 1 to 100, where 100 is maximum (as in the Save for Web & Devices dialog). However, you may find it more reasonable to save your JPEG files a step or two below maximum quality. The reason is that the difference in quality among the near-maximum levels is hard to detect, but the differences in file size are significant. If you have 500 images to upload from an event, you'll probably find that JPEG quality level 10 is indistinguishable from JPEG 12, but the JPEG 10 versions upload much more quickly and consume much less disk space. For JPEG images that are intended to be online masters, we don't advocate dropping below JPEG 10.

Creating Output for Prepress

There may be times when you're called upon to submit images for CMYK output, such as for a magazine or a coffee-table book. If you're not skilled in CMYK editing, it's best for a prepress specialist to tune the image in CMYK after receiving an RGB image from you, but even if you never go into CMYK, it's useful to know what needs to happen to your image.

When used as part of a publication, a photograph is not normally printed straight from Photoshop. Instead it will probably be printed from a page-layout program or a specialized color separation program. In this section we focus on the latter item: page-layout programs, such as InDesign and QuarkXPress. Publications destined for a printing press are typically output to a PostScript-language platesetter, resulting in plates with black-and-white halftoned images. (Older processes use imagesetters to produce film or paper printing plates.) We summarize the recommended file formats for prepress in **Table 12-1**. You'll find more-detailed information about these formats in "File Formats," later in this chapter.

TIP: If you want to save full image metadata (including EXIF data and keywords) with a JPEG file that you intend to send to an online service, create the JPEG file using the Save As command. If you want to strip the metadata, create the JPEG file using the Save for Web & Devices command, and in its Metadata pop-up menu choose the degree of metadata you want to include (or choose None).

TIP: If you use the same layered Photoshop file multiple times in InDesign with different layer settings, make sure you choose Keep Layer Visibility Overrides from the When Updating Link pop-up menu in the Object Layer Options dialog in InDesign. If the images are set to Use Photoshop's Layer Visibility and you update the Photoshop file, all your variations become the same (taking on the last layer visibility settings in Photoshop).

Table 12-1 File formats for prepress.

File format	Notes
Photoshop	Preserves transparency, layers, clipping paths, and layers in InDesign and QuarkXPress
TIFF	Preserves transparency and clipping paths
Photoshop PDF	Preserves vector type and graphics
EPS/DCS	Preserves vector type, graphics, and clipping paths; not color-managed; increasingly being replaced by PDF

Adobe InDesign and QuarkXPress

No matter which page-layout tool you use, it's crucial that you consider how your images will transport from Photoshop to the printed page. There are some basic rules you should follow.

File Formats for Page Layout. When printing from page-layout programs, use TIFF, PDF, DCS, or EPS. With the latest versions of InDesign or QuarkXPress you can also use the native Photoshop (PSD) format.

For straight photography it's reasonably certain that you'll use TIFF or PSD files. Although JPEG is also used, it's discouraged for high-end printing due to its lossy nature. Some online self-publishing book services take only JPEG images; in that case set the Quality value no lower than 10 in the Save As dialog for the JPEG format.

We tend to use the TIFF format for almost all of our files, though we'll occasionally use EPS or DCS for specialized graphic effects such as duotones or custom screening. If your image has vector artwork (like text layers) in it, you should use EPS or (preferably) PDF.

Placing Layered Photoshop Files in InDesign. There are advantages to placing layered Photoshop files into your InDesign layouts. One advantage is speed: You can drag a Photoshop document into an InDesign layout as soon as it's ready, instead of going through another step to create a flattened copy. Also, you can use the Object > Object Layer Options command in InDesign to control which Photoshop layers or layer comps are visible. If you're using layers to create variations on an image, you need to place the

TIP: If you're working with InDesign and have an image that doesn't match the InDesign document profile and doesn't have an embedded profile, select the image on the InDesign layout, choose Object > Image Color Settings, and assign a profile just to that image. This way, it's still possible to save the image without a CMYK profile and still render it correctly.

layered original into InDesign only once, duplicate it on the layout, and change which layers are visible in InDesign (see **Figure 12-4**).

Figure 12-4 Controlling Photoshop document layers in InDesign

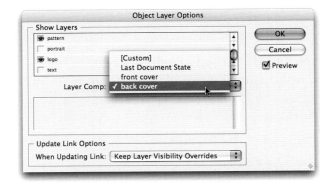

This workflow is not without its costs. Because you aren't locking down the image in a flattened file, there are all sorts of opportunities for things to go haywire. For example, a production person down the line may activate the wrong layer or layer comp. Also, layered Photoshop files take up more disk space, so the final package you deliver to your printer may take longer to transmit or require another DVD. But if you and your production team can stay on top of all that, go ahead and take advantage of the flexibility.

CMYK vs. RGB. For jobs destined for prepress, the choice between importing RGB or CMYK images involves two decision: When do you want to do your separations, and what program do you want to do them in? You can preseparate all your images with Photoshop (or another program), or you can place RGB images in InDesign or QuarkXPress and rely on their color management systems to do the separations for you.

Preseparating has a lot going for it. Images land on pages ready to print; the page-layout program just sends the channels down, with no processing necessary at print time. Placing unseparated RGB files has advantages as well, though. You can use the page-layout program's color management system to produce better proofs using color printers, and you don't have to target the images until the last minute, when you know all your press conditions and are ready to pull final separations. However, when it comes right down to it, we separate almost all our images in Photoshop first. (But we archive the RGB files, just in case we need to reseparate to some other target.)

TIP: If you have problems importing PSD or TIFF files into a layout program, try importing an 8-bit CMYK or RGB duplicate of the file. Some layout programs can't handle higher bit depths or other color modes such as Lab. Also, some programs can't display Photoshop files if the Maximize Compatibility option is off.

Rotating, Scaling, Cropping, Et Cetera. Although you can perform all kinds of wonderful transformations in today's page-layout programs, each rotated, scaled, skewed, and flipped image adds processing overhead. If you want to keep your page-layout workflow as simple and efficient as possible, transform and crop images before you import them into layouts.

Now, this advice is not absolute. If you're on a deadline, staying in your page-layout program and making minor image adjustments can save a lot of time, and if your prepress service provider has up-to-date imagesetters, image adjustments in the layout might not slow down the job so much.

Use care when cropping, though. When you take an 8-megapixel digital SLR frame, crop it down to around 5 megapixels, and send it on to InDesign, InDesign receives 5 megapixels. But if you crop the image in InDesign, InDesign will import and manage 8 megapixels, which can turn out to be an ongoing performance drag on your system and on printers. InDesign and QuarkXPress can be configured to print only the cropped portion, so this won't necessarily slow down output. Still, if you're going to crop out a lot of an image, do it in Photoshop. For this book we saved CMYK copies of our images at the final size and resolution whenever possible.

CREATING IMAGES FOR THE WEB

Just as there are techniques for optimizing an image for paper, there are methods you can use to ensure good quality onscreen (as well as tips for preparing your onscreen image efficiently). For Web capabilities beyond what Photoshop can do on its own, use Adobe Fireworks. But you'll need to go beyond Photoshop only if you're getting pretty deep into Web graphics. If you're a photographer wanting to put images on the Web, Photoshop itself gives you plenty of options.

Tone and Color

At default Mac OS X and Windows display settings, an image displays lighter in Mac OS X than in Windows. The most significant difference is that Mac OS X defaults to gamma 1.8, while Windows defaults to gamma 2.2. There are several strategies for dealing with this mismatch, all involving compromises that we'll discuss. Because the destination monitor is essentially unknown, your images are going to look much better (or worse) on some systems than on others. It's simply impossible to produce images that will look good to every Web user. The best you can do is to aim for a point that will look OK on uncalibrated monitors (which is most monitors) and reasonably good on calibrated monitors. We suggest you choose one of the following alternatives:

- Convert to sRGB. Back in Chapter 4, "Color Settings," we discussed the sRGB color space, developed by several industry giants to describe the general characteristics of a typical PC monitor. While not ideal, converting to sRGB is the easiest way to help ensure that the image appears as consistently as can reasonably be expected on the wide variety of machines out there. Note that this does not mean you have to edit in sRGB. Simply turn on the Convert to sRGB check box in the Save for Web & Devices dialog, which we'll discuss later in this chapter.

- Prepare two sets of images. We know some photographers who care so much about color that they've prepared two sets of their images—one at gamma 1.8 and one at gamma 2.2. Then they code their Web sites so that Mac users see the gamma 1.8 version while Windows users see the gamma 2.2 version. It's a good theory, except that it takes a lot more work, and more professional Mac users now calibrate to gamma 2.2.

- Embed the profile. The ideal solution to the color mismatch problem is to embed an ICC profile in each image, either in the Save As dialog or by using the Edit > Assign Profile command. This approach relies on two conditions: that every person looking at your images has created a custom profile for their monitor, and that his or her browser supports embedded profiles. But let's get real: The vast majority of Web browsers in use today are not color-managed, and of those that are (such as Safari), they're being viewed mostly on monitors that are not calibrated. In a non-color-managed browser, an image uploaded in a relatively large color space, such as AdobeRGB (1998) or ProPhoto RGB, with an embedded profile will actually look much worse than an image uploaded in sRGB, only because sRGB happens to be closer to (but still can't exactly match) the gamuts of most uncalibrated monitors.

Embedding an RGB working space profile usually adds only about 0.5 K to a JPEG image, so file size is a consideration only if you need to upload the smallest possible files.

TIP: If you're a Mac user who wants to more precisely anticipate how Windows users see your images, specify gamma 2.2 the next time you calibrate your monitor. The reasons for setting the Mac to gamma 1.8 are as old as the Mac itself, and thanks to modern color management, those reasons are not really relevant today. Changing the monitor gamma won't change the gamma of your Photoshop working space or your files.

Note that Photoshop does not embed profiles in GIF files because they're always in Indexed Color mode rather than RGB.

Given the maddening interdependencies that get in the way of color-managed Web images, the easiest way out for now appears to be to convert to sRGB before uploading to the Web, and to embed the profile if you and your audience can handle the larger file sizes.

We'll have to resign ourselves to this compromise solution until the day when all major browsers are color-managed by default and most monitors are self-calibrating. Until then, it simply won't be practical to pursue the ideal workflow of preserving maximum image quality by saving Web images in a larger-than-sRGB color space with embedded profiles. The only scenario where that might work today is for a Web site targeting a specific, known audience, all of whom run color-managed browsers on calibrated monitors, such as the internal Web site of a photography studio.

Previewing Online Tone and Color

Not only can you rarely predict tonal shifts in images for the screen, you can't assume anything about color. As we've mentioned, it's pretty likely that your audience's monitors are not calibrated. If you expect your images to be viewed on mobile devices, the quality of the display may vary greatly, possibly displaying a limited range of colors. While monitor calibration is something you can barely hope for on desktop machines, it isn't helpful at all on mobile devices.

When preserving color quality, it's usually more important to retain the contrast between colors than the particular colors themselves. Image details that result from subtle changes in color (like the gentle folds in a red silk scarf) are often lost in translation unless you anticipate and compensate before exporting the image.

Desktop and Notebook Computers. Try looking at your image on a variety of Mac and Windows systems. If it's practical to test only on the system you happen to own, you can choose Windows RGB or Macintosh RGB from View > Proof Setup to approximate how the images will look on the other platform. To see the pure, unproofed view again, turn off the View > Proof Colors command (toggle that command by pressing Command-Y in Mac OS X or Ctrl-Y in Windows).

The Preview Pop-Up Menu. Inside the Save for Web & Devices dialog, the Preview pop-up menu displays how an image will appear under various conditions (see **Figure 12-5**). Like Proof Setup, this setting does not change the image at all—what you're choosing are the conditions under which you want to preview the image. The Macintosh (No Color Management) and Windows (No Color Management) options are the most useful; Monitor Color applies only to the specific monitor in front of you and Use Document Profile shows you only what the image looks like in a program that actually reads profiles (if you choose to embed the profile).

Mobile Devices. If you're asked to optimize your images for use in content for cell phones or other mobile devices, you can click the Device Central button in the Save for Web & Devices dialog. This opens Adobe Device Central, which emulates many handheld devices.

These methods aren't perfect, but they should give you an idea of how the image will look on different systems.

Should You Use Web-Safe Colors? A generation of Web designers was taught that Web graphics should be saved using a Web-safe color palette. The problem is that "Web-safe" really means "Safe for 8 bit/channel monitors," because it's relevant only when viewing images on a display set to 8 bit/channel color (256 colors). That was a rather high-end specification for video cards made in the 1990s, but today, even cell phones and iPods support at least 16 bit/channel color, while computer displays support at least 24 bit/channel color. You may still be concerned about Web-safe color if you are working with an organization with very old equipment. Otherwise, don't restrict yourself to it, especially for photos.

Resolution

One of the wonderful advantages of working on images for screen display is that resolution is measured in pixels, and you need a lot fewer pixels to display an image on a monitor than you do to print it. This makes for very small images (relative to prepress sizes, at least). An 800-by-600-pixel image (rather large for a Web page) saved at JPEG Medium quality weighs in at just 52 K, while an image at roughly the same viewing size saved as an 8-bit ZIP-compressed TIFF for print could occupy 4.5 MB, largely because the print version is set to a much higher resolution, such as 300 pixels per inch.

The smaller file sizes of onscreen graphics mean faster processing times and lower RAM requirements.

You'll notice we didn't specify the resolution of the Web image. That's because it doesn't matter. On the Web, the only dimensions that matter are the pixel dimensions. If you put an 800-by-600-pixel image on a Web page, it doesn't matter whether the image was set to 72 ppi or 2400 ppi—the browser will always display that image at 800 monitor pixels across. Of course, because monitors have different pixel densities that are adjustable, you cannot assume the resolution of your Web audience's monitor; for example, 1440 by 900 pixels results in a different resolution on a 15-inch notebook monitor than on a 13-inch monitor. All you can assume is that the same Web graphic will look larger on lower-resolution monitors (such as a 17-inch monitor set to 1024 by 768 pixels) and smaller on monitors set to higher resolutions (such as a 1680-by-1050-pixel notebook monitor). This is also why we don't repeat the age-old myth that graphics are 72 ppi in Mac OS X and 96 ppi in Windows—that hasn't been true for a very long time. Go ahead, we dare you: Draw a line 72 or 96 pixels across on your monitor, and hold a real-world ruler up to the screen. Chances are, your onscreen line won't match up to 1 inch on your real-world ruler. Your true monitor resolution is simply the number of horizontal or vertical pixels displayed by your monitor divided by its physical display height or width in inches, and of course, that number will be different on someone else's monitor. So for the Web and other onscreen media, pay attention to pixel dimensions, not pixels per inch.

SAVING IMAGES FOR THE WEB

Making images for the Web is a study in compromise: You can have either great-looking images or pictures that download quickly—pick one. The problem is that you need to see all the options to make an informed decision about how much to degrade your image in the name of small file sizes. The solution is the Save for Web & Devices feature.

Save for Web & Devices lets you see exactly what will happen to your images when you convert them to an online format. Better yet, it can display two or four versions at a time and let you tweak each of them until you get just the effect you want. To open this dialog, choose File > Save for Web & Devices or press Command-Option-Shift-S (Mac) or Ctrl-Alt-Shift-S

(Windows). We summarize online file formats in **Table 12-2** and talk about them in more detail in "File Formats," later in this chapter.

Table 12-2 Popular file formats for viewing onscreen.

File format	Notes
JPEG	The standard for photographic images on the Web
GIF	Limited colors, supports 1-bit transparency
PNG	Supports true alpha-channel transparency

The Save for Web & Devices Dialog

TIP: Want to make a Web image gallery? In Photoshop CS4, you now do this from the Output panel in Adobe Bridge (see Chapter 5).

Here are the basic steps you should follow after you open the Save for Web & Devices dialog (see Figure 12-5).

1. Switch to the 2-Up or 4-Up tab of the window. We like 4-Up except when we're almost sure of what settings we're going to use.

2. Leave the first panel set to Original (so you have something with which to compare your tests). Click on the second panel and choose a preset configuration from the Settings pop-up menu. For photographic images a good starting preset is JPEG High. You can choose other presets for any other views; or if you're using 4-Up view, just choose Repopulate Views from the settings pop-up menu in the top right corner to automatically fill the third and fourth views with variations on the second view's settings.

3. Visually check each image's quality, size, and approximate download time (shown under each image).

4. Pick the one that is closest to what you're trying to achieve, and tweak the settings to minimize the size while maintaining quality. The discussion that follows covers each of the settings and how they work.

5. Set other options as needed, such as Metadata and Image Size.

6. When you're ready, click Save (make sure the proper image is highlighted; the one that's highlighted is the one that's saved to disk).

There are a number of settings in the dialog to tweak, many of them obscure. We'll cover the ones that are most relevant to our interests—reproducing photographic images at an efficient file size.

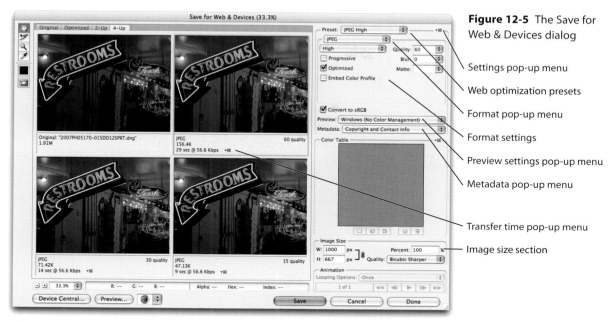

Figure 12-5 The Save for Web & Devices dialog

Settings pop-up menu

Web optimization presets

Format pop-up menu

Format settings

Preview settings pop-up menu

Metadata pop-up menu

Transfer time pop-up menu

Image size section

The colors of the original image look weak because its ProPhoto RGB gamut is too wide for web browsers that don't support color management. The colors in the three Web-optimized views were adjusted by turning on the Convert to sRGB check box.

Presets. The Preset pop-up menu lets you recall saved settings. There's nothing magic about the settings that are already built in; they're only there to get you started. If you don't like the built-in settings, you can delete them by choosing Delete Settings from the settings pop-up menu to the right of the Preset pop-up menu. If you want to add your own group of settings to the list, choose Save Settings instead; make sure the settings are saved in the Optimized Settings folder (inside your Photoshop Presets folder), with an .irs filename extension.

Format. If you prefer to set each option manually, start by choosing a format from the second pop-up menu from the top.

Checking File Size. The file size that Photoshop displays in the lower left corner of the document window doesn't take into account any form of compression that might be applied. The file size you see in the Save for Web & Devices dialog is more accurate, but it's still not perfect. The only way to find an image's true (postcompression) file size is to save it to disk and switch out of Photoshop. In Mac OS X, select the file and choose File > Get Info. In Windows, right-click on the file and choose Properties. If the

TIP: When you have in mind a specific file size for your Web graphics, Photoshop can figure out the compression settings for you. Choose Optimize to File Size from the settings pop-up menu next to the Preset pop-up menu. In the Optimize to File Size dialog, enter the file size you want, select a Start With option, and click OK. You probably don't want to simply accept whatever Photoshop gives you: Even the best images still require some tweaking.

file size is displayed as "27 K on disk (22,045 bytes used)," pay attention only to the second number. The first value actually varies depending on the block size of your hard disk formatting. If your disk uses 32 K blocks, a 2 K file will occupy 32 K on disk, and a 33 K file will use 64 K of disk space. The second number shows the actual amount of data someone must download to see the image, and it's usually smaller than the disk space number.

Image Size. Do you need your final Web graphic to be smaller than the high-resolution version you have? Use the Image Size section to down-sample the image before using Save for Web & Devices, or use the Image Size controls in the Save for Web & Devices dialog. Both do the same thing, except that by its nature, Image Size in Save for Web & Devices always resamples. In Photoshop CS4, Save for Web & Devices now includes the various resizing methods in the Quality pop-up menu.

View-Specific Options. Along the right side of the dialog, the file format options and Preview pop-up menu are specific to the view that's selected with a gray outline. All of the other options apply to all views. For example, if you set Image Size to 600 by 400 pixels, it applies to all views, but you can set Preview separately for each view to proof different output scenarios.

Download Time. Each view in the Save for Web & Devices dialog includes a transfer time pop-up menu (see Figure 12-5) that lists the approximate times it would take to download the image. Of course, it's just an estimate, but it can be a useful reality check.

Metadata. Copyright concerns are more critical than ever for photographers. To ensure that your copyright metadata is sent to the Web with the image, click the Metadata pop-up menu and choose any option other than None. (You did enter copyright metadata in Bridge or File Info, didn't you?) The options distinguish between Copyright, Camera Info, and Contact Info so that you can include as much information as you want. However, be aware that this does not guarantee that metadata will always be with the image—it isn't hard for someone to strip all metadata from the image if they want to, and there's currently no way to prevent that. If you're ultra-paranoid about image theft, you need to (manually) add a visible watermark over the image, keep the image small, or not put it up on the Web at all.

When you choose All, the image also includes metadata such as keywords and captions. For example, many photo Web sites can read an uploaded image's metadata, display its keywords, captions, and shot data next to the

TIP: If you're starting with a very large image, such as a 10-megapixel digital SLR photo, it's faster to resample it using the Image Size dialog rather than using Image Size in the Save for Web & Devices dialog.

TIP: You may think that fast broadband Internet speeds mean a small file size is not the priority it used to be. However, remember that the new frontier of the Internet is mobile, handheld devices like the Apple iPhone, where not all networks are fast and users may be charged per kilobyte. If your Photoshop images will be viewed by this audience, they'll still appreciate small file sizes.

image on a Web page, display the image's GPS coordinates on a map, and make it all searchable. The dark side of this? Before uploading images with metadata, consider auditing that metadata in Bridge for any names, locations, client data, or other information that you intended to be private!

Previewing. At the bottom left of the Save for Web & Devices dialog are three controls. Device Central opens the image in Adobe Device Central so that you can preview the image on a mobile device (this is why Devices is in the name of the dialog). To open the image in your default Web browser, click the Preview button or the globe icon; if you click the arrows next to the globe icon you can choose Edit List to add other browsers that are on your computer, and they'll end up under the globe icon as a pop-up menu.

Saving to Disk. At the bottom right of the Save for Web & Devices are three buttons. To close the dialog and save the image to disk using the file format settings in the selected view, click Save. To close the dialog without making any changes, click Cancel. To close the dialog and save changes to the source document without saving a new file, click Done.

Other Options. We concentrate on photographic images in this book, so we aren't covering the Color Table option, since it's used for controlling the colors in GIF images, which are not optimal for photographic reproduction. We're also not covering the slicing and HTML export options (since those are mostly geared toward Web designers who aren't using Adobe Dreamweaver) or the looping option and Animation panel for creating animated GIF graphics.

TIP: Commands controlling the viewing area are also available on a context menu if you right-click or Control-click (Mac) a view.

Zoomify

The Zoomify feature is a way of displaying high-resolution photos online without letting people download the entire image, and without having it take over the entire screen.

The principle is simple. Zoomify creates an Adobe Flash-based viewer window at the size of your choice, so you can fit it on your Web page. Inside this window is your image (**Figure 12-6**). To zoom in to see details, click the image; this enlarges the image without making the window bigger. To move around in the zoomed image, just drag the image. You can also navigate using the controls at the bottom of the Zoomify object that ends up on your

Web page. It's similar to how Google Maps works. Your audience will need to have Flash installed for their Web browser, but most browsers include it.

Figure 12-6 Zoomify on a Web page

Zoomify zoomed all the way out   Zooming in reveals full-resolution detail.

TIP: The degree of detail at the maximum Zoomify zoom level depends on the size of the image you feed into Zoomify, so to limit the amount of detail use the Image > Image Size command to downsample your image before you open the Zoomify Export dialog.

To create a Zoomify object, start with an 8 bit/channel image, and then choose File > Export > Zoomify to open the Zoomify Export dialog which contains some straightforward options for file export location, quality, and size of the viewer. Zoomify chops up the image into many small tiles and uses its Flash application to reassemble them on the fly; the Image Tile Options control how much compression is applied.

After you've specified the options and clicked OK, you need to copy the table code from the HTML document produced by Zoomify and paste it into the code for your Web page. In the folder Zoomify creates, you can see the image tiles that were generated.

FILE FORMATS

Photoshop can save or export files to a very long list of formats. In this section, we'll guide you through them and the mind-numbing range of options you will encounter.

Photoshop

The Photoshop file format—otherwise known as Photoshop native format, or by its filename extension, PSD—used to be the only way to save everything that Photoshop is capable of producing: multiple layers, adjustment and type layers, layer effects, paths, multiple channels, clipping paths, screening and transfer settings, and so on. (Note that Undo states, histories, and snapshots are not saved in any file format.) The PSD file format is less necessary because almost anything you can save in a Photoshop file you can now also save in either a TIFF or Photoshop PDF file. It's important to note, however, that other applications may not be able to read those formats properly. For instance, you can now save spot colors in a TIFF file, but no other programs currently handle those spot colors properly.

Saving a Composite. By default, Photoshop pretty much insists on saving a flattened composite version of the image in every PSD file. As a result, those of us who have become accustomed to using PSD to save files that consist only of a Background layer and some adjustment layers get a rude shock when we find out how large our Photoshop files are on disk.

You can prevent Photoshop from saving flattened composites in two ways, each tied to the Maximize PSD and PSB File Compatibility pop-up menu in the File Handling pane of the Preferences dialog. By default, this pop-up menu is set to Ask, which means that whenever you try to save a PSD file with layers, you get to choose whether or not you want to "maximize file compatibility." Plus, you get a scary-looking warning (see **Figure 12-7**). The warning is there for two reasons:

- Several other applications claim to be able to read Photoshop files, and although a few can actually read layered files, most just read the flattened composite. Adobe Illustrator, InDesign, and QuarkXPress 6.5 will all attempt to read Photoshop files, even if the composite is not present, so if you're using one of these, you can usually proceed without the composite—if your layered files are relatively straightforward. However, if your layers use any of the new blending modes, such as Pin Light or Vivid Light, the layers will very likely not be read correctly, so it's safer to include the composite. Plus, while InDesign and Illustrator can read 8-bit layered PSD files without a composite, they can't handle 16-bit PSD files without one.

- Future versions of Photoshop may change the layer-blending algorithms, which means that when you opened a layered document, it would look slightly different than it does now. Adobe reasons that with the flattened composite, you'll still be able to retrieve the correct image appearance in future versions. Of course, if you someday open the composite rather than the layered document, you lose all your layers, so the advantage over saving a flattened copy is questionable.

Our advice? The more you use Photoshop native files in other programs, including photo organizers such as Lightroom, the more you want this option to be on, to avoid workflow headaches. If you usually use Photoshop files only within Photoshop, you'll save disk space by turning this off. The way to stop this dialog from being annoying is to open the File Handling pane of the Preferences dialog and choose Always or Never from the Maximize PSD and PSB File Compatibility pop-up menu, depending on your workflow. You'll be nagged only if that pop-up menu is set to Ask, which really means "ask every time."

Figure 12-7 The really annoying "Maximize compatibility" warning

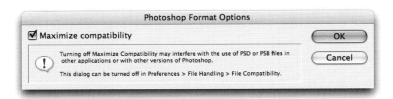

Duotones. Because TIFF and PDF do almost everything that the native Photoshop file format does (and often do it better), we almost never use PSD files anymore. The exception is when using multitone images. InDesign CS and later can import PSD files saved in Duotone mode, and these files are more flexible than PDF, EPS, or DCS files.

Photoshop 2.0 Format. This is an example of the Photoshop team's philosophy of not removing features. This feature is present only for compatibility reasons. It's available only in Mac OS X.

TIFF

The Tagged Image File Format (TIFF, pronounced just as it reads) is the industry-standard bitmapped file format. Nearly every program that works with pixel-based images can handle TIFF files—either placing, printing, correcting, or editing the pixels. A Photoshop TIFF can be any dimension and resolution (at least we haven't heard of any limits). You can save it in Grayscale, RGB, CMYK, or Lab color mode with 8 or 16 bits per channel, as 8-bit RGB indexed color, or as a (1-bit) black-and-white bitmap. Before you get totally carried away, though, bear in mind that TIFF files have a permanent, hard-coded file-size limit of 4 GB.

TIFF was once a very straightforward format—the only information it contained beyond the actual pixels themselves was the output size and resolution. But now, Photoshop can save TIFF files that contain just about everything you can put in a native Photoshop file, including vector data, clipping paths, transparency, spot-color channels, annotations, and adjustment layers. The only exception is that you can't save a duotone as a TIFF. But beware: Just because you can save something as a TIFF doesn't mean a program like InDesign or QuarkXPress can open or print it; you'll see examples later.

Spot Channels. Even though you can save spot channels in a TIFF, we know of no application other than Photoshop that can print them properly from a TIFF. And even though you can save your vector data (type and layer clipping paths) in a TIFF, it will print as a raster (pixels) image from any application other than Photoshop, not a vector image. So be careful.

Ask Before Saving Layered TIFF Files. When you add layers to a TIFF that started out flat and then try to save it, this option forces you to look at the TIFF Options dialog (which we discuss next).

When you save a layered TIFF, Photoshop always includes a flattened composite of the image. As with Photoshop native format, saving layers increases file size significantly. Applications such as QuarkXPress and InDesign import the flattened image, but if you later open the TIFF in Photoshop, it reads the layers.

When you save a TIFF, Photoshop lets you choose from among various options in the TIFF Options dialog (see **Figure 12-8**).

Figure 12-8 Saving TIFF files

Compression. Photoshop lets you save the composite (flattened) information in TIFF files with LZW or ZIP (lossless) or JPEG (lossy) compression. LZW may still give a few antediluvian applications some problems, but it's generally well supported. However, LZW doesn't work well on high-bit files—it actually makes them bigger rather than smaller. The only program (besides Photoshop) we know of that can read TIFF files with ZIP or JPEG compression is InDesign.

If you save your TIFF with ZIP or JPEG compression, you do get a warning that these compression options "are not supported in older TIFF readers"—which really means that they're not supported by any application *except* InDesign, Photoshop, and recent versions of other Adobe programs such as Acrobat. We hope support widens, because ZIP compression is lossless and highly efficient. With layered TIFFs, you have the option of applying ZIP compression only to the layers while leaving the flattened composite uncompressed. We use this option a lot, because compressing the layers makes for a much smaller file and the uncompressed flattened composite is still readable by other applications.

LZW compression is relatively inefficient—and useless on high-bit files—so we generally avoid it (David still uses LZW compression on screen shots, but when pressed, will admit he does so largely out of habit). We use ZIP compression on flattened images destined for InDesign, but if we don't know the final destination, we leave our flattened TIFFs uncompressed.

Pixel Order. Photoshop CS2 introduced a new TIFF option—Pixel Order—which lets you choose between Interleaved (known in neolithic times as "chunky") and Per Channel (also known as "planar"). The difference has to do with how each channel of an image is saved: Interleaved saves a pixel's red channel value, then its green channel value, and then its blue channel value—repeating this cycle for each image pixel. That's how every version of Photoshop before CS2 saved TIFFs. Per Channel saves the entire red channel, followed by the green channel, and finally the blue channel.

Most older programs simply can't read Per Channel TIFFs, so we typically stick with Interleaved. But if you're trying to make your file as small as possible, Per Channel pixel order with ZIP compression produces the smallest file on high-bit images, and Interleaved pixel order with ZIP compression does the same on 8-bit ones.

Byte Order. For some reason, Mac OS X and Windows have different versions of TIFF. It has something to do with the file's byte order and the processing methods of Motorola versus Intel CPUs. These days, no matter what brand of CPU you have in your computer, most programs understand how to read either order. If you find one that doesn't, that program is either old or poorly written.

Image Pyramid. This is basically the contents of the Image Cache, covered in Chapter 1, "Building a Photoshop System." Chances are you'll never use it—it was designed for viewing TIFF files in Web browsers, but the browser support never materialized.

Transparency. When your image has transparency (the file is not flattened and has no Background layer), you can save the transparency in the TIFF file by turning on the Save Transparency check box. Programs that understand transparency (such as InDesign), can read the transparency in these TIFF files. Older programs import the file as if it was flattened.

Layer Compression. Photoshop always compresses the layers in layered TIFF files using either RLE or ZIP. If we're saving layered TIFFs for an application that may not support ZIP compression, we leave the composite data uncompressed, but we choose ZIP compression on the layers (for Photoshop to read). ZIP takes longer to save, but it's a more efficient compression algorithm than RLE, so it results in significantly smaller files.

Compatibility. TIFF is a flexible format, but that flexibility comes at the price of compatibility. Photoshop can easily save TIFFs that either are unreadable by other applications or may not print as expected from other applications. It can read anything it can save in a TIFF, so TIFF is great as a work file format for Photoshop. But as we've shown, other applications may not know what to do with all the features Photoshop can save in a TIFF image. What to do? We offer this guideline: When in doubt, assume that a program using or opening a Photoshop TIFF will read the flattened composite and ignore everything else, and assume that the only widely supported compression option for the flattened composite is LZW.

TIP: You can save even more space by applying ZIP compression to both the layers and the background of a TIFF file, but only a few graphics programs, such as Photoshop and InDesign, will be able to read a TIFF file saved that way.

EPS and DCS

Encapsulated PostScript (EPS) is really an object-oriented file format, but Photoshop can save pixel-based and vector (like text) image data in the EPS format. There are two things you should remember about EPS:

•   The primary use of EPS files is in page-layout software for printed output. They aren't really useful for Web, video, or other types of output.

- EPS is a twentieth-century file format that's being replaced by PDF. Old, second-millennium software such as Adobe PageMaker or Quark-XPress 4 handles EPS files better than PDF files, but for modern software (such as InDesign CS4), PDF is the vector file format of choice, and is even the native file format of Illustrator.

If you're just doing straight photography, you'll rarely, if ever, save files in EPS. If you do, you may be faced with choosing a preview format and other options. Our guideline for those is that current graphic design software (including most Adobe programs) should be able to display an EPS graphic if it doesn't contain a preview. Older or less sophisticated software may not be able to display it without a preview. If you want to be on the safe side, choose TIFF (8 bits/pixel). The Macintosh options use the obsolete PICT format and won't be read in Windows. Don't select any of the other options unless you or your service provider has deemed them necessary for proper output; they certainly won't apply to non-PostScript desktop photo printers.

DCS. Desktop Color Separation (DCS) is a special form of the EPS file format. However, it's weird (and important) enough that Adobe added it as two separate file formats in the Save As dialog: Photoshop DCS 1.0 and Photoshop DCS 2.0. You won't need it in modern prepress workflows; if you do, ask your prepress service provider which settings they work with.

PDF

We like to use PDF (Portable Document Format) whenever an image contains a significant amount of vector data (such as text) that we want to maintain as sharp-edged vectors in the final output. While text is rasterized in TIFFs (making the edges pixelated) and converted to outlines in EPS files (making them slow to print if there's a lot of text), PDF files handle text beautifully. Best of all, you can embed a font into your PDF file, so it will display and print correctly wherever it goes.

PDF is also an excellent format for sending proofs or samples to clients. Not only can you include password protection, but you can create multipage (multi-image) documents very easily by using the Output panel in Bridge (see Chapter 5, "Building a Digital Workflow").

Round-Tripping. Some PDF options (see **Figure 12-9**) actually override the options you chose in the Save As dialog. For example, the Layers check box in the Save As dialog normally determines whether Photoshop will include layered data. However, Photoshop actually ignores that check box and instead pays attention to the Preserve Photoshop Editing Capabilities check box (in the Save Adobe PDF dialog). When you turn on Preserve Photoshop Editing Capabilities, you can keep all of the Photoshop features you used. If you turn this option off and reopen the file in Photoshop, it rasterizes the whole thing, even if you had saved your vector data.

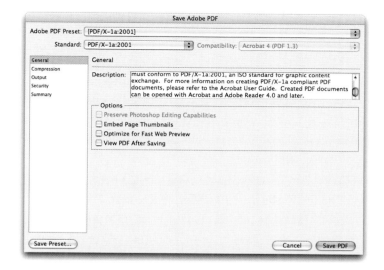

Figure 12-9 Saving a PDF file

In this example, a Photoshop document is an ad being sent to a newspaper that requires ads to conform to the PDF/X-1a standard. Because the Preserve Photoshop Editing Capabilities check box is not part of the PDF/X-1a specification, it's disabled. The ad designer would retain a complete layered copy of the ad in Photoshop format.

PDF Options. The other options in the Save Adobe PDF dialog are virtually identical to the PDF options from Adobe Acrobat Distiller or InDesign or any of the other Creative Suite applications. This includes the Adobe PDF Preset pop-up menu at the top of the dialog, which lets you choose a preset even if the preset was created in another Creative Suite application.

Most important, the options you choose may degrade the image in the PDF, but as long as the Preserve Photoshop Editing Capabilities check box is turned on, these options won't affect the behind-the-scenes PSD data that Photoshop saves with the PDF. For example, if you choose a low-resolution, low-quality JPEG compression in the PDF, the PDF image degrades, but

TIP: If you're using PDF files in a standardized workflow, you can simply choose a preset from the Adobe PDF Preset menu at the top of the Save Adobe PDF dialog. The company receiving your PDF files may also provide PDF presets for you to install. If either is true, choose the right preset instead of editing all the settings.

the layered data does not. That way, when you open it in Photoshop and resave as PDF, you don't recompress (and further degrade) your data.

CompuServe GIF

The Graphics Interchange Format (commonly known as GIF) was once the "house-brand" image file format of the CompuServe online information service. That's why this file format is listed as "CompuServe GIF" in the Save As dialog, even though GIF images have long since broken free of CompuServe's corporate walls and are now a Web standard.

GIF files are designed for onscreen viewing, especially for images where file size is more important than quality and for screens that display only 8-bit color (256 colors). Photoshop GIF files are always 8-bit indexed color images, making them acceptable for onscreen viewing but totally unreasonable for printing and not very usable for reproducing photographs (use JPEG instead). GIFs are automatically compressed using lossless LZW compression (see "Compressing Images," later in this chapter). But we never save a GIF file with the Save As dialog; rather, we use the Save for Web & Devices dialog for much more control.

JPEG

Most JPEG (Joint Photographic Experts Group) images are found on the Web or produced by digital cameras. The only problem with using the JPEG format for printing is that it's lossy (see "Compressing Images," later in this chapter). We don't recommend using JPEG files in a prepress workflow unless you must drastically limit your file sizes.

TIP: If JPEG is not available in the Format pop-up menu in the Save As dialog, make sure your image is in 8 bit/channel mode.

You might have noticed that you can save JPEG files in both the Save As dialog and in the Save for Web & Devices dialog. What's the difference? In the Save for Web & Devices dialog, it's assumed that you want the smallest file possible, so there are no options for features such as embedded previews, and by default, metadata isn't included. If you want to include full metadata and more features, create JPEGs using Save As. If you want smaller files, create JPEGs using Save for Web & Devices.

By the way, don't confuse JPEG with JPEG 2000, which is a newer, more capable format that, unfortunately, has not caught on.

PNG

The Portable Network Graphic (PNG) format was designed as a more fully featured replacement for GIF. For instance, PNG supports both 8-bit indexed color and full 24-bit color. Where GIF can include 1-bit transparency (in which each pixel is either transparent or not), PNG has full 8-bit transparency with alpha channels, so a graphic could be partially opaque in some areas. PNG also includes limited support for color management on the Internet by recording monitor gamma and chromaticity. There are many other features, too (among which is the significant bonus of having a relatively unambiguous pronunciation). Although GIF is still in common use, PNG is gaining ground, thanks to widening Web browser support.

Large Document Format

Large Document Format (PSB) exists to blow past the limitations of the older Photoshop file format. It supports everything that the Photoshop format does, but in addition you can also store files larger than 2 GB and at pixel dimensions up to 300,000 pixels on a side.

So why isn't this the default file format for Photoshop? Because most programs that read Photoshop files don't read PSB files. Also, if you need to send files to people using older versions of Photoshop, keep in mind that PSB files can be opened only using Photoshop CS or later.

Photoshop Raw

The Photoshop Raw option is a way to read or write image data that doesn't appear to be in a Photoshop-supported format. Sometimes these files are simply images that are missing file information that identifies them.

The main reason we're talking about it is to tell you to not confuse Photoshop Raw with the Camera Raw format, which Photoshop can read but not write (see Chapter 5, "Building a Digital Workflow," for more on Camera Raw.)

The only time Photoshop Raw might be useful is if you receive a graphics file that Photoshop can't open, and that's pretty rare. In order to set the right options, you need to have an engineering-level familiarity with the inner

TIP: Is Photoshop missing a file format choice you used to have? Some format support has been removed but is still available as an unsupported free download from Adobe. Go to http://www.adobe.com/support/downloads/ and look for the Optional Legacy Plug-Ins.

workings of graphics file formats. If you don't have that knowledge, the best you can do is click Guess and hope for the best.

WBMP

Photoshop pictures go everywhere these days, as big as billboards and as small as little icons on cell phone screens. If you're trying to make pictures for cell phones and wireless PDAs, we've got just the file format for you: WBMP (Wireless Bitmap). You can save files that are already in Bitmap mode as WBMP format from the Save As dialog, or any file as WBMP from the Save for Web & Devices dialog.

BMP

Windows Bitmap (BMP, pronounced by saying the letters) is the bitmap format native to Windows Paint. It's rarely encountered outside of Windows and is hardly a professional file format. You can store a 1-, 4-, 8-, or 24-bit image of various dimensions and resolutions, but we still prefer TIFF, given its strong support by desktop-publishing applications and compatibility across different computer systems. If you're creating wallpaper for your Windows desktop, this is the format for you!

Uninstalled File Format Plug-Ins

As we noted back in the Introduction, this book covers only a fraction of the potential uses of Photoshop—those centered around print production. People use this program for so many different things that we couldn't hope to cover them all here. In the last two sections, we discussed each of the file formats that are relevant for professionals who are putting images on paper, film, or the Web. You, however, might be doing something interesting, different, or just plain odd. Don't worry; Photoshop can probably still accommodate you. While we won't cover all of the more obscure or just plain obsolete formats in the Save As and Export commands, we'll tell you where they are in case you need them.

On your Photoshop or Creative Suite install disk, look in the folder Goodies\Optional Plug-ins\File Formats. In there, you'll find file format plug-ins such as Alias, ElectricImage, and even good old MacPaint. To install them,

TIP: Some older Mac plug-ins, such as the PhotoCD plug-in, don't work on Intel Macs. To run them, you must switch Photoshop to Rosetta mode. Quit Photoshop, and then in the Finder, select the Photoshop application icon and choose File > Get Info. Turn on the Open in Rosetta check box, and start Photoshop. As long as that option is on, Photoshop will run more slowly because it won't be running natively on Intel CPUs. We recommend that you convert PhotoCD images to a format like TIFF, because Kodak no longer updates PhotoCD software.

open up your Photoshop application folder (the one that's already installed on your computer), go to Plug-ins/File Formats, and drop the plug-ins in the File Formats folder.

The reason the plug-ins aren't installed is that they're provided as a convenience, but they didn't go through the same rigorous testing as the components that were installed. They're the same as what shipped before.

COMPRESSING IMAGES

Bitmapped images are pigs when it comes to hard disk space. In this day and age, when you can buy a 500 GB hard disk as cheaply as a pair of shoes, saving space on disk isn't nearly as important an issue as trying to transfer that data. Whether you have a modestly fast connection to the Web on your handheld device or a T1 line in your office, moving massive files around is somewhat painful.

Our aim, then, is to stretch out the scarce resources we have on hand, and keep files that we need to move around reasonably small. And we've got three methods to accomplish this goal: work with smaller images (no, seriously!), archive our images when we're not using them, and work with compressed file formats.

Lossless Compression

Let's take the example of a 1-bit (black-and-white) bitmap, 100 pixels wide and tall. Without any compression, the computer stores the value (zero or one) for each one of the 10,000 pixels in the image. This is like staring into your sock drawer and saying, "I've got one blue sock and one blue sock and one black sock and one black sock," and so on. We can compress our description in half by saying, "I've got one blue pair and one black pair."

Run Length Encoding. Similarly, we can group the zeros and ones together by counting up common values in a row (see **Figure 12-10**). For instance, we could say, "There are 34 zeros, then 3 ones, then 55 zeros," and so on. This is called Run Length Encoding (RLE), and it's used by fax machines. We call it "lossless" because there is no loss of data when you compress or decompress the file—what goes in comes out exactly the same.

LZW, Huffman, and ZIP. There are other forms of lossless compression. For instance, RLE compresses simple images (ones that have large solid-colored areas) down to almost nothing, but it can't compress more-complex images (like most grayscale images) very much. LZW (Lempel-Ziv-Welch, though you really don't need to know that) and Huffman encoding work by tokenizing common strings of data.

In plain English, that means that instead of just looking for a string of the same color, these methods look for trends. If RLE sees "010101," it can't do any compression. But the LZW and Huffman algorithms are smart enough to spot the pattern of alternating characters and thereby compress that information. ZIP is a considerably smarter version of LZW (smarter means it compresses better, but it may take slightly longer to do so).

Figure 12-10 Run Length Encoding lossless compression

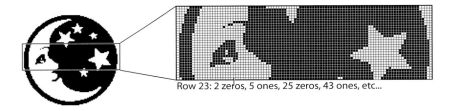

Row 23: 2 zeros, 5 ones, 25 zeros, 43 ones, etc...

Lossy Compression

The table of contents at the front of this book is a way of compressing information. If you ripped the table of contents out of this book and mailed it to someone else, they would understand what the book is about. But they wouldn't actually be seeing the words you're reading now, or all the details. Instead, they'd only get a sampling of each chapter.

Bitmapped images can be similarly compressed, transmitted to someone else, and unpacked. And depending on how the image was compressed, you may not get all the detail from the original image. For example, if 9 pixels in a 3-by-3 square are similar, you could replace them all with a single aver-aged value. That's a nine-to-one compression. But the original data, the variances in those 9 pixels, is lost forever.

This sort of compression is called *lossy* compression because you lose data when compressing it; this creates the possibility of compressing the data further. Where a ZIP-compressed TIFF might be 40 percent of the original size, a lossy-compressed file can be 2 percent or less of the original file size.

Levels of JPEG Compression. Lossy compression schemes typically give you a choice of how tightly you pack the data. With low compression, you get larger files and higher quality. High compression yields lower quality and smaller files. How much quality do you lose? It depends on the level of the compression, the resolution of the image, and the content of the image.

The primary method is JPEG. Different programs implement JPEG differently, and with varying results. Note that JPEG is both a compression method and a file format in its own right, which is why a PDF can contain a JPEG-compressed image.

JPEG Warnings. Images with hard edges, high contrast, and angular areas are most susceptible to artifacts from JPEG compression. Similarly, text (rasterized, not vector) almost always looks terrible after JPEG compression because it has such hard edges. On the other hand, compressing natural, scanned images using JPEG—especially those that are already somewhat grainy or impressionistic—probably won't hurt them much at all, especially if you use the Maximum or High quality setting.

You should use JPEG only for final output after you've finished all editing and correction. Tone or color correction on a JPEG image exaggerates the compression artifacts, and so does sharpening.

INDEX

IMAGE CREDITS AND PERMISSIONS

The following images are © 1992–2008 Conrad Chavez.

Page 55   Steveston X
Page 104   Brockton Point Lighthouse
Page 120   Sidewalkers, Prince St., New York City
Page 143   Sleepy Nathan and Friend
Page 159   Wedding Dinner (detail)
Page 164   Stanley Park Balanced Rocks
Page 200   Amber Fort, Georgetown, and Vivace panoramas
Page 268   Vienna U-Bahn
Page 282   La Push Driftwood
Page 302   Jaipur Vegetable Vendor, Sailboat on Lake Union, Winter Evening on 74th
Page 337   Padova Village Gate
Page 347   Mt. Rainier trail 4690-265
Page 388   Emerging from the Washington, DC Metro
Page 442   French Intersection
Page 465   Old Airplane
Page 552   Würzburg Panorama

Rajasthan, India:
Page 96   Freighter 5190-493
Page 119   Edible Oil
Page 188   Camel, Thar Desert
Page 249   Bell at Brahmin Temple, Pushkar
Page 310   Freight Convoy 5190-500
Page 322   Traditional Dancer
Page 381   Flower Offerings at Brahmin Temple, Pushkar
Page 536   Cow at Vatsalya

Jaipur, Rajasthan, India:
Page 20   Vegetable Market
Page 144   City Palace
Page 145   Danielle and a Camel
Page 152   Marble Sculptor
Page 154   Amber Fort
Page 223   Transport 5180-174
Page 226   Found Collage
Page 241   Transport series
Page 246   By the Polo Ground
Page 246   Govind Dev Ji Temple with Moon
Page 248   Motorcycle and Statue
Page 313   Manju's Spices
Page 331   Street 5190-021
Page 338   Traffic 5190-013
Page 416   Vegetable Market 5180-186
Page 420   City Palace 5180-330

Paris, France:
Page 120   Rooftops
Page 125   Afternoon on the Seine
Page 175   Building 4760-061
Page 232   Gate 4760-062
Page 349   Luxembourg Palace
Page 394   Rue Petion
Page 461   Paris Tower
Page 495   Centre Pompidou Panorama

Versailles, France:
Page 32   Sunday market
Page 305   Rue de Satory

Oporto, Portugal:
Page 411   São Bento Station Clock
Page 414   Red Rooftops 3790-034
Page 486   Layers

Tavira, Portugal:
Page 406   Chimney
Page 458   Dog on Bridge
Page 509   Roof Vents

Seattle, USA:
Page 6   Coffee
Page 18   Car show
Page 104   Orange Balloon 5310-087
Page 118   Orange Balloon 5310-085
Page 124   Paige 4800-207
Page 128   Mt. Baker
Page 140   Orange balloon 5310-104
Page 142   Paige 4800-207
Page 156   More Miles to the Gallon
Page 161   At Bouchee (detail)
Page 163   Henry Art Gallery Elevator
Page 170   Cynthia with Fruit Bowl, Deck
Page 172   Cynthia with Fruit Bowl, Kitchen
Page 206   Heather
Page 247   Do Not Enter
Page 252   Exhibition
Page 361   Green Lake Dock
Page 390   Factory to You
Page 392   University of Washington, Glass Planes
Page 396   Green Lake Rabbit
Page 408   Car for Sale
Page 420   Auto Retrato
Page 424   School Bus near EMP
Page 425   Pike Place Market Capital
Page 431   Fremont Peak Park Hand Shadow
Page 432   Fremont Peak Park Spheres
Page 434   Kelly
Page 443   Paige 4800-096
Page 468   Wooden Spoons
Page 471   Torre de Hercules, A Coruña, Spain
Page 474   The Living Room
Page 488   Georgetown Ruins
Page 491   Seattle Central Library
Page 494   Georgetown panorama
Page 497   Wine Bottles Macro
Page 498   Pike Place Market Vegetables 5230-014
Page 500   Gas Works Park Kite
Page 549   Pike Place Market Neon

Additional image credits

Page 25   Bike Parts ©1991 MacUser Magazine, by Peter Allen Gould
Page 352   Bruce. © 2004 Jeff Schewe
Page 365   Woman in Red Hat ©1990 Eastman Kodak Co., photographer Bob Clemens, Kodak Photo CD Sampler
Page 538   Earth image courtesy National Aeronautics and Space Administration
Page 483   Seattle Sunrise ©2001 Debra Carlson
Page 507   Edna Hassinger courtesy Allee Blatner. Photographer unknown.
Page 518   Birthday Tulips ©2000 Debra Carlson
Page 480   Gabriel © 1995–2004 David Blatner

Courtesy PhotoDisc:
Page 19   From Faces and Hands
Page 21 and 26   From Fine Art and Historical Photos
Page 625   From Object Series 1: Fruits and Vegetables